The
J. K. ROWLING
Encyclopedia

The
J. K. ROWLING
Encyclopedia

Connie Ann Kirk

GREENWOOD PRESS
Westport, Connecticut • London

Library of Congress Cataloging-in-Publication Data

Kirk, Connie Ann.
   The J.K. Rowling encyclopedia / Connie Ann Kirk.
      p.   cm.
   Includes bibliographical references and index.
   ISBN 0–313–33556–7 (alk. paper)
      1. Rowling, J. K.—Encyclopedias.   2. Authors, English—20th century—Biography—
   Encyclopedias.   3. Fantasy fiction, English—Encyclopedias.   I. Title.
   PR6068.O93Z459   2006
   823'.914—dc22   2006001122

British Library Cataloguing in Publication Data is available.

Library of Congress Catalog Card Number: 2006001122
ISBN: 0–313–33556–7

First published in 2006

Greenwood Press, 88 Post Road West, Westport, CT 06881
An imprint of Greenwood Publishing Group, Inc.
www.greenwood.com

Printed in the United States of America

The paper used in this book complies with the
Permanent Paper Standard issued by the National
Information Standards Organization (Z39.48–1984).

10 9 8 7 6 5 4 3 2 1

to John and Ben
with love
&
to Harry Potter fans everywhere—
"Use it well."

Contents

List of Entries

Guide to Related Topics

Beasts, Beings, and Creatures

Abominable Snowman
Abraxan horses
Acromantula
Aethonan horses
Albino bloodhounds
Animagus
Antipodian Opaleye
Aquavirius maggots
Aragog
Arnold
Ashwinder
Augurey
Badger
Bandon Banshee
Bane
Banshee
Basilisk
Beast, Being, and Spirit
    Divisions
Bicorn
Bigfoot
Birds, birdlike, and flying
    creatures
Biting fairy
Blast-Ended Skrewt
Blood-Sucking Bugbear

Boarhound
Boomslang
Bowtruckle
Buckbeak
Bundimun
Bungy
Cats
Centaurs
Chameleon Ghouls
Chimera
Chinese Fireball
Chizpurfle
Clabbert
Common Welsh Green
Cornish pixies
Crookshanks
Crumple-Horned Snorkack
Crup
Dementors
Demiguise
Diricawls
Doxy
Dragon
Dugbog
Dwarfs
Erkling
Errol
Erumpent
Fairy

Fang
Fawkes
Ferret
Fire Crab
Flobberworm
Fluffy
Fox
Fwooper
Ghoul
Giants
Glumbumble
Gnome
Goblins
Granian horses
Graphorn
Gray Centaur
Griffin
Grindylow
Grubs, giant
Gurg
Hag
Hebridean Blacks
Hedwig
Hermes
Hinkypuffs
Hinkypunk
Hippocampus
Hippogriff
Hoppy

Candy and Sweets

Mars Bars
Nosebleed Nougat
Pepper Imps
Peppermint Toad
Puking Pastille
Pumpkin Pasties
Sherbet balls
Skiving Snackboxes
"Special Effects" Sweets
Sugar quills
Ton-Tongue Toffee
Toothflossing Stringmints

Characters

Abbott, Hannah
Abercrombie, Euan
Ackerley, Stewart
Agnes
Agrippa
Alecto
Algie, Great Uncle
Amycus
Anti-Muggle pranksters
Aragog
Archie
Arjeplog
Armenian Warlock
Aubrey, Bertram
Avery
Baddock, Malcolm
Bagman, Ludovic (Ludo)
Bagman, Otto
Bagman, Sr.
Bagnold, Millicent
Bagshot, Bathilda
Bane
Barnabas the Barmy
Baruffio
Bashir, Ali
Basil
Bayliss, Hetty
Belby, Flavius
Belby, Marcus
Belcher, Humphrey
Bell, Katie
Benson, Amy
Big D
Bilius, Uncle

Billywig
Binky
Binns, Prof.
Bishop, Dennis
Black, Elladora
[Black], Phineas Nigellus
Black, Regulus
Black, Sirius
Bletchley, Miles
Bloody Baron
Boardman, Stubby
Bob
Bobbin, Melinda
Bode, Broderick
Bole
Bonaccord, Pierre
Bones, Amelia Susan
Bones, Edgar
Bones's
Bones, Susan
Boot, Terry
Boothby, Gladys
Borgin, Mr.
Bradley
Bragge, Barberus
Brand, Captain Rudolf
Brankovitch, Maximus, III
Branstone, Eleanor
Broadmoor, Kevin and Karl
Brocklehurst, Mandy
Brookstanton, Rupert
  "Axebanger"
Brother Benedict
Brown, Lavender
Bryce, Frank
Bulstrode, Millicent
Bungs, Rosalind Antigone
Burke, Caractacus
Cadogen, Sir
Cadwallader
Carmichael, Eddie
Carrows
Cauldwell, Owen
Celia
Chambers
Chancellor of the Exchequer
Chang, Cho
Chorley, Herbert
Chubb, Agatha

Circe
Clagg, Madame Elfrida
Clearwater, Penelope
Cliodna
Cole, Mrs.
Colonel Fubster
Connolly
Coote, Ritchie
Corner, Michael
Crabbe, Mr.
Crabbe, Vincent
Crapaud
Creevey, Colin
Creevey, Dennis
Cresswell, Dirk
Croaker
Crockford, Doris
Crouch, Bartemius (Barty), Sr.
Crouch, Barty, Jr.
Cuffe, Barnabus
Dagworth-Granger, Hector
Damocles, Uncle
Davies, Roger
Dawlish
Dearborn, Caradoc
Death Eater
Delacour, Fleur
Delacour, Gabrielle
Delaney-Podmore, Sir Patrick
Dennis
Derek
Derrick
Derwent, Dilys
Diggle, Dedalus
Diggory, Amos
Diggory, Cedric
Dimitrov
Dingle, Harold
Dippet, Prof. Armando
Dobbin
Dobbs, Emma
Dobby
Dodgy Dirk
Doge, Elphias
Dolohov, Antonin
Dot
Dumbledore, Aberforth
Dumbledore, Albus Percival
  Wulfric Brian

Dursley, Aunt Marge (Marjory)
Dursley, Aunt Petunia (Evans)
Dursley, Dudley
Dursley, Uncle Vernon
Edgecombe, Madam
Edgecombe, Marietta
Elfric the Eager
Emeric the Evil
Enid, Great Auntie
Eric
Evans, Mark
Everard
The Fat Friar
The Fat Lady
Fawcetts
Fenwick, Benjy
Fergus
Figg, Arabella Doreen (Mrs.)
Filch, Argus
Finch-Fletchley, Justin
Fingal the Fearless
Finnigan, Seamus
Flamel, Nicolas
Flamel, Perenelle
Fleet, Angus
Fletcher, Mundungus
Flint, Marcus
Flitwick, Prof. Filius
Flume, Ambrosius
Fortescue
Fortescue, Florean
Fridwulfa
Frobisher, Vicky
Fudge, Cornelius Oswald
Gaunt, Marvolo
Gaunt, Merope
Gaunt, Morfin
Ghosts
Gibbon
Goldstein, Anthony
Golgomath
Gordon
Goyle, Gregory
Granger, Hermione
Granger, Mr. and Mrs.
Grawp
Greek chappie
Greengrass, Daphne
Grenouille

Greyback, Fenrir
Griffiths, Glynnis
Grimstone, Elias
Grindelwald
Griphook
Grubbly-Plank, Prof. Wilhelmina
Grunnion, Alberic
Gryffindor, Godric
Gudgeon, Davey
Gudgeon, Gladys
Gunhilda
Gwenog
"Hagger"
Hagrid, Rubeus
Half-Blood Prince
Harkiss, Ciceron
Harper
Harpo the Foul
Harris, Warty
Hedwig
Hengist of Woodcroft
Higgs, Bertie
Higgs, Terence
The Hobgoblins
Hogwarts High Inquisitor
Hokey
Hooch, Madam Rolanda
Hooper, Geoffrey
Hopkirk, Mafalda
Hornby, Olive
Horton, Basil
House-elves
Ingolfr the Iambic
Ivanova
Jewkes, Leonard
Johnson, Angelina
Jones, Gwenog
Jones, Hestia
Jordan, Lee
Jorkins, Bertha
Jugson
Karkaroff, Igor
Karkus
Keddle, Gertie
Keitch, Randolph
Kettleburn, Prof.
Kevin
Kirke, Andrew

Kneen, Goodwin
Kreacher
Krum, Viktor
Leanne
Lestrange, Bellatrix Black
Lestrange, Rabastan
Lestrange, Rodolphus
Levski
Llewellyn, "Dangerous" Dai
Lochrin, Guthrie
Lockhart, Gilderoy
Longbottom, Alice
Longbottom, Augusta (Gran)
Longbottom, Neville
Lovegood, Luna
Lovegoods
Lupin, Prof. Remus John
Lynch, Aidan
MacBoon, Quintius
Macdonald, Magnus "Dent-Head"
MacFarlan, Hamish
Macmillan, Ernie
Macnair, Walden
Madley, Laura
Malcolm
Malecrit
Malfoy, Abraxas
Malfoy, Draco
Malfoy, Lucius
Malfoy, Narcissa
Marchbanks, Griselda
Marsh, Madam
Martha
Mason, Mr. and Mrs.
Maxime, Madame Olympe
McCliverts, Dugald
McCormack, Catriona
McCormack, Kirley
McCormack, Meaghan
McDonald, Natalie
McGonagall, Prof. Minerva
McGuffin, Jim
McKinnon, Marlene
McKinnons
McLaggen, Cormac
Meadowes, Dorcas
Mediwizards
Meliflua, Araminta

Tom
Tonks, Andromeda Black
Tonks, Nymphadora
Tonks, Ted
Towler, Kenneth
Travers
Trelawney, Prof. Sibyll
  Patricia
Trevor
Troy
Turpin, Lisa
Twycross, Wilkie
Ugga
Umbridge, Prof. Dolores Jane
Umfraville, Quintius
Uric the Oddball
Urquhart
Vaisey
Vance, Emmeline
Vane, Romilda
Vector, Prof.
Verity
Violet
Voldemort, Lord
Volkov
Vulchanov
Wailing Widow from Kent
Warbeck, Celestina
Warrington
Weasley, Arthur
Weasley, Bill
Weasley, Charlie
Weasley Family
Weasley, Fred and George
Weasley, Ginevra (Ginny)
  Molly
Weasley, Molly Prewett
Weasley, Percy Ignatius
Weasley, "Peter"
Weasley, Ronald (Ron) Bilius
The Weird Sisters
Wendelin the Weird
Whalley, Eric
Whisp, Kennilworthy
Whitby, Kevin
Widdershin, Willy
Wilkes
Will
Williamson

Wimple, Gilbert
Winky
Witch with a hairy chin
Witherwings
Wood, Oliver
Worme, Augustus
Wormtail
Worple, Eldred
Wright, Bowman
Wronski, Josef
Yaxley
"You-Know-Who"
Youdle, Cyprian
Yvonne
Zabini, Blaise
Zamojski, Ladislaw
Zeller, Rose
Zograf

Communication

Birds, birdlike, and flying
  creatures
Books in the series
The Daily Prophet
Evening Prophet
Howler
Mermish
Mersong
Owl Order Service
Paper airplanes
The Quibbler
Quick-Quotes Quill
Self-Inking quills
Singing Valentine
Witch Weekly
Wizarding Wireless Network
  (WWN)

Events

Bonfire Night
Burning Day
Christmas
Death Day Party
Easter
Funeral, Dumbledore's
Halloween
Hurricane

Ilfracombe Incident of 1932
International Confederation
  of Wizards Summit
  Meeting of 1692
Leaving Feast
Quidditch World Cup
1612 Goblin Rebellion
Sorting Hat Ceremony
Start-of-Term Banquet
Triwizard Tournament
Valentine's Day
Warlocks' Convention of
  1709
Wedding
Yule Ball

Food and Beverages

Brother Boniface's Turnip
  Wine
Butterbeer
Candy and sweets
Chipolatas
Corn flakes
Elderflower wine
Elf-made wine
Food and feasts
Fruit 'N Bran breakfast
  cereal
Leaving Feast
Lemons and lemon-flavored
  treats

General Topics

Alchemy
Americanization of the Novels
Americans
Amnesty International
Animals
Astrology
Awards, J. K. Rowling's
The Beatles
Biographies, J. K. Rowling
Bloomsbury, Plc.
Bonfire Night
Book bannings and burnings
Books in the series
Bullies and bullying

Camping, Wizard
Canada
Careers
Castles
Chapters
Chemistry
Children's High Level
  Group
Children's literature, series'
  role in
Christian responses
Clothing
Comic Relief, U.K.
Coming-of-age story
Critical reception
Depression
Dreams in the novels
Fan responses
Films
Fire
Forest of Dean
Games in the series
Ghosts
Ghoul
Giants
Gifts, gift-giving
Goblins
Hero complex
Humor
Illustrations
Killing
Kiss
Latin, use of
Lawsuits
Magic
Merchandising
Money
Multiple Sclerosis Society,
  Scotland
Music
Mystery
Mythology, Use of
Names
National Council for One
  Parent Families
O.B.E. (Order of the British
  Empire)
Pagination
Popular culture

Predictions
Race
Readings, public and
  private
Scars
Scholastic Books
Schools of witchcraft and
  wizardry
Sin
Slavery
Socks
Spies/spying
Timeline of the series
Translations
Tutshill Primary School of
  England
War
Website, J. K. Rowling's
Witches/wizards
Wyedean Comprehensive
  Yate, England

Hogwarts

Ancient Runes
Arithmancy
Armor Gallery
Astronomy
Astronomy Tower
Awards at Hogwarts
Badger
Bloody Baron
Care of Magical Creatures
Careers
Chamber of Secrets
Charm Club
Charms class
Classroom eleven
Coat of arms
Come and Go Room
Defense Against the
  Dark Arts
Defense Against the Dark
  Arts, Harry's class
Detention
Divination
Dormitory
Dueling Club
Dumbledore's Army (DA)

Flying lessons
Gobstones Club
The Great Hall
Gryffindor, Godric
Gryffindor House
Harry Potter Fan Club
Head of House
Herbology
High Table
History of Magic
Hogwarts High Inquisitor
Hogwarts School of
  Witchcraft and Wizardry
The House Championship/
  House Cup
Hufflepuff House
Inter-House Quidditch Cup
The lake
Library, Hogwarts
Muggle Studies
Owlery
Prefect
Ravenclaw House
Remedial Potions
Room of Requirement
School song
Secret passageways
The Slug Club
Slytherin House
S.P.E.W.
"Swish and Flick"
Transfiguration
Troublemakers-in-Chief
West Tower

Incantations

"Accio"
"Alohomora"
"Anapneo"
"Aparecium"
"Avada Kedavra"
"Avis!"
"Colloportus!"
"Crucio"
"Deleterius!"
"Densaugeo!"
"Diffindio!"
"Dissendium"

"Enervate!"
"Engorgio!"
"Episkey"
"Evanesco!"
"Expecto patronum!"
"Expelliarmus!"
"Ferula"
"Finite Incantatem!"
"Flagrate!"
"Furnunculus!"
"Imperio!"
"Incarcerous!"
"Incendio!"
"Langlock!"
"Locomotor Mortis"
"Lumos!"
"Mischief Managed"
"Mobiliarbus!"
"Mobilicorpus"
"Morsmordre!"
"Nox"
"Obliviate!"
"Oddment!"
"Oddsbodikins"
"Oppugno!"
"Orchideous!"
"Peskipiksi Pesternomi"
"Petrificus Totalus!"
"Portus"
"Prior Incantato!"
"Protego!"
"Quietus"
"Reducio"
"Reducto!"
"Relashio!"
"Reparo!"
"Rictusempra!"
"Riddikulus!"
"Scourgify"
"Sectumsempra!"
"Serpensortia!"
"Silencio!"
"Sonorus!"
"Specialis Revelio!"
"Stupefy!"
"Tarantallegra!"
"Tergeo!"
"Waddiwasi!"
"Wingardium Leviosa"

Laws and Decrees

Antiwerewolf legislation
Ban on Experimental Breeding
Ban on Importing Flying
    Carpets
Broom Regulatory Control
Class C Non-Tradeable
    Substance
Code of Wand Use
Council of Magical Law
Decree for the Reasonable
    Restriction of Underage
    Sorcery, 1875
Educational Decree Twenty-
    eight
Educational Decree Twenty-
    five
Educational Decree Twenty-
    four
Educational Decree Twenty-
    nine
Educational Decree Twenty-
    seven
Educational Decree Twenty-six
Educational Decree
    Twenty-three
Educational Decree Twenty-
    two
International Code of
    Wizarding Secrecy
International Magical
    Office of Law
Law Fifteen B
Muggle Protection Act
Reasonable Restriction of
    Underage Sorcery
Statute of Secrecy
Werewolf Code of Conduct,
    1637
Wizengamot Charter of
    Rights

Magical Skills

All-Knowing
Animagus
Apparition
Auror
Curse-Breaker

Dark Magic
Disapparition
Inner Eye
Legilimency
"Legilimens"
Metamorphmagus
Metamorphosing
Occlumency
Occlumens
Parselmouth/Parseltongue
Side-Along-Apparition
Transfiguration

Ministry of Magic

Accidental Magic Reversal
    Squad/Department
Apparition Test Center
Atrium
Auror Headquarters
Beast, Being, and Spirit
    Divisions
Brain Room
British Quidditch League
    Headquarters
Centaur Liaison Office
Committee for the Disposal of
    Dangerous Creatures
Committee of Experimental
    Charms
Council of Magical Law
Courtroom Ten
Death Chamber
Department for the Regulation
    and Control of Magical
    Creatures
Department of International
    Magical Cooperation
Department of Magical
    Accidents and Catastrophes
Department of Magical Games
    and Sports
Department of Magical Law
    Enforcement
Department of Magical
    Transport
Department of Mysteries
Dragon Research and Restraint
    Bureau

Objects

Bulbadox Powder
Calming Draught
Class C Non-Tradeable
  Substance
Confusing and Befuddlement
  Draughts
Deflating Draught
Dr. Ubbly's Oblivious Unction
Dragon blood
Dragon dung
Draught of Peace
Edible Dark Marks
Elixir of Life
Elixir to Induce Euphoria
Enchantments
Everlasting Elixirs
Felix Felicis
Flesh-Eating Slug Repellant
Forgetfulness Potion
Gillywater
Hair-Raising Potion
Hellebore
Hiccuping Solution
Invigoration Draught
Invisible ink
Love potions
Mandrake Restorative
  Draught
Moonstone
Mrs. Skower's All-Purpose
  Magical Mess Remover
Pepperup Potion
Peruvian Instant Darkness
  Powder
Polyjuice Potion
Potions
Rat tonic
Self-Correcting Ink
Shrinking Solution
Skele-Gro
Sleekeazy's Hair Potion
Sleeping Draught
Sleeping Potion
Spine of lionfish
Stinksap
Strengthening Solution
Swelling Solution
U-No-Poo
Undetectable Poisons

Veritaserum
Wartcap powder
Wit-Sharpening Potion
Wolfbane's Potion
Wormwood

Pottermania

The Beatles
Biographies, J. K. Rowling
Christian responses
Critical reception
Fan responses
Films
Merchandising
Popular culture

Publishing Topics

Bloomsbury, Plc.
Book bannings and burnings
Chapters

Quidditch and Magical Sport

Aingingein
Annual broom race
Appleby Arrows
Ballycastle Bats
Banchory Bangers
Barny the fruitbat
Bats (Quidditch)
Beaters
Bigonville Bombers
Blagging
Blatching
Blooder
Bludger
Bludger backbeat
Blurting
Bodmin Moor
Braga Broomfleet
British Quidditch League
  Headquarters
British Quidditch Team
Bulgarian Quidditch Team
Bumphing

Caerphilly Catapults
Catcher
Chaser
Chudley Cannons
Cleansweep Broom Company
Cobbing
The Comet Trading
  Company
Creaothceann
"Dangerous" Dai
  Commemorative Medal
Dom
Dopplebeater Defense
Double Eight Loop
Ellerby and Spudmore
Falmouth Falcons
Fitchburg Finches
Flacking
Flyte and Barker
Gimbi Giant-Slayers
Golden Snitch
Gorodok Gargoyles
Grodzisk Goblins
Gryffindor Quidditch Team
Haileybury Hammers
Haversacking
Hawkshead Attacking
  Formation
Heidelberg Harriers
Herefordshire
Holyhead Harpies
Horton-Keitch braking charm
Hunter
International Association of
  Quidditch
Inverness
Irish International Side
Irish National Quidditch
  Team
Karasjok Kites
Keeper
Kenmare Kestrels
Kwidditch
Mascots
Montrose Magpies
Moose Jaw Meteorites
Moutohora Macaws
Museum of Quidditch
National Squad

Nimbus Racing Broom
    Company
Nimbus 2000
Nimbus 2001
Oakshaft 79
Parkin's Pincer
Patonga Proudsticks
Pennifold Quaffle
Pitch
Plumpton Pass
Porskoff Ploy
Pride of Portree
Puddlemere United
Quaffle
Quaffle-pocking
Quality Quidditch Supplies
Queerditch Marsh
Quiberon Quafflepunchers
Quidditch
Quidditch fouls
Quidditch League
Quidditch rules
Quidditch World Cup
Quijudge
Quodpot
Red card
Referee
Reverse Pass
Scottish Quidditch Team
Second
Seeker
Shuntbumps
Sloth Grip Roll
Snidget
Snidget-hunting
Snitch
Snitchnip
Starfish and Stick
Stitchstock
Stonewall Stormers
Stooging
Sumbawanga Sunrays
Sweetwater All-Stars
Swivenhodge
Tarapoto Tree-Skimmers
Tchamba Charmers
Thundelarra Thunderers
Tinderblast
Toyohashi Tengu

Transylvania
Transylvanian Tackle
Tutshill Tornados
Twigger 90
Universal Brooms Ltd.
Vratsa Vultures
Welsh Quidditch Team
West Ham Soccer Team
Whizz Hard Books
Wigtown Wanderers
Winterbourne Wasps
Woollongong Shimmy
Woollongong Warriors
Wronski (Defensive) Feint

Settings

Apothecary Shop
Armor Gallery
Astronomy Tower
Atrium
Azkaban
Bethnal Green
Blackspool Pier
Bodmin Moor
Borgin and Burke's
Brain Room
Brockdale Bridge
Broomstick shed, Weasleys'
Budleigh Babberton
The Burrow
Cauldron Shop
The Cave
Charing Cross Road
Cokeworth
Courtroom Ten
Dai Llewellyn Ward
Dervish and Banges
Diagon Alley
Dormitory
Elephant and Castle
Eyelops Owl Emporium
Florean Fortescue's Ice
    Cream Parlor
Flourish and Blotts
Forbidden Forest
Gambol and Japes Wizarding
    Joke Shop
Gladrags Wizardwear

Godric's Hollow
Graveyard
The Great Hall
Great Hangleton
Greenhouse One
Greenhouse Three
Gringotts
Grunnings
Hagrid's hut
Hall of Prophecy
The Hanged Man
Hedge
High Street
Hog's Head Inn
Hogsmeade
Hogwarts School of
    Witchcraft and Wizardry
Honeydukes
Hut-on-the-Rock
Invisibility Section
Knockturn Alley
The lake
The Leaky Cauldron
Little Hangleton
Little Whinging, Surrey
Madam Malkin's Robes for
    All Occasions
Madam Puddifoot's Tea
    Shop
Magical Menagerie
Magnolia Crescent
Magnolia Road
Manor, Malfoy
Modesty Rabnott Snidget
    Reservation
Muggle Underground
Museum of Quidditch
North Tower
Norwegian Ministry of
    Magic
Number Four, Privet Drive
Number Twelve, Grimmauld
    Place
Ollivanders
Palace of Beauxbatons
Post Office, Hogsmeade
Prefects' bathroom
Quality Quidditch Supplies
Railview Hotel

The Riddle House
Restricted Section
Room of Requirement
St. Brutus's Secure Center for
    Incurably Criminal Boys
St. Mungo's Hospital for
    Magical Maladies and
    Injuries
Scrivenshaft's Quill Shop
Shrieking Shack
Smeltings
Spinner's End
Stoatshead Hill
Stonewall High
Three Broomsticks
Twilfitt and Tatting's
Weasleys' Wizard Wheezes
Wisteria Walk
Zonko's

**Spells, Charms, and
Curses**

Animagi Transfiguration Spell
Anti-Cheating Charms
Anti-Cheating Spell
Anti–Dark Force Spell
Anti-Disapparition Jinx
Anti-Intruder jinxes
Aquamenti Charm
Armor-bewitching charm
Arrow spell
Babbling Curse
Banishing Charm
Bat bogey Hex
Bluebell Flames
Body-Bind Curse
Boggart Banishing Spell
Bubble-Head Charm
Cheering Charm
Color-Change Charm
Confounding Spell
Confundus Charm
Conjunctivitis Curse
Counterjinxes
Cross-Species Switches
Cruciatus Curse
Curse of the Bogies
Cushioning Charm

Dementor's Kiss
Disarming Spell
Disillusionment Charm
Drought Charm
Engorgement Charm
Enlargement Charm
Entrancing Enchantments
Flame Freezing Charm
Four-Point Spell
Freezing Charm
Full Body-Bind
Growth Charm
Gum shield
Hair-Thickening Charm
Healing Spells
Hormorphus Charm
Horton-Keitch braking charm
Hover Charm
Hurling Hex
Impediment Curse/Jinx
Imperius Curse
Imperturbable Charm
Impervius Charm
Inanimatus Conjurus
Intruder Charm
Invisibility Spell
Jelly-Legs Jinx
Killing Curse
Leg-Locker Curse
Levicorpus
Levitation Charm
Liberacorpus
Memory Charm
Muffliato
Muggle Repelling Charm
Non-verbal Spells
Obliteration Charm
Partial Vanishment
Patented Daydream Charms
Patronus
Permanent Sticking Charm
Petrification
Portable Swamp
Protean Charm
Reductor Curse
Repelling Spells
Severing Charm
Shield Charm
Shock Spells

Silencing Charm
Stealth Sensoring Spells
Stinging Hex
Stretching Jinxes
Stunning Charm
Substantive Charm
Summoning Charm
Switching Spells
Thief's Curse
Tickling Charm
Transfiguration
Trip Jinx
Unbreakable Charm
Unbreakable Vow
Unforgivable Curses
Unplottable
Vanishing Spell

Themes

Choice vs. destiny
Death
Love
Loyalty
Mercy

Transportation

Apparition
Disapparition
Floo Network
Floo Powder
Ford Anglia
Hogwarts Express
InterCity 125
King's Cross Station, London
Knight Bus
Portkey
Portkey Office
Splinching
Summoning Charm

Wizard World

Beauxbatons Academy of
    Magic
Camping, Wizard
Careers

Preface

In working with the Harry Potter series for teaching, writing projects, and moderating online discussions, I have often thought how useful it would be to have a straightforward A–Z reference book to the terms and topics of Harry's world, as well as to related subjects in the author's biography and the world outside the books. Though there are several good websites and readers' companions available, most are categorized into sections that make looking up a character's name, an incantation, or other subject at least a two-step process—the reader must first look in an index, then locate the topic. Many resources leave out the two "schoolbooks," companions to the novels that, though ancillary to some degree to the main storyline of the boy wizard, are still works of fiction (disguised as nonfiction) written by J. K. Rowling. In addition, most of the readers' guides are intended for fans of the series and as such do not include subjects that might be of interest to students, educators, scholars, or others—for example, subjects related to the author's life or the series' critical reception, or its influence on American popular culture at the turn of the millennium. The intent of this book, then, is to provide a quick, "one-stop" reference for the student, educator, scholar, and general reader.

The J. K. Rowling Encyclopedia contains approximately 2,000 alphabetically arranged entries covering three major topic areas—J. K. Rowling, the Harry Potter books, and the Harry Potter phenomenon in world culture. In addition to the thousands of entries, the book also contains a chart and explanation of book abbreviations and the citation system used throughout the reference; a chronology of Rowling's life and work; several appendices listing useful information about Hogwarts School of Witchcraft and Wizardry, The Ministry of Magic, Bertie Bott's Every Flavor Beans, books in the books, and addresses; as well as a selected bibliography and index.

The reader should know that J. K. Rowling has frequently stated that she may write an encyclopedia of the universe she created for Harry Potter, including backstory material that does not appear in the books, after the series is complete. She has said she may compile such a volume for charity. *The J. K. Rowling Encyclopedia* is by no means that book, nor is it a substitute or competitor for such a project, so it should not be regarded as such by readers. It does not attempt to speculate or inform the reader about any inside backstory information, nor does it pretend to compete with the author's encyclopedic knowledge of the original world she created out of her own imagination. Rather, this reference is designed to be a convenient tool for those interested in Harry's magical world, and who may also desire information about matters in our own world surrounding the books, their author, and the phenomenon they have created.

Most of all, I thank J. K. Rowling for reminding readers of what children know but adults often forget—that imagination is power. Thanks also go to my editor, George Butler, at Greenwood Press for his support of this project. Thanks to Barnes & Noble Booksellers and Element K for inviting me to facilitate several Harry Potter Online Reading Groups at the Barnes & Noble flagship website, www.bn.com. These discussions with thousands of readers of all ages from around the world at the release of *Harry Potter and the Half-Blood Prince* supported my belief in the need for an A–Z reference to the series, its author, and the Harry Potter cultural phenomenon, all combined. I also appreciate the insights of fellow writers and editors who have written about the series or otherwise considered the world of Harry Potter, and its place in ours, and with whom I have worked, consulted, or corresponded, over the years.

Most important, thanks to my family, to wizards John and Ben, in particular, for their love and for all that means as the loved one of a writer.

Connie Ann Kirk, Ph.D.
New York

Chronology

1965   Joanne Rowling born on July 31 to Peter James Rowling and Anne Volant Rowling at Cottage Hospital, 240 Station Road, Yate, England.

1967   Sister, Dianne Rowling, born at home in Yate, England.

1970   Begins primary school at St. Michael's Church of England School at High Street, Winterbourne.

1974   Moves to Church Cottage in Tutshill, near Chepstow; begins Tutshill Church of England Primary School.

1976   Begins Wyedean Comprehensive School in Sedbury, beginning the same seven-year period of secondary school the Harry Potter main characters will have at Hogwarts.

1979   Aunt Marian gives her *Hons and Rebels*, by Jessica Mitford; book makes a lasting impression.

1980   Mother diagnosed with multiple sclerosis.

1982   Becomes Head Girl at Wyedean Comprehensive.

1983   Graduates Wyedean Comprehensive; enters Exeter University, majoring in French and the classics; mother makes out her will before disease worsens.

1985   Goes to France for Exeter's Year in France program; teaches English for the first time.

1987   Graduates from Exeter.

1990   Imagines Harry Potter on long train delay and ride from Manchester to London; begins first notes at home. On December 30, mother dies at age forty-five of complications from MS.

1991   Begins teaching English in Oporto, Portugal; continues writing Harry Potter.

1992   Marries Jorge Alberto Rodrigues Arantes on October 16; in *Prisoner of Azkaban*, Prof. Trelawney predicts this as the date Lavender Brown dreads.

1993   Daughter, Jessica, born on July 27; leaves Arantes in December, taking Jessica and Harry Potter manuscript to Edinburgh, Scotland.

1994   Continues work on novel while living on public assistance for a few months and pursuing teaching certification that will allow her to teach French in Scotland.

1995   Completes *Philosopher's Stone*; sends manuscript to agent, Christopher Little, whose name she finds in a market guide.

1997   *Harry Potter and the Philosopher's Stone* published by Bloomsbury in a small print run of 500 copies; Arthur Levine of Scholastic Books bids unprecedented $105,000 for American rights to first novel by unknown children's author.

1998   *Harry Potter and the Chamber of Secrets* published by Bloomsbury. Book 1 published in the United States by Scholastic under the Americanized title, *Harry Potter and the Sorcerer's Stone*.

1999   *Chamber of Secrets* published by Scholastic in the United States; *Harry Potter and the Prisoner of Azkaban* published by Bloomsbury in the U.K. and Scholastic in the United States.

2000   *Harry Potter and the Goblet of Fire* synchronized release at midnight in Britain and the United States; extensive and active promotional campaign ("hype") in full gear.

2001   *Quidditch Through the Ages* and *Fantastic Beasts and Where to Find Them* published. Rowling receives Order of the British Empire (O.B.E.) for work in children's literature. Film, *Harry Potter and the Sorcerer's Stone* premieres in London; breaks ticket sale records for opening day and weekend in the United States. Rowling marries Dr. Neil Murray on Boxing Day, December 26.

2002   Film, *Harry Potter and the Chamber of Secrets* released in theaters.

2003   Son, David Gordon Rowling Murray born on March 23; *Harry Potter and the Order of the Phoenix* published.

2004   Film, *Harry Potter and the Prisoner of Azkaban* released in theaters.

2005   Daughter, Mackenzie Jean Rowling Murray, born on January 23. *Harry Potter and the Half-Blood Prince* published, July 16. Rowling turns 40 on July 31. Film, *Harry Potter and the Goblet of Fire*, released in theaters on November 18.

2006   Commences work on completing the series in Book 7.

Abbreviations
and Citations

Abbreviations

The novels and two schoolbooks from the Harry Potter series are abbreviated throughout *The J. K. Rowling Encyclopedia* according to the notations listed below.

Fantastic Beasts and Where to Find Them (schoolbook)	FB
Harry Potter and the Chamber of Secrets	CS, Book 2, or Year 2
Harry Potter and the Goblet of Fire	GF, Book 4, or Year 4
Harry Potter and the Half-Blood Prince	HBP, Book 6, or Year 6
Harry Potter and the Order of the Phoenix	OP, Book 5, or Year 5
Harry Potter and the Prisoner of Azkaban	PA, Book 3, or Year 3
Harry Potter and the Sorcerer's Stone	SS, Book 1, or Year 1
Quidditch Through the Ages (schoolbook)	QA

Other abbreviations commonly used in the Harry Potter books, or in this reference:

Defense Against the Dark Arts	DADA
Dumbledore's Army	DA
Ministry of Magic	MM
Nastily Exhausting Wizarding Tests (exams)	N.E.W.T.s
Ordinary Wizarding Levels (exams)	O.W.L.s
Quidditch World Cup	QWC
Society for the Promotion of Elfish Welfare	S.P.E.W.
Triwizard Tournament	TT

Citations

For the convenience of readers working with a multivolume series, page citations appear within entries for this reference. These citations follow a book, chapter, and page notation system. For example, a notation such as SS 12:194 signifies that the topic can be found in *Harry Potter and the Sorcerer's Stone*, Chapter 12, page 194. Citations from the schoolbooks use FB (*Fantastic Beasts and Where to Find Them*) or QA (*Quidditch Through the Ages*) as the book signifier with a page number only. Citations for sources of information from within the series directly follow sentences containing the information. Italicized *signifiers* next to many entry names provide quick indicators to the nature of the entries—whether they be characters, incantations, magical creatures, magical spells, and so forth. Cross-references and citations for further reading follow several entries. The Guide to Related Topics should be consulted for inclusive categories, such as Communication; Curses; Spells; and Transportation, which list several individual entries.

Though it is the editorial position of this author that the most authentic editions of the Harry Potter books are the British children's editions since the books were first published in this format in Rowling's mother country, the anticipated audience for this volume is primarily American. For that reason, the edition of the series used throughout this reference is the American Scholastic children's edition. Readers with other English editions as well as translations of Harry Potter should find the book titles and chapter numbers within citations helpful in locating sources.

✦ A ✦

Abbott, Hannah. *Character.* A student in Harry's year; she is sorted into Hufflepuff House (SS 7:119). Abbott has a pink face and blonde pigtails; she is friends with Ernie Macmillan. She stands up for Harry Potter, even when other Hufflepuffs do not (CS 11:199). Abbott becomes a member of Dumbledore's Army (DA). She is made girl prefect of Hufflepuff House in Year 5 (OP 10:188). Abbott is impressed at the first DADA meeting where Harry's accomplishments are discussed (OP 16:342). As O.W.L.s approach in fifth year, Hannah bursts into tears over anxiety for her Herbology exam and is the first student in the year given a Calming Draught from Madame Pomfrey (OP 27:606). In her Transfiguration practical O.W.L., Hannah gets very confused and transforms a ferret into an entire flock of flamingos. Her mistake necessitates the cessation of all exams until the birds can be caught and taken from the room (OP 31:714).

Hannah is one of the DA members who defends Harry against Malfoy, Crabbe, and Goyle during the ride home on the Hogwarts Express after Year 5. The DA's various jinxes and defenses transform the three bullies into oozing slugs that are put out of the way in the luggage rack for the remainder of the trip (OP 38:864).

See also Dumbledore's Army (DA); Hufflepuff House; Macmillan, Ernie

Abercrombie, Euan. *Character.* A Gryffindor House student, four years behind Harry. His physical traits include prominent ears and a terrified expression (OP 11:207).

Abominable Snowman. *Fantastic creature.* From *Fantastic Beasts*. According to *Fantastic Beasts*, this is another name for Yeti and Big Foot (FB 42).

See also Fantastic Beasts and Where to Find Them; Yeti

Abraxan horses. *Fantastic creature.* Giant, winged palomino horses that pull the Beauxbatons Academy of Magic carriage to Hogwarts for the Tri-Wizard Tournament. Those bred by Madame Maxime have red eyes, gigantic hooves, and drink only single-malt whiskey (GF 15:213; FB 42). Hagrid tells Dolores Umbridge that a friend of his breeds these and that he rode one. He tells her this in an attempt to divert her attention from Harry and his friends who are hiding at that moment in his hut (OP 20:437).

See also Fantastic Beasts and Where to Find Them; Winged horse

"Abstinence." *Magic word.* A password for the Gryffindor Common Room. The Fat Lady uses it after she overindulges in wine over the holidays inside the picture of the drunk monks. She drinks with her friend, Violet (HBP 17:331).

Abyssinian Shrivelfigs. *Magical plant.* Figs used in Shrinking Solutions; Prof. Sprout has the class pruning them in Year 2 (CS 15:268). Abyssinia is the old name for modern-day Ethiopia, where figs, a fruit with a shriveled appearance like raisins, are a diet staple.

See also Shrivelfig

Accidental Magic Reversal Squad/Department. *Magical office.* Located on the third level of the Ministry and part of the Department of Magical Accidents and Catastrophes (OP 7:130). These government employees reverse any magic or memories of magic in Muggles who may have been exposed to it by witches and wizards. On the orders of Minister, Cornelius Fudge, the squad goes out and deflates Aunt Marge and erases her memory after Harry blows her up (PA 3:44). They can also resolve instances of splinching during attempted Apparition (GF 6:67).

See also Ministry of Magic

"Accio." *Incantation.* Summoning charm that brings an object to the one who casts the spell. *Accio* is Latin for "to summon, send for, or fetch" (GF 24:18). "Accio" was also the name of a Harry Potter conference held at the University of Reading in the U.K. in July 2005.

See also Fan responses

Achievements in Charming. *Magical book.* Fifth-year textbook for Charms Class at Hogwarts. Hermione studies with Harry and keeps hitting him with this book when she nervously hands it back after checking that she got an answer fully correct (OP 31:709). She continues studying from it at breakfast before the O.W.L. in that subject (OP 31:711).

Acid Pops. *Magical candy.* A wizard candy that burns holes in the tongue. Sold at Honeydukes in Hogsmeade (PA 10:200). Dumbledore tells Harry that he likes them (HBP 9:181).

Ackerley, Stewart. *Character.* Student in Ravenclaw House who is three years behind Harry (GF 12:178).

Aconite. *Magical plant.* A plant used in potions that also goes by the names monkshood and wolfbane. Harry does not know this information when Snape questions him on it during his first Potions class (SS 8:138).

See also Monkshood; Wolfbane

Acromantula. *Fantastic creature.* Entry in *Fantastic Beasts.* Classified 5X by the MM. According to *Fantastic Beasts*, the creature originated in Borneo. It is a giant spider with eight eyes; hairy legs with a span of up to fifteen feet; and pincers. The creature may speak like a human being and it secretes poison. The first recording of a sighting was in 1794. Aragog in CS is an Acromantula. Harry Potter has "handwritten" in *Fantastic Beasts* that he and Ron Weasley confirmed that a colony of Acromantula exists in Scotland. This statement provides strong support that Hogwarts is located in Scotland. Harry, or more likely Ron, has added nine extra X's to the Ministry's danger ranking in their shared copy (FB 1–2). Unknown to Hagrid, Slughorn collects bottles of valuable and marketable Acromantula venom from Aragog before Hagrid buries him (HBP 22:484).

    See also Aragog; *Fantastic Beasts and Where to Find Them*; Mosag; Spiders

Actors in the films. *See* Films

Advanced Potion-Making. *Magical book.* By Libatius Borage. This is the textbook for Potions class, Year 6, and it becomes the most special of all of Harry's textbooks. At first, Harry does not have this book for class. He did not think he would be eligible for the N.E.W.T.-level class in Year 6 after achieving an "E"—Exceeds Expectations—score on his O.W.L. exam rather than an "O" for Outstanding. However, Harry is admitted to the class since Horace Slughorn, rather than Severus Snape, teaches it in Year 6. Prof. McGonagall informs Harry that Prof. Slughorn's eligibility requirements are different from Severus Snape's. Slughorn gets an old copy of the book out of the classroom cabinet for Harry to use, but the book turns out to have more in it than the printed text. It contains valuable handwritten notes in the margins about how to make the potions more effectively, more quickly, or stronger (HBP 9:183–84). The book was once used by the Half-Blood Prince, who turns out to be Snape himself, but it also apparently belonged to Snape's mother, Eileen Prince (HBP 9:193).

    See also Prince, Eileen; Snape, Prof. Severus

Advanced Rune Translation. *Magical book.* Textbook Hermione is reading in Year 6 (HBP 7:129).

The Adventures of Martin Migg, the Mad Muggle. *Magical book.* Ron Weasley's favorite comic book that is in his bedroom at the Burrow when Harry first visits. Given Mr. Weasley's fascination with the Muggle world, it is perhaps not surprising that the main character of Ron's favorite comic book is a Muggle (CS 3:40).

Aethonan horses. *Fantastic creature.* From *Fantastic Beasts*. They are a breed of winged horses that are chestnut-colored and raised mainly in Britain and Ireland (FB 42).

    See also Fantastic Beasts and Where to Find Them; Winged horse

Africa. The continent is mentioned in the series and schoolbooks several times, usually in relation to the distant and the exotic. Bill Weasley is working for Gringotts in Africa (SS 6:107). Prof. Quirrell is said to have acquired his turban from an African prince after Quirrell helped rid the prince of a zombie. Mr. and Mrs. Weasley visit their son, Bill, in Egypt over Christmas during Ron's and Harry's second year at Hogwarts (CS 12:211). The following summer, the entire family goes on vacation in Egypt, and their photograph appears in *The Daily Prophet*. Bill Weasley appears to enjoy working in Africa (PA 1:8–9). Hassan Mostafa of Egypt is Head of the International Association of Quidditch (GF 8:105–6). Some Quidditch referees end up in the Sahara Desert after matches are over (SS 11:181). In *Quidditch Through the Ages*, teams in Africa include the

Patonga Proudsticks of Uganda, the Tchamba Charmers from Togo, the Gimbi Giant-Slayers from Ethiopia (two-time winners of the All-Africa Cup), and the Sumbawanga Sunrays from Tanzania (QA 42–43).

Ron Weasley writes to Harry about the family's trip to Egypt. The pyramids have many curses on them, and Muggles who have broken in to them have not fared well (PA 1:9). At the Quidditch World Cup campground, Harry sees three African wizards in white robes talking seriously about something around a purple fire while roasting a rabbit (GF 7:82). Hermione speculates that perhaps Sirius Black is in hiding in Africa (GF 10:150).

When J. K. Rowling worked for Amnesty International in London after college, she handled files about human rights abuses in Francophone Africa. Francophone African countries include Chad, Congo, Guinea, Rwanda, and Senegal, among others. At the time of the novels' first publications at the turn of the millennium, countries in Africa suffered several problems—genocide in Uganda and Sudan; AIDS; and severe poverty and war. Rowling's efforts at fundraising for Comic Relief, U.K. through the publication of two of Harry's "schoolbooks" lent financial support to battling some of these problems.

According to her website, Rowling has visited Africa at least once, on a safari with her family when her son, David, was five months old. She apparently gained some appreciation for the practice of not speaking a name (à la Voldemort) from cultures she became aware of in Africa and elsewhere, where speaking the name of a person is considered tampering with his or her soul.

See also Amnesty International; Comic Relief, U.K.; Sphinx

Agapanthus. African lily. Albus Dumbledore comments on Vernon Dursley's successful agapanthus plants when he comes to take Harry away from Privet Drive in Year 6 (HBP 3:46). The flower has a circular cluster of blooms atop a straight narrow stem. That Petunia's sister was named Lily may or may not be a coincidence.

Age Line. *Magical object.* Dumbledore draws this gold, thin line on the floor in a ten-foot circle around the Goblet of Fire that sits on the Sorting Hat's tri-legged stool. The purpose of the line is to prevent students under age seventeen from entering their names in the Goblet as candidates for the Triwizard Tournament (GF 16:256, 259). George and Fred Weasley and Lee Jordan take an Aging Potion to try to outsmart the line, but when they attempt to cross it, they are thrown back and given white beards (GF 16:260). Dumbledore tells the students that others who attempted to cross the line are Ravenclaw student, Miss Fawcett, and Hufflepuff, Mr. Summers (GF 16:260).

Aging Potion. *Magical substance.* A potion with unknown ingredients that ages the witch or wizard taking it. The amount of aging varies depending on how much potion is taken. Fred and George Weasley use it in an attempt to cross the Age Line and enter their names in the Triwizard Tournament (GF 12:189; GF 16:260).

See also Age Line

Agnes. *Character.* A patient in St. Mungo's Hospital whose face is covered in fur and who barks like a dog. The nurse gives her some presents and tells her on Christmas that her son has written that he will be visiting her that evening (OP 23:512).

Agrippa. *Character.* A famous witch/wizard card that Ron is missing from his collection and wants to get. The cards come wrapped up with Chocolate Frogs (SS 6:102).

Aids for Magical Mischief Makers. *Magical objects.* The kinds of objects that Arthur Weasley warns Harry about after the diary incident with Ginny in Year 2. Harry at first fears that the Marauder's Map may be another one of them (PA 10:194).

Aingingein. *Magical game.* From QA. One of the fictional games in QA, it is an ancient Irish flying broomstick game. The game involved a Dom, or ball made out of the gallbladder of a goat (QA 4–5).

Albania. The European country is used in the series to represent a faraway and unknown place, useful for hiding. Voldemort hides in the forests of Albania after he kills Harry's parents. He hides there for eleven years, until Harry returns to Hogwarts in Year 2. Prof. Dumbledore's sources tell him Voldemort is still there (CS 18:328). Quirrell helps Voldemort escape from the forest for the first time; Wormtail helps him a second time. Bertha Jorkins' second cousin lives in Albania, and Dumbledore is not surprised when directionless Bertha never returns after going there for a vacation to visit family.

Albania is a small, mountainous country located in southeastern Europe on the Balkan peninsula. Scrub forests cover nearly one-third of the country, and its coastline meets the Adriatic Sea. Tirane is the capital and largest city. Part of the Ottoman Empire for over 400 years, Albania gained its independence in 1912 and was under Communist rule from 1944 until the early 1990s. The government is currently made up of a president, prime minister, and parliament, as well as several regional and local municipalities.

Compared to most European countries, the standard of living in Albania is low. It is one of the least developed countries on the continent. Most people are poor and make their living from farming or fishing. Though incomes are low, the Albanian government provides free health care, social services, and education. Most Albanians are Muslim (70 percent), while others belong to one of the Greek Orthodox churches.

The flag of Albania features a two-headed black eagle on a red background. The official language is *Shqiperia*, which means "The Land of the Eagle."

See also Riddle, Tom Marvolo; Voldemort, Lord

Albino bloodhounds. *Magical creatures.* From *Fantastic Beasts.* A dozen of these dogs are kept by the Pest Subdivision of the Department for the Regulation and Control of Magical Creatures to fend off Nogtails, which leave a location forever if they are chased off by white dogs (FB 31).

See also Fantastic Beasts and Where to Find Them

Alchemy. As a mythical blend of chemistry and the metaphysical, it is small wonder that alchemy plays a large role in Harry Potter's world. Classes at Hogwarts (such as Potions) teach the fine art, and Madam Pomfey, the Hogwarts nurse or "healer," appears to know its curative powers well. The concoctions devised by Rowling in her books entertain readers on a regular basis. Ian Potter, one of the author's childhood friends, claims that Rowling used to prepare concoctions with fascinating pretend ingredients during their backyard play in Winterbourne, England.

Alchemy has roots in ancient civilizations such as Egypt, Arabia, China, and India. The principle aims of alchemy seem to be either the transmutation of stone, metal, or other materials into gold or the development of an elixir to make one immortal. Early efforts at alchemy, though often crude by today's scientific standards, actually developed into our modern-day chemistry and pharmacology, which have supplied the world with valuable materials for every day use, as well as drugs that have saved lives. The most

Alchemist at work in the laboratory. Courtesy of the Library of Congress.

mystical side of alchemy is not concerned with wealth or immortality at all, but rather with discovering the key to understanding life, its meaning, and its purpose.

It is thought that the earliest practice of alchemy may have been the preservation of mummies for the afterlife in ancient Egypt. The Egyptian word *Khem* referred to the "fertile lands" near the Nile. Egyptians' experimentation with chemicals in the mummification process, combined with their belief in the afterlife, is one of history's first examples of mixing substances with the goal of immortality. By the time Alexander the Great conquered Egypt by 332 B.C., Greek philosophers were intrigued by Greek and Egyptian theories of matter being made up of the four elements of Fire, Earth, Air, and Water. They used the word *Khemia* as the word for "Egypt" in Greek. In the seventh century, Arabs took over Egypt and added "al" to the word, translating it to *al-Khemia,* meaning "the Black Land." The Greek word *khumos,* meaning "fluid," may be another root of the present-day word "alchemy." One of the theories of Arabian alchemy was that all metals are made up of sulfur and mercury, and that gold is the most perfect metal of all.

In China, alchemy was studied independently by the Taoist monks who sought the means to make an "outer elixir" and an "inner elixir." The outer elixir would consist of minerals, plants, and other materials used to prolong life. The inner elixir was a form of exercise, such as Qigong, that worked on the life force of the body, called chi. The goal of the inner elixir was to achieve the highest level of purity; the goal of the outer elixir was to achieve longevity to the point that one became immortal.

India also developed alchemy independently. Like the Chinese, Indians worked to develop means to cleanse and purify the body inside and outside and to extend life. One of the Indian contributions to science was the observation that different color flames indicate the presence of different metals. From their work in heating metals, they are also credited with inventing steel long before later Western scientists.

The Arabs brought alchemy to Spain in the eighth century, where it flourished in Western culture. European alchemists worked to change lower metals into the more perfect gold using a material called the Philosopher's Stone. In China, the stone was called the Pill of Immortality. Practices in alchemy eventually led to work in other mixtures and reactions as well as to the development of various devices for making and combining ingredients. By the sixteenth century, practitioners of alchemy had split into two distinct factions—those who followed the scientific method to study elements, compounds, and reactions in what would later become modern-day chemistry, and those who followed a more mystical and metaphysical path that continued to try to turn metal into gold or find the elixir of life (these practices are still referred to as alchemy in the modern world).

Prominent alchemists in history include Zosimus (ca. A.D. 250) who was a Greek born in Egypt. His contribution included the idea that all substances are made up of the four elements of nature—Fire, Water, Air, and Earth. He gathered the knowledge of the time into a twenty-eight-volume encyclopedia on the subject. An Arabian alchemist known as Geber (ca. A.D. 721–815) lived in present-day Iraq. He distilled acetic acid from vinegar and also popularized the idea that all metals contained mercury and sulphur in varying proportions. It was Geber who popularized the notion that a Philosopher's Stone could change lower metals into gold. Geber's full name was Abu Musa Jabir Ibn Hayyan. It is believed that Geber/Jabir was the precursor for the modern-day word "gibberish."

Albert the Great, or Albertus Magnus (ca. A.D. 1200–1280) was a German monk working in alchemy in the Middle Ages. He studied Aristotle and brought the Greek thinker's ideas to the forefront. His student, Thomas Aquinas, also became a monk and alchemist. Paracelsus (whose name means "better than Celsus," a Roman scholar of medicine) was born in Switzerland. His work moved alchemy away from turning metal into gold and into creating compounds that would heal the sick. It was claimed that the French alchemist, Nicolas Flamel, who lived in fourteenth-century Paris, found the Philosopher's Stone that turned metal into gold and also concocted an elixir of life. Legend tells that Flamel left behind books and carvings on his many residences that supposedly give clues to his discoveries. Flamel's legend has never been fully proven. Some scholars say that Flamel made up these fantastic legends to hide the source of his immense wealth, which may have come from lending money with high interest. He appears to have been a philanthropist in France. Flamel's legend remains factually unclear, but its intrigue lives on.

In the Harry Potter series, alchemy is perhaps most prominent in Year 1, when Harry and his cohorts attempt to keep the villain Voldemort from acquiring the Philosopher's Stone (referred to as the Sorcerer's Stone in the novel in the United States, where children are less familiar with alchemy). In the series, Nicolas Flamel is an old friend of Albus Dumbledore's who uses alchemy and the Philosopher's Stone to discover a substance that causes everlasting life. Having used the substance, Flamel and his wife, Perenelle, have lived over 600 years. However, according to Dumbledore, Flamel was never afraid of death, nor did he use the substance because he was greedy for life; rather, Flamel had a higher goal of discovery for its own sake.

See also Chemistry; Flamel, Nicolas; Flamel, Perenelle

Further Reading: Hauck, Dennis William. *Sorcerer's Stone: A Beginner's Guide to Alchemy.* New York: Citadel Press, 2004.

Alecto. *Character.* A female Death Eater who appears at the battle on the Astronomy Tower. Her brother is Amycus (HBP 27:593). As the battle moves downstairs, Prof. McGonagall fights her off (HBP 28:599). In mythology, Alecto is one of the Furies whose head is covered with snakes.

See also Amycus

Algie, Great Uncle. *Character.* Neville Longbottom's great uncle who tries to see whether the boy has magical abilities by putting him through a variety of dangerous tests, including nearly drowning him and dangling him by his ankles out of a window (SS 7:125). Despite his misguided efforts, Algie is a thoughtful relative; he purchased a toad (Trevor) for Neville when he started at Hogwarts. He also gives him the *Mimbulus mimbletonia* plant for his fifteenth birthday (OP 10:186).

See also Longbottom, Neville; Trevor

All-England Best-Kept Suburban Lawn Competition. *Fake contest.* Tonks devises this ruse to get the Dursleys out of the house when the Order wants to pick up Harry at Privet Drive, Year 5. The proud Dursleys think that they have won the prize and thus leave the house quickly (OP 3:48).

All-Knowing. *Magical ability.* Prof. Trelawney tells the unamused Prof. McGonagall that she sometimes pretends not to be all-knowing so that others will not be offended (PA 11:229).

"Alohomora." *Incantation.* A spell to unlock and open doors (SS 9:160).

Americanization of the Novels. When Book 1 was first published in the United States in 1998, Arthur A. Levine (Rowling's American editor at the Arthur A. Levine Books imprint of Scholastic Books) and Rowling changed selected vocabulary from the original British version of the novel into words American children were expected to understand better. For example, the title of the first book is *Harry Potter and the Philosopher's Stone* in Britain, while it appears as *Harry Potter and the Sorcerer's Stone* in the United States. The most frequently used example of a British word that was thought to need clarification in American English is the word "jumper," which means the same thing as the American English word "sweater." A jumper in the United States is a girl's dress that is worn over a blouse. Mrs. Weasley makes jumpers/sweaters for her children— and eventually for Harry—as Christmas gifts each year.

The American "translation" has been criticized by teachers, literary critics, and others. Many educators and literature experts believe American children were denied the opportunity to work out meanings of words for themselves, as well as the chance to enjoy the British flavor in Rowling's original language, thus broadening their understanding of language in general. Perhaps in response to this criticism, the number of such changes from British to American English diminished as the series developed, though the changes did not disappear altogether.

See also Levine, Arthur A.; Translations

Further Reading: Nel, Philip. "You Say 'Jelly,' I Say 'Jell-O'? Harry Potter and the Transfiguration of Language." In Lana A. Whited, ed., *The Ivory Tower and Harry Potter: Perspectives on a Literary Phenomenon*. Columbia: University of Missouri Press, 2002; Vander Ark, Steve, ed., "Differences Between U.K. and U.S. Versions." *The Harry Potter Lexicon*, http://www.i2k.com/~svderark/lexicon/help.html#Language.

Americans. Although the Harry Potter series is set in contemporary England and Scotland, J. K. Rowling has kept the twentieth- to twenty-first-century dominance of the United States on the world stage at a minimum in the series. There are no major or minor American characters, neither Muggle nor magical, though there are a few small references to Americans in the novels and the schoolbooks. In Books 1 through 6, only two references to Americans occurs. One reference appears in *Chamber of Secrets*, when Vernon Dursley asks his boss Mr. Mason to tell Petunia Dursley the funny story about the American plumbers (CS 2:19). There is also one reference in *Goblet of Fire*, at the campground outside the World Cup, where several middle-aged witches camp underneath a star-spangled banner stating that they are from the Salem Witches' Institute (GF 7:82). In *Quidditch Through the Ages*, American Quidditch is mentioned as competing in popularity with the more prevalent sport of Quodpot in North America. American Quidditch teams include the Sweetwater All-Stars from Texas and the Fitchburg Finches from Massachusetts (QA 44–45).

The decision to keep the only superpower in the world at bay within the series may have been deliberate. Rowling insisted on all British actors, no Americans, for the film adaptations of the novels. This is the case even though the films are made and distributed by Warner Bros., an American entertainment company. Despite the enormous success of the books in the United States, Rowling was quoted in a *New York Times* article in July 2000, describing herself as "a very British person." She said in that interview that readers should not expect any American exchange students to suddenly pop up at Hogwarts (CS 1:20; QA 44–45).

Further Reading: Cowell, Alan. "All Aboard the Potter Express." *New York Times*, July 10, 2000.

Amnesty International. J. K. Rowling worked in London for this human rights organization as a research assistant soon after college in the late 1980s. The London office is Amnesty International's research headquarters, where it employs about 300 staff members and 100 volunteers from over 55 countries around the world. Members of the organization who provide financial and other assistance number over 1.8 million in over 150 countries. The organization researches cases of human rights abuses that have been brought to its attention or that it has investigated on its own. The staff includes experts in the areas of law, medicine, media, and technology who apply their skills to work on behalf of human justice. The organization is self-governing and democratic, and it is independent from any one government or religion. Major decisions are made by an International Council made up of representatives from all national areas. Its emblem is a lighted candle encircled with barbed wire.

When J. K. Rowling was employed there in the late 1980s and early 1990s, she worked in an office researching Francophone Africa. She also began her habit of writing in cafés during lunch hours, though she was not yet working on the Harry Potter books. She maintains a link to the organization on her website. The human rights organization's influence on Rowling appears in the novels in the form of Hermione Granger's S.P.E.W. organization, which Hermione founds as a student advocating for the rights of house-elves.

See also Africa; Granger, Hermione; S.P.E.W.

Further Reading: Amnesty International (U.K.) Website: http://www.amnesty.org.

Amortentia. *Magical potion.* According to Hermione, this is the world's most powerful love potion. It has a pearl glimmer and spirals steam. It smells differently to each person, depending on his or her favorite scents. Hermione's favorite scents, as she says in class, include parchment and fresh-mowed grass (HBP 9:185).

Amycus. *Character.* A Death Eater who appears at the Astronomy Tower battle with his sister, Alecto (HBP 27:593). He attacks Ginny Weasley, who manages to evade his Crucio curses. Harry hits him with an Impediment Jinx (HBP 28:599).

In Greek mythology, Amycus is the son of Poseidon. He is a well-known fighter who either kills travelers or throws them into the sea if they choose not to fight.

See also Death Eater

"Anapneo." *Incantation*. Clears the throat. Slughorn casts it on Marcus Belby (HBP 7:144).

Ancient Runes. *Class at Hogwarts*. The ancient runes were Teutonic and Norse alphabets and symbols that were said to have magical and mystical properties. "Rune" comes from Indo-European *ru*, or Norse *runa*, meaning "secret" or "mystery." In Year 2, Easter holidays, Neville Longbottom wonders whether the Ancient Runes class at Hogwarts would be easier or harder than Arithmancy (CS 14:252). Hermione gets upset after an O.W.L. in the subject when she mistranslates *ehwaz*, which means "partnership," as *eihwaz*, which means "defense" (OP 31:715). Ancient Runes is one of the classes that Hermione decides to take but Harry and Ron do not.

Runes originated with early Germanic tribes, but the Scandinavians were the people who made the practice their own. Since the Vikings were seafarers and adventurers, they took their writing system with them and left runes in faraway places, like Greenland. Some runes were practical, labeling the ownership of objects, for example, while others were poetic, telling tales of wars and adventures.

The runic alphabet is called Futhark, and that word is based on the beginning sounds of the alphabet, much the same as the word "alphabet" utilizes the first two letters of the Greek system, alpha and beta. The beginning rune sounds are: "f," "u," "th," "a," "r," and "k." The sounds not only refer to a letter in the rune alphabet but they also frequently bear a connection to Norse mythology. The origin of the runes may be the Etruscan alphabet in Northern Italy, Latin, or early German. Another explanation from the Vikings, however, tells the story of Odin, the chief Norse god, who received the alphabet while hanging from a tree. He had speared himself there in order to learn knowledge about the occult and stayed there for nine windy days and nights, during

Pre-Viking rune stone, the oldest representation of the twenty-four-rune alphabet in Sweden. © Werner Forman/Art Resource, NY.

which he received the runes. Odin passed on the mystery of the runes to the people, and this is why the runes took on their mystical properties.

The literate among the Vikings tended to be the more well-to-do citizens. Many people could write and read runes, but if the divination or sorcery powers of the runes were desired, a specialist in using the runes for this purpose was found. This person was called the Runes Master. The Master would carve runes on an object like a whale bone, for example, and hang it over the bed of a person who was ill in an effort to make the person well. The mystical quality of runes was also frequently used to predict the future. A Runes Master would carve runes on pieces of bark and throw the bark on the ground, choosing three pieces at random from which to read a fortune. Another might carve runes on small stones put into a bag, then fling the stones on a table and read only the runes that turned face up. Soldiers believed runes gave them power in battle and often had their swords or shields engraved with them, sometimes with the name of the Norse god of war, Tyr.

Large rune stones were erected at the graves of loved ones to memorialize the dead. The tall rocks and boulders served another purpose as well, as a kind of last will and testament. The rock would be inscribed with the name of the person who lay in the grave, what land he owned, and who of the dead person's relatives now owned that same measurement and location of land. Few rune stones existed on graves for women, though one that was found tells of the deceased building a bridge to honor her daughter and being very handy throughout her lifetime. Occasionally, rune stones celebrated the accomplishments of people who were still alive at the time, such as the stones that tell about the building of the Jarlabanki causeway in Sweden in the eleventh century.

When Christianity made its way North, runes began to mix with Christian symbols on coffins, memorials, and tombstones in Scandinavia. By the seventeenth century, however, the church banned the use of runes for these purposes in its effort to break the faithful away from what were thought to be pagan practices. Traces of interest in runes have remained throughout history, including among those interested in history, languages and alphabets, the occult, magic, and superstitions. A wide variety of people, from the Nazis in the twentieth century to modern-day New Age followers, have studied the ancient runes. In the twenty-first century, the popularity of the Harry Potter series has brought about another wave of interest in the history and lore of this ancient alphabet.

Further Reading: Pennick, Nigel. *The Complete Illustrated Guide to Runes.* Boston: Element Books, 1999.

Ancient Runes Made Easy. *Magical book.* Third-year textbook for Ancient Runes class at Hogwarts (CS 14:254). Hermione is already reading it in Year 2, once she decides to take all available classes at Hogwarts for her schedule the following year (CS 14:254).

Andorran Ministry of Magic. *Magical office.* Barty Crouch, Sr., moans about hearing from this group when he becomes delusional after being attacked in the woods (GF 28:556). Andorra is a small principality between France and Spain.

Anglesea to Aberdeen. *Muggle places.* The Knight Bus travels to these two places, among others, while Harry rides it. Passengers disembark when they reach their destinations (PA 3:41).

Animagi Registry. *Magical object.* The log of witches and wizards who are Animagi, and their respective animal forms. There are only seven registered Animagi in the twentieth century, but James Potter and his two friends learned how to become Animagi and remain unregistered. Rita Skeeter is an unregistered Animagus who transforms into a beetle (GF 37:727).

Animagi Transfiguration Spell. *Magical spell.* This is the spell that transforms an Animagus into its animal form, or the reverse. The spell causes blue-white light to emit from a wand.

Animagus. *Magical being.* Rowling invented this word by attaching the Latin word for wizard, *magus*, to the English word for animal. The plural form is "Animagi." In the series, an Animagus is a wizard who possesses the power to transform into an animal. Prof. McGonagall is an Animagus who transforms into a cat. Sirius Black can be a black dog, as his constellation name suggests. Harry's father, James Potter, could be a stag, hence his nickname Prongs; Peter Pettigrew turns into Ron's rat, Scabbers. Hermione Granger discovers that Rita Skeeter is an "unregistered" Animagus who can become a beetle (GF 37:727).

The ability of wizards to turn into animals of their choice is common in the world of legends. Rowling, however, has put limits on her wizards and witches. Not all of them have the power to turn into animals, and those who do transform into only one kind of animal. Character traits of the Animagus are reflected in the animal into which he or she transforms (PA 6:108). There are only seven registered Animagi in the twentieth century (PA 17:352).

Animals. The books are filled with animals of all kinds, showing a close connection between the magical world and the natural world. Almost every major character in the series has a pet. Harry has Hedwig the snowy owl; Hermione has Crookshanks the cat; Ron first has Scabbers the rat (who turns out to be Peter Pettigrew in Animagus form), then Pigwidgeon the owl. Neville Longbottom has Trevor the toad; Hagrid has Fang the boarhound.

The most common animals in the series include cats and dogs, but others from the forest also appear. Most animals have magical powers. Harry is frightened by a black dog he sees in the street shadows near Privet Drive in PA. He later learns it may have been a "grim," which is a mysterious dog-shaped creature that foreshadows death. The dog turns out to be Sirius Black in Animagus form. Hagrid's boarhound, Fang, which is a dog like a Great Dane, often greets Harry and his friends when they visit Hagrid at his hut. "Muggle" dogs also appear to exist in Harry's world, such as Aunt Marge Dursley's dogs. Aunt Marge breeds bulldogs, including Ripper, the nasty one she brings with her to Privet Drive (PA 2:25).

Cats are everywhere in the series, as one might expect in books about witches and wizards. Hermione Granger buys a large, orange-colored cat named Crookshanks in Diagon Alley instead of the owl she set out to buy. Mrs. Figg, the Squib who watches out for Harry when he is living at Privet Drive, has several cats. Prof. McGonagall turns into a cat in Animagus form. Rowling has said that she is not particularly fond of cats herself. She is allergic to them and prefers dogs.

The series contains woodland wildlife as well, including the stag Harry sees approaching him out of the mist near the lake in *Prisoner of Azkaban*, reminiscent of the fawn's watchful father in *Bambi*. Lavender Brown laments the loss of Binky, her rabbit back at home. She was told that Binky died on October 16, thus proving Prof. Trelawney's divination. Hogwarts House symbols include two animals, the lion for Gryffindor, and the badger for Hufflepuff.

As in Kenneth Grahame's *The Wind in the Willows* (which Rowling says her father read to her as a child), the author maintains the basic attributes of the animals in the stories even as she endows them with magical or mystical powers. J. K. Rowling had pets as a child, including dogs and guinea pigs. She has often stated that she and her sister longed to have a rabbit when they were younger. She has also acknowledged that her own favorite animal is an otter, and that is why the otter becomes Hermione's Patronus.

The animals in the series provide an important connection between the natural world and the magical world that human witches and wizards cannot. The first strange incident that the reader, along with Vernon Dursley, sees in the Muggle world of Book 1 is a cat reading a map. Somehow, this impossibility comes across as believable to most readers right from the start, perhaps because so many aspects of the natural world remain unknown to human beings.

See also Animagus; Cats

Annual broom race. *Magical game.* A fictional game discussed in QA. Played in Sweden, this was an international ancient broom game where racers flew from Kopparberg to Arjeplog, about 300 miles, through dragon territory. The winner received a silver trophy of a Swedish Short-Snout (QA 4).

See also Sweden; Swedish Short-Snout

An Anthology of Eighteenth Century Charms. *Magical book.* Harry and his friends consult this book to prepare Harry for the second task of the Triwizard Tourament, but they find nothing useful in the book (GF 26:488).

Anti-Burglar Buzzer. *Magical object.* A special built-in feature on a Bluebottle Broomstick that warns against stealing. The Bluebottle is a family-style broomstick, not intended for Quidditch (GF 8:96).

Anti-Cheating Charms. *Magical spells.* Prof. McGonagall notifies students that the O.W.L. examination papers have been given these charms to protect against dishonesty (OP 31:708).

Anti-Cheating Spell. *Magical spell.* Placed on quills during Hogwarts students' final exams (SS 16:262).

Anti–Dark Force Spell. *Magical spell.* A spell cast as protection against the Dark Arts (SS 15:246).

Anti-Disapparition Jinx. *Magical spell.* Keeps a wizard from Disapparating; it is placed on the Death Eaters after the battle in the Hall of Prophecy (OP 36:817).

Anti-Intruder jinxes. *Magical spells.* Tonks tells Harry that Dumbledore put many of these on the gates and doors to Hogwarts over the summer between Years 5 and 6 (HBP 8:159).

Anti-Jinx Varnish. *Magical substance.* The Cleansweep broom that Ron desires after he becomes prefect has a Spanish oak handle stained with Anti-Jinx Varnish that repels unwanted spells (OP 9:173).

Anti-Muggle pranksters. *Characters.* Mischievous wizards and witches who raise havoc on Muggles and their devices. One example of their handiwork is regurgitating toilets that Mr. Weasley must investigate (OP 7:133).

Anti-Umbridge League. *Possible name.* Angelina Johnson suggests this name for the group that will eventually be called Dumbledore's Army (OP 18:391).

Antidotes. *Magical substances.* These are potions made up of various ingredients that reverse the effect of another potion, poison, or other condition. Antidotes often contain mandrakes. The students at Hogwarts learn various antidotes from Prof. Snape in Potions class. They see antidotes applied to reverse many of their own problems, as well as those of their classmates. The Deflating Draught, for example, is the antidote for the Swelling Potion (CS 11:187). Petrification has an antidote in the Mandrake Restorative Draught (CS 9:144). When Mrs. Weasley and the children de-Doxify the draperies at Number Twelve, Grummauld Place at the beginning of *Order of the Phoenix*, Mrs. Weasley has an antidote on hand for Doxy bites. Bezoar provides an antidote to many poisons. Prof. Snape has an antidote on hand to restore Trevor, Neville Longbottom's toad, after he is turned into a tadpole. Dobby finds an antidote for Butterbeer when he brings drunk Winky to the Room of Requirement.

Interestingly, remedies to students' problems almost always appear to be antidotes rather than practices or skills. In the magical world Rowling has created, many of life's nuisances and ailments are cured quickly with magical substances rather than a change of behavior. Some antidotes do take time to make and to take effect.

See also Potions

Antipodian Opaleye. *Magical creature.* From *Fantastic Beasts*. A breed of dragon. Native to New Zealand and Australia, this dragon is of medium size, eats sheep for food, and has pearlized, iridescent scales. It lives in valleys. Its flame is red, and its eyes are multicolored and glittering, with no pupils. Its eggs are pale gray in color and are sometimes mistaken by Muggles for fossils (FB 11).

See also Fantastic Beasts and Where to Find Them

Antiwerewolf legislation. *Magical law.* This is a law drawn up by Dolores Umbridge that makes it difficult for werewolves to find employment. Since Prof. Lupin is a sympathetic character in the novels, this legislation only fuels most readers' dislike of Umbridge (OP 14:302).

"Aparecium." *Incantation. Apareo* is Latin for "appear." A spell that makes invisible ink visible. Hermione's efforts to try the spell on Tom Riddle's diary do not work (CS 13:233).

Apothecary Shop. *Magical place.* A shop on Diagon Alley where Hogwarts students purchase some of the ingredients for their potions. Outside this shop, Harry hears a woman complaining about the cost of dragon liver (SS 5:56). Mrs. Weasley takes her children, Harry, and Hermione there before Year 6, though Harry and Ron do not buy any ingredients because they do not think they are taking Potions that year. It turns out that Harry does indeed take the class (HBP 6:115).

Apparition (aka "Apparation"). *Magical skill.* One of the more sophisticated wizardry skills. Apparition is the ability to disappear ("Disapparate") and reappear ("Apparate") instantly in another location as a form of transportation. If it is not done right, half of one's body can be left behind, a problem known as splinching (GF 6:67). Those who can do it must have a license from the Department of Magical Transportation to practice the skill. Wizards seventeen years of age and older may be licensed. In Year 2 Mr. and Mrs. Weasley take the Ford Anglia to catch the Hogwarts Express with all the children because none of the children are of age to Apparate, though Mr. and Mrs. Weasley can (CS 5:69).

Harry Apparates with Dumbledore from Privet Drive to Budleigh Babberton. The experience makes him feel squished and forced from one dimension to another (HBP 4:58). Wylkie Twycross teaches Harry's class that in order to perform the maneuver, one needs to concentrate on the three Ds: destination, determination, and deliberation (HBP 18:384).

Apparition is not practical in traveling long distances, such as traversing oceans. A broomstick, for example, was used to cross the Atlantic for the first time in 1935. Wizards with great skill are the only ones who should attempt to cross a continent by Apparition (QA 48). A sign advertising lessons for eligible students is posted at Hogwarts when students return from their holiday break in Year 6. Eligibility pertains to age—a student must either be seventeen or must turn seventeen by August 31 to take lessons. The cost is 12 Galleons (HBP 17:354). Ron practices and does not do too well, but he has a successful day in Hogsmeade before the test, going a bit past Madam Puddifoot's Tea Shop to Scrivenshaft's (HBP 21:466). When he takes his test, he fails because he leaves behind half an eyebrow (HBP 22:476). Hermione passes on the first try, of course (HBP 22:475).

Apparition Test Center. *Magical office.* Part of the Department of Magical Transportation, the center issues Apparition licenses for wizards and witches who are of age and have passed the test. It also issues fines to those who Apparate and Disapparate without a license. The test for Harry's year was held on April 21 (HBP 21:448). The center is located on the sixth floor of the Ministry (OP 7:129).

Appleby Arrows. *Magical sports team.* From QA. Professional Quidditch team from Appleby, England, located near the East Coast, southeast of York. The team was founded in 1612 and wears pale blue robes with a silver arrow on the chest. Their fans' practice of firing arrows into the air with their wands during matches was banned in 1894. Close rivals of the Winterbourne Wasps, notable Arrows wins include a defeat of the then-champions Vrasta Vultures in a sixteen-day upset match in 1932 (QA 32). Their match against the Banchory Bangers in 1814 resulted in bad behavior on the part of the Bangers, who eventually disbanded (QA 16–17). The Wasps got their name when they won a game against the Arrows after hitting a bee's nest into the Arrows' Seeker (QA 38).

See also Quidditch Through the Ages

An Appraisal of Magical Education in Europe. *Magical book.* Hermione has read this book, which helps her determine that the people speaking French at the World Cup are probably from Beauxbatons Academy (GF 9:123). She refers to the book in explaining Beauxbatons and Durmstrang to Harry (GF 11:166).

April Fool's Day. Mad-Eye Moody tells Seamus Finnigan about the treatment he gave to a witch who tricked him on this day. His story gives the students more evidence of his paranoid nature (GF 15:233). Rowling has said in interviews that April Fool's Day is Fred and George Weasley's birthday.

Aqua-Lungs. *Muggle objects.* Objects that help people breathe underwater. Ron thinks Harry should cast a Summoning Charm during the second task of the Triwizard Tournament to get Aqua-Lungs from a Muggle to use in the task (GF 26:481).

Aquamenti Charm. *Magical spell.* A spell assigned for practice by Prof. Flitwick in the sixth year (HBP 11:218). The spell brings water or fills a vessel with water. Harry uses it when Dumbledore asks for water in the cave (HBP 26:574).

Aquavirius maggots. *Magical creatures.* Luna Lovegood mentions that her father has told her that the Ministry of Magic is breeding these. She thinks that is what the DA sees in the glass tank in the Department of Mysteries, but Hermione tells her they are brains (OP 34:772).

Aragog. *Magical creature.* Hagrid's Acromantula, an elephant-sized pet spider that lives in the Forbidden Forest. *Aranea* is Latin for "spider"; Gog is a giant from legend. With his mate, Mosag, Aragog has parented thousands of smaller spiders. As time has passed, Aragog has taken on an older appearance with milky-white, blind eyes and gray streaks across his body. As Harry and his friends find out in *Chamber of Secrets*, Aragog and Mosag once regarded humans entering the forest as food for themselves and their offspring. Hagrid has taken care of Aragog for many years. Rowling regards spiders as one of her greatest fears, or her own personal "Boggart." Aragog appears in the vision Tom Riddle shows Harry. In the vision, Aragog crawls over Tom while a large boy (Hagrid) cries for Riddle not to cast a curse on him. The vision leads Harry to believe that Hagrid opened the Chamber of Secrets (CS 13:247).

Aragog calls his own name when Harry and Ron find him in the Forbidden Forest. He also explains his history with Hagrid. Young Hagrid was given the spider as an egg and hatched him and cared for him. Hagrid sent Aragog to live in the Forbidden Forest when he was blamed for killing a female student (Moaning Myrtle) fifty years ago—a crime Aragog did not commit. Hagrid found Aragog a wife, Mosag, and they had many offspring. Out of respect, Aragog has never hurt the giant or any other human being, but he is not afraid of letting his children feed on Harry and Ron now that they have wandered into the forest. Mr. Weasley's enchanted Ford Anglia rescues the boys in time. Aragog provides another clue about the Chamber of Secrets by telling the boys that the beast living in it is the one thing all spiders fear above anything else (CS 15:277–79).

In Year 6, Hagrid thinks that Aragog is on his last legs (HBP 11:230). When the spider dies, Hagrid sends a letter to Harry and friends asking them to come to his burial (HBP 22:470). Harry takes a bit of Luck Potion and goes to the ceremony, where he hopes Prof. Slughorn will give him the memory that Dumbledore has asked him to obtain (HBP 22:484). Hagrid and Slughorn get tipsy drinking toasts to the dead spider. Hagrid says that Aragog was about the size of a Pekingese when he hatched from the egg (HBP 22:486). Slughorn sneaks some of Aragog's valuable venom into vials before the spider is buried (HBP 22:484).

See also Acromantula; Mosag

Arantes, Jorge. J. K. Rowling's first husband. Arantes worked as a Portuguese television journalist. Rowling met and married him in Oporto, Portugal, where she had gone to teach English. Her wedding day, Friday, October 16, 1992, corresponds exactly with the date Prof. Trelawney warns Lavender Brown about in Divination class. Trelawney tells Lavender that this is the date she has been dreading. Arantes and Rowling had one child together—a daughter, Jessica—named after Jessica Mitford, an author Rowling admires. Rowling's relationship with Arantes was tumultuous and ended soon after Jessica was born. Rowling moved to Edinburgh, Scotland, to be near her sister Di. Arantes sold a story in which he claimed that he had influenced the writing of the Harry Potter books, which J. K. Rowling later denied. The author officially divorced Arantes and retained custody of their daughter. On her website, Rowling denies claims made by some journalists that she patterned the character Gilderoy Lockhart after Arantes.

Arbroath. *See* Scotland

Archie. *Character.* An eccentric old wizard who camps at the Triwizard Tournament. He walks around wearing a flowered nightgown because he says he likes the feel of the breeze around his private parts (GF 7:84).

Argyllshire, Map of. *Magical object.* The place on the wall at Hogwarts where the Fat Lady is found hiding after she is attacked (PA 9:165). Argyllshire may have given argyle socks their name.

Arithmancy. *Class at Hogwarts.* Coming from the Greek *arithmo*, meaning "number," and *mancy*, meaning "prophecy," arithmancy is the ancient art of attributing magical meanings and predictions to numbers and names. Arithmancy is the precursor to numerology. Unlike Prof. Trelawney's dubious Divination class at Hogwarts, where students frequently roll their eyes with cynicism as they are asked to analyze tea leaves and images in crystal balls, arithmancy assigns solid meanings to numbers. Meanings are especially attributed to digits 1 to 9, but also to special numbers like 12. Arithmancy looks for appearances of numbers in what others may see as coincidental places and times. In addition, letters are assigned numerical values, and character traits and futures are said to be divined from the numerical value of a name.

Ron thinks it odd that Hermione is taking Arithmancy, which meets at the same time as Divination and Muggle Studies. She resolves the time conflict with Prof. McGonagall, but the reader does not learn how until later in Year 3 (PA 6:98). Hermione prefers her Arithmancy class to Divination, perhaps because arithmancy involves calculation rather than observational skills. She ultimately drops the Divination class. At Hogwarts, the Arithmancy teacher is Prof. Vector. In mathematics, a vector is a quantity that must be expressed in both amount and direction. In Year 2, during the Easter holidays, Neville Longbottom wonders whether Arithmancy would be easier or harder than Ancient Runes (CS 14:252). Hermione claims that Arithmancy is the most difficult course at Hogwarts (OP 31:716).

See also Hogwarts School of Witchcraft and Wizardry

Arjeplog. From QA. The ending place (finish line) in Sweden where the Ancient broom race concluded (QA 4).

See also Quidditch Through the Ages; Sweden

Armadillo bile. *Magical substance.* Substance from the armadillo used in making potions (GF 27:518–19).

Armenian Warlock. *Character.* The real person who saved the village from werewolves. The werewolf encounter is described in Lockhart's book, where Lockhart claims that he saved the village (CS 16:297).

Armor-bewitching charm. *Charm.* As in any good castle, Hogwarts contains several standing suits of armor. The armor-bewitching charm causes armor to sing Christmas carols, whether it knows the words or not. When the singing suits are included as part of the decorations for the Yule Ball in *Goblet of Fire*, Peeves sneaks into them and fills the unknown lyrics with rude replacements (GF 22:395).

Armor Gallery. *Magical place.* This is a room at Hogwarts with a display of standing suits of armor. It is located adjacent to the Trophy Room (SS 9:158). The suits of armor creak as students walk past them, suggesting that they are bewitched in some way.

Arnold. *Magical creature.* Ginny Weasley's purple miniature Pygmy Puff (HBP 7:132).
  See also Pygmy Puffs

Arrow spell. *Spell.* From QA. The Appleby Arrows professional Quidditch team used to cast this spell during matches. The spell makes silver light shaped like arrows shoot into the air from their wands. The practice was banned in 1894 (QA 32).
  See also Appleby Arrows

Ashwinder. *Magical creature.* From *Fantastic Beasts.* Classified 3X in MM's danger ranking. A serpent with pale gray skin and red eyes. It emerges from untended fires and slithers into a dark corner, leaving a trail of ashes behind it. Ashwinders live around the world (FB 2).
  See also Fantastic Beasts and Where to Find Them; Snakes

Asiatic Anti-Venoms. *Magical book.* This book is in the Hogwarts Library. In *Order of the Phoenix*, when Hermione asks Harry if he has thought more about her request that he teach the members of Dumbledore's Army, he pretends to become suddenly interested in this book (OP 16:330–31).

Asphodel. *Magical substance.* One of the ingredients for the Draught of Living Death. Harry does not know this information when Prof. Snape asks him about the substance in his first Potions class (SS 8:137–38).

Astrology. Planet reading, a form of fortune telling, is done by the centaurs in the Forbidden Forest. They take particular interest in the planet Mars, which represents war. Students at Hogwarts are exposed to the subject as a unit in Prof. Trelawney's Divination class. Several names in the series reflect constellation names, but more in astronomical than astrological terms. None of the twelve signs of the zodiac are represented as names in the series through Book 6.
  See also Divination

Astronomical models. *Magical objects.* Models of the universe are for sale or in use in the series. Harry is tempted to buy a moving and perfectly arranged model inside a glass ball on Diagon Alley (PA 4:50). Prof. Trelawney uses a model of the solar system, with nine planets and their moons rotating around the sun under a glass dome, when she teaches Astrology in Divination class (GF 29:575–78).

See also Lunoscope

Astronomy. *Class at Hogwarts.* This class is taught in Astronomy Tower, the tallest tower at Hogwarts, by Prof. Sinistra. The theoretical part of the class seems to be information about the universe, such as Harry and Ron's assigned essay on Jupiter's moons. During O.W.L.s, students have to use telescopes to fill in star charts according to the stars visible in the night's sky. Harry labels Mars and Venus incorrectly, which foreshadows the coming war between good and evil. In Harry's first year, the class meets at midnight on Wednesdays; in fifth year, Gryffindor House students shared the class with those from Hufflepuff House.

Hermione tests Ron in the subject in preparation for first-year exams, and Harry tries to learn Jupiter's moons from a map (SS 15:246–47). For the practical O.W.L. exam in the subject, students are taken to the top of Hogwarts to look at the sky and label star charts. Harry labels Orion and Venus, among other features in the sky. Just as he goes to correct his mislabeling of Venus for Mars, there is a loud bang and movement at Hagrid's hut (OP 31:718–19).

Rowling uses several constellation names as character names in the series. These include: Alphard, Andromeda, Bellatrix, Draco, Regulus, and Sirius.

Astronomy Tower. *Magical place.* The tallest tower at Hogwarts. This is where the Astronomy class is held and where Dumbledore meets his fate at the hand of Snape (HBP 29:596). Umbridge attempts to have Hagrid taken away after she fires him, and the students watch his struggle at the hut from their O.W.L. exam on the tower (OP 31: 718–23).

Atrium. *Magical place.* The entrance hall area in the Ministry of Magic where employees enter and exit using Floo Powder. The Atrium contains a shining dark-wood floor and a peacock-blue ceiling with glimmering gold symbols on it. Along the wooden walls there are several fireplaces from which wizards and witches come and go. Halfway through the Atrium is the Fountain of Magical Brethren, where coins are collected for St. Mungo's Hospital for Magical Maladies and Injuries. The security station where wands and people are checked is also located in the Atrium (OP 7:127). At the other end of the Atrium are about twenty elevators taking employees to various floors (OP 7:129).

See also Floo Powder; Fountain of Magical Brethren; Ministry of Magic

Aubrey, Bertram. *Character.* For detention, Prof. Snape gives Harry the task of working with Snape's files of detentions; one old card tells of James Potter and Sirius Black getting double detention for putting an illegal hex on Bertram Aubrey (HBP 24:532).

Audio books. *See* Dale, Jim; Fry, Stephen

Augurey. *Magical creature.* From *Fantastic Beasts.* Classified 2X by the MM. The creature is an Irish phoenix. Greenish black in color, this bird is a native of Ireland and Britain but can also be found elsewhere in northern Europe (FB 2–3). In his foreword to *Fantastic*

Beasts, Prof. Dumbledore says that readers may find a way to interpret the sad cries of this bird in the book (FB vii). They are also mentioned in *A History of Magic* (FB xi).

See also Fantastic Beasts and Where to Find Them

Aunt Marge. *See* Dursley, Aunt Marge (Marjory)

Aura. *Magical sign.* In Divination class, Prof. Trelawney tells Hermione that she does not see much of an aura around her, which indicates that she does not have "the gift," a good sense of predicting the future (PA 6:107).

Auror. *Magical occupation.* A professional Dark wizard catcher. Harry Potter would like to be an Auror when he leaves Hogwarts. Ron tells him that he would like to be one also. However, Aurors are a superior force of law enforcement, so there is some doubt about that prospect (OP 12:228). Prof. McGonagall tells Harry that Auror training takes three more years of school and testing (OP 29:665). After Umbridge suggests that Harry has no chance of becoming an Auror, Prof. McGonagall pledges to help Harry meet all of the requirements.

Auror Headquarters. *Magical office.* Located on the second floor of the Ministry, it is part of the Department of Magical Law Enforcement (OP 7:130).

British author Jane Austen (1775–1817), one of J. K. Rowling's favorite writers. Courtesy of the Library of Congress.

Austen, Jane (1775–1817). In interviews, J. K. Rowling has frequently named the British novelist Jane Austen as one of her favorite authors. She has mentioned the 1816 novel *Emma* as her favorite among Austen's books. In one interview she claims to have read that novel many times, joking that it may have been as many as twenty. Hogwarts' caretaker Argus Filch's cat, Mrs. Norris, is named after a character in the novel *Mansfield Park*. It is clear that Rowling derives interest from Austen's fiction, though any influence on her work in the Harry Potter novels has yet to be discovered or explored in more depth by literary critics.

Jane Austen is one of the most highly regarded British authors of the nineteenth century, and most of her works are considered classics. In addition to *Emma* and *Mansfield Park*, her masterpieces include the widely read *Pride and Prejudice* and *Sense and Sensibility*. Though these novels and other works were first published centuries ago, they have never been out of print. Among Austen's many strengths as an author are her careful characterization of families in country settings of the period and her quick wit and satire. Themes in Austen's work include timeless subjects such as money, manners, morals, and marriage.

Austen was born on December 16, 1775, at the Rectory in Steventon, a small village in Northeast Hampshire. She was the second daughter and seventh child of Reverend George Austen and his wife, Cassandra Leigh. Among Austen's brothers, two became clergymen, two inherited grand estates in Kent and Hampshire from a wealthy cousin, and the youngest two became admirals in the Royal Navy. Jane Austen's sister, Cassandra, never married and neither did Austen herself. Austen lived with her family in the Rectory at Steventon for the first twenty-five years of her life. While there, she made extensive trips to her brother's home in Kent and to an aunt and uncle's residence in Bath. On these trips, Jane took note of the surroundings and wove them through the settings of two novel manuscripts she was working on at the time—*Pride and Prejudice* and *Northanger Abbey*. She also worked on the manuscript for *Sense and Sensibility* in the 1790s.

When her father retired from the ministry in 1801, he moved his wife and daughters to Bath. While living in Bath, the family often visited the seaside towns of the West Country, including Lyme Regis in Dorset. From this area, Jane picked up background for another work, *Persuasion*. The author's father died in 1805. Following his death, the family moved briefly to Southampton and then to Chawton to one of her brother's estates. They lived there from 1810 to 1817, and it was during this more settled time that Jane revised her first manuscripts and also wrote *Mansfield Park*, *Emma*, and *Persuasion*. In 1816, Jane became ill with what may have been Addison's disease. Her family took her to Winchester for medical treatments; however, the doctor told them nothing could be done. Jane Austen died calmly in Winchester on July 18, 1817 in her sister's arms.

Austen's works appeared in print early in the nineteenth century, well before her famous literary counterparts, the Brontë sisters and Charles Dickens. *Sense and Sensibility* was published in 1811; *Pride and Prejudice* in 1813. *Mansfield Park* appeared in 1814, and *Emma* was published at the end of 1815 or early 1816. *Northanger Abbey* and *Persuasion* were published posthumously in 1817 and 1818.

Rowling's favorite novel, *Emma*, begins: "Emma Woodhouse, handsome, clever, and rich, with a comfortable home and happy disposition, seemed to unite some of the best blessings of existence; and had lived nearly twenty-one years in the world with very little to distress or vex her." Perhaps the opening of *Sorcerer's Stone* echoes this line with the description of Mr. and Mrs. Dursley as "perfectly normal," and an unlikely pair to be associated with anything out of the ordinary. *Emma* goes on to be a story about the title character, her matchmaking successes and failures, and the cleverly hidden plot secret that most readers miss right along with Emma.

In some circles, *Emma* has been called the first detective story, not because it is about murder and criminologists solving a case, but because of its deft interweaving of clues to the plot secret that is revealed at the end of the story. Even after readers discover the secret, rereadings provide increased enjoyment as early clues become recognizable in light of where they lead. Along with the detective nature of the story, Austen's characteristic use of wit is at its sharpest in *Emma*. The title character has a playful mind, yet Emma can also be practical and rational when she needs to be. Together with Mr. Knightley, and despite her many mistakes, Emma proves herself to be a suitable leader in her society. Examining connections between the detective story nature and use of wit in *Emma* and the Harry Potter series may help to establish evidence of Jane Austen's influence on Rowling's writing.

Some critics are beginning to look at *Pride and Prejudice* as it may relate to the Harry Potter series. Draco Malfoy and his family and friends, for example, may be said to be both proud and prejudiced against those with less-than-pure wizard blood. No doubt further explorations of connections between Austen's work and Rowling's will be made once the series is complete.

See also Children's Literature, Series' Role in

Further Reading: Austen, Jane. *The Oxford Illustrated Jane Austen: Emma.* Oxford: Oxford University Press, 1988; Olsen, Kirstin. *All Things Austen: An Encyclopedia of Austen's World.* Westport, CT: Greenwood, 2005.

Authentiticy, challenges to. *See* Lawsuits

Auto-Answer Quills. *Magical object.* A cheating writing device that is banned from the examination hall during O.W.L.s (OP 31:708–9).

"Avada Kedavra." *Incantation.* One of the three Unforgivable Curses, this is the Killing Curse that kills instantly in a flash of green light; there is no countercurse, and Harry Potter is the only victim in wizard history known to have survived it. Voldemort used it to kill Harry's parents. Harry was there when it happened, and although he was an infant, he occasionally has nightmares of flashing green lights. Mad-Eye Moody demonstrates the curse on spiders in DADA, and Harry has a difficult time watching (GF 14:215–17). Snape uses this curse to kill Dumbledore (HBP 27:596). Many readers notice the similarity between this incantation and "abracadabra."

See also Unforgivable Curses

Avery. *Character.* A Death Eater. He was a student in Slytherin House at the time of James and Lily Potter. He was not put in Azkaban because he claimed to be doing Voldemort's bidding under the Imperius Curse (GF 27:531). Voldemort later punishes him with the Cruciatus Curse (GF 33:648–49). Harry has a vision about Avery through the eyes of Voldemort (OP 26:585). In the vision, Avery is present at the attack in the Department of Mysteries (OP 35:788). When Bellatrix Lestrange charges that Snape did not look for Voldemort when he disappeared, Snape counters that neither did other Death Eaters, such as Avery (HBP 2:26). Avery is with Tom Riddle when he goes to see Slughorn (HBP 23:496).

See also Death Eater

"Avis!" *Incantation. Avis* is Latin for "bird." The incantation casts a charm that makes birds fly out of the tip of a wand. Mr. Ollivander uses it in checking out Viktor Krum's wand before the Triwizard Tournament (GF 18:309).

Awards at Hogwarts. Academics, sports, behavior, and service to the school community are areas in which the faculty and staff at Hogwarts give students awards, trophies, and other honors. A key annual award is the House Cup, which is given to the student house that ends the school year with the most points. Throughout the year faculty give and take away points for good and poor behavior and for accomplishments or failures of various kinds. Points may be added or deducted from the total house count for the behavior of individual students and small groups. Examples of behavior that result in deductions include walking around the school halls at night or being too bold with a teacher in class. Points have been granted to students for knowing the answer to a difficult question posed in class, or for standing up to one's peers to do what is right.

There are other distinctions as well. The Quidditch House Cup is awarded each year to the house that scores the most wins in the year. The Triwizard Tournament Cup is awarded to the school and its champion that score the most points over three challenging tasks. A prefect badge goes to one girl and one boy in their fifth year at the school who will help supervise the other students in the house. Prefects have use of an elaborate bathroom and are often in line for Head Boy and Head Girl in seventh year.

Harry Potter and Tom Riddle both earn distinction in their years at Hogwarts by winning the Special Services to the School Award, which is given for an extraordinary accomplishment that benefits the school. Harry wins it for ridding the school of the dangerous threat of the basilisk in the Chamber of Secrets. Riddle's award is tied to his actions surrounding the Chamber as well, but many years earlier.

The End of the Year Feast appears to be the day of reckoning for the awards at the school. At the feast, the winner of the House Cup has its house banner and colors displayed throughout the Great Hall. As readers see in *Sorcerer's Stone*, however, points can be added and taken away from student houses as late as the banquet itself. Prof. Dumbledore appears eager to make sure justice is served by the end of the school year in terms of who has and who has not earned recognition and merit for their achievements.

Awards, J. K. Rowling's. Both Rowling and her books have earned numerous awards around the world. Among the most notable, perhaps, are the author's O.B.E. (Order of the British Empire) award and her honorary doctorate degrees from Exeter University in England (2000); the University of Edinburgh in Scotland (2004); and Dartmouth College (2000) in the United States. The O.B.E. was given to her by Prince Charles in 2001 for the author's work in literature. Rowling has also won recognition for her philanthropic work with the Multiple Sclerosis Society of Scotland and the National

Vice Chancellor Professor Timothy O'Shea of the University of Edinburgh confers an honorary doctorate on Joanne Rowling, July 8, 2004. © David Cheskin/AFP/Getty Images.

Council for One Parent Families. In addition, each of the novels in the series has won several book awards and distinctions.

See also Harry Potter and the Chamber of Secrets; Harry Potter and the Goblet of Fire; Harry Potter and the Half-Blood Prince; Harry Potter and the Order of the Phoenix; Harry Potter and the Philosopher's/Sorcerer's Stone; Harry Potter and the Prisoner of Azkaban; O.B.E. (Order of the British Empire)

Axminster flying carpet. *Magical object.* Before they were banned, Barty Crouch, Sr.'s, grandfather had one of these that could fit twelve people. They were banned because they were considered to be a Muggle object (GF 7:91).

Azkaban. *Magical place.* The wizard prison. Harry first hears of it when disguised with Ron as Crabbe and Goyle. Malfoy tells them that the last person who opened the Chamber of Secrets is probably still in this prison (CS 12:224). The prison is guarded by Dementors and once held Sirius Black until he escaped in *Prisoner of Azkaban*. The prison sounds a bit like Alcatraz, set on an island (PA 10:188). Sirius tells Harry that most prisoners go mad and stop eating; that is how they die (GF 27:529). There is a mass breakout of Voldemort's supporters during Harry's fifth year when the Dementors guarding the prison join Voldemort's ranks (OP 25:544–45). Fudge indicates that the prison is located in the middle of the North Sea (HBP 1:8). The breakout of the Death Eaters took place in January (HBP 1:12). In an online chat in 2000, Rowling said that the prison is located in the northern part of the North Sea, which is very cold.

Further Reading: "Online Chat with J. K. Rowling." Scholastic.com. February 3, 2000.

· B ·

Babbling Curse. *Magical curse.* A curse that keeps a person talking non-stop. Prof. Lockhart claims to have cured a villager from Transylvania who had this ailment. Lockhart forces Harry to play the role of the villager in a reenactment of the cure in DADA class (CS 10:161). Snape mentions that he could administer the curse on Harry if he wants Harry to speak unintelligibly when he tries to communicate with Snape in code in front of Umbridge (OP 32:746).

Baddock, Malcolm. *Character.* A Slytherin student, three years behind Harry (GF 12:178).

Badger. *Magical symbol.* Animal symbol of Hufflepuff House. Badgers are common in the Forest of Dean, near where Rowling grew up.
  See also Hufflepuff House

Bagman, Ludovic (Ludo). *Character.* Department Head of the Department of Magical Games and Sports (GF 5:61). In Latin *ludo* means "to play a sport" and "to deceive." "Bagman" is a slang term for someone who collects money for loan sharks and gangsters, presumably slipping some of it aside for himself. Percy Weasley thinks Ludo Bagman is the wrong person to head the department (GF 5:61).
  Ludo once played professional Quidditch as a Beater for the Winterbourne Wasps and did quite well for England (GF 7:78). In his prime, he was tall and muscular, with bright blue eyes, but when he wears his old uniform to the World Cup, it is evident that some of his attributes have atrophied (GF 7:86). Augustus Rookwood, an old friend of Bagman, Sr., Ludo's father, got Ludo a job at the Ministry (GF 30:592–93). Ludo is a sports commentator at the World Cup, and a commentator and judge at the Triwizard Tournament. He raises his voice too loud while commentating, risking Muggles finding out about the wizard world's sporting events.
  Ludo is a gambler, and he invites the Weasley twins to place a bet at the World Cup; they bet all of their life savings (37 Galleons, 15 Sickles, and 3 Knuts) and a fake wand

for Ireland to win, but they wager that Krum will catch the Snitch (GF 7:87–88). When this actually happens, Ludo pays them off in leprechaun gold, which disappears. When the twins later write to Ludo and ask for their winnings (or at least for their money back), he does not give it to them (GF 37:731–32).

Harry sees Ludo in the Pensieve vision of Igor Karkaroff's hearing. Ludo appears to have passed on information to Rookwood, who was a Death Eater, without knowing that Rookwood was on the Dark Side. It is clear that the witches and wizards on the council admire Ludo's athletic ability, which was at its peak at the time of the hearing years ago (GF 30:592–93). Dumbledore tells Harry that Ludo has not been accused of working for the Dark Side since that time (GF 30:603).

Ludo wrote a blurb that appears in the frontispiece of QA.

Bagman, Otto. *Character.* Ludo Bagman's brother who got in trouble with a lawnmower, apparently giving the Muggle machine magical powers. Mr. Weasley, who is head of the Misuse of Muggle Artifacts Office, gets Otto out of trouble (GF 5:61). In gratitude, Ludo gives Weasley tickets to the Quidditch World Cup (CS 5:61).

Bagman, Sr. *Character.* Ludo and Otto Bagman's father. He helped get Ludo his position at the Ministry through his friend, Augustus Rookwood (GF 30:593).

Bagnold, Millicent. *Character.* The Minister of Magic immediately prior to Cornelius Fudge.

Bagshot, Bathilda. *Character.* The author of *A History of Magic* (SS 5:66). She wrote a blurb that appears in the QA frontispiece.

"Balderdash." *Magical word.* Password into the Gryffindor Common Room, Year 4 (GF 12:191).

Balloons, non-explodable luminous. *Magical objects.* In *Sorcerer's Stone,* Harry receives a packet of these in his Christmas crackers (SS 12:204).

Ballycastle Bats. *Magical sports team.* From QA. Professional Quidditch team from Ballycastle in County Antrim on the northern coast of Northern Ireland. They are mentioned in *Flying With the Cannons.* They are a twenty-seven-time winner of the League Cup. Their mascot is Barny the Fruitbat (QA 32).

Ban on Experimental Breeding. *Magical law.* Legislation written by Newt Scamander and passed in 1965. This law makes it illegal to cross-breed certain species (FB vi).

Ban on Importing Flying Carpets. *Magical law.* Strangely, in the wizard world, magic carpets are considered a Muggle artifact and are banned (GF 7:91).

"Banana fritters." *Magical words.* Password into the Gryffindor Common Room, Year 4 (GF 25:459).

Banchory Bangers. *Magical sports team.* From QA. A historical Quidditch team known for their terrible skills at the game. Their poor behavior after the game eventually led to their disbanding in 1814 (QA 16–17).

Bandon Banshee. *Magical being.* Gilderoy Lockhart claimed to have conquered this creepy creature, but it was actually controlled by a witch with a hairy chin (CS 16:297). In DADA class, Lockhart says he did not conquer it by smiling at it (CS 6:99).

Bane. *Magical creature.* One of the three named centaurs that live in the Forbidden Forest. Bane has black hair, beard, and body, and a wild look about him (SS 15:253). When Bane and Magorian meet Hagrid, Harry, and Hermione in the Forbidden Forest, Bane gives no indication that he remembers Harry, though Harry remembers him. Like Magorian, Bane is disgusted that Firenze has gone to work for Dumbledore to teach humans centaur insights (OP 30:698–99). He comes with Magorian when Umbridge enters the woods in Hermione's ruse to escape her (OP 33:754).

Banishing Charm. *Magical spell.* Sends objects or people away from the one casting the spell; it is the opposite of the Summoning Charm. Harry's class practices the technique in Year 4 Charms class. Neville keeps sending Prof. Flitwick away in different directions due to his poor aim (GF 26:479).

Banshee. *Magical being.* In Prof. Lupin's Year 3 DADA class, when the students work on Boggarts, Seamus Finnegan's takes the form of a banshee (PA 7:137).

From the Irish, *bean sídhe,* and the Scottish Gaelic, *bean sìth,* which literally means "woman of fairyland," a banshee is a female spirit from Gaelic folklore. It is said that to hear the wailing cry of a banshee is a signal that someone in one's family will soon die. Some say the banshee attended five of the old families of Ireland, in particular, and gave them warnings: the O'Neills, O'Briens, O'Connors, O'Gradys, and Kavanaghs. The signal has also been interpreted to mean that the cry itself actually causes the death of the listener. Some say that seeing the banshee portends one's own death, but only hearing it predicts the death of another. Such a figure could hardly be resisted by a British author interested in the history of fantastic beings, so perhaps it is no surprise that Rowling adopts the banshee in the Harry Potter series.

Further Reading: Yeats, W. B., ed. *A Treasury of Irish Myth, Legend, and Folklore.*

Banshee wailing to foretell death in an Irish village. Courtesy of North Wind Picture Archives.

Barnabas the Barmy. *Character.* On the seventh floor of Hogwarts, a tapestry illustrates this character attempting to teach ballet to trolls. It is near the Room of Requirement (OP 18:389). Harry goes there again in Year 6 when he tries to find out what Draco Malfoy is up to (HBP 21:457).

Barny the fruitbat. *Magical mascot.* From QA. The mascot of the Ballycastle Bats Quidditch team from Northern Ireland. The mascot appears in the advertisement for Butterbeer (QA 32–33).

Baruffio. *Character.* Prof. Flitwick tells the students that this wizard transposed "s" and "f" in "swish and flick" and got a buffalo on his chest as a result (SS 10:171). He is likely the character who invented Baruffio's Brain Elixir, though this is uncertain.

Baruffio's Brain Elixir. *Magical substance.* Probably invented by Baruffio. Eddie Carmichael, a sixth-year Ravenclaw student, tries to sell a bottle of it to Harry and Ron for 12 Galleons. He claims it helped him achieve Outstanding scores for nine subjects on O.W.L.s. Hermione takes the bottle away before Ron can figure out how to repay Harry for his half (OP 31:708).

Bashir, Ali. *Character.* Bashir is a flying carpet merchant who wants the Ministry of Magic to lift the embargo on flying carpets (GF 7:91). Later, Percy Weasley says that Bashir was caught smuggling them into the country (GF 23:425).

Basic Blaze Box. *See* Weasleys' Wildfire Whiz-Bangs

Basic Hexes for the Busy and the Vexed. *Magical book.* This is a book that Harry consults as he prepares for the first task of the Triwizard Tournament (GF 20:339).

Basil. *Character.* A wizard who works at the Ministry of Magic and is the keeper of the Portkeys at the Quidditch World Cup. He wears a kilt and a poncho (GF 7:75).
See also Portkey

Basilisk. *Magical creature.* Sometimes called the "king of the snakes," this mythological creature is a giant serpent that can grow up to fifty feet long. It is ranked 5X in the MM system, meaning that it is lethally dangerous. In *Fantastic Beasts and Where to Find Them*, it is said that the snake was bred by Herpo the Foul who was a Greek Dark wizard and Parselmouth (FB 3).

Harry and Ron find out that the Basilisk must be the creature in the Chamber of Secrets. They discover this by putting together clues given to them by Aragog and by studying the information on the piece of paper Hermione clutched in her hand when she was petrified. The Basilisk is born from a chicken's egg hatched underneath a toad. In addition to its poisonous and huge fangs, the creature can kill with its eyes, fixing a lethal stare on its victim. The Basilisk is most afraid of roosters because their crowing can kill the creature (CS 16:290). The *Fantastic Beasts* entry on the Basilisk claims that it has not been seen in 400 years. Either Harry or Ron handwrites his disagreement (FB 4). Basilisks are the one creature feared by all spiders.
See also Fantastic Beasts and Where to Find Them; Snakes

Bat Bogey Hex. *Magical spell.* Ginny Weasley is particularly talented at casting this spell, which covers the victim's face with large-winged bogeys (American translation:

boogers) (OP 6:100). Ginny uses the spell on Malfoy in the escape from Umbridge's Inquisitorial Squad (OP 33:760). Horace Slughorn is so impressed with her talent at casting the spell on Zacharias Smith that he invites her to his luncheon on the Hogwarts Express with the other students he thinks are well connected (HBP 7:146).

See also Weasley, Ginevra ("Ginny")

Bath. *Muggle place.* An old witch from Bath once read a book that made her never stop reading. Ron tells Harry this story as he tries to warn him about the diary he found in Moaning Myrtle's bathroom (CS 13:231).

Bats (Quidditch). *Magical sport equipment.* From QA. These are small, weighty clubs used to hit Bludgers.

Bats, Beater. *See* Bats (Quidditch)

Battle helmet. *Magical clothing.* The giants' Gurg once received this head protection as a gift. It is made by goblins to be indestructible (OP 20:429).

See also Goblins

Bayliss, Hetty. *Character.* A Muggle who spotted the flying Ford Anglia over Norfolk (CS 5:79).

Beaky. *See* Buckbeak

Beast, Being, and Spirit Divisions. *Magical offices.* From *Fantastic Beasts*. Branches of the Department for the Regulation and Control of Magical Creatures at the Ministry of Magic, located on the fourth floor (OP 7:130). Newt Scamander used to work in the Beast Division (FB vi).

See also Quidditch Through the Ages

Beaters. *Magical sport position.* In Quidditch, beaters use bats to hit the two Bludger balls away from players who are trying to score. Fred and George Weasley are Beaters on the Gryffindor Quidditch team during Harry's first year (SS 9:153). Beaters' role has not changed a great deal since they were introduced at the advent of Bludgers; they are to protect their teammates from being hit by Bludgers (QA 24).

The Beaters' Bible. *Magical book.* From QA. This book was written by Brutus Scrimgeour, presumably about the Beater position in Quidditch (QA frontispiece).

See also Quidditch Through the Ages

Beating the Bludgers—A Study of Defensive Strategies in Quidditch. *Magical book.* A book by Kennilworthy Whisp, mentioned in the About the Author page of QA.

See also Quidditch Through the Ages

The Beatles. Rowling once said that the Beatles were her mother's favorite musical group, and the intense global, popularity of the Harry Potter series in the 1990s and 2000s has been compared to the "Beatlemania" phenomenon of the 1960s. Both phenomena originated in Great Britain and were fueled by wide and enthusiastic popularity in the United States before turning into worldwide sensations. Harry Potter has been described as the "fifth Beatle," wearing the dark-haired mop-top that the four musicians sported in their younger days. Rowling read from the novels to record-breaking crowds in North American stadiums. The events were somewhat reminiscent of Beatles concerts. Her books have been banned for inviting young people to worship the devil, just as the Beatles' rocking melodies and lyrics moved some concerned parents a generation before her to forbid the playing of Beatles' music in their homes. Critics of both literature and music have raved about the Harry Potter series and Beatles albums. Other critics have panned both creators for what some see as their sell-out to film and commercialism.

On promotional tours, such as the one in England for *Goblet of Fire*, where Rowling rode through towns on a mock-up version of the Hogwarts Express, the crowds were large and enthusiastic. However, most people left disappointed because the author was not allowed to disembark the train and meet with them or sign their books, and they only caught a glimpse of her from the window. The commotion left Rowling as unhappy as her fans. John Lennon reportedly had a similar reaction after the first American Beatles concert at Yankee Stadium in 1964. Lennon and the other members of the band noted that the screaming frenzy of the audience was so loud and chaotic that there was little chance the fans could have actually heard the music. "Hype" had been discovered as a new entity in the world, and it is a charge leveled every time a new Harry Potter book or film is released.

While Rowling has said that she is quite capable of going to the grocery store without being recognized or mobbed, that is probably not the case, even now, for Paul McCartney or Ringo Starr, the only surviving members of the "fab four" who have stood somewhere in the spotlight of the world stage for over four decades. The Beatles have gained some respect in the music community for their influence and longevity. Time will tell if the Harry Potter series endures in the same way.

Further Reading: Kirk, Connie Ann. "Is Harry Potter 5th Beatle?" *Harrisburg Patriot-News* (PA), July 2003: A7.

Beauxbatons Academy of Magic. *Magical school. Beauxbaton* means "beautiful wand" in French. Readers first hear of the school at the Quidditch World Cup when Hermione tells Harry that the French-speaking witches they pass by probably go to this school. She tells him that she read about the school in *An Appraisal of Magical Education in Europe* (GF 9:123). Their method of transportation is a huge, powder-blue carriage pulled by a dozen winged palomino horses (GF 15:242–43). The carriage stays parked near Hagrid's hut where a paddock has been set up for the horses to graze (GF 16:263). Fleur Delacour tells Harry and friends that the students take exams in their sixth year, not the fifth as at Hogwarts (HBP 5:101).

A Beginner's Guide to Transfiguration. *Magical book.* A first-year textbook by Emeric Switch (SS 5:66). Lucius Malfoy mocks the Weasleys about Ginny's tattered copy in their Flourish and Blotts encounter (CS 4:62).

Belby, Flavius. *Character.* From *Fantastic Beasts.* A wizard who wrote the earliest known account of an encounter with a Leithifold; the attack occurred in Papua, New Guinea, in 1782 (FB 25–27).
See also Fantastic Beasts and Where to Find Them

Belby, Marcus. *Character.* A fellow student at Hogwarts, he has lunch with Slughorn, Harry, and others aboard the Hogwarts Express in Year 6. Slughorn tells Harry that he taught Marcus's Uncle Damocles (HBP 7:143–44).

Belch powder. *Magical object.* In Year 3, Filch asks Harry why he is not going to Hogsmeade to buy this and other joke products (PA 8:153).

Belcher, Humphrey. *Character.* Dumbledore tells Harry he may be as wrong about future theories about Voldemort as Humphrey Belcher, who thought cheese cauldrons were a good idea (HBP 10:197).

Bell jar. *Magical object.* A hummingbird hatches, flies up, and drops back down into its jeweled egg inside a bell jar in the Department of Mysteries (OP 34:776–77).

Bell, Katie. *Character.* Gryffindor student who is a Chaser on the Quidditch team (SS 11:186). She is nearly asleep at Oliver Wood's predawn practice in Year 2 (CS 7:108). Katie points out that Umbridge thinks Hagrid has been putting nifflers in her office, and that is one reason why Umbridge fires him (OP 31:723). In Year 6, Katie is the only member of the Gryffindor Quidditch team who was there when Harry joined in his first year (HBP 9:175). Katie is attacked when she accidentally touches an opal necklace in a package given to her in the bathroom at the Hogs Head (HBP 12:248–52).

Belladonna, Essence of. *Magical substance.* While everyone is at the World Cup, Mrs. Weasley replaces Harry's low supply of Essence of Belladonna during her shopping trip to Diagon Alley (GF 10:155).

Benson, Amy. *Character.* One of the orphans Tom Riddle tortured in a cave (HBP 13:268).

Bertie Bott's Every Flavor Beans. *Magical candy.* This is one of the first candies Harry Potter is treated to when he meets Ron Weasley on the Hogwarts Express (SS 6:101, 103–4). The candies are mentioned frequently throughout the series, mostly in terms of additional flavors and how characters may respond when they try them. The slogan of the candy is "A Risk with Every Mouthful" (GF 8:102). Flavors include normal candy flavors such as chocolate, peppermint, marmalade (SS 6:103), but also include others like spinach, liver, and tripe. Ron bites into a green sprouts bean while sharing with Harry and tells him that Fred and George claim they have eaten a booger once. On his first try, Harry's bean flavors include: toast, coconut, baked bean, strawberry, curry, grass, coffee, sardine, and a gray bean he shares with Ron that tastes like pepper (SS 6:104). Other flavors that come up later in the series include those Prof. Dumbledore says he tasted or thought he had tasted: earwax, toffee, and vomit (SS 17:300–301). The candies are advertised on the flashing board at the Quidditch World Cup (GF 8:102).

A commercially available version of Bertie Bott's Beans was made by Jelly Belly in the United States and sold in small drawstring bags. Most of the flavors were more savory to the palate than the beans Harry and his gang enjoyed, though some were more bitter than sweet.

See also Appendix C; Candy and Sweets; Merchandising

Bethnal Green. *Muggle place.* Anti-Muggle pranksters have rigged public toilets near Bethnal Green so that they flush up instead of down. The phenomenon is called "regurgitating toilets." The pranksters need to be taken care of by the Magical Law

Enforcement Patrol (OP 7:133). After the hearing Mr. Weasley offers to take Harry back to Grimmauld Place on his way to Bethnal Green to check out the toilet (OP 9:153).

Bezoar. *Magical substance.* This is a stone found in a goat's stomach. It is useful as an antidote to many poisons. Harry does not know this information on his first day in Potions class when Prof. Snape asks him about Bezoars (SS 8:137–38). In Year 6 when he benefits from the notes in his Potions textbook, Harry uses the Bezoar quickly, which impresses Prof. Slughorn (HBP 18:377–78).

Bicorn. *Magical creature.* Hermione needs powdered horn from a bicorn for the Polyjuice Potion (CS 10:165).

Big D. *Muggle nickname.* Dudley Dursley's friends nickname him Big D after he wins a boxing championship (OP 1:12).

Bigfoot. *Magical creature.* From *Fantastic Beasts*. Another name for Yeti.
See also Fantastic Beasts and Where to Find Them; Yeti

Bigonville Bombers. *Magical sports team.* From QA. A professional Quidditch team from Luxembourg (QA 41).
See also Quidditch Through the Ages

Bilius, Uncle. *Character.* Ron Weasley tells Harry that his Uncle Bilius once saw a Grim and died within twenty-four hours (PA 6:110). Rowling has said in interviews that Bilius is Ron's middle name.

Billywig. *Magical creature.* From *Fantastic Beasts*. Ranks 3X in MM classification, meaning that a wizard with normal abilities should be able to handle any complications concerning it. The Billywig is an insect about one-half-inch long and bright blue in color. Its wings are like propellers on top of its head, and its stinger is at the bottom of its body. Dried Billywig stingers may be a component of Fizzing Whizbees; stings cause the victim to hover above the ground after a period of laughter. Ron or Harry writes that he will not eat anymore Fizzing Whizbees after seeing what may be in them (FB 4–5).
See also Fantastic Beasts and Where to Find Them

Binky. *Magical animal.* Lavender Brown's rabbit at home. On October 16 she hears that the rabbit was killed by a fox and she relates this to Prof. Trelawney's prediction that something she has been dreading would happen on that day (PA 8:148). The date coincides with the wedding date of Rowling's first marriage.
See also Animals

Binns, Prof. *Character.* This History of Magic professor at Hogwarts is the only ghost on the faculty. He died by falling asleep near the fireplace in the staff room, leaving his body behind, but he returns to class each morning and goes on teaching anyway (SS 8:133).

Through Binns, Rowling may be poking fun at teachers who have fallen into old habits and who absentmindedly instruct their students as though dead. Binns's classes are boring and monotonous; his voice and manner match. Binns is forgetful of students' names (he once called Harry "Perkins"), and he looks like a turtle. His name suggests a rubbish bin, which is where most of his students might wish to place his teaching methods.

Biographies, J. K. Rowling. Biographies of the author have so far fallen into two major categories, depending on their purpose; these are: biographies for fans and biographies for students. To date, there is no full-length literary biography of J. K. Rowling in print. The only biographical treatments the author has cooperated with have been *Conversations with J. K. Rowling* with Lindsey Fraser, which is a short book written in question-and-answer format for younger readers; and a BBC/A&E video interview program, *Harry Potter and Me*. Rowling has written an autobiographical sketch, "Biography," on her website, www.jkrowling.com. Readers desiring facts about the author's life from the most credible source should seek out this account.

All other biographies have been written by popular culture journalists or authors for the school library and reference market. Examples of the former include *J. K. Rowling* by Marc Shapiro, which came out quickly and very early in the Potter phenomenon and has been known to contain several errors. *J. K. Rowling: A Biography* by Sean Smith is the most extensive of all of the biographies so far and includes interviews with people who knew Rowling in her youth, as well as a contact who worked at the Christopher Little Literary Agency when the manuscript for Harry Potter first arrived in that office. Rowling later dispelled some of the information in the book, saying it was untrue.

Of the biographies written for use by students for research, Connie Ann Kirk's *J. K. Rowling: A Biography* is geared toward lower-division college undergraduates and high school students, as well as the interested adult general reader. *Triumph of the Imagination: The Story of Writer J. K. Rowling* by Lisa A. Chippendale is appropriate for ages nine to twelve; and *J. K. Rowling* by Cari Meister provides information with colorful maps and photographs for elementary school students.

With the publication of the author's website in early 2004, Rowling has had a worldwide medium with which to discount rumors and false information, as well as to put her own interpretation on events. This information is also accessible to readers, fans, and students, who may wish to check other published biographies of Rowling's life against the website for consistency. Published biographies of the popular author, even though occasionally labeled "unauthorized," are often relevant for the objective perspective they bring to the telling of the story. An unauthorized biography of J. K. Rowling is the same as a biography of any other author, alive or dead, who has not supplied information through an interview or other direct means to the biographer. "Unauthorized" simply demonstrates Rowling's careful insistence that readers, who may be young, are sure to know the difference between a biography with which she cooperated (gave interviews and materials), and one with which she did not.

Birds, birdlike, and flying creatures. Witches and wizards on brooms are not the only living things that fly in the Harry Potter books. Each book is filled with flying creatures from the real world (with a twist) and the world of mythology. Owls bring the mail; a hippogriff takes off with Harry on its back; and a group of thestrals takes Harry and other members of Dumbledore's Army to the Ministry when they need to get there in a hurry. Birds, birdlike, and flying creatures play an important role in the series, particularly as a means of communication and transportation, but also as another link between the magical and natural worlds. Prof. Dumbledore's phoenix, Fawkes, even brings an element of the spiritual to the skies over Hogwarts.

Owls of all breeds, sizes, and colors bring the mail that keeps the magical community in touch. Harry is good to his snowy owl, Hedwig; Ron is thrilled when he receives Pigwidgeon, a small Scops owl, from Sirius Black. Errol, the Weasleys' old owl, does not deliver quite as quickly or as reliably as he probably did in the past, and he is showing the signs of being used by a large family. Percy's owl, Hermes, is a screech owl, perhaps fittingly. The school has an owlery where hundreds of owls stay, waiting to be sent out on communication or package delivery missions. Sirius Black sends messages to Harry during the summer before Year 4 with tropical birds instead of owls. This indicates to Harry that Black is in hiding in an exotic place (GF 2:24).

Fawkes, the phoenix, occupies a special place in the skies over Hogwarts and in the heart of Dumbledore's love for Harry. A feather from Fawkes occupies the center of both Harry's and Voldemort's wands, making them brothers. Fawkes's tears have healing qualities that Harry benefits from in the Chamber of Secrets. Dumbledore tells Harry that Fawkes will come and protect those who remain loyal to him, and the phoenix helps Harry fight off the Basilisk by striking out its death-causing eyes and bringing the Gryffindor sword to Harry.

Other than birds, creatures small and large bear wings and fly, running the gamut from the Cornish pixies in Prof. Lockhart's DADA class, to Bucky the hippogriff, part horse and part eagle; from Madame Maxime's Abraxan horses that pull the Beauxbatons blue carriage, to the thestrals that pull the Hogwarts coaches for second- through seventh-year students at Hogsmeade Station at the start of the school year.

While objects such as broomsticks and Ford Anglias also fly in the series, they do not have the same spirit and sweep of wings pumping air that seem to symbolize hope and freedom when performed by a bird or other winged creature in the books.

See also Abraxan horses; Hippogriff; Phoenix; Pixy

Birmingham. Stan Shunpike, the Knight Bus conductor, tells Harry that he is from outside of Birmingham (OP 24:525).

Bishop, Dennis. *Character.* One of the orphans Tom Riddle tortured in a cave (HBP 13:268).

Biting fairy. *Magical creature.* Another name for a Doxy, this creature is small, covered with black hair, and has sharp teeth. It is a household pest that may nest in the curtains and needs to be fumigated with Doxycide. It is advisable to keep Doxy bite antidote on hand at all times. Mrs. Weasley recommends that Grimmauld Place be cleared of them (OP 6:102).

See also Doxy; *Fantastic Beasts and Where to Find Them*

Black, Elladora. *Character.* One of Sirius Black's unsavory aunts, she beheaded house-elves once they were too old to carry tea trays. She handed down this practice as a family tradition (OP 6:113).

Black Family Tapestry. *Magical object.* In *Order of the Phoenix*, Sirius Black shows Harry the tapestry in Number Twelve, Grimmauld Place that dates back to the Middle Ages and contains the Black family tree. Sirius points out and talks about various family members who are and are not on the tapestry. If a family member has disagreed with the family's traditional position that pure-blood wizards are superior to Muggles or half-bloods, his or her name has been stricken from the wall hanging (OP 6:113).

Phineas Nigellus, whose portrait hangs in Dumbledore's office, is Sirius's great-great-grandfather and was the least favored of all of Hogwarts' headmasters. Araminta Meliflua is Black's mother's cousin who tried to make hunting Muggles legal. His Aunt Elladora beheaded house-elves once they became too old to carry trays of tea, and she passed on this practice as a family tradition. Bellatrix and Narcissa are sisters who married other pure-blood wizards, so their names are present. Their other sister, Andromeda, married a Muggle, Ted Tonks, so she is not on the tapestry. Narcissa Black married Lucius Malfoy and had one child, Draco. This makes Sirius Black related to Draco Malfoy, much to Harry's surprise (OP 6:111–13).

[Black], Phineas Nigellus. *Character.* Sirius Black's great-great-grandfather and a former headmaster of Hogwarts. He was the least popular of all of the headmasters (OP 6:113). His portrait hangs in Dumbledore's office. Dumbledore sends him on a mission which it is his duty to perform as a former headmaster. Phineas performs his task reluctantly since he is of the house of Black. Dumbledore wants Phineas to inform Sirius of Arthur Weasley's attack and to let Sirius know that Harry and the Weasleys will be staying at the Order's headquarters, which is closer to the hospital. Phineas is to do this by appearing in his portrait at Grimmauld Place (OP 22:472). When he accomplishes his task, he informs Dumbledore that Sirius has strange taste in houseguests; he then returns to his portrait in front of the Slytherin banner (OP 22:474). Harry recognizes Phineas's voice from the empty picture frame in his room at Grimmauld Place. He appears at Grimmauld Place and gives Harry a message from Dumbledore at Christmas that he is to stay there. When Harry gets angry at the thought of staying put, Phineas yells at him that this is why he hated teaching—because so many of the students think they know everything and are sure they are right (OP 23:493–96). After Dumbledore escapes Cornelius Fudge and the others who want to forcibly remove him from Hogwarts, Phineas says that although he does not agree with Dumbledore on several subjects, he does admire Dumbledore's style (OP 27:623). After the battle in the Hall of Prophecy, Harry does not want to tell Phineas's portrait that Sirius has died (OP 37:821).

Black, Regulus. *Character. Regulus* means "prince" or "little king" in Latin. It is the twenty-fifth brightest star and is located at the heart of the constellation Leo, the lion. At the end of *Half-Blood Prince*, the initials "R.A.B." become important (HBP 28:609; HBP 29:631). Readers ponder whether they might belong to this former Death Eater who turned against Voldemort and was killed as a result. That his name represents a star at the heart of Leo the lion suggests that he may provide some kind of benefit to the students of Gryffindor House, whose mascot is the lion.

Regulus is Sirius Black's younger brother. He was a Death Eater who turned to the other side and was killed fifteen years before Harry's Year 5 at Hogwarts. His name appears at the bottom of the Black family tapestry, where Sirius points it out to Harry. Sirius tells Harry that Regulus was the "better son" and was probably killed by one of Voldemort's supporters since it is doubtful that he would have been considered important enough to have been killed by Voldemort himself (OP 6:112). Dumbledore tells Harry that Regulus died before Sirius and, like his brother, was without children (HBP 3:50). At Harry's birthday celebration at the Burrow, Mr. Weasley tells everyone that Regulus lived only a few days after leaving the Death Eaters (HBP 6:106).

Black, Sirius. *Character. Sirius* in Latin and *seirios* in Greek mean "glowing." Sirius is a star located at the eye of the constellation Canis Major, so Sirius is known as the dog star. It is the brightest star in the sky and can be seen from all locations on the earth. To find Sirius, viewers locate the three stars that make up the belt of the constellation Orion, then look below and to the left of the trio's first star to spot the brightest star.

Sirius Black is Harry Potter's godfather, and his father James's best friend. The first reference to the wizard is when Hagrid speaks of borrowing Sirius's motorcycle to deliver infant Harry to Privet Drive on Prof. Dumbledore's orders (SS 1:14). Then, on the Muggle television news, there is a report of someone named Black who is on the run and is armed and dangerous. Uncle Vernon comments on his shaggy appearance on the television news (PA 2:16–17). Aboard the Knight Bus, Stan Prang shows Harry a *Daily Prophet* article about Sirius's breakout (PA 3:37–38). Sirius Black was in prison for the murder of a wizard and twelve Muggles on an open street (PA 3:38). Harry overhears Molly and Arthur Weasley discussing Sirius Black and finds out that he may be after Harry (PA 4:65). Worse, he hears Cornelius Fudge discuss with some of the Hogwarts faculty in the Three Broomsticks that Sirius was James Potter's best friend and is Harry's godfather (PA 10:204).

When Harry finally meets Sirius Black, he hears his story. Sirius explains that he is not sure how he stayed sane in Azkaban Prison except by remembering that he was an innocent man (PA 19:371). He escapes by becoming a dog in his Animagus form (PA 19:371). He admits to Harry that he is his godfather and asks Harry if he would ever consider living with him when things calm down (PA 20:379). Black played a trick on Snape that would have sent him down Hogwarts' secret passageway to the Shrieking Shack where Lupin lay in werewolf form. However, James Potter prevented Snape from going to the Shrieking Shack, thereby saving his life (PA 21:391; PA 18:357). Mrs. Weasley accuses Sirius of confusing Harry with Harry's father and thinking he has a new friend rather than a godson to look out for (OP 5:89). Hermione wonders if Mrs. Weasley might be right (OP 9:159). When Harry does not want Sirius to take risks in an effort to protect him, Sirius immaturely accuses him of being less like his father than he thought (OP 14:305).

Harry learns at the Black mansion that Sirius ran away from home due to his family's bigotry. He lived with James Potter's parents, who took him in (OP 6:111). Sirius was an original member of the Order of the Phoenix (OP 9:174). While seeing off Harry at the train platform, he behaves too humanlike in his dog form and causes Hermione to think he may have attracted too much attention (OP 10:183). Sirius appears to Harry in the Gryffindor Common Room with his head in the fire (OP 14:300). He gives Harry a small package after the holidays at Grimmauld Place to take back to Hogwarts with him. Harry does not open the two-way mirror until it is too late, but it is supposed to be a way for him to contact Sirius if he has any problems with Snape in Occlumency lessons (OP 24:523).

Sirius is killed in battle by his own Death Eater cousin, Bellatrix Lestrange, the same Death Eater who drove Neville Longbottom's parents insane with the Cruciatus Curse. He falls "behind the veil" on the dais (OP 35:806). In Book 6, the Muggle Prime Minister misconstrues his name when he hears it from Fudge as "Serious" Black (HBP 1:7). Prof. Dumbledore informs Harry that Sirius willed all that he had to him, including Number Twelve, Grimmauld Place, and the Black family house-elf, Kreacher (HBP 3:49, 53).

Blackspool Pier. *Magical place.* This is the pier off of which Neville Longbottom's Great Uncle Algie pushed him, in hopes that any latent magical powers might appear (SS 7:125).

"Bladvak." *Magical word.* The word means "pickax" in the Goblins' language of Gobbledegook (GF 24:446).

Blagging. *Magical sports penalty.* From QA. In Quidditch, this foul is committed when a player grabs the tail-twigs of another player's broom to slow the player down or manipulate his or her moves (QA 29).
See also Quidditch Through the Ages

Blast-Ended Skrewt. *Magical creature.* Hagrid bred these creatures illegally by crossing Manticores with Fire Crabs. They look like pale lobsters without their shells, with legs poking out at different angles, and no apparent head. They smell like rotting fish and move by blasting sparks out of one end. The males have stingers and the females have suckers on the bottom. Hagrid introduces his students to six-inch skrewts that were just hatched in his first Care of Magical Creatures class, Year 4 (GF 13:196). They start killing each other off as they grow, and there are fewer of them each time Harry and friends see them throughout the novel (GF 16:264). Hagrid has his students put a leash over the armor of the remaining three-foot-long skrewts and take them for a walk (GF 18:294).
See also Fantastic Beasts and Where to Find Them

Blatching. *Magical sports penalty.* From QA. A Quidditch foul where one player flies with the intent of crashing into another player (QA 29).
See also Quidditch Through the Ages

Bletchley, Miles. *Character.* Slytherin student, one or two years older than Harry. He is the keeper on the Slytherin Quidditch team (SS 11:186). Before a Gryffindor-Slytherin Quidditch match, he hits Alicia Spinnet with a jinx, but Snape refuses to blame him or believe the fourteen eyewitnesses who said he did it (OP 19:400).

Blibbering Humdinger. *Magical myth.* Luna Lovegood tells Harry that people used to believe in the Blibbering Humdinger and the Crumple-Horned Snorkack, and Hermione reminds her that there are no such things (OP 13:262).

Blood-flavored lollipops. *Magical candy.* Just what they sound like, they are most likely enjoyed by vampires (PA 10:197).
See also Candy and sweets

Blood Blisterpod. *Magical candy or plant.* Fred and George offer to take Katie Bell to the castle after her run-in at the Quidditch practice leaves her bloody. They say she may have swallowed a Blood Blisterpod (OP 14:294).

Blood-Replenishing Potion. *Magical substance.* Arthur Weasley takes Blood-Replenishing Potion every hour to resupply his body with blood until the Healers can find an antidote for the snakebite he received (OP 22:488).

Blood-Sucking Bugbear. *Magical creature.* In Harry's second year at Hogwarts, Hagrid wonders if this creature might be killing the roosters at the school. In folklore, bugbears ate poorly behaved children. They represent fears based more on imagination than reality (CS 11:201).

Blooder. *Magical sports equipment.* From QA. An old name for Bludger (QA 9).
See also Quidditch Through the Ages

Bloody Baron. *Character.* The Slytherin House ghost (SS 7:124). He is covered with silver blood and never speaks. No one knows where the blood came from. Harry impersonates him with a hoarse whisper. Peeves obeys and looks up to the Bloody Baron, calling him "Your Bloodiness" and "Mr. Baron."

See also Ghosts

Bloomsbury, Plc. Rowling's British publisher. Headquartered at Soho Square, London, Bloomsbury was founded in 1986 as an independent publisher interested in bringing books of high literary quality to the public. In 1995 the company added paperbacks and children's books to its list. It was into this new environment that agent Christopher Little queried Bloomsbury's Barry Cunningham with the manuscript for a long children's novel, *Harry Potter and the Philosopher's Stone,* by an unknown writer at the time named Joanne Rowling. Bloomsbury took on the book in its new children's department and published a very limited print run of just 500 hardcover copies in 1997. Later hardcover first print runs included: 10,150 for *Chamber of Secrets*; 10,000 for *Prisoner of Azkaban*; and 1 million for *Goblet of Fire.* Bloomsbury stopped releasing first print run numbers after *Goblet of Fire* but reported that over 2 million copies of *Half-Blood Prince* were sold over the course of the release weekend in July 2005. As the series' popularity grew, subsequent reprintings of all of the novels soared into the millions.

Bloomsbury continues to invest and grow, using its successes to build business. In 1998 Bloomsbury USA was created. It is located on Fifth Avenue in New York City. In August 1999 Bloomsbury published the popular *Encarta World English Dictionary* in print and electronic editions. The publisher continues to publish fiction, nonfiction, and reference books for adults and children, both in the U.K. and the United States.

Besides J. K. Rowling, Bloomsbury authors include such well-known and respected writers as: Al Alvarez, Margaret Atwood, Russell Banks, Nora Ephron, Carlos Fuentes, Mavis Gallant, Nadine Gordimer, Ethan Hawke, John Irving, Alice McDermott, Jay McInerney, Michael Ondaatje, Peter Taylor, Tobias Wolff, and many others. Rowling may have named her minor character Urquhart Rackharrow after Jane Urquhart, a fellow author whose work is also published by Bloomsbury.

See also Cunningham, Barry; Rackharrow, Urquhart

Bloomslang skin. *Magical substance.* One of the potion ingredients that Snape keeps locked up in his office (GF 27:516).

"Blubber!" *Word.* One of the "few words" Prof. Dumbledore speaks before the Start-of-Term Banquet in Harry's first year. The other few words are "Nitwit!" "Oddment!" and "Tweak!" (SS 7:123).

See also Dumbledore, Albus Percival Wulfric Brian

Bludger. *Magical sports equipment.* Used in Quidditch, these are two black, heavy balls made of iron that try to knock players off their brooms during play. They are smaller than the Quaffle, about ten inches across, and made of iron (QA 22). Beaters knock them away with their bats (SS 10:168). A Bludger becomes bewitched during a match in Year 2 to go after Harry only; finally, it strikes his elbow and breaks his arm (CS 10:169). In years past, a Bludger was known as a "Blooder" and used to consist of flying rocks (QA 21).

See also Quidditch Through the Ages

Bludger backbeat. *Magical sports play.* From QA. A Bludger backbeat occurs when a Beater hits the Bludger with a backswing, sending it behind him or her (QA 52).
See also Quidditch Through the Ages

Bluebell Flames. *Magical spell.* This spell casts blue flames in a certain direction. Hermione uses the spell to catch Snape's robes on fire during the Quidditch match in *Sorcerer's Stone* (SS 11:191).

Bluebottle Broomstick. *Magical object.* A family broomstick, rather than a racing broomstick, advertised at the Quidditch World Cup. It is said to be safe and reliable and features a burglar alarm (GF 8:96).

Blume, Judy (1938–). Judy Blume offered crucial early support to Rowling's series when the tide of popularity began to backfire, and when educators and parents began questioning the value of the books for children. Talk had begun to circulate among concerned parents that the books promoted interest in the occult among young people, and the books began to evaporate from school libraries and classroom shelves in states such as Minnesota, Michigan, New York, California, and South Carolina. In an Op-Ed piece in the October 22, 1999, issue of the *New York Times* (during Rowling's American book tour for *Harry Potter and the Prisoner of Azkaban*), Blume defended Rowling against charges of occultism. Blume compared the banning of Rowling's fantasy series to her own experience; Blume's books have been banned in various places for over twenty years, primarily for dealing with mature themes. Ironically, the problem in her case was not with fantasy, but rather with "reality that's seen as corrupting." Blume argued that Rowling must have been confused by the negative reaction to her fantasy books; she writes, "After all, she was just trying to tell a good story."

Further Reading: Blume, Judy. "Is Harry Potter Evil?" *New York Times*, October 22, 1999.

Blurting. *Magical sports penalty.* From QA. Knocking broom handles in an effort to veer the opponent out of one's flying direction (QA 29).
See also Quidditch Through the Ages

Blyton, Enid (1897–1968). In the 2005 "Cub Reporter" interview on British ITV, Rowling stated that her mother gave her books by Enid Blyton when she was a child and that she read some of *The Famous Five* series. However, Blyton was not Rowling's favorite author. Blyton was a British children's book author who wrote over 600 books, many in series. Her most popular series were the *The Famous Five*, *Secret Seven*, and the *Noddy* books. She also wrote poetry and nonfiction. Blyton's work has been criticized as unimaginative, elitist, and racist. Other readers approve of her stand against violence in children's books and films and what they see as her support of Christian morality through her books. Blyton's birth name was Enid Mary Waters; she also published under the name Mary Pollock.

Further Reading: Edinburgh "Cub Reporter" Press Conference, ITV. July 17, 2005. http://news.bbc.co.uk/cbbcnews/hi/newsid_4690000/newsid_4690800/4690885.stm.

Boa constrictor. This is the snake with magical powers that Harry speaks to at the zoo and that scares Dudley when it bursts out of its display (SS 2:27–28).

Boardman, Stubby. *Character.* Lead singer of the Hobgoblins who was struck by a turnip at a concert in Little Norton Church Hall and left show business afterwards. Though it is said he retired, at least one fan of the group says this is untrue. Mrs. Doris Purkiss and *The Quibbler* claim that Sirius Black and Stubby are one in the same and that Stubby was with Purkiss the night of the Potters' murders. Purkiss, a somewhat delirious character, says that Sirius is innocent of the crime and wrote to Cornelius Fudge asking for a pardon for him (OP 10:191–92).

See also Black, Sirius; Purkiss, Mrs. Doris

Boarhound. *Magical pet.* Hagrid's dog, Fang, is a black Boarhound. Something like a Great Dane, the Boarhound is said to be large and bred to hunt boars. Fang accompanies Harry, Draco, and Hagrid into the Forbidden Forest for the boys' detention, where Hagrid tells them the dog is too cowardly to offer much protection (SS 15:251).

See also Animals

Bob. *Character.* Mr. Weasley speaks to Bob, a Ministry employee who is holding a box, while he and Harry wait for the elevator in the Ministry Atrium. When Arthur asks, Bob says he is not sure what the creature inside the box is, but it is apparently a fire-breathing chicken and may be unlawful as a result of the Ban on Experimental Breeding (OP 7:129).

Bobbin, Melinda. *Character.* Slughorn invites Harry to dinner with some other students, including Melinda, whose family owns a sizable chain of apothecary stores (HBP 11:233).

See also Slughorn, Horace

Bode, Broderick. *Character.* Broderick Bode is an employee of the Department of Mysteries at the Ministry. Mr. Weasley tells Harry and friends that Bode is an Unspeakable, meaning that his work is top secret; no one knows what he does (GF 7:86). Mr. Weasley speaks to Bode as he and Harry go to Harry's hearing in Courtroom Ten at the Ministry. When Bode mentions that he does not often see Mr. Weasley on the first level, Mr. Weasley responds that he is there on important business; Bode then sees Harry and understands (OP 7:135).

Later, Bode is a patient at St. Mungo's; he had supposedly been injured in a work-related accident. When Harry and the Weasleys are at St. Mungo's to see Arthur, a visitor ahead of them in line tells the clerk that he is there to see Broderick Bode. The clerk tells him that Bode has lost his mind and thinks he is a teapot, so the visitor is wasting his time (OP 22:486). The nurse says that he is regaining some of his speech, though he talks in languages no one recognizes (OP 23:511). He is sent a hippogriff calendar as well as a potted plant for Christmas (OP 23:512). At age forty-nine, he is killed in his hospital room by a Devil's Snare plant, which Healer Strout mistook for a Flitterbloom (OP 25:546). Harry has a vision through Voldemort's eyes that Bode was under the influence of the Imperius Curse put on him by Lucius Malfoy (OP 26:587). Bode was sent to steal the prophecy from the Ministry when his "accident" apparently occurred (OP 35:787).

See also St. Mungo's Hospital for Magical Maladies and Injuries

Bodmin Moor. *Magical place.* From QA. In 1844 a live Golden Snitch bird escaped to Bodmin Moor and avoided being caught for at least six months, resulting in the two

Quidditch teams deciding to give up; legend has it the snitch is still living somewhere on the moor (QA 23).

See also Quidditch Through the Ages

Bodrod the Bearded. *Fake magical name.* Ron Weasley makes up this name during his History of Magic exam in Year 4. He says that Bodrod the Bearded is one of the goblins in the Goblin Rebellion.

Body-Bind Curse. *Magical curse.* The incantation for this curse is "Petrificus Totalus!" Though the victim remains conscious, his or her body is petrified (SS 16:273; HBP 28:597–98).

See also "Petrificus Totalus!"

Boggart Banishing Spell. *Magical spell.* In order to drive off a Boggart, one must use the incantation "Riddikulus!" While casting the spell, one must laugh and think of something humorous related to his or her worst fear (PA 7:134–38).

Boggarts. *Magical beings.* No one knows what the Boggart looks like on its own, but it likes to be in dark places such as closets, cupboards, and under beds; it is a shape-shifter. When found, it comes out of its hiding place and takes on the form of the thing most feared by the one who sees it (PA 7:133). Prof. Lupin takes the DADA class into the teachers' lounge where a Boggart has taken up residence in a wardrobe where old robes are kept. He uses the Boggart to teach the students to defeat it should they ever come upon one. The best antidote to its effects is laughter.

Neville Longbottom's Boggart is Prof. Snape. Lupin teaches Neville to imagine Snape dressed up in his grandmother's clothes and to say the incantation "Riddikulus!" Parvati Patil's Boggart is a mummy; Seamus Finnigan's is a banshee; Ron's is a spider; Dean Thomas's is a cut-off hand (PA 7:134–38). Harry's turns out not to be Voldemort, as Lupin had expected, but a Dementor (PA 8:155). Boggarts are part of Prof. Lupin's DADA final exam in Year 3 (PA 16:318). Mad-Eye Moody reviews the Boggart lesson from DADA class before he teaches the students the Unforgivable Curses (GF 14:211).

There is a Boggart in the writing desk at Twelve Grimmauld Place (OP 6:102). When Molly tries to get rid of it, it keeps changing into the dead bodies of all of the Weasley children and Harry. Molly become helpless against it, and Lupin drives the Boggart away (OP 9:176).

Bole. *Character.* Bole is a Beater on the Slytherin Quidditch team (PA 15:308). By Harry's fifth year, he has left the school and is replaced by Goyle (OP 19:405).

Bonaccord, Pierre. *Character.* The first Supreme Mugwump of the International Confederation of Wizards (OP 31:725–26).

Bones, Amelia Susan. *Character.* Head of the Department of Magical Law Enforcement at the Ministry of Magic. Tonks tells Harry that she is fair and will listen to his story during the hearing about the Dementors, Dudley, and his expulsion from Hogwarts (OP 7:123). She is one of the Interrogators for Harry's expulsion hearing (OP 8:138). She is later murdered sometime in the summer between Harry's fifth and sixth year at Hogwarts (HBP 1:4; HBP 4:73). Fudge tells the Prime Minister that due to her skill as a witch she may have been targeted and killed by Voldemort himself. Evidence showed that she put up a fight (HBP 1:13).

Bones, Edgar. *Character.* A member of the original Order of the Phoenix. He was a great wizard, but both he and his family were killed by Death Eaters. He is the brother of Amelia Bones (OP 9:174).

Bones's. *Characters.* Hagrid tells Harry that Voldemort managed to kill these people, who were among the best witches and wizards of their time; yet Harry, as an infant, survived Voldemort's attack (SS 4:56).

Bones, Susan. *Character.* Student in Harry's year; she is sorted into Hufflepuff (SS 7: 119). She comes to Harry's DADA class and asks him about conjuring a Patronus. She says her Aunt Amelia told her that Harry can make a Patronus; Amelia learned this at Harry's hearing (OP 16:342). Susan lost an aunt, uncle, and cousins to Death Eaters who escaped Azkaban (OP 25:550).

Susan is one of the DA members who defends Harry against Malfoy, Crabbe, and Goyle during the ride home on the Hogwarts Express after Year 5. The DA's various jinxes and defenses leave the three bullies in the form of oozing slugs that are put in the luggage rack for the remainder of the trip (OP 38:864). Susan has a bit of trouble Apparating during beginning lessons with the hoop; her left leg does not go with the rest of her body (HBP 18:385).

Bonfire Night. *Muggle event.* The weatherman suggests that the shooting stars people saw were actually people celebrating Bonfire Night early (SS 1:6). In England, Bonfire Night is celebrated on November 5 of each year. It marks the anniversary of Guy Fawkes's plot to burn up the Houses of Parliament. Fireworks go off across the country to celebrate the survival of the British government.

See also Fawkes

Book bannings and burnings. In the United States, the Harry Potter novels fall in the top ten among the most challenged titles in school districts and public libraries across the country from 1990 to 2000. A challenge to a book means that parents or other concerned adults have cited a problem they have with their children having access to the book in school, or to the book being taught or read in school as part of the curriculum. They state their concerns at school board meetings, through conferences with teachers or librarians, or by some other means, and they express a desire that the book be removed. Some of the reasons people give for challenging books include offensive language; occult theme or promotion of Satanism; unsuitability to the age group in question; violence; advocation of a religious viewpoint or homosexuality; racism; or sexual explicitness. The most frequent grounds cited for challenging the Harry Potter novels is the perception that they promote the occult and Satanism or that they are age-inappropriate.

Since school districts are locally run, the local community sometimes challenges a book in such numbers that books are voted to be banned from the classroom, school, or public library. A challenge is an expression of the wish for a book to be banned; a banned book is one that has actually been removed from the shelf. Sixty percent of the reported challenges to books in the last decade of the twentieth century were made by parents. Such bannings have occurred since the Harry Potter books were first published in the United States in 1998.

The American Library Association ranked the Harry Potter novels seventh of the 100 most challenged books in the country in the decade of 1990 to 2000, and Rowling the fourth most challenged author from 1990 to 2004. On the list of 100, Harry Potter sits between *Of Mice and Men* by John Steinbeck (at number six) and *Forever* by Judy Blume (at number eight). Other books in the top ten of the list include *Adventures of Huckleberry Finn* by Mark Twain and *I Know Why the Caged Bird Sings* by Maya Angelou.

Not only have the Harry Potter books been challenged and banned in some places over the years, they have also been ceremonily burned. In one incident in New Mexico that made the national news, Jack Brock, pastor and founder of Alamogordo, New Mexico's Christ Community Church, led his congregation in a burning of the books during the December holidays of 2001. Participants threw books into a bonfire while singing "Amazing Grace." In another incident in Maine, the fire department would not grant the group a fire permit, so the books were instead cut up while an anti-banning group protested nearby.

Interestingly, in the year 2004, Rowling's name did not appear on the list of banned authors, and her books did not appear on the challenged list. After several years of battle against censorship, something shifted in 2004 that kept the books off the list. One reason could be that those who were once concerned about the books promoting Satanism were now hearing that the books may have a completely opposite message compatible with Christian or other theologies.

Books in the series. *Magical objects.* Books are a large part of the Harry Potter series. There are well over 100 individual titles mentioned in the first six novels, including two schoolbooks. Books are stacked three-deep on the mantelpiece of the Burrow (CS 3:34). When Harry finds the diary in Moaning Myrtle's bathroom, Ron warns Harry that books can be dangerous (CS 13:230). When Harry goes to tell Gilderoy Lockhart about the Basilisk in *Chamber of Secrets*, Lockhart tells Harry that books can be deceiving and admits that he has not done all the heroic deeds he has written about in his many books (CS 16:297). Rowling clearly depends on the deception possible in books; she built plotlines throughout Harry's story that lead readers a short way down false paths, much as detective novels do.

Readers see most of the main characters reading at some point in the novels. Hermione is a bookworm of the highest order, choosing large reference books for a little "light reading." She is rarely part of a scene where there are no books present. Harry consults books on his own when he is trying to figure out a problem. Ron may be a reluctant reader who reads comic books at home, but he gets through his schoolwork fairly successfully. Books fill Hogwarts, in the student house common rooms, dormitories, classrooms, and professors' offices.

Interestingly, most of the books in the series are nonfiction rather than fiction or poetry. Besides Ron's comic book, there is one play mentioned, *Hélas, Je me suis Transfiguré Les Pieds* ("Alas, I've Transfigured My Feet") by Malecrit (QA 39), and one book of poetry, *Sonnets for a Sorcerer* (CS 13:231). At least one effect of this within the series is that books are regarded as keepers of history, information, and secrets, and are not generally read for escape, entertainment, or enlightenment beyond that which can be provided by factual knowledge. Other purposes for reading, beyond the acquisition of knowledge, seem to be met in other ways, such as playing games; doing research to solve problems; practicing, playing, or watching Quidditch; and talking with other students and the Hogwarts professors and staff. Harry learns about life through his own experiences and adventures rather than vicariously through the experience of a character in a novel or the feelings and impressions of a poet.

The shortage of imaginary literature at Hogwarts causes the reader of the series to remain focused on the magical and imaginary world in which the characters live. Expanding the fictional dimension into yet another realm of the imagination would only complicate that world. An irony of the series is that Vernon Dursley is portrayed unsympathetically in the Muggle world because he has little or no imagination, yet the students and adults in the magical world live in a world of the imagination but do not show a great deal of it themselves (other than the kind of expansive thinking that is required to solve problems).

See also Appendix D

Further Reading: Kirk, Connie Ann. "Imagi(c)nation in *Harry Potter and the Philospher's Stone*." In Steve VanderArk, ed., *The Harry Potter Lexicon*. http://www.hp-lexicon.org/essays/essays-imagicnation.html.

Boomslang. *Magical creature.* Hermione needs shredded skin from a Boomslang for the Polyjuice Potion. Harry tells Hermione that this ingredient is not in Snape's classroom cabinet and wonders if they will have to steal into his private collection of ingredients (CS 10:165).

Boot, Terry. *Character.* Student in Harry's year; sorted into Ravenclaw (SS 7:119). Terry Boot attends Harry's DADA class and asks him if he killed a Basilisk with the sword in Dumbledore's office; a portrait told Terry that Harry did this (OP 16:342). Terry is one of the DA members who defends Harry against Malfoy, Crabbe, and Goyle during the ride home on the Hogwarts Express after Year 5. The DA's various jinxes and defenses leave the three bullies in the form of oozing slugs that are put in the luggage rack for the remainder of the trip (OP 38:864). During Potions class in Year 6, Boot asks Prof. Slughorn why people do not take the Luck Potion every day (HBP 9:187).

Boothby, Gladys. *Character.* From QA. Inventor of the Moontrimmer broomstick in 1901 (QA 48–49).
See also Quidditch Through the Ages

Borgin and Burke's. *Magical place.* A wizard's shop on Knockturn Alley. Harry accidentally arrives there on his first trip by Floo Powder (CS 4:49). Borgin and Burke's is filled with objects and contraptions related to the Dark Arts, such as glass eyes, human bones, bloody cards, and rusty instruments (CS 4:49). Tom Riddle worked at the shop right after he left Hogwarts. Many believed he was wasting his many talents, but he spent much of his time convincing people to give up their valuable goods to sell at the store (HBP 20:432–33).

Borgin, Mr. *Character.* The owner of Borgin and Burke's. He agrees to buy some of Lucius Malfoy's illegal Dark Arts loot (CS 4:51). When Draco Malfoy goes into Mr. Borgin's store in Year 6, Borgin shows more deference to a teenager than most elders would, which gives Harry evidence for his claim that Draco is a Death Eater (HBP 6:124).

Boris the Bewildered. *Magical statue.* Cedric Diggory tells Harry to use the prefect's bathroom to help him understand the clues in the golden egg for the second task of the Triwizard Tournament. He tells him the bathroom is located four doors down to the left of the statue of Boris the Bewildered. The password is "pine fresh" (GF 23:431). The figure of Boris has a confused expression, and his gloves are on the wrong hands (GF 25:459).

See also Statues

Bottle Puzzle. *Magical puzzle.* The logic puzzle at the end of Year 1, which Hermione solves so she, Harry, and Ron may keep looking for the Sorcerer's Stone (SS 16:285). Viewers of the film were disappointed that this was left out of the movie because scenes showing a young female using logic forcefully and successfully are so rarely depicted in fiction or film. It is impossible for the reader to discern the answer to the puzzle from the facts given in the novel, since the location of the different-sized bottles is not defined.

Bouncing Bulb. *Magical plant.* One of these plant parts bops Harry in the face during Herbology (GF 18:293).

Bowtruckle. *Magical creature.* Bowtruckles are classified 2X by the MM, which means they are safe and tameable. A Bowtruckle can grow to eight inches and it clings to trees; it is shy, eats insects, and is only threatening when its tree is approached for purposes such as getting wood for wands. It can be pacified during such an operation by being fed woodlice (FB 5). Hermione earns five points for Gryffindor when she identifies Bowtruckles by name in Prof. Grubbly-Plank's Care of Magical Creatures class. She also states that they will eat fairy eggs (OP 13:259).

See also Fantastic Beasts and Where to Find Them

"The Boy Who Lived." *Magical nickname.* Wizards and witches toast the infant Harry Potter with this moniker the night his parents are killed as he miraculously survives. He is later known by this name in other places (SS 1:17).

"The Boy Who Scored." *Magical slur.* Draco Malfoy says this mockingly to Harry in Year 6 (HBP 19:412).

Boyhood. *See* Coming-of-Age Story

Bradley. *Character.* Slytherin Quidditch player whom Ron successfully blocks as Keeper (OP 31:703).

Braga Broomfleet. *Magical sports team.* From QA. A professional Quidditch team from Portugal (QA 41).

See also Quidditch Through the Ages

Bragge, Barberus. *Character.* From QA. The Chief of the Wizards' Council in 1269. He instituted Snidget-hunting as part of Quidditch, as chronicled by Modesty Rabnott in a letter to her sister, Prudence. Bragge fined Modesty 10 Galleons after she rescued a Snidget from the game she was watching. Bragge's idea stayed with the game for some time, adding 150 points to whichever team's "Hunter" caught the Snidget (QA 11–14).

See also Quidditch Through the Ages

Brain Room. *Magical place.* A section of the Department of Mysteries at the Ministry (OP 35:797).

Brains. The Department of Mysteries has a tank with these floating inside (OP 34:772).

Brand, Captain Rudolf. *Character.* From QA. The Seeker of the Heidelberg Harriers who asks his opposing Seeker, Gwendolyn Morgan of the Holyhead Harpies, to marry him at the end of a match. She says neither "yes" nor "no," but instead hits him over the head with her Cleansweep Five broomstick (QA 34–35).
See also Quidditch Through the Ages

Brankovitch, Maximus, III. *Character.* From QA. Seeker on the Fitchburg Finches American Quidditch team; he has been the captain of the American Quidditch team at the World Cup over the two years previous to the publication of QA (QA 45).
See also Quidditch Through the Ages

Branstone, Eleanor. *Character.* A Hufflepuff student, three years behind Harry (GF 12:178).

Brazil. Ron Weasley is leary of foreigners at the Quidditch World Cup campground partly because of a bad experience his brother Bill had with a pen pal from Brazil. The friend asked Bill to come to his country to visit, but Mr. Weasley said they could not afford it. When Bill wrote to say that he could not come, the Brazilian pen pal sent him a hat with a curse on it that made Bill's ears shrivel (GF 7:85).

Break With a Banshee. *Magical book. Break With a Banshee* is a second-year "textbook" written by Gilderoy Lockhart (CS 4:43).
See also Banshee

"Bring-and-Fly Sale." *Fake ad/event.* Rita Skeeter mocks Luna Lovegood because her father probably runs a newspaper that tells the dates of a "Bring-and-Fly Sale" (OP 25:568).

Bristol, England. Perhaps as a nod to the town where her father worked while she was growing up, Rowling has infant Harry Potter fall asleep in Hagrid's care as they fly on Black's motorcycle over this village on their way to Privet Drive (SS 1:15).

British Quidditch League Headquarters. *Magical place.* This office is located in the Department of Magical Games and Sports on the seventh level of the Ministry (OP 7:129).

British Quidditch Team. *Magical sports team.* The British Quidditch Team lost badly to Translyvania in the running for the World Cup. The score was 390 to 1 (GF 5:63). The British Quidditch League Headquarters is located in the Department of Magical Games and Sports on the seventh level of the Ministry (OP 7:129).

Broadmoor, Kevin and Karl. *Characters.* From QA. Quidditch Beaters for the Falmouth Falcons from 1958 to 1969 who were known for playing rough and received at least fourteen suspensions (QA 34).
See also Quidditch Through the Ages

Brockdale Bridge. *Muggle object.* A bridge less than ten years old that broke in half and sent about a dozen cars to the water below. It is a problem that the Muggle Prime Minister thinks he alone is having, until he is visited by Cornelius Fudge (HBP 1:2, 4).

Brocklehurst, Mandy. *Character.* Student in Harry's year; sorted into Ravenclaw (SS 7:119).

Broken Balls: When Fortunes Turn Foul. *Magical book.* Harry sees this book at Flourish and Blotts (PA 4:53).

Brookstanton, Rupert "Axebanger." *Character.* Hermione seeks somebody with the initials "R. A. B." She is trying to identify the author of the note left in the locket Dumbledore was carrying when he died. Although she finds Brookstanton's name in the library, she does not think he is the author of the note (HBP 30:636).

Broom Regulatory Control. *Magical office.* Located in the Department of Magical Transport on the sixth floor of the Ministry (OP 7:129).

Broomstick Servicing Kit. *Magical object.* Hermione sends Harry a Broomstick Servicing Kit for his thirteenth birthday. It contains a jar of Fleetwood's High-Finish Handle Polish, Tail-Twig Clippers, a brass compass for long trips, and a *Handbook of Do-It-Yourself Broomcare* (PA 1:12).

Broomstick shed, Weasleys'. *Magical place.* A small storage building at the Burrow where the Weasleys keep their brooms. This is where Dumbledore discusses Sirius Black's death with Harry and informs him of his upcoming private lessons with Dumbledore in his sixth year (HBP 4:76–78).

Broomsticks. *Magical objects.* Much is made in the series of this traditional symbol of witches. In folklore, it was thought that witches were homemakers who flew out of their houses through the chimneys on their brooms. Rather than providing the chief means of transportation for the magical characters in the Harry Potter books, however, broomsticks of various makes and models are employed primarily in playing the popular sport of Quidditch. Wizards and witches drool over the latest and fastest models in store windows at Diagon Alley, and the most recent model is always thought to be superior to those that came before. Having the latest Nimbus racing broomstick as part of a player's or team's equipment is believed to give a Quidditch player or team an advantage in the game.

In Book 1, Harry Potter sees Draco Malfoy and a group of boys admiring the Nimbus 2000 in a window on Diagon Alley. Later, Harry proves during Flying Lessons that he has a talent for flying quickly on a broom; shortly thereafter, an anonymous donor sends Harry a Nimbus 2000 broomstick. He is recruited to be the Seeker on the Gryffindor team, a position rarely held by a first-year student. Harry becomes the envy of his peers when he is found to possess this latest, most fashionable and expensive broomstick. The Weasleys, by contrast, still have older Cleansweep Fives or Sevens.

The Nimbus 2000 has a shiny mahogany handle, gold lettering, and long, straight twigs. The main attraction of the Nimbus racing broom, however, is its performance— they reach speeds of up to 100 miles an hour, they are able to turn 360 degrees in mid-air from a stopped position, and they are reliable and easy to handle.

In QA, at least two chapters are devoted to the broomstick and its history, including the development of the "racing broom." According to QA, models of the broom used chiefly for sport include: Cleansweep One (the first mass-marketed racing broom in 1926), the Comet 140 of 1929, the Timberblast of 1940, the Swiftstick of 1952, and the

Shooting Star developed in 1952. In 1967 the Nimbus company formed to manufacture high-end racing brooms and continued to dominate the market well into Harry Potter's time at the turn of the twentieth century. Its only competition, the Twigger 90, proved to have manufacturing defects that involved warping. In Book 2, Lucius Malfoy, not to be outdone by the Gryffindor House Quidditch team, buys the entire Slytherin House team a set of Nimbus 2001 broomsticks so that his son, Draco, may be made Seeker.

The broomsticks in the series require maintenance by the Quidditch players who own them to keep them in top operating condition. Hermione gives Harry a Broomstick Servicing Kit for his thirteenth birthday that includes a jar of Fleetwood's High-Finish Handle Polish, Tail-Twig Clippers, a brass compass, and a *Handbook of Do-It-Yourself Broomcare.*

Critics see the series' attention to brand names and material objects such as the racing brooms as feeding into, and encouraging, the materialistic culture and class conflicts of children. Others argue that material culture is already well embedded in children as it is in adults, and the series simply portrays the world in figurative terms as many children in civilized countries live it today. They say young readers benefit from seeing consumerism brought out into the open for consideration.

When Ron is made prefect, his mother tells him he can have a new broomstick, and he chooses the latest model of Cleansweep since it is less costly than a Firebolt. He looks at the Cleansweep in a catalog, which advertises it as going from 0 to 70 miles per hour in 10 seconds (OP 9:170). The catalog also describes it as having a Spanish oak handle complete with anti-jinx varnish and vibration control (OP 9:173). Umbridge confiscates Harry's Firebolt and Fred and George's Cleansweeps when she bans them from playing Quidditch. She keeps them chained and padlocked to her office wall (OP 28:629). Fred and George's lifetime ban from Quidditch and the confiscation of their brooms seems to be the last straw for the twins. They leave Hogwarts soon afterwards.

The broom is perhaps one of the most recognizable symbols of witchcraft. The origin of the association between the two is cloudy. One source of the connection may be the custom in the fifteenth through seventeenth centuries of a woman leaving her broom on the porch by the door or sticking it out of the chimney to signal that she is not at home. This practice may have also led to stories of women flying out of their chimneys on brooms. Another source may be a pagan fertility rite that involved men and women straddling broomstick and pitchfork handles like hobbyhorses and running and leaping in the air about the fields.

Further Reading: Guiley, Rosemary Ellen. *The Encyclopedia of Witches and Witchcraft.* New York: Facts on File, 1999; Russell, Jeffrey B. *A History of Witchcraft.* London: Thames and Hudson, 1980.

Brother Benedict. *Character.* From *Fantastic Beasts.* Franciscan monk from Worcestershire whose manuscript fragment survives to give proof that Muggles did notice fantastic beasts many years ago, but may have mistaken what they were (FB xiv).
See also Fantastic Beasts and Where to Find Them

Brother Boniface's Turnip Wine. *Muggle drink.* From *Fantastic Beasts.* Brother Benedict mentions this in his manuscript fragment (FB xiv).
See also Fantastic Beasts and Where to Find Them

Brown, Lavender. *Character.* Student in Harry's year; the first student in his year sorted into Gryffindor House (SS 7:119). Parvati Patil tells Lavender Brown that she heard Hermione crying in the girls' bathroom on the night of the Halloween Feast in Year 1 (SS 10:172). She is impressed at the first DADA meeting where Harry's accomplishments are discussed (OP 16:342). She and Ron spend much of Year 6 "snogging" (HBP 14:300).

Bryce, Frank. *Character.* The Riddles' gardener in Little Hangleton. He returned from the war with a leg that resisted bending and a discomfort with crowds and loud sounds. Fifty years ago he was accused of the murders of Mr. and Mrs. Riddle and their son Tom, but he insisted on his innocence. He claimed that the only person he had ever seen around the house was a pale, dark-haired teenage boy (GF 1:2). Bryce is going on seventy-seven years old in Book 4 (GF 1:5). Voldemort kills him when Nagini informs Voldemort that a Muggle is outside his room listening to his conversation with Wormtail (GF 1:15).

Bubble-Head Charm. *Magical spell.* This spell puts a large bubble of clean air around the head of the one who casts it. Students frequently use the charm to avoid the foul odors of Dung Bombs and Stinkpellets (OP 30:677).

Bubotubers. *Magical plant.* Plants that look like black slugs. They have swollen nodules all over them that are full of pus. In Prof. Sprout's Herbology class, the students squeeze the nodules and collect the pus. The substance is used to cure acne (GF 13:194–95). After a Rita Skeeter article appears in *Witch Weekly* wrongfully accusing Hermione of being mean to Harry Potter, Hermione receives hate mail with undiluted pus in it that puts yellow boils all over her hands (GF 28:541).

Buckbeak. *Magical creature.* Hagrid's pet hippogriff. Harry makes friends with Buckbeak in Hagrid's first Care of Magical Creatures class in Year 3. Harry rides on the creature as it flies around the paddock. It has a twenty-four-foot wingspan (PA 6:115–17). Unfortunately, Draco Malfoy is not as careful meeting Buckbeak and ends up being deeply scratched. This results in Draco's father calling for not only the removal of Hagrid as teacher and Dumbledore as headmaster, but the execution of Buckbeak (PA 6:118). Buckbeak is scheduled to be executed on June 6 at sundown, but is saved by Harry and Hermione with the use of a Time-Turner (PA 21:400). Buckbeak flies off with Sirius Black on his back as they both escape at the end of *Prisoner of Azkaban*. For a while, they live in the mountains. When they return to London to work for the Order, Sirius keeps Buckbeak upstairs in Number Twelve, Grimmauld Place in his mother's bedroom (OP 6:102). After Sirius's death, Dumbledore and the Order send Buckbeak to Hagrid to look after, and he is renamed Witherwings to protect him from the Ministry. Dumbledore tells Harry that the hippogriff now belongs to him, since he was part of the Grimmauld Place estate that Harry inherited from Sirius. Harry prefers that Buckbeak stay with Hagrid because he thinks Buckbeak will be happy there (HBP 3:53).
See also Hippogriff

Budleigh Babberton. *Magical place.* Muggle village where Horace Slughorn is living in retirement. He keeps moving about, and he has occupied a house during a Muggle's vacation to the Canary Islands (HBP 4:59).

Bulbadox Powder. *Magical substance.* Bulbadox Powder causes boils. Fred Weasley puts some powder in Kenneth Towler's pajamas in their fifth year (OP 12:226).

Bulgarian Quidditch Team. *Magical sports team.* This team plays against Ireland in the Quidditch World Cup and has Viktor Krum as a star player (GF 5:63). Their campsite features blinking posters of a moving Viktor Krum over each tent (GF 7:83).

Bullies and bullying. Students and teachers alike at Hogwarts intimidate others whom they perceive to be weaker than themselves. These individuals also bully those whom they view as competition, a threat, or whom they simply do not like for some other reason. Certainly, Draco Malfoy and his cohorts, Vincent Crabbe and Gregory Goyle from Slytherin House, fit this category. Likewise, Severus Snape, the Potions teacher, bullies Harry and others in his classes. Dolores Umbridge bullies everyone in her path. Harry sees that bullying extends back in time, and in people whom he would rather not think engaged in the practice; when he sees Snape's memory in the Pensieve, Harry discovers that Snape was bullied as a youth by a classmate—James Potter.

The Scottish press picked up on the bullies in the books because bullying was an issue of public concern in Scottish and British schools when the books first came out. Rowling has said that she had one sadistic teacher in school who seemed to take pride in making students feel inadequate. It was reported that at least one female bully at Wyedean Comprehensive pushed Rowling up against her locker when she was a student there. She struggled to hold her ground as the locker was the only thing holding her up. Rowling avoided the girl in the halls for some time afterwards. Another account stated that Rowling witnessed a very fair young male student in her school getting harassed often. These and other incidents sensitized Rowling to the very real and all too common experience of school bullies that her young readers, even now, must endure on a daily basis.

In a 2000 *Time* magazine interview, Rowling admitted that one of the things she was doing with bullies in the novels was exploring how other people behave around them and why. Weaker children tend to want to hang around bullies, for example, because they make them feel safe or important, and everyone wants to feel safe and important. She has also said elsewhere that Dudley Dursley is a physical bully who beats up on kids in his neighborhood just because he is bigger, not smarter. Draco Malfoy, however, has the brains to figure out just what buttons to push to hurt those he chooses to pick on most. The implication is that this quality makes Draco even more sinister.

The profile of bullies in the novels, and Rowling's public concern over them in children's lives, is great enough that a question related to them from a fan is answered on Rowling's website. The fan asks what young people who encounter a bully should do. Rowling's advice is to tell someone—a parent, teacher, or other adult—and keep telling other people if the first person does not believe the incident happened or does not do anything about it. Rowling clearly sees bullying as a real and present problem for young people, many of whom are her readers.

Bulstrode, Millicent. *Character.* Student in Harry's year; she is sorted into Slytherin (SS 7:119). Millicent is Hermione's partner during the Dueling Club lesson (CS 12:214). She becomes of member of Umbridge's Inquisitorial Squad and holds Hermione up against Umbridge's wall (OP 32:742).

Bumphing. *Magical sports penalty.* From QA. A foul in Quidditch committed when a Beater hits a Bludger toward the crowd, resulting in halt of play. The move is occasionally made by an unsavory player in an attempt to keep a Chaser from scoring (QA 29).

See also Quidditch Through the Ages

Bundimun. *Magical creature.* From *Fantastic Beasts.* Classified 3X by the MM, meaning that a wizard with reasonable skills can deal with any of the Bundimun's complications. It looks like green fungus and is a pest that infests houses and makes a smelly odor as it rots wood. Its secretions are used in various magical cleaning solutions (FB 5–6).
See also Fantastic Beasts and Where to Find Them

Bungs, Rosalind Antigone. *Character.* Hermione finds this name in the library in her search to identify the author—"R.A.B."—of the note left in the locket Dumbledore was carrying when he died (HBP 30:636).

Bungy. *Bird.* A parakeet-like bird ("budgie") living in Five Feathers in Barnsley that has apparently been taught to water-ski and will soon be featured on the news as reported by Mary Dorkins. Harry hears the announcement that this report is coming up when he is hiding outside the Number Four, Privet Drive window, trying to hear anything on the news about Voldemort (OP 1:4).

Burke, Caractacus. *Character.* One of the founders of Borgin and Burke's. Dumbledore takes Harry into one of Burke's memories in the Pensieve. In the memory, Burke is telling someone about the Slytherin locket that he bought from Merope Riddle for 10 Galleons (HBP 13:261).

Burning Day. *Magical event.* The day that a phoenix bursts into flames and is reborn from the ashes. Harry first sees Fawkes on one such day in Dumbledore's office (CS 12:207).

The Burrow. *Magical place.* The Weasley family residence, located outside of Ottery St. Catchpole (CS 3:31–32). The Burrow is a stone cottage that may have begun as a pigpen with several additions and levels; it has a red roof with four or five chimneys. Chickens scuttle about the lawn. It is the first wizard's residence Harry has seen. Magical things happen at the Burrow as a matter of course. Dishes get washed when Molly Weasley waves her wand in their direction; the clock indicates when it is time to do different chores.
Ron's room is upstairs and has a sloping ceiling. Nearly everything in it is orange, the color of his favorite professional Quidditch team, the Chudley Cannons. His bedspread has the Cannons logo on it, two black C's, and a racing cannonball on a bright orange background. He owns a tank with frogspawn in it, messy stacks of books, and several comic books of the character Martin Miggs, the Mad Muggle. The tattered walls are lined with posters, and a ghoul lives in the attic above the room (CS 3:40). When Ron seems a bit uncertain in showing Harry his house and small room, Harry assures him that the Burrow is the best house he has ever visited (CS 3:41). Harry stays with the Weasleys at the Burrow for one month before Year 2 at Hogwarts (CS 5:66). Because of the trees and layout of the grounds, the Weasleys are able to practice Quidditch in the orchard (GF 10:150).

Bust, Medieval Wizard. *Magical statue.* The bust is located near the hallway to Dolores Umbridge's office at Hogwarts. It mumbles to itself (OP 32:738).

Butterbeer. *Magical drink.* A popular drink served at the Three Broomsticks pub in Hogsmeade. It can be served either hot or cold (PA 10:201). Fans of the series have made their own versions of the sweet drink with cream soda and butterscotch syrup.

✦ C ✦

Cabbage. When a location has a foul smell in the series, it often bears the odor of cabbage. Mrs. Figg's house smells like it (SS 2:22).

Cadogen, Sir. *Character.* The spritely knight on a gray pony in one of the portraits on Hogwarts' walls. Sir Cadogen goes on an entertaining quest to help Harry and Ron find the North Tower where Divination class is held (PA 6:99–101). When the Fat Lady's portrait is attacked, he is the only one who volunteers to take her place guarding Gryffindor Tower (PA 9:167). Cadogen unintentionally allows an intruder into Gryffindor Tower because the person has all of the week's passwords (stolen from Neville Longbottom) written down on a slip of paper (PA 13:268). Cadogen gets fired as guard as a result (PA 14:269). Harry must pass Cadogen's portrait frequently on his way to the North Tower and Divination class (OP 12:236).

Cadwallader. *Character.* Chaser on the Hufflepuff team in Harry's sixth year. Luna Lovegood cannot remember his name as she commentates the game (HBP 19:414).

Caerphilly Catapults. *Magical sports team.* From QA. The Welsh Quidditch team that originated in 1402. "Dangerous" Dai Llewellyn was its most famous player (QA 33). The Catapults were the opponents in the game where Seeker Roderick Plumpton set the record for the fastest Snitch catch at three and a half seconds (QA 37).
  See also Quidditch Through the Ages

Calming Draught. *Magical substance.* Madam Pomfrey administers a Calming Draught to Hannah Abbott when she becomes distraught and anxious about her upcoming Herbology O.W.L. exam (OP 27:606).

Camping, Wizard. The tents the wizards use at the Quidditch World Cup have special features that do not make them blend in with the standard Muggle tent (as they are supposed to do to avoid detection). Special features include: three floors, turrets, weathervanes, chimneys, bell-pulls, fountains, peacocks stationed at the entrance, a birdbath, and a sundial (GF 7:78). The Weasley tent is borrowed from Perkins, an office colleague of Arthur Weasley, and it looks like an old, two-person tent on the outside. Inside, it is actually a three-room apartment with bunk beds and a kitchen and bath. It reminds Harry of Mrs. Figg's house, complete with crocheted furniture covers and cat odor (GF 7:80). Cooking seems to be another area in which the magical world finds it difficult to imitate the Muggle world. Mr. Weasley insists on cooking outside on a fire, even though they have a full kitchen in their tent (GF 7:80). Though some wizards make fire from their wands, others struggle to light their fires with matches the Muggle way (GF 7:81).

Wizard children wander outside the tents and get hold of their parents' wands. Some ride a small broomstick inches above the ground (GF 7:81). Clearly, a wizard campground would not escape the notice of any Muggle, regardless of how fancy or fully equipped his or her own recreational vehicle might be.

Canada. For *Goblet of Fire*, J. K. Rowling made a book tour to Canada in 2000. She did a reading at the Skydome in Toronto to approximately 12,000 screaming fans. She had to wear earplugs to muffle the noise while she read, and when the reading was over, she pulled one plug out as she was taking her bows just so that she could hear what the crowd really sounded like before she left the stage. Just twenty-four hours later, she read before 10,000 people as part of the International Writers and Readers Festival in Vancouver. She has described these stadium appearances as something like rock concerts.

Canada has embraced the Harry Potter books, published there by Raincoast Books, from the beginning. A contest was sponsored asking young readers to write about how Harry Potter had changed their lives. Rowling met with the finalists at a special breakfast that was arranged during the *Goblet of Fire* book tour and was moved by the experience of hearing their essays, though she says she felt somewhat embarrassed by the topic and the contest in general.

One Canadian fan, in particular, became well known in Harry Potter lore. Natalie McDonald and her mother had written to J. K. Rowling in July 1999. Natalie was dying and it was one of her final wishes to meet the famous author on her next trip to Canada. Just before Rowling's reply reached the girl's mother, Natalie died. Rowling memorialized her by using her name in *Goblet of Fire* as a new student whom the Sorting Hat chooses for Gryffindor House. She is the only person from real life to be incorporated into the series entirely as herself.

Rowling has said that her father once had an opportunity to be transferred to Canada when she was young. She says she looked forward to it at the time, but the transfer did not occur.

In QA, the Canadian Quidditch teams are said to be among the best in the world. They are: the Moose Jaw Meteorites, the Haileyburg Hammers, and the Stonewall Stormers (QA:43).

See also Readings, public and private

Canary Creams. *Magical candy.* Fred and George Weasley invent these and sell them for 7 Sickles apiece at Hogwarts (GF 21:367).

Candy and sweets. *Magical food.* If Rowling's readers enjoy sweets, they have more than enough to satisfy their appetites in the Harry Potter series. Harry begins to see the splendor of his new life when the vendor cart appears on the Hogwarts Express, and he looks for Mars Bars that are not there, but finds that the cart is loaded with fascinating treats such as Chocolate Frogs with wizard collector cards, Bertie Bott's Every Flavor Beans, Droobles Best Blowing Gum, Pumpkin Pasties, Cauldron Cakes, and Licorice Wands. Harry buys several of each and shares his loot with Ron Weasley. It is Harry's generosity and their first sharing experience that begin their important friendship (SS 6:101–2).

Sweets continue to marvel and delight the participants at Hogwarts, at feasts, in Honeydukes at Hogsmeade, and other places. Fred and George Weasley are involved in making treats of various kinds, such as Canary Creams, some with tricks and some not. Even Albus Dumbledore enjoys a Bertie Bean or two and has a known fondness for lemon drops (or sherbet lemons, actually a different kind of candy, in the British edition). Desserts at Hogwarts' feasts include treacle tart, spotted dick (a steamed suet pudding with raisins or currants), and chocolate gateau (GF 12:183).

Chocolate has magical properties beyond satisfying the sweet tooth in Harry's world. Prof. Lupin has Harry eat some chocolate after he is attacked by the Dementor on the Hogwarts Express, and Madame Pomfrey offers Honeydukes' best chocolate as an antidote on other occasions. She keeps large chunks of it on hand in the hospital wing. If Dementors symbolize depression, then chocolate can be seen in the wizarding world as lifting one's spirits, perhaps as much as it does for many people in the Muggle world.

Rowling was asked in an interview which of the candies in her magical world would be her favorite. She answered that it would be the Chocolate Frogs because she would like to collect the cards, but in another interview she named Cockroach Clusters. Both varieties are a nod on Rowling's part to one of her favorite entertainments—the British comedy *Monty Python*. There was once a popular *Monty Python* sketch about a candy maker who made revolting chocolates.

"Caput Draconis." *Magical password.* The first password Harry learns to get into the Gryffindor Common Room through the entrance behind the portrait of the Fat Lady (SS 7:130).

Care of Magical Creatures. *Magical class.* This class at Hogwarts introduces students to various magical creatures and teaches them how to feed and care for them. Fred and George Weasley feed a Filibuster Firework to a salamander, much to Percy Weasley's dismay (CS 8:131–32). Hagrid fills in for a while teaching this class. Prof. Kettleburn used to teach it. Percy Weasley advises Harry in planning his schedule for Year 3 that his older brother Charlie chose this class because of his interest in the outdoors (CS 14:252). Prof. Dumbledore writes in his foreword to *Fantastic Beasts* that Hogwarts' students consistently earn high marks in this class, perhaps due to *Fantastic Beasts* being assigned regularly as a textbook (FB vii).

For Harry's practical O.W.L. in the subject (held on the grounds near the Forbidden Forest), he is asked to pick out the Knarl from a group of hedgehogs; then he must properly handle a Bowtruckle, feed and clean a Fire Crab, and choose the proper food for a sick unicorn (OP 31:717).

Careers. Over their Easter holiday in Year 5, Hogwarts students have what amounts to a guidance counselor meeting about what kind of job they might eventually want. They are then advised on what O.W.L.s and N.E.W.T.s are required for obtaining that position. The various careers mentioned in the flyers that Harry and his friends look at include: Healer, Muggle Relations, Wizard banking, training security trolls, and working in the Department of Magical Accidents and Catastrophes (OP 29:656–57).

Harry discusses his desire to become an Auror with Prof. McGonagall. She tells him the requirements in terms of O.W.L.s and N.E.W.T.s, plus the other exams given to Auror candidates by the Ministry. However, Umbridge interferes many times in McGonagall's advising session, playing down Harry's chances of becoming an Auror. She says Harry is as likely to become an Auror as Dumbledore is to return to Hogwarts. With that, McGonagall proclaims that it is a sure thing that Harry will become an Auror, and she says that she will prepare him herself so that he meets all of the requirements (OP 29:662–65).

Carmichael, Eddie. *Character.* A Ravenclaw sixth-year student in Harry's fifth year who tries to sell Harry and Ron a bottle of Baruffio's Brain Elixir (OP 31:708).

Carrows. *Characters.* Death Eaters, perhaps siblings or a couple. Bellatrix Lestrange charges that Snape did not look for Voldemort when he disappeared, so Snape counters with the claim that neither did other Death Eaters, such as the Carrows (HBP 2:26).

Cartomancy. Cartomancy involves reading the constellations in conjunction with a deck of cards. Trelawney tells Harry that Firenze does not know this area of Divination (HBP 25:544).

Castles. From Hogwarts to Edinburgh to Chepstow, J. K. Rowling has not only imagined castles, but has lived in a region of the world where she can see them on a fairly regular basis. Two of the towns she lived in for many years are overlooked by prominent

Rear view of Edinburgh Castle as seen from the street, between 1860 and 1890. Courtesy of the Library of Congress.

castles on cliffs and can be seen and felt as important aspects of the communities' histories and atmospheres.

The construction of the Castle of Chepstow began in 1067, the year after the battle of Hastings. Situated defensively on a cliff overlooking the River Wye, J. K. Rowling saw it frequently when she lived in Tutshill and attended Wyedean Comprehensive—the same seven years of her life that her students spend attending Hogwarts. The castle includes Marten's Tower, Outer Gatehouse, the East Chamber Block, the Great Tower, and the Great Hall. The castle's long and varied history includes various terms as a fortification, a role in a British Civil War when it was held for the King and fell, and a term as a prison. Eventually, the armaments were taken out and the castle was left to ruin until it was purchased by the state in the 1950s. Visitors can tour its ruins along the River Wye and take pictures of its ragged beauty reflected in the water from the opposite shore.

Another prominent castle in J. K. Rowling's life is Edinburgh Castle. Edinburgh Castle has a long and important role in Scottish history. Many say studying the history of the castle is learning the history of Scotland. It is also situated upon a cliff and overlooks the city of Edinburgh. J. K. Rowling moved to Edinburgh with her young daughter in 1993 and has kept the city and its surrounding countryside as her main residence ever since.

The Scots are so proud of the castle and link it so intimately with their long history that they say the beginning of the castle dates back millions of years. They link it to a volcano that once existed in the rock on which the castle was built, and to a Bronze Age fort built on the spot in 1000 B.C. Malcolm III and Queen Margaret built a hunting lodge at the site around A.D. 1000, which began its existence as a fortress for royalty. The castle includes St. Margaret's chapel built in Queen Margaret's memory, the Great Hall, the Portcullis Gate, the Gatehouse, Mills Mount, and Crown Square. Interestingly, the Palace has only recently regained the Stone of Destiny from England's Westminster Abbey. The stone is a symbolic object that is important to the Scottish people because it was the seat where royalty received their coronations. Scottish kings were crowned on the stone for 400 years, then English monarchs for another 300, and both Scottish and English for the last 400 years, since 1603.

Readers of the Harry Potter series know that Hogwarts School of Witchcraft and Wizardry is a castle with mysterious passageways, dungeons, a Great Hall, moving staircases, and towers where the students live. Knowing that many of J. K. Rowling's long-term residences have been dominated by castles in their skylines may help readers understand why it is perhaps natural for her to write about these magical settings.

Catcher. *Magical sports position.* From QA. An old name for a Chaser in "Kwidditch," the old form of Quidditch (QA 9–10).
See also Quidditch Through the Ages

Catherine Wheels. *Magical object.* A kind of firework that Fred and George Weasley set off at the school in protest of Umbridge taking over (OP 28:632).
See also Weasleys' Wildfire Whiz-Bangs

Cats. *Magical creatures.* There are several cats in the series, as one might expect in books about witches and wizards. In ancient Rome, cats were a symbol of liberty since they dislike confinement so intensely. In ancient Egypt, cats were sacred, and there was a penalty of death to anyone who killed one even accidentally. In mythology, the goddess Diana was thought to take the form of a cat, which brought about the fury of the Giants.

In medieval times, a cat was called a "familiar," meaning that Satan preferred to take the form of a cat. The latter is probably what has led to current superstitions about cats, including the belief that one will have bad luck if a black cat crosses one's path.

Among the many cats in the series is the tabby cat Mr. Dursley spots reading a map on his way to work (SS 1:2, 5) and Mrs. Figgs' cats: Tibbles, Snowy, Mr. Paws, and Tufty (SS 2:22). Prof. McGonagall turns into a cat as an Animagus. Hermione Granger owns Crookshanks, a cat said to have been at the store for a long time before she bought him. Argus Filch's cat, Mrs. Norris, has protruding eyes like his and is dust-colored (SS 8:132).

One thing seems to be certain, and that is that cats, with their rich history and folklore, warrant close scrutiny in the Harry Potter books.

See also Animals

Cauldron. *Magical object.* A mixing pot that wizards and witches use to make potions and other concoctions. These are the first magical products Harry sees when he arrives at Diagon Alley for the first time. He sees a stack of

As might be expected, cats play an important role in J. K. Rowling's magical series. Courtesy of the Dover Pictorial Archive.

cauldrons and a sign over them advertising items in copper, brass, pewter, silver, as well as those that stir themselves and collapse flat (SS 5:71). Harry needs to buy a Pewter #2 model for his first year at Hogwarts, though he likes a gold one he sees better (SS 5:80). Hagrid makes sure he gets the right kind. Harry gives the full set of Lockhart's books to Ginny Weasley by dropping them into her cauldron in Flourish and Blott's; Ron puts his books in, too, and much commotion over books in the cauldron ensues, which results in Ginny unknowingly receiving Tom Riddle's diary from Lucius Malfoy (CS 4:61).

After he leaves Hogwarts, Percy Weasley joins the Ministry of Magic, working for Barty Crouch. One of his first assignments is to write a report on standardizing the thicknesses of cauldron bottoms for the Department of International Magical Cooperation (GF 5:56).

Although Cauldrons in Hogwarts' Potions class are used to make unharmful substances, one potion makes the largest cauldron Harry has ever seen all the more terrifying at the Little Hangleton graveyard. Voldemort concocts a potion that includes Pettigrew's arm, blood from Harry, and other ingredients. The potion allows Voldemort to rise again (GF 32:639–40).

Throughout the folklore of many cultures, cauldrons have been associated with witches and witchcraft. Bizarre potions of animal and insect parts and blood mixed with exotic roots, plants, powders, or other substances were thought to be stirred and cooked in them over a blazing fire. Many works of folk art depict witches sitting or standing in a circle around a black iron cauldron. One story tells of a witch stirring her potion with the

Hermione Granger (Emma Watson) using a cauldron to concoct the Polyjuice Potion in *Harry Potter and the Chamber of
Secrets* (2002). Courtesy of Photofest.

skull of a beheaded robber. Other stories tell of children being boiled in cauldrons. Still others tell of witches dumping the contents of their cauldrons into the ocean to cause storms.

The cauldron itself has magical powers in different cultures. In ancient Ireland, for example, the Celts thought that special cauldrons never ran out of food for a feast. Cauldrons also represented fertility, plenty, and rebirth of those who had died. This is one way in which the rise of Voldemort from a large cauldron fits with folklore. In Norse mythology, the god Odin drank blood from a cauldron of wisdom in order to receive divine powers. Cauldrons were also a tool of the alchemist who mixed and cooked ingredients with the hope of obtaining good health, longevity, purity, or immortality. Ironically, one story tells of a Scottish wizard in the fourteenth century who was boiled to death in a cauldron for his wicked use of magic.

Probably the most famous cauldron in literature is the boiling pot the three witches dance around in Shakespeare's *Macbeth*, Act IV, Scene 1. As they add strange and exotic ingredients to their potion, they sing: "Double, double toil and trouble / Fire burn and cauldron bubble."

> *Further Reading:* Guiley, Rosemary Ellen. *The Encyclopedia of Witches and Witchcraft*, 2nd ed. New York: Facts on File, 1999.

Cauldron Cakes. *Magical treat.* One of the treats sold on the Hogwarts Express Candy Cart that Harry buys and shares with Ron on their first meeting (SS 6:101). The witch who sells them leaves some with Harry to give to Prof. Lupin if he wakes up (PA 5:79).
  See also Candy and sweets

Cauldron Shop. *Magical place.* A shop on Diagon Alley. Harry sees the display of cauldrons outside this shop on his first visit to Diagon Alley (SS 5:71).

Cauldwell, Owen. *Character.* Hufflepuff student, three years behind Harry (GF 12:179).

The Cave. *Magical place.* Dumbledore takes Harry with him on a quest to find a Horcrux of Voldemort's that he thinks he has traced to this spot. First they Apparate to a cliff, then they slide from a rock into the sea and swim to a cave. The cave is the place where Dumbledore thinks Tom Riddle brought the two orphan children to terrorize them. It contains a lake that has been cursed with jinxes (HBP 26:555–60).

In the cave Dumbledore makes Harry promise to keep him drinking the potion that will allow him to grasp the locket he believes to be the Horcrux. The chapter has prompted intense scrutiny from close readers of the series and has come to be known as "the cave chapter." One reason it receives such attention is that Prof. Dumbledore mumbles mysterious and provocative words while fighting the effects of the potion. Another reason is that the reader sees Dumbledore—a mentor to Harry for many books—now sorely at Harry's mercy. He has instructed Harry to do something that will hurt the great wizard physically and Harry emotionally. The locket that Dumbledore works so diligently through the maze of jinxes to retrieve turns out to have its Horcrux missing, supposedly taken already by someone with the mysterious initials, "R.A.B." It is unknown whether the potion Dumbledore drank in the cave had more of an effect on his life than he first revealed to Harry, but there is no doubt that the entire cave incident weakened the wise wizard more than he expected it would.

Celia. *Character.* A young female accompanying Tom Riddle, Sr., when he drives by the Gaunt shack on the other side of the valley from the land he owns. She notices a snake has been nailed to the door of the shack (HBP 10:209).

Censorship. *See* Book bannings and burnings

Centaur Liaison Office. *Magical office.* From *Fantastic Beasts*. This office was set up to facilitate relations between the wizard and centaur communities, but the centaurs have never used it. Being "sent" to this office has become an inside joke in the Ministry, meaning that the person in question was fired (FB xiii).

See also Fantastic Beasts and Where to Find Them

Centaurs. *Magical creatures.* Ranked 4X in the MM classification system due to the respect they deserve rather than any danger they cause. In *Fantastic Beasts* and in the series, centaurs are as intelligent as human beings (FB x). A centaur has a human form to the waist and a horse's body from the waist down. They should not be confused with the mythological figure Pan, which is half man, half goat. In the series, centaurs live in forests and stay away from wizards and Muggles to take care of their own affairs (FB 6).

A Greek mythological creature that is half man and half horse, the centaur was said to live in Thessaly of ancient Greece, where the horsemanship of its inhabitants was probably excellent and where the myth began.

Pallas and the Centaur by Sandro Botticelli (1482). The centaurs that live in the Forbidden Forest are intelligent and proud. © Erich Lessing/Art Resource, NY.

One myth tells the story that centaurs were invited to a wedding feast, but they tried to abduct the bride and were therefore driven out of the land.

In the series, several centaurs are said to live in the Forbidden Forest. Harry meets three of them—Bane, Firenze, and Rowan—in detention with Hagrid in Year 1. Firenze saves Harry from Voldemort in that encounter (15:252–57). About fifty centaurs converge on Umbridge, Harry, and Hermione when they end up in the Forbidden Forest. Since centaurs resent being called "half-humans," Umbridge quickly makes a mistake in addressing them as such, much to her disadvantage (OP 33:753).

The centaur herd appears at Dumbledore's funeral, just inside the woods, with their bows aimed down. At some point in the ceremony, arrows shoot into the sky and this is the centaurs' tribute to the great wizard who always treated them with respect (HBP 30:645–46).

See also Fantastic Beasts and Where to Find Them; Firenze; Mythology, Use of

Chamber of Secrets. *Magical place.* In *Chamber of Secrets*, Harry and his friends see writing on the walls of the school that the chamber has been opened by the Slytherin heir. They try to find out what the chamber is, why it is significant, and where it is located. It turns out that it is beneath Hogwarts, possibly even below the lake, and it holds a Basilisk that does battle with Harry Potter. Malfoy tells Harry and Ron disguised as Crabbe and Goyle that the last time the chamber was opened, a Mudblood (Moaning Myrtle) died (CS 12:223).

See also Hogwarts School of Witchcraft and Wizardry

Chambers. *Character.* Slytherin Quidditch player whom Ron successfully blocks as Keeper (OP 31:704).

Chameleon Ghouls. *Magical creatures.* Hermione has read about these beings that can take on different disguises (CS 11:184).

See also Ghoul

Chancellor of the Exchequer. *Character.* Among others, this Muggle dignitary tried to remove the portrait of the Muggle Prime Minister from the wall of his office (HBP 1:7).

Chang, Cho. *Character.* A year older than Harry, Cho is Seeker on the Ravenclaw Quidditch team and the only girl on the team (PA 13:259). Oliver Wood tells Harry that Cho rides a Comet Two Sixty broomstick, which can be easily outridden by Harry's new Firebolt. Harry thinks Cho is pretty; she flies well on her broom (PA 13:254, 260). Harry spots her at the Quidditch World Cup campground (GF 7:84). Prof. McGonagall tells Harry that as a Triwizard Tournament champion, he is expected to have a partner at the Yule Ball. Harry wants to ask Cho to go with him, but she already said she would go with Cedric Diggory (GF 22:397).

Harry is embarrassed when Cho sees him covered with Stinksap from Neville's new plant on the Hogwarts Express (OP 10:187). Ron butts in on Harry's attempt at conversation with her, asking her about her Tutshill Tornados badge; she tells him she has supported the Quidditch team since she was six years old (OP 12:230). She tells Harry in the Owlery that she admires him standing up to Umbridge (OP 14:283). Cho is impressed at the first DADA meeting where Harry's accomplishments are discussed (OP 16:342). After a bit of confusion, Harry asks her to Hogsmeade with him on Valentine's Day (OP 24:528–29). Though things do not go well when Harry mentions that he is meeting Hermione at the Three Broomsticks at noon, Cho makes up with him after she reads the article in *The Quibbler* about him and the rise of Voldemort (OP 26:583).

Cho tries to apologize to Harry after Dumbledore's Army is caught and Dumbledore leaves Hogwarts, but Harry does not understand her compassion for Marietta Edgecombe. When Cho mentions to him that it is hard for Marietta to have her mother working at the Ministry, Harry reminds her that Ron's father is working there as well. When she disapproves of Hermione jinxing the document that Dumbledore's Army signed, Harry tells her he thought it was a brilliant idea. Cho leaves in a huff as Harry warns her not to start crying again (OP 28:637). On the Hogwarts Express on the way home, Cho sees Harry but blushes and keeps on walking. When Ron asks, Harry tells him that there is nothing between them anymore (OP 38:865). Ginny tells Harry and Ron that Cho is now seeing Michael Corner (OP 38:866).

Chapters. Each of the books (except for *Fantastic Beasts*, which contains entries on beasts listed alphabetically) is divided into titled chapters. The American editions contain illustrations on each chapter title page. The total number of chapters from Book 1 through Book 6 is 162, or an average of 27 chapters per novel. The number of chapters per book is as follows: *Sorcerer's Stone*, 17; *Chamber of Secrets*, 18; *Prisoner of Azkaban*, 22; *Goblet of Fire*, 37; *Order of the Phoenix*, 38; *Half-Blood Prince*, 30. The schoolbook, *Quidditch Through the Ages*, has 10 short chapters.

Most chapters are written in third person, limited to Harry's point of view. However, there are four chapters up through Book 6 in the series in which this is not so because Harry is not in them. These are Chapter 1 of *Sorcerer's Stone*, "The Boy Who Lived"; Chapter 1 of *Goblet of Fire*, "The Riddle House"; and Chapters 1 and 2 of *Half-Blood Prince*, "The Other Minister" and "Spinner's End."

See also Illustrations

Charing Cross Road. *Muggle place.* The Knight Bus travels along this road on its way to taking Harry to Diagon Alley (PA 3:41). The Leaky Cauldron is located on this street (HBP 6:109).

Charm Club. *Magical student organization.* Angelina Johnson tells Harry that Vicky Frobisher would put Charm Club ahead of Quidditch, so she accepts Ron as Keeper over Vicky, even though Vicky showed more talent during try-outs (OP 13:276).

A Charm to Cure Reluctant Reversers. *Magical book.* When cruel Aunt Marge visits, Harry tries to avoid putting a spell on her by imagining page twelve from this book as a diversion for his mind (PA 2:27).

Charm Your Own Cheese. *Magical book.* Book in the Burrow (CS 3:34).

Charms class. *Magical class.* Class at Hogwarts taught by Prof. Flitwick. There is a marble staircase that leads up to the classroom (PA 15:294). Hermione is particularly talented in this class. Prof. Flitwick told her privately in Year 1 that she received a 112 on his exam (SS 16:271). In Year 3, when she is overscheduled and uses the Time-Turner to get to all of her classes, she forgets to go to one Charms class and misses the lesson on Cheering Charms (PA 15:295).

Chaser. *Magical sports position.* Position in Quidditch. Oliver Wood explains to Harry that the Chasers make up three of the seven players on each team. It is their job to throw and catch the Quaffle and get it through one of six hoops to score a goal. Goals are worth ten points (SS 10:167). It is the first position in the history of the game (QA 25).

Cheering Charm. *Magical spell.* This is the subject matter that Hermione misses in Year 3 when she forgets to attend Charms class because her schedule is overloaded. Ron comments happily to Harry on the way to lunch that Hermione could have used a little cheering up from the stress of her coursework (PA 15:294). Hermione is not sure she did as well she could have on the Cheering Charm part of the Theory of Charms O.W.L. exam because she ran out of time (OP 31:712).

Chemistry. J. K. Rowling did not take a class in Potions, but she did have challenges in John Nettleship's chemistry class at Wyedean Comprehensive. Her mother worked at the school as a lab technician, and Mr. Nettleship used to call on Rowling to answer questions in class even though he knew she was struggling with the subject. Some of Rowling's former classmates see connections between Prof. Snape and Rowling's chemistry teacher. Potions class at Hogwarts equate with chemistry in today's high schools.
See also Alchemy

Chepstow, Wales. This is the nearest town of any size to Tutshill, which is where J. K. Rowling lived from the time she was nine years old until she went off to college. Chepstow Castle overlooks the River Wye in this town.
See also Castles; Tutshill, England

Children's High Level Group. This is one of J. K. Rowling's chosen charities, an organization established to help Europe's institutionalized children. The children involved are being cared for by the state because they are orphaned, abandoned, disabled, or poor, or for some other reason because they cannot or are not cared for by parents, relatives, or foster families. J. K. Rowling began her involvement in the organization in Romania in January 2006 at the invitation of Baroness Emma Nicholson of Winterbourne. The Children's High Level Group seeks to protect children's rights. Rowling was first moved to act on the issue after reading an article by Justin Sparks in a June 2004 issue of the *Sunday Times*. The article described how many institutionalized children in Czechoslovakia are kept in cage beds, literally restrained and caged like animals. Not only did the horror of the children's plight affect Rowling, but it also particularly touched her because her greatest fear is not of spiders, as she is so famous for saying, but actually of being confined in a small space, much like Harry Potter's cupboard under the stairs at the Dursleys. After she read the article, Rowling wrote a letter to politicians and others and enclosed a copy of the article. One of the people contacted was the baroness, who was already at work on the issue; her invitation to Rowling to join the Children's High Level Group followed.

Further Reading: Rowling, J. K. "My Fight by J. K. Rowling." *The Sunday Times* (London), February 5, 2006. http://www.timesonline.co.uk/article/0,,2092-2025101_1,00.html.

Children's literature, series' role in. J. K. Rowling did not initially set out to write a series of books for children. She simply thought up the story and started writing. When she mailed the *Sorcerer's Stone* manuscript to an agent, however, she clearly labeled it as a middle-grade novel for ages nine to twelve. This was one reason the book may have been passed over at first. Christopher Little's literary agency did not handle children's books. When the readers at the firm started reading the manuscript, however, they were hooked, and the sweep of the Harry Potter phenomenon was set in motion.

It is too early to tell what the lasting influence of the series will be on children's literature. The seven books in the series are not all published, and time has not had a chance to sift and sort through both the criticism and the high praise. In the midst of the phenomenon, however, it is possible to determine influences that are contemporary to the publication of the first six books.

As a series with a strong male protagonist, the books have opened doors to reading, particularly for reluctant young male readers. Boys who would rather be out playing ball have hidden under the covers in their beds with flashlights, staying up late to read what happens to Harry next. In this result, teachers, parents, and J. K. Rowling have taken great pleasure. Children's literature, like all literature, should be compelling and draw readers to enjoy the elements of language and story. In its time, then, the series' influence on children's literature has been that it opened up the possibility for many people to enjoy literature who may not have enjoyed it in the past. This means that a concentrated generation of readers has grown up appreciating at least one form of children's literature. Fantasies have enjoyed a rebirth of interest as a result, and copycat writers try to outdo each other with more and more fantastic tales. Readers move from Rowling's books to other fantasy writers like J.R.R. Tolkien, C. S. Lewis, and Philip Pullman.

J. K. Rowling's influence on children's and young adult literature extends beyond her own titles to include recommendations of books by others. *The Little White Horse* by Elizabeth Goudge, for example, saw its way back into print after Rowling named it as one of the books she read as a child that most influenced her writing of Harry Potter. The Royal Society of Literature asked J. K. Rowling and other British authors for their list of top 10 books that schoolchildren should read. Rowling's list contained several children's or young adult titles. Published in *The Guardian* in early 2006, the list was made up of the following: *Wuthering Heights* by Emily Brontë; *Charlie and the Chocolate Factory* by Roald Dahl; *Robinson Crusoe* by Daniel Defoe; *David Copperfield* by Charles Dickens; *Hamlet* by William Shakespeare; *To Kill a Mockingbird* by Harper Lee; *Animal Farm* by George Orwell; *The Tale of Two Bad Mice* by Beatrix Potter; *The Catcher in the Rye* by J. D. Salinger; and *Catch-22* by Joseph Heller.

With the greater appreciation of children's literature in light of the success of Harry Potter, it did not take long for business to realize a large market was waiting to be tapped. Unfortunately, children's literature suddenly became big business—really big business—and this has had both positive and negative effects on the quality of writing being targeted to young audiences. While doors have opened for other talented writers because of the success of the series, other previously guarded gates have opened as well, and children's literature professionals, such as teachers, critics, and librarians, are concerned about their young charges being taken advantage of for profit. Children's literature once opened the imaginations of young readers; now, some of these professionals fear, it is opening their piggy banks and bank accounts as well. Many feel that children are pressured to get swept up in Pottermania or risk being rejected as an outcast. Peer pressure, these professionals argue, has no place in the enjoyment of literature, and children need protection from exploitation for profit.

Another effect of the series is that it has thrust children's literature front and center into the spotlight of world culture. There is a current focus on what children's literature is and should be, what it has been in the past, and what it will become as a result of the Harry Potter phenomenon. Scholars and others study the phenomenon from a variety of disciplines such as children's literature, education, child culture, popular culture, marketing, and others, trying to discern what the right questions are to ask and to begin researching appropriate and viable answers. In this way, children's literature has perhaps gained credibility, to an extent it has never previously enjoyed, as an art form worthy of serious attention, research, and debate.

Despite these and other influences the series has had thus far on children's literature, its creation, and its reception, J. K. Rowling has cautioned that the later books in the series do not come across to some readers as appropriate for younger children. The books get darker and more complex, and some younger readers may stop reading them until they become older or can appreciate the plot developments with more maturity. On the other hand, and for readers of a certain age, the series may mark the first time in literary history that a story, its protagonist, and its themes have aged and matured in close to real time with its audience, and the effects of that phenomenon, when all is said and done, are perhaps the most intriguing of all.

See also Coming-of-age story

Further Reading: Higgins, Charlotte. "From Beatrix Potter to Ulysses... What the Top Writers Say Every Child Should Read." *The Guardian* (London), January 31, 2006. http://www.guardian.co.uk/uk_news/story/0,,1698548,00.html.

Chimera. *Magical creature.* From *Fantastic Beasts.* Ranked 5X by MM as lethally dangerous. The creature has a lion's head, goat's body, and the tail of a dragon. Their eggs are a nontradeable item (FB 7). Hermione says that Hagrid might have had a Chimera if he had been able to find its eggs (OP 21:442). "Dangerous" Dai Llewellyn was eaten by a Chimera while on vacation in Greece (QA 33).

See also Fantastic Beasts and Where to Find Them

Chinese Chomping Cabbage. *Magical plant.* Hermione diagrams this plant for Herbology (OP 16:332).

Chinese Fireball. *Magical creature.* From *Fantastic Beasts.* This dragon is red with gold spikes around its face (FB 11–12). It is one of the many dragons that comes to Hogwarts for the Triwizard Tournament (GF 19:327). Viktor Krum chooses to get past this breed for the first task (GF 20:350).

See also Fantastic Beasts and Where to Find Them

Chipolatas. Sausages served at the small Christmas Feast in Year 3. Dumbledore offers some to first-year student Derek (PA 11:230).

Chizpurfle. *Magical creature.* From *Fantastic Beasts.* Classified 2X by the MM; they are low risk. They are a bit like fleas in that they bother other magical creatures, but they also eat away at magical objects. Chizpurfles are treated with various lotions (FB 7).

See also Fantastic Beasts and Where to Find Them

Chocoballs. *Magical candy.* Candy available from Honeydukes in Hogsmeade. Some are filled with strawberry or cream (PA 5:77).

Chocolate Cauldrons. *Magical candy.* Candy with firewhiskey in it. Romilda Vane gives a box of these to Harry, claiming that she received them from her grandmother and does not like them (HBP 15:309). Ron eats several from a box given to him for his birthday and Harry discovers that they are the same candies Romilda Vane laced with love potion. Ron thinks he loves Romilda Vane. Slughorn tells the boys that the older the potion, the more potent it gets (HBP 18:393, 395).

Chocolate Frogs. *Magical candy.* One of the treats sold on the Hogwarts Express Candy Cart that Harry buys and shares with Ron on their first meeting (SS 6:101–2). Ron shows Harry the collector cards inside that have pictures of famous witches and wizards. Ron has collected about five hundred of them but is missing Agrippa and Ptolemy. In interviews, Rowling has named Chocolate Frogs as one of the candies she would like best if she could have them.

See also Candy and sweets

Choice vs. destiny. When Prof. Dumbledore tells Harry that it is our choices, rather than our abilities, that show us who we really are, he articulates one of the major themes of the series (CS 18:333). In his tribute to Cedric Diggory, Dumbledore praises the Hufflepuff student as a hero and asks that the Hogwarts community remember him as one who took the right path when given the choice of doing what was right or what was easy (GF 37:724). Harry is often presented with this choice; he has chosen to be brave and help those around him as best he can. By the sixth novel, news of his courageous efforts have reached beyond Hogwarts, and the *Daily Prophet* calls him "the Chosen One" who will diminish the force of evil in the world that is personified by Lord Voldemort.

Dumbledore presents Harry with the prophecy that neither Voldemort nor Harry can live while the other survives. He also tells Harry that Voldemort has chosen to live out this prophecy, but Harry need not accept it as inevitable. Voldemort will try to kill Harry because he thinks he has to in order to achieve his goal of eternal life. Harry, Dumbledore instructs him, need not be bound by the same set of rules, but only by the rules that he sets for himself. If he confronts Voldemort, Dumbledore tells him, it should be on his own terms and for his own reasons. Harry recognizes that the difference is comparable to fighting willingly for a good cause versus fighting simply because one sees no other way out of a situation.

Some Christian readers of the series find religious meaning in the theme of the importance of choice. They see the theme as an expression of free will to live one's life moving toward or away from God. Others read the choice theme as an argument for or against fate, or as an argument for the empowerment of the individual versus society or other forces.

On her website, Rowling has discussed the topic of the prophecy and choice. She does so especially in terms of the possibility that Neville Longbottom is the character the prophecy refers to as the one who could fight Voldemort. Neville and Harry both meet the requirements specified by the prophecy: both sets of parents confronted the villain three times and their birthdays both occur as the month of July ends. However, Voldemort decided that it would be Harry who was his threat, not Neville. Rowling points out that the prophecy parallels the one in Shakespeare's play *Macbeth*, where witches make a prophecy to the title character. Had they not made the prophecy in the first place, events of the plot may not have occurred as they did.

In an interview in *The Vancouver Sun* in 2000, Rowling admitted to having her first cry in writing the series when she wrote Dumbledore's tribute to Cedric Diggory at the end of *Goblet of Fire* (not when she wrote the poignant scene in *Sorcerer's Stone* about Harry seeing his parents in the Mirror of Erised). Dumbledore's tribute touched her because it was about making the choice between what is good and what is easy. Rowling said that tyranny finds fertile ground in a society that has grown apathetic and that takes the easy way out until it suddenly realizes that a tyrant has taken over. By the time this realization is made, people are already in serious trouble.

When the series is complete and all of the novels are available to readers, analysis of the full story will begin in earnest, and the theme of choice is surely one that will be discussed in depth.

See also Shakespeare, William

Further Reading: Max Wyman. "'You Can Lead a Fool to a Book But You Can't Make Them Think': Author Has Frank Words for Religious Right." *The Vancouver Sun* (B.C.), October 26, 2000.

Chorley, Herbert. *Character.* One of the Muggle Prime Minister's junior ministers who acted so strangely that he was removed from office to spend more time with his family (HBP 1:2). Fudge tells the Prime Minister that Chorley's family would be in less danger if he were not with them and that the Ministry of Magic will be sending him to their hospital, St. Mungo's (HBP 1:10). Rufus Scrimgeour informs the Prime Minister that Chorley was the victim of an Imperius Curse that has affected his brain. The Prime Minister informs Rufus that Chorley has been quacking but hears from Scrimgeour in return that he has lately tried to strangle three of the staff at St. Mungo's (HBP 1:18).

"The Chosen Captain." *Magical slur.* Draco Malfoy says this mockingly to Harry in Year 6 (HBP 19:412).

"The Chosen One." *Magical nickname.* People call Harry "the Chosen One." The *Daily Prophet* refers to him by this name after the fight at the Hall of Prophecy (HBP 3:39; HBP 7:136). Harry matures a lot in the moment when he leans toward Slughorn and tells him that he is the Chosen One, that he must kill Voldemort, and that he needs Slughorn's memory to help him do it (HBP 22:490).

See also Choice vs. destiny; The prophecy; Shakespeare, William

Christian responses. Since the series revolves around witches and wizards, most people in the United States could predict that the Harry Potter books would ruffle the feathers of some concerned with keeping their children clear of the devil. There is a long history in the United States, especially among Christians, of suspicion of the occult, ranging all the way back to the Salem witch trials among the Puritans in New England. The reaction to the Harry Potter books among some Christian conservatives has been no exception. Responses have ranged from defenders who say the series contains a Christ figure and backs Christian doctrine by preaching good triumphing over evil, to those who burn the books without reading them simply because they have heard that they contain witches as characters.

That said, there have been some serious attempts by careful Christian thinkers to study the books from a Christian perspective. Interestingly, the number of books published about the series so far is greatest from those offering spiritual responses to the series. This number will soon be overtaken, perhaps, by reading guides and literary criticism once the series is published in full, but the Christian response was one of the first and most dominating readings and is likely to continue to be so for some time. Two books that praise the series from a Christian perspective are John Granger's *Looking for God in Harry Potter* and Connie Neal's *The Gospel According to Harry Potter: Spirituality in the Stories of the World's Most Famous Seeker.*

Harry does pray. In *Prisoner of Azkaban*, he prays that the Dursleys are asleep when he tries to get his troublesome *Monster Book of Monsters* out from under his desk (PA 1:13). Peter Pettigrew goes into a prayer posture before Sirius Black in the Shrieking Shack scene (PA 19:372). For the most part, however, religious practices are not part of the series. Characters do not attend religious services, nor do they preach or hear about God at Hogwarts or anywhere else. If they address it at all, the books address spirituality in terms of moral behavior and feelings rather than explicit dogma or theology.

For her part, Rowling has admitted in interviews that she is a Christian. She has said that the moral elements of the stories have always seemed obvious to her, and she has been surprised over the years that they were not more obvious to some of the Christians who have attacked the books and accused her of being an atheist. She has also said that if she spoke more about her Christian beliefs, intelligent readers of all ages would be able to guess what is coming in the books. To protect her audience's experience of reading each new book for themselves as the books become available, she has been just as glad not to have interviewers dig deeper into questions about her faith.

See also Book bannings and burnings

Further Reading: Granger, John. *Looking for God in Harry Potter*. Wheaton, IL: Tyndale House Publishers, 2004; Neal, Connie. *The Gospel According to Harry Potter: Spirituality in the Stories of the World's Most Famous Seeker*. Louisville, KY: Westminster John Knox Press, 2002.

Christmas. Students may stay at Hogwarts over the Christmas holiday if their families are traveling or if there is another good reason for them not to go home. Harry does not want to go back to the Dursleys, who never acknowledge his presence other than to punish or ridicule him, so he remains at Hogwarts. His first year, he has his best Christmas ever, complete with friendship, food, things to do, and of course, presents. Ron Weasley also stays at Hogwarts in his first year since his parents are going to Romania to visit his brother Charlie (SS 12:195).

When Harry and Ron wake up on Christmas morning, Harry finds presents at the foot of his bed. The presents include: a homemade-looking wooden flute from Hagrid that sounds like an owl when he blows it; a 50 pence coin from Aunt Petunia and Uncle Dursley; an emerald-green sweater and homemade fudge made by Mrs. Weasley; and his father's Invisibility Cloak from an unknown giver who turns out to be Prof. Dumbledore (SS 12:200–201).

The Great Hall is decorated gaily with holly and mistletoe and twelve large trees that Hagrid has brought. Many of the trees are decorated with candles and icicles (SS 12:196). The Christmas Feast is the best dinner Harry has ever had for the holiday, complete with roast turkey, buttered peas, and Wizard Crackers full of toys (SS 12:203). During Harry's second year the Great Hall is also decorated with enchanted snow (CS 12:212). In his third year there are only twelve students who stay for Christmas, and the Great Hall is set up with just one table in the center of the room (PA 11:227).

In Year 5, Harry spends Christmas at Number Twelve, Grimmauld Place and in Year 6 he stays at the Burrow. Though Christmas is celebrated in the series as a cultural rather than a religious holiday, it should be noted that Halloween, Christmas, Valentine's Day, and Easter are all mentioned and celebrated in the series. Roots for all of these holidays can be traced back to both Christian and pagan holidays and celebrations that took place at similar times of the year.

See also Gifts, gift-giving

Chronicles of Narnia (Lewis). *See* Lewis, C. S.

Chubb, Agatha. *Character.* Witch who noted the existence of at least twelve lead Bludgers from the early sixteenth century in the peat bogs of Ireland and in British marshes (QA 22).

Chudley Cannons. *Magical sports team.* Ron Weasley's favorite professional Quidditch team. Their colors are orange and black; he has a bedspread with their logo on it in his room at the Burrow (CS 3:40). The players in the posters on Ron's bedroom walls keep moving (GF 5:56). Apparently the Cannons lose a lot; Dumbledore alludes to their desperate fans in his foreword to QA (QA vii). Though the Cannons won the League twenty-one times, they have not won since 1892 (QA 33).

Church Cottage. J. K. Rowling's home in Tutshill, England, from the time she was about nine years old until she went to college. The house was originally a school in the 1800s, and Pete Rowling liked the idea of maintaining an older home while at the same time equipping it with modern conveniences. The house was made of stone, and it had a history of being not only a school but also the facility where church services were held from 1848 until 1853. It sits beside St. Luke's Church and a graveyard. J. K. Rowling found the graveyard an interesting place to collect names.

Rowling revisited Church Cottage for the BBC documentary *Harry and Me* in 2001. Standing outside of the house, she talks about spending a great deal of time writing in her room, which, she points out, had the window at the top right floor. She also hung out her window many a late night smoking cigarettes behind the curtain and dropping the butts down to the ground below. In the morning, she would tell her father that patrons of the pub had thrown their cigarette butts in the garden again.

The house, the church, and the graveyard were all beside the school that she and her sister Di attended, Tutshill Church of England Primary School.

See also Tutshill, England; Tutshill Primary School of England

Circe. *Character.* One of the figures on the Famous Witches and Wizard Cards found in Chocolate Frogs (SS 6:103).

See also Chocolate Frogs

Clabbert. *Magical creature.* From *Fantastic Beasts.* Classified 2X by the MM. It lives in trees and looks like a cross between a frog and monkey. The Clabbert is native to the southern states of America (FB 8).

See also Fantastic Beasts and Where to Find Them

Clagg, Madame Elfrida. *Character.* The Chief of the Wizards' Council who came after Burdock Muldoon (FB xi). Everard moves into Madame Elfrida Clagg's portrait at the Ministry to catch a better view of Arthur Weasley after he is attacked and to report back to Dumbledore (OP 22:471). Clagg made Golden Snidgets a protected species, which means that they can no longer be hunted or used in Quidditch matches (QA 14).

Class C Non-Tradeable Substance. *Magical substance.* A substance that is illegal to buy or sell (OP 9:171).

Classroom eleven. *Magical place.* Dumbledore gives Firenze this classroom on the ground floor of Hogwarts since he cannot climb stairs to the Tower to teach Divination. The classroom is decorated like a forest to make the centaur feel more at home. It is located off the entrance hall on the opposite side of the Great Hall (OP 27:600).

Cleansweep Broom Company. *Magical business.* From QA. Begun by Bob, Bill, and Barnaby Ollerton in 1926, this was the first company to mass-produce racing brooms, beginning with the Cleansweep One (QA 49).
See also Broomsticks; *Quidditch Through the Ages*

Cleansweep Eleven. *Magical object.* This is the new racing broomstick Ron asks for and receives from his parents as a gift when he becomes prefect (HBP 11:225).
See also Broomsticks

Cleansweep Five. *Magical object.* Older racing broomstick model owned by Fred and George Weasley (CS 7:111).
See also Broomsticks

Cleansweep One. *Magical object.* From QA. The first mass-produced broom sold particularly for racing, it was manufactured by the Cleansweep Broom Company and purchased by every Quidditch team in the nation at the time (QA 49).
See also Broomsticks; *Quidditch Through the Ages*

Cleansweep Seven. *Magical object.* Oliver Wood recommends either a Cleansweep Seven or a Nimbus 2000 to Prof. McGonagall for Harry Potter's new broom as Seeker (SS 9:152).
See also Broomsticks

Cleansweep Three. *Magical object.* From QA. Racing broom manufactured by the Cleansweep Broom Company in 1937 (QA 50).
See also Broomsticks; *Quidditch Through the Ages*

Cleansweep Two. *Magical object.* From QA. Racing broom manufactured by the Cleansweep Broom Company in 1934 (QA 50).
See also Broomsticks; *Quidditch Through the Ages*

Clearwater, Penelope. *Character.* A Ravenclaw prefect who is petrified in Harry's Year 2 (CS 14:258). Ginny accidentally catches Percy kissing her (CS 18:341). Percy accuses Ron of spilling tea on Penelope Clearwater's photograph (PA 5:69). Penelope congratulates Harry on his new Firebolt broomstick and asks if she can hold it (PA 13:257). She and Percy make a 10 Galleon bet on the Gryffindor-Ravenclaw match in Year 3 (PA 13:257).

Cliodna. *Character.* A druidess found in the collection of Famous Witches and Wizards Cards that come in Chocolate Frogs. She is scratching her nose when Harry sees her card for the first time (SS 6:103). Clio was one of the nine muses who were daughters of

Zeus and Mnemosyne. She is the muse of History, and her symbols are the wreath and scroll.

See also Chocolate Frogs

Clocks. *Magical objects.* Dumbledore likes Molly Weasley's clock that notifies her of the whereabouts of her family at all times, regardless of whether or not they are in any danger (OP 22:471). The clock has a hand for each member of the Weasley family and locations where they can normally be found, such as school and work. It also has a reading for traveling and one for danger. When Harry goes to the Burrow before Year 6 at Hogwarts, all hands of the clock are on the danger signal (HBP 5:88).

Clothing. Attention is paid in the novels to what characters are wearing, and the description of clothing or unusual outfits is often humorous or telling. School uniforms are described in some detail. For example, first-year students at Hogwarts are sent a list of requirements for their uniforms. These include three black plain work robes, a pointed black hat, dragon hide gloves, and a black winter cloak (SS 5:66). Each of these items is to be labeled with the student's name.

When traveling for the Quidditch World Cup, the wizarding world is told to dress like Muggles to try to stay incognito while traveling. This causes some problems. Basil, the Portkey manager, wears a kilt and a poncho; another wizard wears plus-fours (baggy, knicker-style pants with four inches of extra material in them that golfers used to wear) (GF 7:77). Archie, an old wizard, prefers a flowered nightgown (which he says Muggles wear) because he prefers to have air circulation around his privates (GF 7:83–84).

Ron is unhappy about all the hand-me-downs he must wear from his brothers, but he positively revolts when it comes to the dress robes Mrs. Weasley buys second-hand for him in Year 4. He says that he will never wear them. They have lace at the collar and cuffs (GF 10:155). Because Mrs. Weasley has Harry's money to buy his dress robes, she buys him new green ones that she says will bring out the color of his eyes. Harry feels guilty about the difference in wealth, but he knows that the Weasleys would not take money if he offered it to them (GF 10:156).

In the series, clothing is used as a colorful clue to a character's personality. When Lupin gives the DADA class the lesson in boggarts, he has Neville imagine the clothing his Gran wears and then tells him to envision this clothing on his boggart, Snape. The resulting vision that appears before the class is amusing, indeed, to all of them (PA 7:135–37). Clothing does not seem to be the typical status symbol in the series among Hogwarts' adolescents, and this might be partly because of the school uniforms they wear.

Clothing is mentioned primarily in terms of accessories, such as Luna Lovegood's lion's hat that she wears to a Quidditch match; clothing also becomes a focus when new characters or situations are introduced. Dumbledore's robes are often described when Harry sees him in a new environment, such as in his office late in the evening when he is wearing a dressing gown. Hermione guesses that the Durmstrang students who go to Hogwarts for the Triwizard Tournament in *Goblet of Fire* come from somewhere up north because they wear furs over their uniforms. At the Yule Ball, when students and professors wear their dress robes, the robes are described in terms of color, material, and pattern, if any. Hermione's dress robe is described as periwinkle blue, for example (GF 23:414); Percy Weasley attends in new navy blue robes (GF 23:415); and Prof. McGonagall wears a tartan red robe with an unbecoming thistle wreath around the brim of her hat (GF 23:413).

Coat of arms. The Hogwarts coat of arms is a large H with a lion, eagle, badger, and snake around it (GF 15:237).

Cobbing. *Magical sports penalty.* From QA. A foul in Quidditch caused by elbowing an opponent too much (QA 29).
See also Quidditch Through the Ages

Cockroach Clusters. *Magical candy.* Ron shows these to Hermione at Honeydukes before they know Harry has arrived (PA 10:197). Rowling mentioned Cockroach Clusters in one interview when she was asked which of the candies in the series were her favorites.
See also Candy and sweets

Code of Wand Use. *Magical law.* Amos Diggory cites clause three of this code that forbids the use of wands by nonhumans (GF 9:132).

Coins, enchanted. *Magical objects.* Draco Malfoy gets the idea to communicate using coins with Madam Rosmerta who is under the Imperius Curse from Hermione who used them with the DA (HBP 27:589).

Cokeworth. *Muggle place.* The location of the Railview Hotel where Uncle Vernon takes the family to escape the letters arriving for Harry from Hogwarts (SS 3:42).

Cole, Mrs. *Character.* The head of the orphanage where Tom Riddle lived as a boy (HBP 13:264).

"Colloportus!" *Incantation.* Hermione says this, which results in a door sealing (OP 35:788). *Portus* is Latin for "harbor."

Colonel Fubster. *Character.* The retired man who looks after Aunt Marge's bulldogs while she stays with Vernon and Petunia Dursley for a week in the summer before Harry's third year at Hogwarts (PA 2:23).

Color-Change Charm. *Magical spell.* Harry confuses the incantation for the Color-Change Charm with the Growth Charm in his practical Charms O.W.L. exam (OP 31:713).

Columbus, Christopher. *See* Films

Come and Go Room. *Magical place.* Another name for the Room of Requirement (OP 18:386).
See also Room of Requirement

Comet 140. *Magical object.* From QA. The first racing broom sold by the Comet Trading Company. The founders tested 140 designs in their effort to find this first model to offer for sale (QA 49).
See also Broomsticks; Quidditch Through the Ages

Comet 180. *Magical object.* From QA. Racing broom manufactured by the Comet Trading Company in 1938 (QA 50).
See also Broomsticks; Quidditch Through the Ages

The Comet Trading Company. *Magical business.* From QA. Racing broom company begun in 1929 by Randolph Keitch and Basil Horton, players for the Falmouth Falcons (QA 49).

See also Broomsticks; *Quidditch Through the Ages*

Comet Two Sixty. *Magical object.* Broomstick model that Draco Malfoy has at home; an old model (SS 10:165).

See also Broomsticks; *Quidditch Through the Ages*

Comic Relief, U.K. *Organization.* In his forewords to *Fantastic Beasts* and QA, Albus Dumbledore relates that Comic Relief, U.K. has raised more than $250 million, or £174 million, since 1985. These figures translate, he says, into magical money as 34,000,872 Galleons, 14 Sickles, and 7 Knuts (FB vii–viii). The organization was cofounded by Richard Curtis and others on Christmas Day 1985 in a live broadcast from Safawa, Sudan, in a fund-raiser to relieve famine in that country. Since then, it has broadened its mission to relieve hunger and poverty all over Africa as well as throughout the U.K. The charity is headquartered in London and is not associated with Comic Relief in the United States.

In 2001 J. K. Rowling made a major donation to Comic Relief, U.K. when she agreed to write and publish two of "Harry's books," *Fantastic Beasts and Where to Find Them* and *Quidditch Through the Ages*. Rowling gave her royalties to the charity.

See also Curtis, Richard; *Fantastic Beasts and Where to Find Them*; *Quidditch Through the Ages*

Further Reading: Comic Relief Website. http://www.comicrelief.com.

Coming-of-age story. The Harry Potter series, with its protagonist maturing from age eleven to seventeen, joins many other novels for young people and adults in a genre called the coming-of-age story. The narrative arc of a character maturing from childhood or adolescence into adulthood has an inherent drama that authors have used in fiction for many years. Rowling's story is perhaps unique in the genre because it ages Harry exactly one year in each book and chronicles his experiences at school in that one year.

Albus Dumbledore tells the Dursleys that the age of maturity for wizards is seventeen (HBP 3:54). When readers first meet Harry, he is a one-year-old infant in a basket left on the doorstep of the Dursleys. When we meet him again, he is ten going on eleven and is about to embark on a wild and fantastic adventure. The adventure will extend past his seventeenth birthday and by that time he will not only have grown up, but he will also have come to terms with one of the most evil forces the world has ever seen. Such is the stuff of fantasy fiction.

Although the fantasy takes place mostly in the world of magic, Harry, his friends, and the other students at Hogwarts go through many of the same phases of development as other young people. Harry becomes frustrated and angry with the adults in charge of his care when he thinks they do not listen to him or they do not understand or care about his views. He begins noticing girls at Hogwarts and receives his first kiss from Cho Chang in a mixture of confusion, blundering, and excitement. He leaves one relationship and feels uneasy about another but comes to find one with Ginny Weasley that seems right to him. All the while, his body, knowledge, and skills are growing in size and strength, and his ideas about the world and his place in it are developing as well, deepening in complexity and maturity. He not only values his mentor, Dumbledore, for what he has taught him but he also begins to question his mentor's advice when comparing it with his own experience and view of the world.

Realistic fiction in the United States that has addressed the theme of coming-of-age often explores the ending of this long process, or the period of awkward shift from adolescence into adulthood, and often involves serious issues with psychological or social problems. Novels such as *The Bell Jar* by Sylvia Plath and *The Catcher in the Rye* by J. D. Salinger are two of the more complex and well known of these books. Karen Hesse's *Out of the Dust* is a more contemporary example.

The later novels in the series of seven come closest to the traditional coming-of-age story for young adults, but Rowling would perhaps be the first person to argue that it took all seven books for Harry to mature to the place where he will be in the final chapter.

Committee for the Disposal of Dangerous Creatures. *Magical office.* The group in the Ministry of Magic that ruled against Buckbeak (PA 11:218).

Committee of Experimental Charms. *Magical office.* A group in the Ministry of Magic that is charged with investigating reports of new charms being invented or tried (CS 3:38).

Common Apparition Mistakes and How to Avoid Them. *Magical pamphlet.* Given by the Ministry to Apparition students to study before their tests (HBP 22:469). Apparition manuals, lessons, tests, and licensing echo the steps a teenager follows in learning to drive a car in the Muggle world.

Common Magical Ailments and Afflictions. *Magical book.* Harry imagines Hermione advising him to consult this book when his scar hurts him very badly in the summer before Year 4 (GF 2:21).

Common Welsh Green. *Magical creature.* Though this is the dragon involved in the Ilfracombe Incident, it is one of the least dangerous to human beings (FB 12). It is found wild in Britain (SS 14:231). The breed is one of the many that comes to Hogwarts for the Triwizard Tournament (GF 19:327). Fleur Delacour chooses a miniature version of this dragon from the bag, so she has to get past a Common Welsh Green for the first task (GF 20:350).
See also Fantastic Beasts and Where to Find Them

Company car. *Muggle object.* By *Prisoner of Azkaban*, Uncle Vernon has apparently earned himself use of a company car from Grunnings (PA 1:3).

A Compendium of Common Curses and Their Counter-Actions. *Magical book.* This book is in the Room of Requirement when Harry uses it for Dumbledore's Army lessons (OP 18:390).

Conferences/conventions, Harry Potter. *See* Fan responses

Confounding Spell. *Magical spell.* Hermione blushes when Ron says that Cormac McLaggen looked confounded during try-outs for Keeper (HBP 11:227). She later admits to Harry that she did cast the spell on Cormac to help Ron, but also because Cormac has a bad temper that Harry would not want on the team (HBP 11:232).

Confronting the Faceless. *Magical book.* Hermione quickly puts this book into her bag when Snape comes in to the DADA classroom (HBP 9:177).

Confundus Charm. *Magical spell.* This spell apparently confuses the victim or causes him or her to believe the opposite of what is logical (PA 21:386). Mad-Eye Moody guesses that it would take a powerful one of these charms to confuse the Goblet of Fire into choosing four champions rather than the traditional three (GF 17:279).

Confusing and Befuddlement Draughts. *Magical substances.* Apparently these are potions to confuse and befuddle the recipient by making the brain warm. Harry reads about them for homework when he becomes a bit befuddled himself. He is then wakened by Dobby returning Hedwig to him (OP 18:384).

Conjunctivitus Curse. *Magical spell.* Affects the victim's eyes; effective against dragons since their eyes are their weakest attribute (GF 23:406).

Connolly. *Character.* Player on the Ireland National Quidditch Team in the World Cup (GF 8:105).

"Constant vigilance!" *Magical expression.* Mad-Eye Moody, the ex-Auror, says this continuously to students to remind them to stay on the alert for Dark wizards and Dark Magic (GF 14:213; GF 29:571). "Constant vigilance!" became a catchphrase among fans of the series who combed the books for clues about what will happen in future books of the series.

Coote, Ritchie. *Character.* A new Beater on the Gryffindor Quidditch team the year Harry captains. He has good aim (HBP 11:225). Zacharias Smith accuses him of not having the bulky build of most Beaters (HBP 14:296).

Corn flakes. *Muggle food.* Several students at Hogwarts eat this common Muggle cereal for breakfast (PA 14:272).

Corner, Michael. *Character.* Michael Corner is impressed at the first DADA meeting held at the Hog's Head where Harry's accomplishments are discussed (OP 16:342). He is a boyfriend of Ginny's (OP 16:347). She dumps him later because he was a sore loser when Gryffindor beat Ravenclaw at Quidditch, and he takes up with Cho Chang (OP 38:866; HBP 6:121). Michael asks Prof. Slughorn in Potions class if he has ever taken Felix Felicis (HBP 9:187).

Cornish pixies. *Magical creatures.* Harry's class with Lockhart does not take these small creatures seriously until the professor unleashes them in the classroom. They are about eight inches long, blue, and make a shrill cry. They shoot and fly all around the room and are very difficult to catch (CS 6:101–2).

See also Fantastic Beasts and Where to Find Them; Pixy

Council of Magical Law. *Magical organization.* A group of witches and wizards who make judgments on the actions of others. The council had the hearing of Karkaroff years ago, which Harry witnesses in the Pensieve (GF 30:594).

Counterjinxes. *Magical spell.* The textbook *Defensive Magical Theory* says that this term is misnamed, but Hermione debates this claim. She thinks that counterjinxes can be used defensively (OP 15:317).

Courtroom Ten. *Magical place.* On the first level (or dungeon level) in the Ministry of Magic, this is where the full court of the Wizengamot meets to try cases and hold hearings. Courtroom Ten is where Harry sees the Lestranges tried through Dumbledore's memory in the Pensieve. It is also where Harry himself has his expulsion hearing. The walls are dark and made of stone, lit only by a few torches. There are benches rising along each side and very tall benches at one end, where fifty or more judges sit (OP 7:134, 137).

Covers, book. *See* Illustrations

Crabbe, Mr. *Character.* A Death Eater who attends Voldemort's rising at the Little Hangleton graveyard (GF 33:651). He is also present at the attack on the Department of Mysteries (OP 35:788).

Crabbe, Vincent. *Character.* One of Draco Malfoy's croneys at Hogwarts. Draco introduces Vincent Crabbe to Harry on the Hogwarts Express (SS 6:108). Vincent is described as tall with a thick neck and a page-boy haircut (PA 5:80). He is the Slytherin Beater in fifth year (OP 19:405). Vincent is in the train compartment with Draco when Harry spies on him with his Invisibility Cloak; Harry gets caught spying (HBP 7:149–54).

Crackers, Wizard. *See* Cribbage's Wizarding Crackers

Crapaud. *Character.* From QA. A character in French playwright Malecrit's play, *Hélas, Je me suis Transfiguré Les Pieds* ("Alas, I've Transfigured My Feet") (QA 39).
  See also Quidditch Through the Ages

Creaothceann. *Magical sport.* From QA. The ancient Scottish flying broomstick game. Considered the most dangerous of the old games, it involves players wearing a cauldron on their heads and trying to catch rocks falling from the sky. The number of fatalities from the game resulted in its banning in 1762. The Ministry did not make the game legal again after Magnus "Dent-Head" Macdonald tried to make it so in the 1960s (QA 5–6).

Creevey, Colin. *Character.* In Harry's second year at Hogwarts, young Colin Creevey is a first-year student who is also sorted into Gryffindor House and who is very taken with the famous boy wizard. He follows him around the school and tries to take his picture all the time so that he can prove to people back home that he knows Harry. Colin's father is a milkman (CS 6:96). Colin wants to take Ron's picture when he is belching slugs (CS 7:113). He fusses over Harry all the time. He is the second petrification in *Chamber of Secrets* (CS 10:180). He is impressed at the first DADA meeting where Harry's accomplishments are discussed (OP 16:342).

Creevey, Dennis. *Character.* Colin's younger brother by two years. He begins Hogwarts in Harry's fourth year and falls in the lake on his way to the castle (GF 12:174, 176). Colin tells Dennis that the thing that grabbed him in the lake was probably the giant squid and this makes Dennis even more excited to be at Hogwarts. The Creeveys both clearly enjoy Hogwarts (GF 12:179).

Cresswell, Dirk. *Character.* Head of the Goblin Liaison Office at the Ministry and former student of Horace Slughorn's; muggle-born; gives Slughorn inside information on happenings at Gringott's (HBP 4:71).

Cribbage's Wizarding Crackers. *Magical objects.* Paper party favors that open when two people pull on the ends; lots of candy and toys fall out. Crackers are a typical favor left on the tables in the Great Hall at Christmas (GF 23:410). Harry receives several during his first Christmas at Hogwarts. When he pulls one with Fred Weasley, an explosion occurs, smoke billows, and an admiral's hat and a few live white mice fall out (SS 12:203). From other crackers he gathers Non-explodable, luminous balloons; a Grow-Your-Own-Warts kit; and a Wizard Chess set (SS 12:204).

Critical reception. Though the series has clearly won the popular vote of readers around the world by a wide margin, critical reception of the literary and lasting quality of the novels remains mixed and undecided. Reviews of the books tend to be favorable as they are released. In a February 14, 1999, review of *Sorcerer's Stone* in the *New York Times*, Michael Winerip called the book "a wonderful first novel" that is "as funny, moving and impressive as the story behind its writing." In 2005 Michiko Kakutani wrote of *Half-Blood Prince* and the series in the *New York Times*, "The achievement of the Potter books is the same as that of the great classics of children's literature, from the Oz novels to *The Lord of the Rings*: the creation of a richly imagined and utterly singular world, as detailed, as improbable and as mortal as our own." The books are praised for their plotting and characterization and externally for their accomplishment in getting reluctant young readers to stay up reading an eight-hundred-page novel under their bedcovers by flashlight.

Detractors do exist, however. Many find problems with the writing in the books as well as with the Potter Phenomenon the series has created. The structure of each novel following one school year after another has been tiresome for some readers; even Rowling herself seemed relieved in one interview that she would not be writing about another Quidditch match in the later books. Rowling's propensity for using adverbs in dialogue tags ("'Go,' said Hagrid *fiercely*" [PA 16:330, italics added] and "'It's liquid luck,' said Hermione *excitedly*" [HBP 9:187, italics added]) looks to some sophisticated readers like a lazy and annoying writer's tic, marking Rowling as an amateur whose work should have been better edited. In the *Wall Street Journal* in 2000, longtime literary critic Harold Bloom wrote a scathing article about the books despite their huge popularity, saying that Rowling's "prose style, heavy on cliché, makes no demands upon her readers." Critic Jack Zipes, in his 2001 *Sticks and Stones: The Troublesome Success of Children's Literature from Slovenly Peter to Harry Potter*, calls the Potter books "formulaic and sexist" (171).

By the time the sixth novel was published, there were already three collections of criticism about the unfinished series, containing several essays each: *Reading Harry Potter: Critical Essays*, edited by Giselle Liza Anatol; *Harry Potter's World: Multidisciplinary Critical Perspectives*, edited by Elizabeth E. Heilman; and *The Ivory Tower and Harry Potter: Perspectives on a Literary Phenomenon*, edited by Lana A. Whited. Rather than argue for or against the series' quality, these essays tend to discuss topics such as Harry's literary ancestors and context; magic as modern-day technology; gender issues;

censorship and the novels; class and Harry Potter; the law; the hero and Harry Potter; and many others.

One thing is certain about the critical response to the series—once the seventh book is available, more studies, analyses, articles, and books are bound to appear. These works, and that most important quality—time—will determine whether the books will come to be called "classics" of world literature or simply a short-lived, literary moment in world culture.

See also Christian responses

Further Reading: Bloom, Harold. "Can 35 Million Book Buyers Be Wrong? Yes." *Wall Street Journal*, July 11, 2000, A26; Kakutani, Michiko. "Harry Potter Works His Magic Again in a Far Darker Tale." *New York Times*, July 16, 2005. http://www.nytimes.com; Zipes, Jack. *Sticks and Stones: The Troublesome Success of Literature from Slovenly Peter to Harry Potter*. New York: Routledge, 2001.

Croaker. *Character.* Employee of the Department of Ministries at the Ministry; he is an Unspeakable (GF 7:86).

Crockford, Doris. *Character.* The first witch to recognize Harry Potter in the Leaky Cauldron in London, Year 1. She is proud of him; meeting him apparently throws her into a tizzy (SS 5:69).

Crookshanks. *Magical pet.* Hermione Granger's large, ginger-orange cat. He is bow-legged and has a scowling, smushed-in looking face. He has been in the store for a long time without someone wanting to purchase him. The cat senses that something is not quite right with Scabbers and is befriended by Sirius Black in his Animagus dog form (PA 4:60; PA 8:146; PA 15:303; PA 16:336). Sirius says that the cat is the most intelligent one he has ever seen (PA 19:364). When he is at the Burrow, Crookshanks likes chasing the garden gnomes (GF 5:57). Rowling has said in interviews that the cat is part kneazle.

Cross-Species Switches. *Magical spell.* A technique in Transfiguration in which animals are transformed into other animals (for example, a guinea fowl turns into a guinea pig) (GF 22:385).

Crouch, Bartemius (Barty), Sr. *Character.* Head of the Department of International Magical Cooperation. When Ludo Bagman says that he speaks over 150 languages, Percy Weasley speaks up and claims that Barty Crouch, Sr., speaks over 200, including Mermish, Gobbledegook, and Troll (GF 7:89). Barty Sr. is a distinguished older man who obviously conducted a good amount of research on what to wear to look like a Muggle for the World Cup. He arrives wearing a suit and tie, a trim mustache, and straight gray hair (GF 7:90). Prof. Dumbledore introduces Barty Sr. at the Triwizard feast (GF 16:254). Barty used to be Head of the Department of Magical Law Enforcement and sent Sirius Black to Azkaban (GF 27:526). He gave Aurors permission to use Unforgivable Curses against those they found to be on the Dark Side (GF 27:527). He was passed over for the Minister position that Cornelius Fudge originally slated him to claim (GF 27:530). He is killed by his son, Barty Jr., and transfigured into a bone that Barty Jr. buries in soft earth in front of Hagrid's cabin (GF 35:691).

Crouch, Barty, Jr. *Character.* Son of Barty Crouch, Sr. Barty Jr. was accused of being a Death Eater and was sent to Azkaban Prison by his own father (GF 27:528). Sirius Black tells Harry that Barty Jr. and his mother both died at the prison, and that he saw

Dementors bury Barty Jr. outside (GF 27:529). When Harry witnesses the hearing in the Pensieve, he sees Barty Jr. accused of putting the Cruciatus Curse on the Aurors (Frank Longbottom and his wife) and of torturing them (GF 30:595). Barty Jr. did not die at Azkaban, however, but remained alive under his father's protection. Barty Jr. devises a plan to switch identities with the Auror Mad-Eye Moody in order to ensure that Harry Potter wins the Triwizard Tournament. Touching the Cup, which Barty Jr. has made into a Portkey to the graveyard where Voldemort is waiting to come alive again, sends Harry out of the maze of the third task and into a scene of horror.

Cruciatus Curse. *Magical Dark Magic spell.* One of the three Unforgivable Curses, the Cruciatus Curse tortures the victim in a variety of ways. The incantation is "Crucio!" Mad-Eye Moody demonstrates it in DADA on spiders (GF 14:214). Prof. Umbridge threatens to use the Cruciatus Curse on Harry to find out whom he has been communicating with in the fires at Hogwarts (OP 32:746).

"Crucio." *Incantation.* Incantation for the Cruciatus Curse (GF 31:626). *Crucio* is Latin for "torture." Harry tries to use it for the first time (OP 36:810) against Bellatrix Lestrange in the attack in the Room of Prophecy, but she tells him that a curse cast in anger for good purposes will not affect her for long. The Cruciatus Curse is one of the Unforgivable Curses and does not work on her. Draco Malfoy tries to put it on Harry, but Harry gets to him first with another spell (HBP 24:522).

Crumple-Horned Snorkack. *Magical myth.* Luna Lovegood tells Harry that people used to believe in the Crumple-Horned Snorkack and the Blibbering Humdinger, and Hermione reminds her that there are no such things (OP 13:262). Luna says her father was expecting an article on Crumple-Horned Snorkack for *The Quibbler* at the same time that Harry's interview came in (OP 26:570). Luna says her father is pleased with Harry's article, which is even more popular than the one on the Snorkack and has prompted another printing (OP 26:583). Luna tells everyone that the Snorkack does not fly (OP 33:762). The summer after Year 5, Luna Lovegood's family plans to go to Sweden to try to catch a Crumple-Horned Snorkack (OP 38:848).

Crup. *Magical creature.* Classfied 3X by MM. Except for a forked tail, this creature could be taken for a Jack Russell terrier. It favors wizards but is mean to Muggles (FB 8–9). Prof. Grubbly-Plank plans to review Crups before Harry's O.W.L.s (OP 15:323). Hagrid, while under Umbridge's probation, shows the class nothing more dangerous than Crups (OP 25:552).
See also Fantastic Beasts and Where to Find Them

Crystal ball. *Magical object.* Prof. Trelawney teaches students how to use this device for predicting the future in third-year Divination class. She explains that one must relax the external eyes and conscious mind, allowing the Inner Eye to "See" and to activate the super-conscious (PA 15:297).
See also Divination; Orb

Crystalized pineapple. *Magical treats.* Slughorn likes this sugary treat and is often swayed by those who bring it to him (HBP 23:494).

Cuarón, Alfonso. *See Films*

Cuffe, Barnabus. *Character.* Editor of *The Daily Prophet* and former student of Horace Slughorn. Slughorn claims that Barnabus is always interested in his opinions on news of the day (HBP 4:71).

Cunningham, Barry. As the founding publisher of children's books at Bloomsbury, Cunningham was the first person to purchase any Harry Potter manuscript for publication. In a famous meeting with J. K. Rowling, he told her that there was no money to be made in writing children's books, and she told him that she had several sequels in mind, six of them in fact, for the manuscript he was purchasing.

When he first read the manuscript the evening he received it, he did not know that several others had passed on it and that Rowling was getting discouraged. He has said in interviews that he thinks the book was turned down by other publishers of children's books because it was longer than most middle-grade novels (for ages nine through twelve); that it had a strange title; and it ventured into some dark territory. It was not a children's novel in the traditional sense, Cunningham says. He recalls trying to figure out the rules of Quidditch in his first reading that evening and liking the friendship among the three main characters. He recognized that it was a book that a child would cling to with his or her imagination, and that made the difference to him in deciding to acquire the rights to publish it. He offered Rowling a contract with a few thousand pounds' advance and scheduled the book for a limited initial print run of five hundred copies.

Born in the early 1950s, Cunningham may have been able to relate in some way to Harry's plight in the first book. His own father, George, came from Leith and joined the army, then worked as an engineer. George Cunningham smoked heavily and died at the age of forty-four from lung cancer, when Barry was just six years old. Barry Cunningham was a great reader as a child, especially enjoying books such as *Treasure Island* and the excitement of checking books out of the adult section of the library. Later, when he started working in publishing, he worked with Roald Dahl, the author he maintains is the best children's novelist. He now ranks J. K. Rowling among his top five favorites; the others include Dahl, C. S. Lewis, Philip Pullman, and Enid Blyton.

The publisher says he almost dreaded the publication of new Harry Potter books because the press pursued him knowing that they would not obtain an interview with Rowling. As part of the promotional campaign for *Half-Blood Prince*, for example, Cunningham agreed to appear on American television's *Oprah* show.

Cunningham recently sold his new company, Chicken House Children's Books, to Scholastic.

See also Bloomsbury, Plc.; Scholastic

Further Reading: Cunningham, Barry. "Discovering Harry Potter." *Fortune Magazine*, June 27, 2005; Dick, Sandra. "That Magical Day When Barry Met Harry." *The Scotsman*, September 15, 2005.

Curse-Breaker. *Magical skill.* Bill Weasley is a Curse-Breaker; he likes adventure (HBP 5:93). One of his tasks in working for Gringotts is to break curses on areas where treasure lies, such as in the pyramids in Egypt, so that entry is possible.

Curse of the Bogies. *Magical curse.* Prof. Quirrell taught the Curse of the Bogies to Harry's class, but Ron has not yet perfected it (SS 9:157).

Curses and Countercurses. *Magical book.* Book written by Prof. Vindictus Viridian. Harry sees this intriguing book on his first trip to Flourish and Blotts; Hagrid nearly has to pull him away from looking at it. The subtitle is *Bewitch Your Friends and Befuddle Your Enemies with the Latest Revenges: Hair Loss, Jelly-Legs, Tongue-Tying and Much, Much More* (SS 5:80).

Curtis, Richard. The cofounder of Comic Relief, U.K. who wrote to J. K. Rowling asking if she would be interested in cooperating with a fund-raising project. The letter resulted in Rowling's writing and publishing the two Harry Potter "schoolbooks," *Fantastic Beasts and Where to Find Them* and *Quidditch Through the Ages* and donating all of her royalties from those two books to the agency. Curtis is a screenwriter, actor, and director in the film and television industry. His screenplays include *Bridget Jones: The Edge of Reason* (2004); *Love Actually* (2003); *Bridget Jones's Diary* (2001); *Notting Hill* (1999); and *Four Weddings and a Funeral* (1994).

See also Comic Relief, U.K.

Cushioning Charm. *Magical spell.* From QA. Invented by Elliot Smethwyck in 1820, the charm makes the witch or wizard feel like he or she is sitting on a cushion while on a broomstick (QA 47).

See also Quidditch Through the Ages

· D ·

Dagworth-Granger, Hector. *Character.* Prof. Horace Slughorn asks Hermione if she is related to this person who founded the Most Extraordinary Society of Potioneers. She tells him that she was born a Muggle (HBP 9:185).

Dahl, Roald (1916–1990). Rowling has often been compared to Roald Dahl, who is the British author of popular children's novels such as *Charlie and the Chocolate Factory* (1964) and *James and the Giant Peach* (1961). Other popular works include *Fantastic Mr. Fox* (1970), *The BFG* (1982), and *Matilda* (1988). Dahl's fantasies are characterized by difficult themes such as death; they portray complex, eccentric, and often unflattering characters. Dahl adapted his novel *Charlie and the Chocolate Factory* for the film *Willy Wonka and the Chocolate Factory* (1971); another film adaptation appeared in 2005.

Dahl was born near Cardiff, Wales, and his father died when he was four years old. Several of his books concern the loss of parents, and this is one area where readers find similarities between Dahl and Rowling. Dahl's most popular novels are fantasy, as is Harry Potter. Dahl's and Rowling's books are both highly imaginative. Dahl, however, did not write series books.

Comparisons between Rowling and Dahl began early in Rowling's career as an author. In a 1997 article in *The Herald* of Glasgow, Rowling's agent, Christopher Little, made one of the first comparisons. By 1999, when the Harry Potter books were selling well and the comparison to Dahl was fairly common, Rowling downplayed it. She is quoted in a 1999 article in *The Independent* of London as saying, "While I think Dahl is a master at what he did, I do think my books are more moral than his. He also wrote very overblown comic characters, whereas I think mine are more three-dimensional."

Further Reading: "Book Written in Edinburgh Cafe Sells for $100,000." *The Herald* (Glasgow), July 8, 1997. http://www.theherald.co.uk; Williams, Rhys. "The Spotty Schoolboy and Single Mother Taking the Mantle from Roald Dahl." *The Independent* (London), January 29, 1999. http://www.independent.co.uk.

British author Roald Dahl (1916–1990). Early on, J. K. Rowling's Harry Potter books were compared to Dahl's fantasy novels *James and the Giant Peach* (1961) and *Charlie and the Chocolate Factory* (1964). Courtesy of the Library of Congress.

Dai Llewellyn Ward. *Magical place.* Arthur Weasley is moved to this ward at St. Mungo's. It is a special ward for the treatment of dangerous and serious bites. It is located on the first floor, which is the treatment floor for injuries caused by creatures (OP 22:487). Kennilworthy Whisp's book *He Flew Like a Madman* is a biography of "Dangerous" Dai Llewellyn (QA v).

The Daily Prophet. *Magical publication.* The wizard newspaper. Hagrid reads a copy while in the boat on his and Harry's way back to shore from the Hut-on-the-Rock (SS 5:64). At Flourish and Blotts, the magical bookstore on Diagon Alley, popular author Gilderoy Lockhart poses with Harry for a picture for the front page (CS 4:60). Like people in portraits and in book pictures in the magical world, people in *The Daily Prophet* photos move as well.

Other stories appearing in the paper include: Arthur Weasley's fine for bewitching a Muggle car (CS 12:221); "Mystery Illness of Bartemius Crouch"; "Ministry Witch Still Missing—Minister of Magic Now Personally Involved" (GF 27:522); "Harry Potter: 'Disturbed and Dangerous'" (GF 31:611–12). Hermione takes out a subscription in Year 5 so that she can know what the paper is saying about members of the Order of the Phoenix without trying to find a copy somewhere (OP 12:225).

Prophet may be a pun on "profit." The inclusion of a newspaper in the series may offer some insight into Rowling's attitude toward the press. Articles frequently contain errors, for example, and the most notable reporter in the series is Rita Skeeter, whose name is a playful turn on the "skeeter" slang term for mosquito, the annoying insect that bites.

See also Skeeter, Rita

***Daily Prophet* Grand Prize Galleon Draw.** *Magical prize.* Arthur Weasley wins this prize of 700 gold Galleons in the summer before Year 3, and the whole family goes to visit Bill in Egypt with the winnings. Ron writes to Harry that most of the money was spent on the trip, but his parents are also going to buy him a new wand (PA 1:8–9).

Dais. *Magical object.* A dais is in the center of the circular room in the Department of Mysteries and has a black veil hanging on it from a stone archway (OP 34:773).

Dale, Jim. Actor Jim Dale has had more accomplishments than his Grammy award–winning vocal performances of over 200 speaking roles in the audio books of the Harry

British actor Jim Dale holds up a copy of *Harry Potter and the Order of the Phoenix* at a Toys "R" Us store in New York, June 21, 2003, shortly after it went on sale at midnight. Dale narrates the American books-on-tape version of the Harry Potter series. According to Dale, it took 145 hours and about 10,000 edits to record the 870-page book at a studio in New York. © Henny Ray Abrams/AFP/Getty Images.

Potter series. Dale received a Tony Award in 1981 for his portrayal of P. T. Barnum in the Broadway musical *Barnum* and an Academy Award nomination in 1966 for writing the lyrics to the song "Georgy Girl." He also earned three Tony Award nominations for his roles on and off Broadway in *Scapino, Joe Egg,* and *Candide*. A versatile artist, Dale has worked as a dancer, comedian, Shakespearean actor (with Laurence Olivier), disc jockey, pop singer, host of a television show in England, playwright, songwriter, and actor on stage, film, and television. His many film credits include: *The Hunchback* (1997); *Carry On Columbus* (1992); *Adventures of Huckleberry Finn* (1985); *Adolf Hitler—My Part in His Downfall* (1972); and *The Winter's Tale* (1967). His television work in the United States includes: *Adventures of Huckleberry Finn* (PBS); *The Cosby Show; The Ellen Burstyn Show;* and *The Dinah Shore Show*. In England, he has hosted *Sunday Night at the London Palladium; Six Five Special;* and *Thank Your Lucky Stars*.

Dale's career, spanning over forty years in the entertainment industry, has likely never reached the height of notoriety that it has more recently attained as the reader of the American audio editions of the Harry Potter books. Dale reads the books cover to cover without abridgment. He not only reads the narration, he also alters his voice slightly for each of the speaking characters, from those with the smallest parts to Harry Potter himself. Listeners have asked Dale how he differentiates the characters' voices as he works on the recordings, and he has explained that he underlines the dialogue in colored pencils according to a key he keeps beside him. He indicates that there are many re-recordings of times when he has made mistakes.

When asked where the inspiration for each character's voice originates, he has explained the following: Hagrid's voice is that of Dale's rather large uncle; Dobby's is from a small person (whom Dale met in an elevator) playing a dwarf in a musical version of *Snow White* (Dale claims the man said from behind him in a small voice, "Excuse me Sir, you're wiping my nose with your bum"). Prof. McGonagall's voice comes from his aunt who lives in Edinburgh, Scotland; Hermione, his first girlfriend who spoke very quickly so as not to leave any words behind; Prof. Dumbledore, deceased great actor and friend, John Houseman; Prof. Snape, one of his teachers whom his class disliked so much that they fastened a raw fish under his desk (the source of the smell was never discovered); Moaning Myrtle, a girl he heard telling her mother that her brother had swallowed her goldfish; and Draco Malfoy, the voice of a boy who has just tromped through dog excrement.

Goblet of Fire took the actor ten days to complete, reading twenty pages per hour for seven hours each day, then coming back to re-record mistakes. *Order of the Phoenix* takes up seventeen cassette tapes and twenty-three compact discs, with twenty-six hours and thirty minutes of listening time, or the rough equivalent of nine major league baseball games. For his work in 2000, Dale won a Grammy for his recording of *Goblet of Fire*, and he has earned three Grammy nominations for his work on the series. Random House claims the recorded books have sold a combined total of 575,000 copies, the largest number in the history of the format. They compare this number to the average run of 15,000 to 20,000 copies for audio books of other popular children's books, or 250,000 for an adult audio best-seller.

See also Fry, Stephen

Further Reading: Jim Dale website: http://www.jim-dale.com.

Damocles, Uncle. *Character.* The uncle of Marcus Belby. Damocles invented the Wolfsbane Potion (HBP 7:144).

"Dangerous" Dai Commemorative Medal. *Magical sports award.* From QA. A Quidditch League medal awarded at the end of the season to the player who took the most risks during games (QA 33).

See also Quidditch Through the Ages

The Dark Arts Outsmarted. *Magical book.* The book is one of a collection in the Room of Requirement. Harry uses it for Dumbledore's Army lessons (OP 18:390).

Dark Detectors. *Magical objects.* Harry sees some of these in Moody's office. They include a large Sneakoscope; something like a television antenna; and a mirror with dark, blurry figures in it (GF 20:342–43).

The Dark Forces: A Guide to Self-Protection. *Magical book.* In Year 4, Mad-Eye Moody tells his DADA students that they will not be needing this textbook (GF 14:210).

The Dark Lord. *See* Voldemort, Lord

Dark Magic. *Magical skill.* Involves using magical talents for evil or sinister purposes. Hagrid suspects someone has used Dark Magic to cast a spell on Harry's broomstick during his first Quidditch match (SS 11:190).

The Dark Mark. *Magical sign.* It is the sign placed in the sky when Voldemort or his followers have killed someone (GF 9:142). The sign usually appears in the night sky and consists of stars forming a green skull with a large serpent coming out of the mouth. It appears on the night of the Quidditch World Cup (GF 9:128). Mr. Weasley tells Harry and his friends that before that night, it had not been seen in thirteen years. Hermione tells Ron that she read about it in *The Rise and Fall of the Dark Arts* (GF 9:141). Only Death Eaters can conjure the Dark Mark (GF 9:143). The Death Eaters wear a tattooed Dark Mark on their forearms (GF 33:645). Harry thinks that Draco Malfoy has been branded with the Dark Mark over the summer, making him a Death Eater while his father is back in Azkaban (HBP 7:135).

Dark Side. *Magical group and philosophy.* Voldemort has gone over to the Dark Side. Hagrid describes the Dark Side to Harry for the first time at the Hut-on-the-Rock (SS 4:55). The Dark Side is a group of witches and wizard who believe in using their magical talents and abilities for evil purposes.

David Copperfield. See Dickens, Charles

Davies, Roger. *Character.* Ravenclaw Quidditch Captain in Year 4 (GF 23:413). Harry and Cho Chang see him kissing a blonde girl at Madam Puddifoot's Tea Shop in Hogsmeade on Valentine's Day (OP 25:559).

Dawlish. *Character.* An Auror who attends the meeting about DA in Dumbledore's office. Dumbledore informs Dawlish that if he tries to bring him in by force, Dumbledore will have to hurt him (OP 27:620). Dawlish tries to stun Hagrid when Hagrid is sacked by Umbridge and comes to take Hagrid away (OP 31:721). Cornelius Fudge asks Dawlish to go to the Department of Mysteries to check on the Death Eaters Dumbledore has put in the Death Chamber (OP 36:817). Nymphadora Tonks tells Harry that Dawlish is at Hogwarts when he arrives at school in Year 6 (HBP 8:158).

Dearborn, Caradoc. *Character.* A member of the original Order of the Phoenix; his body was never found (OP 9:174).

Death. Rowling has said that she wrote the *Sorcerer's Stone* chapter "The Mirror of Erised" shortly after arriving in Oporto, Portugal, after her mother's death in 1990 at the age of forty-five. It was not until later, however, when she reread the chapter, that she realized she had infused it with much of the sadness she felt from her own personal loss, and it became her favorite chapter of the book. With characters such as ghosts, poltergeists, and Death Eaters at Hogwarts, and the evil Lord Voldemort always searching for eternal life in the background, death and the possibility of death is present in all of the novels. Harry is heralded as "The Boy Who Lived" after his parents are murdered by Voldemort on Halloween night. Cedric Diggory is dramatically killed in *Goblet of Fire*; Sirius Black meets his fate in *Order of the Phoenix*; and Harry's beloved mentor and grandfather figure dies in *Half-Blood Prince*. Rowling has stated in interviews that death is perhaps the most important theme of the novels, and most readers are likely to agree.

Prof. Dumbledore tells Harry that the Flamels do not mind dying, that to older people death can seem like going to sleep after a very long day. Death, he says, is like the next great adventure to one who has a well-organized mind (SS 17:297). He tells Voldemort at the Hall of Prophecy that there are worse things than death and other ways to beat a man (OP 36:814). Despite the magic that can do so much in the new world in which Harry finds himself, Dumbledore tells Harry clearly and firmly that no spell can bring someone back from the dead (GF 36:697). However, another piece of wisdom that Dumbledore passes on to Harry about death is that those we love are always with us, even after they die. When we need them, their presence is stronger than ever (PA 22:427).

Despite these talks with Dumbledore, Harry is still struggling with the meaning of death when he experiences the loss of Sirius Black. Harry goes to see the Gryffindor ghost, Nearly Headless Nick, about death after Sirius falls behind the veil. Nick has expected Harry to come, since, he says, many do after they have suffered a loss. Nick tells Harry that Sirius is gone. When Harry presses him about the meaning of death and what happens after one dies, Nick says that the Department of Mysteries studies this topic, and he quickly excuses himself to attend the Year-End Feast (OP 38:859–62).

Harry finds perhaps his best relief from Sirius's death in talking with Luna Lovegood. When Luna was nine, she saw her mother die in an accident with an experimental spell. She tells Harry that she will see her mother, and he will see Sirius because they could hear their voices behind the veil. Although Luna presents some strange theories at times, Harry finds comfort in this suggestion because he did indeed hear voices behind the veil (OP 38:863).

Some adult readers and parents have been uneasy about children reading books that deal so directly with the subject of death and the questions it leaves for the living. Others praise the books for the same reason.

Death Chamber. *Magical place.* A room in the Ministry at the Department of Mysteries where the escaped Death Eaters are taken after the battle in the Hall of Prophecy (OP 36:817).

Death Day Party. *Magical event.* Nearly Headless Nick invites Harry, Ron, and Hermione to his 500th Death Day Party on Halloween night in their second year. He is hoping that if they pretend that he is a very scary ghost, Sir Patrick Delaney-Podmore will allow him to join the Headless Hunt. The Hunt is an event that he seems to think is a lot of fun, and from which he has been excluded because he is only nearly—not completely—headless (CS 8:130).

At the party, the dungeon decorations include long, black candles, a chilly temperature, and a grating sound that is probably supposed to be ghost music. The refreshments include moldy cheese, smelly salmon, burned cakes, haggis with maggots all over it, and a large cake in the shape of a tombstone with Nick's name and death date (October 31, 1492) on it. This date is used by many readers to place the timing of the scene at October 31, 1992. At the party, hundreds of ghosts float about, waltzing. While the Fat Friar seems to be having a good time talking with another ghost, most of the others leave the Bloody Baron to himself. Peeves is dressed in a party hat and bow tie. Nick's guests from out of town include the Wailing Widow from Kent; he is honored that she made the trip.

Moaning Myrtle is also at the party, and this is where Harry and Ron first meet her, though she has been talking with Hermione in the girls' bathroom. She is easily offended, and gets hints from Peeves that Hermione was talking about her. When Sir Patrick does arrive, it is with great flourish and with hundreds of ghosts on horses. The ghosts scatter the dancers at Nick's party and begin a feisty game of Head Hockey. All the party-goers stop partying to watch the match. Harry tries to tell Sir Patrick how frightening Nick is, but Sir Patrick has Nick's number and says that Nick probably told Harry to say that. When Sir Patrick's takeover makes it obvious that Nick has lost control of his own party, Harry and his friends leave the festivities (CS 8:131–37).

Death Eater. *Magical being.* Death Eaters are what Voldemort calls his supporters (GF 9:142). Ten of them escape Azkaban in Harry's fifth year (OP 25:544–45). Since Voldemort's goal is to escape death and to live for all eternity, his followers eat death, presumably to conquer it. Each one has the Dark Mark branded onto his or her forearm. The mark burns when Voldemort has strengthened and wants them to come to him.

The Death Eaters in the various novels include: Alecto; Amycus; Avery; Regulus Black (who redeemed himself from the Dark Side before he was killed by Voldemort or Death Eaters); the Carrows; Mr. Crabbe; Barty Crouch, Jr.; Antonin Dolohov; Gibbon; Mr. Goyle; Fenrir Greyback; Jugson; Igor Karkaroff; Bellatrix Black Lestrange; Rabastan Lestrange; Rodolphus Lestrange; Walden Macnair; possibly Draco Malfoy; Lucius Malfoy; Mulciber; Nott; Peter "Wormtail" Pettigrew; Augustus Rookwood; Evan Rosier; Severus Snape (perhaps a spy working for Dumbledore); Travers; Wilkes; and Yaxley, among others.

In a BBC interview in 2003, Rowling began discussing the origins of the Death Eaters and said that they were once called the Knights of Walpurgis. The name was a wordplay on Walpurgis Night, April 30, the eve of St. Walpurga's Feast Day of May 1, and the opposite day in the year from Halloween. St. Walpurga is the patron saint of witches. In witch folklore, witches met in the highest parts of the Harz mountains on Walpurgis Night and feasted and danced.

Death Omens: What to Do When You Know the Worst Is Coming. *Magical book.* Harry sees this book at Flourish and Blotts, but the manager warns him not to read it because he will start seeing death omens in everything. Harry finds the book unsettling because the cover shows a big black dog which looks strikingly like the one he thinks he may have seen in the hedge on Magnolia Crescent (PA 4:54).

Decoy Detonators. *Magical objects.* Black, horn-like objects that walk off of shelves on their own; they are a product sold in the Weasley brothers' shop. They make a noise from a distance, creating a diversion when one needs one. Harry takes out his money bag to buy some, but the brothers tell him he can have anything in the shop for free because of the start-up loan he gave them from his Triwizard Tournament winnings (HBP 6:119).

Decree for the Reasonable Restriction of Underage Sorcery, 1875. *Magical legislation.* Snape also calls this legislation the Decree for the Restriction of Underage Wizardry (CS 5:81). Mafalda Hopkirk cites Paragraph C of this law in her letter to Harry about the Hover Charm that Dobby casts with the pudding at Privet Drive (CS 2:21). Harry knows that he has broken this law when he blows up Aunt Marge in the summer before Year 3 (PA 3:31, 45). Paragraph C of the decree apparently also concerns conjuring a Patronus Charm in the presence of Muggles, and it is this segment of the law that Harry is supposed to have broken when the Dementors attack him and Dudley Dursley in Little Whinging (OP 8:140).

Defense Against the Dark Arts. *Magical class at Hogwarts.* This is a class where students learn techniques to protect themselves against wizards and witches who have gone over to the Dark, or evil, Side. Dark Side witches and wizards use magic for evil purposes. Durmstrang Institute teaches the Dark Arts, thereby making the school rather suspect. Hogwarts teaches defensive techniques only. However, in Year 4, Barty Crouch, Jr., who is disguised as Mad-Eye Moody, teaches the students all three of the Unforgivable Curses so that they will know what they are up against.

During Harry's first year, the class is taught by Prof. Quirrell. In subsequent years the teachers are: Year 2, Prof. Gilderoy Lockhart; Year 3, Prof. Remus Lupin; Year 4, Mad-Eye Moody/Barty Crouch, Jr.; Year 5, Prof. Dolores Umbridge; and Year 6, Prof. Severus Snape. It is significant that Prof. Snape teaches the class in Year 6, because he knows a lot about the Dark Arts and has coveted that position for many years. Dumbledore tells Harry that the school has never been able to keep a teacher in the position for more than one year since the job was refused to Tom Riddle (HBP 20:446).

See also Hogwarts School of Witchcraft and Wizardry

Defense Against the Dark Arts, Harry's class. *Magical class.* Hermione puts Harry up to teaching practical skills in Defense Against the Dark Arts in fifth year, since Prof. Umbridge is bent on only teaching them theory. At the first meeting of the group in the Hog's Head, the following students appear: Harry, Ron, and Hermione; Neville Longbottom; Dean Thomas; Lavender Brown; Parvati and Padma Patil; Cho Chang and a friend; Luna Lovegood; Katie Bell; Alicia Spinnet; Angelina Johnson; Colin and Dennis Creevey; Ernie Macmillan; Justin Finch-Fletchley; Zacharias Smith; Hannah Abbot; Anthony Goldstein; Michael Corner; Terry Boot; Ginny, Fred, and George Weasley; and Lee Jordan (OP 16:337–38). Hermione tells Sirius Black that there are twenty-eight members of the group (OP 17:372).

Defense Association. *Name.* This name—DA for short—is suggested by Cho Chang before Dumbledore's Army is decided upon as the final name (OP 18:392).

Defensive Magical Theory. *Magical book.* Book by Wilbert Slinkhard. It is a fifth-year textbook (OP 9:160). Prof. Umbridge makes the students read the book, but never lets them practice the techniques (OP 12:240).

Deflagration Deluxe. *See* Weasleys' Wildfire Whiz-Bangs

Deflating Draught. *Magical substance.* Antidote to Swelling Solution (CS 11:187).

Delacour, Fleur. *Character.* Fleur Delacour is engaged to Bill Weasley and is irreverently called "Phlegm" by Ginny, who does not like her. She works part-time at Gringotts to improve her English (HBP 5:91, 93). Fleur attended Beauxbatons school and was chosen as their champion for the Triwizard Tournament (GF 16:269). She attends the Yule Ball with Roger Davies (GF 23:413–14).

Delacour, Gabrielle. *Character.* Fleur's sister; she is the person Fleur would least want to lose, so she is tied in the village of the merpeople in the lake at Hogwarts for the second task of the Triwizard Tournament. Harry rescues her (GF 26:502). She never stops talking about Harry. She will be at Fleur's wedding in Book 7 (HBP 5:92).

Delaney-Podmore, Sir Patrick. *Character.* Sends the letter to Nearly Headless Nick refusing his participation in the Headless Hunt. Nick sarcastically refers to him as "Sir Properly Decapitated-Podmore" (CS 8:124). He crashes Nick's Death Day Party (CS 8:131–37).

"Deleterius!" *Incantation.* This incantation causes something to delete or disappear. Amos Diggory uses it to make the remaining shadow of the Dark Mark vanish on the night of the World Cup (GF 9:136).

"Dementoids." *Wrong word.* Vernon Dursley mistakenly calls Dementors "Dementoids" when he is listening to Petunia's and Harry's explanations of them (OP 2:34).

Dementors. *Magical beings.* The guards at Azkaban. They are tall, dark-hooded beings in long robes; they have no faces. Their hands look gray, old, and scabby (PA 5:83). When they arrive, the air feels cold, and all life seems to freeze. People feel as though they may never feel happy again in their lives. Harry hears his mother's screams at her death when the Dementors come around him, and this causes him to faint in the train (PA 5:84). Prof. Lupin recommends chocolate as an antidote to the depressed feelings the Dementors leave with their victims (PA 5:84). They have mouths that they use to kiss their victims to suck out their souls. After the breakout of Sirius Black from Azkaban Prison, they are stationed outside Hogwarts by the Ministry in order to protect Harry and the other students. Prof. Dumbledore is not pleased, but accepts the Ministry's orders (PA 4:66).

Madam Poppy Pomfrey, the school nurse, agrees that Dementors are a terrible thing, and comments that they particularly prey on the delicate, which Harry objects to being called (PA 5:89). Dumbledore tells the students at Hogwarts about the Dementors guarding the school from escaped prisoner Sirius Black, and warns them that the beings are not fooled by such attempts at diversion as disguises, tricks, or Invisibility Cloaks. Dumbledore also tells the students that Dementors do not have it in their nature to stop for pleas of mercy or for reasons why someone crosses their path (PA 5:92). About 100 Dementors get onto the Quidditch field and distract Harry, resulting in his falling from his broom and losing the match (PA 9:182). Harry calls the sight of them the scariest thing he has ever seen (PA 9:179). Lupin explains to Harry that he is more bothered by the Dementors than the other students because Harry has a more tragic past (PA 10:187). A Dementor kills Barty Crouch, Jr., with the Killing Kiss before Barty can stand trial or give testimony against Voldemort and the Death Eaters (GF 36:703). Two Dementors attack Harry and Dudley in Little Whinging (OP 1:17–19).

Many readers interpret the Dementors as representing depression, or those who would leave their victims demented. Rowling has admitted in interviews that she thought them up when she was depressed over her first marriage failing, and over finding herself without a job and with a young daughter to support. She has said they mimic the dead feeling that one experiences, as though one will never be cheerful again.

See also Depression

Dementor's Kiss. *Magical action.* Dementors suck the soul out of their victims with a kiss, leaving their victims with no chance of recovery (PA 12:247).

Demiguise. *Magical creature.* From *Fantastic Beasts.* Classified 4X by the MM. A furry beast with large eyes that can make itself invisible. Its silvery fur may be used in Invisibility Cloaks. It lives in the Far East and eats plants (FB 9).

See also Fantastic Beasts and Where to Find Them

Dennis. *Character.* One of Dudley Dursley's gang (SS 3:31).

"Densaugeo!" *Incantation.* Causes teeth to enlarge. Draco Malfoy accidentally puts the jinx on Hermione when it misses his intended target, Harry (GF 18:299).

Department for the Regulation and Control of Magical Creatures. *Magical office.* Newt Scamander worked in this department (FB vi); it is the second largest department in the Ministry (FB xviii). It is located on the fourth level and contains the Beast, Being, and Spirit Divisions, the Goblin Liaison Office, and the Pest Advisory Bureau (OP 7:130).

Department of International Magical Cooperation. *Magical office.* Percy Weasley gets a job in this department at the Ministry of Magic (GF 3:36). It is located on the fifth floor and includes the International Magical Trading Standards Body, the International Magical Office of Law, and the British Seats of the International Confederation of Wizards (OP 7:130).

Department of Magical Accidents and Catastrophes. *Magical office.* Located on the third level of the Ministry of Magic, it includes the Accidental Magic Reversal Squad, the Obliviator Headquarters, and the Muggle-Worthy Excuse Committee (OP 7:130).

Department of Magical Games and Sports. *Magical office.* Department at the Ministry of Magic that is responsible for putting on the Quidditch World Cup. Ludo Bagman is the head (GF 5:61). It is located on the seventh level at the Ministry and also contains the British and Irish Quidditch League Headquarters, the Official Gobstones Club, and the Ludicrous Patents Office (OP 7:129).

Department of Magical Law Enforcement. *Magical office.* The largest department at the Ministry and the one to which the other six, except possibly the Department of Mysteries, report in some way (FB xviii). It is located on the second level of the Ministry offices and includes the Improper Use of Magic Office, Auror Headquarters, and the Wizengamot Administration Services (OP 7:130).

Department of Magical Transport. *Magical office.* Located on the sixth level of the Ministry, it encompasses the Floo Network Authority, Broom Regulatory Control, Portkey Office, and Apparition Test Center (OP 7:129).

Department of Mysteries. *Magical office.* Located on the first level of the Ministry. Luna Lovegood tells Harry that Cornelius Fudge is having poison made there (OP 18:395). Harry tries to ask Snape what is there that Voldemort wants so badly (OP 24:537). The people who work at the Department of Mysteries are called Unspeakables (OP 24:539).

Depression. Rowling has admitted in interviews that the Dementors she created for the series probably rose from her own depression after the failure of her first marriage and the difficulties she faced when she first brought her infant daughter, Jessica, to Edinburgh, Scotland. She sought professional counseling and at the same time tried to finish her novel, get trained as a teacher, find child care while at school, and locate a job. No doubt some of her feelings about her mother's early death also plagued her thoughts.

Within the series, the Dementors make their biggest performance in Book 3, which many readers find to be the most introspective and, to some, the most intriguing of the novels. In this book, Harry does not confront Voldemort in person but rather deals with his own inner demons—the loss of his parents, the strangeness of his situation in the magical world as a famous child survivor, and his situation in the Muggle world as an unwanted child. Prof. Lupin helps him acknowledge and encounter his fear of fear. Lupin serves as a kind of therapist to Harry in their private lessons on Boggarts, and he helps Harry cope with the ferocity of the Dementors as well as his fear of them. It is a testament to Harry's strength as a character that he is willing to tackle this weakness head-on. By the end of the novel, the reader sees that he has succeeded in addressing his fear by performing his own Patronus—the stag—which makes him feel particularly close to his father.

Derek. *Character.* First-year student who attends the Hogwarts Christmas Feast when there are only twelve in attendance (PA 11:230).

Derrick. *Character.* Beater on the Slytherin Quidditch team (PA 15:308). He has left by Harry's fifth year and is replaced by Vincent Crabbe (OP 19:405).

Dervish and Banges. *Magical place.* Store in Hogsmeade where wizard instruments and implements are sold (PA 5:76).

Derwent, Dilys. *Character.* A witch with silver ringlets in one of the portraits of old headmasters and -mistresses on Dumbledore's office wall. Dumbledore sends her out to sound the alarm after Arthur Weasley is attacked. He tells her to make sure that Arthur is taken care of by friends, not foes. She is sent because she and Everard are two of the most renowned Hogwarts Heads; both have portraits in other significant wizard institutions to which they can travel for help or information (OP 22:468–69). She comes back and reports to Dumbledore that Arthur was carried past her portrait at St. Mungo's Hospital and that he did not look good (OP 22:471). When Harry and the others go to the hospital to visit Arthur, they see her portrait, which has a label indicating that she was headmistress of Hogwarts from 1741–1768 and a Healer at St. Mungo's from 1722–1741 (OP 22:485).

Destination, Determination, Deliberation. *Magical mantra.* The witch or wizard who wishes to Apparate must concentrate on these three words (HBP 18:384).

Detachable Cribbing Cuffs. *Magical object.* A cheating device that is banned from the O.W.L. examination room (OP 31:708).

Detention. *Magical punishment.* Detentions at Hogwarts are unpleasant, but Harry's detentions often provide more information about his new world and the people in it. In Book 1, when he gets detention for being out of his room at night, he must go to the Forbidden Forest with Hagrid to help find what is killing the unicorns (SS 15:250). When he is attacked by Voldemort there, he learns more about the evil forces that are out for him, and he learns about the possible kindness from unicorns. In Year 2, Ron is charged with polishing trophies with Mr. Filch, and Harry has to help Prof. Lockhart answer his fan mail (CS 7:118–19). Ron must clean bedpans in the hospital wing for Snape without using magic in Year 3 (PA 9:173). Probably the worst detention Harry ever endures is with the cruel Prof. Umbridge who makes him write lines about not telling lies, and these words get cut over and over into the back of his hands (OP 13:266–67). Harry learns not to let cruelty break his will.

See also Hogwarts School of Witchcraft and Wizardry

Devil's Snare. *Magical plant.* One of the barriers Harry, Ron, and Hermione must overcome to get to the Sorcerer's Stone. Hermione remembers from Herbology that the plant reacts to heat and light (SS 16:277–78). The plant later kills Broderick Bode in his room at St. Mungo's (OP 25:546).

Devon. From QA. Shuntbumps, the ancient broomstick game, was especially popular here (QA 6).

See also Quidditch Through the Ages

Diagon Alley. *Magical place.* The main shopping street for Hogwarts students and families of the magical world. Hagrid takes Harry on his first trip here. They reach it by tapping three bricks up and two across in the courtyard behind the Leaky Cauldron in London; this brick-tapping opens an archway to the magical street. The street is full of magical shops and products of all kinds, including cauldrons, an apothecary, stores selling broomsticks, robes, telescopes, spell books, potion bottles, bat spleens and eels' eyes, moon globes, and more (SS 5:72).

Stores and other establishments most frequently mentioned in the series include: Madam Malkin's Robes for All Occasions (SS 5:76); Flourish and Blotts (bookstore) (SS 5:80); Ollivanders (wands) (SS 5:81); Quality Quidditch Supplies (CS 4:58); and also Gambol and Japes Wizarding Joke Shop (CS 4:58). In Year 5 the Weasley twins announce the location of their new store at Number 93 Diagon Alley (OP 29:675).

See also Flourish and Blotts; The Leaky Cauldron; Madam Malkin's Robes for All Occasions; Ollivanders; Weasleys' Wizard Wheezes

Diary, Tom Riddle's. *Magical object.* The first mention of a diary is when Harry and the Weasley family try to leave the Burrow at the end of the summer to catch the Hogwarts Express. The family has to turn the Ford Anglia around and go back because Ginny has forgotten her diary (CS 5:66). Moaning Myrtle tells Harry that the diary fell on her head while she was in her U-Bend thinking about death (CS 13:230). Harry sees "T. M. Riddle" written in ink on the first page (CS 13:231). The name of a variety store on Vauxhall Road, London, is printed on the back of Tom Riddle's diary. This is a clue to Ron that Tom must have been Muggle-born (CS 13:231–32). The diary must be fifty years old because that is when Tom attended the school. Harry and his friends discover this when Ron polishes Tom's award in the Trophy Room during detention (CS 13:231–32). Harry has a written conversation with the diary, which leads him to see a vision that Tom Riddle wants to show him (CS 13:240–48). The diary is stolen when Harry's room is ransacked (CS 14:253).

Dickens, Charles (1812–1870). As one of the world's major and most important authors, it is important to remember that Charles Dickens was also an immensely popular British author who enjoyed unprecedented worldwide fame during his lifetime. His vivid characterization, frequent theme of young orphans improving themselves through the kindness of others, and use of humor make comparisons between Rowling and Dickens not unfounded. Over the years, critical debates about the nature of Dickens's books have addressed whether the books are literature or simply entertainment. These debates, seemingly settled in the literature camp by the early twenty-first century, bring to mind similar debates over Rowling's series in contemporary literary circles. Dickens's lecture tours increased his fame and notoriety around the world, much as Rowling's appearance on the global scene at the blossoming of the Internet and the electronic age increased her recognition across continents.

Dickens wrote twenty novels, including five short Christmas books, and other works such as travel books, sketches, and more. Among his most significant, popular, and enduring novels are *Great Expectations, David Copperfield, Oliver Twist, A Tale of Two Cities, A Christmas Carol,*

British author Charles Dickens (1812–1870). J. K. Rowling's success mirrors his in a few ways. Chapters from Dickens's popular books came out in installments that were eagerly awaited by readers. Fans became so attached to his characters that they anticipated what would happen to them next with great emotion. Courtesy of the Library of Congress.

The Pickwick Papers, and *The Old Curiosity Shop.* Several of his works were published serially, with each new chapter published in periodicals before the entire book was written. The great anticipation for each new book in the Harry Potter series can be compared with excitement over Dickens's *Old Curiosity Shop,* which was published serially. Some stories have said that when the next installment arrived in New York Harbor, readers lined the docks urgently asking those on board whether or not their favorite character, Little Nell, was still alive. Likewise, readers of the Harry Potter series will not know until they reach the end of the seventh novel whether or not Harry survives. By the time the seventh novel appears, readers of the series from the beginning will have waited 10 years or more to find out how the story ends.

"Diffindio!" *Incantation.* This incantation cuts open a bag or other container (GF 20:340). *Differo* is Latin for "scatter."

Diggle, Dedalus. *Character.* The excitable wizard whom Prof. McGonagall says has little sense and whom she blames for the shooting stars over Kent the night that Harry Potter is left on the Dursleys' doorstep (SS 1:10). Dedalus Diggle meets Harry in the Leaky Cauldron, where Harry remembers seeing Dedalus bow to him in a store. Dedalus is pleased that Harry remembers the incident (SS 5:69). He is a member of the original Order of the Phoenix (OP 9:173) and comes with other members of the Order to pick up Harry at Privet Drive; he keeps dropping his hat (OP 3:49).

Stephen Dedalus is the famous narrator of Jame Joyce's *Portrait of the Artist as a Young Man*. In mythology, Dedalus was an aviator and inventor. He designed the famous Minos labyrinth. He made wings out of feathers and wax for himself and for Icarus, but Icarus flew too close to the sun and fell when the sun melted off the wings.

Diggory, Amos. *Character*. Cedric Diggory's father who works for the Department for the Regulation and Control of Magical Creatures (GF 6:71). At the Portkey for the World Cup, he meets Harry Potter and brags about Cedric staying on his broom and beating Harry in the Quidditch match where Harry fell (GF 6:72–73). He wants to charge Winky with making the Dark Mark appear when she is found with a wand in her hand after the appearance (GF 9:134).

Diggory, Cedric. *Character*. Hufflepuff Quidditch captain and Seeker; the girls on the Gryffindor team say that he is tall and very good-looking (PA 9:168). He is two years ahead of Harry at Hogwarts (PA 9:174). Cedric is a fair player and requests a rematch when Harry falls off his broom during a Dementor attack. Harry's fall resulted in Cedric catching the snitch. It was the first Quidditch match Harry did not win (PA 9:180). Cedric congratulates Harry when he gets his new Firebolt broomstick (PA 13:257). Cedric is also friendly when he and his father meet Harry and the Weasleys at the Portkey on the way to the Quidditch World Cup (GF 6:71). He is chosen as the Hogwarts champion for the Triwizard Tournament, which leads many at the school to call him the real champion of the school since Harry is not the right age (GF 16:270). In the third task of the tournament, Cedric and Harry both grab the Triwizard Cup together at the center of the maze. The Cup turns out to be a portkey to the Little Hangleton Graveyard. Soon after they arrive, Cedric is killed with the "Avada Kedavra" curse by Wormtail (GF 32:638). Dumbledore leads a tribute to Cedric after the Triwizard Tournament and asks students to remember Cedric when confronted with the choice of doing what is right versus doing what is easy (GF 37:725). Cho Chang, who went to the Yule Ball with Cedric, has mixed feelings about his loss and about her renewed interest in Harry in fifth year. She asks Harry if Cedric mentioned her before he died (OP 25:561). Cedric Diggory's name may or may not be an allusion to the character Digory Kirke in C. S. Lewis's *The Lion, the Witch, and the Wardrobe*.

"Dilligrout." *Magic word*. Password to get past the Fat Lady in Year 6 (HBP 12:256; HBP 14:289).

Dilys. *See* Derwent, Dilys

Dimitrov. *Character*. Chaser on the Bulgaria National Quidditch Team who plays in the World Cup (GF 8:108).

Dingle, Harold. *Character*. Hermione confiscates this student's powdered dragon claw, which is really dried doxy dung, before Ron or Harry can buy any. Harold was selling the substance as a brain stimulant before O.W.L.s (OP 31:708). Seamus Finnegan and Dean Thomas ask Harry if he wants to chip in some money for firewhiskey, which they say Harold can get for them (OP 32:738).

Dippet, Prof. Armando. *Character*. The headmaster of Hogwarts fifty years before Harry's time, when Tom Riddle was a student (CS 13:241). Moaning Myrtle says that Olive Hornby came into the bathroom telling her that Prof. Dippet was looking for her

(GF 25:465). From his portrait, Dippet reprimands Phineas Nigellus for his foul mood about having to help Dumbledore; Dippet reminds Phineas of his duty (OP 22:473). He is aghast at seeing Harry's anger and frustration at Dumbledore after Sirius Black's death (OP 37:825). Tom Riddle asked him if he could join the faculty, but Prof. Dippet told him he was too young at the age of eighteen and said that he should come back in a few years to apply again (HBP 20:432).

Diricawls. *Magical creatures.* From *Fantastic Beasts*. Classified 2X by the MM. Diricawls are mentioned in *A History of Magic* (FB xi). The creature is a bird that can disappear at will and reappear somewhere else (FB 9–10).
See also Fantastic Beasts and Where to Find Them

Disapparition. *Magical transportation.* Disappearing through a magical spell and reappearing elsewhere. Arthur Weasley offers to fix the Dursley fireplace before he Disapparates to join his family at the Quidditch World Cup (GF 4:45).
See also Apparition

Disarming Spell. *Magical spell.* The incantation for the Disarming Spell is "Expelliarmus!" It knocks the victim off his or her feet, taking away his or her wand. Snape uses this spell on Lockhart during the first Dueling Club lesson (CS 11:190). Harry has known how to do it for a long time, so Hemione says they do not need to review it for the third task in the Triwizard Tournament (GF 29:574). Harry does use the spell on the spider in the maze (GF 31:632). Harry begins his DADA classes with the DA with a review of this spell (OP 18:392). Ron uses it in the escape from the Inquisitorial Squad (OP 33:760).

Disillusionment Charm. *Magical spell.* This spell disguises the victim, making him or her chameleon-like. Moody casts it on Harry before they leave Privet Drive with the guard of the Order (OP 3:54). It distorts the vision of Muggles who may see something magical. Its effects do not last long, so it may be conjured daily, as needed (FB xix). Harry has the spell placed on him again when he is taken to the Ministry of Magic for his hearing caused by using magic against the Dementors in Little Whinging (OP 7:123).

"Dissendium." *Incantation.* This incantation allows entry to the secret passage from Hogwarts to Hogsmeade. The entrance is in the hump of a statue. The person climbs into the statue and descends, sliding down a hole until he or she reappears in a cellar under a trap door in the floor of Honeydukes (PA 10:195–96).

Dittany. *Magical plant.* Harry looks up this term in *One Thousand Magical Herbs and Fungi* while studying for his Herbology exam (SS 14:229).

Divination. *Magical class at Hogwarts.* A class at Hogwarts taught by Prof. Trelawney that teaches how to predict the future using tea leaves, crystal balls, and other items. Prof. McGonagall and Hermione Granger have strong opinions against it as an imprecise science. Percy Weasley recommends the class to Harry as he plans his schedule for the next year over Easter holidays in Year 2 (CS 14:252). The classroom looks like an attic and a tea store, and there is a constant fragrance in the room. The first term is about reading tea leaves; the next term is about the crystal ball, then fire omens (PA 6:103–4).

Prof. Trelawney predicts events in the students' futures that are usually unpleasant. In the first class, for example, she tells Parvati Patil to watch out for a red-haired man (PA

6:103) and predicts that an event that Lavender Brown has been dreading will occur on Friday, October 16 (PA 6:104). She tells Harry that his tea leaves show a Grim, which is an omen of death (PA 6:107). Prof. McGonagall does not think very highly of Divination because she considers it rather imprecise; she says that true Seers are rare, and she implies that Prof. Trelawney is probably not one (PA 6:109). Trelawney's final exam involves seeing each student individually and asking them what they see in the crystal ball. Harry, knowing about Buckbeak's impending execution, says that he sees a hippogriff flying away (PA 16:323). Following his exam, Prof. Trelawney goes into a trance and makes a prediction about Lord Voldemort rising again (PA 16:324). Prof. Dumbledore never took Divination (HBP 20:427).

See also Hogwarts School of Witchcraft and Wizardry

"Do a Weasley." *Expression.* The Weasley twins' departure from Hogwarts became the stuff of legend around the school almost immediately. Students often threatened to follow their lead and jump on their brooms and fly away from school (OP 30:676).

Dobbin. *Character.* Prof. Trelawney tells Luna Lovegood that she prefers to think of Firenze by this name (HBP 15:317).

Dobbs, Emma. *Character.* In Year 4, Harry looks at the Sorting Hat while Emma Dobbs is sorted; he does this to avoid looking at the Creevey brothers who are talking excitedly about him (GF 12:179).

Dobby. *Character.* Lucius Malfoy's house-elf who comes to warn Harry about trouble at Hogwarts and tries to make sure that Harry will not return the second year (2:13). He is impressed with Harry's kindness in treating him like an equal. Though he is trying to save Harry, Dobby's efforts make life more complicated for him. It is Dobby who prevents him from getting through to Platform 9¾; and Dobby enchants the Bludger in the Quidditch match that breaks Harry's arm so that he might be sent home (CS 10:176–77). Later in *Chamber of Secrets*, Harry manages to free Dobby by making it so that Lucius Malfoy inadvertently gives him a sock (being given clothing of his own is what sets Dobby free) (CS 18:338). After he is free, Dobby travels for two years trying to find a job before he is hired by Dumbledore to work at Hogwarts. Dumbledore offers him 10 Galleons a week with weekends off, but Dobby requests 1 Galleon a week with one day off a month (GF 21:378–79).

Dodgy Dirk. *Character.* From *Fantastic Beasts*. "Dodgy Dirk" is the nickname of a Muggle who supposedly did not receive the Mass Memory Charm of the Ilfracombe Incident of 1932. He visits pubs along the south coast telling stories of seeing a great, large lizard (FB xvi).

See also Fantastic Beasts and Where to Find Them

"Dogbreath and Dunghead." *Fake mantra.* When Apparition lessons get frustrating for the students, they begin to make fun of Wilkie Twycross's three D's (Destination, Determination, Deliberation) for performing the feat. They change two of the words to "Dogbreath and Dunghead" (HBP 18:389).

Doge, Elphias. *Character.* A member of the original Order of the Phoenix; he has a wheezy voice (OP 3:49). He used to wear a crazy hat (OP 9:174).

Dogs. *See* Animals

Dolohov, Antonin. *Character.* Igor Karkaroff revealed this Death Eater's name in his hearing years ago. Harry witnesses this through the Pensieve. Karkaroff saw Antonin Dolohov torturing Muggles and others who did not support Voldemort; Barty Crouch, Sr. tells Karkaroff that Dolohov was caught soon after him (GF 30:589). Dolohov was convicted of the murders of Gideon and Fabian Prewett (OP 25:543). He is present at the attack on the Department of Myteries (OP 35:788). He is one of Voldemort's original Death Eaters (HBP 20:444).

Dom. *Magical sports equipment.* From QA. The ball used in the ancient Irish flying broomstick game Aingingein; it was made out of the gallbladder of a goat (QA 4–5).
  See also Aingingein; *Quidditch Through the Ages*

Dopplebeater Defense. *Magical sports play.* From QA. The Dopplebeater Defense involves two Beaters whacking a Bludger at the same time, making its strike at an opposing player doubly effective (QA 52).
  See also Quidditch Through the Ages

Dormitory. *Magical place.* The sleeping quarters in the houses at Hogwarts. Dormitories are divided into male and female rooms, and each bedroom has five beds. Harry's roommates are Ron Weasley, Dean Thomas, Seamus Finnigan, and Neville Longbottom.

Dorset. *Muggle place.* From *Fantastic Beasts.* Dorset is where Newt Scamander and his wife Porpentina have retired to live (FB vi).

Dot. *Character.* A woman in the Hanged Man Pub in Little Hangleton who says that Frank Bryce had a bad temper (GF 1:3).

Double Eight Loop. *Magical sports play.* From QA. The Keeper tries to defend the goals during a penalty play by flying quickly around all of them (QA 52).
  See also Quidditch Through the Ages

Doxy. *Magical creature.* Classified 3X by the MM. Another name for a Biting Fairy, this creature is small and covered with black hair; it has sharp teeth and four arms and four legs (FB 10). It is a household pest that may nest in the curtains and needs to be fumigated with Doxycide (OP 6:102). Since their teeth are poisonous, it is advisable to keep Doxy bite antidote on hand at all times. Mrs. Weasley recommends Grimmauld Place be cleared of them and has Sirius and others helping her do so (OP 6:101). To rid the house of Doxies, they must be sprayed until they do not fly, then dumped in a bucket; one must take care all the while not to get bitten (OP 6:103).
  See also Biting Fairy; *Fantastic Beasts and Where to Find Them*

Doyle, Roddy (1958–). Doyle is an Irish novelist, dramatist, and screenwriter perhaps best known for his Barrytown Trilogy, which includes: *The Commitments* (1987), *The Snapper* (1990), and *The Van* (1991). *The Commitments* was made into a film in 1991 that was popular in the United States. In a 2001 BBC online chat, Rowling stated that *The Van* was one of her favorite books. The trilogy concerns the working-class Babbitte family of Dublin. In *The Van*, Jimmy Babbitte, Sr., loses his job and misses going to the pub to visit his chums. He goes into business with his best friend, Bimbo, selling fish and chips from an old van. The book is the final installment of the trilogy, which takes a humorous look at friendship and family from a distinctly Irish point of view.

Dr. Filibuster's Fabulous Wet-Start, No-Heat Fireworks. *See* Filibuster's Fabulous Wet-Start, No-Heat Fireworks

Dr. Ubbly's Oblivious Unction. *Magical substance.* Madam Pomfrey applies this to patients who are suffering after the battle at the Hall of Prophecy. She uses it to ease the scars on their thoughts (OP 38:847).

"*Draco dormiens nunquam titillandus.*" *School motto.* The phrase is Latin for "Don't tickle a sleeping dragon." It is the school motto of Hogwarts School of Witchcraft and Wizardry and it appears in the crest. Albus Dumbledore signs off his foreword to *Fantastic Beasts* with this motto (FB viii).

Dragon. *Magical creature.* Classified 5X by the MM. *Fantastic Beasts* states that the female dragon is larger, and the creature is always nearly impossible to conceal. Most of its parts have magical qualities. Dragon varieties discussed in *Fantastic Beasts* include: Antipodean Opaleye, Chinese Fireball, Common Welsh Green, Hebridean Black, Hungarian Horntail, Norwegian Ridgeback, Peruvian Vipertooth, Romanian Longhorn, Swedish Short-Snout, and the Ukrainian Ironbelly (FB 10).

Hagrid tells Harry that he has heard dragons guard the most secure vaults at Gringotts and that he has wanted one of his own ever since he was a child (SS 5:64–65). Ron informs Harry that keeping dragons is against magical laws, since it would be impossible to hide the magical world's existence from Muggles if dragons were allowed. Dragon breeding was voted against the law by the Warlocks' Convention of 1709 (SS 14:230). Hagrid explains that the Common Welsh Green and Hebridean Blacks are found wild in Britain (SS 14:231).

There are over thirty dragons at the Triwizard Tournament, and the champions randomly select which breed they will be challenged by for the first task (GF 19:326).

See also Fantastic Beasts and Where to Find Them

In *Fantastic Beasts and Where to Find Them*, Newt Scamander (J. K. Rowling) describes ten different breeds of dragon. Courtesy of the Dover Pictorial Archive.

Dragon blood. *Magical substance.* Dumbledore is known for finding a dozen uses for this substance. Hermione tells her friends that the blood is very useful, though one would not want a dragon as a pet (GF 13:197). Dumbledore asks Horace Slughorn what kind of blood is on his wall in Budleigh Babberton, and Slughorn replies that it is dragon blood (HBP 4:65).

Dragon Breeding for Pleasure and Profit. *Magical book.* Hagrid uses this book to identify the kind of dragon egg he has (SS 14:233).

Dragon dung. *Magical substance.* This is Prof. Sprout's favorite fertilizer for plants (OP 13:263).

A Dragon Keeper's Guide. *Magical book.* A book Hagrid is looking at in the Hogwarts Library, Year 1 (SS 14:230).

Dragon Research and Restraint Bureau. *Magical office.* From *Fantastic Beasts.* Newt Scamander worked with this group that allowed him to research *Fantastic Beasts* in lands abroad (FB vi).
See also Fantastic Beats and Where to Find Them

Dragon Species of Great Britain and Ireland. *Magical book.* A book Hagrid is looking at in the Hogwarts Library, Year 1 (SS 14:230).

Draught of Peace. *Magical substance.* A potion that is often on the O.W.L. exam. It has a calming effect on anxiety and helps prevent anger and frustration. Ingredients include powdered moonstone and syrup of hellebore (OP 12:232).

Dreadful Denizens of the Deep. *Magical book.* Harry and friends consult this book to prepare Harry for the second task of the Triwizard Tournament. They find nothing of use in the book (GF 26:488).

The Dream Oracle. *Magical book.* A reference book written by Inigo Imago that is used in Divination class, fifth year (OP 12:237).

Dreams in the novels. Harry has many dreams throughout the series, and many foretell the future or reflect the past (or some aspect of the past). He dreams of a flying motorcycle and tells his Uncle Vernon about it (SS 2:25). Harry dreams of his Firebolt when someone slashes through Ron's bed curtains (PA 13:265). Harry dreams that he oversleeps for a Quidditch match, and Slytherins appear riding dragons (PA 15:302). Before the second task of the Triwizard Tournament, Harry dreams about a mermaid who has taken his Firebolt broomstick (GF 26:489). He dreams the entire episode of Frank Bryce's murder in Divination class (GF 29:576) and in the next year, he dreams about long corridors and Cedric Diggory (OP 1:9). He dreams about Hagrid and weapons in Book 5 (OP 6:101).

Throughout *Order of the Phoenix*, Harry frequently has foreshadowing dreams about long corridors and locked doors. The dreams are often accompanied by pain or another sensation in his scar (OP 6:118; OP 15:329; OP 31:726–28). One of his strangest dreams occurs when he envisions himself as a large snake that bites Arthur Weasley. He knows this is something that has actually happened, and his warning to Ron and others afterward saves Arthur's life (OP 21:462).

In Divination class, Prof. Trelawney has the class keep dream journals and attempt to interpret one another's dreams using the book *The Dream Oracle* (OP 15:312–13). Harry pays attention to his dreams, a strategy which works for him, for they are rarely unimportant.

Droobles Best Blowing Gum. *Magical candy.* One of the treats on the Hogwarts Candy Cart (SS 6:101). It is also sold at Honeydukes candy shop in Hogsmeade. The bubbles are blue and can get as large as a room without popping for several days (PA 10:197). Alice Longbottom, who is insane, gives her son Neville a Droobles gum wrapper at Christmas when he visits with his grandmother at St. Mungo's. Neville keeps the wrapper, even though his grandmother claims that his mother has given him many of them before (OP 23:514–15).

Drought Charm. *Magical spell.* This charm dries up bodies of water like ponds and puddles (GF 26:486).

Dueling Club. *Magical student organization.* A student club started by Lockhart in which students are given lessons in wizard duels. Lessons are given by Snape and Lockhart in the Great Hall (CS 11:188–89). In the first lesson, Neville is paired with Justin Finch-Fletchley; Ron is with Seamus Finnegan; Hermione is with Millicent Bulstrode; and Harry is paired with Draco Malfoy (CS 11:191).

Dugbog. *Magical creature.* Classified 3X by the MM. When not moving, the creature looks like a log, but it actually has sharp teeth and paws with fins. Its favorite food is Mandrake (FB 15). Ron mistakenly writes "Dugbog" instead of "Dementor" in his essay when his Spell-Check quill is running out (HBP 21:449).
See also Fantastic Beasts and Where to Find Them

Dumbledore, Aberforth. *Character.* Prof. Dumbledore's brother. He was once prosecuted for putting improper charms on a goat. Dumbledore says he is not sure his brother can read, but Aberforth held his head high and went about his normal affairs after the goat incident was publicized in the papers (GF 24:454). Aberforth Dumbledore was a member of the original Order of the Phoenix and is in the photograph of the Order that Mad-Eye Moody shows Harry at Grimmauld Place. Moody says he only met Aberforth at the time of the photo and found him strange (OP 9:174). It may be that Aberforth is the mysterious unnamed bartender at the Hog's Head pub in Hogsmeade. Dumbledore says that he is friends with barmen, and this bartender has the odor of goats around him, which connects his identity with his brother Aberforth (HBP 20:445).

Dumbledore, Albus Percival Wulfric Brian. *Character.* Headmaster of Hogwarts and (grand)father figure to Harry. *Albus* means "white" in Latin, and white is a color associated with the great wizard. *Dumbledore* is Old English for "bumblebee." J. K. Rowling has said that she pictures the wizard always busy, going about the castle humming to himself since he likes music. In witchcraft history, bees held special meaning. It was believed by those who conducted witch-hunts that a witch who ate a queen bee before being questioned could endure tortures of all kinds without breaking down and confessing.

Dumbledore is tall and thin with a long, crooked nose, a long, silver beard, and twinkling blue eyes behind half-moon spectacles (SS 1:8). Dumbledore's titles and credentials in addition to being headmaster of Hogwarts, include: Order of Merlin, First Class; Grand Sorcerer; Chief Warlock; and Supreme Mugwump, International Confederation of Wizards (SS 4:51). Percy Weasley describes him as a genius who is the world's best wizard, but who is at least slightly mad (SS 7:123).

Harry first sees Dumbledore on a Chocolate Frog collector card on the Hogwarts Express (SS 6:102). The card describes Dumbledore's accomplishments as defeating the dark wizard Grindelwald in 1945 and discovering the twelve uses of dragon's blood. The card also mentions his alchemy work with Nicolas Flamel. It indicates that Dumbledore's hobbies include listening to chamber music and tenpin bowling (SS 6:103).

Michael Gambon as Prof. Albus Dumbledore in *Harry Potter and the Goblet of Fire* (2005). Prof. Dumbledore provides wisdom and guidance to Harry throughout the series. Courtesy of Warner Bros./Photofest.

A younger Dumbledore shows up in the vision Tom Riddle shows to Harry in *Chamber of Secrets*. He is very tall and has long, auburn hair (CS 13:245). He taught Transfiguration at that time (CS 17:312). In *Prisoner of Azkaban*, Harry's affection and esteem for the Headmaster runs deeper. Just seeing him at the Head Table at Hogwarts calms him down more than anything else after Harry's first experience with the Dementors (PA 5:91). Even so, Dumbledore tells Harry that he has no power to make people see the truth or to overrule the Minister of Magic (PA 21:393).

Harry continues to learn more about his mentor from others who also hold him in high regard. Hagrid, for example, tells Harry that Dumbledore gives people second chances and trusts in the basic goodness of people. This sets him apart from other leaders. Despite the opinions of others, Dumbledore will allow anyone into Hogwarts who has shown that he or she has magical talent. Hagrid tells Harry that Dumbledore took Hagrid in when his father died (GF 24:455). Mad-Eye Moody tells Snape that Dumbledore is trusting and gives people second chances, but Moody thinks that some people never lose their spots, referring to Snape's Death Eater tattoo (GF 25:472).

In *Order of the Phoenix*, when Dumbledore is not believed by the Ministry for the first year after the rise of Voldemort, he is demoted from Chief Warlock of the Wizengamot and voted out of his position as Chairman of the International Confederation of Wizards. His Order of Merlin, First Class is at risk. He is asked to leave the Wizengamot (OP 8:149). Bill Weasley says jokingly that he does not mind any of these demotions as long as the great wizard remains on Chocolate Frog cards (OP 5:95). Throughout *Order of the Phoenix*, Dumbledore avoids Harry, and when they are together, he avoids meeting Harry's eyes. Harry does not learn until very late in the novel that Dumbledore engaged in this practice to keep Voldemort from being able to interfere in any way with Dumbledore's mind as Voldemort already had with Harry's.

Dumbledore's office is guarded by a large stone gargoyle. An escalator-type spiral staircase leads up several levels to the office. The door is oak with a griffin-shaped brass knocker (CS 11:204). The room is circular, with portraits of former headmasters and headmistresses of Hogwarts lining the walls. It has magical silver instruments, apparently working constantly, since many are moving, or issuing smoke. A very large desk with claw feet occupies the room. The Sorting Hat sits on a shelf. On a gold perch sits a large phoenix, Fawkes, who was not looking well the day Harry first sees it (CS 12:205–6). Dumbledore's office is also apparently his living quarters at Hogwarts. When Harry and Prof. McGonagall go to his office after Arthur Weasley is attacked in *Order of the Phoenix*, Dumbledore is wearing a finely embroidered gold-and-purple robe over a bright white nightshirt (OP 22:467).

Dumbledore helps Harry to understand his history and his future calling by telling him bits of this information as he matures. He is also a protective force that helps Harry through difficult situations at just the right time and in just the right way. In *Sorcerer's Stone*, for example, it is Dumbledore who gives Harry his father's Invisibility Cloak. Dumbledore tells Harry later that James Potter had asked him to hold onto it for a while (SS 17:299). It is Dumbledore's spell on the stone and the Mirror of Erised that drops the stone in Harry's pocket just when Voldemort is looking for it (SS 17:300). In addition, it is also Dumbledore who rescues young Harry from Quirrell/Voldemort after their struggle (SS 17:297). In *Chamber of Secrets*, Dumbledore tells Harry that is was his great loyalty to Dumbledore that brought Fawkes to the Chamber to help Harry and Ginny Weasley against Tom Riddle (CS 18:332). In *Prisoner of Azkaban*, Dumbledore encourages Harry and Hermione to use the time-turner to help reverse the fate of Sirius Black and Buckbeak (PA 21:393).

Dumbledore's protection and Harry's trust of that protection is an important and deepening aspect of the series. Harry's development into a young man and wizard capable of protecting himself grows from the security he feels from Dumbledore's love. Following Harry's handling of the Triwizard Tournament in *Goblet of Fire*, Dumbledore appears to stand back a bit and allow Harry to continue to handle matters himself. However, he is available to step in when events require it. In *Order of the Phoenix*, for example, though Dumbledore remains aloof from Harry because of Voldemort's use of Legilimency on Harry, he advocates on Harry's behalf at the Ministry (OP 8:139). After Harry's training of Dumbledore's Army and their attempt to rescue Sirius Black, whom they are led to believe is in the Hall of Prophecy, Dumbledore arrives to save them during their battle with the Death Eaters (OP 35:805). In *Half-Blood Prince*, Dumbledore puts the Freezing Charm on Harry, who is under the Invisibility Cloak, to protect him from the Death Eaters who are storming the tower at Hogwarts (HBP 27:584).

In *Half-Blood Prince*, both Harry and the reader see more of Dumbledore than before. Dumbledore has injured his wand hand; it looks burned (HBP 3:48). When Harry asks how it happened, Dumbledore tells him that it is an exciting story that he will explain later (HBP 4:61). He tells Harry to be careful of imposters; he reveals that his favorite jam flavor is raspberry, and that Harry can use this knowledge to test for a Dumbledore impostor (HBP 4:62). When Dumbledore takes Harry to Horace Slughorn's and allows Harry to persuade the retiree to teach at Hogwarts, Dumbledore comes back from the bathroom sometime later saying that he was reading Muggle magazines, enjoying the knitting patterns (HBP 4:73). This is interesting because Dumbledore claimed previously that if he looked into the Mirror of Erised, he would see himself holding a pair of woolen socks (SS 12:214). Soon after his death, Dumbledore appears sleeping peacefully in a new portrait on the wall of the new Headmistress, Prof. McGonagall (HBP 29:626).

In his foreword to the schoolbook *Quidditch Through the Ages*, Dumbledore refers to Madam Pince, the school librarian. He claims that she suggested that they tell a story to Comic Relief, U.K., as a way of avoiding allowing the organization to duplicate a Hogwarts Library book (QA viii). Dumbledore "writes" that, in the end, he needed to pry the book from her hands so that it might be reprinted for the benefit of Comic Relief.

As one of the most beloved characters of the series, Dumbledore's death at the hand of Prof. Severus Snape in *Half-Blood Prince* was deeply mourned by readers. The fact that the great wizard has a brother, Aberforth Dumbledore (GF 24:454), offers some hope to fans. That fact and the lament of the phoenix suggest that neither Harry nor the reader has seen the last of Dumbledore's goodness, nor of his strong influence on the final outcome of events. Dumbledore told Harry that Dumbledore will never really be gone from the school as long as someone there remains loyal to him. At the close of Book 6, his longevity seems assured when Harry says he is "Dumbledore's man, through and through" (HBP 30:649).

Dumbledore's Army (DA). *Magical organization.* Hermione asks Harry if he will teach his classmates more advanced skills in Defense Against the Dark Arts since Dolores Umbridge is only teaching them theory (OP 15:325–26). In their search for a group name, Ginny Weasley comes up with "Dumbledore's Army" after several others are suggested, including the Anti-Umbridge League, Ministry of Magic Morons, and Defense Association (OP 18:391–92). Cornelius Fudge is fooled into thinking that Dumbledore formed the DA himself; Dumbledore tells him this to protect Harry and the other students (OP 27:618). A few members of the DA go with Harry, Ron, and Hermione to the Department of Mysteries to look for Sirius Black (OP 33:760–61).

Several members of the DA display their newly acquired skills on the Hogwarts Express after Year 5. Harry has taught them how to deal with the pranks of Draco Malfoy, Vincent Crabbe, and Gregory Goyle. Ernie Macmillan, Hannah Abbott, Susan Bones, Justin Finch-Fletchley, Anthony Goldstein, and Terry Boot all show that they have learned well from Harry. Their various jinxes and defenses leave Draco, Vincent, and Gregory in the form of oozing slugs that Harry, Ernie, and Justin put in the luggage rack for the remainder of the trip (OP 38:864).

Dundee. On the night that Harry is left on Mr. Dursley's doorstep, weather forecaster Jim McGuffin reports that people have seen a downpour of shooting stars as far away as Dundee, rather than the rain showers he predicted (SS 1:6).

Dung. *Magical nickname.* Nickname for Mundungus Fletcher (OP 5:81).

Dungbomb. *Magical object.* During their first year, Fred and George Weasley set off a dungbomb and get in trouble with Argus Filch. During their detention, they find the Marauder's Map in Filch's office (PA 10:191). Harry and Ron purchase some dungbombs at Zonko's (PA 14:278). Ginny sends dungbombs toward the door at Order headquarters when she, Harry, and the others try to hear the meetings of the Order, but the dungbombs do not work (OP 4:69). Filch comes after Harry in the Owlery, accusing him of sending out an order for dungbombs (OP 14:284). After Fred and George Weasley leave Hogwarts, many students set off dungbombs in an effort to raise more havoc in their protest against Prof. Umbridge (OP 30:677).

Durmstrang Institute. *Magical school.* Another school of witchcraft and wizardry, presumably in Russia, though its location is not officially known. The school teaches the Dark Arts, not just defensive measures against them, so Durmstrang bears some suspicion. Draco Malfoy's father wanted him to go there, but his mother said it was too far away (GF 11:165). Hermione guesses that the school is located quite far North, since the students' uniforms include fur capes (GF 11:167). The students arrive for the Triwizard Tournament in a dramatic way, their wrecked-looking ship rising magically up out of the Hogwarts lake (GF 15:246). Their headmaster is Prof. Karkaroff (GF 15:247) and their uniforms are a blood-red color (GF 16:251).

The name of the school comes from the German phrase *Sturm und Drang*, which means "storm and stress." The phrase describes a kind of literature in the nineteenth century involving spectacle and rebellion. Composer Richard Wagner wrote an opera in this mode called *The Flying Dutchman*. In the story, a ship must sail the seas without stopping because its captain cursed God during a storm. Rowling's use of a ship to transport Durmstrang Institute students to Hogwarts provides an allusion to this opera. Another connection is that Wagner was known to be Hitler's favorite composer, and the *Sturm und Drang* movement was popular with the Nazis. In the Harry Potter novels, the Institute teaches the Dark Arts; it will not enroll Muggle-borns; and it has some unsavory faculty, making it a place not to be trusted.

Dursley, Aunt Marge (Marjory). *Character.* Uncle Vernon's sister. When the reader first hears of her, she is vacationing on the Isle of Wight. A postcard arrives from her the same day as Harry's first letter from Hogwarts (SS 3:34). Marge comes to visit in the summer between Years 2 and 3. She is a large woman, like her brother, but even more cruel to Harry, if that is possible. When he was five, she hit his legs with her walking stick because he was beating Dudley at a game of musical statues. Another year at Christmas she bought a computer robot for Dudley and dog biscuits for Harry. The last time she visited, the year before Harry first went to Hogwarts, her favorite dog, Ripper, chased Harry up a tree after he accidentally stepped on his tail, and she left him there with the dog standing watch at the bottom until after midnight. She raises bulldogs in a large house in the country and does not visit her brother very often because she cannot leave the dogs alone. In *Prisoner of Azkaban*, Harry is informed that she will stay for a week on her latest visit, and he wonders how he will cope (PA 2:18).

Aunt Marge finally crosses the line with Harry when she begins comparing his parents to dogs, explaining how a bad pup is the result of bad breeding (PA 2:25). Her glass breaks, and eventually, despite Harry's efforts to the contrary, she is puffed up and floats away as a result of Harry's anger (PA 2:29).

Dursley, Aunt Petunia (Evans). *Character.* Harry's mother's sister, Petunia, appears to be jealous of her sister Lily (Harry's mother), who was a witch. Petunia describes Lily in more detail in front of Harry at the Hut-on-the-Rock (SS 4:53). Petunia is thin and bony with the face and teeth of a horse (CS 1:4; GF 3:26). She has spoiled her only son and mistreated Harry principally by showing preference for Dudley and allowing her husband Vernon to be as mean to her nephew as possible. Petunia is very tidy and does not like dirt (CS 6:89). She is nosy and watches her neighbors' goings-on from her windows (PA 2:17). After Harry and Dudley are attacked by Dementors in Little Whinging, Uncle Vernon does not believe Harry's story, but Petunia reveals that she has heard of Dementors and of Azkaban (OP 2:31–32). When she receives a Howler, she is reminded quite forcefully that she must keep her promise to allow Harry to stay (OP 2:39–41). Harry later confirms that Dumbledore sent the Howler (OP 37:836).

Petunia seems as much embarrassed as scared when she sees several members of the Order of the Phoenix accompany Harry to talk with her and Vernon; she seems especially bothered by Nymphadora Tonks's pink hair (OP 38:868–69). There are hints in *Half-Blood Prince* and in interviews with Rowling that Petunia's knowledge of the wizarding world becomes important in Book 7.

Dursley, Dudley. *Character.* Harry's cousin (his mother's sister's son). Dudley's mother calls him various pet names, such as: "Duddy" (SS 2:19); "popkin" (SS 2:21); "Dinky Duddydums" (SS 2:23); "Ickle Dudleykins" (SS 3:32); "sweetums" (CS 1:2); "Diddy darling" (GF 3:26); "Diddy" (OP 2:24). Aunt Marge calls him "Dudders" and "neffy-poo" (PA 2:22). When Harry hears Dudley's gang members call him "Big D," Harry tells him that he is still "Ickle Diddykins" to him (OP 1:13).

Dudley is overweight, blond, and spoiled, with a personality to match. He complains that he has received thirty-six presents for his birthday, which is two less than he received the year before (SS 2:21). He is mean and careless. A few weeks after his birthday, he had already broken his new video camera and remote control plane, and he ran into Mrs. Figg on her crutches with his new racing bike (SS 3:31). When the boy gets on Hagrid's nerves in the Hut-on-the-Rock, the giant casts a spell, giving him a pig's tail (SS 4:59). Dudley puts up with his Aunt Marge's hugs because she gives him a twenty-dollar bill in the exchange (PA 2:22).

After he spends three years at Smeltings, the school nurse sends Dudley home on a diet. The whole family goes on the diet because Petunia thinks it will be easier that way (GF 3:27). Dudley wins the Junior Heavyweight Inter-School Boxing Championship of the Southeast (OP 1:11). Harry saves himself and Dudley from two Dementors at the beginning of *Order of the Phoenix*, but he is threatened with expulsion from Hogwarts as a result (OP 1:16–19; OP 2:26–27). In Book 6, Petunia tells Dumbledore that Dudley is one month older than Harry (HBP 3:54).

Dursley, Uncle Vernon. *Character.* In a fantasy with so many colorful characters who possess magical abilities and who live in fanciful places, it is ironic that Vernon Dursley is actually the first character the reader meets in the entire series (SS 1:1). He is the director of Grunnings, a factory that makes drills, and he does not care much for imagination (SS 1:5). Dursley is a large man, overweight to the point where he barely has a neck, and he wears a mustache (SS 1:1). Vernon joins Petunia in spoiling Dudley by buying him many gifts, while he treats Harry with contempt. He sends Dudley to his old school Smeltings but pretends to send Harry to a school for delinquents. Vernon is ambitious; he wants to advance his career and make a large deal with Mr. Mason on drills. The dinner party at which he plans to do this is held on Harry's twelfth birthday. Vernon makes no acknowledgement of the day's importance to his nephew (CS 1:7).

Even the wizards in Harry's new world do not like Vernon. At King's Cross, Vernon asks Mad-Eye Moody if he looks like a man who can be intimidated. He falls back when Moody shows him his frightful eye, and Moody tells him that he does look like someone who can be intimidated (OP 38:869–70).

In *Half-Blood Prince*, Prof. Dumbledore tells Vernon that he has been cruel and neglectful of Harry. He says the best thing he and Petunia did for Harry was to not raise him to be a boy like Dudley (HBP 3:55).

Rowling found the name Dursley on a map of England; it is a town not far from where she grew up.

Dwarfs. *Magical beings.* Harry sees dwarfs during his two weeks at the Leaky Cauldron before Year 3 (PA 4:49).

◆ E ◆

Easter. *Holiday.* Hogwarts students have a holiday during Easter (CS 14:251). It is treated in the books as something more like a spring break—classes are not held, but all students stay at the school (PA 15:299). Mrs. Weasley sends Easter eggs in Year 4. Harry's and Ron's are as large as dragon eggs, but Hermione's is smaller than the egg of a chicken. Mrs. Weasley has apparently read the untrue article about Hermione's poor behavior toward Harry in *Witch Weekly* (GF 28:549). Hermione spends much of the Easter holiday in fifth year putting together study schedules for their O.W.L.s exams that are six weeks away (OP 29:651). Mrs. Weasley sends Easter eggs again in Year 5, including one to Harry that is decorated with Snitches (OP 29:654).

"Eckeltricity." *Wrong word.* Mr. Weasley mispronounces "electric" when discussing the electric fireplace that blocks the real fireplace in the Dursleys' living room. He mentions to Vernon that he collects plugs and batteries (GF 4:46).

"Eclectic." *Wrong word.* Mr. Weasley mispronounces "electric" when Harry tries to explain the electric fireplace that his blocking his family's entrance into the Dursley house (GF 4:43).

Edgecombe, Madam. *Character.* She is an employee at the Department of Magical Transportation and has been watching the Floo Network, particularly the fires at Hogwarts. She is Marietta Edgecombe's mother (OP 27:612).

Edgecombe, Marietta. *Character.* Marietta Edgecombe is Cho Chang's curly-haired friend who comes to Dumbledore's Army meetings without much interest. Cho pressured her to join (OP 18:394–95). She turns in the DA, so Hermione puts a hex of boils on her face that even Prof. Umbridge has not been able to counter (OP 27:613). On the way home from Year 5, she and Cho walk past Harry on the Hogwarts Express. Marietta is wearing a balaclava (OP 38:865).

Edible Dark Marks. *Magical substance.* Another product from Weasleys' Wizard Wheezes. The Marks come in a tub and make people sick. A small boy is caught trying to shoplift a tub of them when George Weasley warns him that he will pay in more than Galleons if he tries to steal from them (HBP 6:118).

Edinburgh. *See* Scotland

Educational Decree Twenty-eight. *Magical law.* Signed by Cornelius Fudge, this document makes Umbridge Head of Hogwarts after Dumbledore is demoted (OP 28:624).

Educational Decree Twenty-five. *Magical law.* Dolores Umbridge makes this rule that gives the High Inquisitor the power to take privileges away from students. She uses it to ban Harry, Fred Weasley, and George Weasley from Quidditch for life (OP 19:416).

Educational Decree Twenty-four. *Magical law.* This law disbands all student organizations at Hogwarts and orders that those who wish to reorganize must obtain permission from Dolores Umbridge (OP 17:351–52).

Educational Decree Twenty-nine. *Possible magical law.* Argus Filch tells Harry and others that when this law is made by Prof. Umbridge, he will be able to whip students if they use stink pellets or Fanged Frisbees; he has always thought that Dumbledore was too soft on them (OP 28:628).

Educational Decree Twenty-seven. *Magical law.* This rule by Prof. Umbridge says that students with copies of *The Quibbler* will be expelled. The rule does not upset Hermione because it ensures that every student at Hogwarts will read Harry's article about the rise of Voldemort (OP 26:581).

Educational Decree Twenty-six. *Magical law.* Dolores Umbridge makes this rule that teachers cannot disseminate any information to students except course material. Lee Jordan comments that this must also apply to Umbridge scolding Fred and George Weasley for playing Exploding Snap in the back of class (OP 25:551).

Educational Decree Twenty-three. *Magical law.* This law creates the position of Hogwarts' High Inquisitor. Umbridge is appointed to the post (OP 15:307).

Educational Decree Twenty-two. *Magical law.* A rule that says that if the headmaster cannot find a faculty member to fill a post, the Ministry will fill it (OP 15:307).

Egg song. *Magical song.* The golden egg for the second task of the Triwizard Tournament sings to Harry when he opens it in the tub in the prefects' bathroom. Its song gives a clue to what the task will be (GF 25:463).

Egypt. *See* Africa

"Ehwaz"/"eihwaz." *Ancient runes.* Hermione mixes up these runes in her Ancient Runes O.W.L. *Ehwaz* means partnership; *eihwaz* means defense (OP 31:715).

Elderflower wine. *Magical drink.* Percy Weasley drinks this wine at his family's picnic before their trip to the Quidditch World Cup (GF 5:62).

Elephant and Castle. *Magical place.* An area where the Magical Law Enforcement Squad has to clear up a backfiring jinx; the incident makes Mr. Weasley late in arriving at the Burrow on the day Harry arrives in Year 6 (HBP 5:87).

Elf-made wine. *Magical drink.* Snape serves elf-made wine to Narcissa Malfoy and Bellatrix Lestrange when they visit him at Spinner's End (HBP 2:24).

Elfric the Eager. *Character.* Hermione is glad she did not have to know about the uprising concerning Elfric the Eager for her Year 1 History of Magic exam (SS 16:263).

Elixir of Life. *Magical substance.* Nicolas Flamel made this eternal-life potion from the Sorcerer's Stone (SS 13:220). Dumbledore explains to Harry why this elixir alone would not satisfy Voldemort's desire for immortality. The substance must be drunk at intervals for the rest of one's life in order to be effective. Dumbledore thinks that dependence on a substance that could be tampered with drove Voldemort to think of other ways to stay alive, especially since his effort to obtain the Sorcerer's Stone failed (HBP 23:502).

Elixir to Induce Euphoria. *Magical substance.* Harry makes this potion in Potions class the day there are only three students in attendance; most of the other students are taking their Apparition tests. Prof. Slughorn is impressed that Harry has added peppermint to the elixir to counteract the usual side effects of singing and nose-tweaking. Slughorn says that Harry has inherited his mother's genes for Potions. In reality, Harry found this tip written in his *Advanced Potion-Making* book by the Half-Blood Prince (HBP 22:474–75).

Ellerby and Spudmore. *Magical business.* From QA. Racing-broom manufacturers in the Black Forest area of Europe. They made the Tinderblast and Swiftstick racing brooms (QA 50).
  See also Quidditch Through the Ages

Emeric the Evil. *Character.* Prof. Binns teaches about this historical figure in the History of Magic (SS 8:133).

Emma **(Austen).** *See* Austen, Jane

Enchantment in Baking. *Magical book.* Book in the Burrow (CS 3:34).

Enchantments. *Magical spells.* The words spells and enchantments are frequently used interchangeably in the series. Hagrid tells Harry that anyone would be insane to try to rob Gringotts because it is guarded by enchantments (SS 5:64).

Encyclopedia of Toadstools. *Magical book.* Lucius Malfoy is hit in the eye with this book during the scuffle at Flourish and Blotts (CS 4:63).

"Enemies of the Heir, Beware." *Magical words.* Words written on Hogwarts' walls during the Chamber of Secrets mystery; the "heir" is the heir of Salazar Slytherin, who is the only person who can open the chamber (CS 11:199).

"Enervate!" *Incantation.* This incantation brings a victim back to consciousness from a stunning spell. Barty Crouch, Sr., performs it on his house-elf Winky (GF 9:133); Dumbledore performs it on Viktor Krum (GF 28:560).

Engorgement Charm. *Magical spell.* This spell causes swelling and rapid growth. The incantation is "Engorgio!" Seeing Dudley Dursley's foot-long tongue, Mr. Weasley tells Vernon Dursley that this charm was probably put on Dudley by Weasley's son Fred, who is a practical joker. However, Dudley had actually eaten one of the Weasley twins' Ton-Tongue Toffees (GF 4:49; GF 5:51). Ron used to think that Hagrid had an Engorgement Charm put on him as a child (GF 23:430). Hagrid uses this charm to make his pumpkins grow large (CS 7:118).

"Engorgio!" *Incantation.* This is the incantation for the Engorgement Charm. Barty Crouch, Jr., posing as Mad-Eye Moody, places the charm on spiders which he brings to DADA class to demonstrate the Cruciatus Curse to the students (GF 14:214).

Enid, Great Auntie. *Character.* Neville Longbottom's great aunt, presumably married to his Great Uncle Algie. She offered the meringue to Algie that caused him to accidentally drop Neville when he was dangling him out a window to test his magical abilities (SS 7:125). Enid may have been named after author Enid Blyton, whose work Rowling has said she enjoys.
  See also Algie, Great Uncle; Longbottom, Neville

Enlargement Charm. *Magical spell.* Fred and George Weasley put this spell on *The Quibbler* to make a poster out of the cover with Harry's picture and article (OP 26:584).

Entrancing Enchantments. *Magical spells.* On Valentine's Day in Harry's second year, Lockhart recommends that the students entice Prof. Flitwick to show them some of these charms (CS 13:236).

"Episkey." *Incantation.* Nymphadora Tonks uses this incantation to repair Harry's nose after Draco Malfoy steps on it on the Hogwarts Express (HBP 8:157).

Eric. *Character.* Security employee at the Ministry. He inspects Harry and his wand when he goes to the Ministry for his hearing (OP 7:128).

Erkling. *Magical creature.* From *Fantastic Beasts*. Classified 4X by the MM. The Erkling comes from the Black Forest in Germany and is elf-like in appearance. A six-year-old wizard child named Bruno Schmidt survived an attack from an Erkling by hitting it with his father's collapsible cauldron (FB 15).
  See also Fantastic Beasts and Where to Find Them

Errol. *Magical creature.* Ron Weasley's owl that is old and worn out and does not always fulfill his deliveries as quickly as other owls (CS 3:30). Errol delivers the Howler that Ron receives from his mother after the Ford Anglia incident (CS 6:87).

Erumpent. *Magical creature.* From *Fantastic Beasts.* Classified 4X by the MM. This large beast looks like a rhinoceros from far away. It is from Africa. Its hide deflects most spells (FB 16).
  See also Fantastic Beasts and Where to Find Them

"Evanesco!" *Incantation. Evanesco* is Latin for "vanish." Bill Weasley says these words to make the scrolls from the Order's meeting disappear (OP 5:80). Snape uses the incantation to clear out Harry's cauldron after he botches his first try at the Draught of Peace (OP 12:234).

Evans, Lily. *See* Potter, Lily Evans

Evans, Mark. *Character.* A ten-year-old boy who was the recipient of a beating from Dudley Dursley and his gang (OP 1:13). Rowling later claimed that the name had nothing to do with Lily Evans and regretted not thinking of it beforehand when fans diligently searched for connections.

Evening Prophet. *Magical newspaper.* The evening edition of *The Daily Prophet.* The paper reports Muggles's sightings of the flying Ford Anglia (CS 5:79).

Ever-Bashing Boomerangs. *Magical objects.* Dumbledore tells students at the Start-of-Term Banquet in Year 4 that Argus Filch has banned these from Hogwarts (GF 12:183).

Everard. *Character.* One of the old headmasters who appears in a portrait on Dumbledore's office wall; his black hair is trimmed in bangs. After Arthur Weasley is attacked, Dumbledore asks Everard to sound the alarm and be sure that Arthur is rescued by friends, not foes. Everard is sent because he and Dilys Derwent are two of the most renowned Hogwarts Heads; both have portraits in other wizard institutions to which they can travel for help or information (OP 22:468–69). He gives a report to Dumbledore that Arthur is covered in blood and does not look good. He goes to Elfrida Cragg's portrait to get a better view (OP 22:471). After Dumbledore dies, it is Everard who informs Prof. McGonagall that the Minister is on his way (HBP 29:627).

Everlasting Elixirs. *Magical substance.* Potions class works on making these (HBP 15:305).

Exeter University. Rowling graduated from Exeter in 1987 with a degree in French and was given an honorary doctorate degree from the university in 2000. She said in a 2002 interview in *The Scotsman* that Exeter was not what she expected at first. She thought she would find more "radical" kinds of students there, and it took her awhile to find a few classmates who thought more like herself. As the former Head Girl at Wyedean, grades became less important to the future author in college. She admitted in *The Scotsman,* "I don't think I worked as hard as I could have." Instead, she spent more time playing her guitar, sketching, and telling stories to her friends at the Black Horse pub in town and the Devonshire House coffee bar on campus. She also wrote stories.

Unlike so many British universities like Oxford and Cambridge that have long and prestigious histories, Exeter is a relatively new college—it was not established until 1955. Set on a hill overlooking the town of Devon, its buildings have the rather nondescript brick look of the period instead of the inspired, ornate structures of Oxford and Cambridge. When Rowling attended, there were approximately 5,000 students. While attending Exeter, Rowling spent one year in Paris teaching English as a second language.

The Greek and Roman mythology courses that Rowling took at Exeter (in addition to her language studies) surely represent some of the most significant influences of the school on Rowling and the Harry Potter series.

Further Reading: Fraser, Lindsay. "Harry Potter—Harry and Me." *The Scotsman*, November 2002.

"Expecto patronum!" *Incantation.* These are the magic words for the Patronus charm (PA 12:238). Harry uses them during a Quidditch match in third year when "Dementors" plague him—they turn out to be Draco Malfoy, Vincent Crabbe, Gregory Goyle, and Marcus Flint in hooded black cloaks (PA 13:262). After the Shrieking Shack scene, Harry uses this incantation on Sirius Black by the lake (PA 20:383).

See also Patronus

"Expelliarmus!" *Incantation.* This is the incantation for the Disarming Charm, which knocks the victim off his or her feet and takes away his or her wand. Snape uses this incantation on Gilderoy Lockhart during the first Dueling Club lesson (CS 11:190). Harry uses the same spell on Lockhart later (CS 16:298). He also uses it on the spider in the third task of the Triwizard Tournament (GF 31:632). Draco Malfoy casts this spell on Dumbledore at the same time that Dumbledore, who could have used the moment to defend himself, instead puts a nonverbal Freezing Charm on Harry (HBP 27:584).

"Explain Why Muggles Need Electricity." *Magical assignment.* Essay assigned in Hermione's Muggle Studies class (PA 12:250).

Exploding Bonbons. *Magical candy.* They are sold at Honeydukes (PA 10:197).

Exploding Snap. *Magical game.* A card game played by students at Hogwarts (CS 12:211; CS 18:340). Fred and George Weasley play it in the back of class (OP 25:551).

Expressions. Characters in the series frequently use colorful expressions when they are surprised or taken aback by events. For instance, Hagrid's expressions include: "Gallopin' Gorgons" (SS 4:52); "Gulpin' gargoyles" (SS 4:54); "Codswollop" (SS 4:57); "Blimey" (SS 5:65); "Crikey" (SS 5:65); "Merlin's beard" (OP 20:421). Prof. Lockhart says "Great Scott" (CS 7:121). Amos Diggory says "Merlin's beard" (GF 6:72) and so do Mad-Eye Moody (GF 25:475) and Arthur Weasley (OP 24:521). Prof. Tofty says "Galloping gargoyles" when she sees Prof. McGonagall harmed in her attempt to rescue Hagrid (OP 31:721). Horace Slughorn says "Merlin's beard" (HBP 22:480). The expressions add to the humor of the series and make the adult characters more real to child readers.

Extendable ears. *Magical object.* An invention of Fred and George Weasleys', these are long, flesh-colored strings that allow one to hear what is going on inside from outside a closed room. They first use them at Number Twelve, Grimmauld Place to try to overhear what the Order of the Phoenix is planning (OP 4:67–68). Ron has extendable ears when Draco Malfoy goes into Borgin and Burkes (HBP 6:124).

Eyelops Owl Emporium. *Magical place.* An owl shop on Diagon Alley. On his first visit to the street, Harry sees a sign outside advertising owls of different varieties, including: tawny, screech, barn, brown, and snowy (SS 5:72). It is here that Hagrid buys Harry his snowy owl for his eleventh birthday (SS 5:81). Harry and friends buy nuts at Eyelops for Hedwig and Pigwidgeon when shopping for Year 6 (HBP 6:115).

✦ F ✦

Fainting Fancies. *Magical candy.* A treat invented by Fred and George Weasley; they try them out on first-year students who fall over their desks and out of their chairs in the Gryffindor Common Room (OP 13:253).

See also Candy and sweets

Fairy. *Magical creature.* From *Fantastic Beasts*. Classified 2X by the MM. Muggles have written about these in fairy tales. They are small—between one and five inches—and humanlike in appearance. Fairies cannot talk (FB 16–17). They are also mentioned in *A History of Magic* (FB xi).

See also Fantastic Beasts and Where to Find Them

"Fairy lights." *Magical password.* Password to Gryffindor Tower, Year 4 (GF 22:398).

Falmouth Falcons. *Magical professional sports team.* From QA. Players Randolph Keitch and Basil Horton formed the Comet Trading Company and started the line of Comet racing brooms (QA 49). The Falcons are known as hard, tough players (QA 34).

See also The Comet Trading Company; *Quidditch Through the Ages*

Famous Witches and Wizards Cards. *Magical object.* The collector cards found in Chocolate Frogs (SS 6:103). The cards were also marketed for collectors in the real world and introduced some witches and wizards not mentioned in the any of the books.

See also Chocolate Frogs

Fan responses. Readers of the Harry Potter series have found various ways to share their enthusiasm for the books since the novels first appeared in the late 1990s. The Internet provides a ready and convenient medium for fan communities to communicate and discuss the books, plan events, and keep informed about the latest book and film releases, interviews with the author, and other areas of interest. Fan websites—written by fans for fans—such as the Harry Potter Lexicon, the Leaky Cauldron, and Muggle.net.com, post intricate and catalogued details about the books, quotations, timelines, links, essays, news, and other information. Online discussion forums, such as Harry Potter for Grown-Ups, discuss the series at length and present various theories of how Harry's story will end. Fan fiction written by readers appears on some websites, which takes the characters Rowling created and moves them into different plots and relationships of the fans' designs (those who argue for the pairing of different characters in relationships are called "shippers").

An outgrowth of the online communities are fan conventions and conferences. A fan group based in Texas called Harry Potter Education Fanon, Inc. (HPEF) has sponsored two conventions to date, including "Nimbus 2003" in Orlando, Florida, at Disney World and "The Witching Hour" in Salem, Massachusetts, in 2005. "Lumos—2006" takes place in Las Vegas and is also sponsored by HPEF. "Phoenix Rising" is another meeting that will take place in New Orleans in 2007. Other meetings include "Convention Alley" held in Ottawa, Canada, in 2004, and the first academic conference about the series in Britain—called "Accio!"—which took place at the University of Reading in 2005, shortly after the release of the sixth novel. Fan conventions typically feature a combination of fan events with academic lectures, readings by authors and other speakers, as well as games, film showings, book sales, costumes, and other activities.

In Harry Potter's world, a fairy cannot speak and possesses little magical talent. Courtesy of the Dover Pictorial Archive.

Fans respond to the series by not only communicating with one another on the Internet and at conventions, but also by joining book clubs, taking college classes in Harry Potter (some from perspectives other than literature, such as the study of popular culture or marketing), collecting Harry Potter merchandise, collecting the books in translation, or sharing original artwork that depicts scenes or characters from the books.

Fang. *Magical beast.* Hagrid's dog. Fang is a very large, black boarhound (SS 8:140). He accompanies Hagrid, Harry, Draco Malfoy, and Neville Longbottom into the Forbidden Forest during the boys' detention in Year 1. Draco says he wants him to go with Fang when they split up, but Hagrid informs him that Fang is a coward (SS 14:251). After Umbridge fires Hagrid, Harry sees Fang try to defend Hagrid when Dawlish comes to take him away (OP 31:721).

Fanged Frisbees. *Magical object.* Dumbledore tells students at the Start-of-Term Banquet in Year 4 that Argus Filch has banned Fanged Frisbees from Hogwarts (GF 12:183). Filch threatens to hang students up by their ankles if they use Fanged Frisbees when

Dolores Umbridge takes over Hogwarts (OP 28:628). Hermione confiscates one from a fourth-year student and tells him they are banned (HBP 9:172).

Fanged Geranium. *Magical plant.* Harry gets bitten by one of these during his Herbology O.W.L. exam (OP 31:714).

Fantastic Beasts and Where to Find Them. *A schoolbook.* Written under the tongue-in-cheek pseudonym Newt Scamander, Rowling wrote this "textbook" to benefit Comic Relief, U.K. It was published with its companion schoolbook, *Quidditch Through the Ages,* in March 2001. Both books came out in the interim period between the publication of *Goblet of Fire* in 2000 and *Order of the Phoenix* in 2003.

The fictional story of the book's publication within Harry's world is as follows: Newt Scamander was working for the Ministry when he was asked by Augustus Worme of Obscurus Books whether he might like to research and write the book. In Harry's world, the book is now in its 52nd edition (FB ix). The book is a standard textbook for the Care of Magical Creatures class at Hogwarts.

The actual book is a slim volume of approximately 15,000 words and is a facsimile of Harry's personal copy, including claw marks and a sticker with his name on the cover. It contains a section about the author and a foreword by Albus Dumbledore. It also includes an introduction by Newt Scamander which outlines the history of the study and classification of magical beasts and creatures. There is a chart and description of the classifications of beasts from 1X to 5X by the Ministry of Magic (the classifications refer to the level of danger the beasts represent to humans—the greater the number, the greater the danger). Following this material are seventy-five alphabetized entries, from Acromantula to Yeti, describing beasts of various kinds with additional subentries on ten different breeds of dragon. Most entries include physical descriptions, place of origin and/or where the creature can be found, a brief history of sightings and interactions with the wizarding world, diet, and characteristic behaviors. Occasionally, entries mention if some part of the creature, such as a powdered horn or venom, is valuable in potions or for other magical uses. Footnotes refer to other fictional references or events concerning the creatures.

Throughout the book are hand-scribbled doodles, drawings, and notes by Harry Potter or Ron Weasley. The latter tells the reader in a scribble on the bookplate page that he shares Harry's book because his fell apart. The hand-written notes frequently refer to events in the novels that involve creatures described in *Fantastic Beasts*, including the Acromantula, Basilisk, and various dragons. The notes add humor to the book for readers who are familiar with the plot connections to the series.

In the first four years of sales, *Fantastic Beasts and Where to Find Them*, along with *Quidditch Through the Ages*, raised over $28.7 milllion (£15.7 million) for Comic Relief, U.K.

See also Comic Relief, U.K.; *Quidditch Through the Ages*

The Fat Friar. *Character.* The Fat Friar is the friendly Hufflepuff House ghost. In Book 1 he greets the first-year students in the Entrance Hall before they are sorted into their houses (SS 7:115). After the night Dumbledore leaves Hogwarts, he tells Ernie Macmillan that Prof. Umbridge tried to get into Dumbledore's office but could not get past the gargoyle (OP 28:625).

The Fat Lady. *Character.* The Fat Lady is the subject of a portrait at Hogwarts. The location of her portrait is where students must give their password to enter the Gryffindor

Common Room. The password changes frequently, and the lady occasionally makes comments on events or disappears altogether from her frame into another picture on the wall. She wears a pink silk dress (SS 7:129). During Year 3 the Fat Lady disappears. Some believe that her painting was cut to shreds by Sirius Black when she would not give out the password for Gryffindor Tower (PA 8:160). She is later found hiding on the second floor in the map of Argyllshire (PA 9:165). She returns to her guarding post after Sir Cadogen allows an intruder into Gryffindor Tower. When she returns she is guarded by several trolls (PA 14:269). The only time she allows passage without a password is the night that Dumbledore dies (HBP 29:630).

Fawcetts. *Characters.* Amos Diggory tells Arthur Weasley that the Fawcetts could not get tickets for the World Cup, so they do not need to wait for them at the Portkey (GF 6:73). Snape catches a Fawcett girl from Ravenclaw running out of the bushes after the Yule Ball (GF 23:426).

Fawkes. *Magical creature.* Prof. Dumbledore's phoenix. Harry sees a phoenix in Dumbledore's office and the professor explains how they die in flames only to be born again from their ashes. Fawkes has beautiful gold and red feathers, which also happen to be the Gryffindor colors. Dumbledore says phoenixes make faithful pets (CS 12:207). When Fawkes arrives in the Chamber of Secrets, he is preceded by music. He drops the Sorting Hat with the Gryffindor sword in it to Harry. He also fights the Basilisk with Harry, pecking out its eyes so that it cannot kill Harry with its stare. Then Fawkes heals Harry's poisonous wound and gives Harry the diary so that he may jab the poisonous fang into it and overcome Voldemort's current challenge (CS 17:315–22). The phoenix feathers in Harry's and Voldemort's wands both came from Fawkes. Fawkes's tears heal Harry once again when his leg is injured in the graveyard (GF 36:698). The night Dumbledore dies, Fawkes leaves his perch in the headmaster's office and sings a long, beautiful lament outside the castle before flying away (HBP 29:611–32).

Fawkes gets his name from Guy Fawkes, a conspirator in English history who wanted to burn the Houses of Parliament. On November 5 each year, Brits celebrate Guy Fawkes' Day, or Bonfire Night, when they light fireworks to celebrate the survival of their government.

See also Bonfire Night; Dumbledore, Albus Percival Wulfric Brian; Phoenix

Felix Felicis. *Magical substance.* Liquid luck. Prof. Slughorn explains to his Potions class that this substance makes one lucky, but taken in excess it can make one overconfident and it can be toxic (HBP 9:187). Harry gives Ron a pair of socks that have Felix Felicis wrapped in them in case he or Hermione needs it (HBP 25:552).

"Fellytone." *Wrong word.* Ron Weasley's mispronunciation of "telephone," a Muggle device (PA 22:431). Arthur Weasley pronounces it the same way to the Dursleys, but he is corrected by Hermione (OP 38:869).

Fenwick, Benjy. *Character.* A member of the original Order of the Phoenix who was killed the last time Voldemort was in power; only small pieces of his body were ever found (OP 9:174).

Fergus. *Character.* Seamus Finnigan's cousin who Apparates all the time to show off in front of Seamus (HBP 17:355).

Ferrari. *Muggle car.* Harry thinks that his Uncle Vernon, who is normally impressed by people who drive fancy cars, would not appreciate Arthur Weasley even if he had a Ferrari. It is one of the rare instances in the series, along with Ford Anglia and PlayStation, that a brand name from the world outside the books is mentioned (GF 4:41).

Ferret. Barty Crouch, Jr. (in the form of Mad-Eye Moody) turns Draco Malfoy into a white ferret after he catches him picking on Harry Potter for not knowing his mother. He seems to delight in tossing the Malfoy-ferret up and down in the air (GF 13:204).

"Ferula." *Incantation. Ferula* is Latin for "stick." This incantation wraps the victim or desired part of a victim in bandages and a splint. Prof. Lupin uses this incantation to help Ron's broken leg in the Shrieking Shack (PA 19:376).

Fever Fudge. *Magical candy.* Another of Fred and George Weasley's concoctions. They have not mastered it yet. When it is first mentioned they say it causes boils in addition to fever that they do not know how to get rid of (OP 18:378–79).

Figg, Arabella Doreen (Mrs.). *Character.* Mrs. Figg is an old woman who lives two streets over from the Dursleys and is often charged with watching Harry while his aunt and uncle take Dudley out to do something fun. Harry dislikes going to see her because Mrs. Figg's house smells of cabbage and she is always showing him photo albums of all the cats she has owned (SS 1:22). She is walking the neighborhood the night the Dementors come to Little Whinging (OP 1:2). The night Harry and Dudley are attacked by the Dementors, she is wearing a hairnet, plaid slippers, and she is carrying a shopping bag (OP 1:19). She later tells Harry that she is a Squib (OP 2:20). She appears at the expulsion hearing on behalf of Harry as a witness to the events of August 2. She is called by Harry's advocate, Albus Dumbledore. She tells the Wizengamot that she is a Squib and that Squibs can see Dementors (OP 8:143).
See also Cats

Filch, Argus. *Character.* He is the caretaker of Hogwarts (SS 7:127). He owns a beloved cat, Mrs. Norris. Harry suspects he may be a Squib when he discovers that Filch is taking a correspondence course in Magic called Kwikspell (CS 8:127). Filch later admits his Squib status in front of Harry (CS 9:142). Filch is delighted to be courted by Prof. Umbridge into cooperating with her as she attempts to rule the school. He is hoping that she will pass another Educational Decree allowing him to whip students who do not obey the rules and expelling Peeves from the premises (OP 28:628). In Greek mythology, Argos had 100 eyes and was assigned to watch Io for the jealous Juno.

Filibuster's Fabulous Wet-Start, No-Heat Fireworks. *Magical objects.* These fireworks are popular with Fred and George Weasley (CS 4:58). They celebrate the last night of summer with fireworks at the Burrow during the month that Harry stays with them (CS 5:65). They need to go back to the Burrow in the Ford Anglia when Fred forgets a box of them (CS 5:66). Harry uses one to create a diversion when Hermione needs to get ingredients from Snape's private stores for the Polyjuice Potion (CS 11:187). Fred makes sure to use the last of these fireworks before they head home for the summer (CS 18:340).

Films. Almost as soon as the first book appeared, people began talking about how well the story could be adapted to the medium of film. The books contain much visual

Madam Hooch (Zoe Wanamaker) leads Harry's first flying lesson in this still from *Harry Potter and the Sorcerer's Stone* (2001). Shown: Neville Longbottom (Matthew Lewis, in flight); just below him are Ron Weasley (Rupert Grint), Harry Potter (Daniel Radcliffe), and Hermione Granger (Emma Watson). Courtesy of Warner Bros./Photofest.

imagery, and the fantasy world Rowling created was a welcome potential challenge for many film directors and special effects artists. Rowling was concerned about the film adaptations of her books and maintained unprecedented control over the rights when they were initially sold to Warner Bros. Just like the books, the films have reached blockbuster status with each release. One of the gifts that the films offer to cinema is that the three main child actors who play Harry, Ron, and Hermione have virtually grown up on-screen. In the films, the actors mature in close to real time with their characters. Actors have played the same characters in film sequels before, but this may be the first time a child actor aged with his character on-screen year by year through a sequence of as many as seven films.

Harry Potter and the Sorcerer's Stone was released in 2001. Steven Kloves wrote the screenplay and the film was directed by Chris Columbus. It is 152 minutes long and was rated PG for scary moments and mild language. It stars Daniel Radcliffe as Harry; Rupert Grint as Ron; and Emma Watson as Hermione. Robbie Coltrane, who was a Rowling choice, plays Hagrid; Tom Felton plays Draco Malfoy. Richard Harris plays Prof. Dumbledore; Maggie Smith plays Prof. McGonagall; and Alan Rickman plays Prof. Snape. Vernon and Petunia Dursley are played by Richard Griffiths and Fiona Shaw, respectively. Rowling had her wish fulfilled in that the complete cast is made up of British actors, and the film follows the book very closely. The movie was nominated for three Academy Awards: Best Art-Set Direction; Best Costume Design; and Best Music, Original Score. The film grossed over $90 million on opening weekend in the United States. One of the notable features of the film is that the scene of Hermione solving the bottle logic puzzle was left out. This disappointed many viewers who wanted to see

Hermione's strong female character work this kind of task—an accomplishment so rarely seen on screen performed by a young girl.

Harry Potter and the Chamber of Secrets was released in 2002. The screenplay was written by Steven Kloves; Chris Columbus was the director. The film is 161 minutes long and was rated PG for scary moments, some creature violence, and mild language. The same actors portray the main trio of characters. Most of the other major characters are portrayed by the same actors as well. New characters include: Dobby (voice) by Toby Jones, and Prof. Lockhart portrayed by Kenneth Branagh. This film was not nominated for an Academy Award. It grossed over $88 million on opening weekend in the United States. An interesting fact about the *Chamber of Secrets* film is that fourteen Ford Anglias were destroyed in the effort to re-create the scene of Harry and Ron crashing into the Whomping Willow.

Harry Potter and the Prisoner of Azkaban was released in 2004. Steven Kloves wrote the screenplay again, but this film was directed by Alfonso Cuarón. Chris Columbus remained involved as one of the producers. The movie is 141 minutes long and is rated PG for frightening moments, creature violence, and mild language. Since Richard Harris died between films, Prof. Dumbledore was played by Michael Gambon. New characters include Prof. Lupin played by David Thewlis, and Prof. Trelawney played by Emma Thompson. On opening weekend in the United States, this third film in the series grossed over $93 million. The film was nominated for two Academy Awards: Best Achievement in Music Written for Motion Pictures, Original Score; and Best Achievement in Visual Effects. Many viewers appreciate Cuarón's departure from strict faithfulness to the books and his use of a more cinematic interpretation of the original story. There are more exterior scenes, and the main trio of characters is dressed frequently in contemporary clothing (jeans and so forth) and not always in Hogwarts robes. The film also has a darker appearance, capturing the increasing maturity of the story line and the fact that this segment of the overall plot concerns more of Harry's interior life.

Harry Potter and the Goblet of Fire was released in 2005. The screenplay was again written by Steven Kloves, and this film was directed by Mike Newell. It is 157 minutes long, and the film was rated PG-13 for sequences of fantasy violence and frightening images. Characters and their casting include: Lord Voldemort played by Ralph Fiennes; Cedric Diggory played by Robert Pattinson; Viktor Krum played by Stanislav Ianevski; and Cho Chang played by Katie Leung. Opening weekend sales in the United States were $101.4 million.

Harry Potter and the Order of the Phoenix is slated for a 2007 release, and *Harry Potter and the Half-Blood Prince* is expected in 2008. However, these dates may be subject to change.

Finch-Fletchley, Justin. *Character.* Student in Harry's year; sorted into Hufflepuff (SS 7:120). He is friendly with Harry and his friends during the Mandrake lesson in Herbology in Year 2. Justin tells them that he was bound for Eton until he received his invitation to Hogwarts (CS 6:93–94). During the Dueling Club lesson, the snake that Draco Malfoy produces goes toward Justin, and Harry speaks Parseltongue to get it away. Justin thinks Harry's odd speech made the snake go near him rather than away (CS 11:194). Unfortunately, Justin winds up being the third petrification (CS 11:202). He ignores Harry after Harry is chosen as a second Hogwarts champion for the Triwizard Tournament (GF 18:293), but he is impressed at the first DA meeting where Harry's accomplishments are discussed (OP 16:342).

Justin is one of the DA members who defends Harry against Draco Malfoy, Vincent Crabbe, and Gregory Goyle during the ride home on the Hogwarts Express after Year 5.

The DA's various jinxes and defenses leave the three bullies in the form of oozing slugs that Justin, Ernie Macmillan, and Harry put in the luggage rack for the remainder of the trip (OP 38:864).

Fingal the Fearless. *Character.* From QA. An Aingingein champion (QA 4).
See also Aingingein

"Finite Incantatem!" *Incantation. Finis* is Latin for "end." The incantation ends the effects of the previous incantation. Draco Malfoy uses this incantation to stop his earlier "Tarantallegra!" incantation on Harry during their Dueling Club lesson (CS 11:192). The incantation can be shortened to "Finite!" (OP 36:808).

Finnigan, Seamus. *Character.* A student in Gryffindor House in Harry's year. He has sandy-colored hair and asks Nearly Headless Nick how he can be nearly headless; Nick demonstrates how (SS 7:124). Seamus tells Harry and friends that he is half magical, half Muggle. His mother did not tell his father she was a witch until after they were married (SS 7:125). He is Harry's partner in Charms class when they begin to learn to use their wands (SS 10:171). Seamus Finnigan is among those who congratulate Ron and Harry for their brilliant entrance to Hogwarts in the Ford Anglia in Year 2 (CS 5:85). He chuckles and does not think the Cornish pixies in Lockhart's class look very dangerous until they are released into the room; then they prove difficult to catch (CS 6:101). Prof. Binns erroneously calls Seamus "O'Flaherty" in History of Magic class (CS 9:151). Seamus greets Harry and friends at the World Cup campground where his tent is covered with shamrocks. He wants to make sure they are supporting Ireland in the Cup (GF 7:82). His mother does not want him to return to Hogwarts after reading lies about Harry in the *Daily Prophet* (OP 11:217). After Dumbledore dies, Seamus argues with his mother in the hall about wanting to stay for the funeral. She agrees to stay but has difficulty finding lodging in Hogsmeade with all the witches and wizards arriving in town to pay their respects (HBP 30:633).

Fire. Dumbledore tells Harry that the forces of evil cannot tolerate light and heat. When all seems lost in the cave with Dumbledore, Harry forgets this tip, and Dumbledore somehow revives to create a ring of fire that protects him and Harry and lets them escape the cave (HBP 26:576). Hagrid gives the gift of an everlasting fire to the giant chief when trying to win him over (OP 20:430).
See also Gubraithian fire

Fire Crab. *Magical creature.* From *Fantastic Beasts.* Classified 3X by the MM. The Fire Crab looks like a large tortoise with jewels on its shell. Fire Crab shells are sometimes used as cauldrons. It defends itself by blasting fire out of its tail area when attacked (FB 17).
See also Fantastic Beasts and Where to Find Them

Firearms/Firelegs. Arthur Weasley and Kingley Shacklebolt get together in a cubicle at their office in the Ministry under the ruse of correcting the misuse of firelegs for firearm in a report. They do this in order to talk in secrecy about the Order (OP 7:132).

Firebolt. *Magical object.* This broomstick model is so expensive that its price is not even listed in the window of Quality Quidditch Supplies. It features an ash handle that is treated with a special polish. Every twig in the broom is made from a birch tree and has been aerodynamically designed for excellent flying and balance. It also has a charm on it to prevent it from breaking and can go up to 150 miles an hour in ten seconds. The new broom is on display in the summer before Harry's third year at Hogwarts (PA 4:51). Harry mysteriously receives a Firebolt after his Nimbus 2000 crashes. Prof. McGonagall takes it to Prof. Flitwick, who makes sure that it is not bewitched. After Sirius Black has gone back into hiding, he tells Harry in a note that it was he who sent it (PA 22:432). Prof. Umbridge confiscates Harry's Firebolt after the Gryffindor-Slytherin match; she bars Harry from playing and locks the Firebolt in her office with a chain and padlock on her wall (OP 28:629).

See also Broomsticks

Firenze. *Magical creature.* Firenze is the Italian word for "Florence," one of Italy's most beautiful cities. In the Harry Potter series, Firenze is one of the three centaurs that Harry meets. He lives in the Forbidden Forest. Firenze has a palomino body, white-blond hair, and pale blue eyes. He appears younger than the other two centaurs. He saves Harry from an early encounter with Voldemort in Year 1 (SS 15:256). He is compassionate and more open to contact with humans than the other centaurs. Firenze eventually becomes a Divination teacher at Hogwarts with Prof. Trelawney. He arrives in Harry's fifth year when Prof. Trelawney is fired by Dolores Umbridge (OP 26:598).

Firenze tells the students that the centaurs have divined from watching the planets that the last decade has really been a calm interim between two wars. He says that Mars is shining brightly again, indicating that the second war is about to begin (OP 27:603). He again shares the class with Prof. Trelawney in Harry's sixth year (HBP 9:174). Prof. Trelawney resents Firenze's presence on the faculty.

Fitchburg Finches. *Magical sports team.* From QA. A professional Quidditch team from Massachusetts. They have won the U.S. League seven times. Their Seeker, Maximus Brankovitch III, was the captain of the American team for the two most recent World Cups (QA 45).

Fizzing Whizbees. *Magical candy.* Fizzing Whizbees are balls of sherbet that make one rise from the ground (PA 10:197). Mrs. Weasley sends some to Harry over the Easter holidays (OP 29:654).

Flacking. *Magical game penalty.* From QA. If a Keeper puts an arm or leg through a goal hoop to push out a Quaffle, he or she receives a penalty for Flacking (QA 30).

"Flagrate!" *Incantation.* Flagro is Latin for "fire" or "burn." Hermione uses this incantation to mark doors with an X or a cross after the DA checks them while looking for Sirius Black in the Department of Mysteries (OP 34:772).

Flame Freezing Charm. *Magical spell.* Harry reads about this spell in *A History of Magic.* Witches and wizards being burned used this charm on themselves to feel a tickling sensation rather than heat (PA 1:2).

Flamel, Nicolas. *Character.* A colleague of Prof. Dumbledore's in alchemy. Flamel made the Philosopher's/Sorcerer's Stone, which also creates the Elixir of Life (SS 11:193). Flamel is over 665 years old and his wife Perenelle is 658 (SS 13:220). Harry discovers that Flamel and his wife will die since the Sorcerer's Stone was destroyed (SS 17:297).

See also Alchemy

Flamel, Perenelle. *Character.* Nicolas Flamel's wife; she is 658 years old (SS 13:220). She dies with Nicolas when he and Dumbledore decide to destroy the Sorcerer's Stone (SS 17:297).

See also Alchemy

Flanders. *Place.* From QA. The Quidditch World Cup between Flanders and Transylvania was recorded as the most violent in history (QA 40).

Fleet, Angus. *Character.* A Muggle who reported seeing the flying Ford Anglia over Peebles (CS 5:79). Angus is a kind of beef.

Flesh-Eating Slug Repellant. *Magical substance.* This is what Hagrid says he is buying at Knockturn Alley when he runs into Harry, who arrives there by mistake after using Floo Powder from the Burrow (CS 4:55).

Flesh-Eating Trees of the World. *Magical book.* Hermione consults this book to get a better idea of how to juice Snargaluff pods (HBP 14:283).

Fletcher, Mundungus. *Character.* This old wizard tries to hex Mr. Weasley during a raid by the Ministry for misuse of Muggle artifacts (CS 3:38). Mrs. Figg is very unhappy with Mundungus Fletcher when she discovers that two Dementors attacked Harry and Dudley Dursley at Little Whinging when he was supposed to be guarding them (OP 1:19–20); he was out buying stolen cauldrons instead (OP 2:23). Fletcher's nickname is "Dung" (OP 5:81). He hides in a witch's get-up in the Hog's Head when Harry's DADA class first meets; he then informs Sirius Black of what is going on (OP 17:370). Molly Weasley does not think very highly of Mundungus Fletcher's integrity (HBP 5:85). Harry tries to stop him when he sees him outside the Three Broomsticks picking up the contents of a fallen suitcase. Harry presumes the objects are stolen goods from Grimmauld Place (HBP 12:245).

An interpretation of the legendary alchemist Nicolas Flamel in his library; anonymous woodcut. Rowling's Flamel was a friend and colleague of Albus Dumbledore. Courtesy of the Library of Congress.

"Flibbertigibbet!" *Magical password.* One of the Fat Lady's passwords into Gryffindor Tower, Year 3 (PA 15:295).

See also Passwords

Flint, Marcus. *Character.* During Harry's first year at Hogwarts, Marcus Flint was a sixth-year Slytherin student and captain of the Slytherin Quidditch team. Harry thinks he is so big that he may be part troll (SS 11:185). Marcus moves in front of Draco Malfoy to defend him against Fred and George Weasley, who attack Draco for calling Hermione a Mudblood (CS 7:112).

Flitterbloom. *Magical plant.* Healer Strout mistakes a Devil's Snare plant for a Flitterbloom when one is delivered to Broderick Bode at St. Mungo's at Christmas (OP 25:546–47).

Flitwick, Prof. Filius. *Character.* Prof. Flitwick is the Charms teacher. Flitwick is a very small wizard who must stand on a pile of books in his chair for his students to see him. During roll call in Harry's first year, he squeaks and topples off the pile when he comes to Harry's name (SS 8:133). He is the one who cleans up the Weasley twins' Portable Swamp in no time once Dumbledore returns as Head of Hogwarts. He leaves a small puddle roped off as a monument to the twins' good magic (OP 38:848).

Flobberworm. *Magical creature.* Classified 1X by the MM. It is a worm up to ten inches long that likes to live in ditches. Both ends exude a substance used to thicken some potions. It likes to eat lettuce (FB 17–18).

Some flobberworms die under Hagrid's care when he feeds them too much lettuce (PA 11:220). For the final exam in Care of Magical Creatures in Year 3, Hagrid gives the students a tub of these worms; they must still be alive at the end of one hour. Since the worms survive best when left to themselves without interference, the exam was particularly easy (PA 16:317). Snape has Harry sort decayed ones from good ones for his detention (HBP 22:236).

See also Fantastic Beasts and Where to Find Them

Floo Network. *Magical transportation system.* A series of connected fireplaces that allow wizards to travel from one to the other using Floo Powder. Muggle homes are not supposed to be on the network, but Arthur Weasley requests special use from the Floo Regulation Panel in order to pick up Harry for the Quidditch World Cup (GF 4:45).

Floo Network Authority. *Magical office.* Located in the Department of Magical Transport on the sixth floor of the Ministry (OP 7:129).

Floo Network Regulator. *Magical occupation.* Dolores Umbridge says there is a Floo Network Regulator looking over all of the fires at Hogwarts (OP 28:631).

Floo Powder. *Magical substance and transportation.* Floo Powder is a substance that provides a method of transportation. One steps up in front of a fireplace, tosses a pinch of the glittery powder into the fire, and says very clearly where one wants to go. Elbows must stay tucked; eyes closed; and the traveler must watch for the correct fireplace grate from which to leave and not get out too early. The process is a bit complicated, and Harry winds up on his first try at Knockturn Alley rather than Diagon Alley (CS 4:47–49, 53). The Weasley family tries to pick up Harry at the Dursleys using this method, but gets caught behind Vernon's electric fireplace, which blocks their way (GF 4:43).

Floo Regulation Panel. *Magical office.* Arthur Weasley requests that the Floo Regulation Panel attach the Dursleys' fireplace to the Floo Network for one afternoon; he wants to pick up Harry for the Quidditch World Cup (GF 4:45).

Florean Fortescue's Ice Cream Parlor. *Magical place.* Harry gets free sundaes every half hour at Florean Fortescue's while working on his essays for Hogwarts at the end of the summer before Year 3. Florean also helps him with his work since he happens to know a lot about medieval witch burnings (PA 4:50).

Flourish and Blotts. *Magical place.* Bookstore on Diagon Alley (SS 5:80). Prof. Dumbledore tells readers of *Fantastic Beasts* that the book will be sold at Flourish and Blotts (as well as Muggle bookstores) to benefit Comic Relief, U.K. (FB viii).

Fluffy. *Magical creature.* Hagrid's enormous, drooling three-headed dog with yellow fangs. Fluffy guards the Sorcerer's Stone in Hogwarts (SS 9:160). He stays asleep as long as there is music playing. In Roman mythology, a three-headed dog is called Cerberus and guards the entrance to Hell. Orpheus put Cerberus to sleep with his lyre. It was the custom in ancient Egypt to have dogs guard graves.

Flume, Ambrosius. *Character.* Ambrosius Flume is the head of Honeydukes and a former student of Horace Slughorn (HBP 4:71).

Fluxweed. *Magical plant.* An ingredient in the Polyjuice Potion (CS 10:165).

Flying carpets. *Magical/Muggle objects.* The Ministry has defined the carpets as Muggle Artifacts in the Registry of Proscribed Charmable Objects; they are banned from the wizarding world as a result (GF 7:91).
See also Bashir, Ali

Flying lessons. *Magical class at Hogwarts.* Madam Hooch, the referee for Quidditch matches, is also in charge of teaching first-year students to fly on broomsticks (SS 9:146).
See also Hogwarts School of Witchcraft and Wizardry

Flying With the Cannons. *Magical book.* Harry is reading this book during the summer before Year 4 (GF 2:18). He rereads it at Christmas for about the tenth time, which annoys Hermione because he is not working on the second task for the Triwizard Tournament (GF 22:392).

Flyte and Barker. *Magical business.* From QA. Flyte and Barker created the Twigger 90 racing broom to compete with the Nimbus brooms, but they made it too expensive, faulty, and with too many useless features (QA 51).

Foe-Glass. *Magical object.* A mirror-like tool of Moody's (Crouch, Jr.) that shows him his enemies. He tells Harry he is not in danger from his enemies until he can see the whites of their eyes; once they get this close, he gets out his trunk of other tools to catch them (GF 20:343). Three figures—Dumbledore, Prof. McGonagall, and Snape—eventually show themselves clearly in Moody/Crouch's glass, telling Harry that something must be wrong since they would not be enemies of Mad-Eye Moody's (GF 35:678–79). There is a large broken Foe-Glass in the Room of Requirement for use by Dumbledore's Army (OP 18:390).

Food and feasts. Rowling has said in interviews that she remembers reading about food in books as a child and she wanted to include descriptions of food in her writing. She recalls *The Little White Horse*, in particular; as a hungry young reader, she relished reading about the foods described in this book. In the Harry Potter series, food is a comfort to Harry, who apparently was neither fed as much, nor presumably as well, as his overweight cousin at the Dursley residence.

One of the first marvels Harry encounters at Hogwarts is the Start-of-Term Banquet in Year 1. Food of all kinds magically appears on the tables, heaped high to the point of overflowing. Harry also enjoys the abundance of treats on the Hogwarts Express snack cart. Feasts occur with some regularity throughout the school year—there is one at Christmas and a last one at the end of the term, with occasional special meals in between. Meals are served in the Great Hall, and the students appear to eat three meals a day—breakfast, lunch, and dinner—as part of their regular school-day routine.

More than one observer has noticed that the food at Hogwarts tends to be on the heavy side. Rather than salads of fruits and vegetables served with bottles of water, menus bend toward meats and potatoes, sausage, bacon, breads, puddings, pies, and casseroles, with pumpkin juice and butterbeer for beverages. In *Goblet of Fire*, students are served a hundred turkeys and puddings for Christmas lunch, and pork chops at the Yule Ball (GF 23:416); Harry has goulash (GF 23:418). Fleur Delacour complains about the heavy Hogwarts food that will surely expand her waistline so that she will not fit in her dress robes for the ball (GF 23:404).

Food offered outside of Hogwarts in private wizard residences tends to be about the same. Mrs. Weasley offers Harry breakfast before his hearing at the Ministry, with choices including toast, bacon and eggs, porridge, muffins, and kippers (OP 7:122). Hagrid, who keeps trying to cook despite mixed results, offers rock cakes and other questionable tidbits to Harry and his friends. The trio knows to be cautious around Hagrid's generous hospitality. Hermione, for example, finds a large claw in her helping of Hagrid's beef casserole (GF 16:265).

Forbidden Forest. *Magical place.* The forest next to Hogwarts is a dark and mysterious place where students are forbidden to go. Harry first visits the forest with Hagrid during his detention. They go to find what is killing the unicorns (SS 15:250).

Ford Anglia. *Enchanted Muggle object.* Mr. Weasley's turquoise and white flying car. He adapts the Muggle car to make it fly. The irony is that his job is to make sure wizards do not misuse Muggle artifacts. Ron and his brothers use the car to rescue Harry from the Dursleys. They take him to their house, the Burrow, in the summer before Harry's second year at Hogwarts (CS 3:24–28). When they take the car to catch the Hogwarts Express, Mrs. Weasley does not notice that the car has magically expanded to fit Ron, Harry, Fred, George, and Percy in the backseat. Mr. Weasley has done this, again, against his own rules at the Ministry of Magic (CS 5:66). After they start out, they must return three times to retrieve items the children have forgotten: Fred forgets his Filibuster Fireworks; George forgets his broomstick; and Ginny forgets her diary (CS 5:66).

Harry and Ron fly the car to Hogwarts when they cannot break through the barrier at Platform 9-3/4. One of the features that Arthur Weasley has modified in the car is the

Invisibility Booster, which makes the car invisible to Muggles (CS 5:67). The car winds up in the Forbidden Forest, which turns it rather wild (CS 15:274).

The Ford Anglia is an actual car. Ford made the model from 1959 to 1968. The car was a four-cylinder, manual transmission, two-door car that seated four people. Its most distinguishing feature was the upright, tall rear windshield that allowed more headroom for rear passengers. The Super Ford Anglia was made from 1962 to 1968. A Super model could go up to 82 miles per hour with gas mileage at about 31 miles per gallon. The Anglia was replaced by the Ford Escort in 1968. Ford sold just over one million Anglias for sport and family use.

Forest of Dean. The Forest of Dean encompasses 203 square miles between the rivers Severn and Wye in southwest England on the northern side of the Bristol Channel. The southern section of the forest is made up of 27,000 acres of ancient forest dating back before the Romans lived in England. Rowling lived near and visited the Forest of Dean from the time she was about nine years old until she left home for college. The magical and natural qualities of the forest may have influenced her writing of fantasy.

Rowling has said that she and her sister Di used to play for days along the River Wye. The forest nearby is home to much flora and fauna that may have fueled the imagination of a young J. K. Rowling. Native birds include coot, heron, gray wagtail, reed warbler, mute swans, welducks, and peregrine falcons. Animals include fox, badger, mink, polecats, brown rats, and shrew. Plants and flowers include daffodils, violets, and bluebells but also ivyleaved toadflax and germander speedwell. Fungi that grow in the forest bear Rowling-esque names such as dead man's fingers, dung roundhead, scarlet elfcup, stinkhorn, parrot wax cap, brain purple-drop, amethyst deceiver, and fairy parasol.

Forgetfulness Potion. *Magical substance.* Harry tries to remember how to make this potion for his Year 1 Potions exam while Snape looks over his shoulder (SS 16:262).

Fortescue. *Character.* A former headmaster at Hogwarts, Fortescue has a portrait on Dumbledore's office wall. He hears questioning about the DA in Dumbledore's office and he objects to the corruption that is obvious in the Ministry (OP 27:614).

Fortescue, Florean. *Character.* The wizard who ran the ice cream parlor at Diagon Alley. For his History of Magic exam in Year 3, Harry tries to remember the tips that Florean Fortescue gave him about medieval witch hunts (PA 16:318). It is assumed that Florean was taken away from Diagon Alley by Death Eaters (HBP 6:106).

"Fortuna Major!" *Magical password.* *Fortuna* is Latin for "fortune" or "fate." "Fortuna Major!" is a password into the Gryffindor Tower during Harry's third year at Hogwarts (PA 5:94).

See also Passwords

Fountain of Magical Brethren. *Magical object.* Located in the Atrium at the Ministry of Magic, the large fountain contains statues of a wizard, witch, centaur, house-elf, and goblin spouting water from various places. Coins thrown into the fountain are donated to St. Mungo's Hospital for Magical Maladies and Injuries (OP 7:127). Harry silently promises to give 10 Galleons to the fountain as he passes it if he wins in his hearing (OP 7:178). On his way out of the hearing, free and clear, he does not forget his promise—he not only gives 10 Galleons, but deposits all of the money from his bag into the fountain

(OP 9:156). During the attack at the Room of Prophecy, Dumbledore appears out of the wizard in the fountain, and the other statues in the fountain come to life to help him defend Harry against Death Eater Bellatrix Lestrange (OP 36:813).

Four-Point Spell. *Magical spell.* This spell makes a wand point due north (GF 31:608).

Fowl or Foul? A Study of Hippogriff Brutality. *Magical book.* Ron reads this book in his efforts to help Hagrid with Buckbeak's appeal before the Ministry (PA 15:300).

Fox. Thinking it may have been an Auror in Animagus form, Bellatrix Lestrange kills a tawney fox along the river near Spinner's End, which is where she and her sister go to find Snape (HBP 2:20).

France. Hermione Granger visits France with her parents in the summer before Year 3. She writes Harry a letter from France (accompanied by his birthday present), saying that there is a lot of witchcraft history there. She says that she has rewritten her entire summer essay about the History of Magic as a result of what she has found (PA 1:11). Hagrid and Madam Maxime pretend they are going to France when they go to visit the giants in the mountains; they do so because they know they are being followed by a spy from the Ministry. They lose the spy somewhere around Dijon (OP 20:425–26). When Dolores Umbridge asks Hagrid if he visited the mountains while he was away from Hogwarts, Hagrid tells her that he went to the south of France for the sunshine and water (OP 20:438).

Freezing Charm. *Magical charm.* This charm causes alarms and other objects to freeze. Hermione uses it to catch two Cornish pixies at once in DADA in Year 2 (CS 6:103). Prof. Slughorn uses it on Muggle burglar alarms when he wishes to stay in a house while in hiding during his retirement (HBP 4:68).

Fridwulfa. *Character.* Hagrid's mother who ran off when he was young. She is a giantess. She was not found among those who were caught turning to the Dark Side and may be living in the mountains of another country (GF 24:439).

Frobisher, Vicky. *Character.* Vicky Frobisher tries out for Keeper on the Gryffindor team, but loses to Ron Weasley because captain Angelina Johnson thinks she is too involved in other extracurricular activities and will not make Quidditch a priority (OP 13:276).

Frog Spawn Soap. *Magical object.* Harry and Ron buy some of this soap at Zonko's in Hogsmeade (PA 14:278).

From Egg to Inferno. *Magical book.* A book that Hagrid is looking at in the Hogwarts Library, Year 1 (SS 14:230).

Fruit 'N Bran breakfast cereal. *Muggle food.* Harry hears an ad for this Muggle product while listening to the television news from behind the hydrangea bushes at the Dursleys (OP 1:2).

Fry, Stephen. Stephen Fry is the narrator of the audio books in the British edition. Fry is an actor, writer, director, and producer whose career in the entertainment industry spans over twenty years. His films include *The Hitchhiker's Guide to the Galaxy* (2005); *Gosford Park* (2001); and *The Wind in the Willows* (1996). His writing credits include an episode of *Dr. Who* for television in 2005; and *Pushing Up Daisies* in 1984. He received a Tony Award nomination in 1987 for cowriting a revision of the play *Me and My Girl*. Besides narrating the Harry Potter audio books, he is best known in England for his television roles in *Blackadder II* (1987) and *Jeeves and Wooster* (1990).

Fry was born in 1957 and makes his home in London and Norfolk. He grew up in Norfolk and attended Uppingham School, then Stout's Hill. After a three-month incarceration at Pucklechurch prison for credit card fraud (which received a notable amount of publicity), Fry attended Queens College in Cambridge, majoring in English. He has published four novels and several other works.

Rowling has not only said that she enjoys Fry's reading of her books but that her oldest daughter does also. At one point when she was at home working on *Goblet of Fire* in the evenings, she could hear Fry's voice on tape coming from her daughter's room, reading to her from one of Harry's earlier adventures. The experience, she said, was slightly disconcerting at the time, but she enjoys his performance as much as her daughter.

Fry works carefully to devise different voices for the characters, including accents from the appropriate parts of the country where characters grew up. He has said that he wished he had given Prof. McGonagall a Scottish accent, but he started out thinking of her as a cat and forgot that she would transform back into a human being, so now he is stuck with the original voice he created. When he began recording the first novel, Rowling was late getting to the studio to hear his first attempts at voices. When she arrived, he mentioned to her that he performed Hagrid as though he were from Somerset in the West Country,

British actor Stephen Fry on stage with J. K. Rowling at London's Royal Albert Hall on June 26, 2003. Fry narrates the British books-on-tape version of the Harry Potter novels. © Getty Images/ Handout.

and Rowling was delighted. Accent is an important aspect of Hagrid's character, and she had been concerned that she would not reach the studio in time to let Fry know what it should be.

When asked in an interview which character he enjoys performing most in the audio books, Fry first said Dumbledore, then several other characters including Harry, Ron, Hermione, Prof. McGonagall, and Mrs. Weasley. He stated that choosing one was too hard a decision. He finds the books to be a good blend of humor, fun, and fright for listeners of all ages.

See also Dale, Jim

Further Reading: Stephen Fry website: http://www.stephenfry.com.

Fudge, Cornelius Oswald. *Character.* The Head Minister of the Ministry of Magic. He was given the position when Albus Dumbledore turned it down in order to remain at Hogwarts (SS 5:65). After the petrifications at Hogwarts in Harry's Year 2, Lucius Malfoy and the board of governors pressure Fudge to fire Dumbledore. As a result, he arrives at Hagrid's hut to put him under arrest and he suspends Dumbledore from his post as headmaster (CS 14:261–63). Harry meets Fudge at the Leaky Cauldron when the Knight Bus drops him off. Fudge makes sure that Harry is well protected; he has erased Aunt Marge's memory of Harry's offense and makes sure that innkeeper Tom has a room for him. Fudge says that Harry may go to Diagon Alley, but that is all; he is not to be out at night. Tom will keep an eye on him (PA 3:42–46). Fudge comes to Hogwarts as the required witness to Buckbeak's execution; he was already going there on business about Sirius Black (PA 16:320). He and Dumbledore part ways when Fudge will not believe that Voldemort has risen to full power again. He refuses to enact the plan for defensive measures that Dumbledore says is necessary (GF 36:709). As Minister, Fudge is in charge of Harry's expulsion hearing (OP 8:138). Dumbledore thinks that Fudge is acting on his own accord rather than under the influence of the Imperius Curse when he mistreats Dumbledore and others and when he refuses to believe in the rise of Voldemort (OP 9:155). Fudge is in Dumbledore's office when Harry is brought in about the DA (OP 27:610).

Fudge Flies. *Magical candy.* A treat at Gryffindor's party for their win over Ravenclaw at Quidditch (PA 13:265).

Full Body-Bind. *Magical spell.* This spell locks the entire body in a stiff position. Its incantation is "Petrificus Totalus!" Hermione casts it on Neville to keep him from following her, Ron, and Harry when they go to look for the Sorcerer's Stone (SS 16:273).

Funeral, Dumbledore's. *Magical event.* Since Dumbledore always wished for Hogwarts to be his final resting place, Prof. McGonagall agrees to allow students to stay for his funeral on the school grounds. They will be transported homeward by the Hogwarts Express one hour after the ceremony.

Those who attend the ceremony include, of course, Harry, Ron, Hermione, and Ginny Weasley; Seamus Finnigan and his mother; the Minister of Magic and a delegation of officials. Rufus Scrimgeour sits in Snape's chair in the Great Hall at breakfast; Prof. McGonagall leaves Dumbledore's headmaster chair vacant. Percy Weasley is there, as are Vincent Crabbe and Gregory Goyle. Other attendees include: Horace Slughorn; Madam Pince; Kingsley Shacklebolt; Mad-Eye Moody; Tonks and Remus Lupin (holding hands); Mr. and Mrs. Weasley; Bill Weasley, aided by Fleur Delacour; Fred and George

Weasley in black dragon-skin jackets; Madame Maxime; Tom, the Leaky Cauldron landlord; Arabella Figg; the bass player from the Weird Sisters; Ernie Prang; Madam Malkin; the Hog's Head barman (who may be Aberforth Dumbledore, his brother); and the witch who serves candy on the Hogwarts Express. All of the ghosts from the castle attend, as do Neville Longbottom and Luna Lovegood, sitting together. Additional attendees are: Cornelius Fudge; Rita Skeeter; Dolores Umbridge; Firenze; and a chorus of merpeople and the centaur herd. The herd keeps their bows to their sides until after Dumbledore's tomb appears, then they shoot arrows into the sky in tribute. Hagrid carries Dumbledore's body to the front, then sits down beside his half-brother, Grawp, who seems much more human than before (HBP 30:639–46). The finality of Dumbledore's passing hits Harry hard during the funeral, but he also begins to make plans about what he must do next.

"Furnunculus!" *Incantation.* This incantation causes boils (GF 18:298–99). In Latin, *furnus* means "an oven."

Fwooper. *Magical creature.* From *Fantastic Beasts.* Classified 3X by the MM. Fwoopers are also mentioned in *A History of Magic* (FB xi). A Fwooper is an African bird with bright feathers; its song can drive a listener insane (FB 18).
   See also Fantastic Beasts and Where to Find Them

·G·

Gadding With Ghouls. *Magical book.* Gilderoy Lockhart wrote this second-year "text-book" (CS 4:43). Hermione refers to the book when she asks Lockhart to sign the form that will allow her to check out a book in the Restricted Section of the Hogwarts Library. She plays into his vanity by complimenting him on catching the last ghoul with a tea strainer (CS 10:162). Harry wants to throw this book at Lockhart after Hagrid is taken away in Year 2, and Lockhart suspects him of causing the troubles the school has been having (CS 15:270).

Galleons. *Magical money.* Gold coins. There are 17 Sickles to a Galleon (SS 5:75). Galleons are also used as a means of communication. Hermione devises fake ones to show the date and time of the next DA meeting. Hermione's Galleons will grow hot in DA members' pockets when the information about the meetings changes (OP 19:398).
See also Money

Gallico, Paul (1897–1976). Paul Gallico is one of the authors Rowling frequently mentions in interviews as among her favorites. Gallico was born in New York City and worked as a sports journalist and editor for many years at the New York *Daily News*. He wrote fiction and articles for other periodicals such as the *Saturday Evening Post* and *Vanity Fair*. After the wide popularity of his 1941 short story "The Snow Goose," Gallico moved to Europe and wrote full time (predominantly fiction).

Rowling mentions Gallico principally in connection with his 1968 children's novel *Manxmouse*, which she read and enjoyed. The story is about a blue ceramic mouse with no tail that magically comes to life and has various adventures, including a brave quest for a confrontation with the Manx Cat, whose destiny appears to be bound with his. The subtitle of the story is *The Mouse Who Knew No Fear*. The book has long been out of print and is difficult to find.

Gambol and Japes Wizarding Joke Shop. *Magical place.* A store on Diagon Alley. This is where Fred and George Weasley buy their load of Dr. Filibuster's Fabulous Wet-Start, No-Heat Fireworks (CS 4:58).

Games in the series. *Magical games*. The witches and wizards of Hogwarts engage in many other games besides Quidditch for entertainment. For example, Ron teaches Harry to play Wizard Chess on the first Christmas holiday at the school. They play Hangman on paper, a card game called Snap, and a game like marbles called Gobstones (PA 4:50).

Gargoyles. *Magical statues*. One stone gargoyle guards the entrance to Prof. Dumbledore's office. Two talking gargoyles are located on either side of the staff room (OP 17:357).

Stone gargoyle water spouts are often found on medieval churches and cathedrals. They are frequently located at the top of exterior walls and carved in the shape of dragons' heads. The dragon comes from the legend of Garouille, a large dragon that supposedly resided in the Seine and raised havoc in Rouen. The dragon was said to have been slain in the seventh century by St. Romanus, Bishop of Rouen. Draco Malfoy's sidekick, Gregory Goyle, may be said to share brutish traits with Gargouille.

See also Statues

A gargoyle, perhaps similar to this one overlooking Paris, guards Prof. Dumbledore's office. Gargoyles are a familiar sight throughout Europe. Courtesy of Getty Images/PhotoDisc.

Garroting Gas. *Magical "substance."* To create a diversion so that Harry might communicate with Sirius Black, Ginny Weasley tells people not to go to a certain area of the school because it has been filled with Garroting Gas. It was something Fred and George had planned to do (OP 32:737). She tells students the gas is colorless, and that they cannot see it (OP 32:739).

Gaunt, Marvolo. *Character*. Voldemort's maternal grandfather. Mr. Gaunt is a Parseltongue. He and his family are the last direct decendants of Salazar Slytherin. He wears a ring that has been handed down through the Slytherin family for generations. It bears the Peverell coat of arms. Mr. Gaunt is sentenced to six months in Azkaban for attacking Ministry employees. He is violent and shabby in appearance in part because the Gaunts before him squandered their money and married their cousins (HBP 10:202–16).

A gauntlet is a protective glove. In the Middle Ages, when a knight threw his gauntlet on the ground, he was challenging another knight. If the challenge was accepted, the other knight picked up the gauntlet, and the duel was on. To "run the gauntlet" means to race between two lines of soldiers or sailors or others who hit the runner with clubs or paddles.

The Gaunts may also derive their name from their gaunt—or lean, haggard, and grim—appearance.

Gaunt, Merope. *Character.* Voldemort's mother. She is a Squib, an abused daughter made to serve like a slave for her father, Marvolo Gaunt. She wears a locket that was a Slytherin heirloom. She liked a Muggle, Tom Riddle, which did not sit well with her father (HBP 10:203–16).

In mythology Merope is part of the Pleiades cluster of stars. Merope is duller than the other stars because she married a mortal. She left her sisters in the Pleiades and can no longer be seen in the sky.

Gaunt, Morfin. *Character.* Voldemort's maternal uncle. Morfin Gaunt speaks Parsel-tongue. He is being sought by Bob Ogden for putting a hives hex on a Muggle who turns out to be Tom Riddle. Morfin is sentenced to three years in Azkaban (HBP 10:202–16). He is later stupefied by Voldemort, who steals his wand and Marvolo Gaunt's ring. After Voldemort kills his father and grandparents in Little Hangleton, he returns to Morfin and alters his memory to make him think that he committed the murders; Voldemort then returns Morfin's wand to his side. Morfin confesses to the murders and is sentenced to Azkaban (HBP 17:366–67).

Ghosts. *Characters.* Hogwarts is full of ghosts. About twenty of them glide through the back wall of the Entrance Hall in Harry's first year when he and the others are waiting to be led into the Sorting Ceremony (SS 7:115). Each student house appears to have its own ghost. Gryffindor's is Nearly Headless Nick; Hufflepuff's is the Fat Friar; Ravenclaw's (as deduced by readers) is the Grey Lady; and Slytherin's is the Bloody Baron.

Ghosts seem to function in the series as overseeing aids, companions, and advisors to the houses they inhabit. Nearly Headless Nick welcomes first-year Gryffindors at the Start-of-Term Banquet (SS 7:124). He counsels Harry after the death of Sirius Black (OP 38:859–62). The Bloody Baron can apparently keep Peeves in line, but that merely suggests that he has the same intimidation skills as his house of Slytherin. The Fat Friar is very friendly and welcomes first-years. The twenty ghosts who show up for the feast are white and transparent (SS 7:115–16). None of the ghosts at Hogwarts seem to have bad or evil intentions.

The popular fear of ghosts may come from religious beliefs that the soul leaves the body at death to live eternally in either heaven or hell. A soul, in that case, is in trouble if it is seen roaming the earth. This may explain Nick's comment that he is neither here nor there. Souls returning to earth are thought to be frightening, possibly the work of the devil. In folklore and fiction, ghosts often return to take care of unfinished business. The ghosts of Christmas Past, Present, and Future in Charles Dickens's classic novel, *A Christmas Carol*, come back to teach Ebenezer Scrooge a lesson about life. Ghosts can either take a visible form, such as an apparition, or a sensory form, such as a presence sensed through sounds, a breeze, or a particular smell that seems out of place. Contrary to widespread belief, reports of ghost sightings are not most common in graveyards, but in buildings.

In some cultures it is believed that ghosts are not here intentionally but are trapped between worlds. Mediums work to rid a house of a troublesome ghost by helping the ghost move on. Visiting ghosts are said to express many reasons for returning, including a desire to avenge their own death with the death of an enemy; relive their death; protect or warn loved ones; give advice; or reward those left alive. Superstitions about ghosts also vary by culture and location. In European folklore, for example, one should not touch a ghost; ghosts cannot pass through running water; they appear at night only; and they have distinct smells.

Gray ladies are a special kind of ghost. They frequently appear in houses and wear gray clothing. They also appear in white, brown, or black. What is most characteristic about a gray lady is that she supposedly died a violent death for the sake of a loved one, or else she died from having no love at all. When they haunt houses, gray ladies want to be reunited with their loved ones. There have been several famous accounts of gray ladies in England but they have also been reported around the world.

Thus far, the ghosts in the Harry Potter series are the friendly type, though according to Nearly Headless Nick, they may not be especially happy being "neither here nor there."

Further Reading: Guiley, Rosemary Ellen. *The Encyclopedia of Ghosts and Spirits.* New York: Facts on File, 2000.

Ghoul. *Magical being.* From *Fantastic Beasts.* Classified 2X by the MM. Ogre-like in appearance, the ghoul is not very dangerous and likes to lives in barns or attics. It eats spiders and moths. It can be removed from Muggle homes by the Ghoul Task Force, but most wizards do not bother to have them taken out of their homes (FB 18).

A ghoul lives in the attic of the Burrow, over Ron's bedroom; it is mostly an annoyance that makes noise by dropping pipes and howling when it thinks the house has gotten too quiet (CS 4:42). Another ghoul lives in an upstairs toilet at Number Twelve, Grimmauld Place (OP 6:118).

In Islamic folklore, a ghoul is a demon that eats human beings. It particularly likes travelers, children, and bodies stolen out of graves. Ghouls frequently take the form of women who feed on men whom they stalk as prey.

See also Fantastic Beasts and Where to Find Them

Ghoul Task Force. *Magical group.* From *Fantastic Beasts.* A group of wizards at the Department for the Regulation and Control of Magical Creatures at the Ministry charged with removing ghouls from Muggle dwellings (FB 18–19).

See also Fantastic Beasts and Where to Find Them

Giants. *Magical creatures.* Hagrid is a half-giant and tries to get Madame Maxime to acknowledge that she must be one also. She insists that she is simply "big boned" (GF 23:429). Ron tells Harry that giants are quite mean; they like to kill, like trolls. Giants live in the mountains. Aurors killed many giants (GF 23:430). Hermione says full-blood giants are about twenty feet tall (GF 24:434). Hagrid and Madam Olympe Maxime go to the mountains to try to enlist giants into Dumbledore's Order of the Phoenix, but they are not very successful (OP 20:422–40).

Hagrid tells Harry and friends that full-blood giants are about twenty feet tall with the tallest standing up to twenty-five feet. There are only about eighty giants left in the world. Wizards killed some, but for the most part they killed off each other. The chief of the giants is called a Gurg. The first Gurg that Hagrid and Maxime meet is named Karkus, but he is soon overtaken by another Gurg named Golgomath (OP 20:426–27, 30).

Gibbon. *Character.* Gibbon is a Death Eater who shows up at the battle of the Astronomy Tower; he sets the Death Mark in the sky at the top of the tower and is hit by a Killing Curse when he comes back down (HBP 29:618). A gibbon is an ape with long arms found in Southeast Asia.

Gifts, gift-giving. Gifts are given at Hogwarts for birthdays and Christmas. The gifts Harry receives at Hogwarts contrast strongly with those he receives from the Dursleys on Privet Drive. As of his thirteenth birthday, Harry had never received even a birthday card (PA 1:5). His new life at Hogwarts changes that.

Harry's birthday presents include: a coat hanger and a pair of Uncle Vernon's old socks for his tenth birthday (SS 3:43); a chocolate cake (SS 4:48) and Hedwig the snowy owl from Hagrid for his eleventh. For his twelfth birthday no gifts are mentioned, but for his thirteenth, he receives: from Ron, a pocket Sneakoscope and his first birthday card (PA 1:9–10); from Hermione, a card and Broomstick Servicing Kit; from Hagrid, a card and the book *The Monster Book of Monsters*. For his fourteenth birthday, he receives four birthday cakes—one each from Hagrid, Hermione, Ron, and Sirius Black (GF 3:28). For his fifteenth birthday, Harry receives an assortment of Honeydukes sweets from Ron and Hermione, as well as a card from Hermione (OP 1:8).

For Harry's first Christmas at Hogwarts, he receives: a homemade-looking wooden flute from Hagrid that sounds like an owl when he blows it; a 50 pence coin from Aunt Petunia and Uncle Dursley; an emerald-green sweater and fudge made by Mrs. Weasley; and the Invisibility Cloak from an unknown giver who turns out to be Prof. Dumbledore (SS 12:200–201).

For his second Christmas, the Dursleys send Harry a toothpick; Hagrid gives him treacle fudge; Ron gives him a book, *Flying With the Cannons*; Hermione gives him an eagle-feather quill; Mrs. Weasley gives him a card, another sweater, and a plum cake (CS 12:212).

In Year 3, Harry receives a red sweater with a Gryffindor lion on the front from Mrs. Weasley, as well as a dozen mince pies, Christmas cake, peanut brittle, and a new pair of maroon socks. He also receives his Firebolt broomstick from Sirius Black—an expensive gift, Sirius says, to make up for all the years he was in Azkaban and never gave his godson a present (PA 11:223).

Harry's Christmas presents in Year 4 include: one red sock with Quidditch brooms on it and one green sock with Golden Snitches on it, hand-knit from Dobby (who does not realize that socks come in pairs); *Quidditch Teams of Britain and Ireland* from Hermione; a bag of Dungbombs from Ron; a penknife that can unlock locks and unknot knots from Sirius Black; and a box of his favorite kinds of candy from Hagrid (Bertie Bott's Every Flavor Beans, Chocolate Frogs, Droobles Best Blowing Gum, and Fizzing Whizbees). From Mrs. Weasley he receives his usual hand-knit sweater, this one with a dragon on it to represent the Horntail he went past in the Triwizard Tournament, and an assortment of mince pies (GF 23:410).

In Year 5, Harry spends Christmas at Grimmauld Place with the Weasleys, and he receives a set of books called the *Practical Defensive Magic and Its Use Against the Dark Arts* from Sirius Black and Prof. Lupin. He receives from Hagrid a brown fur wallet with fangs that bite his hands when he tries to put money in it (rather than guarding his money against theft). He also receives a miniature model of the Firebolt broomstick from Tonks; a huge box of Bertie Bott's Beans from Ron; a sweater and mince pies from Mrs. Weasley; and a painting by Dobby (OP 23:501).

In Year 6, Harry receives a sweater from Mrs. Weasley with a Golden Snitch knitted into it, a box of Weasleys' Wizard Wheezes products, and a package of maggots from Kreacher (HBP 16:339).

Harry is not the only character in the books who receives gifts. In Year 5, Hermione receives the book *New Theory of Numerology* from Harry and an unusual-smelling perfume from Ron (OP 23:503). In the hospital, Mr. Weasley receives fuse wire and screwdrivers from Harry (OP 23:506). Ron receives a necklace from Lavender Brown that says "My Sweetheart" (HBP 16:338). Mrs. Weasley receives a blue witch's hat with twinkling stars on it and a substantial gold necklace from Fred and George (HBP 16:339).

Harry gives Ron a Keeper's glove for his seventeenth birthday on March 1 (HBP 18:389). Harry also receives two broomsticks as gifts at times other than Christmas or his birthday—he gets the Nimbus 2000 from Prof. McGonagall in Year 1, and the Firebolt in Year 5 from Sirius Black.

Gifts are also used in the series to make bargains. They are an important negotiating tool for giants. When Hagrid and Madame Maxime try to recruit giants for Dumbledore, they offer the chief a battle helmment made by goblins and a branch of Gubraithian fire; they give the second chief a roll of dragon skin (OP 20:428–30).

Giving or receiving a multitude of gifts, such as Dudley Dursley receives for his birthday in Book 1, is frowned upon in the series as excessive. However, gift-giving in terms of a meaningful gift exchange between friends and loved ones is clearly regarded as part of the ritual of friendship and family relationships in the series.

Gilderoy Lockhart's Guide to Household Pests. *Magical book.* This book is in the Burrow (CS 3:36). Although Prof. Lockhart proves to be a fraud, his book on pests is apparently useful. Mrs. Weasley consults it for getting rid of Doxies at Number Twelve, Grimmauld Place (OP 6:103).

Gillywater. *Magical substance.* Romilda Vane offers Harry some Gillywater to drink, but Hermione has already tipped him off that Romilda may have put Love Potion in it (HBP 15:308).

Gillyweed. *Magical plant.* Gillyweed is something like seaweed. Eating it allows one to breathe underwater. Dobby brings Harry some Gillyweed, and Harry uses it to help him with the second Triwizard Tournament task (GF 26:491). The weed causes the one who eats it to grow gills and long, webbed feet (GF 26:494).

Gimbi Giant-Slayers. *Magical sports team.* From QA. Quidditch team from Ethiopia; they won the All-Africa Cup twice (QA 43).

Ginger Newt. A treat Prof. McGonagall keeps in her office (OP 12:248). She keeps them in a plaid tin. After Harry punches Draco Malfoy at a Quidditch match, Prof. McGonagall slams her fist on her desk, causing her tin to fall and her Ginger Newts to spill.

"Give her hell from us, Peeves." *Expression.* Fred and George Weasley call out to Peeves as they fly over and away from Hogwarts. The scene takes place after Dolores Umbridge has taken over, and Peeves salutes the twins while the student body stands looking up at them in awe. Their call is such a strong expression of rebellion against corruption that it became a popular catch phrase among readers of the series (OP 29:675).

Gladrags Wizardwear. *Magical place.* A store advertised on the flashing board at the Quidditch World Cup. The store has locations in London, Paris, and Hogsmeade (GF

8:97). This is the store where Harry buys his reward (socks) for Dobby for helping him with the Triwizard Tournament (GF 27:520).

Glumbumble. *Magical creature.* From *Fantastic Beasts.* Classified 3X by the MM. The Glumbumble is a furry insect that flies. It can infest beehives and affect their honey. It eats nettles (FB 19).
See also Fantastic Beasts and Where to Find Them

Gnome. *Magical creature.* Classified 2X by the MM. This pest is about a foot tall. It gets into gardens in Europe and North America (FB 19). Its head is something like a potato, and it has a small body with leatherlike skin and horned feet. To de-gnome, or weed, a gnome out of the garden, one must pull it up and whirl it about one's head several times, then fling it out of the yard. This makes the gnome dizzy so it does not remember its way back to its gnomehole in the garden.

Gnomes are not the most intelligent creatures; when they hear a de-gnoming process going on, they rise to the surface to have a look, and they are, of course, plucked out of the earth more easily. Mr. Weasley thinks they are funny and is not hard enough on them. A gnome bites Harry on the finger when he helps Ron and his brothers de-gnome the Weasley garden (CS 3:36–37).

In mythology, gnomes were earth spirits that guarded quarries and mines.

Gobbledegook. *Magical language.* The language of goblins. Ludo Bagman is frustrated because they do not know English, and he only knows "Bladvak," the word for "pickax" in their language (GF 24:446).

Goblet, Black. *Magical object.* Mundungus Fletcher eyes a silver goblet engraved with the Black family crest that he claims could be polished off (for resale). Sirius Black tells him it is from the fifteenth century and was cast by goblins (OP 5:83).

Goblet of Fire. *Magical object.* At the Triwizard Tournament Feast, Prof. Dumbledore approaches a wooden chest with jewels on it, brought to him by Filch. With three taps of his wand, he opens the chest and takes out a large, roughly carved cup that is filled with blue-white flame. Students who are of age (seventeen and older) put their names in the cup as candidates to compete for their school in the Triwizard Tournament. The Goblet then shoots out one name from each school who will perform in the three tasks of the competition (GF 16:255–56). Once it has done this, its fire goes out until the next tournament (GF 16:277).

Goblin Liaison Office. *Magical office.* This office is located on the fourth floor of the Ministry and is part of the Department for the Regulation and Control of Magical Creatures (OP 7:130).

Goblins. *Magical beings.* Goblins run Gringotts Bank. Luna Lovegood tells Harry that Cornelius Fudge has had some goblins assassinated (OP 18:395). Goblins are short with large heads and long, pointy noses, ears, and fingers. Goblins are said to make quality artifacts, such as the helmet Hagrid and Madam Maxime present to the chief of the giants, and the family tiara Mrs. Weasley offers to Fleur Delacour for her wedding.

In French folklore, goblins live in grottoes but occasionally attach themselves to households where they are either helpful or a pest. A hobgoblin is a good goblin. They like houses where many children live and where there may be a good quantity of wine. They take care of children by giving them presents when they are good and punishing them when they are not. They like to do chores around the house as well. Goblins can make noise at night by banging pots and pans and raising other kinds of havoc. Sometimes they may be gotten rid of by sprinkling flaxseed on the floor. They will clean the flaxseed each night, but eventually they get tired of doing so and leave the premises for another house that is less messy.

Goblins in England and Scotland are frequently called brownies; in Russia they are called *domoviks*; in Germany they are called *kobolds*. They are said to be out and about on Halloween.

Further Reading: Guiley, Rosemary Ellen. *The Encyclopedia of Ghosts and Spirits*. New York: Facts on File, 2000.

Gobstones. *Magical game.* Gobstones is somewhat like marbles. However, when a player loses a point, the stones squeeze an odorous liquid in the player's face (PA 4:50).

Gobstones Club. *Magical student organization.* A second-year student asks if Dolores Umbridge's decree 24 disallowing student organizations applies to this, too (OP 17:352).

Godric's Hollow. *Muggle place.* The location of James and Lily Potter's house; this is where they were murdered (SS 1:12). Harry says that he will go back there in order to explore his roots and visit his parents' graves. Ron tells him that he and Hermione will go to Privet Drive and Godric's Hollow with him (HBP 30:650–51).

Golden egg. *Magical object.* The champions of the Triwizard Tournament needed to pick this up and get past a dragon for the first task; there is a clue inside the egg about what the second task will be; the egg is heavy (GF 21:365).

Golden Snitch. *Magical sports equipment.* The Golden Snitch was invented by Bowman Wright of Godric's Hollow. It is the size of a walnut and the weight of a Snidget bird. It has wings that move it in all directions (QA 14–15). The team whose Seeker catches it gets 150 points added to its score, and the game ends. As Gryffindor Seeker, Harry has many glorious, as well as dangerous, moments flying after and catching the Golden Snitch.

Golden watch. *Magical object.* Prof. Dumbledore's watch has twelve hands with no numbers. There are small planets turning around the outside edge (S 1:12).

Goldstein, Anthony. *Character.* Ravenclaw classmate in Harry's year; he is made boy prefect of his house in fifth year (OP 10:189). He likes the idea of Harry teaching Defense Against the Dark Arts (OP 16:339). Goldstein takes his practical Charm O.W.L. exam at the same time as Hermione (OP 31:713). He is one of the DA members who defends Harry against Draco Malfoy, Vincent Crabbe, and Gregory Goyle during the ride home on the Hogwarts Express after Year 5 (OP 38:864).

Golgomath. *Character.* The second giant chief Hagrid meets in his efforts to negotiate for Dumbledore (OP 20:430).

Golpalott's Third Law. *Magical property.* This principle states that an antidote to a mixed poison will equal more than the sum of its components (HBP 18:374).

Gordon. *Character.* One of Dudley Dursley's gang (SS 3:31; OP 1:12).

Gorodok Gargoyles. *Magical sports team.* From QA. A professional Quidditch team from Lithuania (QA 45).
    See also Quidditch Through the Ages

Goudge, Elizabeth (1900–1984). When interviewers ask Rowling which authors were her favorites as a child, she invariably mentions British fantasy author Elizabeth Goudge, and, in particular, her novel *The Little White Horse* (1946). Rowling claims that this book, more than any other she has read, had the greatest influence on her writing of Harry Potter.
    The Little White Horse is about a plain, red-haired orphan girl, Maria Merryweather, who finds out that she has a special place in a magical world about which she was previously unaware. She is rescued from her dull life and taken to the West Country. There she is led through a door in a rock to a tunnel and out to a magical kingdom. At the castle, she discovers that she is the princess of Moonacre Valley. All of the people she runs into already know who she is. If the plot sounds familiar to readers of Harry Potter, so will other devices such as Goudge's detailed descriptions of food at feasts. She also uses interesting names such as "Marmaduke Scarlet"; and animals that have special gifts, such as the dog Wrolf that turns out to be a lion that protects Maria.
    In a November 2002 interview in *The Scotsman*, Rowling said of *The Little White Horse*, "It is a very well-constructed and clever book and the more you read it, the cleverer it appears."

Goyle, Gregory. *Character.* One of Draco Malfoy's croneys at Hogwarts. Draco introduces him to Harry on the Hogwarts Express (SS 6:108). He is described as having long, thick arms and a brushcut (PA 5:80). There is a Death Eater named Goyle at Voldemort's rising at the Little Hangleton graveyard (GF 33:651). The young Gregory Goyle is a Slytherin Beater in fifth year (OP 19:405). He is called at the same time as Hermione to do his practical Charm O.W.L. exam (OP 31:713). He is in the train compartment with Draco when Harry spies on him with his Invisibility Cloak and gets caught (HBP 7:149–54). In Year 6, Draco gives him Polyjuice Potion and turns him into an eleven-year-old girl who stands watch outside the Room of Requirement (somewhat like the gargoyles that guard the staff room) (HBP 21:464).
    See also Gargoyles

Grandfather clock. *Magical object.* Harry enjoys this Weasley clock at the Burrow. It contains nine hands that represent each of the Weasleys. Around its face are places they might normally be found, such as home, school, and work, as well as more unusual circumstances such as traveling, lost, hospital, prison, and mortal danger (GF 10:151).

GrandPré, Mary. *See* Illustrations

Granger, Hermione. *Character.* (Pronounced Her-MY-oh-NEE.) The reader first meets young Hermione when she tries to help Neville Longbottom find his toad and ends up in Harry's and Ron's compartment on the Hogwarts Express in Year 1 (SS 6:105). She is described as having bushy brown hair, a bossy-sounding voice, and big front teeth. She is an overeager student and already wears her new robes when she meets Ron and Harry on the train. She watches Ron fail at casting a spell on his rat Scabbers in an attempt to turn it yellow. She tells Ron and Harry that she was surprised to get her invitation letter to Hogwarts because her parents are not magical. She has since read and memorized all of Hogwarts' textbooks, along with some other books for background, and has practiced doing spells, which have all worked out pretty well so far. She introduces herself to the boys, giving them all of this information very quickly (SS 6:105–106). During the Sorting Ceremony, she is quickly sorted into Gryffindor House after eagerly putting the Sorting Hat on her head (SS 7:120). Her birthday is in September (PA 4:57).

One of the first charms Hermione creates on her own involves lighting a bright blue fire in a jar to keep herself, Ron, and Harry warm (SS 11:181). She uses this same skill in lighting Snape's robes on fire during Harry's first Quidditch match. After the incident with the troll in the girls' bathroom, Hermione begins checking Ron's and Harry's homework for them, though she refuses to do the work for them (SS 11:182)—she does not approve of copying (PA 8:146). Prof. Flitwick tells her in secret at the end of the first year that she received a 112 on her Charms exam (SS 16:271). In fact, Hermione receives the best grades of all of the students in her year (SS 17:307).

Hermione is petrified in Year 2 (CS 14:257). At the beginning of Year 3, Hermione has a meeting with Prof. McGonagall. Readers later learn that this must have been when she received special permission to take classes that meet at the same time, using the Time-Turner to help her do it (PA 5:90). Like Harry and Ron, Hermione feels repulsion for Draco Malfoy. Her disgust seems to reach a climax when she slaps him for calling Hagrid a pathetic Care of Magical Creatures teacher (PA 15:293). Her courseload becomes so heavy in Year 3 that she ends up dropping Divination class when Prof. Trelawney tells her that she is "hopelessly mundane" (PA 15:298).

In order to deal with the difficulty some readers have in pronouncing Hermione's name, Rowling has her explain the pronunciation to a character in *Goblet of Fire*. Viktor

Hermione is clever, adept at magic, and a steadfast friend. Shown from left: Ron Weasley (Rupert Grint), Hermione Granger (Emma Watson), and Harry Potter (Daniel Radcliffe) in *Harry Potter and the Prisoner of Azkaban* (2004). Courtesy of Warner Bros./Photofest.

Krum pronounces her name "Hermy-own," and she corrects him, "Her-my-oh-nee" (GF 23:418–19). He has not yet learned it when he speaks to Harry about her and pronounces her name "Hermy-own-ninny" (GF 28:552). Hermione is made prefect of Gryffindor in her fifth year. She receives her letter announcing this at Grimmauld Place (OP 9:162). That same year, she begins making hats for the house-elves over the summer, knitting them without magic and then making them magically at Hogwarts. She leaves them out in the Common Room for the elves to take (OP 13:255). Terry Boot asks her why she was sorted into Gryffindor and not into Ravenclaw since she is so smart. She says that the Sorting Hat did consider her intelligence, but then put her in Gryffindor (OP 19:399). For the Christmas holiday in fifth year, she goes skiing with her parents (OP 21:451).

Rowling has said in interviews that Hermione's character is based on herself at Hermione's age. She tended to be booksmart, but took less time to develop friendships than Hermione. She has also admitted that the name Hermione comes from the strong female protagonist in Shakespeare's play *The Winter's Tale*.

See also Shakespeare, William

Granger, Mr. and Mrs. *Characters.* Hermione's Muggle parents; they are both dentists (SS 12:199). Mr. Weasley is especially pleased to make their acquaintance on Diagon Alley (CS 4:57).

Granian horses. *Magical creatures.* From *Fantastic Beasts*. Winged horses that are gray in color and plump in stature (FB 42).
See also Fantastic Beasts and Where to Find Them; Winged horse

Graphorn. *Magical creature.* From *Fantastic Beasts*. Classified 4X by the MM. A purple creature with a hump on its back. Trolls sometimes ride Graphorns. Their powdered horns are an expensive but useful ingredient in some potions (FB 19–20).
See also Fantastic Beasts and Where to Find Them

Graveyard. *Magical place.* Harry and Cedric are transported by Portkey to this place where Voldemort is waiting. The Portkey is the Triwizard Cup which they touch at the same time in the center of the hedge maze (GF 31/32:635–36). The graveyard in Little Hangleton is overgrown and has a church behind a large yew tree (GF 32:636). Tom Riddle's house is visible on top of a hill (GF 33:646). Almost immediately after they arrive, on Voldemort's order, Wormtail runs up and kills Cedric Diggory with the Killing Curse. Harry is pulled along and thrown against a marble headstone that is marked "Tom Riddle" (GF 32:638).

Grawp. *Character.* Hagrid's giant half-brother; they share the same mother. Hagrid found Grawp in the mountains and brought him back to Hogwarts. Hagrid tries to teach him English. Grawp is sixteen feet tall—small for a giant—so Hagrid suspects that is why his mother left Grawp behind, just as she did Hagrid (OP 30:691). Grawp is violent and catches his own food, which includes birds and deer (OP 30:693). Firenze has tried to warn Hagrid that his efforts at training Grawp are not working, but Hagrid insists on keeping him in the Forbidden Forest (OP 30:693). Hagrid asks Harry and Hermione to visit Grawp and to keep trying to teach him English if Hagrid gets sent away by Dolores Umbridge (which everyone expects will happen) (OP 30:694). Grawp comes to the rescue when Harry, Hermione, and Umbridge run into the centaurs in the Forbidden

Forest (OP 33:158–59). At the end of Year 5, Hagrid tells Harry and friends that Grawp has calmed down quite a bit (OP 38:854). He tells them in Book 6 that Grawp has moved to the mountains to a cave prepared for him by Dumbledore, where Grawp is much more content (HBP 8:170).

Gray Centaur. *Magical creature.* Hermione is held by the Gray Centaur when she leads Dolores Umbridge out to the Forbidden Forest in a ruse to escape her. Hermione is not saved from the centaur until Grawp comes on the scene (OP 33:756–57).

The Great Hall. *Magical place.* The main dining room and gathering room at Hogwarts. Harry first sees the Great Hall during the Sorting Ceremony at the start of his first year. Thousands of candles are suspended in midair over long tables where hundreds of students sit. There is a High Table at the front of the room where the headmaster and faculty members sit. The black ceiling has stars on it, as though open to the night sky. Golden plates and goblets line the tables (SS 7:114).

The night Beauxbatons and Durmstrang arrive at Hogwarts, the Great Hall is decorated with the silk banners of each of the four houses: red and gold with a lion (Gryffindor); blue with a bronze eagle (Ravenclaw); yellow with a black badger (Hufflepuff); and green with a silver snake (Slytherin). Behind the High Table hangs a banner with the Hogwarts coat of arms—a large "H" with a lion, an eagle, a badger, and a snake around it (GF 15:237).

Yule Ball decorations include everlasting icicles, lighted holly berries, and gold owls. The suits of armor sing carols (GF 22:395).

See also Hogwarts School of Witchcraft and Wizardry

Great Hangleton. *Magical place.* Great Hangleton is the next town over from Little Hangleton, where the Riddles lived and where Frank Bryce was questioned at the police station for the murder of the Riddles (GF 1:3).

The Great Humberto. *Muggle television program.* This is the television program Dudley Dursley wants to watch when his father keeps the Dursley family away from home; Mr. Dursley wants to escape the letters coming from Hogwarts for Harry (SS 3:43).

Great Wizards of the Twentieth Century. *Magical book.* Harry and friends go searching for information about Nicolas Flamel in this book (SS 12:197).

"Gred and Forge." *Magical nicknames.* Fred and George Weasley play with the idea of interchanging their names; the idea comes up in speaking about their mother's habit of making them sweaters with their initials each Christmas (SS 12:202).

Greece. From QA. "Dangerous" Dai Llewellyn was eaten by a Chimera during his vacation in Mykonos (QA 33).

Greek chappie. *Character.* Hagrid bought Fluffy from a person in a pub; Hagrid describes this person as a "Greek chappie" (SS 11:192).

Green light, flashing. *Magical phenomenon.* Harry sees this blinding light several times in the series as he starts to remember Voldemort killing his parents (SS 4:56).

Greengrass, Daphne. *Character.* Daphne Greengrass is called to do her practical Charm O.W.L. exam at the same time as Hermione (OP 31:713).

Greenhouse One. *Magical place.* Greenhouse One is where Prof. Sprout's Herbology class is held at Hogwarts. Less dangerous plants are grown in this greenhouse (CS 6:90).

Greenhouse Three. *Magical place.* Mandrakes and other dangerous plants are grown in Greenhouse Three at Hogwarts. Harry's Herbology class is held here at the beginning of Year 2; the class usually meets in Greenhouse One. Greenhouse Three has huge umbrella-shaped plants hanging from the ceiling (CS 6:90).

Gregory the Swarmy. *Magical statue.* During their first week at Hogwarts, Fred and George Weasley found a secret passageway behind this statue in the east wing (SS 9:153). They tell Ron to go there in Year 5 so that Harry can try to talk to Sirius in the fire (OP 29:659).

Grenouille. *Character.* Grenouille is a character in a play written by French playwright Malecrit. The play is titled *Hélas, Je me suis Transfiguré Les Pieds* ("Alas, I've Transfigured My Feet") (QA 39).

Greyback, Fenrir. *Character.* When Bellatrix Lestrange charges that Snape did not look for Voldemort when he disappeared, Snape counters that neither did other Death Eaters, such as Greyback (HBP 2:26). Draco Malfoy tells Mr. Borgin that Greyback is a friend of his family (HBP 6:125). Prof. Lupin tells Harry that Greyback is one of the most dangerous werewolves alive; Greyback is the one who bit Lupin (HBP 16:334–35). It is said that Greyback is the one who attacked the little Montgomery boy and killed him; he especially likes attacking children (HBP 22:473). Greyback has blood on his face and teeth when he appears at the Astronomy Tower battle. He tells Dumbledore that he could not resist the opportunity to come to Hogwarts where there are so many children. He says that he has taken on a taste for flesh that needs to be satisfied more than once a month (HBP 27:593).

Griffin. *Magical creature.* From *Fantastic Beasts.* Classified 4X by the MM. These creatures have the head and front legs of an eagle and the body and hind legs of a lion. They like raw meat and often guard treasure for wizards (FB 20).
See also Fantastic Beasts and Where to Find Them

Griffiths, Glynnis. *Character.* From QA. A Seeker on the Holyhead Harpies professional Quidditch team who finally caught the Snitch at the end of a game that lasted seven days (QA 34).
See also Quidditch Through the Ages

Grim. *Magical sign.* An omen of death that Prof. Trelawney sees while reading Harry's tea leaves in Divination class. She tells him that the Grim is a giant dog that hangs around graveyards (PA 6:107). She sees it again when she looks in the crystal ball (PA 15:298).

Grimmauld Place, Number Twelve. *See* Number Twelve, Grimmauld Place

Grimstone, Elias. *Character.* From QA. Inventor of the Oakshaft 79 broomstick in 1879; he lived in Portsmouth (QA 47).
See also Oakshaft 79; *Quidditch Through the Ages*

Grindelwald. *Character.* The dark wizard defeated by Dumbledore in 1945 (SS 6:103). The year 1945 coincides with the end of World War II, an event and time frame that Rowling has said she kept in mind in writing the series. Grendel was a monster killed by Beowulf in the Anglo-Saxon tale *Beowulf*.

Grindylow. *Magical creature.* From *Fantastic Beasts.* Classified 2X by the MM. These are water creatures that eat fish and menace humans and merpeople. Their long fingers are easily broken (FB 20).
Lupin tells Harry when his friends are at Hogsmeade to come look at his new shipment of Grindylow. They are green and their long fingers like to grip. Like Kappas, they live in water (PA 8:153–54). They are part of Prof. Lupin's DADA final exam in Year 3 (PA 16:318). Mad-Eye Moody makes sure that the students have gone over Grindylows in DADA class before he teaches them the Unforgivable Curses (GF 14:211). Harry sees Grindylows in the lake during the second Triwizard Tournament task (GF 26:495).
See also Fantastic Beasts and Where to Find Them

Gringotts. *Magical place.* The wizard bank. It is run by goblins, and Hagrid tells Harry that it is the safest place to keep anything. The bank is located hundreds of miles beneath the city of London on Diagon Alley. Dragons guard the vaults with the highest security (SS 5:63–64). Hagrid goes there with Harry to retrieve the "You-Know-What" (Philosopher's/Sorcerer's Stone) for Prof. Dumbledore out of Vault 713 (SS 5:73, 74–75). Harry has money in this bank that was left to him by his parents. Dumbledore tells readers of *Fantastic Beasts* that if they wish to make a further donation to Comic Relief, U.K., they may take their money to this bank and ask for Griphook (FB viii).
See also Goblins

Griphook. *Character.* A goblin who works at Gringotts (SS 5:73). If readers wish to make a further donation to Comic Relief, U.K., Dumbledore advises them (in the foreword to *Fantastic Beasts*) to take their money to Gringotts and ask for Griphook (FB viii).

Grodzisk Goblins. *Magical sports team.* From QA. Professional Quidditch team from Poland; Josef Wronski was their Seeker (QA 41).
See also Quidditch Through the Ages

Grow-Your-Own-Warts kit. *Magical object.* Harry receives this kit in his Wizard Crackers at Christmas in Year 1 (SS 12:204).

Growth Charm. *Magical spell.* Harry mixes up the incantation for the Growth Charm with the Color-Change Charm in his practical Charm O.W.L. (OP 31:713).

Grubbly-Plank, Prof. Wilhelmina. *Character.* Prof. Grubbly-Plank is a substitute teacher for Hagrid's Care of Magical Creatures class. She is an old witch with short gray hair and a protruding chin. She gives her students one of their best lessons ever, in unicorns (GF 24:435–36). She is still teaching the class at the beginning of Year 5 (OP 10:196). She tells Dolores Umbridge during her evaluation that Dumbledore initially sent her an owl asking if she would teach for two weeks (OP 15:322–23). She examines Hedwig for Harry in the staff room when the owl is injured (OP 17:358–59).

Grubs, giant. *Magical creatures.* Hagrid feeds these to Aragog (HBP 11:230).

Grunnings. *Muggle place.* The drill-making firm where Harry's Uncle Vernon Dursley works as director (SS 1:1). *Grunnio* is Latin for "to grunt like a pig."

Grunnion, Alberic. *Character.* One of the figures on the Famous Witches and Wizards Cards found in Chocolate Frogs (SS 6:103).
See also Chocolate Frogs

Gryffindor, Godric. *Character.* The founder of Gryffindor House at Hogwarts. Harry fights the Basilisk in the Chamber of Secrets with his sword, given to him by Fawkes with the Sorting Hat. Prof. Dumbledore tells Harry that he need not worry that the hat once tried to sort him into Slytherin House; only a true Gryffindor would have been given the sword to use when in trouble (CS 18:333).

Gryffindor House. *Magical school organization.* One of the four student resident houses at Hogwarts. It was founded by Godric Gryffindor, and its current head is Prof. Minerva McGonagall, who teaches Transfiguration. Its ghost is Nearly Headless Nick. The house's students are characterized by courage and loyalty. The house colors are red and gold; its emblem is a gold lion on a red shield. Quidditch robes are red. The entrance to Gryffindor Tower is on the seventh floor of the castle. The common room is circular and filled with cushioned armchairs. The bedroom quarters at the top of the spiral staircase in Gryffindor House contain five four-poster beds with heavy red velvet curtains around them (SS 7:130).
    Since this is Harry Potter's house, most of the major characters in the series come from Gryffindor. Some of them are: Hermione Granger; all of the Weasleys; Neville Longbottom; Lavender Brown; Oliver Wood; Dean Thomas; and Seamus Finnigan, among others.
See also Hogwarts School of Witchcraft and Wizardry

Gryffindor Quidditch Team. *Magical sports team.* In Year 3, at the Gryffindor-Slytherin match, Lee Jordan commentates and says that this year's Gryffindor team is one of the best in some time. The team that year consisted of Harry Potter, Katie Bell, Angelina Johnson, Alicia Spinnet, Fred Weasley, George Weasley, and Oliver Wood (PA 15:305).

Gubraithian fire. *Magical fire.* Hagrid gives this everlasting fire to a giant chief in his effort to negotiate with him for Dumbledore (OP 20:430).

Gudgeon, Davey. *Character.* Davey Gudgeon was a student at Hogwarts during Lupin's days as a Hogwarts student. The year the Whomping Willow was planted, Davey Gudgeon tried to touch the trunk and almost lost an eye. Ever since, students have been forbidden to go near the tree (PA 10:186).

Gudgeon, Gladys. *Character.* Gladys Gudgeon is a big fan of Gilderoy Lockhart. During his detention in Year 2, Harry has to address Lockhart's response to Gladys's fan mail (CS 7:120). At St. Mungo's, where Lockhart is institutionalized, Lockhart insists that she still writes to him each week (OP 23:511).

A Guide to Advanced Transfiguration. *Magical book.* This book falls out of Cedric Diggory's bag when Harry stops him to tell him about the dragons in the first task of the Triwizard Tournament (GF 20:340).

A Guide to Medieval Sorcery. *Magical book.* Harry and friends consult this book to prepare him for the second task of the Triwizard Tournament, but they find nothing of use in it (GF 26:488).

Guidelines for the Treatment of Non-Wizard Part-Humans. *Magical guidelines.* Rita Skeeter writes an article about the Ministry's involvement in the World Cup incident. Percy Weasley complains about her article and cites this document (GF 10:147).

Gulping Plimpies. *See* Gurdyroot

Gum shield. *Magical spell.* A spell that protects the gums (HBP 14:279).

Gun. A gun is described in the magical world as a type of metal wand that Muggles use to kill one another (PA 3:38).

Gunhilda. *Character.* From QA. A relative, perhaps the wife, of Goodwin Kneen; she is sick with dragon pox when he writes his cousin Olaf about a "Kwidditch" game (QA 8–10).
   See also Kneen, Goodwin; *Quidditch Through the Ages*

Gurdyroot. *Magical plant.* Gurdyroot looks something like an onion; Luna Lovegood has some Gurdyroot and gives some to Ron when he asks. She says they are helpful in keeping away Gulping Plimpies (HBP 20:425).

Gurg. *Magical being.* The chief of a tribe of giants is called a Gurg (OP 20:427). *Gurges* in Latin means "abyss."

Gwenog. *Character.* From QA. Gertie Keddle has a record of this witch in her diary. Gwenog visited Gertie to have some nettle tea and to watch players at Queerditch Marsh. Gwenog told Gertie that she often played Quidditch herself (QA 7–8).
   See also *Quidditch Through the Ages*

· H ·

Hag. *Magical being.* Harry thinks he sees a hag order a dish of raw liver at the Leaky Cauldron during his stay there before Year 3 (PA 4:49). A dish popular in Scotland called "hag's dish" is made of organ meats. In Old Norse folklore, priestesses lived in *hagi*, or a "sacred grove." *Haggen* means "to chop to pieces."

In Greek mythology, Hecate is most like a hag and is the goddess of witchcraft and crossroads. A hag is generally thought to be an old and ugly witch.

"Hagger." *Nickname.* This is the way Grawp pronounces Hagrid's name (OP 33:758).

Hagrid, Rubeus. *Character.* The name comes from an Old English word, *hagridden*, which means "to have had a bad night." Rowling has said that Hagrid likes to drink and has had a bad night or two in his time. This half-giant is one of the most likeable characters in the series. Hagrid is twice as tall as a normal man and three times as wide (OP 20:421). Readers meet him when he brings infant Harry Potter to Privet Drive on Prof. Dumbledore's orders. He arrives on a motorcycle he borrowed from young Sirius Black. Hagrid is very loyal to Dumbledore, who says he would trust the giant with his life (SS 1:14). Hagrid is Keeper of Keys and Grounds at Hogwarts (SS 4:48).

It is Hagrid who first informs Harry that he is a wizard (SS 4:50). Though he was expelled in his third year at Hogwarts, Dumbledore allowed Hagrid to stay on as Keeper of Keys and Grounds (SS 4:59). Hagrid's possessions include a crossbow and galoshes as well as a copper kettle and a large bed covered with a patchwork quilt (SS 8:140). He often wears a moleskin coat and balaclava (CS 11:201). Hagrid has Dumbledore's full trust (CS 14:261).

Harry and Ron find out after they visit Aragog in the Forbidden Forest that Hagrid is innocent of opening the Chamber fifty years ago (CS 15:281). Hagrid always wanted to teach Care of Magical Creatures, and Dumbledore gives him his chance after Prof. Kettleburn's retirement in Harry's third year (PA 5:94).

In the overheard conversation between Hagrid and Madam Maxime, readers learn (along with Harry) quite a bit of Hagrid's background. His mother was one of the last giants in Britain; his father was a small wizard. Hagrid's mother left her family, as giants tend to do, and Hagrid was raised by his father (GF 23:427–28). Rita Skeeter writes in her article that Hagrid's mother is Fridwulfa. Fridwulfa remains missing because she was not caught years ago among the giants who were working for the Dark Side (GF 24:439).

Hagrid tells Harry that he reminds him of himself because his mother ran away and his father died; Hagrid was taken in at Hogwarts by Dumbledore, just like Harry (GF 24:456). Hagrid and Harry are both orphans, so to speak, who originally came from good families (OP 25:563–64). Hagrid was a member of the original Order of the Phoenix (OP 9:174).

Perhaps not surprisingly, Dolores Umbridge puts Hagrid on probation (OP 25:549). When Umbridge fires him, he is ambushed at night by Dawlish and others, but he is not stunned because his giant blood makes him immune. Hagrid takes Fang and runs away (OP 31:722). Harry finds him back in his hut after the battle at the Hall of Prophecy (OP 38:853). After Dumbledore's death, Prof. McGonagall consults Hagrid's opinion in deciding whether or not to keep Hog-

Robbie Coltrane as Hagrid in *Harry Potter and the Prisoner of Azkaban* (2004). Courtesy of Warner Bros./Photofest.

warts open or whether to refer the matter to the board of governors (HBP 29:628). Hagrid serves as the one and only pall bearer at Dumbledore's funeral. Hagrid carries Dumbledore's covered body in his arms to the table where the tomb will appear (HBP 30:643).

Hagrid's flute. *Magical object.* The homemade wooden flute that Hagrid made for Harry for Christmas in Year 1. Harry plays the flute to make Fluffy fall asleep so that he and his friends can find the Sorcerer's Stone (SS 16:274).

Hagrid's hut. *Magical place.* Hagrid's home. It is a small wooden house on the edge of the Forbidden Forest that faces Hogwarts Castle. It has only one room (SS 8:140).

Haileybury Hammers. *Magical sports team.* From QA. Quidditch team from Canada (QA 43).
See also Quidditch Through the Ages

Hair-Raising Potion. *Magical substance.* One ingredient in Hair-Raising Potion is rats' tails (CS 13:228).

Hair-Thickening Charm. *Magical spell.* Snape says Alicia Spinnet must have had this spell put on her to make her eyebrows grow so thick and long that she cannot see. Fourteen witnesses tell Snape that Miles Bletchley, the Slytherin Keeper, put a jinx on Alicia in the library (OP 19:400).

Hairy Snout, Human Heart. *Magical book.* From *Fantastic Beasts*. This book was written by an anonymous author and was published in 1975 by Whizz Hard Books. The book tells the story of a werewolf's struggle of constantly transitioning back and forth between being a warm and caring human being and a cold, killing animal (FB 41).

See also Fantastic Beasts and Where to Find Them; Werewolf

Half-Blood Prince. *Character.* For much of Half-Blood Prince, the identity of the owner of this name is unknown. He or she used Harry's copy of the Potions textbook, *Advance Potion-Making*, and inserted handwritten directions alongside the recipes. These directions explain how to make the potions better and more quickly (HBP 9:193). Just before Snape Apparates, he tells Harry that he is the Half-Blood Prince (HBP 28:604).

Hall of Prophecy. *Magical place.* The area at the Ministry in the Department of Mysteries where the Prophecy is kept (OP 35:789; HBP 4:78).

Halloween. *Magical event.* Hagrid tells Harry that Voldemort killed his parents on Halloween when Harry was one year old (SS 4:55). As might be expected, Halloween is a day of celebration at a school of witchcraft and wizardry. The Great Hall is decorated with a thousand bats and pumpkins with candles (SS 10:172). Harry, Ron, and Hermione miss the festivities in Year 2, when they are invited to Nearly Headless Nick's Death Day Party. The arrangements in the Great Hall include live bats, dancing skeletons scheduled by Dumbledore, and Hagrid's mammoth pumpkins carved into lit-up lanterns (CS 8:131).

All Hallow's Eve occurs the night before All Saints' Day, November 1, which is a Christian holiday when saints are remembered and celebrated; All Souls' Day falls on November 2 and is the day when all the deceased are remembered. The customs that American children, in particular, practice on Halloween night evolved over time. They began in the Middle Ages as pagan celebrations through Christian church congregations. The celebrations took place in Europe and beyond. In the mid-1800s, Irish immigrants brought to America some of the Halloween traditions known to Americans today.

The ancient Celts celebrated New Year's around November 1, which they marked as the end of summer. In Ireland the festival was called *Samhein* or *La Samon*, for "Festival of the Sun." In Scotland, it was called *Hallowe'en*. Halloween was thought to be the night when the veil between the living and the dead is the thinnest. As the last harvest of the year took place, the dead were believed to rise and raise havoc on fields and in homes. At the darkest hour of night, the Lord of the Dead was thought to call together all souls and send them back to their rightful places. The Celts made offerings to the Lord of the Dead on behalf of the lost souls, and they wore disguises so that the souls would pass them by. Bonfires were lit to honor the sun god who was leaving his prime time of the year.

Christianity made use of the pagan practices as a way to help spread their own. The church encouraged praying for the lost souls. Cakes were given out to the poor who prayed for the dead. Masquerading was allowed as a tribute to saints, not to ward off evil spirits. In Ireland, poor people went door to door collecting cakes. They frequently carried lanterns made out of hollowed-out gourds and turnips with candles inside of them. These were called jack-o-lanterns. Over time, young men and boys began a musical tradition called "souling songs." They went door to door singing in trade for food and ale.

Popular Halloween practices in the United States were influenced by Irish immigrants, but also by Day of the Dead rituals from Mexico and other immigrant traditions. Halloween parties, costumes, trick-or-treating, and ghost stories all have roots in centuries-old traditions that were practiced at the same time of the year as Halloween.

Further Reading: Guiley, Rosemary Ellen. *The Encyclopedia of Witches and Witchcraft,* 2nd ed. New York: Facts on File, 1999.

The Hand of Glory. *Magical object.* In Borgin and Burkes in Knockturn Alley, there is a shriveled hand on a cushion that gives light only to the holder if one puts a candle into the hand. Draco Malfoy asks his father if he can have it (CS 4:52). In British folklore, the fingers of the Hand of Glory light up like candles and put a house's occupants to sleep, giving burglars the opportunity to rob a house without being detected (HBP 7:129). Ginny Weasley says Draco Malfoy carried the hand out of the Room of Requirement the night Dumbledore died (HBP 29:618).

In folklore, the Hand of Glory was the severed hand of a murderer who had been hanged. The right arm would be cut off while the corpse was still hanging, or perhaps at an eclipse of the moon. The arm was wrapped in a shroud, the blood squeezed out of it, and then it was pickled for two weeks in an earthen jar with salt, long peppers, and saltpeter. Then it was dried in an oven with vervain, an herb that was thought to repel demons. Candles were inserted between the fingers, or sometimes the arm was preserved in wax, and the fingers themselves were lit as candles.

It was thought that the Hand of Glory helped burglars break into dwellings and businesses, but it had additional powers as well. If the thumb did not burn, it was believed that someone in the house was not sleeping and could not be influenced by charms. According to folklore, once the hand was lit, the only thing that could extinguish the flame was milk. Counterjinxes to ward off the hand's power included screech-owl blood and the bile of black cats smeared on thresholds.

Further Reading: Guiley, Rosemary Ellen. *The Encyclopedia of Ghosts and Spirits.* New York: Facts on File, 2000.

Handbook of Do-It-Yourself Broomcare. *Magical book.* This book comes with the Broomstick Servicing Kit that Hermione gives Harry for his thirteenth birthday (PA 1:12).

Handbook of Hippogriff Psychology. *Magical book.* Ron reads this book in his efforts to help Hagrid with Buckbeak's appeal before the Ministry (PA 15:300).

The Hanged Man. *Magical place.* The pub in Little Hangleton (GF 1:2).

Hangman. Ron and Harry play this game instead of taking notes in their History of Magic class (OP 12:229).

Hangman's Rope. *Magical object.* A rope in Borgin and Burke's that bears a sign saying that it has killed nineteen Muggles who have owned it so far (CS 4:52).

Harkiss, Ciceron. *Character.* A former student of Prof. Slughorn's. The professor claims that Ciceron Harkiss gave Ambrosius Flume his job at Honeydukes after being introduced to Ambrosius by Slughorn (HBP 4:71).

Harp. *Magical object.* A harp plays constantly to keep Fluffy asleep while guarding the Sorcerer's Stone (SS 16:275). A harp, not a shamrock, is the national symbol of Ireland.
    See also Fluffy

Harper. *Character.* Harper is a Seeker on the Slytherin Quidditch team in Year 6 (HBP 14:295).

Harpo the Foul. *Character.* From *Fantastic Beasts.* A Greek Dark wizard and Parselmouth who first bred a Basilisk (FB 3).
    See also Fantastic Beasts and Where to Find Them

Harris, Warty. *Character.* Mundungus Fletcher talks about his business colleague, Will, stealing goods from Warty Harris (OP 5:86).

Harry Hunting. *Muggle activity.* Dudley Dursley's favorite sport—getting his gang to pile up on his cousin, Harry Potter (SS 3:31).

Harry Potter and the Chamber of Secrets. *Book 2.* The second novel in the series was first published in the U.K. by Bloomsbury in 1998, and in the United States by Scholastic in 1999. It is approximately 85,000 words long and contains eighteen chapters. The book is dedicated to Rowling's friend from high school, Seán P. F. Harris, who owned a Ford Anglia in which he used to take her for rides. Principle settings in the novel include: Number Four, Privet Drive; the Burrow; Diagon Alley; Mr. Weasley's Ford Anglia; and Hogwarts School of Witchcraft and Wizardry. Major characters newly introduced in *Chamber of Secrets* include: Dobby the house-elf; Gilderoy Lockhart, the new DADA teacher; Moaning Myrtle; and Cornelius Fudge, the Minister of Magic. Ginny Weasley's character is developed as a first-year student at Hogwarts. Creatures that play an important role include Aragog the giant spider, and the Basilisk in the Chamber of Secrets. Principle magical substances or objects important to the plot of *Chamber of Secrets* include the Polyjuice Potion and Tom Riddle's diary.

Plot Summary Harry spends his twelfth birthday at the Dursleys, staying out of sight in his room, while the Dursleys entertain Mr. and Mrs. Mason. The Masons are there for a dinner party that Vernon hopes will result in a large order for Grunnings' drills. Dobby the house-elf arrives in Harry's room making a ruckus when Harry is supposed to be quiet for the party. Dobby warns Harry not to return to Hogwarts; it is too dangerous for him. Dobby makes a dessert fall on Mrs. Mason's head, and Harry is confined to his room, but he is rescued by the Weasleys. Fred, George, and Ron come to get him in their father's flying Ford Anglia, and Harry escapes out the window with his Hogwarts belongings.

Harry visits the Burrow for the first time, where he sees his first wizarding residence and experiences the warm life that Ron enjoys with his large family. On Diagon Alley, Harry and friends meet Gilderoy Lockhart and Lucius Malfoy and have memorable encounters with both. Lockhart poses with Harry for a picture for the *Daily Prophet*, and

Lucius has a run-in with Arthur Weasley. Harry and Ron cannot get through the barrier to Platform 9¾, so they take the Ford Anglia to Hogwarts, where it crashes into the Whomping Willow. They get detention for their means of arrival, though they are celebrated throughout the school by their classmates. Lockhart, who is the new DADA teacher, keeps talking to Harry about how he could better handle his fame.

It turns out that Draco Malfoy's father has purchased new racing brooms for the entire Slytherin Quidditch team, in return for making Draco the Seeker on the team. Harry catches the Snitch in the game against Slytherin, but not without suffering a broken arm. Lockhart puts a spell on the arm that dissolves all of the bones rather than mending them, and Harry must go to the hospital to recover. A student is petrified in the hall, and a strange message about the Chamber of Secrets is written in blood on the wall. Lockhart starts a Dueling Club. Harry speaks Parseltongue to a snake that was about to go after another student in dueling practice. His classmates misunderstand, thinking that only Slytherin heirs can speak to snakes and that it is a Slytherin heir who must open the Chamber of Secrets. They think Harry is the one who is petrifying students and leaving messages in blood on the wall.

On Halloween night, Harry, Ron, and Hermione are invited to Nearly Headless Nick's 500th Death Day Party. Hermione concocts a Polyjuice Potion that takes a long time to make, but that will turn Harry and Ron into Vincent Crabbe and Gregory Goyle. Disguised as Crabbe and Goyle, they hope to find out if Draco Malfoy is behind the attacks in the school. They learn that Malfoy is not the Slytherin heir. In the girls' bathroom, Moaning Myrtle leads Harry to the diary where he sees Tom Riddle's past. Riddle has accused Hagrid of being the one to open the Chamber of Secrets. Later, Hermione and a Ravenclaw girl are also petrified, Hermione with a piece of paper in her hand.

With so many petrifications at the school, Cornelius Fudge and Lucius Malfoy arrive to remove Dumbledore and Hagrid from their posts. Before Hagrid leaves, he tells Harry and Ron to follow the spiders. They do this and discover the Acromantula in the Forbidden Forest, a friend of Hagrid's named Aragog. It is through Aragog that they learn that Moaning Myrtle was killed by Tom Riddle and that Hagrid was innocent of opening the Chamber of Secrets long ago. From the note in Hermione's stiff hand, they discover that the beast in the Chamber must be a Basilisk.

Ginny Weasley has been taken hostage in the Chamber, and Harry, Ron, and Lockhart go to find her. Lockhart does so unwillingly; he has been a fraud all along, and the acts of courage he writes about in his books are fake. They all go down to the Chamber, where Harry encounters Tom Riddle and the Basilisk. Riddle magically unscrambles the letters of his name to reveal that he is Lord Voldemort. Dumbledore's phoenix, Fawkes, flies into the Chamber when Harry makes a statement of loyalty to Dumbledore. The bird puts out the deadly eyes of the Basilisk and brings Harry the Gryffindor sword in the Sorting Hat. Harry kills the Basilisk with the sword, then drives a poisonous fang into the diary, defeating Voldemort. Ginny wakes up and is fine.

Lockhart has suffered a backfire of his own Memory Charm, and he has forgotten who he is. He is sent to St. Mungo's. When Dumbledore returns, Harry tells him what happened, and the great wizard praises him, saying that Fawkes will only help those who are very loyal to Dumbledore. Lucius Malfoy is manipulated into freeing Dobby, his house-elf, who can only be freed by being given clothing of his own by his master. Lucius does this by accidentally giving Dobby a sock.

Harry gives Ron his telephone number as they go off the Hogwarts Express. When Hermione asks Harry if his aunt and uncle will be proud of what he accomplished for the school, Harry replies that they will be disappointed he did not die. With that, the summer holiday begins until the next adventure.

Distinctions American Library Association Best Book for Young Adults, 1999; British Book Awards Children's Book of the Year, 1999; Nestlé Smarties Book Prize Gold Award, 1998; Scottish Arts Council Children's Book Award, 1999; short-listed for the Whitbread Children's Book of the Year Award, 1999.

Harry Potter and the Goblet of Fire. *Book 4. Goblet of Fire* was the first novel to have a simultaneous printing in the U.K. and the United States, celebrated by a highly publicized midnight release that occurred in July 2000. The novel was the longest of the series up to that point, with approximately 180,000 words in thirty-seven chapters. It is dedicated to the author's father, Peter Rowling; to a friend of the family, Mr. Ridley; and to another friend, Susan Sladden. Major settings in the novel include: the Riddle House in Little Hangleton; Number Four, Privet Drive; the Burrow; the Quidditch World Cup; the Hogwarts Express; Hogwarts; and the Little Hangleton graveyard. Significant characters introduced or newly developed in Book 4 include: Mad-Eye Moody; Ludo Bagman; Bartemius Crouch, Jr. and Sr.; the Death Eaters; and Rita Skeeter. Magical substances, objects, or creatures critical to the plot include: the Dark Mark; Portkeys; the Goblet of Fire; and the Pensieve.

Plot Summary *Goblet of Fire* begins in a setting where Harry is not present—Little Hangleton, in the ancestral home of Tom Riddle's family. Wormtail (Peter Pettigrew) has gone to Voldemort after escaping from Sirius Black and Remus Lupin outside the Shrieking Shack in Hogsmeade. Wormtail tells Voldemort what he knows. Nagini, Voldemort's snake, apparently gives his owner nourishment, but Voldemort is still in a diminished physical state. Voldemort murders Frank Bryce, the Riddle gardener who was wrongly accused fifty years earlier of killing Tom Riddle's father and grandparents. Harry's scar pains him greatly when Bryce's murder occurs, and he sees visions of it in his mind. Over the summer, Harry is invited by the Weasley family to attend the Quidditch World Cup. After a series of adventures that include a win by the Ireland team and an appearance of the Dark Mark over the night sky, they catch the Hogwarts Express and arrive at Hogwarts, where most of the remaining action takes place.

A Triwizard Tournament involving two other wizard schools, Beauxbatons and Durmstrang, results in Harry's winning the Triwizard Cup and the 1,000 Galleon prize. The tournament takes a backseat, however, to the rise of Voldemort, which occurs after a series of complicated deceits, adventures, mysteries, and maneuvers in the third and final task of the contest. Cedric Diggory, a noble and kind student from Hufflepuff House, ends up dying at Wormtail's hand under Voldemort's direction during the third and final task of the tournament. Though Harry is shaken up by the intense events, including seeing his parents emerge out of Voldemort's wand, he has informed Prof. Dumbledore of all that has happened. Dumbledore assembles allies for the struggle that will ensue, beginning in Book 5. Unfortunately, a split in allegiance occurs among those who should be working together against Voldemort's power; this occurs when Cornelius Fudge, the Minister of Magic, fails to believe Harry and Dumbledore when they tell him that Voldemort is alive and has come back to power. At the Leaving Feast, Dumbledore warns everyone that Voldemort's power to divide is great and that they must stick together through the hard times that are to come. Harry gives his winnings to the Weasley twins so that they may start their joke shop—he says that he and most everyone else could use a few laughs.

Distinctions American Library Association Notable Children's Book, 2000; Hugo Award; Scottish Arts Council Book Award, 2001.

Harry Potter and the Half-Blood Prince. *Book 6.* Simultaneously published at midnight July 16, 2005 in the U.K., the United States, and other English-speaking countries. The book is approximately 160,000 words long and contains thirty chapters. It is dedicated to Mackenzie Rowling Murray, the author's daughter who was born a few months before the book's publication. Principle settings in the novel include: the Prime Minister's office; Spinner's End; Budleigh Babberton; the Burrow; Weasleys' Wizard Wheezes and Diagon Alley; the Hogwarts Express; Hogwarts; Big and Little Hangleton; and the cave. New or significantly developed characters in the novel include the Prime Minister; Rufus Scrimgeour; Horace Slughorn; Tom Riddle; Merope Gaunt Riddle; Morfin Gaunt; and Marvolo Gaunt. The most important magical objects in the novel are the Pensieve and Horcruxes.

Plot Summary Harry is not present in the first two chapters of this novel. The first chapter has the Minister of Magic speaking with the Prime Minister about all the strange goings-on in the country. The second chapter is set at Spinner's End where Narcissa Black Malfoy and her sister visit Snape. Snape makes an Unbreakable Vow with Narcissa that he will protect Draco Malfoy and do the deed that Voldemort has committed Draco to doing if Draco cannot carry it out. Prof. Dumbledore takes Harry away from Privet Drive himself this time. They enlist the help of Horace Slughorn to teach at Hogwarts. However, Slughorn will not be the new DADA teacher; he is teaching Potions, and Snape has finally been given the coveted DADA job. Harry's O.W.L. results do not seem good enough for him to take Potions class, so he does not get the Potions book. When it turns out that Harry does qualify for the class under Slughorn's requirements, Slughorn gives him a book from the classroom cupboard. The book turns out to have been used before by the Half-Blood Prince, who has put notes in the margins about how to make potions better and more quickly. After a Quidditch match in which Ron does very well, Harry kisses Ginny Weasley, and their relationship blossoms.

Much of the novel is spent with Dumbledore showing Harry memories (his own and others') of Tom Riddle's/Lord Voldemort's past. Harry finally extracts the memory from Slughorn that Dumbledore needs to prove his theory that Voldemort used Horcruxes (objects which hold pieces of the soul) to re-create himself. Dumbledore and Harry go to the cave where Dumbledore thinks there may be a Horcrux. Harry helps Dumbledore retrieve it, but Dumbledore is sorely weakened. Back at Hogwarts, the Dark Mark can be seen over the castle. Draco Malfoy has been doing his duty as a new Death Eater working for Voldemort, though he is afraid and has not carried out his task to completion. When he confronts Dumbledore at the top of Astronomy Tower, he cannot kill him, and Snape arrives. Snape kills Dumbledore, and he and Draco escape.

The end of the novel features Dumbledore's funeral, which is a sad event for almost all of the characters. Harry knows the torch has been passed, and it is now his duty to rid the world of Voldemort's evil power. Bill Weasley and Fleur Delacour will marry the following summer. Harry tells Ginny that he must do his duty alone and not risk Voldemort going after her, but Ginny, Ron, and Hermione say that they will all be with him.

Distinctions Within the first twenty-four hours of release, the book sold 6.9 million copies in the United States and 2 million copies in the United Kingdom, beating the previous sales record set by its own predecessor, *Order of the Phoenix*, by 13 percent in the U.K. The $100 million sales from the book were higher than the combined box office sales of the two highest-grossing movies showing that same weekend in the United States.

Harry Potter and the Order of the Phoenix. *Book 5.* The fifth and longest book of the series, *Order of the Phoenix* was published in 2003. It is approximately 218,000 words long and contains thirty-eight chapters. The book is dedicated to Rowling's husband Neil, daughter Jessica, and son David. Principle settings in the novel are: Number Four, Privet Drive; Number Twelve, Grimmauld Place; the Ministry of Magic; Hogwarts; Hogsmeade; and St. Mungo's Hospital for Magical Maladies and Injuries. New or more fully developed characters in the novel include: Cho Chang; Tonks; Mad-Eye Moody; Mundungus Fletcher; Kingsley Shacklebolt; Emmeline Vance; Dedalus Diggle; Luna Lovegood; Dolores Umbridge; and Kreacher, the Black family house-elf. Magical creatures, substances, or objects of importance in the novel include: The veil in the Hall of Prophecy at the Ministry; the Prophecy.

Plot Summary Two Dementors try to kill Harry and Dudley on Privet Drive until Harry manages to conjure the Patronus and drive them away. Harry is sent a message from the Ministry expelling him from Hogwarts for using magic outside of school. Several members of the Order come to fetch Harry at Privet Drive and take him to Order headquarters, which is at Number Twelve, Grimmauld Place, the old Black family mansion. There, he meets other members of the Order. Arthur Weasley takes him to his hearing at the Ministry, where Dumbledore advocates on his behalf but will not look at him or speak to him. Harry is cleared of the charges against him.

At Hogwarts, the new DADA teacher is Dolores Umbridge, a cruel woman who makes Harry write lines for detention that actually get cut into the backs of his hands. She becomes the Hogwarts High Inquisitor and attends classes where she evaluates the professors in a cruel, unfair, and domineering way. Conditions at the school go from bad to worse. Hermione and some of the other students begin a group they call Dumbledore's Army, which has Harry training them practical DADA skills in secret. Umbridge gives Harry and the Weasley twins a lifetime ban from Quidditch. In a spectacular display of fireworks and rebellion against her tyranny at the school, the Weasley twins raise havoc and then fly away, off to start their joke shop.

Dumbledore has asked Snape to teach Harry the skill of Occlumency, which is the ability to keep someone from reading your mind. Harry has been having many dreams about a long corridor. He also dreams that he is a snake that bites Arthur Weasley. Harry then tells everyone that Arthur was attacked. Arthur goes to St. Mungo's, and Harry and the Weasleys visit him there over Christmas. By threatening to reveal Rita Skeeter's Animagus status, Hermione gets Rita to write a truthful article about Harry's witness to Voldemort's rise. The article gets published in Luna Lovegood's father's paper, *The Quibbler*. People finally begin to believe that Harry has told the truth about the rise of Voldemort. Before the students take their important O.W.L. exams, Harry and friends learn that Hagrid has returned from a mission to enlist the giant community in helping to fight the Dark Side. He has found his half-brother, Grawp, and brought him home with him. Firenze is hired to take Prof. Trelawney's place when Umbridge fires her. This has made the centaur community angry with humans.

Umbridge's Inquisitorial Squad, including Draco Malfoy, finds out about the DA and brings Harry and the others to a hearing in Dumbledore's office. Dumbledore is threatened and escapes. Hermione finds a way to lead Umbridge to the forest, where Umbridge's bigotry against half-humans is dealt with by the centaurs, and the centaurs are dealt with by Grawp. Harry is convinced that Sirius Black is at the Department of Mysteries and that he needs help. He goes there with several others on thestrals that Hagrid has been raising in the woods. There they encounter the Death Eaters, who are seeking the Prophecy for Voldemort. A battle ensues, with the Order of the Phoenix arriving as reinforcement. However, Sirius Black (who was not there earlier as Harry had feared) is struck by his cousin, Bellatrix Lestrange. Sirius falls through the veil and dies. Dumbledore arrives through the Fountain of Magical Brethren and saves Harry. Dumbledore explains the Prophecy to Harry and accepts his blame for his indirect role in Sirius's death. A welcoming committee of several members of the Order meets Harry at King's Cross. They will make sure that the Dursleys will not cause him any trouble while he remains in danger and is grieving the loss of his godfather.

Distinctions The book sold over 1.6 million copies on the first day in the U.K., breaking publishing records to that date.

Harry Potter and the Philosopher's/Sorcerer's Stone. *Book 1.* The first Harry Potter book was published in a limited print run of only five hundred copies in the U.K. by Bloomsbury in 1997. It was published in the United States in 1998. The book contains approximately 77,000 words and seventeen chapters. It is dedicated to Rowling's daughter Jessica; her mother Anne; and her sister Di. The principle settings are Number Four, Privet Drive; the Hut-on-the-Rock; Diagon Alley; Platform 9¾; the Hogwarts Express; and Hogwarts School of Witchcraft and Wizardry. The book introduces Harry Potter and the wizarding world to readers. Magical objects significant to the plot include Harry's magic wand; his broomstick; his father's Invisibility Cloak; and the Mirror of Erised.

Plot Summary Everything is pretty normal at Vernon and Petunia Dursley's house at Number Four, Privet Drive, except that Vernon notices a cat reading a map and other strange occurrences on his way to work at the Grunnings drill company. The arrival that evening of an old wizard who begins putting out the streetlights with an odd device adds to the strangeness, but he is not seen. Neither is the cat that transforms into a witch, nor the giant who rides from the sky on a motorcycle carrying a baby with a lightning-shaped scar on his forehead. After these events, things will never be the same again. The wizard, Albus Dumbledore, leaves a note with the baby and puts him on the Durleys' doorstep. He assures the witch, Minerva McGonagall, and the giant, Rubeus Hagrid, that the boy will be protected from harm. The baby's parents, Mr. and Mrs. Potter, have been killed, but this little baby is "the boy who lived."

Ten years pass, and it is clear that the orphaned boy, Harry Potter, has not had an easy life at his aunt and uncle's. He stays in a closet under the stairs instead of in a proper bedroom. His cousin Dudley, who is only a few months older than Harry, is an overweight and overindulged boy with a bratty personality to match his father's, and a careless attitude toward Harry that matches his mother's. When owls begin bringing mail for Harry, Vernon Dursley refuses to allow Harry to read the letters; but the letters arrive with increasing frequency and ferocity, chasing the Dursleys to the Hut-on-the-Rock, where they still cannot escape them. Hagrid finds Harry at the Hut-on-the-Rock and notifies him that he is a wizard. Hagrid tells Harry that now that he is eleven, he is due at Hogwarts School of Witchcraft and Wizardry in September to begin his proper magical education.

The giant takes Harry shopping for his school robes, books, and supplies on the magical street in London, Diagon Alley. On Diagon Alley Harry also discovers that he has a lot of wizard money in Gringotts Bank that was left to him by his parents. While at the bank, Hagrid fulfills a mission for Dumbledore by taking a small package out of a vault. For Harry's birthday, Hagrid gives him a pet snowy owl that Harry later names

Hedwig. Harry goes shopping for his magic wand. While at Ollivander's Wand Shop, he learns that the wand that chose him has a brother; this brother wand is Voldemort's wand, which killed Harry's parents.

As instructed by Hagrid and his letter, Harry catches the Hogwarts Express, a scarlet steam engine and train that leaves from Platform 9¾ at King's Cross Station. A matronly woman helps him find the mysterious missing platform, and Harry meets members of the large and friendly Weasley family for the first time. On the train, Ron Weasley shares the treats that Harry buys for them and begins to tell him what it is like to be a wizard. Hermione Granger joins their compartment. She is the child of Muggles, non-magical people, and she seems to have already read all of their textbooks for the year. She seems to be a snotty know-it-all. At the same time, she begins to make friends with Harry by fixing his broken glasses with a flick of her wand. A boy named Draco Malfoy tries to befriend Harry at first, until Harry notices that Draco is snobby about people's backgrounds and heritage. He does not like him very much.

As a first-year student at Hogwarts, Harry participates in the Sorting Hat Ceremony, where he is sorted into Gryffindor House, a student house that is also home to all of the Weasley children and Hermione. There are three other student houses that are also named after the founders of the school; they are called Ravenclaw, Hufflepuff, and Slytherin. Mysteries begin to unfold gradually as Harry learns that his lightning bolt scar was made by a villain named Voldemort who killed his parents. Harry's aunt and uncle had told him that his parents died in a car accident. Harry also learns that the name of the villain, Voldemort, is a name that others dare not say. However, Dumbledore tells him that people only grow more afraid of what they cannot say aloud, so Harry learns to be brave and to say the name of this villain, even though it causes other people around him to flinch.

As school progresses, Harry grows concerned about his Potions teacher, Prof. Severus Snape. Snape appears to have it out for Harry from day one for reasons the boy does not understand. On the other hand, Harry learns to fly his broomstick, and he is recruited for the Gryffindor Quidditch team by Prof. McGonagall. Since he is an excellent flyer, an exception is made and he is allowed to play Seeker on the team, even as a first-year student. Prof. McGonagall sends him a Nimbus 2000 broomstick as a gift. For Christmas, Harry stays at Hogwarts and receives an Invisibility Cloak that once belonged to his father. While using the cloak one night, Harry finds a strange and large mirror, called the Mirror of Erised, in which he sees his parents and other family members looking back at him—this is his heart's desire. His mentor, Prof. Dumbledore, appears behind him and warns him not to avoid living by thinking too much about desires that cannot be fulfilled.

When he must serve detention with Hagrid and Draco Malfoy in the Forbidden Forest, Harry has his first run-in with Voldemort. The villain is in the forest killing unicorns and drinking their blood. Unicorn blood has magical properties that Voldemort is using to try to come back to life in full form. It turns out that this is not the only substance Voldemort seeks; he is also after a Sorcerer's Stone that is hidden and guarded inside Hogwarts. Through an elaborate plan, Harry, Ron, and Hermione find their way to the stone, and Harry gets hold of it. The climactic scene finds Harry holding the stone in his pocket while facing Prof. Quirrell, the Defense Against the Dark Arts teacher, who has been possessed by Voldemort. When Harry touches Quirrell's face, it burns and disintegrates, and Voldemort is too weak to fight. Voldemort dissolves and disappears.

Harry is in the hospital wing recovering from his shocking adventure when Dumbledore visits him again. Harry also reunites with Ron and Hermione, and all is well.

Harry rides back to the Dursleys on the Hogwarts Express for the summer, but not before Hagrid gives him a photo album containing pictures of his parents.

Distinctions American Booksellers Book Award, 1999; American Library Association Best Book for Young Adults, 1998; British Book Awards Children's Book of the Year, 1998; short-listed for the Carnegie Medal (Commended), 1998; Nestlé Smarties Book Prize Gold Medal for children 9–11, 1997.

Harry Potter and the Prisoner of Azkaban. *Book 3.* The third novel in the series was published in 1999 in the U.K. by Bloomsbury and in the United States by Scholastic. The book contains approximately 109,000 words and twenty-two chapters. It is dedicated to two of Rowling's friends in Oporto, Portugal, who frequently went with her to a disco called Swing—Jill Prewett and Aine Kiely. Principle settings include: Number Four, Privet Drive; Magnolia Crescent; the Knight Bus; the Leaky Cauldron and Diagon Alley; Hogwarts; and Hogsmeade and the Shrieking Shack. Characters introduced or newly developed in *Prisoner of Azkaban* include: Sirius Black; Remus J. Lupin; Peter Pettigrew; Sibyll Trelawney; Aunt Marge Dursley; and Stan Shunpike. Creatures or beings particularly important in the book include Buckbeak; the Dementors; Boggarts, and the Patronus. Several characters also take important animal forms: the black dog, "Padfoot" Sirius; werewolf, "Moony" Lupin; Scabbers the rat as "Wormtail" Pettigrew; and the stag, "Prongs" James Potter. Principle magical objects include the Marauder's Map and the Time-Turner.

Plot Summary Aunt Marge Dursley visits Privet Drive and crosses the line when she begins comparing Harry's mother to the dogs she raises. Harry's anger blows her up until she inflates into a balloon and floats away. Harry is so angry that he runs away from Privet Drive. While he is outside in the night, he thinks he sees a black dog staring at him from the shadows. Harry is picked up by the Knight Bus and taken to the Leaky Cauldron. There he is met by Cornelius Fudge, Minister of Magic, who makes sure he is taken care of for the short time that is left in the summer before school starts. The Weasleys and Hermione shop with Harry on Diagon Alley. He learns that Sirius Black has escaped from Azkaban Prison and that he may be after him. He also learns that Sirius is his godfather. On the Hogwarts Express, Harry and friends sit in a compartment with the sleeping Prof. Lupin. A Dementor attacks the compartment, causing Harry to faint; Prof. Lupin chases the Dementor away and revives Harry with chocolate.

Dementors have been charged by the Ministry to protect Harry and the others at Hogwarts. Prof. Lupin teaches DADA, including a lesson in Boggarts. Harry finds that he is most afraid of Dementors, not of Voldemort. When Harry is not allowed to go to Hogsmeade with his friends, Prof. Lupin gives him private lessons in performing a Patronus, which gets rid of Dementors. A series of events leads to a climactic scene in the Shrieking Shack in Hogsmeade. Harry and friends confront old friends of Harry's father—Peter Pettigrew, Remus J. Lupin, Sirius Black, and Severus Snape. James Potter and the former three men were the originators of the Marauder's Map. The map was given to Harry by Fred and George Weasley. It shows the location of everyone in the castle at any one time. Hermione has been dealing in time herself, using a Time-Turner so that she may attend extra classes. From the occurrences in the Shrieking Shack, Harry discovers that Pettigrew was actually Scabbers in Animagus form; it turns out that Pettigrew was the one who led Voldemort to his parents, not Sirius Black. Sirius was falsely imprisoned and he convinces Harry that he is on his side as his godfather. He says he would never have betrayed Harry's father, who was his best friend.

Hagrid, as teacher of Care of Magical Creatures, has introduced the students to Buckbeak, a hippogriff. Harry makes friends with the hippogriff enough to ride it, but Draco Malfoy's careless actions result in Draco getting scratched quite badly. Draco's father finds out about the matter and presses charges. After a few mock hearings, Buckbeak's neck is scheduled for the chopping block. Harry and Hermione use the Time-Turner to save Sirius Black from being recaptured and Buckbeak from being executed. The stag that Harry sees driving off the Dementors from Sirius Black and himself is not his father, as he first thought, but rather his own Patronus. Dumbledore tells Harry that his father is alive within him.

Distinctions American Library Association Best Book for Young Adults, 2000; British Book Awards Children's Author of the Year, 2000; short-listed for the Carnegie Medal, 2000; Nestlé Smarties Book Prize Gold Award, 1999; Whitbread Children's Book of the Year Award, 2000.

Harry Potter Fan Club. *Magical non-club.* Ron warns Harry that Colin Creevey and Ginny Weasley may get together and start one of these (CS 6:99).

The Harry Potter Phenomenon. *See* Popular culture

Haversacking. *Magical game penalty.* From QA. This penalty occurs if the Chaser's hand is still on the Quaffle when it flies through the goal hoop (QA 30).

Hawkshead Attacking Formation. *Magical game play.* From QA. A move where Chasers fly close together; the Irish Chasers do this during the World Cup, and the play shows up on Harry's Omnioculars as "Hawkshead Attacking Formation" (GF 8:106). The formation is shaped like an arrow and effectively works like one in piercing the defense of the opposing team (QA 52). The maneuver was invented by Darren O'Hare of the Kenmare Kestrels (QA 35).
See also Quidditch Through the Ages

"He-Who-Must-Not-Be-Named." *See* Voldemort, Lord

Head of House. *Magical position.* The Head of House is the faculty member who leads each student house at Hogwarts (GF 13:206). While Harry is there the heads are: Gryffindor, Prof. McGonagall; Slytherin, Prof. Snape; Hufflepuff, Prof. Sprout; and Ravenclaw, Prof. Flitwick. Prof. Slughorn becomes Head of Slytherin House at Snape's departure (HBP 29:625).

Headless hats. *Magical objects.* Fred and George Weasley sell these hats with a pink feather at Hogwarts for 2 Galleons each. Fred demonstrates by putting on the hat; both the hat and his head disappear. When he removes the hat, his head reappears. Hermione tries to figure out how they work in relation to the Invisibility Spell (OP 24:540).

The Healer's Helpmate. *Magical book.* Mrs. Weasley consults this book's section on "Bruises, Cuts, and Abrasions" as she tries to help Hermione find an antidote for a bruised eye. Hermione needs the antidote after a run-in with the Weasley twins' punching telescope in their room at the Burrow (HBP 5:100).

Healing Spells. *Magical spells.* Harry trusts Madam Pomfrey with Healing Spells more than Nymphadora Tonks, but Tonks heals his nose anyway (HBP 8:157).

Hebridean Blacks. *Magical creatures.* These dragons can grow up to thirty feet long; they eat mostly deer (FB 12). They are found wild in Britain (SS 14:231). When they were a team, the Banchory Bangers tried to catch one of these as their mascot (QA 16–17).
See also Fantastic Beasts and Where to Find Them

Hedge. *Muggle place.* The hedge outside Number Four, Privet Drive seems to be staring back at Harry as he daydreams (CS 1:7–8). The eyes Harry sees in it foreshadow the dog he will meet in *Prisoner of Azkaban*.

Hedwig. *Magical pet.* Hedwig is Harry's snowy owl given to him by Hagrid for his eleventh birthday (SS 5:81). While waiting at Privet Drive for school to start, Harry found the name for his pet in *A History of Magic* (SS 6:88). In the summer between Years 1 and 2, Uncle Vernon will not allow Hedwig out of her cage, and Harry tells him that she is bored from not being allowed to fly outside (CS 1:1). She is a good companion for Harry, and he is normally good to her. When Sirius Black writes to Harry that he is coming back north because Harry's scar has been hurting, Harry becomes unhappy and he takes out his grumpiness on Hedwig (GF 14:226–27). It does not take long, however, for Hedwig to forgive him. Her pride makes her go out on another messenger mission for Harry soon after the incident (GF 15:229). Harry overhears Lavender Brown say to Parvati Patil that she always thought Hedwig was a beautiful owl (OP 17:356).
    Rowling has said that she found Hedwig's name in a book of saints. St. Hedwig lived from 1174 to 1243. She was the daughter of a duke of Croatia. She married another duke and had seven children. With her husband, she worked many acts of benevolence, including funding the building of a monastery and tending to the sick and forgotten. When her husband died she gave her fortune to charity and joined a convent. She was canonized in 1266 by Pope Clement IV. The Sisters of St. Hedwig were established in 1859. They work in Germany, Austria, and Denmark, and their principle mission is educating orphaned children, a cause not far removed from the story of Harry Potter.

Heidelberg Harriers. *Magical sports team.* From QA. A seven-day Quidditch game between this German team and the Holyhead Harpies is regarded as one of the finest in the game's history (QA 34, 41).
See also Quidditch Through the Ages

***Hélas, Je me suis Transfiguré Les Pieds* ("Alas, I've Transfigured My Feet").** *Magical play.* This is a play written by a French wizard playwright named Malecrit (QA 39).

Heliopaths. *Magical beings.* Fire spirits. Luna Lovegood tells the DADA class at the Hog's Head that Cornelius Fudge has his own private army of Heliopaths (OP 16:345).

Hellebore. *Magical substance.* The syrup of Hellebore is an ingredient in the Draught of Peace (OP 12:234). In mythology, Helle was the daughter of Athamas and Nephele who rode off on a ram with golden fleece but fell into a body of water that now bears her name.

Hengist of Woodcroft. *Character.* One of the figures on the Famous Witches and Wizard Cards found in Chocolate Frogs (SS 6:103).
See also Chocolate Frogs

Heptomology. *Magical ability.* Students in Divination break into Prof. Trelawney's lectures to ask her questions about heptomology, which may be a way of predicting the future by reading plants (OP 25:552).

Herbology. *Magical class.* Prof. Sprout teaches this class at Hogwarts. The class focuses on the growth and use of plants for potions and other magical purposes (SS 8:133). There are greenhouses and vegetable gardens on the Hogwarts grounds (OP 9:159). Neville does particularly well in the class. Some of the magical plants the class learned about include: Devil's Snare, Mandrakes, and Bubotubers.

Herefordshire. From QA. The ancient broomstick game of Swivenhodge began in Herefordshire.
See also Swivenhodge

Hermes. *Magical creature.* Hermes is the owl that Mr. and Mrs. Weasley buy Percy the year he is made prefect at Hogwarts (CS 3:30). Hermes is a screech owl (PA 5:70). In mythology, Hermes is called Mercury by the Romans and is a son of Zeus and Maia. He is a messenger of the gods.

"Hermy." *Nickname.* Hagrid asks Hermione if Grawp can call her this, since it is easier for him to say (OP 31:705).

Hero complex. When Harry wants to go to the Department of Mysteries to rescue Sirius, Hermione warns him that he too often wants to be the hero. She calls it his "saving-people-thing" (OP 32:733). Hermione may be correct in her judgment; Lucius Malfoy later says in the Department of Mysteries that Voldemort knows Harry has this weakness (OP 35:782).

Hiccup Sweets. *Magical candy.* Harry and Ron buy some of these at Zonko's in Hogsmeade (PA 14:278).
See also Candy and sweets

Hiccuping Solution. *Magical substance.* Draco Malfoy gets little attention from Slughorn with this potion (HBP 22:475).

Higgs, Bertie. *Character.* Bertie Higgs went Nogtail hunting with Cormac McLeggan's Uncle Tiberius and Rufus Scrimgeour (HBP 7:144–45).

Higgs, Terence. *Character.* Slytherin Seeker in Quidditch during Harry's first year (SS 11:187).

High-Finish Polish. *Magical substance.* Material used to polish broomsticks; it comes in the Broomstick Servicing Kit (PA 11:232).

High Inquisitor. *See* Hogwarts High Inquisitor

High Street. *Magical place.* The road in Hogsmeade where the shops are (PA 14:278). Harry walks up High Street to the edge of town when he is supposed to meet Sirius Black (GF 27:520).

High Table. *Magical object.* The head table in the Great Hall at Hogwarts where the headmaster and faculty sit (SS 7:122).

Hinkypuffs. *Magical creatures.* On the day Prof. Snape substitutes for Prof. Lupin in DADA class, Hermione tells him that Hinkypuffs are the next subject they are supposed to discuss (PA 9:171).

Hinkypunk. *Magical creature.* One-legged, smoky creature with a lantern that leads travelers into bogs (PA 10:186). Hinkypunks are on Prof. Lupin's DADA final exam in Year 3 (PA 16:318). Mad-Eye Moody makes sure that the students have gone over Hinkypunks in DADA class before he teaches them the Unforgivable Curses (GF 14:211).

Hippocampus. *Magical creature.* From *Fantastic Beasts.* Classified 3X by the MM. This blended creature originated in Greece. It has the head and front legs of a horse with the back legs and tail of a fish. It is normally found in the Mediterranean (FB 20–21).
See also Fantastic Beasts and Where to Find Them

Hippogriff. *Magical creature.* Classified 3X by the MM. A hippogriff is a creature that is half horse, half bird (FB 21). Hagrid describes them as proud and easily offended. To befriend them, one must wait for them to make the first move and try to make eye contact without blinking (PA 6:114). In mythology, the hippogriff is the offspring of a male griffin and a female horse (a filly). In Greek, *hippos* means "horse"; *gryphos* means "griffin." The hippogriff is a symbol of love.

Madam Modesty Rabnott of Kent had a hippogriff. After objecting to Snidget-hunting becoming part of Quidditch, Madam Rabnott lost her house, but she did not lose her hippogriff (QA 13).
See also Fantastic Beasts and Where to Find Them

History of Magic. *Class at Hogwarts.* This is the only class at Hogwarts that is taught by a ghost, Prof. Binns (SS 8:133). Many of the students find the class boring, mostly because Prof. Binns recites dates and events in a dry, monotone voice. He comes into the classroom through the blackboard, then proceeds to read from his notes. In Year 2, Hermione leaves her copy of *Hogwarts, A History* at home, and the library copies are all checked out while students try to figure out the mystery of the Chamber of Secrets. She convinces Binns one day to speak to the class about the Chamber, and he tells a bit of the legend, including the factual information about the founding of Hogwarts (CS 9:150). For his exam in Year 3, Harry tries to remember the tips that Florean Fortescue, the ice cream vendor on Diagon Alley, gave him about medieval witch hunts (PA 16:318).

For the History of Magic O.W.L., Harry needs to write about the Statute of Secrecy breached in 1749; the formation of the International Confederation of Wizards; and the Supreme Mugwump of the International Confederation and his opponent (OP 31:725–26). Harry receives a D on his History of Magic O.W.L. exam.

A History of Magic. *Magical book.* This book was written by Bathilda Bagshot and published by Little Red Books in 1947. It is the textbook for the Hogwarts class of the same name (PA 1:1).

The Hobgoblins. *Magical singing group.* Doris Purkiss claims that Sirius Black was a member of this group (OP 10:191–93).
  See also Boardman, Stubby

Hog's Head Inn. *Magical place.* A pub and inn in Hogsmeade (SS 16:265). The Hog's Head Inn is where Hermione has her meeting for those who want to study Defense Against the Dark Arts techniques with Harry. The inn is made up of one room that is dark and dirty. It is where Hagrid gets the dragon's egg from a stranger in a hood (OP 16:335–36). According to Sirius Black, the bartender has a long memory (OP 17:370). Dumbledore hears the Prophecy in a room above the pub (OP 37:840).

Hogsmeade. *Magical place.* Third-year Hogwarts students are allowed to visit Hogsmeade on select weekends during the school year. It is the only village in Britain with an all-magical population (PA 5:76). Students need written permission from a parent or guardian to go there, however, and Uncle Dursley refuses to sign the form for Harry (PA 1:14). Sirius Black later writes Harry a permission slip as his godfather. The Hogwarts Express pulls into Hogsmeade Station where all students except first-years are picked up by carriage and taken to the school (HBP 8:159).

Hogwarts, A History. *Magical book.* Hermione has read this book before her first year at Hogwarts. In Year 2, all the library copies are checked out as the students try to make sense of the Chamber of Secrets and the writing on Hogwarts walls (CS 9:147). Hermione keeps telling Harry and Ron that they must read it (GF 11:166). She gives the book different names when she is disappointed to discover that the house-elves are not mentioned in it anywhere; these other names include: *A Revised History of Hogwarts* and *A Highly Biased and Selective History of Hogwarts, Which Glosses Over the Nastier Aspects of the School* (GF 15:238). Hermione mentions that the book states that Hogwarts founders considered girls more worthy of trust than boys (OP 17:353).

Hogwarts Express. *Magical object.* The magical train pulled by a big crimson-red steam engine that takes students from Platform 9¾ at King's Cross Station to Hogwarts School of Witchcraft and Wizardry (SS 6:93). The train appears to go directly north from London (CS 5:71; PA 5:80).

Hogwarts Express Candy Cart. *Magical object.* The cart brings treats to students riding the train on their way to Hogwarts (SS 6:101). Seeing that Ron cannot afford to buy any candy, Harry splurges and buys a generous sampling of everything for them to share (SS 6:101). The trolley also carries cold pumpkin juice (CS 5:72).
  See also Candy and sweets

Hogwarts High Inquisitor. *Magical position.* Dolores Umbridge manages to get herself a job at the Ministry as Hogwarts High Inquisitor, which gives her complete power over every affair at Hogwarts. One of her responsibilities is to evaluate the faculty by sitting in on their classes, much to the faculty's displeasure, and she can fire anyone she wishes

(OP 15:306). The position was created by Educational Decree Twenty-Three (OP 15:307). In just one of her acts of intrusion in the post, she has all the mail checked and inspected (OP 29:654).

Hogwarts School of Witchcraft and Wizardry. *Magical place.* The reader is introduced to Hogwarts' existence when Harry reads his invitation letter to attend the school (SS 4:51). One of the clues that the school is in Scotland is that the Hogwarts Express is directly north of London, which Ron and Harry learn by following it in the flying Ford Anglia in Year 2 (CS 5:71). The school is invisible to Muggles. All they see are ruins with a sign over the door telling them it is too dangerous and unsafe to enter. It is also unplottable, meaning that it is enchanted so that it cannot be marked anywhere on a map (GF 11:166).

In History of Magic class, Prof. Binns gives readers some of the background surrounding the founding of the school. It was founded over 1,000 years ago by four of the greatest witches and wizards of the age—Godric Gryffindor, Helga Hufflepuff, Rowena Ravenclaw, and Salazar Slytherin. The castle was built far away from where Muggles might see it, since at that time Muggles were a threat to all magical people.

For some time things went well, but after a few years Slytherin began to believe that only pureblood magical people should be accepted for admission. He separated from the others, who thought that it was fine to enroll children of Muggle or mixed bloods. Eventually his disagreement with the others was so great that he left the school altogether.

Legend had it that before he left, Slytherin built a Chamber of Secrets beneath the castle or the grounds; it was said that he kept a monster in the Chamber. Only one of his heirs would be able to open it and let loose the monster that would eradicate all Muggles

The Great Hall at Hogwarts School of Witchcraft and Wizardry from *Harry Potter and the Sorcerer's Stone* (2001). Courtesy of Warner Bros./Photofest.

and mixed-blood people from the school. Over the hundreds of years since that time, many faculty, staff, and students searched for the Chamber, but it was never found. Prof. Binns then concluded that it did not exist at all but was simply an old legend intended to scare people.

Indeed, the Chamber of Secrets does exist, and Tom Riddle (aka Lord Voldemort) turns out to be the Slytherin heir who will open it. The monster within is a giant Basilisk, but Harry Potter defeats it, saving the school. For his efforts, he earns a Special Award for Service to the School.

First-years arrive at the school and are taken four-each in small boats across the lake to Hogwarts Castle. Students in other years wait on a platform, then board nearly 100 stagecoaches to the castle. The coaches do not appear to have horses, or if they do, they are invisible (GF 11:170). Harry later learns that they are pulled by thestrals. The Hogwarts gates are wrought iron with a stone column on each side topped with statues of boars with wings. Once on the grounds, the coaches pick up speed as they wind their way up the sloping road toward the castle with its turrets and towers (PA 5:87). The gates have statues of winged boars on each side, and the large main doors are made of oak (GF 12:171). The Entrance Hall has a long marble staircase and is lit by torches (GF 12:171).

By the third year, Harry has come to regard the school as his home (PA 5:95). The bedroom quarters at the top of the spiral staircase in Gryffindor House contain five four-poster beds with heavy red-velvet curtains around them (SS 7:130). There is a Common Room for studying and talking which has a fireplace, tables, and cushioned chairs. Students need the password to get by the Fat Lady in the portrait to enter Gryffindor Tower. Hermione keeps reminding Harry and Ron that Hogwarts is protected by many kinds of enchantments, and Apparition does not work within its walls (PA 9:164).

Hogwarts' grounds include the lake where the merpeople and the giant squid live. Slytherin House quarters are believed to be somewhere under the lake. The Forbidden Forest borders the grounds. The centaur herd lives there and Hagrid has friends he keeps there, including Aragog and Mosag; the thestrals; and his half-brother, Grawp. In Year 2, the Ford Anglia rode off into the forest somewhere after getting tangled with the Whomping Willow, a tree that does not like to be wrestled with.

The staircases at Hogwarts move, sometimes taking students to places they may not want to go. The corridors are lined with portraits of people who can travel from one portrait to another. Special rooms at the school include the Room of Requirement, which becomes whatever room the first person entering it wants it to be; the Armor Gallery, where suits of armor are lined up; and the Trophy Room, which holds the school awards.

See also The Great Hall; Appendix A

Hokey. *Character.* Dumbledore tells Harry that Hokey is an old house-elf. They enter one of Hokey's memories in the Pensieve (HBP 20:430). Hokey is charged and convicted with poisoning her mistress, Hepzibah Smith, when it was really Tom Riddle who killed her because he wanted her treasures (HBP 20:438).

Holidays with Hags. *Magical book.* This is a second-year "textbook" written by Gilderoy Lockhart (CS 4:43). One of the Slytherin girls reminds Harry of a picture he has seen in this book (CS 11:191).

Holyhead Harpies. *Magical sports team.* A Welsh Quidditch team, in existence since 1203. It was the first professional team to include witches as players (QA 34; HBP 4:71).

Home Life and Social Habits of British Muggles. *Magical book.* Hermione reads this book instead of joining the Gryffindor party after their Quidditch win over Ravenclaw in Year 3. She is desperate with her overloaded schedule and has 422 pages left to read (PA 13:264).

Honeydukes. *Magical place.* Candy shop in Hogsmeade (PA 5:77). Harry, Ron, and Hermione are glad to see that it is still open in Year 6, when so many other stores and shops are closed (HBP 12:243).
See also Candy and sweets

Hooch, Madam Rolanda. *Character.* Flying Lessons instructor and Quidditch referee (SS 7:127). She casts an Impediment Jinx on Harry when he hits Draco Malfoy in the stomach during a Quidditch match; Harry hit Draco for making nasty comments about his and Ron Weasley's mothers (OP 19:413).

Hooper, Geoffrey. *Character.* Angelina Johnson tells Harry that Geoffrey Hooper had more talent as Keeper than Ron during try-outs, but Geoffrey is a whiner, so she took Ron on the Quidditch team instead (OP 13:276).

Hopkirk, Mafalda. *Character.* The employee at the Ministry's Improper use of Magic Office who sends Harry a letter accusing him of using a Hover Charm at Privet Drive, though it was really Dobby who did it (CS 2:20–21). She sends another letter after Harry conjures the Patronus that saves him and Dudley Dursley from two Dementors in Little Whinging. Her second letter states that due to his previous warning and the severity of the latest use of magic he has been expelled from Hogwarts and his wand will be broken (OP 2:27).

Hoppy. *Magical creature.* From *Fantastic Beasts.* The name of one of Newt and Porpentina Scamander's pet kneazles (FB vi).
See also Fantastic Beasts and Where to Find Them

Horcruxes. *Magical objects.* In Latin *horreo* means "to be rough" and *crux* means "cross." Tom Riddle tries to find out more from Slughorn about what Horcruxes are and about their capabilities. Harry sees this in the memory that he and Dumbledore watch in the Pensieve (HBP 17:370–71). Slughorn explains to Tom Riddle that they are objects that contain a part of a person's soul so that if the body is ill or damaged, at least part of the soul will live on, though in a diminished state that is worse than death (HBP 23:497). Dividing the soul is an act against nature, however, so it takes an act of evil, such as murder, for the soul to split. Tom Riddle finds out that it is theoretically possible to split the soul seven times, since seven is the most magical number (HBP 23:498).
If there are seven Horcruxes, Dumbledore tells Harry what some of them must be. Tom Riddle's diary is one, and Harry destroyed that (HBP 23:500). Marvolo Gaunt's ring was another, and Dumbledore himself destroyed the Horcrux in it when he found it in the ruins of the Gaunt family shack. Snape helped Dumbledore's burning hand resulting from the ring, and now the Horcrux is no longer in the ring (HBP 23:503). Dumbledore guesses that two of the remaining Horcruxes are the Slytherin locket and the Hufflepuff cup (HBP 23:505). He also conjectures that Nagini, the snake, is another. That leaves a Horcrux representing Ravenclaw or Gryffindor Houses to discover and destroy. Since the only

known artifact of Godric Gryffindor is the sword kept protected in Dumbledore's office, a Gryffindor object is more uncertain (HBP 23:504–5).

Horklumps. *Magical creatures.* Classified 1X by the MM. Something like a mushroom, the creature is pink with wiry black hair (FB 21–22). Prof. Dumbledore mentions in his foreword to *Fantastic Beasts* that readers may find a way to get Horklumps out of their lawn by reading the book (FB vii). Newt Scamander admits to taking them apart in his room at the age of seven (FB ix). Gnomes like to eat this mushroom-like creature that has tentacles that spread through a lawn like roots (FB 21–22).
See also Fantastic Beasts and Where to Find Them

Hormorphus Charm. *Magical spell.* This charm brings a werewolf back to human form. In DADA class, Harry must help Prof. Lockhart demonstrate how he used this charm. Lockhart supposedly rescued some villagers from the Wagga Wagga Werewolf (CS 10:162).

Hornby, Olive. *Character.* Olive Hornby is a girl who made fun of Moaning Myrtle about her glasses before she died. The incident made Myrtle go into the girls' bathroom to cry, where Myrtle met her fate (CS 16:299). Moaning Myrtle used to haunt Olive and tells Harry in the prefects' bathroom about a time she did so at Olive's brother's wedding. Olive went to the Ministry to get Myrtle to stop bothering her, and that is when Myrtle retreated to her toilet at Hogwarts (GF 25:465–66).

Horton, Basil. *Character.* One of the founders of the Comet Trading Company, broomstick makers, in 1929 (QA 49).
See also The Comet Trading Company

Horton-Keitch braking charm. *Magical spell.* This spell gave Quidditch players using Cleansweep Comet broomsticks an advantage; they could stop more quickly, for example, in trying to make an accurate goal. The feature made the Cleansweep Comet broomstick dominant in the sporting market for many years (QA 50).

Hourglasses. *Magical objects.* There are giant hourglasses at Hogwarts that hold stones representing the house points (OP 28:626). A large hourglass is also used at the desk of the O.W.L.s examiner during the theoretical part of the exams (OP 31:712). The Gryffindor hourglass is hit with a hex during the battle at Hogwarts, and it crashes to the floor (HBP 28:601).

The House Championship/House Cup. *Magical honor.* One student house at the end of each school year at Hogwarts wins the House Cup. Points are added to houses for students' good behavior, academics, and other achievements. Points are taken away when students are caught breaking the rules, talking back in class, or doing anything else a faculty member deems to be worth punishment (SS 7:114). Slytherin won the House Cup seven years in a row until Harry's first year. That year, Gryffindor won the Cup when Dumbledore gave the house more points at year's end. These points were added for the heroic deeds performed by Harry (sixty points for courage), Ron (fifty points for the best game of wizard chess seen at Hogwarts in several years), Hermione (fifty points for staying calm under pressure and using logic), and Neville Longbottom (ten points for standing up to his friends) during the Sorcerer's Stone adventure (SS 17:306). The evening they won the House Cup is described as the best night of Harry's life up to that point (SS 17:307). Gryffindor wins it Year 2, especially with the extra points Harry and Ron win for the house with their work solving the Chamber of Secrets mystery (CS 18:339).

House-elves. *Characters.* Hogwarts has the most house-elves of any single living space in Britain. Hogwarts has about a hundred of them. They live under the castle and provide the food for all meals and clean and tend the castle fires at night; they are never seen, which is part of their pride in their work. When Nearly Headless Nick tells Hermione about the house-elves working at Hogwarts, she gets angry and will not finish her dinner (GF 12:182).

Hover Charm. *Magical spell.* Harry is accused by the Ministry of Magic of casting this charm while on Privet Drive; however, it is really Dobby who caused Aunt Petunia's pudding to rise up in the air and fall on the floor (CS 2:20–21). When the Wizengamot points out this previous citation at Harry's hearing, Harry tells them that a house-elf was responsible for the incident (OP 8:148).

Howler. *Magical letter.* An angry letter in a red envelope. When opened, the voice of the sender rants and raves loudly at the recipient until the letter finally bursts into flames. Molly Weasley sends one to Ron after the Ford Anglia incident in Year 2 (CS 6:87–88). After Neville Longbottom leaves the list of passwords to Gryffindor Tower lying in a place where they get stolen, Neville's grandmother sends him a Howler (PA 14:271). Prof. Dumbledore sends one to Petunia Dursley to remind her that Harry must stay with her and Vernon (OP 2:40).

Hufflepuff, Helga. *See* Hufflepuff House

Hufflepuff House. *Magical school organization.* Harry first hears of Hufflepuff House when Draco Malfoy speaks to him at Madam Malkin's on Diagon Alley (SS 5:77). It is one of the four student resident houses at Hogwarts. It was founded by Helga Hufflepuff and is currently headed by Prof. Pomona Sprout, who teaches Herbology. The house ghost is the Fat Friar. Students of the house are characterized as hard workers who are patient and loyal. House colors are 'yellow and black, and the house emblem is a black badger on a gold field. Their Quidditch robes are yellow. The location of Hufflepuff quarters is unknown; however, they may be reached by stairs leading down from the main hall of the castle. Notable Hufflepuff characters include Cedric Diggory, Hannah Abbott, Ernie Macmillan, Susan Bones, and others.

Humor. Rowling has said that she likes working in fantasy because of the opportunities it gives her to write humor. The books are nothing if not funny, and many readers point to Rowling's use of humor, combined with her meaningful story lines, as one of her greatest talents as a writer.

Perhaps the surest source of humor lies with certain characters. Neville Longbottom is humorous at the beginning of the series with his fumbling and bumbling, but his situation is also poignant when readers begin to learn his full story. Ron Weasley is clearly the funniest of the major trio. Characters who represent humor through and through are certainly Fred and George Weasley, the school tricksters, who may be relied upon in almost any scene to provide much-needed comic relief. Harry gives them his Triwizard Tournament earnings to open their joke shop so that they may continue their mission beyond Hogwarts. He tells them that he and many others could use a good laugh once in awhile. Even characters such as Dumbledore, Hagrid, and others on the faculty and staff at Hogwarts are not without their jokes and humorous actions.

Beyond characters who can laugh at themselves, Rowling pokes fun at institutions and other entities. She makes fun of the press, education, teachers, political officials, magic, and just about any established institution or practice with which Harry comes into contact. The result is a book that readers young and old can appreciate on several levels, even as they recognize themselves among the pages that have them laughing.

Humpbacked One-eyed Witch. *Magical statue.* A statue on the third floor; a secret passageway is located beneath her hump and she is never guarded (PA 10:190). The way to enter the passageway is to tap the hump and say "Dissendium" (PA 16:326).
See also Statues

Hungarian Horntail. *Magical creature.* Of all the dragon species, this may be the most dangerous. The dragon looks like a lizard with black scales. It eats goats, sheep, and will also eat human beings (FB 13). Charlie Weasley shows Harry this breed of dragon (GF 19:327). It ends up being the one Harry chooses out of the bag to get past for the first task of the Triwizard Tournament (GF 20:350).
See also Fantastic Beasts and Where to Find Them

Hunter. *Magical sports position.* "Hunter" was the early name for the Seeker in Quidditch history (QA 13).

Hurling Hex. *Magical spell.* Prof. Flitwick wants to check out Harry's new Firebolt broomstick to make sure it does not have a Hurling Hex on it (PA 12:245).

Hurricane. One of the Muggle Prime Minister's difficulties is what he describes as a hurricane that hit the West Country (HBP 1:2). Cornelius Fudge explains that it was not a hurricane but a ruckus caused by the Death Eaters and a possible giant. The Ministry was trying to erase the memories of Muggles who saw what happened (HBP 1:13).

Hut-on-the-Rock. *Muggle place.* When Uncle Vernon is trying to escape the letters arriving for Harry from Hogwarts, he sails the family in a little boat out to sea, and they stay in an old shack on a rock. Their only provisions are a bag of potato chips and four bananas. The two-room cabin smells of seaweed and wind blows through the cracks in the walls. Vernon is not able to start a fire in the fireplace. Most of all, his ploy to escape does not work, since Hagrid finds Harry at the Hut-on-the-Rock (SS 3:44).

Hydrangea bush. *Muggle plant.* Harry hides behind a hydrangea bush outside the window of Number Four, Privet Drive in order to listen to the television news inside (OP 1:1).

· I ·

"I must not tell lies." *Magical detention*. Prof. Umbridge makes Harry write this sentence over and over during his detention in her office. However, instead of writing the words on paper, they are cut into the back of his hand (OP 13:266).

"I solemnly swear that I am up to no good." *Incantation*. This incantation makes the Marauder's Map reveal its secrets (PA 10:192). The phrase began appearing on T-shirts not long after the book and film were released.

Ice Mice. *Magical candy*. The treat is sold at Honeydukes and makes one's teeth chatter and squeak (PA 10:197).
See also Candy and sweets

Ilfracombe Incident of 1932. *Magical event*. From *Fantastic Beasts*. A Welsh Green dragon flew down on Muggles on a beach. Catastrophe was averted by a vacationing wizard family that cast the largest number of Memory Charms in the twentieth century (FB xvi).
See also Fantastic Beasts and Where to Find Them

Ilkley. From QA. The Kwidditch team from Ilkley played Goodwin Kneen's team (QA 9).
See also Kneen, Goodwin; *Quidditch Through the Ages*

Illness, Injuries, and Maladies. *See* St. Mungo's Hospital for Magical Maladies and Injuries

Illustrations. Though Rowling can sketch and did so in her notes and on her website, different illustrators were contracted to depict the covers and inside illustrations of most of the Harry Potter books. The exception is that Rowling illustrated *Quidditch Through the Ages* with small diagrams and sketches of broomsticks, Quidditch pitches, plays, and so forth. The British editions of the novels do not contain chapter opening illustrations, but the American editions do. Covers of the novels in translation illustrate almost as much about the country and its culture as they do about Harry and the story line of the novel.

Bloomsbury has used different illustrators for the covers of the British children's and adult editions of the books. The illustrators for the children's editions are: *Philosopher's Stone*, Thomas Taylor; *Chamber of Secrets*, Cliff Wright; *Prisoner of Azkaban*, Cliff Wright; *Goblet of Fire*, Giles Greenfield; *Order of the Phoenix*, Jason Cockcroft; and *Half-Blood Prince*, Jason Cockcroft. The adult British editions of the early books use black-and-white photographs of a steam locomotive, a Ford Anglia, and so forth. The covers for OP and HBP are constructed from images by Michael Wildsmith and are designed by William Webb.

The American edition covers, both children's and adult's, have been illustrated by artist Mary GrandPré. Rowling told GrandPré the only time they met (which was around the publication of *Prisoner of Azkaban*) that her drawings depict the fantasy nature of the books in the way that the author had envisioned them, and they look similar to Rowling's own sketches. The artist also illustrated each of the chapter opening pages, and the drawings add to the pleasure of the books for many readers.

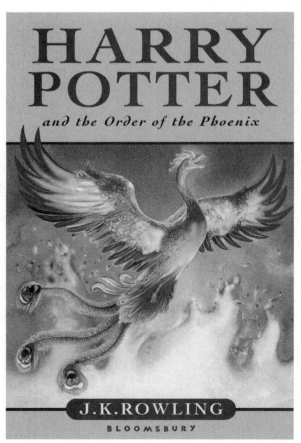

British cover of *Harry Potter and the Order of the Phoenix* (2003) illustrated by Jason Cockcroft and published by Bloomsbury. © Bloomsbury/AFP/Getty Images.

In a September 2005 interview in the *Herald Today* (Bradenton/Sarasota, FL), GrandPré described how the first Harry Potter manuscript came to her and how, when she first said that she had too much other work to do and did not think she could take it on, David Saylor of Scholastic asked her if she might try to "squeeze" the Potter book into her schedule. The former Minnesotan who now lives in Florida is one of the few people who reads the new Harry Potter novels before they are published. She said she looks for scenes that might make a good cover and highlights them in the manuscript. These tend to be scenes that are exciting and feature Harry in intriguing atmospheres. She then sketches several different possibilities, which she sends on to Scholastic. Scholastic chooses one, and GrandPré completes the art in color with pastels. The process of doing the color cover takes about four weeks; it takes another four weeks to do the chapter opening illustrations. Though GrandPré has not disclosed her salary for doing the artwork, she is paid a flat fee, not royalties, and she says she has not become rich from illustrating the Potter books.

When asked about her feelings that the Harry Potter series is about to come to an end, GrandPré said that, as an artist she will have mixed feelings: "The Potter phenomenon has taken over parts of my career and it's sometimes frustrating. It will be kind of like getting a kid off to college and out of the house when he's 18. I'll miss him in a good way." GrandPré's artwork has appeared in magazines such as *The Atlantic* and *The New Yorker*; in books and other materials for publishers such as Penguin, Dell, Random House, and McGraw-Hill; on the Nickelodeon television network; and in the Dreamworks animated feature film *Antz.*

Editions other than the English-language books have been illustrated with motifs that express an interpretation of Harry Potter in that culture. Rowling once said that she particularly liked the Japanese covers. The Japanese cover of *Sorcerer's Stone* features a small figure of Harry flying his broomstick against a large, full moon hanging in a midnight-blue sky over Hogwarts. The Argentinian cover is very similar to the American design, with some of the elements removed. The Icelandic edition features a rugged-looking Harry in a suit jacket, white shirt, and striped tie standing in front of the Hogwarts Express, which is billowing overhanging clouds of gray and black smoke against a blood-red background. This Harry looks at the reader with large, Prof. Trelawney–like eyes behind his glasses, and his scar is thick and prominently red, as though fresh. The Ukrainian cover of HBP shows Dumbledore and Harry in the boat in the cave in vibrant colors of gold, purple, and blue with faces of near-portrait quality in their intricate detail.

Further Reading: Hartman, Donna. "Imagining Harry: Sarasota Artist Mary GrandPré Brings Boy Wizard to Life Through Book's Illustrations." *Herald Today* (Bradenton/Sarasota, FL), September 25, 2005. http://www.bradenton.com/mld/bradenton/entertainment/12724363.htm.

Imp. *Magical creature.* From *Fantastic Beasts.* Classified 2X by the MM. This creature is native to Britain and Ireland and is often confused with the pixy; it lives near riverbanks (FB 22).
See also Fantastic Beasts and Where to Find Them

Impediment Curse/Jinx. *Magical spell.* This spell slows down or obstructs an attacker (GF 29:574). The incantation is "Impedimenta!" Madam Hooch uses the curse on Harry during a Quidditch match when Harry hits Draco Malfoy in the stomach (OP 19:413). James Potter puts the curse on Snape in Snape's worst memory (OP 28:646). Neville uses it in the escape from the Inquisitorial Squad (OP 33:760). Harry uses it in the cave against the Inferi (HBP 26:575).

"Imperio!" *Incantation.* This incantation is used to cast for the Imperius Curse, which gives the caster complete control over the victim (GF 14:213).
See also Imperius Curse; Unforgivable Curses

Imperius Curse. *Magical spell.* The curse gives the caster complete control over another witch or wizard. It is one of the Unforgivable Curses. Mad-Eye Moody teaches it to his DADA class in Year 4. The incantation is "Imperio!" Moody demonstrates it on spiders. To counter the curse takes strength of will and character (GF 14:213). In another class, Moody casts the spell on several students to give them a sense of what it feels like to be controlled by another wizard. He makes Dean Thomas hop and sing the national anthem; Lavender Brown behave like a squirrel; and Neville Longbottom perform gymnastics. Harry successfully resists the curse (GF 15:231–32). Snape tells

Harry that the skill needed for this spell is similar to what he needs for Occlumency (OP 24:534).

Imperturbable Charm. *Magical spell.* This spell makes entry impossible; it also makes it impossible to use other spells that allow entry (OP 4:69).

Imperturbable door. *Magical object.* This type of door does not allow entry or charms that would make entry possible (HBP 6:125).

Impervius Charm. *Magical spell.* Keeps eyeglasses from fogging up in the rain or presumably other natural effects from happening. Incantation: "Impervius!" (OP 18:379).

Important Modern Magical Discoveries. *Magical book.* Harry and friends go searching for information about Nicolas Flamel in this book (SS 12:198).

Improper Use of Magic Office. *Magical office.* Located on the second floor of the Ministry, this office is part of the Department of Magical Law Enforcement (OP 7:130). Molly Weasley fears that Fred and George will be required to appear at this office for their experiments with unusual candy and joke products (GF 5:59).

Inanimatus Conjurus. *Magical spell.* Use of this spell is assigned as homework by Prof. McGonagall in Transfiguration class (OP 14:289).

"Incarcerous!" *Incantation.* This incantation puts ropes around its victim (OP 33:755). Harry uses it in the cave against the Inferi (HBP 26:575).

"Incendio!" *Incantation.* This incantation causes fire. Mr. Weasley makes the spell put a fire back in the Dursleys' fireplace (GF 4:47). *Incendo* is Latin for "set fire."

Inferi. *Magical beings.* Corpses that have been forced through magic to do a Dark wizard's wishes. They were rare before Voldemort's time (HBP 4:62). Unlike a ghost, which is transparent, an Inferius still has its body (HBP 21:460).

Ingolfr the Iambic. *Character.* From QA. A Norwegian poet who wrote a verse in the early 1400s that mentioned the game of Quidditch (QA 39). Iambic pentameter is the most frequent metrical line in English speech and is used often in Shakespeare.
See also Quidditch Through the Ages

Inner Eye. *Magical skill.* Prof. Trelawney tells her students in Divination class that some people have the gift of a more developed Inner Eye than others; these people will be better able to predict the future (PA 6:103).

Inquisitorial Squad. *Magical student organization.* Draco Malfoy is a member of this group that was set up by Dolores Umbridge to spy on fellow students at Hogwarts. The group has been given authority to take points away from student houses (OP 28:626). Hermione suggests that Draco chose to stay with this group and gave up his prefect job at Hogwarts, but Harry thinks that Draco is no longer a prefect because he has become a Death Eater (HBP 7:141).

Instant Darkness Powder. *Magical substance.* A product sold at Weasley's Wizard Wheezes. The substance makes escapes easier. The Weasley twins import the powder from Peru (HBP 6:119).

Inter-House Quidditch Cup. *Magical award.* This cup is given to the Hogwarts house with the most Quidditch points by the end of the school year. The contest is cancelled in Year 4 because of the Triwizard Tournament (GF 12:183).

InterCity 125. *Muggle train.* Mr. Weasley becomes interested in this train that arrives at Platform 9 at King's Cross (PA 5:71).

Intermediate Transfiguration. *Magical book.* Harry needs this third-year textbook for Hogwarts (PA 4:54). Hermione uses the book to study a diagram of an owl turning into opera glasses for O.W.L.s (OP 31:705).

International Association of Quidditch. *Magical office.* Referee Hassan Mostafa from Egypt is chairwizard of this office (GF 8:106).

International Ban on Dueling. *Magical rule.* Percy Weasley tells Harry and friends about how the Ministry has tried to get Transylvania to sign this ban. He says that he is meeting with Transylvania's Head of Magical Cooperation the following year (GF 23:425).

International Code of Wizarding Secrecy. *Magical law.* Harry knows that using a Muggle Aqua-Lung is not possible for the second task in the Triwizard Tournament under Hogwarts' lake; it would break the International Code of Wizarding Secrecy and he would be disqualified (GF 26:482). Clause 73 was adopted into the code in 1750. This clause ordered all segments of the wizarding world to keep magical creatures secret, cared for, and controlled within its own borders. If a creature from any area causes harm or attention from Muggles, then that segment of the wizarding world will be prosecuted by the International Confederation of Wizards (FB xvi). The number of species was later increased as success of the code widened (FB xvi). The Confederation imposes fines on nations that defy Clause 73. Tibet with its Yeti and Scotland with its Loch Ness Kelpie sightings are frequent offenders (FB xvii).
See also Fantastic Beasts and Where to Find Them

International Confederation of Warlocks' Statute of Secrecy. *See* Statute of Secrecy

International Confederation of Wizards, British Seats. *Magical office.* This office is located on level five of the Ministry as part of the Department of International Magical Cooperation (OP 7:130).

International Confederation of Wizards' Conference. *Magical event.* Rita Skeeter asks Dumbledore if he saw her article on this conference (GF 18:307).

International Confederation of Wizards' Statute of Secrecy. *See* Statute of Secrecy

International Confederation of Wizards Summit Meeting of 1692. *Magical event.* From *Fantastic Beasts.* Representatives from the wizard, centaur, merpeople, and goblin communities gathered to discuss magical creatures. Agreement among all but the goblins was made to designate twenty-seven species of magical creatures to keep hidden from Muggles or presented in a fashion as to suggest they never actually existed (FB xv).
 See also Fantastic Beasts and Where to Find Them

International Federation of Warlocks. *Magical organization.* Something like the United Nations for the wizarding world, the Confederation is displeased with the Minister of Magic, Cornelius Fudge, for telling the Muggle Prime Minister about Sirius Black's escape from Azkaban Prison (PA 3:37).

International Magical Office of Law. *Magical office.* This office is located on level five of the Ministry as part of the Department of International Magical Cooperation (OP 7:130).

International Magical Trading Standards Body. *Magical office.* This office is located on level five of the Ministry as part of the Department of International Magical Cooperation (OP 7:130).

International Statute of Secrecy. *See* Statute of Secrecy

Interrogators. *Magical position.* The Wizengamot hearing about Harry's expulsion from Hogwarts contains several people who ask questions while the other judges preside over the proceedings. Harry's Interrogators are: Cornelius Fudge, Minister of Magic; Amelia Susan Bones, Head of the Department of Magical Law Enforcement; and Dolores Jane Umbridge, Senior Undersecretary to the Minister (OP 8:138–39).

Intruder Charm. *Magical charm.* This charm makes a warning sound if an intruder approaches (HBP 4:67).

Inverness. From QA. The Ministry of Magic caught the unruly Banchory Bangers Quidditch team over Inverness and disbanded the team in 1814 (QA 17).
 See also Quidditch Through the Ages

Invigoration Draught. *Magical potion.* When Snape leaves Harry alone and does not intimidate him in Potions class, Harry is able to concoct this potion well (OP 29:660).

Invisibility Booster. *Magical object.* Arthur Weasley has added this silver button to the dashboard (CS 5:70) of the Ford Anglia to make it suitable for wizards to fly; it makes the car invisible to Muggles, though it does not always function properly (CS 5:67).

Invisibility Cloak. *Magical object.* One of the most magical and important items Harry owns at Hogwarts is the silvery and watery cloak he receives from an unknown giver during his first Christmas. A note comes with the cloak explaining that it was once owned by Harry's father, James Potter, who gave it to this gift-giver for safekeeping. Harry is advised to "use it well" (SS 12:201–2). He later finds out that he was given the cloak by Prof. Dumbledore (SS 17:299). Anything covered by the cloak becomes invisible. Harry takes it to Hogsmeade and uses it "well" in many of his adventures (PA 14:276).

Invisibility Section. *Magical place.* Section in the Hogwarts Library where some books are hidden (CS 11:198).

Invisibility Spell. *Magical spell.* A charm to make an object invisible (OP 24:540).

Invisible Book of Invisibility. *Magical book.* The manager of Flourish and Blotts bookstore tells Harry that they once lost track of two hundred copies of these expensive books, and he will never order them again (PA 4:53).

Invisible ink. *Magical substance.* Hermione suggests that perhaps Tom Riddle's diary was written in Invisible ink (CS 13:233).

Ireland. There are several references to Ireland in the series. Ireland's Quidditch team wins the World Cup after playing well against Peru in the semi-finals (GF 5:63). The Irish camp outside the field is a delight in green. The tents are covered in sod and shamrocks that makes them look like sod houses (GF 7:82). Seamus Finnegan is of Irish descent.

Irish International Side. *Magical team.* From QA. The professional Quidditch team from Ireland. They ordered seven Firebolt broomsticks for the team before the Quidditch World Cup (PA 4:51).
  See also Quidditch Through the Ages

Irish National Quidditch Team. *Magical sports team.* Ireland played well against Peru in the semi-finals that won them their place in the Quidditch World Cup (GF 5:63).

Irish Quidditch League Headquarters. *Magical place.* This office is located in the Department of Magical Games and Sports on the seventh level of the Ministry (OP 7:129).

Isle of Drear. *Muggle place.* From *Fantastic Beasts.* An island off northern Scotland made unplottable because of the presence of a magical creature called a Quintaped (FB 34–36).
  See also Fantastic Beasts and Where to Find Them; Quintaped

Isle of Skye. From *Fantastic Beasts.* The Pride of Portree professional Quidditch team is from Isle of Skye (QA 36).

Ivanova. *Character.* Chaser on the Bulgarian National Quidditch Team who plays in the World Cup (GF 8:105).

· J ·

Janus Thickey Ward. *See* Thickey, Janus

Jarvey. *Magical creature.* From *Fantastic Beasts.* Classified 3X by the MM. The jarvey looks like a ferret and is found in Britain, Ireland, and North America. They eat gnomes, moles, rats, and voles (FB 22).
   See also Fantastic Beasts and Where to Find Them

Jelly-Legs Jinx. *Magical spell.* Makes the victim's legs rubbery like jelly (GF 31:608).

Jelly Slugs. *Magical candy.* This candy is sold at Honeydukes; Harry hears a clerk ask for a box of them when he arrives by secret passageway under the trapdoor (PA 10:196).
   See also Candy and sweets

Jewkes, Leonard. *Character.* From QA. Leonard Jewkes invented the Silver Arrow broomstick (QA 49).
   See also Quidditch Through the Ages

Jinxes for the Jinxed. *Magical book.* This book is in the Room of Requirement when Harry uses it for Dumbledore's Army lessons (OP 18:390).

Jobberknoll. *Magical creature.* From *Fantastic Beasts.* Classified 2X by the MM. The Jobberknoll is a small blue bird that eats insects. Its feathers are ingredients in Truth Serums and Memory Potions (FB 22–23).
   See also Fantastic Beasts and Where to Find Them

Johnson, Angelina. *Character.* She is a Chaser on the Gryffindor Quidditch team in Harry's first year (SS 11:185). She is nearly asleep at Oliver Wood's pre-dawn practice in Year 2 (CS 7:108). She turned seventeen in October in Year 4 and enters her name into the Goblet of Fire, but she is not chosen as the Hogwarts champion who will compete (GF 16:261). In Harry's fifth year, Angelina is the Gryffindor Quidditch team captain (OP 12:224). She gets frustrated with all of Harry's detentions with Prof. Umbridge when she tries to find a new Keeper to replace Oliver Wood (OP 13:269). Hagrid was teaching better in Year 5 than in the previous year, so Angelina wonders why Umbridge fires him. Hermione tells her that Umbridge hates half-humans (OP 31:723).

Joke cauldron. *Magical object.* In Year 6, Verity, a young witch with short blonde hair, tells the Weasley twins in their joke shop that someone is looking for the joke cauldron. Harry thinks it strange to hear Verity call the twins by the formal, adult name of "Mr. Weasley" (HBP 6:120).

Jones, Gwenog. *Character.* A former student of Horace Slughorn's; she is captain of the Holyhead Harpies (HBP 4:71).

Jones, Hestia. *Character.* A member of the Order of the Phoenix who arrives with others at Privet Drive to take Harry to Headquarters. She has pink cheeks and black hair and waves at Harry from near the toaster in the kitchen when she is introduced (OP 3:49). Hestia is the Greek goddess of hearth and home.

Jordan, Lee. *Character.* Lee Jordan surfaces in the series at King's Cross Station on Harry's first trip aboard the Hogwarts Express; Lee is showing a large tarantula to others around him (SS 6:94, 98). He wears dreadlocks. Lee Jordan finds a new secret passageway out of the school during Harry's first year, but Fred and George Weasley think it is probably the same one they found their first year (SS 9:153). Lee is a friend of the twins and commentates a little less than objectively for Quidditch matches during Harry's first year (SS 11:186). Lee congratulates Ron and Harry on their brilliant entrance to Hogwarts in the Ford Anglia in Year 2 (CS 5:84). He commentates the Gryffindor-Slytherin match in Year 3 and gets scolded by Prof. McGonagall for being biased in his commentary in favor of his Gryffindor friends (PA 15:308). Lee is the first student to notice something unusual in the lake right before Durmstrang arrives (GF 15:246). Lee gets in trouble with Prof. Umbridge when he suggests that Educational Decree 26 must keep teachers from scolding students about playing games in the back of classrooms. He has to do detention with Umbridge, and Harry advises the essence of murtlap bath for his hands, which get carved in detention (OP 25:551). Lee admits that it was he, not Hagrid, who was putting nifflers in Umbridge's office (OP 31:723).

Jorkins, Bertha. *Character.* An employee of the Ministry, Bertha Jorkins sets out to visit relatives in Albania and never returns. She was killed by Voldemort (GF 1:10–11). Arthur and Percy Weasley discuss her disappearance and Percy complains about how Ludo Bagman has done nothing about it. He says that Ludo jokes about Bertha's sense of direction and how she may have mistaken Australia for Albania on a map (GF 5:61–62). Sirius Black warns Harry that perhaps she told Voldemort about the Triwizard Tournament; this would allow Voldemort to get Harry's name in the Goblet so that he could participate in the Tournament (GF 19:334). It is known that Bertha visited her second cousin, then headed south to see her aunt, but she never made it (GF 24:447). Sirius Black insists that when she was a student at Hogwarts, Bertha was not forgetful as people were trying to make her out to be later. She had a good memory for gossip (GF 27:533).

She turns up as a student in Dumbledore's Pensieve when he and Harry share the Pensieve for the first time (GF 30:599).

See also Albania

Jugson. *Character.* A Death Eater who helps Lucius Malfoy (OP 35:788).

See also Death Eater

Junior Assistant to the Minister. *Magical position.* Percy Weasley has this position working for Cornelius Fudge at the Ministry. Percy's father is not impressed with his son's job because Fudge has been giving Dumbledore a hard time since Voldemort's return; Fudge and the Ministry do not believe that Voldemort has returned (OP 4:71).

Junior Heavyweight Inter-School Boxing Champion of the Southeast. *Muggle sports title.* Dudley Dursley achieves this title competing for Smeltings (OP 1:11).

Jupiter. Ron makes up a prediction about this planet for Divination homework (GF 14:221). Hermione helps Ron with his essay about Jupiter's moons, including Ganymede (the largest), Callisto, Io (the one with volcanos), and Europa (covered with ice) (OP 14:295, 300).

⋆ K ⋆

"Kacky Snorgle." *Wrong name.* Ron mistakenly calls Crumple-Horned Snorkacks "Kacky Snorgle" (OP 33:762).

Kappas. *Magical creatures.* From *Fantastic Beasts.* Classified 4X by the MM. Kappas are water creatures from Japan with webbed hands and monkey faces that strangle those who wade into the ponds where they live (PA 8:141). The Kappa drinks human blood, but it can be placated by being fed a cucumber with the victim's name on it (FB 23). Snape claims they are found most often in Mongolia (PA 9:172). Mad-Eye Moody makes sure that the students have gone over Kappas in DADA class before he teaches them the Unforgivable Curses (GF 14:211).
  See also Fantastic Beasts and Where to Find Them

Karasjok Kites. *Magical sports team.* From QA. A Norwegian Quidditch team that was beaten in a famous match of the European Cup in 1956 by the Caerphilly Catapults (QA 33).
  See also Quidditch Through the Ages

Karkaroff, Igor. *Character.* Igor Karkaroff was a Death Eater in Azkaban Prison when Sirius Black was there. Karkaroff was released when he made a deal with the Ministry to give them the names of more Death Eaters. Mad-Eye Moody was the Auror who originally caught him and put him in Azkaban (GF 19:332). Karkaroff shows Snape that the Dark Mark tattoo on his arm is getting darker and more distinct (GF 27:519). After Karkaroff deserts the Death Eaters, his body is found in a shack up north; people see the Dark Mark in the sky above the shack (HBP 6:106).

Karkus. *Character.* The first giant chief that Hagrid negotiates with to recruit the giants' help for Dumbledore (OP 20:427).

Keddle, Gertie. *Character.* From QA. The witch who lived on the edge of Queerditch Marsh in the eleventh century and wrote in her diary about watching fools playing a game with a leather ball (QA 7–8).
   See also Quidditch Through the Ages; Queerditch Marsh

Keeper. *Magical sports position.* The goalie in Quidditch (SS 10:168). The position has been a part of Quidditch since the thirteenth century (QA 23).
   See also Quidditch

Keitch, Randolph. *Character.* From QA. One of the founders of the Comet Trading Company, broomstick makers, in 1929 (QA 49).
   See also The Comet Trading Company; *Quidditch Through the Ages*

Kelpie. *Magical creature.* From *Fantastic Beasts*. Ranked 4X by the MM. The Kelpie is another water demon. *Fantastic Beasts* relates that the Kelpie takes different forms but often looks like a horse (FB 23–24).
   See also Fantastic Beasts and Where to Find Them

Kenmare Kestrels. *Magical sports team.* Seamus Finnigan adjusts his poster of this Quidditch team in the Gryffindor dormitory while talking to Harry about his mother not wanting him to return to school that year (OP 11:217). The Irish team was founded in 1291 and they are famous for their leprechaun mascots and their spectacular displays (QA 35).

Kent. On the night Harry is left on the Dursleys' doorstep, weather forecaster Jim McGuffin reports that people have been seeing a downpour of shooting stars as far away as Kent, rather than the showers he predicted (SS 1:6). Prof. McGonagall tells Prof. Dumbledore that the Kent shower was probably the doing of careless Dedalus Diggle (SS 1:10). Madam Modesty Rabnott, an important figure in Quidditch history from the thirteenth century, was from Kent (QA 12).

Kettleburn, Prof. *Character.* A teacher who retired, leaving the position of Care of Magical Creatures professor open for Hagrid to take over at Dumbledore's invitation (PA 5:93).

Kevin. *Character.* The very small wizard boy Harry sees at the campground for the Quidditch World Cup. He has gotten hold of his father's wand and is making slugs swell to several times their size when his mother comes out of the tent and steps on them and scolds him (GF 7:81).

Killing. Much is made in the series about killing and murder, and the desire or lack of desire to do so. The first time Harry wants his wand to kill somebody is in the Shrieking Shack when he confronts Sirius Black, whom he believes contributed to Voldemort's killing of his parents (PA 17:339). However, Harry is unable to kill Sirius when he is given the chance (PA 17:343). Draco Malfoy is unable to kill Dumbledore when given his chance as well (HBP 27:594–95).

Killing Curse. *Magical Dark spell.* The incantation for the Killing Curse is "Avada Kedavra." It is one of the Unforgivable Curses. Mad-Eye Moody demonstrates it on spiders in DADA class (GF 14:215–20). The Potters and Dumbledore die from it.

King, Stephen (1947–). The best-selling American thriller writer from Maine endorsed the Harry Potter series in a highly visible review that appeared in *The New York Times Book Review* in July 2000. In the review King admitted that the first three novels in the series helped him move through the pain he suffered after his famed 1999 accident when he was out walking and was severely injured after being hit by a car. He wrote, "The fantasy writer's job is to conduct the willing reader from mundanity to magic. This is a feat of which only a superior imagination is capable, and Rowling possesses such equipment." Coming amid the intense promotional campaign of *Goblet of Fire* that left some readers wondering if any book could live up to such high expectations, King's positive review provided reinforcement. Stephen King is the award-winning popular author of such novels as *Carrie* (1974); *The Shining* (1977); *Cujo* (1981); *Misery* (1987); and the Dark Tower series. Like Rowling, he has had many of his books made into films.

Further Reading: King, Stephen. "Wild About Harry: The Fourth Novel in J. K. Rowling's Fantastically Successful Series about a Young Wizard." *New York Times Book Review*, July 23, 2000, 13–14.

King's Cross Station, London. *Muggle place.* Hogwarts students are instructed to leave from Platform 9¾ at 11:00 A.M. on September 1 at this station to catch the Hogwarts Express to Hogwarts School of Witchcraft and Wizardry (SS 5:87; SS 6:89).

The station was the location of one of four London terrorist bombings on the morning of July 7, 2005. The event occurred nine days before Rowling's reading at Edinburgh Castle and resulted in her choosing a different chapter to read; instead of reading the opening chapter about the Muggle Prime Minister, she opted for the chapter on the Weasley twins' new joke shop. Rowling has admitted that she mistakenly remembered

London's King's Cross Station during the promotional tour for *Harry Potter and the Goblet of Fire*, July 2000. © Hugo Philpott/AFP/Getty Images.

Euston Station for King's Cross when she wrote the first account of Platform 9¾ in Book 1.

Kirke, Andrew. *Character.* Andrew Kirke becomes a Beater on the Gryffindor team when Prof. Umbridge bans Fred and George Weasley from playing (OP 21:453). Ron says Andrew Kirke has even less talent than he has (OP 25:556).

Kiss. Harry receives his first kiss from Cho Chang under the mistletoe before Christmas in his fifth year. Hermione guesses this is the reason for the goofy look on his face later. When Ron asks how it went, Harry describes it as wet, since Cho was crying. Ron wonders if Harry is such a bad kisser that he could make Cho cry; this thought gets Harry wondering the same thing. Hermione assures Harry that Cho cries all the time over her confused feelings for Cedric Diggory (who has died) and her attraction to Harry. Hermione tries to explain the complexity of Cho's feelings to a befuddled Harry and Ron (OP 21:457–58).

Klein, Cheryl. The Continuity Editor for *Harry Potter and the Half-Blood Prince* at Arthur A. Levine Books of Scholastic. She is an editor of other books at the imprint as well, such as *Millicent Min, Girl Genius* by Lisa Yee and *The Book of Everything* by Guus Kuijer, translated from the Dutch by John Nieuwenhuizen.
  See also Levine, Arthur A.

  Further Reading: Arthur A. Levine Books website: http://www.arthuralevinebooks.com.

Kloves, Steven. *See* Films

Knarl. *Magical creature.* From *Fantastic Beasts.* Classified 3X by the MM. Muggles see this creature and confuse it with a hedgehog. When given food, the knarl becomes offended and attacks the home owner's garden (FB 24). Prof. Grubbly-Plank plans to review knarls before Harry's O.W.L.s (OP 15:323). Harry is able to tell a knarl from a hedgehog for his practical O.W.L. by offering it milk. The knarls will behave in an agitated manner out of fear of being poisoned (OP 31:717).
  See also Fantastic Beasts and Where to Find Them

Kneazle. *Magical creature.* From *Fantastic Beasts.* Classified 3X by the MM. Furry, catlike creatures with large ears and lionlike tails. They make good pets, guard their homes, and can interbreed with cats (FB 24–25). Newt Scamander and his wife, Porpentina, have three kneazles as pets; they are named Hoppy, Milly, and Mauler (FB vi). Prof. Grubbly-Plank plans to go over kneazles before Harry's O.W.L.s (OP 15:323). In interviews, Rowling has said that Crookshanks is part kneazle.
  See also Fantastic Beasts and Where to Find Them

Kneen, Goodwin. *Character.* Goodwin Kneen writes to his cousin Olaf in Norway about "Kwidditch" a century after Gertie Keddle's diary was written (QA 8–10).

Knickerbocker Glory. *Magical treat.* The treat Dudley Dursley does not finish at the zoo because he complains that there is not enough ice cream topping on it; Harry is allowed to finish eating it (SS 2:26).

Knight Bus. *Magical object.* The bus stops on Magnolia Crescent, picking up Harry after he runs away from the Dursleys. It is an emergency transportation system for witches and wizards who are lost or stranded. It is a triple-decker bus that is bright purple with gold letters over the windshield identifying its name (PA 3:33). The bus can go anywhere the riders want to go, as long as it is on land; it cannot go underwater (PA 3:34). The fare is 11 Sickles for the ride alone; it costs 13 Sickles to have chocolate during the ride; or 15 Sickles for a hot water bottle and toothbrush in the rider's choice of color. There are beds instead of seats (PA 3:35). When Harry asks why the Muggles do not see the bus, the driver tells him it is because Muggles do not listen well and notice very little as a result (PA 3:36). Hagrid makes a reservation for two seats to go to London for Buckbeak's trial (PA 14:273). Harry and friends go back to Hogwarts from the holiday at Grimmauld Place aboard the Knight Bus (OP 24:522).

Knobbly stick. *Muggle object.* The Knobbly stick is also called a Smelting stick. Each student at Smeltings private school receives a stick to whack fellow students with when the teachers cannot see them. Dudley Dursley practices on Harry (SS 3:32).

Knockturn Alley. *Magical place.* Knockturn Alley is the Dark Arts version of Diagon Alley. Stores include Borkin and Burkes, which contains instruments and other objects related to the Dark Arts (CS 4:53). Knockturn Alley is a side street off of Diagon Alley (HBP 6:123).

Knotgrass. *Magical plant.* An ingredient in the Polyjuice Potion (CS 10:165).

Knuts. *Magical money.* Small bronze coins used in the magical world (SS 5:62).
   See also Money

Kopparberg. From *Fantastic Beasts.* Kopparberg is the starting place of the ancient broom race in Sweden (QA 4).
   See also Sweden

Kreacher. *Character.* Kreacher is the Black family house-elf at Grimmauld Place (OP 4:76). He demonstrates the Black family's bigotry toward individuals with mixed bloodlines. For example, he calls Hermione Granger a Mudblood (OP 6:108). For Christmas Hermione gives him a quilt for his space under the boiler beside the kitchen (OP 23:503). Kreacher disappears several times while the Order of the Phoenix occupies Grimmauld Place, and he is usually found in the attic (OP 29:669). However, when Kreacher is missing at Grimmauld Place before Christmas, he is not at the house at all but serving another master, Narcissa Black Malfoy (OP 37:830). Sirius Black tells Kreacher to inform Dumbledore that Harry was looking for Sirius at the Department of Mysteries (OP 37:830). Harry inherits Kreacher's house-elf services when Sirius dies (HBP 3:51).

Krum, Viktor. *Character.* Viktor Krum is the star player on the Bulgarian Quidditch Team. He is still very young and attends Durmstrang Institute for Witches and Wizards (GF 5:63). Ron calls him one of the best Seekers in the world (GF 16:248). He is chosen by the Goblet of Fire to be the champion of Durmstrang in the Triwizard Tournament (GF 16:269). For the second task of the Triwizard Tournament, he can be seen diving into the cold lake (GF 24:443). After Viktor takes Hermione to the Yule Ball, Ron breaks apart his Viktor Krum action figure and throws it under his bed (GF 24:444). Hermione is pen pals with Viktor in her fifth year (OP 16:332). Viktor Krum has told

Hermione that he was impressed with Harry's abilities in the Triwizard Tournament. Harry knows skills that Viktor still does not know in his seventh year at Durmstrang (OP 16:331).

Kwidditch. *Magical sport.* From QA. An old spelling for Quidditch, used in Goodwin Kneen's letter to his Norwegian cousin Olaf (QA 8–10).
  See also Quidditch Through the Ages

Kwikspell. *Magical course.* This is a correspondence course for beginning magic lessons. Harry sees the materials for it on Argus Filch's desk and surmises that he is a Squib. The material includes endorsements by Madam Z. Nettles of Topsham and Warlock D. J. Prod of Didsbury (CS 8:127). One of the lessons is about how to hold a magic wand (CS 8:128).

ᐧ L ᐧ

Lacewing flies. *Magical creature.* An ingredient in the Polyjuice Potion (CS 10:165).

Lachlan the Lanky. *Magical statue.* This statue is located near the entrance to Gryffindor Tower on the seventh floor of Hogwarts.

The lake. *Magical place.* There is a black lake on the Hogwarts School grounds with the castle sitting on a high mountain on the other side (SS 6:111). Hagrid meets first-year students getting off the Hogwarts Express and takes them across the lake toward the castle in boats that fit no more than four students each. The merpeople live in the lake and Slytherin House is thought to be underneath it.
   See also Hogwarts School of Witchcraft and Wizardry

"Langlock!" *Incantation.* This incantation makes one's tongue stick to the roof of the mouth, making speech impossible. Harry learned it from the Half-Blood Prince's book and performs it on bothersome Peeves (HBP 19:420).

Languages, use of. *See* Latin, Use of; Translations

Latin, use of. Though there are small phrases of French and German in the series, the principle language next to English would surely have to be Latin. Names of characters, slogans, incantations, and other notable phrases have Latin roots that are either left alone or manipulated by Rowling with further wordplay. The inclusion of Latin words and phrases has sent children to dictionaries and other research quests to find the "hidden" meanings of these words. Some say that children and others have become interested in studying Latin in more depth because of the books.
   In an interview for CBC in 2000, Rowling said that when she went back to Exeter (her alma mater where she earned a degree in French and classics), she commented in a speech that she is one of the few people she knows who ever made practical use of her classics degree. The comment was met with laughter from the audience, some of whom

were Latin professors and scholars. She has said that she finds it amusing to think of the wizarding world still using Latin (which is considered a "dead" language; that is, it is read but rarely spoken), but bending it for their own purposes, including the way they use it in incantations. She actually bends the language the same way her characters do in the series. She has said that for her, Latin (the small amount of it she knows) is basically a self-taught language.

See also Translations

Further Reading: Rogers, Shelagh. "Interview: J. K. Rowling." Canadian Broadcasting Co., October 23, 2000.

Law Fifteen B. *Magical law.* Dolores Umbridge begins to cite this law about creatures with near-human intelligence when she is approached by the displeased centaurs (OP 33:754).

Lawsuits. Once a book becomes highly successful, lawsuits regarding plagiarism and the origin of the story and intellectual property frequently arise. Rowling's experience with the Harry Potter series has been no exception. The most troubling of these suits for Rowling was one brought by Nancy (N. K.) Stouffer of Pennsylvania. Stouffer's book, *Legend of Rah and the Muggles*, was reportedly published in 1984. That book, and the books following, which, it was said, appeared from 1984 through 1988, contained a main character named Larry Potter who has wavy black hair and glasses similar to Harry Potter's. Larry's mother's name is Lilly, similar to Lily Potter of Rowling's creation. The most potentially harmful claim was Rowling's use of the word "Muggle," which Stouffer claims in her title and throughout her books. Muggles in Stouffer's books are hairless creatures who take care of an orphan. The case battled its way through court until judgment was finally handed down late in 2002 that Stouffer's case did not prove a reasonable connection between her book and Rowling's. Rowling won the case. Stouffer lost an appeal in early 2004.

Rowling and her representatives have also filed several lawsuits of their own. They have done so in efforts to protect readers and others from pirated or falsified copies of the books (both before and after publication), from forged "autographed" copies that were being sold or auctioned for exhorbitant amounts, and for other matters concerning Rowling's rights as author and Warner Bros.' rights to the films and merchandising.

The Leaky Cauldron. *Magical place.* This is a small, dingy pub in London where witches and wizards can pass from the Muggle world to the magical world. The old bartender is named Tom. If one goes out the back door of the pub, there is a courtyard with nothing else but weeds and garbage cans. Tapping on the brick wall above the garbage cans in a certain configuration makes a large archway appear which leads to Diagon Alley. Once the people are through, the wall closes up again (SS 5:68–71). Harry taps on the third brick from the left over the garbage can (PA 4:50).

Leanne. *Character.* A friend of Katie Bell's who argues with her in Hogsmeade about a package Katie is holding (HBP 12:248).

Leaving Feast. *Magical event.* The dinner and celebration at the end of the school year. At the end of Year 4, the event in the Great Hall is subdued, with black decorations in memory of Cedric Diggory. Dumbledore leads the school in a toast to him (GF 37:720–21).

Leeches. *Magical creatures.* An ingredient in the Polyjuice Potion (CS 10:165).

Leg-Locker Curse. *Magical curse.* This curse freezes one's legs so that they are stuck straight out together (SS 13:217). The incantation is "Locomotor Mortis" (SS 13:222). Harry tries to put this curse on Draco (HBP 24:522).

Legilimency. *Magical ability.* The skill to take feelings and memories from the mind of someone else (OP 24:530). The incantation is "Legilimens" (OP 24:534). One who has this skill is also called a Legilimens; Dumbledore tells Harry that he is a reasonably accomplished one of these himself (OP 37:832). Snape tells Bellatrix Lestrange that Voldemort is the most skilled Legilimens in world history (HBP 2:26).

"Legilimens." *Incantation.* This is the incantation for Legilimency (OP 24:534).

Leith Academy. One of Scotland's oldest schools that dates back to 1560, Leith employed Rowling briefly before the publication of *Sorcerer's Stone*. It is a six-year comprehensive school located in Academy Park in Edinburgh, not far from where the author used to live. Her position there as a teacher was particularly beneficial for her, not only because of the school's location (she did not have to find transportation), but also because the school had on-site day care for her daughter.

Lemons and lemon-flavored treats. The taste of lemon comes up frequently in the series. One of Prof. Dumbledore's favorite Muggle treats is lemon drops (called sherbet lemons in *Philosopher's Stone*) (SS 1:10). Aunt Petunia looks like she has swallowed a lemon when Harry mentions that perhaps he could stay home alone on Dudley's birthday to watch television and use Dudley's computer (SS 2:23). At the zoo, Harry enjoys the inexpensive lemon ice pop the Dursleys buy for him (SS 2:26). A password into Dumbledore's quarters is "Lemon drop" (CS 11:204).

Leprechauns. *Magical beings.* From *Fantastic Beasts.* Classified 3X by the MM. *Fantastic Beasts* says that the leprechaun is smarter than a fairy and not as mean as creatures like imps, pixies, or Doxies; however, leprechauns can still cause trouble. Ron's "handwritten" note in *Fantastic Beasts* indicates that he is not amused by the fact that leprechaun gold disappears (FB 25).

Leprechauns are the Ireland National Quidditch Team mascots at the Quidditch World Cup. Thousands of them appear in the stadium, making a huge rainbow across the sky from which thousands of leprechaun gold coins spill into the audience (GF 8:104).

In folklore, leprechauns are tiny shoemakers. Irish *leith-bhrogan*, from *leigh-brog*, means "one-shoe maker." The leprechauns work on the same shoe over and over.

See also Fantastic Beasts and Where to Find Them

Lestrange, Bellatrix Black. *Character.* Sirius Black's cousin. She married pure-blood Rodolphus Lestrange, thus staying in the family's graces and keeping her name on the tapestry showing the family line (OP 6:114). The couple are both Death Eaters in Azkaban Prison (GF 27:531). Harry remembers seeing Bellatrix Lestrange in Dumbledore's Pensieve; she is tall and dark with heavy eyelids and is a proud supporter of Voldemort (OP 6:114). Kreacher keeps a photograph of her in his cupboard (OP 23:504). After Harry and his friends see Neville Longbottom's parents at St. Mungo's,

Harry tells them that Bellatrix made them insane with a Cruciatus Curse, and that is why she is in Azkaban (OP 23:515). She is present at the attack in the Department of Mysteries (OP 35:788) and she kills Sirius Black (OP 35:806). She tells Snape that although Voldemort appears to trust him, she does not (HBP 2:25).

Lestrange, Rabastan. *Character.* Rodolphus Lestrange's brother. He went to Azkaban at the same time as Barty Crouch, Jr., and Rodolphus and Bellatrix Lestrange (OP 6:114). He is at the attack in the Department of Mysteries (OP 35:788).

Lestrange, Rodolphus. *Character.* A Death Eater imprisoned with his wife, Bellatrix, in Azkaban (OP 6:114). He is at the attack in the Department of Mysteries (OP 35:788). One of the Lestranges was with Tom Riddle when he went to ask Slughorn more about Horcruxes, but Riddle was asked to leave (HBP 23:496).

Lethifold. *Magical creature.* From *Fantastic Beasts.* Classified 5X by the MM. The Lethifold is also known as Living Shroud. It is rare and lives in the tropics. The Lethifold resembles a Dementor in that it looks like a black cloak. It attacks victims at night and eats them immediately. As with Dementors, wizards protect themselves against them through the use of a Patronus (FB 24–27).
See also Fantastic Beasts and Where to Find Them

Levicorpus. *Magical spell.* In Latin, *levo* means "to lift up"; *corpus* means "body." The Levicorpus is a nonverbal jinx that the owner of *Advanced Potions* seemed to have trouble using. Harry tries it in bed one night and ends up dangling Ron upside down in the air by his ankles. The counter-jinx is "Liberacorpus" (HBP 12:238–39). Prof. Lupin tells Harry that the jinx was very popular in his time at Hogwarts but hints that it may not have been documented yet as a jinx at that time (HBP 16:336).

Levine, Arthur A. Levine is Rowling's American editor at Scholastic Books, Inc., under the Arthur A. Levine imprint. Levine helped launch Rowling's career onto the world stage by offering an unheard-of sum of $105,000 as an advance for a children's novel from an unknown author. Levine believed in Harry Potter. He liked Harry's underdog quality; after his first ten miserable years of life, Harry finds out that he is actually special—not only to one person, but to many people. Levine thought back to his own childhood; he had been interested in music, but he grew up in a town that honored athletics above all else. Harry reminded Levine of himself and of all the other artistic or otherwise gifted children who were not recognized for their merits.

In a talk at Yale in September 2005, Levine said that he had a personal goal before he had ever heard of Harry Potter. His goal was to publish a children's novel that would remain important to readers into their adult years. He said that themes like love and its protection are very real and add to the story of Harry Potter, making it more than a collection of special effects. Levine surprised his audience by saying that though his work on the Potter novels will end soon with the publication of the last book, he and Rowling plan to continue to work together on future projects.

Further Reading: Levine, Arthur A., with Doreen Carvajal. "Why I Paid so Much." *New York Times,* October 13, 1999: C14; Mangino, Andrew. "'Harry Potter' Editor Comes to Silliman." *Yale Daily News,* September 27, 2005; Arthur A. Levine Books Official Website: http://www.arthuralevinebooks.com.

Levitation Charm. *Magical spell.* Harry has to perform the Levitation Charm for his Charms practical O.W.L. (OP 31:713).

Levski. *Character.* Levski is a Chaser on the Bulgaria National Quidditch Team in the World Cup (GF 8:105).

Lewis, C. S. (1898–1963). C. S. Lewis's *Chronicles of Narnia* is a fantasy series that is embraced as a classic of children's literature. The Harry Potter books are sometimes compared to *Narnia*, either favorably or unfavorably. Like the Harry Potter series, *Narnia* is a septology. The seven novels in their narrative sequence are: *The Magician's Nephew* (1955); *The Lion, The Witch, and the Wardrobe* (1950); *The Horse and His Boy* (1954); *Prince Caspian: The Return to Narnia* (1951); *The Voyage of the "Dawn Treader"* (1952); *The Silver Chair* (1953); and *The Last Battle* (1956). *The Last Battle* won the Carnegie Medal of 1957.

Lewis is said to have had a series of nightmares about lions that started him thinking about the story. As he thought more about it, he wanted to write a fantasy that contained the principle elements of the story of Christ. The story would change the characters and setting but otherwise would follow the life, death, and resurrection of Jesus as told in the Bible and church teachings. While some label the septology as allegory, others point out that Lewis joined J.R.R. Tolkien and other Inkling thinkers in the belief that myth and story have the power to directly nurture one's spiritual growth. Whether allegory or not, what Lewis achieved became one of the most highly regarded, sustained fantasies of the twentieth century and a classic of children's literature.

The Harry Potter books have been compared to *The Chronicles of Narnia* in that both are series that portray a character slipping into a fantasy world to undergo a series of moral adventures. In a 2005 *Time* magazine article, Rowling said that she has read some but not all of the *Narnia* books. She is bothered by Lewis's portrayal of Susan, who becomes lost to Narnia because she begins using lipstick. Rowling is quoted as saying, "She's become irreligious basically because she found sex. I have a big problem with that." Though the authors may have different views on the nature of growing up, critics have begun to argue that Rowling's and Lewis's works bear much more in common that should be explored once the Potter series is completed.

See also Tolkien, J.R.R.

Further Reading: Granger, John. *Looking for God in Harry Potter.* Wheaton, IL: Tyndale House, 2004; Grossman, Lev. "J. K. Rowling Hogwarts And All." *Time*, July 27, 2005.

Liberacorpus. *Magical spell.* The Liberacorpus spell is the counter-jinx to the Levicorpus spell (HBP 12:238–39). In Latin *liber* means "free"; *corpus* means "body."

Library, Hogwarts. *Magical place.* Snape makes up a rule that no library books are to be taken outdoors (SS 11:182). Madam Irma Pince is the librarian.

Licorice Wands. *Magical candy.* One of the treats sold on the Hogwarts Express Candy Cart that Harry buys and shares with Ron on their first meeting (SS 6:101).

See also Candy and sweets

Liechtenstein. The wizarding community of this country has a disagreement with Pierre Bonaccord over trolls' rights. Harry tries to write an essay about the issue in his History of Magic O.W.L.s (OP 31:726).

See also Bonaccord, Pierre

Little, Christopher. Rowling's literary agent. When she completed *Sorcerer's Stone*, she looked through a market guide of agents and publishers and decided she liked the sound of Little's name, so she sent off a portion of the manuscript to his office in London. Little sent back a letter asking to see the rest of the manuscript. Rowling has said that this short letter was the best she had ever received. She quickly sent the rest of the book, and Little took her on as a client. Little did Little know then that his association with the tenuously employed single mother was about to change his life.

Little Hangleton. *Magical place.* The town where the Riddle family lived; they are buried in the churchyard there (GF 1:1, 4).

"Little Miss Question-All." *Nickname.* Prof. Umbridge calls Hermione "Little Miss Question-All" (OP 32:747).

Little Norton Church Hall. *See* Boardman, Stubby

Little Whinging, Surrey. *Muggle place.* Where Number Four, Privet Drive is located (SS 3:34).

Little White Horse **(Goudge).** *See* Goudge, Elizabeth

Llewellyn, "Dangerous" Dai. *Character.* From QA. A Welsh Quidditch player who was killed on vacation in Mykonos, Greece, by a Chimera; a medal was initiated in his honor (QA 33).
See also Quidditch Through the Ages

Lobalug. *Magical creature.* From *Fantastic Beasts*. Classified 3X by the MM. The Lobalug is ten inches long and is poisonous. Merpeople sometimes use them as weapons (FB 27).
See also Fantastic Beasts and Where to Find Them

Lochrin, Guthrie. *Character.* From QA. The first wizard to write of a flying broomstick in 1107. A Scottish wizard, he complains of having splinters in his bottom and hemorrhoids (QA 2).

Locket. *Magical object.* There is a heavy locket that cannot be opened at Number Twelve, Grimmauld Place (OP 6:116). The Slytherin locket has the Slytherin "S" on it (HBP 20:437). The locket found in Dumbledore's robes after he dies contains a note from someone with the initials "R.A.B." saying that he had already destroyed the Horcrux that was inside the locket (HBP 28:609). The opal necklace that hurts Katie Bell is a different necklace from the one in Dumbledore's robes (HBP 12:250). Which necklace/locket is which in terms of Book 7 remains to be clarified for many readers.

Lockhart, Gilderoy. *Character.* Gilderoy Lockhart is a vain and corrupt author who teaches Defense Against the Dark Arts in Year 2. In his first class, he makes the students take a quiz about himself that they should be able to answer after reading the full collection of his works, which he assigned as required textbooks. When the students go over the quiz in class, the reader learns that Lockhart's favorite color is lilac, which is written in *Year with the Yeti*. His favorite birthday gift, which he says is written in chapter twelve of *Wanderings with Werewolves,* is peace between Muggles and magical people, though he adds that he would not mind a large bottle of Odgen's Old Firewhisky as well. His secret ambition is to eradicate the world of evil while simultaneously starting his own brand of hair care potions (CS 6:100). His awards and qualifications, as listed in a get-well message to Hermione Granger, include: Order of Merlin, Third Class; Honorary Member of the Dark Force Defense League; and five-time winner of *Witch Weekly's* Most Charming Smile Award (CS 13:228).

Lockhart does not limit his "knowledge" to the classroom, either. He visits Hagrid's hut and tries to advise him on how to get rid of Kelpies from a well and goes on about how he banished the banshee (CS 7:114–15). Among his other claims, he tells Harry that he was a Seeker and was invited to try out for the National Squad but turned it down (CS 10:163). Instead of healing Harry's broken arm after a Quidditch match, he inadvertently removes the bones entirely (CS 10:173).

Lockhart's office is in the second floor corridor (CS 7:119). It is filled with portraits of himself (CS 9:141). Lockhart admits to Harry that an Armenian warlock was the actual person to save the village from werewolves described in Lockhart's book, and a witch with a hairy chin was the one who banished the Bandon Banshee (CS 16:297). Near the Chamber of Secrets, he tries to put a Memory Charm on Harry and Ron, but it backfires on him (CS 17:324). He does not return as DADA teacher the following year because he must get his memory back (CS 18:340). Harry and friends see Lockhart at St. Mungo's in the Spell Damage ward, where he is still working on getting his memory back. The nurses say he never gets any visitors (OP 23:508–509). Lockhart provides a blurb for *Quidditch Through the Ages* (QA frontispiece).

Rowling denies that Lockhart is drawn from her first husband, but admits that his character is drawn from a real person she has met. She has never identified the person's name for what she considers to be obvious reasons.

"Locomotor Mortis." *Incantation.* This is the incantation for the Leg-Locker Curse (SS 13:222). In Latin, *loco* means "to put" and *mors* means "death."

Logic Puzzle. *Magical puzzle.* The bottle puzzle at the end of Year 1, which Hermione solves so she, Harry, and Ron may keep looking for the Sorcerer's Stone (SS 16:285). There is not enough information given for the reader to solve the logic puzzle because the location of the different-sized bottles in relation to one another is not completely defined. Viewers of the first film were disappointed that this scene was left out of the movie. They argue that it depicts an intelligent young girl solving a problem using logic, an act that is not often portrayed in books or films.

Longbottom, Alice. *Character.* Neville Longbottom's mother. She was an Auror who was attacked by Voldemort's supporters and was driven insane. She permanently resides at St. Mungo's. At Christmas, when Harry and friends visit Arthur Weasley in the hospital, she motions to Neville, who is there visiting with his grandmother, and puts a Droobles Blowing Gum wrapper in his hand. Neville keeps it (OP 23:514–15).

Longbottom, Augusta (Gran). *Character.* Neville Longbottom's grandmother. She believes Dumbledore when he says that Voldemort has returned; she does not believe the false stories in the *Daily Prophet* about Dumbledore and Harry (OP 11:219). Harry and friends see her at St. Mungo's when they visit Arthur Weasley at Christmas. She wears a green dress with fox fur on it that has been damaged by moths, along with a pointy hat with a stuffed vulture on it. When she meets Harry she tells him that Neville speaks very highly of him. She is kind to Ron and Ginny Weasley, telling them she knows their parents, though not well. She recognizes Hermione and tells her that Neville has told her she has helped him many times and that he is a good boy but not the talent that his father was. She tells Neville's friends that her son and his wife were Aurors who were tortured by Voldemort's followers and that they were left insane (OP 23:512). She is quoted in an article in the *Daily Prophet* about Neville fighting with Harry against the Death Eaters in the Hall of Prophecy (HBP 3:41). Prof. McGonagall tells Neville that she will write Gran that just because she failed her own Charms O.W.L. it is no reason to call the subject worthless for Neville to continue on in N.E.W.T.s (HBP 9:174).

Longbottom, Neville. *Character.* Readers first encounter Neville at Platform 9¾ when he has lost his toad and is asking his Gran to help him find it (SS 6:94). As with Harry, the Sorting Hat takes a long time to decide where to place Neville, but he is finally sent to Gryffindor House (SS 7:120). Neville's family thought he was Muggle, but his Great Uncle Algie kept testing his magical abilities and finally saw them emerge (SS 7:125). Neville's bumbling continues, unfortunately, at Hogwarts. In his first Potions class, Snape gets angry at Neville for melting a cauldron and getting potion all over himself, resulting in boils on his arms and legs (SS 8:139).

Neville is among those who congratulate Ron and Harry for their brilliant entrance to Hogwarts in the Ford Anglia in Year 2 (CS 5:85). He fears that he is almost a Squib, due to his small magical ability (CS 11:185). He does not get to go to the World Cup because his grandmother did not want to go and did not buy tickets (GF 11:167). Neville melts at least six cauldrons in his time at Hogwarts (GF 14:209). Neville can see thestrals because he saw his grandfather die (OP 21:449). He gets a new wand from his grandmother after the battle at the Hall of Prophecy; it is cherry with a unicorn-hair center and is the last wand Mr. Ollivander sold before disappearing (HBP 7:137).

See also Algie, Great Uncle; Longbottom, Alice; Longbottom, Augusta (Gran)

***Lord of the Rings* trilogy (Tolkien).** *See* Tolkien, J.R.R.

"Loser's Lurgy." *Fake ailment.* Luna Lovegood commentates the Quidditch match with little regard for plays and scores. Instead, she focuses on cloud formations and refers to Zacharias Smith's failure to score as "Loser's Lurgy" (HBP 19:415).

Lovage. *Magical plant.* Lovage is used in Confusing and Befuddlement Draughts (OP 18:383).

Love. One of the themes of the books is that love is stronger than hate; that love can conquer evil, or at least keep it from winning all the time. Dumbledore explains to Harry at the end of Year 1 that his mother did not have to die, but she put herself in danger out of love so that he might be saved (SS 17:298). Dumbledore tells Harry that love is a force that Voldemort does not know and a power he underestimates. Despite the early tragedy in his life and his trials since, Harry remains uninterested in the Dark Arts, which Dumbledore reads as a sign that he has basic goodness in his heart.

Dumbledore clearly loves Harry. In *Order of the Phoenix*, when Dumbledore explains why he waited to tell Harry about the prophecy, he indicates that one of his mistakes was caring more for Harry's happiness than for Harry knowing the truth. He valued Harry's peace of mind over his own strategy to defeat Voldemort, and he valued Harry's life over the lives of others. He says his actions played into Voldemort's hands because he acted "exactly as Voldemort expects we fools who love to act" (OP 37:838). Voldemort is aware of Dumbledore's insistence on using old magic that depends on love. However, there is an implication in the series that since Voldemort does not know love firsthand (either loving someone himself or being loved by another), he is not fully knowledgeable of its powers. Love is likely to have a major effect on how Harry's story is eventually resolved.

Love potions. *Magical substances.* Love potions are popular items at Weasleys' Wizard Wheezes (HBP 6:120). On Valentine's Day in Harry's second year, Lockhart recommends that students ask for Love potions in Prof. Snape's class (CS 13:236). In a Rita Skeeter article, Pansy Parkinson is quoted accusing Hermione of making a Love potion to get Viktor Krum to like her (GF 27:512).

Lovegood, Luna. *Character.* In Latin *luna* means "moon." Harry and friends meet Luna on the Hogwarts Express when she is sitting in a cabin reading a magazine called *The Quibbler* upside down. Luna has bulgy eyes and brown-blonde hair down to her waist. She seems rather befuddled and wears a necklace of butterbeer caps; she keeps her wand tucked behind her ear (OP 10:185). She believes Harry when he says that Voldemort is back (OP 13:261). For a Gryffindor Quidditch match in her fifth year, she wears a hat with a lion's head on it that really roars (OP 19:403). The summer after Year 5, her family plans to go to Sweden to try to catch a Crumple-Horned Snorkack (OP 38:848).

Harry finds perhaps his best consolation after Sirius Black's death in talking with Luna. She tells him that she saw her mother die in an accident with an experimental spell when she was nine. She tells Harry that she will see her mother, and he will see Sirius; she reminds him that they are just beyond the veil and that they could hear their voices. Somehow, though Luna presents some strange theories, Harry finds hope in this one. He did, indeed, hear voices behind the veil that hangs from the archway on the dais (OP 38:863). Harry asks Luna to go to Slughorn's Christmas party with him as a friend (HBP 15:310–11).

Lovegoods. *Characters.* At the Portkey near where the Lovegoods live, Amos Diggory tells Arthur Weasley that the Lovegood family has been gone to the World Cup for a week already (GF 6:73). Luna Lovegood is not mentioned at the time, but this reference may be to her family.

Loyalty. Loyalty is certainly one of the themes of the series. Albus Dumbledore tells Harry that the phoenix is one of the most loyal pets. When the board of governors suspends Dumbledore from his position as headmaster of Hogwarts, he mentions before he is taken away that he will remain at Hogwarts as long as there is someone there who is loyal to him. He surely knows that Harry and Ron are within earshot beneath the Invisibility Cloak when he says this (CS 14:264). Fawkes comes to Harry's aid in the Chamber of Secrets, so Prof. Dumbledore thanks Harry for what must have been real loyalty shown to him; Fawkes only comes to those who are loyal to Dumbledore (CS 18:332). When Rufus Scrimgeour tries to lure Harry away from Hogwarts to work for the Ministry, Harry makes it clear that he is Dumbledore's man, through and through.

Ludicrous Patents Office. *Magical place.* This office is located in the Department of Magical Games and Sports on the seventh level of the Ministry (OP 7:129).

"Lumos!" *Incantation.* This incantation lights the end of one's wand so that one can see (CS 15:272). *Lumen* means "light" in Latin.

Lunoscope. *Magical object.* On Diagon Alley, Harry hears someone discussing how, with a Lunoscope, one need not bother with moon charts anymore (PA 4:50).

Lupin, Prof. Remus John. *Character.* Readers meet Prof. Lupin at the same time that Harry meets him. He is found sleeping next to the window in Harry's cabin aboard the Hogwarts Express (PA 5:74). Unlike the other faculty members, Lupin seems to have only ragged clothing (PA 5:92). Like Harry, he is not afraid to say Voldemort's name (PA 8:155). The students consider him the best DADA teacher they ever had (PA 9:170). For their final exam in the class during Year 3, Lupin makes an obstacle course of several hazards that the students need to outwit and make spells to get past. Lupin is proud of Harry when he emerges from the exam and he tells Harry that he will receive full marks (PA 16:318).

It is revealed in the Shrieking Shack scene that Lupin is a werewolf (PA 17:345). He was bitten by a werewolf when he was a boy and suffered a miserable childhood as a result. Prof. Dumbledore allowed him to come to Hogwarts, and he planted the Whomping Willow with the secret passageway to Hogsmeade and the Shrieking Shack underneath it. Lupin became friends with James Potter, Sirius Black, and Peter Pettigrew. The first two became Animagi in order to be with Lupin when he transformed. Pettigrew was not as smart, but with James Potter's and Sirius Black's help, he was able to transform into a rat (PA 18:354). Lupin transforms into a werewolf on the night of the Shrieking Shack incident and he attacks Sirius Black in dog form (PA 20:381).

Prof. Lupin leaves Hogwarts when Snape reveals to everyone at Hogwarts that Lupin is a werewolf (PA 22:423). Lupin is a faithful member of the Order of the Phoenix that guards Harry and lives in the headquarters at Grimmauld Place. When Harry returns to King's Cross Station after Year 5, Lupin is among those in the Order who are there to meet him and protect him. Harry sees that his face is pale, his hair looks even more gray, and he wears a long, tattered overcoat. He is no doubt also in mourning with Harry over the loss of Sirius (OP 38:867).

In mythology, Remus is the son of Mars and Rhea Silvia and the twin brother of Romulus. The twins were thrown into the Tiber River while young but they were rescued and raised by a she-wolf. In an argument about building Rome, Remus is killed by Romulus.

Lupin is one of Rowling's favorite characters; one reason is because of his "disability," which she relates to her mother's illness with multiple sclerosis.

Lynch, Aidan. *Character.* Seeker on the Ireland National Quidditch Team in the World Cup (GF 8:105, 108).

·M·

***Macbeth* (Shakespeare).** *See* Choice vs. dentiny; Shakespeare, William

MacBoon, Quintius. *Character.* From *Fantastic Beasts.* A Scottish wizard who was chief of the MacBoon clan; he dueled and killed the wizard clan chief, Dugald McCliverts. He and all the MacBoons were transformed into hairy, five-legged creatures by the McCliverts in retribution. The MacBoons would not return to human form, thinking they were more dangerous in their new form; they wreaked havoc on the McCliverts. Soon afterward, however, they realized that there was no one left with a wand to transform them back to human form. Over time they evolved into beasts that would not allow themselves to be captured in order to be changed back (FB 34–36).
  See also Fantastic Beasts and Where to Find Them; McCliverts, Dugald; Quintaped

Macdonald, Magnus "Dent-Head." *Character.* From *Fantastic Beasts.* A Scottish wizard who tried to make the ancient game of Creaothceann legal again in the 1960s, but failed (QA 6).

MacFarlan, Hamish. *Character.* From QA. A Seeker on the Montrose Magpies team and captain from 1957 to 1968. He worked as Head of the Department of Magical Games and Sports (QA 35–36).

Mackled Malaclaw. *Magical creature.* From *Fantastic Beasts.* Classified 3X by the MM. The Mackled Malaclaw looks like a lobster but should not be eaten by humans because it causes a green rash and fever and it makes its victim unlucky (FB 28).
  See also Fantastic Beasts and Where to Find Them

Macmillan, Ernie. *Character.* Hufflepuff student who thinks Harry is dangerous in Year 2; he believes that Harry is the heir of Slytherin and is causing people to get petrified (CS 11:203). He changes his view of Harry after Hermione gets petrified. Harry sees Ernie at the Quidditch World Cup campground, where Ernie waves to Harry cheerily (GF 7:84). Ernie is excited about Hufflepuff Cedric Diggory entering the Tri-wizard Tournament (GF 15:235) and gets angry at Harry again when he is also chosen (GF 18:293). He is made boy prefect in his fifth year (OP 10:188). Ernie tells Harry that he believes what he says about Voldemort coming back (OP 13:262). He says that learning DADA from Harry is the most important thing the students will do that year (OP 16:344).

After Dumbledore escapes from Cornelius Fudge and leaves Hogwarts, Ernie tells Harry and friends that the Fat Friar said that Prof. Umbridge tried to get into the Headmaster's office but could not get past the gargoyle (OP 28:625). When he prepares for O.W.L.s Ernie asks fellow students how long they are studying (OP 31:706). He points out that Hagrid's nighttime ambush was to try to avoid a scene like Prof. Tre-lawney's in front of the whole school (OP 31:723). Ernie is one of the DA members who casts spells on Draco Malfoy, Vincent Crabbe, and Gregory Goyle during the ride home on the Hogwarts Express after Year 5. The DA's various jinxes and defenses leave the three bullies in the form of oozing slugs that Ernie, Justin Finch-Fletchley, and Harry put in the luggage rack for the remainder of the trip (OP 38:864).

Macnair, Walden. *Character.* The executioner who comes to chop off Buckbeak's head as punishment for hurting Draco Malfoy in Hagrid's Care of Magical Creatures class. Walden Macnair is a friend of Lucius Malfoy (PA 16:328; PA 21:400). He is a Death Eater who attends Voldemort's rising at the Little Hangleton graveyard (GF 33:651). He spies on Hagrid and Madame Maxime when they try to negotiate with giants to help Dumbledore (OP 20:432). He is present at the attack in the Department of Mysteries (OP 35:788).

Madam Malkin's Robes for All Occasions. *Magical place.* The store on Diagon Alley where Hogwarts students frequently buy their robes (SS 5:76). Harry buys his robe at Madam Malkin's. Madam Malkin does not approve of Draco Malfoy's foul language when Hermione comes into the store in Year 6. Draco and his mother leave to go to a competitor's store (HBP 6:112–14).

See also Clothing; Diagon Alley

Madam Puddifoot's Tea Shop. *Magical tea shop.* Cho takes Harry to Madam Puddi-foot's Tea Shop on their Valentine's Day date in Hogsmeade. The shop is lacy and is decorated for the holiday with cherubs that fly about throwing pink confetti down on couples paired up at small circular tables (OP 25:559). Harry thinks that Ginny Weasley and Dean Thomas are there on a visit to Hogsmeade in Year 6 (HBP 12:248).

See also Hogsmeade; Valentine's Day

Madcap Magic for Wacky Warlocks. *Magical book.* Harry and friends consult this book to prepare him for the second task of the Triwizard Tournament, but they find nothing of use in it (GF 26:488).

Madley, Laura. *Character.* A Hufflepuff student three years behind Harry (GF 12:180).

Magic. The word "magic" comes from the Greek *megus*, meaning "great," or *magein*, which was the science and religion of Zoroaster, a Persian prophet. One definition of magic is to change the physical world or human consciousness completely at will. Divination, because it seeks to predict and not change the future, is not considered magic. Belief or exploration of magic is known to have occurred as early as the Paleo-lithic Age. Cave paintings suggest that rites of magic were peformed to ensure good hunts. Magic, among those who believe in it, is thought to have no morality in and of itself, but its uses can be symbolized by the colors white, black, and gray. White magic signifies magical powers used for good purposes; black for evil; and gray for ambiguous reasons.

The ancient Greeks divided magic into "high" and "low." High magic, called *theurgy*, or *theourgia* (meaning "working things pertaining to the gods") was performed by priests for the goodness of all in conjunction with religious practices. Low magic, *mageia* or sorcery, was performed by fake magicians for unsavory purposes and who charged a fee. The Romans employed sorcery and counter-sorcery in their efforts to thwart political rivals and others. By 364, the Christian Church was working to separate magic from religion. Priests could not become magicians, and church leaders were not allowed to consult with sorcerers or diviners. Later, witches and sorcerers were executed. Magical orders in the form of secret societies became prevalent in the seventeenth and eighteenth centuries in Europe, when ritual or ceremonial magic became popular with believers.

It was believed that in order for magic to take place, it must be initiated by a witch or wizard under an altered state of consciousness. This state may be induced by a trance brought on by a variety of means, including sounds, gestures, symbols, colors, smells, and images. The timing of the trance was also important, and this was often dictated by astrology. Contemporary magic employs symbols of the four elements: the athame, or sword, for fire; the pentacle for earth; the chalice for water; and the wand for air.

In the Harry Potter series, magic is not taken as seriously as it has been by believers throughout history. It is the underlying skill of those in the magical world and it enables witches and wizards to communicate, move about, defend themselves, and go about their daily lives more easily than Muggles. The only time magic is considered evil is when it is used for bad purposes; this magic is referred to in the series as the Dark Arts. Students at Hogwarts, like Harry, are only educated in Defense Against the Dark Arts. Neither Headmaster Dumbledore nor the school condones the teaching of Dark Arts.

One of the principle uses of magic in the series is to point out the differences between Harry's new world and his old world with the Dursleys. Maintaining the parallel lives of the magical world and Muggle world is the source of much effort and curiosity on both sides. Uncle Vernon does not allow Harry to say the "M word" in his house at Privet Drive (CS 1:2). He is afraid of the new magical powers that Harry has learned; Vernon does not know in the summer between Harry's first two years that his nephew is not allowed to practice magic in a Muggle neighborhood. He calls Harry's magical ability an "abnormality" (PA 2:19). In the cave scene in *Half-Blood Prince*, Dumbledore tells Harry that magic always leaves a trace (HBP 26:563).

When Rowling was asked in interviews if she believes in magic with wands and spells, she said that she does not. She does, however, believe in figurative magic, such as the magic of children learning to read. Critics considering the series are beginning to in-terpret Rowling's figurative use of magic in the books. Critic Margaret Oakes has argued that magic in the series represents technology in the late twentieth and early twenty-first century. Connie Ann Kirk has argued that magic represents the power of imagination.

Further Reading: Guiley, Rosemary Ellen. *The Encyclopedia of Witches and Witchcraft*, 2nd ed. New York: Facts on File, 1999; Kirk, Connie Ann. "Imagi(c)nation in *Harry Potter and the Philosopher's Stone.*" In Steve VanderArk, ed. *The Harry Potter Lexicon.* http://www.hp-lexicon .org/essays/essay-imagicnation.html; Oakes, Margaret J. "Flying Cars, Floo Powder, and Flaming

Torches: The Hi-Tech, Low-Tech World of Wizardry." In Giselle Liza Anatol, ed., *Reading Harry Potter: Critical Essays*, Westport, CT: Praeger, 2003.

Magical fire. *Magical element.* From *Fantastic Beasts*. Regular fire that has had a magical substance added to it (FB 2).

Magical Hieroglyphs and Logograms. *Magical book.* Hermione is reading this book when she stops to explain why Ginny Weasley can fly so well on her broomstick (OP 26:574).

Magical Law Enforcement Squad/Patrol. *Magical organization.* When Harry visits Mr. Weasley's office, he asks if Aurors will be required to go after Anti-Muggle pranksters who have made Muggle toilets flush up rather than down. Mr. Weasley reports that the Magical Law Enforcement Squad takes care of these less severe infractions rather than Aurors. In Year 6, he reports that this group handled a backfired jinx at Elephant and Castle before he arrived at the Burrow (HBP 5:87).

Magical Maintenance. *Magical employees.* Since the entire Ministry is underground, these employees determine what weather the false windows will depict in all of the offices. Mr. Weasley tells Harry that they once depicted a hurricane for two months straight when maintenance was looking for a raise (OP 7:131).

Magical Me. *Magical book.* This book is Gilderoy Lockhart's newest release. It is his autobiography (CS 4:58). In DADA class, he offers an autographed copy to the student author of the best poem about his defeating the Wagga Wagga Werewolf (CS 10:162). In his blurb for *Quidditch Through the Ages*, *Magical Me* is the book that is listed beside his name (QA frontispiece).

Magical Menagerie. *Magical place.* A store on Diagon Alley that sells magical creatures and animals, such as snails, toads, tortoises, rabbits, ravens, and rats. Hermione buys Crookshanks here (PA 4:58).
  See also Diagon Alley

Magical Water Plants of the Mediterranean. *Magical book.* This is the book that Mad-Eye Moody gives to Neville Longbottom after scaring him in DADA class (GF 14:220). It turns out that "Moody" was actually Barty Crouch, Jr., who planted the book in Harry's dormitory so that Harry would find it and discover how to beat the second Triwizard Tournament task using gillyweed. The goal was to get Harry to win the Triwizard Tournament so that he would touch the cup that was the Portkey to the graveyard where Voldemort was waiting to rise again (GF 35:677).

Magick Moste Evile. *Magical book.* This book contains only a very brief mention of Horcruxes, to Hermione's annoyance as she tries to find out about them for Harry (HBP 18:381).

Magizoology. *Magical science.* From *Fantastic Beasts*. The study of magical beasts (FB vi, x).

Magnolia Crescent. *Muggle street.* A street several blocks away from Privet Drive where the Knight Bus picks Harry up after he runs away from the Dursleys. Magnolia

Crescent is where he first sees the black dog that turns out to be Sirius Black (PA 3:31). He crosses this street on his way to Magnolia Road, which is where the play park is located in *Order of the Phoenix* (OP 1:9).

Magnolia Road. *Muggle street.* The play park is located here; it is near the Dursley residence. The street is very similar to Privet Drive, with square houses and manicured, orderly lawns (OP 1:9).

Magorian. *Magical creature.* One of three centaurs Harry meets that lives in the For-bidden Forest. Magorian has a chestnut body, black hair, and high cheekbones. His face shows a proud expression. He is not pleased that Firenze has gone to work for Dumbledore, and Hagrid stops him from harming Harry. He lets Hagrid free, even though the centaurs made an agreement that they could kill any other human being who entered the forest; on that particular day, Hagrid has Harry and Hermione with him, and it is a crime among centaurs to harm the young (OP 30:697–98). Magorian approaches Dolores Umbridge with his bow raised when she enters the Forbidden Forest with Hermione (OP 33:754).

See also Centaurs

Majorca. This is the place where Aunt Petunia Dursley's friend Yvonne is vacationing, which makes her unable to watch Harry on Dudley's birthday (SS 2:23).

Malcolm. *Character.* One of Dudley Dursley's gang members (OP 1:12).

Malecrit. *Character.* From QA. A French playwright wizard who wrote *Hélas, Je me suis Transfiguré Les Pieds* ("Alas, I've Transfigured My Feet") (QA 39).

Malfoy, Abraxas. *Character.* Trying to impress Prof. Slughorn, Draco Malfoy asks him if he has ever heard of his ancestor Abraxas Malfoy. Unimpressed, Slughorn says it was too bad that Abraxas Malfoy died of dragon pox (HBP 9:189–90).

Malfoy, Draco. *Character.* Harry first sees Draco Malfoy in Madam Malkin's robe shop on Diagon Alley in Year 1, where the boy speaks about Quidditch and Slytherin House. Draco later introduces himself to Harry on the Hogwarts Express (SS 6:108). He tries to warn Harry about hanging around the wrong sort of wizards and initially appears to want to be friends with him; However, Harry clearly shows that he does not approve of Malfoy's snobby attitude toward the Weasleys and Hagrid. Malfoy flies well on a broomstick (SS 9:148). His father donates new broomsticks (Nimbus 2001s) to the Slytherin team, and Draco is made Seeker in his second year as a result (CS 7:111). He is made prefect in fifth year (OP 10:188). From observing Draco on Knockturn Alley, Harry deduces that he has become a Death Eater (HBP 7:130).

When Draco's father gets imprisoned in Azkaban after the battle at the Hall of Prophecy, Draco is charged by Voldemort to kill Dumbledore. He is not able to do it, so Snape does it instead (HBP 27:596).

Malfoy, Lucius. *Character.* Ron Weasley informs Harry on the Hogwarts Express that the Malfoys came back to the good side from the Dark Side after the disappearance of Voldemort. He tells Harry that Lucius Malfoy never needed a reason to go to the Dark Side and he does not believe their family's claim that they were bewitched to do so (SS 6:110). Lucius Malfoy loses his place on the board of governors after it is revealed that he threatened all the other members with violence if they did not sign the suspension notice on Dumbledore (CS 18:340). Lucius is a Death Eater who arrives when Voldemort calls the Death Eaters to the Little Hangleton graveyard (GF 33:650).

Lucius lives in a mansion in Wiltshire and is forty-one years old in Harry's fifth year (OP 15:307). When Bellatrix Lestrange charges that Snape did not look for Voldemort when he disappeared, Snape counters that neither did other Death Eaters, including Lucius Malfoy (HBP 2:26).

Malfoy Manor. *Magical place.* The Malfoy family home. Draco indicates that his father has several Dark Arts products and supplies hidden away underneath the drawing-room floor (CS 12:224).

Malfoy, Narcissa. *Character.* Readers first see Draco's mother, Narcissa Malfoy, at the World Cup in *Goblet of Fire.* She is tall, thin, and pretty, except that she has a foul look on her face as though she were always smelling something odorous (GF 8:101). She and her sister visit Snape at Spinner's End where she makes an Unbreakable Vow with him. Snape swears that he will protect Draco for her and that he will perform Draco's assigned deed if Draco cannot (HBP 2:36). Narcissa Malfoy is at Madam Malkin's robe shop in Year 6 where Harry, Ron, and Hermione see her. She warns Harry that Dumbledore will not always be around to defend him (HBP 6:113).

Mallowsweet fire. *Magical fire.* In Divination class, Firenze has his students make a Mallowsweet fire and sage fires and look for certain things in the flames (OP 27:603).

Manchester, England. Rowling lived and worked in Manchester in the early 1990s. The town is relevant to Harry Potter in that the author has said the idea for Harry Potter fell into her imagination on a train ride from Manchester to London. Rowling also has said that she thought up the game of Quidditch in a Didsbury hotel after having a disagreement with her then-boyfriend. Another significant event in Rowling's life that occurred in Manchester was that her apartment was robbed not long after her mother's death; the burglars ran off not only with valuables but also with mementoes of her mother. The event convinced Rowling that a change of scenery was necessary in her life. Not long afterwards, she was on her way to Oporto, Portugal. While she was in Manchester, Rowling worked brief stints as a secretary at the University of Manchester and the Chamber of Commerce.

Manchester is located in Northwest England and is the country's second-largest city. It was primarily known as an industrial center, particularly of textiles, until the 1950s or 1960s. Manchester and its vicinity still manufacture more than half of England's goods.

Mandrake Restorative Draught. *Magical substance.* An antidote to heal the petrified and those with other ailments (CS 9:144).

Mandrakes. *Magical plants.* Mandrakes are also known as Mandragora. Harry and his class replant these at the beginning of Year 2 in Prof. Sprout's Herbology class. Mandrakes restore people who have been transfigured back to their original form, and they are an important ingredient in many other antidotes. Mandrakes are like babies with leaves on top of their heads. They cry loud cries, and when they are mature these cries can kill the listener. The class has to wear earmuffs when they repot them to muffle the sound of their cries. The mandrakes are young, so their cries cannot yet kill, but they could knock the listener unconscious. When they are teething, their teeth are poisonous (CS 6:92–93). Prof. Sprout proclaims that they are mature when they try to jump out of their pot into another's (CS 14:251).

The mandrake is a poisonous perennial herb that grows in the Mediterranean region. Ancient Arabs and Germans believed that Mandragoras, a small man with no beard, was a demon spirit who lived in the plant. In ancient Greece, the witch goddess Circe made juice of the mandrake and turned Odysseus's men into swine. The herb was also believed to contain properties of fertility and virility. In Genesis, Rachel, the barren wife of Jacob, ate the root and conceived Joseph.

Manticore. *Magical creature.* From *Fantastic Beasts.* Classified 5X by the MM. The manticore has a human-like head, a lion-like body, and a scorpion tail. Its sting causes instant death, and its skin wards off most charms (FB 28). Hermione reads about a manticore that killed a person in 1296; the beast got off because no one dared go near it (PA 11:222).
See also Fantastic Beasts and Where to Find Them

***Manxmouse* (Gallico).** *See* Gallico, Paul

Maori art. From QA. The New Zealand Ministry of Magic worked hard to keep Muggles from learning about Quidditch through Maori art (QA 41).

Marauder's Map. *Magical object.* Fred and George Weasley give this map to Harry as an early Christmas gift in Year 3, when Harry cannot go to Hogsmeade because Vernon Dursley would not sign his permission form. The map on old parchment reveals the entire layout of Hogwarts and indicates where people are; it also shows them moving. Fred and George find the map in a drawer in Argus Filch's office that is labeled "Confiscated and Highly Dangerous" (PA 10:192). The incantation to get the blank parchment to reveal its secrets is "I solemnly swear that I am up to no good" (PA 10:192); to make the map go blank again, the incantation is "Mischief managed" (PA 10:194). The map was made by four friends and former students at the school, Moony (Remus Lupin), Wormtail (Peter Pettigrew), Padfoot (Sirius Black), and Prongs (James Potter) (PA 14:287).

Marchbanks, Griselda. *Character.* Griselda Marchbanks is one of the elder Wizengamot members who resigns in protest over the decree that allows the Ministry control over Hogwarts (OP 15:308). She is the head of the Wizarding Examinations Authority (OP 31:707). She is very old, small, hunched over, and partially deaf. Her face is creased with wrinkles. She tells Dolores Umbridge that she remembers examining Dumbledore in Transfiguration and Charms for N.E.W.T.s and that if he does not want to be found, he will not be. He performed spells with his wand that she had never before seen (OP 31:710).

Marietta. *See* Edgecombe, Marietta

Mars. Ron makes up a prediction about Mars for Divination homework (GF 14:221). The centaurs say that Mars has been indicating for some time that a second war is coming. In mythology, Mars is the god of war.

Mars Bars. *Muggle candy.* Harry is ready to buy lots of Mars Bars from the Hogwarts Candy Cart, but they do not carry them; they carry many mysterious and new treats instead (SS 6:101). The candy may also allude to Mars and war.

Marsh, Madam. *Character.* Another rider on the Knight Bus the night Harry rides it. She must be awoken to get off in Abergavenny (PA 3:36).

Martha. *Character.* An employee of the orphanage where Tom Riddle spent his child-hood (HBP 13:264).

Mascots. *Magical beings.* At the Quidditch World Cup, each team brings mascots to the game. Bulgaria brings Veela and Ireland brings leprechauns. The mascots get out of hand. The leprechauns make a rude hand gesture to the Veela, who charge at them with fire (GF 8:111–12).
 See also Leprechauns; Veela

Mason, Mr. and Mrs. *Characters.* These are the dinner party guests who visit the Dursleys on Harry's twelfth birthday at the beginning of *Chamber of Secrets.* Vernon Dursley is having them over for the sole purpose of securing a business deal for Grun-nings' drills; he claims that the deal will make his career (CS 1:7).

Mass Memory Charm. *See* Ilfracombe Incident of 1932

Mauler. *Magical creature.* From *Fantastic Beasts.* Mauler is the name of one of Newt and Porpentina Scamander's pet kneazles (FB vi).

Maxime, Madame Olympe. *Character.* The headmistress of Beauxbatons, Madame Maxime is half-giant and very large. She speaks with a French accent and wears silk clothing and lots of jewelry (GF 15:244). Hagrid likes her, so he dresses up and wears eau de cologne to spend some time with her (GF 16:266). After the Yule Ball, Harry and Ron overhear Hagrid talking privately with Madame Maxime about being a half-giant. She will not admit that she is a half-giant and is offended that Hagrid assumes she is; she says only that she is big-boned (GF 23:429). She goes with Hagrid to the mountains to try to win over the giants so that they will fight with Dumbledore against Voldemort (OP 20). Hagrid says that she can get fired up when she is excited (OP 20:432).

McCliverts, Dugald. *Character.* From *Fantastic Beasts.* A Scottish wizard who was chief of the McCliverts. He got drunk and died while dueling with Quintius MacBoon, chief of the MacBoon clan. After his death, the McClivert clan transformed all the members of the MacBoon clan into five-legged, hairy creatures. They would not return to human form, thinking they were more dangerous in their new form, and they wreaked havoc on the McCliverts. Soon afterward, however, the MacBoons realized that there was no one left with a wand to transform them back to human form. Over time they evolved into beasts that would not allow themselves to be captured and tested so that they might be turned back into human form (FB 34–36).
 See also Fantastic Beasts and Where to Find Them; MacBoon, Quintius; Quintaped

McCormack, Catriona. *Character.* From QA. A Chaser on the Pride of Portree pro-fessional Quidditch team. She was the captain of the team for its two League champi-onships in the 1960s (QA 36).

McCormack, Kirley. *Character.* From QA. The son of Catriona McCormack who plays lead guitar for the Weird Sisters (QA 36).

McCormack, Meaghan. *Character.* From QA. Catriona McCormack's daughter who is a Keeper for the Pride of Portree (QA 36).

McDonald, Natalie. *Character, also a real person.* A Gryffindor student three years behind Harry. Natalie McDonald is the only character in the series drawn entirely from a real person, including her name (GF 12:180). Rowling bestowed the distinction on a young Canadian girl she heard about who wanted to meet her. McDonald was terminally ill. Rowling agreed to meet her on a future trip to Canada but the girl died before the author could fulfill her promise.

See also Canada

McGonagall, Prof. Minerva. *Character.* Readers first see Prof. McGonagall in her animagus form as a tabby cat on Privet Drive (SS 1:9). In her duties as deputy headmistress, it is she who sends the letter of invitation to Harry to attend Hogwarts (SS 4:51). Hagrid presents the first-year students to her when they first arrive at the school, and she explains the Sorting Ceremony and the four student houses to them (SS 6:113). She is described as having square spectacles, a strict expression, and wearing her hair in a bun (PA 5:88). She has taught at Hogwarts for thirty-nine years by Harry's Year 5 (OP 15:321). When Prof. Umbridge fires Hagrid, Prof. McGonagall runs to try to stop him from being taken away (OP 31:721, 723). She is levitated and put on her back from four Stunners to the chest, after which she is transferred to St. Mungo's (OP 32:730). She comes back out good as new after

the battle at the Hall of Prophecy (OP 38:852). After Dumbledore's death, McGonagall takes over as headmistress of Hogwarts. She exemplifies Dumbledore's philosophy when she consults, as he would have done, with representatives of the faculty, staff, and student body in deciding what to do immediately following his death. She informs Hagrid that Dumbledore respected his opinion, and so does she (HBP 29:628).

In mythology, Minerva is the Roman name of the Greek goddess Athena. Born out of the head of Zeus and one of the twelve Olympians, Athena is the goddess of wisdom, skill, and warfare.

McGuffin, Jim. *Character.* The Muggle weather forecaster that Mr. Dursley watches after dinner on the night that infant Harry Potter is left on his doorstep (SS 1:6).

Maggie Smith as Prof. Minerva McGonagall in *Harry Potter and the Goblet of Fire* (2005). Courtesy of Warner Bros./Photofest.

McKinnon, Marlene. *Character.* A member of the original Order of the Phoenix. She was killed two weeks after the photograph of the original Order (which Mad-Eye Moody shows to Harry) was taken. Her entire family was murdered (OP 9:173).

McKinnons. *Characters.* Hagrid tells Harry that Voldemort killed these people, who were among the best witches and wizards of their time; yet Harry, as an infant, survived Voldemort's attack (SS 4:56). In the Pensieve vision of Igor Karkaroff's hearing, Harry hears Karkaroff say that someone named Travers aided in the McKinnons' killing (GF 30:590). Marlene McKinnon was a member of the original Order of the Phoenix (OP 9:173).

McLaggen, Cormac. *Character.* A student at Hogwarts. He has lunch with Prof. Slughorn, Harry, and others on the Hogwarts Express in Year 6 (HBP 7:143). He tries out for Keeper for the Gryffindor Quidditch team the year Harry is captain (HBP 11:225). Hermione goes with him to Slughorn's Christmas party for the sole purpose of making Ron jealous (HBP 15:313). After she finds herself fighting him off under the mistletoe, she escapes (HBP 15:317).

Meadowes, Dorcas. *Character.* A member of the original Order of the Phoenix. She was killed by Voldemort (OP 9:174).

Medal for Magical Merit. *Magical award.* Tom Riddle won this award, which is stored in the Trophy Room (CS 23:234).

"The Medieval Assembly of European Wizards." *Magical assignment.* Prof. Binns assigns the students a three-foot-long composition on this topic in History of Magic. Hermione's essay is four feet, seven inches long in tiny handwriting; Ron's is eight inches too short (CS 9:147).

Mediwizards. *Characters.* The mediwizards are medical staff that help Ireland's Seeker, Aidan Lynch, recover from Viktor Krum's Wronski Feint during the World Cup. They administer a potion that gets Aidan back in the game (GF 8:108–109).

Mega-Mutilation Part Three. *Muggle video game.* Harry writes to Sirius Black about Dudley Dursley throwing his PlayStation out the window in frustration over his diet. Dudley cannot play Mega-Mutilation Part Three to avoid thinking about the diet (GF 2:25).

Meliflua, Araminta. *Character.* Sirius Black's mother's cousin who tried to make hunting Muggles legal (OP 6:113).

Memory Charm. *Magical spell.* This spell erases the victim's memory (CS 3:31). Prof. Lockhart has used the spell on the heroes of his books, who were actually the ones to defeat all the entities Lockhart takes credit for defeating (CS 16:298). The charm can be reversed by a powerful wizard. Voldemort used the Memory Charm on Bertha Jorkins before he killed her (GF 1:12).

Men Who Love Dragons Too Much. *Magical book.* Harry consults this book to help him with the Triwizard Tournament's first task (GF 20:338).

Merchandise, wizard. *Magical products.* At the Quidditch World Cup, there are several souvenirs available that entice the crowd to buy; Harry and his friends buy several items. Products include: light-up rosettes that scream the names of players on each team; green hats with shamrocks that dance; flags that play the Bulgarian and Irish national anthems when they are waved; Bulgarian scarves with lions that roar; small flying Firebolts; and moving action figures of players. Ron buys a shamrock hat, a green rosette, and an action figure of Viktor Krum. Harry buys Omnioculars for himself and his friends for 10 Galleons each. Ron is overcome and embarrassed with Harry's generosity, but Harry promises Ron that he won't give him anything for Christmas (GF 7:93).

See also Merchandising; Omnioculars

Merchandising. Though Rowling was initially against merchandise associated with her characters, she agreed to allow it once Warner Bros. began producing films from the books. In a 2003 interview with *BBC Newsnight* for *Order of the Phoenix*, she said that she meets with Warner Bros. twice a year to discuss which merchandise should be made and which should not. The interviewer asked her if she is concerned that Harry Potter will be better known as a doll, and Rowling said that she thinks the books will outlast all the merchandising that has been associated with the release of each film.

Harry Potter merchandise tends to come out anew with each film release and ties in with scenes from the movie. Merchandise includes, but is not limited to: wands, broomsticks (including some that vibrate), video games, play sets, Lego building sets, action figures, wizard chess sets, witch and wizard collector cards, pens, leather briefcases, calendars, blank journal books, folders, bookbags, and other school and stationery supplies, Halloween masks and costumes, tapestry throws, Harry's glasses, scarves, pewter figurines, a Time-Turner, computer games, Sorting Hats, sheet music to the film scores, T-shirts, jewelry, train sets, figurines, games, puzzles, and more.

Rowling indicated in the same 2003 interview that the high volume of merchandise sales works to offset some of the expense of making the films, which are filled with special effects. In 2005 BBC News reported that worldwide sales of Harry Potter merchandise have topped $1.75 billion (£1 billion).

Further Reading: Paxman, Jeremy. "JK's OOTP Interview." *BBC Newsnight*, June 19, 2003.

Merchieftainess Murcus. *Character.* The head of the merpeople. She tells Dumbledore that Harry tried to save all of the hostages rather than just his own hostage during the second task of the Triwizard Tournament (GF 26:506).

Mercury. Ron and Harry make up predictions based on Mercury and other planets in order to speed up their Divination homework (GF 14:222). In mythology, Mercury is the god of commerce and gain, and he is a messenger of the gods.

Mercy. Mercy is an important motif in the novels. Harry shows mercy to Peter Pettigrew. Rather than allowing Sirius Black and Prof. Lupin to kill Pettigrew for betraying Harry's parents to Voldemort, Harry insists that they take him to the castle and plans to see him go to Azkaban Prison. He says that his act of mercy on Pettigrew is not for the Pettigrew's sake, but because he believes his father would not have wanted Sirius Black and Prof. Lupin to become killers on behalf of such a low-life (PA 19:375–76). Dumbledore tells Harry that his decision to save Pettigrew's life was a good act that will no doubt be repaid in the future (PA

22:426–27). A bond is created when one wizard saves the life of another (PA 22:427). Draco Malfoy and Dumbledore discuss mercy at the Astronomy Tower. Dumbledore tells Draco that it is he and not Draco who is in the position to grant it.

Merlin. *Character.* Merlin is one of the figures on the Famous Witches and Wizard Cards found in Chocolate Frogs (SS 6:103). Merlin was one of the most famous wizards in all of British folklore. Dumbledore is a First Class member of the Order of Merlin, which appears to be an honor.

See also Chocolate Frogs

Mermish. *Magical language.* The language of the merpeople. Dumbledore understands and speaks it (GF 26:505).

Merpeople. *Magical beings.* Classified 4X by the MM in *Fantastic Beasts*. Like centaurs, merpeople share some commonalities with human beings but prefer to remain separate from human communities. They speak their own language, Mermish. Their ancestors were called Sirens in ancient Greece, where the most beautiful merpeople live. Those in Scotland and Ireland are called selkies and Merrows, respectively. Ron has crossed out that these are "less beautiful" than those living in warmer water and scribbled in that they are "ugly" (FB 28–29).

Harry discovers that there are merpeople living at the bottom of the Hogwarts lake when he opens the golden egg in the prefects' bathroom (GF 25:464). Harry is the first to find the merpeople in the second task of the Triwizard Tournament. They live in rough stone houses. They have gray skin and long green hair like seaweed. They have yellow eyes and their teeth are broken. For jewelry, they wear strands of chipped pebbles; their tails are silver. Their village includes a large statue of one of their kind (GF 26:497–98). Albus Dumbledore communicates with them. The merpeople come to his funeral, floating just below the surface of the lake in tribute.

Mermaids and mermen have been part of folklore ever since people took to the seas. In aquatic folklore they are the equivalent of fairies. Merpeople's cries had the power to predict bad events, serving as omens.

See also Fantastic Beasts and Where to Find Them

This statue depicting Hans Christian Andersen's Little Mermaid was sculpted by Edvard Eriksen and is located at Langelinie Pier in Copenhagen, Denmark. In the Harry Potter series, merpeople live at the bottom of the lake at Hogwarts. Prof. Dumbledore communicates with them in their language, Mermish. Courtesy of Corbis.

Merrows. *Magical beings.* From *Fantastic Beasts*. Merpeople of Ireland (FB 29).

See also Fantastic Beasts and Where to Find Them; Merpeople

Merrythought, Prof. Galatea. *Character.* A Hogwarts professor in Tom Riddle's days at the school. Tom asks Prof. Slughorn whether or not she is retiring in one of the memories Dumbledore and Harry visit in the Pensieve (HBP 17:369). She taught DADA for nearly fifty years (HBP 20:432).

Mersong. *Magical song.* The singing of the merpeople at the bottom of the Hogwarts lake (GF 26:497).

Metamorph-Medals. *Counterfeit magical objects.* Wearers are told they will be able to change their appearance one hundred thousand different ways for the price of 10 Galleons, but the medals actually turn people orange and some people grow tentacle-like warts (HBP 5:87). This is the kind of object Arthur Weasley is charged with eradicating in his new job at the Ministry (HBP 5:87).

Metamorphmagus. *Magical ability.* A witch or wizard who can change his or her appearance, such as hair color or other traits, at will. It is a rare, inborn trait. Nymphadora Tonks tells Harry that she is a Metamorphmagus (OP 3:52).

Metamorphosing. *Magical skill.* The ability to change one's appearance. Hermione tells Harry that Nymphadora Tonks has been having trouble with metamorphosing ever since Sirius Black died; she feels guilty as an Auror for not saving Sirius (HBP 5:95).

Midgen, Eloise. *Character.* Hannah Abbott tells Prof. Sprout that Eloise Midgen tried to curse her pimples off of her face. Prof. Sprout calls Eloise silly, saying that Madam Pomfrey had to fix her nose afterwards (GF 13:195). Ron says that he would rather attend the Yule Ball alone than go with Eloise, but Hermione sticks up for her and says that her acne is better, and that she is a nice girl (GF 22:394).

Miggs, Martin. *Character.* The Lead character in Ron's comic books, *The Adventures of Martin Miggs, the Mad Muggle*, at the Burrow (CS 3:40).

Milly. *Magical creature.* From *Fantastic Beasts.* The name of one of Newt and Porpentina Scamander's pet kneazles (FB vi).

Mimbulus mibletonia. *Magical plant.* Neville Longbottom returns to school in Year 5 with this plant. It looks like a small gray cactus, but it has boils on it where the spines would be. Neville wants to see if he can breed it in Herbology. When Harry asks if the plant does anything, Neville makes it work its defense mechanism of shooting slimy green Stinksap out of its boils. The Stinksap gets all over Harry, Ginny Weasley, and Luna Lovegood on the train just as Cho Chang walks by to say hello to Harry. Neville says his great uncle Algie got the plant for him for his birthday (OP 10:186–87). *Mimbulus mibletonia* is one of the Gryffindor Common Room passwords in Year 5 (OP 13:251). On the way home after Year 5 on the Hogwarts Express, Neville pets his plant, which has grown quite a bit over the year, and which croons at his touch (OP 38:865).

Mimsy-Porpington, Sir Nicholas de. *Character.* This character is also known as Nearly Headless Nick. He is the Gryffindor ghost (SS 7:124).
  See also Death Day Party; Nearly Headless Nick

Ministry of Agriculture and Fisheries. *Muggle office.* After announcing that some-one named Black is on the loose, armed, and dangerous, the television news broadcast aired on the Dursleys' television goes into a report from this office (PA 2:17).

Ministry of Magic. *Magical office.* Hagrid comments that the Ministry has been dis-rupting the world again as he reads *The Daily Prophet* on the boat from the Hut-on-the-Rock. He explains to Harry that it is the Ministry's job to keep Muggles unaware of the existence of the magical world (SS 5:64–65).

The Ministry is reached through a telephone booth in the center of London. One gets into the booth and dials the numbers 62442. This brings a voice that asks the visitor's name and purpose and the machine deposits a visitor's badge. The floor of the booth then lowers to the Atrium of the Ministry, where one's wand is searched for security.

The Atrium is a long hall with polished dark-wood flooring. The ceiling is peacock blue with gold stars. Several fireplaces line the walls; employees come and go from these fireplaces using Floo Powder. A large fountain called the Fountain of Magical Brethren sits in the center of the Atrium. Elevators take employees and visitors up and down to the various floors. Since the entire complex is belowground, the Magical Maintenance department puts images of weather events in the windows. The numbers of the floors are reversed. On the tenth floor, the furthest floor down, is Courtroom Ten. This courtroom can only be reached by taking stairs down from the ninth floor, which is the location of the Department of Mysteries. The eighth floor is the Atrium; the seventh holds the Department of Magical Games and Sports; the sixth is the Department of Magical Transportation; the fifth is the International Magical Cooperation; the fourth is Regu-lation and Control of Magical Creatures; the third is Magical Accidents and Catastro-phes; and the second is Magical Law Enforcement. The first floor is presumably the street level at the phone booth.

When Harry visits the Ministry for his hearing in Courtroom Ten, he sees a busy office facility. Paper airplanes shoot about, and Mr. Weasley tells him that these are interoffice memos (OP 7:121–136).

See also Appendix B

Ministry of Magic Are Morons Group. *Suggested name.* Fred Weasley suggests this name for what will become Dumbledore's Army (OP 18:392).

Ministry of Magic Classifications. *Magical ranking system.* The Ministry ranks the potential danger of magical creatures on a scale of 1 to 5 Xs (5 being the most dan-gerous); a ranking is given for each creature discussed in *Fantastic Beasts*. The rankings mean the following: 5 = lethal; 4 = dangerous to the point that a trained and skilled wizard must deal with the creature; 3 = a wizard with normal abilities may handle any complications arising from this creature; 2 = safe and capable of being domesticated; and 1 = downright uninteresting (FB xxii).

Minsk. Hagrid tells Harry and friends that he had a run-in with a vampire in a pub in Minsk on his way to recruit giants for Dumbledore (OP 20:426). It is the capital of the Republic of Belarus, which is located east of Poland and north of Ukraine.

Mirror of Erised. *Magical object.* Harry discovers the mirror in Hogwarts Castle and finds that when he looks in it, he sees his parents and his entire family. He notices that his eyes are just like his mother's in shape and color. He longs to sit in front of the mirror forever so that he may be with his family. Over the top of the mirror is inscribed, *"Erised stra ehru oyt ube cafru oyt on wohsi."* In reverse, this reads: "I show you not your face but your hearts desire." Harry convinces Ron to come look with him, but Ron does not see Harry's family—he sees himself winning the House Cup and other glories. Finally, Dumbledore sees Harry staring at the mirror again. He warns Harry not to waste away his life in front of it. When Harry asks Dumbledore what he would see in the mirror, he says he would see a pair of socks (SS 12:214).

Mirror, Sirius Black's. *See* Two-Way Mirror

"Mischief Managed." *Incantation.* This incantation makes the Marauder's Map go blank again (PA 10:194).

Mistletoe. Luna Lovegood points out mistletoe over Harry's head, but when he skirts out from under it, she tells him that it was a good idea because it is frequently loaded with nargles (OP 21:453).

Misuse of Muggle Artifacts Office. *Magical office.* Arthur Weasley works in this office, which is ironic since he is fascinated with Muggles and their artifacts, such as Ford Anglias (CS 3:30). The office is located through wooden double doors at the end of the Ministry's second floor, in a dark and dingy corridor. It is a small, shabby office with no window (OP 7:132).

Mitford, Jessica (1917–1996). Jessica Mitford is one of Rowling's favorite authors and human rights activist heroines. She was born in Gloucestershire, England, into an eccentric and wealthy family. She was one of six sisters. Schooled at home, Mitford became interested in the Loyalist cause in the Spanish Civil War. She risked losing family ties by running away to the front where she met and married her first husband, journalist Esmond Romilly. Romilly was a nephew of Winston Churchill's and later died in World War II. Mitford moved to the United States, joined the Communist Party, and later married an attorney. She left Communism but continued to write as a muckraker journalist. Her subjects included the American funeral industry, the NAACP, and others.

At fourteen, Rowling was given Mitford's book *Hons and Rebels* by her great-aunt Marian. The book is an autobiography of Mitford's youth and early years of leaving her family to work for a political cause in Spain. Rowling was so taken with Mitford's courage and with her activism that she named her first daughter after the author and gave her a copy of *Hons and Rebels* as a christening gift. In a 2002 interview in *The Scotsman*, Rowling said about Mitford, "I love the way she never outgrew some of her adolescent traits, remaining true to her politics . . . throughout her life."

In the United States, Mitford is best known for her exposé of the American funeral industry, *American Way of Death* (1963). An essay from that book is frequently anthologized in college textbooks.

Further Reading: Fraser, Lindsay. "Harry Potter—Harry and Me." *The Scotsman*, November 2002.

Moaning Myrtle. *Character.* The ghost of a student killed by Voldemort years ago, Myrtle lives in the U-bend of the pipes in one of the girls' bathrooms. She tells Harry and Ron about a boy that she visits in the boys' bathroom who is sad and talks to her—the boy is Draco Malfoy (HBP 21:462). Myrtle first appears in *Chamber of Secrets*. She has been hiding in the bathroom since she went there to cry after Olive Hornby teased her about her glasses. There, she heard a boy's voice and went to tell him to get out of the girls' bathroom, when she met a Basilisk and was killed. She haunted Olive for some time afterwards until the Ministry made her stop. She has haunted the girls' bathroom ever since. Myrtle is sensitive and easily offended.

Myrtle provided information in *Chamber of Secrets* that helped Harry figure out where the entrance to the Chamber was. She also helped him in *Goblet of Fire* with the clue of the golden egg in the prefects' bathroom. Myrtle was in the Hogwarts lake, leading Harry toward the Mervillage in the second task of the Triwizard Tournament.

"Mobiliarbus!". *Incantation.* This incantation moves an object. Harry uses it in the Three Broomsticks to make a Christmas tree move in front of his table to keep him hidden (PA 10:201). In Latin, *mobilis* means "easy to move."

"Mobilicorpus." *Incantation.* This incantation moves a body in its upright position by making it float low above the ground. Prof. Lupin casts this spell on Snape in order to move him from the Shrieking Shack to Hogwarts (PA 19:377). In Latin, *corpus* means "body."

Mockridge, Cuthbert. *Character.* Head of the Goblin Liaison Office (GF 7:86).

Modesty Rabnott Snidget Reservation. *Magical place.* From *Fantastic Beasts.* A preserve for Snidgets established in Somerset in honor of Modesty Rabnott's efforts at saving the Golden Snidget (QA 14).
See also Rabnott, Madam Modesty; Snidget-hunting

Moke. *Magical creature.* From *Fantastic Beasts.* Classified 3X by the MM. The Moke is a greenish-silver lizard, ten inches long. It is unseen by Muggles because it can shrink at will (FB 29).
See also Fantastic Beasts and Where to Find Them

"Mollywobbles." *Magical nickname.* Molly Weasley's pet name for her husband Arthur when they are alone together. They use it as a password in Year 6, and Molly blushes when Arthur makes her say it in front of everyone before she opens the door to allow them into the Burrow (HBP 5:86).

Money. Currency is mentioned early in the series when Uncle Vernon Dursley refuses to pay for Harry to go to private school to learn "magic tricks" (SS 4:59). Harry fears that he will not have money to buy his equipment and supplies for his first year at Hogwarts until Hagrid shows him his vault at Gringotts with the mounds, columns, and heaps of gold (Galleons), silver (Sickles), and small bronze (Knuts) coins. Harry is rich. Hagrid explains the conversion factor for magical money as 17 Sickles to a Galleon and 29 Knuts to a Sickle (SS 5:75). Under Hagrid's supervision, Harry pays 7 gold Galleons for his magic wand (SS 5:85).

The first time he is on his own to spend any of his money is on the Hogwarts Express, where he buys himself and Ron Weasley some of everything from the candy cart for a total of 11 Sickles and 7 Knuts (SS 6:101). The Weasleys do not have much money; in fact, the reader is made aware of their bank "account," which includes only 1 Galleon and a small stack of Sickles (CS 4:57).

Money differences between the Muggle and wizarding worlds become a source of humor in the books. Mr. Weasley does not quite know how to pay Mr. Roberts for his campsite at the Quidditch World Cup, so Harry helps him with the fives and twenties. Mr. Roberts comments that there must be a lot of foreigners traveling these days because someone just tried to pay him with gold coins the size of hubcaps a while ago (GF 7:77).

Harry is generous to his friends with his money. At the Quidditch World Cup, he buys himself, Ron, and Hermione a pair of Omnioculars at 10 Galleons each. Ron is embarrassed by the large gift and later pays Harry back with leprechaun gold. When Ron later learns that those coins disappeared and that Harry never told him, he gets angry (GF 28:546). Harry gives his winnings from the Triwizard Tournament to the Weasley twins to start up their business. Rowling was surprised when readers first pointed out to her that money is mentioned frequently in the books. When she thought about it, she said it did not surprise her because she had so little money when she began writing the series.

Monkshood. *Magical plant.* A plant used in potions. It also goes by the names aconite and wolfbane. Harry does not know this information when Snape questions him on it during his first Potions class (SS 8:138).

The Monster Book of Monsters. *Magical book.* Hagrid sends this book to Harry for his thirteenth birthday; it is also his textbook for Care of Magical Creatures class in Year 3. The book bites (PA 1:13).

Montague. *Character.* Player on the Slytherin Quidditch team (PA 15:306). He is captain of the team in Harry's fifth year; his body is a lot like Dudley Dursley's (OP 19:405). Fred and George Weasley put him into the Vanishing Cabinet when he tries to dock points from Gryffindor as a member of the Inquisitorial Squad (OP 28:627).

Montgomery sisters. *Characters.* Hermione tells Harry and Ron that the Montgomery sisters' five-year-old brother died in St. Mungo's after being attacked by a werewolf (possibly Fenrir Greyback) when their mother would not help the Death Eaters (HBP 22:472–73).

Montrose Magpies. *Magical sports team.* From QA. This popular Quidditch team has won the League Cup thirty-two times (QA 35).

Moody, Alastor "Mad-Eye." *Character.* Arthur Weasley asks Amos Diggory what Mad-Eye is saying at the Ministry about the happenings at the World Cup (GF 11:159). Mad-Eye Moody is an old Auror, a Dark wizard catcher, who was a strong wizard in his day. His face is scarred, his skin is leathery, and he has a wooden leg. He has one good dark eye and one large blue eye that roams around in all directions, even backwards until it shows all white, seemingly at its own devices (GF 12:184–85). He caught half of the prisoners in Azkaban. As he has gotten older, Mad-Eye has come across so many families of prisoners who have it out for him that he has become paranoid and sees Dark wizards everywhere; he appears to be slightly mad. He is an old friend of Dumbledore's (GF 11:161–62). He joins Hogwarts as the DADA teacher in Year 4 (GF 12:185). Dumbledore calls him by his first name, Alastor, for the first time when Mad-Eye speaks to Igor Karkaroff, insinuating prior wrongdoing (GF 17:280). The reader later learns that Mad-Eye Moody through much of Goblet of Fire is actually Barty Crouch, Jr., in disguise.

Mad-Eye gives Harry advice for the first Triwizard Tournament task: "play to your strengths" (GF 20:344). He can see through Harry's Invisibility Cloak (GF 25:471). The one thing he hates above all else is a Death Eater who did not go to Azkaban but went free (GF 25:477). Mad-Eye suggests that Harry might be a good Auror (GF 25:477). He shows him a photograph of the original Order of the Phoenix at Grimmauld Place and joins the fight at the Hall of Prophecy (OP 9:173). He is at King's Cross to welcome and guard Harry with some of the others from the Order on Harry's way home from Year 5 (OP 38:867).

In mythology, Alastor is one of Pluto's horses that Pluto uses to abduct Persephone.

Moon. *Character.* A student in Harry's year (SS 7:121).

Mooncalf. *Magical creature.* From *Fantastic Beasts*. Classified 2X by the MM. This very shy creature only comes out of its burrow during full moons. It is gray with four legs and large, flat feet. The Mooncalf does an unusual dance in the moonlight (FB 29–30).
See also Fantastic Beasts and Where to Find Them

Moonstone. *Magical substance.* Powdered moonstone is one ingredient in the Draught of Peace (OP 12:234).

Moontrimmer. *Magical object.* From QA. A broomstick invented by Gladys Boothby in 1901; its advantage was that it could fly higher than any before it (QA 48–49).
See also Broomsticks

Moony. *Character.* The nickname of Remus Lupin, James Potter's contemporary who turns into a werewolf when the moon is out (PA 14:287). He is one of the creators of the Marauder's Map.

Moose Jaw Meteorites. *Magical sports team.* From QA. Quidditch team from Canada (QA 43).

Moran. *Character.* The Chaser on the Ireland National Quidditch Team in the World Cup (GF 8:105).

Moran, Gwendolyn. *Character.* From QA. A Seeker on the Holyhead Harpies who clobbered her opposition Seeker, Captain Rudolf Brand of the Heidelberg Harriers, when he proposed marriage to her at the end of a seven-day game in 1953 (QA 34–35).

Morgana. *Character.* Ron has about six of this witch's collector cards from Chocolate Frogs, so he gives his newest one to Harry to begin his collection (SS 6:103).

"Morsmordre!" *Incantation.* This incantation makes the Dark Mark appear in the sky (GF 9:128). In Latin, *mors* means "death."

Mortlake. *Character.* A wizard who is taken in for questioning at the Ministry for performing some kind of strange magic on ferrets (CS 3:38).

Mosag. *Magical creature.* Aragog the giant spider's wife (CS 15:278).

Most Charming Smile Award. *Magical award.* Gilderoy Lockhart has received this award from *Witch Weekly* five times in a row (CS 6:91).

Mostafa, Hassan. *Character.* A Quidditch referee from Egypt. He is chairwizard of the International Association of Quidditch (GF 8:106).

Moste Potente Potions. *Magical book.* Located in the Restricted Section of the library, the book contains the recipe for the Polyjuice Potion (CS 9:159–60). Hermione gains access to it by getting Prof. Lockhart to sign the required form (CS 10:163). The title is French for "Most Potent Potions."

Moutohora Macaws. *Magical sports team.* From QA. New Zealand Quidditch team (QA 42).

Mr. Tibbles. *Magical pet.* One of Mrs. Figg's cats that helps her guard Harry while he is at Number Four, Privet Drive. She puts him under a car, and she tells Harry that Mr. Tibbles informed her that Harry was in trouble (OP 2:20).

Mrs. Norris. *Magical animal.* Argus Filch's cat. It has protruding eyes like Filch and is dust-colored (SS 8:132). Mrs. Norris is the first to be petrified during the time of the Chamber of Secrets adventure (CS 8:139). Rowling has admitted borrowing the name from Mrs. Norris in Jane Austen's novel *Mansfield Park*.
See also Austen, Jane; Cats; Filch, Argus

Mrs. Skower's All-Purpose Magical Mess Remover. *Magical substance.* Filch tries to clean the writing on the walls of Hogwarts in Year 2 with this substance (CS 9:146).
Advertised on the flashing sign in the Quidditch World Cup stadium, it apparently causes pain while cleaning (GF 8:96). Rita Skeeter sets up her Quick-Quotes Quill on a crate of this substance in the closet when she interviews Harry Potter before the first task of the Triwizard Tournament (GF 18:304).

Mudblood. *Type of character.* A derogatory term for a witch or wizard of Muggle or mixed magical and Muggle ancestry. The bloodline is not considered "pure" by racial bigots, but is thought instead to be "muddied" through intermarrying. Draco Malfoy uses the term frequently when addressing or talking about Hermione Granger. Readers first encounter the term when Hermione accuses Draco of buying his way onto the Slytherin Quidditch team (CS 7:112).
Ron informs Harry about the meaning of the term. He explains that most wizards are no longer "pure" but are only half magical as a result of several generations of intermarriage with Muggles. Wizards have had to marry Muggles to keep from dying out (CS 7:115–16).
See also Race

Muffliato. *Magical spell.* This spell muffles sound into a buzzing noise in a nearby classmate's ear so that he or she cannot hear a conversation (HBP 12:238).

Muggle. *Character.* A Muggle is a non-magical person. A small man speaks with Vernon Dursley about being one, and this is the first time readers come across the term

(SS 1:5). Hagrid explains the term to Harry at the Hut-on-the-Rock (SS 4:53) and mentions that he does not know how Muggles survive in the world without magic (SS 5:67). Hermione Granger was born of Muggle parents, yet she is widely regarded as the brightest witch of her year at Hogwarts.

Rowling invented the word. In a 1999 interview in the *Boston Globe*, she describes beginning with the word "mug," which in England means someone who is easily fooled. She changed the word to "Muggle" to make the word sound softer and less unkind. Good wizards and witches are interested in Muggles and do not treat them unkindly. The word was challenged in a lawsuit brought by Nancy Stouffer of Pennsylvania, who claimed that she invented the word in a book she wrote. Stouffer lost her case.

See also Lawsuits

Further Reading: Loer, Stephanie. "All about Harry Potter from Quidditch to the Future of the Sorting Hat." *Boston Globe*, October 18, 1999.

Muggle-baiting. *Magical offense.* Bothering Muggles with annoying uses of magic that make their lives puzzling or frustrating. Arthur Weasley gives the example of a wizard putting a charm on a Muggle's keys that makes the keys keep shrinking. Because Muggles do not believe in magic, they never report these odd occurrences and chalk them up to some other cause, making the wizard offender difficult to catch and convict (CS 3:38). Arthur thinks that the practice goes beyond mischief and instead comes from a sinister place (OP 9:153).

Muggle magic tricks. *Objects.* Fred Weasley says the card and rope tricks are novelties that he sells in his shop. They do not sell a lot of them, but they are popular with people interested in Muggle (non-magical) life, like his father (HBP 6:118).

Muggle marked playing cards. *Objects.* A Muggle magic trick that Mr. Weasley looks at while visiting Weasleys' Wizard Wheezes (HBP 6:123).

Muggle money. *Muggle object.* Hagrid hands Harry some bills for their train ride to London since he does not understand Muggle money (SS 5:65).

Muggle Protection Act. *Magical law.* Lucius Malfoy speaks to Mr. Borgin about a rumor that the Muggle Protection Act may become a new law; he suspects Arthur Weasley is behind it (CS 4:51).

Muggle Repelling Charm. *Magical spell.* This spell keeps Muggles unaware and away (GF 8:95). It also keeps Muggles out of the forests where centaurs and unicorns are, and away from water where merpeople live (FB xviii–xix).

Muggle Studies. *Magical class.* Percy Weasley recommends this class to Harry as he plans his schedule for the next year over Easter holidays in Year 2 (CS 14:252). Hermione's schedule in Year 3 starts out with this class at 9:00, the same time she has Divination and Arithmancy (PA 6:98). Hermione is assigned to write an essay in Muggle Studies on the topic "Explain Why Muggles Need Electricity" (PA 12:250). After a difficult year balancing all of her classes, Hermione decides at the end of Year 3 that she will drop Muggle Studies the following year (PA 22:430).

Muggle Underground. *Muggle place.* The subway, or Underground, in London (PA 4:64).

Muggle-Worthy Excuse Committee. *Magical organization.* This organization is located on the third floor of the Ministry as part of the Department of Magical Accidents and Catastrophes (OP 7:130).

Muggles Who Notice. *Magical book.* From *Fantastic Beasts.* This book, written in 1972 by Blenheim Stalk, states that some Muggles did not have their memories altered in the Ilfracombe Incident. Muggle Dodgy Dirk frequents pubs on the south coast, telling tales of seeing a large lizard (FB xvi).
See also Fantastic Beasts and Where to Find Them

Mulciber. *Character.* Name given up by Igor Karkaroff during the hearing that Harry sees in Dumbledore's Pensieve. Mulciber's specialty was the Imperius Curse, which he used to make people do dastardly deeds (GF 30:590). He is a Death Eater who appears at the Department of Mysteries during the attack (OP 35:788). He is one of Voldemort's original Death Eaters (HBP 20:444).

Muldoon, Burdock. *Character.* From *Fantastic Beasts.* During the fourteenth century, Burdock Muldoon was Chief of the Wizards' Council (the government before the Ministry); he made a distinction between beings and beasts. He said beings are those who walk on two legs and beasts are all others (FB x).
See also Fantastic Beasts and Where to Find Them

Mullet. *Character.* Chaser on the Ireland National Quidditch Team in the World Cup (GF 8:105).

Multiple Sclerosis Society, Scotland. In tribute to her mother who died of multiple sclerosis at the age of forty-five, Rowling is patron of this organization. It is part of the MS Society of Great Britian and Northern Ireland. Rowling is a spokesperson and benefactor. She attended the opening of the Stuart Resource Center in Aberdeen in 2001. The Society serves over 10,000 people in Scotland who have been diagnosed with MS. It has over forty branch offices and its national headquarters is located in Edinburgh. The Society funds research, offers a hotline, facilitates respite care and specialized vacations for MS sufferers and their families, produces publications, and provides grants, education, and training in the disease and its management.

One of the startling facts about MS that Rowling's participation has helped to highlight is that the disease is more common in Scotland than in any other country in the world. Approximately 1 in 500 Scots have MS or will get it in their lifetime, compared with 1 in 700 in the U.K. It is estimated that the world has approximately 2.5 million cases.
See also Rowling, Anne Volant

Further Reading: MS Society (Scotland) website: http://www.mssocietyscotland.org.uk.

Mumps, Zacharias. *Character.* From QA. A wizard who wrote about Quidditch for the first time in some detail in 1398 (QA 15).

Munch, Eric. *Character.* Night-watch wizard at the Ministry (OP 14:287).

Muriel, Great Auntie. *Character.* Ginny Weasley teases Ron that the only kiss he has ever received is from the Weasleys' aunt (HBP 14:287). Molly Weasley tells Fleur

Delacour that their Great-Auntie Muriel owns a beautiful goblin-made tiara; Molly thinks she can convince Muriel to let Fleur borrow the tiara for her wedding day with Bill. Auntie Muriel is fond of Bill (HBP 29:623).

Murray, David Gordon Rowling. J. K. Rowling's second child; he was her first with her second husband, Dr. Neil Murray. The boy was born on March 23, 2003.

Murray, Dr. Neil. J. K. Rowling's second husband. The couple was married on Boxing Day, December 26, 2001. He practices in Edinburgh, Scotland.

Murray, Eunice. *Character.* The Seeker on the Montrose Magpies who died in 1942. She thought the Snitch was too easy and slow and asked that it be made to fly faster (QA 35). The book in which the name appears was published in 2001; later that year Rowling married Neil Murray.

Murray, Mackenzie Jean Rowling. Born January 23, 2005, at the Edinburgh Royal Infirmary, Mackenzie is Rowling's third child and her second with husband Dr. Neil Murray. Rowling announced her new daughter's birth and name on her website two days after the baby was born. *Half-Blood Prince* is dedicated to Mackenzie as her twin in paper and ink since Rowling turned in the completed manuscript to her editor about a month before her daughter's birth.

Murtlap. *Magical creature.* From *Fantastic Beasts*. Classified 3X by the MM. Somewhat like a rat, the murtlap has a bulge on its back that is useful as an antidote to curses (FB 30). Hermione makes a potion using murtlap tentacles to help soothe Harry's hands after Prof. Umbridge's detention (OP 15:324). Apparently the essence of murtlap remedy works well enough that Harry recommends it to Lee Jordan, who gets the same detention later in the year (OP 25:551). Lee passes along information about the murtlap's recuperative properties to Fred and George Weasley, who use it in their Skiving Snackboxes (OP 26:574).
  See also Fantastic Beasts and Where to Find Them

Museum of Quidditch. *Magical place.* From QA. Located in London, the Museum of Quidditch has a knobby medieval broomstick on display (QA 2). The museum's other artifacts include: Gertie Keddle's diary describing players engaged in a game near Queerditch Marsh (QA 7); the 1269 letter from Madam Modesty Rabnott of Kent to her sister Prudence in Aberdeen describing Snidget-hunting.

Music. Prof. Dumbledore proclaims that music is a magic beyond all that is performed at Hogwarts (SS 7:128). One of the reasons Rowling gave Dumbledore his name, which means "bumblebee," was because she knew he enjoyed music, and she envisioned him walking about the castle humming to himself all the time. The wizarding community does listen to music and also performs. The Weird Sisters are a professional rock band that plays at the Yule Ball in Year 4. In Book 1, Fluffy, the three-headed dog guarding the Sorcerer's Stone, must be placated by music; Hagrid makes a wooden flute for Harry as a gift. Mrs. Weasley listens to her favorite singer, Celestina Warbeck, over Christmas on the wizard radio station, WWN. At Grimmauld Place, the Order of the Phoenix finds a sinister music box that puts people to sleep.
  Rowling is said to play guitar, which she learned from her mother, and enjoys music herself. When she was younger, she enjoyed the Beatles and the Smiths. The classical

music she enjoys, and used to play while writing, includes Beethoven's Appassionata Piano Sonata; Tchaikovsky's Violin Concerto in D Major; and, perhaps fittingly for the subject matter of her books, Mozart's Requiem Mass in D Minor.

As much as she enjoys music and wrote in many cafés where music was playing, the author has said on her website that the music in her ideal café cannot be played too loudly, since loud music is the only noise that distracts her from writing.

See also Warbeck, Celestina; Weird Sisters

Further Reading: Kirk, Connie Ann. *J. K. Rowling: A Biography*. Westport, CT: Greenwood, 2003.

Mykonos, Greece. From QA. Welsh Quidditch player "Dangerous" Dai Llewellyn died in Mykonos, Greece, where he was eaten by a Chimera (QA 33).

Mystery. Certainly one of the literary genres to which the Harry Potter series belongs is the mystery novel and its subgroup, the detective novel. Mystery novels involve curiosity and intrigue. They contain at least one incident, often a series of them, for which an explanation is unknown. The explanation gets carefully deduced through unraveling clues that the author places in various positions in the plot. The author also cleverly plants distractions throughout the plot to divert attention away from the solution to the mystery and to propel the story and mystery forward. Examples of mysteries for ages nine through eleven, the original marketed audience for the first Harry Potter novel, include E. L. Konigsburg's Newbery Award–winning *From the Mixed-Up Files of Mrs. Basil E. Frankweiler* and Ellen Raskin's *The Westing Game*. Adult mysteries include the novels of Stephen King and Agatha Christie.

The genre is particularly popular in series fiction, since the same major characters reappear in novel after novel and the main focus may be kept on plot (that is, collecting clues and attempting to answer questions) rather than on introducing and developing characters. Best-selling mystery series for young people in the United States have included the Hardy Boys and Nancy Drew novels. Popular adult versions include those featuring famous detectives like Sherlock Holmes or contemporary criminologists such as Kinsey Mallone in Sue Grafton's A–Z series.

There is a major mystery in each of the Harry Potter novels, in addition to the overall mystery of Harry's existence and his apparent role in defeating or pushing back the force of evil in the world. The main mystery in *Sorcerer's Stone* involves the Sorcerer's (Philosopher's) Stone and the form and whereabouts of the villain, Lord Voldemort. *Chamber of Secrets* is concerned with what is in the Chamber and why it is important enough to be heavily guarded, as well as what is happening at the school to cause students to be petrified. Other mysteries concern the messages in blood appearing on the walls and a trail of tiny spiders leading outside. *Prisoner of Azkaban* contains the mystery of the black dog that Harry keeps seeing in the shadows and the strange behavior of Ron's rat, Scabbers. In *Goblet of Fire*, the Dark Mark in the sky after the Quidditch World Cup and Harry's inclusion in the Triwizard Tournament both require explanation. The main mystery in *Order of the Phoenix* is taken up in Harry's dreams of the Hall of Prophecy and the appropriately named Department of Mysteries at the Ministry. The identity and goals of the Half-Blood Prince create suspense in the sixth novel; Snape's loyalty and unexplained murder of Dumbledore add to the mystery in *Half-Blood Prince*. The concept of Horcruxes and where and what the remaining Horcruxes may be sets up one of the remaining mysteries for the final novel.

In detective fashion, Harry, Ron, and Hermione often use the Hogwarts Library as their source of information when they try to research a problem or solve a mystery. They also go to Hogwarts faculty and staff, particularly those advisors who are closest to them, such as Hagrid or Prof. Dumbledore. They keep their ears and eyes open and make connections from one event or bit of information to another, and even from one school year to another. By the end of each school year at Hogwarts, the trio has solved the one major mystery developed in the book and they have placed a few more pieces in the puzzle of the overarching plot that connects the books. Other mysteries from the overall plot remain.

The connecting plot among all of the novels (Harry's growing up, and the struggle between Harry and Voldemort) are the key feature that sets the Harry Potter novels apart from most mystery or detective series. The suspense that is an integral part of the mystery genre has been a useful tool in maintaining interest in the series as it has developed over a decade. The fact that millions of readers around the world who found Harry Potter in 1997 and 1998 remained interested for a decade in how his story would eventually end when the final book would be published is a testament to the strength of Rowling's plotting technique, as well as to the lure of mystery on readers' imaginations.

Mythology, use of. One of the delights of the series for many readers is its frequent allusions to Greek, Roman, and other mythologies. These allusions are particularly prominent in the names of creatures that fly and walk in Harry's magical world, as well as in the names of characters. Rowling became familiar with mythology in her studies of the classics at Exeter University. Mythological creatures in the series include: the cereberus (Fluffy) the three-headed dog; the Basilisk; the phoenix; and the hippogriff. Names used in the series that come from world mythology include, but are not limited to: Minerva, Hermes, Hestia, Dedalus, and Narcissa. Many other beings, beasts, and names in the series also come from folklore. It is important in reading the mythological allusions in the series to know that Rowling uses parts of mythology for her own purposes, so she may not represent a concept faithfully to its original story or characterization.

Further Reading: Brewer, E. Cobham. *The Dictionary of Phrase and Fable*. New York: Avenel Books, 1978; Colbert, David. *The Magical Worlds of Harry Potter*. New York: Penguin, 2004.

· N ·

Nagini. *Magical creature.* Voldemort's snake friend from which he draws milk and nourishment in his diminished state (GF 1:7).

Names. Rowling has admitted in interviews that as a writer she has collected names for many years. Creative names in the series are clearly one of the novelties of the books for young and old readers alike. The author has said she obtains names from maps, gravestones, books, mythology, and languages such as Latin, French, and German. She also invents names and puts parts of names together for her own purposes.

Examples of Rowling's creativity with names include: Dursley, which is a town in England, as are Snape and Flitwick; Beauxbaton means "beautiful wand" in French. Ludo Bagman's first name means "to play" in Latin; "Dumbledore" is Old English for "bumblebee." Occasionally, Rowling uses a real name in the series. Nicolas Flamel, for example, was a real alchemist in France, and his wife was named Perenelle. Natalie MacDonald was a real little girl in Canada, a fan of Harry Potter who died before she was able to meet Rowling in a promised rendezvous.

Nargles. *Magical creatures.* Luna Lovegood points out mistletoe over Harry's head, but when he skirts out from under it, she tells him that it was a good idea because mistletoe is frequently loaded with nargles (OP 21:453). When Cho Chang points out the mistletoe to Harry and he mentions nargles, he says he does not know what they are and that Cho would have to ask Luna about them (OP 21:456).

National Council for One Parent Families. One of the British charitable organizations that Rowling supports as a result of her own difficult experience as a single parent. Rowling explains her own trying times that gave rise to her involvement as ambassador/patron of the organization in an article that was published in London's *Daily Telegraph* in 2002. In the article, she describes going to the store Mothercare, not to buy clothes for Jessica, but to slip into the restroom to take one of the free diapers they offered to customers. She also recalls counting out change for a can of baked beans and coming up two pence short, then pretending in embarrassment in front of the bored sales clerk that she had misplaced a ten-pound note. She disliked depending on relatives for Jessica's new shoes, buying her clothes at charity stores, and trying very hard not to envy Jessica's friends' decorated bedrooms.

Headquartered in London, the National Council for One Parent Families offers information and support to families with only one parent due to divorce, death, or other causes. It also works to dispel the social stigma associated with single parenting. Rowling has been a donor since 2000 and in 2004 was made president. She has also supported the organization by writing forewords to several of their publications, including their book *Families Just Like Us*; two fund-raising story collections, *Magic* and *Summer Magic*; and articles in leading newspapers such as the *Sunday Times*.

Further Reading: Rowling, J. K. "A Kind of Magic." *The Daily Telegraph* (London), June 9, 2002.

National Squad. *Magical sports team.* The Quidditch team that Prof. Lockhart was supposedly invited to join as Seeker (CS 10:163).

Nature's Nobility: A Wizarding Genealogy. *Magical book.* At Grimmauld Place, Sirius Black uses this book to smash a silver spiderlike object that is crawling up Harry's arm and appears ready to sting him (OP 6:116).

Nearly Headless Nick. *Character.* Also known as Sir Nicholas de Mimsy-Porpington, he is the Gryffindor ghost (SS 7:124). Nick believes that getting hit in the neck forty-five times with a blunt axe should qualify him for the Headless Hunt, but his participation has been denied again in Harry's second year because his head is still slightly attached (CS 8:124). Halloween in Harry's second year is the 500th anniversary of Nick's Death Day (CS 8:129). He invites Harry, Ron, and Hermione to his party so that they might tell Sir Patrick how frightening he is as a ghost and win him points toward joining the Headless Hunt (CS 8:130). Nick is petrified in Year 2 (CS 11:202). Nick tells Harry and his friends that he has heard the Sorting Hat give the school warnings about uniting against foes. Harry suggests that the Sorting Hat may hear about danger to the school because it is kept in Dumbledore's office. Nick says he is not afraid (OP 11:209).

Harry goes to Nick after Sirius Black's death to ask whether he might see Sirius again as a ghost. Nick explains that he is present in ghost form because he was afraid of death and chose to stay; most wizards move on, and Nick wonders whether he should have done so as well, because now he is caught between two realms and he is neither really alive, nor really dead. When Harry presses him about the meaning of death and what happens after one dies, Nick says that they study this subject at the Department of Mysteries and quickly excuses himself to attend the Year-End (or Leaving) Feast (OP 38:859–62).

Neptune. Ron and Harry joke about this and other planets in Divination class (GF 13:201).

Nesbit, E. (Edith) (1858–1924). Nesbit was a British children's book author who wrote under the name E. Nesbit to keep her name genderless, much as J. K. Rowling was asked to do by Bloomsbury. Rowling has frequently mentioned Nesbit's books among those she admires. At the Edinburgh Book Festival in 2004, Rowling said, "I love

E. Nesbit—I think she is great and I identify with the way that she writes. Her children are very real children and she was quite a groundbreaker in her day." She has recommended any book by Nesbit to children who ask for titles to read.

Nesbit was born in London and grew up in France, Germany, and Kent. She wrote more than sixty books for children. Among her most well-known books are: *The Railway Children*; *Five Children and It*; and *The Phoenix and the Carpet*. She was involved in politics in the Fabian Society, a late-nineteenth-century precursor to the Labor Party in England. Rowling admires not only Nesbit's work but also her life.

Further Reading: Fraser, Lindsay. "J. K. Rowling at the Edinburgh Book Festival." August 15, 2004. http://www.jkrowling.com/textonly/en/news_viewicfm?id=80.

New Theory of Numerology. *Magical book.* Hermione receives this book from Harry for Christmas in their fifth year (OP 23:503).

New Zealand Ministry of Magic. *Magical organization.* This organization puts a lot of time and money into preventing Muggles from discovering Quidditch through its portrayals in Maori art (QA 41).

N.E.W.T.s. *Magical tests.* N.E.W.T.s stands for Nastily Exhausting Wizarding Tests. These tests are given in seventh year and they provide the highest qualifications for wizard abilities at Hogwarts (PA 16:314).

Nicolson's Café. One of the reasons J. K. Rowling became an intriguing figure before her books were even read was because she wrote a novel that garnered over $100,000 in American rights as a single mother in a café in Scotland. That café was Nicolson's, an establishment partly owned by her brother-in-law Roger. It was located near the corner of South Bridge and Royal Mile, not far from her apartment in Edinburgh. The story goes that when Rowling lived on public assistance for six months and had no job or available child care, she would push her baby daughter Jessica around Edinburgh in her stroller until she fell asleep; then Rowling would slip the stroller into Nicolson's, order a cup of coffee, and write Harry Potter's story in longhand until Jessica woke up. Rowling has said that while this story is essentially true, it became exaggerated through retellings in the press. Reports in the press said that Rowling's apartment was unheated; these stories also gave the impression that Rowling was on welfare for an extended period of time rather than just a few months. One story claimed she wrote on napkins.

Once the story of Nicolson's became well known, Rowling still attempted to write there but was eventually driven away by people coming to watch or stare at her. The café became a favorite tourist stop for those visiting Edinburgh, though new ownership and renovations over the years have left the place unlike it was when Rowling frequented it.

Nifflers. *Magical creatures.* From *Fantastic Beasts*. Classified 3X by the MM. A niffler is a British creature that lives up to twenty feet below ground and is born in litters of six to eight (FB 30).

Nifflers are flat, furry black creatures with long snouts. They like sparkly objects and are often used to find gems or treasure in mines. Hagrid brings them to Care of Magical Creatures class and has each student choose one to dig and find coins he has buried. The student with the niffler that finds the most coins wins a prize. Hagrid says that despite their cuddly nature, nifflers do not make good pets because they tear a house apart. Ron's niffler finds the most coins, so he wins Hagrid's class prize of a large piece of Honeyduke's chocolate (GF 28:543–44).

See also Fantastic Beasts and Where to Find Them

Nigellus, Phineas. *See* [Black], Phineas Nigellus

Nimbus Racing Broom Company. *Magical business.* From QA. Established in 1967, this company took over the racing broom market with its Nimbus 1000, which could fly up to 100 miles per hour and turn in a complete circle from a stopped position. Professional Quidditch teams have kept the company in business, buying many of its 1001, 1500, and 1700 models (QA 51).

See also Quidditch Through the Ages

Nimbus 2000. *Magical object.* Hogwarts students covet this new model of Quidditch broomstick displayed in a storefront window on Diagon Alley (SS 5:72). Oliver Wood recommends this model to Prof. McGonagall when she recruits Harry to be the new Gryffindor team Seeker (SS 9:152). Harry receives one as a gift after he is recruited to join the Gryffindor team his first year (SS 9:164). The assumption is that the broom came from Prof. McGonagall, who noticed Harry's potential as Seeker when she witnessed his first flying lesson. When she admires his Firebolt broomstick, Madam Hooch tells Harry that the Nimbus brands have had a tendency to turn a bit off center in the back (PA 13:254).

See also Broomsticks

Nimbus 2001. *Magical object.* Lucius Malfoy donates these racing brooms to the Slytherin Quidditch team; this buys Draco Malfoy a spot as Seeker on the team (CS 7:111).

See also Broomsticks

Ninety-seven. *Magical number.* Harry has dreamed that Sirius Black will be in trouble at the end of row ninety-seven at the Department of Mysteries (OP 34:777). The year 1997 was the year that the first Harry Potter book was published in Britain.

"Nitwit!" One of the "few words" Prof. Dumbledore speaks before the new school year Start-of-Term Banquet in Harry's first year. The other few words he utters are "Blubber!" and "Oddment!" (SS 7:123).

The Noble Sport of Wizards. *Magical book.* From QA. This book was written by Quintius Umbraville and was published in 1620. It features a diagram of the seventeenth-century Quidditch pitch (QA 18–19).

Nogtail. *Magical creature.* From *Fantastic Beasts.* Classified 3X by the MM. Nogtails are somewhat like piglets. They are found in European, Russian, and American rural areas (FB 30–31). Cormac McLaggen tells Horace Slughorn that he went hunting for them with his Uncle Tiberius, Bertie Higgs, and Rufus Scrimgeour (HBP 7:144).

See also Fantastic Beasts and Where to Find Them

Non-explodable, Luminous Balloons. *Magical objects.* Harry receives these in his Wizard Crackers at Christmas in Year 1 (SS 12:204).

Non-verbal Spells. *Magical spells.* Snape tells the DADA students in his first class that Non-verbal Spells are important skills to know (HBP 9:178–79). Once sixth-year students begin using them, they are supposed to use them in many of their classes, such as DADA, Charms, and Transfiguration (HBP 11:217). Hermione becomes very good at them, as one might expect (HBP 18:376).

Norbert. *Magical creature.* The illegal dragon Hagrid hatches from a large black egg in his hut. The dragon is a Norwegian Ridgeback (SS 14:233). Hagrid names it Norbert and babies it like a child (SS 14:236). When it becomes obvious from Norbert's habits and appetite that Hagrid will not be able to keep him, Ron suggests that he give the dragon to his brother Charlie in Romania, who is studying dragons (SS 14:236). This makes Hagrid sad, but they then devise a scheme to make it happen; the plan involves a crate, the Invisibility Cloak, and meeting Charlie's colleagues at the top of the Astronomy Tower. Hagrid packs brandy, rats, and Norbert's teddy bear in the crate in case Norbert gets lonely. Charlie's friendly colleagues have a special harness made for the dragon and they manage to take him away (SS 14:241).

Norfolk. Location where Muggle Hetty Bayliss saw a flying car while hanging out her wash (CS 5:79). Quidditch referee Cyprian Youdle, who died during a match, came from Norfolk (QA 30).

North Tower. *Magical place.* The tower at Hogwarts where Divination class is held (PA 6:99). Students get to it by climbing a spiral staircase, then a silver stepladder to a round trapdoor in the ceiling (GF 13:199).

Norway. Percy Weasley thinks that the dragon dung his twin brothers sent to his office as a prank is actually a sample of fertilizer from Norway (GF 5:64).

Norwegian Ministry of Magic. *Magical place.* This office has in its holdings the letter from Goodwin Kneen to his cousin Olaf describing·an old form of Quidditch (QA 9).

Norwegian Ridgeback. *Magical creature.* From *Fantastic Beasts*. This is the breed of dragon that is Hagrid's pet, Norbert (SS 14:236). It has ridges rather than spikes along its back, and young dragons of this variety breathe fire at a younger age than many other breeds (FB 13).
   See also Fantastic Beasts and Where to Find Them

Nose-Biting Teacup. *Magical object.* Harry and Ron each buy one of these at Zonko's (PA 14:278).

Nosebleed Nougat. *Magical food.* The most popular kind of Skiving Snackboxes sold at Weasleys' Wizard Wheezes. Harry notices that there is only one beat-up box left at his first visit to the store in Year 6 (HBP 6:117).

Notable Magical Names of Our Time. *Magical book.* Harry and friends go searching for information about Nicolas Flamel in this book (SS 12:197).

Nott, Mr. *Character*. A Death Eater at the Little Hangleton graveyard (GF 33:651). He joins Lucius Malfoy at the Department of Mysteries, and Malfoy tells the other Death Eaters to leave him when he is attacked (OP 95:788). Draco Malfoy tells his friends that Horace Slughorn asked him about Mr. Nott (HBP 7:150–51). Mr. Nott is one of Voldemort's original Death Eaters (HBP 20:444).

See also Death Eaters

Nott, Theodore. *Character*. A student in Harry's year (SS 7:121). Harry and Hermione see him with Vincent Crabbe, Gregory Goyle, and other sons of Death Eaters in the library (OP 26:583).

Nottingham. *Muggle place*. Mr. Weasley asks Bill if he remembers the goblins Voldemort killed near Nottingham the last time he was in power (OP 5:85).

Nottinghamshire. From QA. Kennilworthy Whisp lives here when he is not traveling to see Quidditch games played by the Wigtown Wanderers (QA v).

See also Quidditch Through the Ages

"Nox." *Incantation*. In Latin *nox* means "night." The opposite of "Lumos!"; the spell puts out the light created at the end of a wand (PA 17:338).

Number Four, Privet Drive. *Muggle place*. The address where Harry's Aunt Petunia and Uncle Vernon Dursley live with their son, Dudley, and where Harry spent ten of the first eleven years of his life. It is located in Little Whinging, Surrey (SS 3:34). Professor Dumbledore has Harry placed at Privet Drive after the death of his parents in order to protect him from Voldemort, his parents' murderer (SS 1:1). The houses in the neighborhood are large and square-shaped (OP 1:1).

Number Seven, Mrs. *Muggle neighbor*. One of the Dursleys' neighbors (OP 1:5).

Number Twelve, Grimmauld Place. *Magical place*. The Headquarters for Albus Dumbledore's Order of the Phoenix. The house is the old Black family home in London. It is reached by standing between Numbers Eleven and Thirteen and thinking about Number Twelve when a door appears (OP 4:59). The house has not been used for years. Since Sirius Black is the last descendant of the family, he owns it and offers it to Dumbledore as the headquarters for the Order (OP 5:79). It is full of cobwebs and dust, as well as magical insects and infestations of other pests. The wallpaper is peeling off the walls, the carpet is thin, and portraits hang at odd angles (OP 4:60). The house is unplottable so that Muggles cannot find it (OP 6:115).

The Weasleys, Sirius Black, Harry, and friends all work at cleaning out the house before the start of Year 5 at Hogwarts. They find several items, including: a heavy locket; several old seals, including Sirius's father's Order of Merlin, First Class, given to him for Services to the Ministry (which Black claims meant giving the Ministry lots of money); Sirius's father's black ring with the family crest on it; snuff boxes; books; and unusual silver instruments. Harry thought of the cleaning operation as doing battle with the house (OP 6:116–17). Other items they found included a grandfather clock that threw bolts whenever one of them walked by, and purple robes that tried to strangle Ron (OP 6:118).

Numerology and Gramatica. *Magical book.* Hermione's Arithmancy textbook in Year 3 (PA 16:315).

Nundu. *Magical creatures.* From *Fantastic Beasts*. Classified 5X by the MM. A giant leopardlike beast, it lives in East Africa and is likely the most dangerous beast in the world (FB 31).

See also Fantastic Beasts and Where to Find Them

Oakshaft 79. *Magical object.* From QA. A broomstick invented in 1879 (hence the number) by Elias Grimstone; its thick oak handle was useful in high winds. An Oakshaft was used in the first crossing of the Atlantic by broom (QA 47–48).

See also Broomsticks

O.B.E. (Order of the British Empire). Rowling received this award in 2001 from Prince Charles, the Prince of Wales. The O.B.E. recognizes British citizens who have given "valuable service" to the empire. Honorary awards are also given to non-British citizens. There are an estimated 100,000 living O.B.E. honorees in the world.

The award was initiated in 1917 during World War I by King George V, who wished to honor military and civilian citizens who helped in the war effort. For the first time, women were included in an order of chivalry. Every four years approximately 2,000 members gather at the official Chapel of the Order, St. Paul's Cathedral in London, to celebrate the Order. The motto of the Order is "For God and the Empire." The medal of the 1917–1937 era was composed of a center gilt medallion of Britannia surrounded by the motto in red enamel. The medallion was mounted on a silver-gilt cross enameled in pearl-gray. On the back of the medallion were the letters "GRI" inscribed inside a gilt imperial crown. The letters stand for "George Rex Imperator." The medal was later adapted for Queen Elizabeth II.

Rowling was initially supposed to receive the Order from Queen Elizabeth II in December of 2000, but the BBC reported that the ceremony was postponed until the following spring because Rowling's seven-year-old daughter Jessica was ill.

See also Awards, J. K. Rowling's

Oblansk/Obalonsk, Mr. *Character.* The Bulgarian Minister of Magic. Cornelius Fudge attempts to introduce him to the Malfoys, but Mr. Oblansk has trouble with their name (GF 8:101).

Obliteration Charm. *Magical spell.* Hermione casts this spell on the snow to dissolve their footprints outside of Hagrid's cabin (OP 20:440).

"Obliviate!" *Incantation.* The magic words to work the Memory Charm. This spell to erase one's memory makes an explosion in the tunnel to the Chamber of Secrets, causing rocks to fall in the tunnel (CS 16:303). Arthur Weasley uses the incantation on Mr. Roberts, the campsite manager, after Arthur has obtained a site for the World Cup (GF 7:77).

Obliviator. *Magical occupation.* From *Fantastic Beasts.* Obliviators are wizards and witches who are trained to wipe out the memories of Muggles who have seen something of the magical world (FB xx).
See also Fantastic Beasts and Where to Find Them

Obliviator Headquarters. *Magical office.* Located on the third level of the Ministry as part of the Department of Magical Accidents and Catastrophes (OP 7:130).

Obscurus Books. *Magical press.* From *Fantastic Beasts.* This is the imaginary publishing house that "published" *Fantastic Beasts and Where to Find Them* in cooperation with Scholastic. The title page information indicates it is located at 18a Diagon Alley, London (FB iii).
See also Fantastic Beasts and Where to Find Them

Occamy. *Magical creature.* From *Fantastic Beasts.* Classified 4X by the MM. These are located in India and the Far East and have a snakelike body with wings and two legs (FB 31).
See also Fantastic Beasts and Where to Find Them

Occlumency. *Magical skill.* This is a defensive skill used to block someone who is trying to read one's mind (OP 24:519). *Occulto* in Latin means "to conceal or hide"; *mens* means "mind." Prof. Dumbledore assigns Snape the task of giving Harry lessons in Occlumency in his fifth year, but neither Harry nor Snape is happy working with the other (OP 24:519). In Year 6, Dumbledore tells Harry that Voldemort is probably using Occlumency on him and that is why his headaches and visions of flashing green light have eased (HBP 4:59).
See also Legilimency

Occlumens. *Person with magical ability.* One skilled with the power of Occlumency. Prof. Lupin tells Harry that Snape is a very good Occlumens, and he should study hard with him for his own protection (OP 24:527).

"Oddment!" One of the "few words" Prof. Dumbledore speaks before the Start-of-Term Banquet in Harry's first year. The other few words are "Blubber!," "Nitwit!," and "Tweak!" (SS 7:123).

"Oddsbodikins." *Magical password.* Password to Sir Cadogan's portrait for entry into Gryffindor Tower (PA 12:249).

Odgen's Old Firewhisky. *Magical drink.* Along with world peace between magical and non-magical people, Gilderoy Lockart says he would not mind a large bottle of Odgen's Old Firewhisky as a birthday present (CS 6:100).

Odo. *Character.* In their drunken state at Aragog's burial, Hagrid and Slughorn sing an old ballad about a wizard named Odo who died (HBP 22:487).

Office for House-Elf Relocation. *Magical office.* Newt Scamander used to work in this office at the Ministry (FB vi).

Office for the Detection and Confiscation of Counterfeit Defensive Spells and Protective Objects. *Magical office.* Arthur Weasley's new job in Year 6 is head of this new office in the Ministry. The Metamorph Medal is an example of such a counterfeit object (HBP 5:84, 87).

Office of Misinformation. *Magical office.* From *Fantastic Beasts.* A segment of the Ministry that works with the Muggle Prime Minister in the case of a large magical accident. They decide on a mutual untrue explanation to give to Muggles to keep them unaware of the wizarding community (FB xx).

Official Gobstones Club. *Magical organization.* Located in the Department of Magical Games and Sports on the seventh level of the Ministry (OP 7:129).

Ogden, Bob. *Character.* Bob Ogden was an employee of the Department of Magical Law Enforcement. Dumbledore extracted a memory from him about the Gaunts before he died (HBP 10:198).

Ogden, Tiberius. *Character.* Elder Wizengamot member who resigned in protest over the decree that allowed the Ministry control over Hogwarts (OP 15:308). He is a friend of Prof. Tofty (OP 31:714).

Ogg. *Character.* The caretaker at Hogwarts in Arthur and Molly Weasley's time as students there (GF 31:617).

O'Hare, Darren. *Character.* From QA. A Keeper who played for the Kenmare Kestrals from 1947 to 1960. He invented the Chaser Hawkshead Attacking Formation (QA 35).
  See also Quidditch Through the Ages

Olaf. *Character.* Goodwin Kneen's Norwegian cousin to whom he writes about "Kwidditch," an old form of Quidditch (QA 8–10).

Olde and Forgotten Bewitchments and Charmes. *Magical book.* Hermione consults this book for Harry's second task in the Triwizard Tournament (GF 26:486).

Ollerton, Bob, Bill, and Barnaby. *Characters.* From QA. The Ollerton Brothers started the Cleansweep Broom Company in 1926 (QA 49).
  See also Quidditch Through the Ages

Ollivander, Mr. *Character.* The elderly owner and proprietor of Ollivanders magic wand shop (SS 5:82). He sells Harry his magic wand and makes the famous statement that the wand chooses the wizard. Mr. Ollivander checks the weight of all the wands of the four champions for the Triwizard Tournament. He remembers Harry's wand (GF 18:308–309). He has disappeared from Diagon Alley when Harry is at the Burrow on his sixteenth birthday (HBP 6:106).
  See also Ollivanders; Wands

Ollivanders. *Magical place.* The magic wand shop on Diagon Alley. Ollivanders has sold wands since 382 B.C. (SS 5:82). Harry buys his 11-inch phoenix feather–filled holly wand at Ollivanders on his first trip to Diagon Alley. The last wand sold at Ollivanders before Mr. Ollivander disappeared was to Neville Longbottom's grandmother for Neville; Mr. Ollivander was missing the next day (HBP 7:137).

See also Diagon Alley; Wands

Omnioculars. *Magical object.* Somewhat like binoculars, Omnioculars include special features like slow motion, instant replay, and play-by-play action (GF 7:93).

One Minute Feasts—It's Magic! *Magical book.* A book in the Burrow (CS 3:34).

One Thousand Magical Herbs and Fungi. *Magical book.* This book was written by Phyllida Spore. It is the Potions class textbook for first-years (SS 8:138). As he studies for his year-end exam, Harry looks up "Dittany" in it (SS 14:229). Ginny Weasley repairs her copy at the Burrow when it is damaged by a Howler sent to the Burrow (GF 10:150). The book is still apparently used as the Potions class textbook in fifth year (OP 17:362).

Oona. *Character.* From QA. A person from the inn who gave Goodwin Kneen's "Kwidditch" team barrels to use for goals and gave them mead when they won (QA 9).

See also Kneen, Goodwin; *Quidditch Through the Ages*

Opal necklace. *Magical object.* Katie Bell is put under a spell and given a package in the bathroom of the Three Broomsticks to take to Hogwarts. The package contains an Opal necklace when she opens it she is raised up off the ground, then she screams and falls, writhing in a sort of seizure. At Hogwarts, Prof. McGonagall tells Argus Filch to take the necklace to Snape (HBP 12:249). Dumbledore tells Harry that if Katie had touched more of the necklace she would have died (HBP 13:259).

Oporto (Porto), Portugal. J. K. Rowling went to this city to teach English at Encounter Schools in 1991. It is the second-largest city in Portugal and is best known for its tourist industry centered on its port wineries, including Taylor's and Graham's. The explorer Henry the Navigator came from the city; Ferdinand Magellan may have been from Oporto as well.

Rowling continued to work on her Harry Potter manuscript while she taught at the school. She typically taught night school, which left her days free to write. She shared an apartment with two other women—Aine Kiely and Jill Prewett—and often socialized at clubs after work with them. During one of the evenings, she met the man who would become her first husband, Jorges Arantes. After the birth of her daughter Jessica, Rowling's marriage broke up, and she left Portugal in 1993.

"Oppugno!" *Incantation.* In Latin *oppuguo* means "attack." Hermione uses this incantation after witnessing Ron kissing Lavender Brown. Her spell makes a group of birds surround Ron and begin pecking at him (HBP 14:302).

Orb. *Magical object.* Prof. Trelawney calls a crystal ball an "Orb" in Divination class. The class begins using Orbs early because, as she informs them, the Orb will be on their final exam (PA 15:296).

"Orchideous!". *Incantation.* This incantation makes orchids appear out of the end of a wand. Mr. Ollivander performs the spell on Fleur Delacour's wand during the wand-weighing for the Triwizard Tournament (GF 18:308).

Order of Suspension. *Magical document.* Cornelius Fudge has an Order of Suspension signed by all twelve members of the board of governors to remove Prof. Dumbledore from his post as Hogwarts Headmaster. Fudge has the order because people keep getting petrified at the school during Year 2 (CS 14:262).

Order of the British Empire (O.B.E.). *See* O.B.E. (Order of the British Empire); Awards, J. K. Rowling's

Order of the Phoenix. *Magical society.* Dumbledore founded this secret society. It is composed of the people he trusted in the last fight against Voldemort. Ron tells Harry that they have seen at least twenty Order members during their stay at the Order's Headquarters (located at Number Twelve, Grimmauld Place, London). The house is the Black ancestral home (OP 4:67). Only wizards who are age seventeen or older may belong to the Order (OP 5:97).

Members include: Sirius Black; Elphias Doge; Dedalus Diggle; Mundungus Fletcher; Hestia Jones; Remus Lupin; Alastor "Mad-Eye" Moody; Sturgis Podmore; Severus Snape; Nymphadora Tonks; Emmeline Vance; Arthur, Bill, Charley, and Molly Weasley (OP 9:173–74).

Mad-Eye Moody shows Harry a photograph of the original Order of the Phoenix that includes himself, James and Lily Potter, Peter Pettigrew, Dedalus Diggle, Sirius Black, Aberforth Dumbledore, Albus Dumbledore, Sturgis Podmore, Marlene McKinnon, Frank and Alice Longbottom, Rebius Hagrid, Emmeline Vance, Benjy Fenwick, Edgar Bones, Caradoc Dearborn, Elphias Doge, Gideon and Fabian Prewett, and Dorcas Meadows (OP 9:173–74).

Ornithomancy. *Magical ability.* Ornithomancy is the art of predicting the future from the flight patterns of birds. Students break into Prof. Trelawney's lectures with questions about ornithomancy after she is put on probation by Dolores Umbridge (OP 25:552).

Ottery St. Catchpole. The town just outside where the Weasley residence, the Burrow, is located (CS 3:31).

Ouagadogou. *Magical place.* Gilderoy Lockhart claims to have seen attacks similar to the one that Mrs. Norris endured. He claims that the attacks took place in Ouagadogou, and that he gave the townspeople amulets to ward them off (CS 9:142).

Owl Order Service. *Magical mail order.* Weasleys' Wizard Wheezes sends products to students at Hogwarts via Owl Order Service. When Argus Filch bans purchase of their goods, they disguise products like love potions as bottles of perfume and cough potions (HBP 15:306).

Owl treat. *Magical pet food.* Pigwidgeon nearly chokes on an extra large owl treat when Ron objects to wearing the used dress robes his mother buys for him at Diagon Alley (GF 10:157). Ron feeds owl treats to Hedwig and Pigwidgeon at Grimmauld Place because they have to stay in at night so as not to draw attention (OP 6:99).

Owlery. *Magical place.* The area of Hogwarts castle where the owls live in between flying on mail missions for their witches and wizards. Hedwig is offended when Harry tells her to go to the Owlery to find food after her long journey bringing Sirius Black's letter (GF 14:226). The Owlery is a circular room located in the West Tower with glassless windows. On the floor are straw and owl droppings and the spit-up bones of mice and voles. Hundreds of messenger owls live there, waiting to be sent out on messenger duty (GF 15:229).

Owls. *Magical creatures.* As the primary messengers in the magical world of Harry Potter, there are several kinds of owls in the series. The first mention of owls comes during the evening news Mr. Dursley watches at the beginning of the first novel. The news anchor, Ted, reports that owls all over Britain have changed their sleeping pattern and are now flying about in large numbers in all directions during the day (SS 1:6). Hagrid buys Harry a snowy owl as a birthday gift on Harry's first trip to Diagon Alley (SS 5:81). Draco Malfoy has an eagle owl (SS 9:144); Neville Longbottom receives mail from a barn owl in Year 1 (SS 9:145) and a big tawny owl in Year 4 (GF 13:194). Sirius Black gives Ron Weasley a little Scops owl (PA 22:431–32, 434) to replace Errol, the weary and worn family owl that has trouble making ordinary journeys, never mind long and difficult ones. Percy Weasley gets a screech owl, Hermes, as a gift from his parents when he is made a prefect (PA 5:70).

Harry Potter's friend Hedwig is a snowy owl like this one. Courtesy of Getty Images/PhotoDisc.

In Greek mythology the owl was a symbol of Athens because there were so many owls in the city. The owl is the symbol of the goddess Athena (Minerva in Roman mythology) because she shares her name with the city.

O.W.L.s. *Magical examinations.* O.W.L.s stands for Ordinary Wizarding Levels. Students who are fifteen years old must pass examinations to be awarded levels of academic accomplishment (GF 5:55). Bill Weasley passed twelve O.W.L.s, which is a high number (CS 4:46). The scores are discussed among the students at lunch after one of Snape's Potions classes. They say that P is for Poor; D is for Dreadful; and T is for Troll. All of these are failing grades. The passing grades are: O for Outstanding; E for Exceeds Expectations; and A for Acceptable, which is the last passing grade (OP 15:310–11). The test results are mailed to students by owl sometime in July (OP 31:709).

Harry is pleased with his O.W.L. results; he earns seven. He did not pass History of Magic or Divination, but this does not surprise him or Ron, who does not pass them either. Harry's O.W.L. grades are: Astronomy, A; Care of Magical Creatures, E; Charms, E; Defense Against the Dark Arts, O; Divination, P; Herbology, E; History of Magic, D; Potions, E; and Transfiguration, E. Ron earns no Outstanding grades. Hermione earns ten Outstandings and one E for Defense Against the Dark Arts, which leaves her a bit disappointed (HBP 5:102–3).

✦ P ✦

Paddington Station. *Muggle place.* This is the train station in London where Hagrid takes Harry to catch his train back to Privet Drive after their first shopping trip to Diagon Alley (SS 5:86).

Padfoot. *Magical nickname.* Sirius Black's nickname from his Animagus form as a black dog (PA 14:287). Harry uses this nickname when he tries to communicate to Snape in front of Prof. Umbridge that Sirius is in trouble (OP 32:745).

Pagination. One of the difficulties that students, teachers, and others who work with the series must contend with is the different pagination for the novels in different editions. For example, the pagination is different between the children's British and American editions and between the children's and adult editions (the adult editions contain the same story with a different cover). The pagination is affected in each case by trim size, the presence or absence of chapter opening illustrations, type size, margins on the page, and so forth. In the future, consistent pagination for an accepted scholarly edition of the series will be essential for serious, long-term work in the books. Lacking that, individuals writing about the series should always indicate which edition they are using. It is also helpful to readers using translations from English if writers indicate the chapter their source material comes from in the novels, since page numbers will likely be different.

In the American children's edition (which this reference uses), the page counts are as follows: Book 1 = 309; Book 2 = 341; Book 3 = 435; Book 4 = 734; Book 5 = 870; and Book 6 = 652. *Quidditch Through the Ages* and *Fantastic Beasts and Where to Find Them* are 56 and 42 pages, respectively.

Palace of Beauxbatons. *Magical place.* The Palace of Beauxbatons at Beauxbatons Academy is equivalent to the Great Hall at Hogwarts. Fleur Delacour tells Roger Davies that its Christmas decorations, which include ice sculptures that do not melt, are superior to those at Hogwarts (GF 23:418).

Paper airplanes. *Magical object.* Paper airplanes are used as interoffice memoranda at the Ministry of Magic. Mr. Weasley tells Harry that they used to use owls but the bird droppings got too messy in the office (OP 7:129–30).

Paracelsus. *Character.* One of the figures on the Famous Witches and Wizard Cards found in Chocolate Frogs (SS 6:103). A statue of Paracelsus is located on the seventh floor of Hogwarts, near the entrance to Gryffindor Tower. Nearly Headless Nick tells Harry that Peeves is planning to drop the statue on the next person to walk by it (OP 14:281). Paraclesus (1493–1541) was a Swiss physician and mystic.

See also Chocolate Frogs

Parkin, Walter. *Character.* From QA. A wizard butcher whose seven offspring established the Wigtown Wanderers Quidditch team in 1422 (QA 37).

Parkin's Pincer. *Magical sports play.* From QA. A Chaser move in which two Chasers fly on either side of a Chaser from the other team; a third flies directly at the player. The move was named for players on the Wigtown Wanderers team (QA 53).

Parkinson, Pansy. *Character.* A Slytherin student in Harry's year (SS 7:121). She has a face that looks like a pug dog. Pansy speaks up to Parvati Patil when she crosses Draco Malfoy for making fun of Neville Longbottom during their first Flying Lesson (SS 9:148). She teases Harry about his trouble with Dementors at the beginning of their third year (PA 6:96) and is concerned about Draco after Buckbeak cuts him (PA 7:123). Pansy is the girl prefect for Slytherin in Year 5 (OP 10:188). She makes fun of Cho Chang and Harry when she sees them together (OP 25:558). A member of the Inquisitorial Squad, she grows antlers after the Weasley twins leave and the school rebels against Dolores Umbridge (OP 30:677). She is called to take her practical Charm O.W.L. at the same time as Harry (OP 31:713). Pansy is in the train compartment with Draco's head on her lap when Harry spies on him with his Invisibility Cloak (HBP 7:149–54).

"Parry Otter, the Chosen Boy Who . . ." When Horace Slughorn is drunk at Aragog's burial, he mixes up Harry Potter's nicknames, "the Chosen One" and "the Boy Who Lived" (HBP 22:487).

Parselmouth/Parseltongue. *Magical person/magical ability.* One who can speak to snakes is called a Parselmouth; the snake language itself, which makes a hissing sound, is called Parseltongue. The ability is rare and is often associated with those involved in the Dark Arts. Harry has this ability, but Dumbledore says he received it when Voldemort transferred some of his skills to Harry at the time of his parents' death and the making of his scar. Salazar Slytherin was a Parselmouth, and that is why the Slytherin House symbol is a serpent (CS 11:195–96). Rita Skeeter announces Harry's "skill" in an article in the *Daily Prophet* (GF 31:612).

Partial Vanishment. *Magical spell.* Harry looks for a book in the library on this subject (OP 26:583).

Passwords. *Magical words.* One of the entertaining features of the series is the password that keeps changing for admission to the Gryffindor Common Room and Tower. These words, which must be said to the Fat Lady portrait that swings open to allow admittance, include: "Caput Draconis" (SS 7:130); "Pig snout" (SS 9:156); "Fortuna Major!" (PA 5:94); "Flibbertigibbet!" (PA 15:295); "Balderdash" (GF 12:191); "Fairy lights" (GF 22:398); "Banana fritters" (GF 25:459); *"Mimbulus mibletonia"* (OP 13:251); "Dilligrout" (HBP 12:256); "Abstinence" (HBP 17:351); "Tapeworm" (HBP 23:493); "Quid agis" (HBP 24:533).

When Sir Cadogen takes the Fat Lady's place, the passwords are: "Scurvy cur" (PA 11:230) and "Oddsbodikins" (PA 12:249).

A password into Dumbledore's quarters is "Lemon drop" (CS 11:204). When Harry needs to find Dumbledore quickly in Year 4, he tries "Lemon drop," but it does not work, so he starts guessing several other possibilities—"Pear drop"; "Licorice Wand"; "Fizzing Whizbee"; "Drooble's Best Blowing Gum"; "Bertie Bott's Every Flavor Beans"; "Chocolate Frog"; "Sugar Quill"—but none of them work. Finally, he guesses "Cockroach Cluster," and the gargoyle moves aside (GF 29:579). Prof. McGonagall uses the password "Fizzing Whizbee" in Year 5 when she takes Harry to Dumbledore's office after his dream about the attack on Arthur Weasley (OP 22:466–67). Dumbledore's password is "toffee éclairs" in Year 6 (HBP 23:493).

The password into the prefects' bathroom near the statue of Boris the Bewildered is "pine fresh" (GF 23:431).

Patented Daydream Charms. *Magical charms.* A product sold at Weasleys' Wizard Wheezes (HBP 6:117).

Patil, Padma and Parvati. *Characters.* Twins in Harry's year (SS 7:120). Parvati tells Draco Malfoy to shut up during Flying Lessons when he makes fun of Neville Longbottom (SS 9:147). Harry and Ron also overhear her telling Lavender Brown that Hermione was crying in the bathroom before the Halloween Feast in Year 1 (SS 10:172). Parvati gets called Miss Pennyfeather by Prof. Binns in History of Magic class (CS 9:152). Ron goes to the Yule Ball with Padma, and she is made girl prefect of Ravenclaw House in her fifth year (OP 10:189). The twins are called at the same time as Harry to be examined for their practical Charms O.W.L. (OP 31:713). Parvati tells Harry that she was almost sent home from Hogwarts after the attack on Katie Bell in Year 6 (HBP 15:312–13). After Dumbledore dies, the twins leave the school before breakfast the following day (HBP 30:633).

Patonga Proudsticks. *Magical sports team.* From QA. A Quidditch team from Uganda (QA 42).
See also Quidditch Through the Ages

Patronus. *Magical charm.* In Latin *patronus* means "protector, defender." A difficult spell to conjure, a Patronus acts as a kind of shield between the caster and a Dementor. The shape a Patronus takes is different with every wizard. It is conjured by concentrating on a very happy memory. It is advanced magic, and not all wizards can successfully conjure it (PA 12:237). The incantation is "Expecto patronum!" (PA 12:238). Harry works a Patronus to rescue himself and Sirius Black from about 100 Dementors around the Hogwarts lake; Harry thinks the Patronus is his father (PA 21:406). He conjures another one to save himself and Dudley Dursley from two Dementors in Little Whinging (OP 1:18). Harry impresses his examiner for his DADA O.W.L. when he is able to conjure a Patronus when asked (OP 31:714–15). Amelia Bones is impressed with Harry's ability when he confirms that he is able to conjure a full, corporeal Patronus at the

Wizengamot court hearing for his expulsion (OP 8:141). He tells Amelia that his Patronus always takes the form of a stag (OP 8:141). Cho Chang's Patronus takes the form of a swan (OP 27:606). Hermione's is a silver otter (OP 27:607). The Order of the Phoenix uses a Patronus to communicate, as Nymphadora Tonks does when she tends to Harry's nose and sends word to Hogwarts Castle that she has him in her care (HBP 8:158).

Prof. Lupin tells Harry that it is possible for a witch or wizard's Patronus to change, especially when the person has undergone a shock. He tells Harry that Tonks's has done this (HBP 16:340).

Payne, Mr. *Character.* The Muggle in charge of campsites in the second field for the Quidditch World Cup (GF 7:76).

Peacock Quill. *Magical object.* The huge pen Prof. Lockhart uses for book signings (CS 10:163).

Peakes, Jimmy. *Character.* Jimmy Peakes becomes a Beater on the Gryffindor Quidditch team the year that Harry captains. He hits a Bludger so hard that it accidentally hits Harry on the back of the head raising a giant bump (HBP 11:225). Later, he brings Harry a parchment message from Dumbledore telling Harry to come see him as soon as possible (HBP 25:540).

Peasegood, Arnold (Arnie). *Character.* An Obliviator with the Accidental Magic Reversal Squad (GF 7:86).

Peebles. The location of Angus Fleet's sighting of the flying Ford Anglia, which he reports to the police (CS 5:79).

Peeves. *Character.* The Hogwarts poltergeist (SS 7:129). Rowling has described Peeves as a nuisance in the castle that no one can get rid of. He is a pest that comes with the building, and most have found a way to live with his irritating and meddlesome ways. The only presence he seems afraid of is the Bloody Baron, the Slytherin House ghost (SS 7:115). One of his pranks is putting chewing gum into keyholes (PA 7:131). He makes a mocking rhyme about Harry's anger after his hearing (OP 12:247). Argus Filch hopes that Dolores Umbridge will expel Peeves after she takes over the school (OP 28:629).

Pennifold, Daisy. *Character.* From QA. Daisy Pennifold put a spell on a Quaffle that would cause it to fall slowly, giving Chasers time to catch it (QA 21).
See also Quidditch Through the Ages

Pennifold Quaffle. *Magical sports equipment.* From QA. A Quaffle with Daisy Pennifold's spell that makes it fall slowly so that Chasers can catch it (QA 21).
See also Quidditch Through the Ages

Pensieve. A large, shallow stone bowl with carvings along the side; it holds a bright silver substance that is something between a liquid and a gas. The substance swirls and clouds over. When Harry first sees it, he looks inside and feels a falling sensation. He arrives in a courtroom in a dungeon he does not recognize and witnesses the trial of Barty Crouch, Jr. (GF 30:584–96).

Dumbledore tells Harry that the Pensieve stores memories and thoughts that crowd one's mind. He touches his wand to his temple, and a silvery hair attaches to it. He then drops the hair into the Pensieve to look at later at his convenience (GF 30:597).

Using the Pensieve, Harry sees Snape's worst memory of James Potter bullying him and in *Half-Blood Prince* Dumbledore shows him much about Voldemort's/Tom Riddle's past.

Pepper Imps. *Magical candy.* Those who eat Pepper Imps will have smoke coming out of their mouths (PA 5:77).

See also Candy and sweets

Pepper, Octavius. *Character.* Hermione reads in the *Daily Prophet* about Octavius Pepper's disappearance, which is a sign that trouble is brewing now that Voldemort is back (HBP 21:457).

Peppermint Toad. *Magical candy.* Ron eats one of these at the start of the holidays in Year 3 (PA 11:213). George Weasley tosses them around at the Gryffindor party after they beat Ravenclaw in Quidditch (PA 13:264).

Pepperup Potion. *Magical substance.* Madam Pomfrey concocts this potion to help students get over colds in Harry's second year. It works well except that it leaves some students with smoke coming out of their ears (CS 8:122). She gives Pepperup Potion to the people brought up from the mervillage in the second task of the Triwizard Tournament (GF 26:505).

Perkins. *Character.* An ancient warlock who works with Arthur Weasley in the Ministry's Misuse of Muggle Artifacts Office (CS 3:31). Arthur Weasley borrows his shabby old tent for the Quidditch World Cup; the tent turns out to be a three-room apartment on the inside (GF 7:80). When Harry visits Mr. Weasley's office before his hearing, he sits at Perkins's desk. Then old Perkins arrives and tells Mr. Weasley that Harry's hearing has been moved up ten minutes (OP 7:133–34). Prof. Binns calls Harry by the name Perkins by mistake (OP 17:357).

Perks, Sally-Anne. *Character.* A student in Harry's year (SS 7:121).

Permanent Sticking Charm. *Magical spell.* This spell keeps something fastened to a wall or another location. Sirius Black thinks his mother may have put the spell on her portrait at Grimmauld Place because he cannot get it down (OP 5:79).

Peru. The Irish Quidditch team beat Peru in the semifinals to win their place at the Quidditch World Cup (GF 5:63). Peru has the most successful Quidditch team in South America (QA 45). The Weasley twins import the Instant Darkness Powder they sell in their store from Peru (HBP 6:119).

Peruvian Instant Darkness Powder. *Magical substance.* This substance is sold at Weasleys' Wizard Wheezes. Draco Malfoy uses it to disguise his movements on the night Dumbledore dies. When Ron hears about the incident, he says he is going to have a talk with his brothers about who buys their products (HBP 29:618).

Peruvian Vipertooth. *Magical creature.* From *Fantastic Beasts.* A breed of dragon (MM Classification 5X) that grows to only fifteen feet long; it eats goats, cows, and especially humans (FB 13–14).
See also Fantastic Beasts and Where to Find Them

"Peskipiksi Pesternomi." *Incantation.* Prof. Lockhart tries this spell on the Cornish pixies when they will not be recaptured in his DADA class in Year 2. The spell does not work (CS 6:102).

Pest Advisory Bureau/Pest Sub-Division. *Magical office.* This office is located on the fourth level of the Ministry in the Department for the Regulation and Control of Magical Creatures (OP 7:130; FB 30–31).
See also Fantastic Beasts and Where to Find Them

Petrification. *Magical spell.* Several animals, ghosts, and students are petrified in the halls of Hogwarts by Voldemort acting through Ginny Weasley during Year 2. Those who get petrified include: Mrs. Norris, Justin Finch-Fletchley, Nearly Headless Nick, and Hermione. Ginny is the last to suffer but is revived in the Chamber of Secrets after Harry temporarily defeats Voldemort (CS 17:322–23).

"Petrificus Totalus!" *Incantation.* This is the incantation for the Full Body-Bind. The spell locks the entire body in a stiff position. Hermione casts it on Neville Longbottom to keep him from following her, Ron, and Harry when they go to look for the Sorcerer's Stone (SS 16:273). Draco Malfoy puts this spell on Harry when he catches him spying on him in the luggage of his Hogwarts Express compartment (HBP 7:153). Harry uses it against an Inferus in the cave (HBP 26:575).

Pettigrew, Peter. *Character.* A Hogwarts student at the time of James Potter, Sirius Black, and Remus Lupin. Pettigrew had less talent than Sirius Black and James Potter, so he admired them (PA 10:207). It turns out that Pettigrew was a double agent for Voldemort and sold his friends out to him. Since the Potters' murder, he has been hiding in Animagus form as Ron's rat, Scabbers. After the murders, Pettigrew's mother received his Order of Merlin award and one of her son's fingers. Scabbers's missing toe is one indication to Sirius and Lupin that the rat is actually Pettigrew (PA 11:215). Sirius Black made Pettigrew the Potters' Secret-Keeper, which gave him the ability to lead Voldemort to the Potters and to kill them (PA 19:369). Pettigrew was a member of the original Order of the Phoenix but he betrayed them, which resulted in the death of Harry's parents. In the photograph of the original Order of the Phoenix, Harry's parents sit on either side of Pettigrew (OP 9:174).

Pets. Ironically, of all the characters in the series, it is Hagrid who observes that people can sometimes behave foolishly when it comes to matters concerning their pets (PA 14:274).
See also Animals

The Philosophy of the Mundane: Why the Muggles Prefer Not to Know. *Magical book.* From *Fantastic Beasts.* This book was written by Prof. Mordicus Egg (Dust & Mildeewe, 1963). It discusses the Muggle habit of passing off obvious evidence of the existence of magical creatures (FB xvii).

Philpott, Arkie. *Character.* Arkie Philpott had the misfortune of having a Probity Probe stuck up his bottom during a security search for Voldemort after the villain's second rise to power (HBP 6:108).

Phineas. *See* [Black] Phineas Nigellus

"Phlegm." *Magical nickname.* Ginny Weasley's nickname for Fleur Delacour after she becomes engaged to Bill Weasley (HBP 5:94).

Phoenix. *Magical creature.* Harry sees a phoenix in Dumbledore's office, and the professor explains how they live to die in flames only to be born again from their ashes. He tells Harry that they can carry heavy loads, heal wounds with their tears, and are extremely loyal pets. Dumbledore's phoenix is named Fawkes (CS 12:207).

In *Fantastic Beasts*, the phoenix is classified 4X by the MM. It has a high classification number not because it is dangerous, but because very few wizards have tamed them. A phoenix, according to *Fantastic Beasts*, is red with a long gold tail, beak, and claws. It is peaceful and eats herbs. Its song gives courage to those with pure hearts and fear to those with evil motives (FB 32).

After Dumbledore dies, the surviving faculty, students, and members of the Order of the Phoenix hear the long, lamenting song of Fawkes outside the castle (HBP 29:614–15, 621). In medieval times, the phoenix was often depicted in signs over alchemists' shops; it is a symbol of alchemy.

See also Fantastic Beasts and Where to Find Them; Fawkes

Pig. *Magical creature.* Ron Weasley's small gray owl given to him by Sirius Black. The name is short for "Pigwidgeon" (GF 3:35).

See also Pigwidgeon

"Pig snout." *Magical password.* This password is used for admission into Gryffindor Tower, Year 1 (SS 9:156).

See also Passwords

Pigwidgeon. *Magical creature.* Ron's tiny owl, given to him by Sirius Black. The owl brings Sirius Black's message to Harry at the end of *Prisoner of Azkaban*, when Black goes back into hiding. The young owl flies excitedly and is proud of itself for carrying messages (PA 22:431–32, 434). Ginny Weasley named him (GF 5:57). Ron keeps him in his room because his quick and constant flying bothers the other family owls, Errol and Hermes (GF 5:57).

Pince, Madam Irma. *Character.* Hogwarts librarian. She is more of a guardian of books than one who encourages use of them (SS 12:198). She is described as thin, with vulturelike features (CS 10:163). She chases Harry and Ginny Weasley out of the library when she sees that they have chocolate (OP 29:655–56).

Pink umbrella. *Magical object.* Hagrid carries his broken wand in a pink umbrella and performs magic on occasions, though he is not supposed to do so (SS 4:56).

See also Wands

Pitch. *Magical sports playing area.* From QA. The playing field in Quidditch. It is oval-shaped with a length of five hundred feet and width of eighty feet. In the center is a small circle about two feet across where the flying balls are let go. At both of the narrow ends of the oval are three goals on poles with a scoring area in front of them (QA 17–19).

See also Quidditch Through the Ages

Pittiman, Radolphus. *Character.* Radolphus Pittiman is a biographer of Uric the Oddball. He writes about Uric having a ten-day concussion after trying to walk through walls (Uric thought he was a ghost) (FB 3).

Pixy. *Magical beings.* From *Fantastic Beasts*. Classified 3X by the MM. In Ron and Harry's copy of *Fantastic Beasts*, they note that the pixy should be ranked 7X for Prof. Lockhart. A pixy flies without wings, is blue in color, and is found predominantly in Cornwall, England (FB 32). They are also mentioned in *A History of Magic* (FB xi).

Platform 9¾. *See* King's Cross Station, London

PlayStation. *Muggle game.* Harry writes to Sirius Black that Dudley Dursley got angry from being on a diet and threw his PlayStation out of the window (GF 2:25). PlayStation is an actual video game system and is one of the few references in the entire series to the popular culture of contemporary young readers.

"Please-men." *Wrong word.* Mr. Weasley's mispronunciation of "policemen" (GF 11:159).

Plimpy. *Magical creature.* From *Fantastic Beasts*. Classified 3X by the MM. The Plimpy is a round fish with two legs and webbed feet; it searches the bottom of bodies of water looking for snails (FB 32–33).

Plumpton Pass. *Magical sports play.* From QA. In 1921 Seeker Roderick Plumpton of the Tutshill Tornados caught a Snitch in his sleeve. He says this was intentional, though many people later wondered. The maneuver was afterwards called the Plumpton Pass (QA 53).

See also Quidditch Through the Ages

Plumpton, Roderick. *Character.* Seeker for the Tutshill Tornados who was the captain when the team won the League Cup five years in a row. He has the record for the fastest Snitch catch at three and a half seconds. The catch was made in a game against the Caerphilly Catapults in 1921 (QA 37). The Plumpton Pass play is named after him.

Pluto. In Divination class Prof. Trelawney discusses the interferences in life caused by Pluto. The students snicker at the subject (GF 21:371).

Pocket Sneakoscope. *Magical object.* Harry receives the Pocket Sneakoscope for his thirteenth birthday from Ron. It is a smaller version of the device that flashes when something untrue is said or happening nearby (PA 1:10).

Podmore, Sturgis. *Character.* A member of the original Order of the Phoenix who arrives with others at Privet Drive to take Harry to Headquarters. He has a square jaw and thick hair the color of straw. He winks at Harry when he is introduced (OP 3:49). Mad-Eye Moody says that Podmore borrowed and kept his best Invisibility Cloak (OP

9:173). He is missing at Headquarters when he is supposed to help guard Harry on the way to King's Cross at the beginning of the school year (OP 10:180). Mad-Eye says that he will report Podmore's second absence that week to Dumbledore (OP 10:181). The *Daily Prophet* lists Podmore's address as Number Two, Laburnum Gardens, Clapham, in the article charging him with trespassing at the Ministry (OP 14:287). Podmore is arrested for trespassing, quite possibly at the Department of Mysteries (OP 24:539). Podmore tried to steal the Prophecy under Voldemort's power (OP 35:787).

Pogrebin. *Magical creature.* From *Fantastic Beasts.* Classified 3X by the MM. The creature is a native of Russia; it resembles a rock that likes to follow human beings in their shadows, then eats them when they become exhausted and upset (FB 33).
See also Fantastic Beasts and Where to Find Them

Point of view. *See* Chapters

Poland. Hagrid tells Harry and friends that he and Madame Maxime ran into a couple of trolls on the border of Poland in their quest to recruit giants for Dumbledore (OP 20:426).

Poliakoff. *Character.* Durmstrang student who wants mulled wine when Prof. Karkaroff offers it only to Viktor Krum (GF 16:257).

Polkiss, Piers. *Character.* Dudley Dursley's best friend. He is scrawny and has a ratlike face. He holds people's arms behind their backs so Dudley can hit them (SS 2:23). Dudley told his parents he was going to Piers Polkiss's house the night the Dementors caught up with him and Harry in Little Whinging (PA 1:3).

Polyjuice Potion. *Magical substance.* This potion turns a person into someone else. Hermione concocts some to get information out of Draco Malfoy in Year 2. Harry and Ron turn into Vincent Crabbe and Gregory Goyle. Hermione makes a mistake and puts a cat hair in her potion and ends up in the hospital wing with fur on her face. The recipe is in *Moste Potente Potions* in the Restricted Section of the library. Hermione says it is the most difficult potion she has ever seen (CS 10:165). The ingredients take months to prepare, and the procedure is very tricky (CS 9:159–60). Among the ingredients are: lacewing flies, leeches, fluxweed, knotgrass, powdered horn of bicorn, shredded skin of boomslang, plus something that belongs to the person you are trying to become, such as a hair (CS 10:165). There is also a waiting period for some of the ingredients. The fluxweed needs to be harvested at the full moon; lacewings need to be stewed for twenty-one days (CS 10:166).
Barty Crouch, Jr., turns into Mad-Eye Moody for the events of the Goblet of Fire (GF 35:682) and may have used Polyjuice Potion to do so. Harry thinks he got full credit for knowing the ingredients of this potion on his Potions O.W.L. (OP 31:716).

Pomfrey, Madam Poppy. *Character.* The Hogwarts nurse. Prof. Dumbledore first speaks of her when saying that she complimented him on his new earmuffs and made him blush (SS 1:11).

Pontner, Roddy. *Character.* Roddy Pontner makes a bet with Ludo Bagman on who will score first in the World Cup; Ludo brags to Mr. Weasley that he has good odds on his bet on Ireland, since Ireland has its strongest team in years (GF 7:88).

Popular culture. It could be argued that anyone over the age of reason who was alive in Western society from 1997 to 2007 would have heard of the name Harry Potter. Prof. McGonagall's prophecy that everyone will know Harry Potter's name came true for the previously unknown writer who first penned those words. The words proved to be more true than even Rowling, with her vivid imagination, could have envisioned at the time. While books are certainly part of popular culture, Harry's influence stretched beyond books once they began selling so widely and then the story made its way in installments into blockbuster films. Merchandising, advertising, newspaper articles, reviews, interviews, soundtracks, video and computer games, translations, websites, posters, costumes, books of criticism, fan events, documentaries, Halloween parties, readings, book and film release parties—the infiltration of Harry Potter into popular culture was hard for anyone living near a bookstore, computer, or television screen to miss.

The phenomenon became so hard to miss, in fact, that the series risked backlash against what is the most enduring legacy of any work of literature—the continual printing, reading, and discussion of the book. In short, the influence of the books on popular culture was so strong in the early years of the new millennium that their popularity jeopardized the serious regard of the series by the people who would later be charged with keeping the books alive. Librarians, teachers, professors, scholars, and others began to be less than impressed by the characters and plot and were turned off by what came to be called the "Harry Potter Phenomenon." It may take several years after

Young Harry Potter fans dressed in costume in Tokyo, Japan, at a promotional event for the film *Harry Potter and the Goblet of Fire*, November 2005. Harry Potter books and films have influenced popular culture around the world. © Yoshikazu Tsuno/AFP/Getty Images.

the publication of the last book and the release of the last film for the phenomenon to cool so that it may be studied more clearly for what it was.

What remains to be seen is whether the Harry Potter cultural moment will be studied longer than the Harry Potter books themselves after the current generation encourages their children to read and share them. Will the books still be widely enjoyed by the grandchildren of today's children? Only time, something popular culture has never been able to keep hold of, will tell.

Porlock. *Magical creature.* From *Fantastic Beasts.* Classified 2X by the MM. The Porlock grows to be about two feet tall and likes to guard horses; it eats grass (FB 34). They are also mentioned in *A History of Magic* (FB xi). Prof. Grubbly-Plank plans to cover Porlocks before Harry's O.W.L.s in his fifth year (OP 15:323).

Porskoff Ploy. *Magical game play.* From QA. Harry sees the Ireland National team make this play against Bulgaria during the World Cup (GF 8:106). One Chaser flies up with the Quaffle, appearing to be about to score, but then passes it quickly down to another Chaser. The move was named for Russian Chaser Petrova Porskoff (QA 53).
  See also Quidditch Through the Ages

Portable Swamp. *Magical spell.* Fred and George Weasley make a Portable Swamp on the fifth floor to cause a diversion so that Harry may speak with Sirius Black. They will offer the swamp for sale at their store (OP 39:675). No one knows how to dry it up after the Weasleys leave, so Argus Filch ends up punting students across it so they may get to class (OP 30:676). After the return of Dumbledore to Hogwarts, Prof. Flitwick cleans up the swamp quickly, except for a small patch left as a monument to Fred and George because of the good magic that it represents (OP 38:848).

Portkey. *Magical transportion.* Portkeys are usually simple, everyday objects that turn into a form of transportation when one touches them at a scheduled time. To move thousands of magical people around the world to the Quidditch World Cup, the host country of Britain established two hundred Portkeys around the country (GF 6:70). The Burrow has one near it that Harry and the Weasleys use to get to the World Cup; it is at the top of Stoatshead Hill and is an old boot (GF 6:70–71). Other Portkeys include: an empty drink can; a popped football; and an old newspaper (GF 7:75). Mr. Weasley and everyone who goes with him to the World Cup return via an old tire (GF 10:145). The golden head of the statue from the Fountain of Magical Brethren becomes a Portkey. Dumbledore hands this Portkey to Harry to get him back to Hogwarts after the battle in the Hall of Prophecy (OP 36:819).

Portkey Office. *Magical office.* Located in the Department of Magical Transport on the sixth floor of the Ministry (OP 7:129).

Portsmouth. From QA. Elias Grimstone, inventor of the Oakshaft 79 broomstick, lived here (QA 47).
  See also Quidditch Through the Ages

"Portus." *Incantation.* In Latin *portus* means "port, harbor, or haven." This incantation turns an object into a Portkey for transportation. Dumbledore turns a kettle into a Portkey in his office after Arthur Weasley is attacked (OP 22:472).

Post Office, Hogsmeade. *Magical place.* Harry and Ron visit the post office in Hogsmeade. There are over three hundred owls of all sizes, from the Great Gray size to little, palm-sized Scops that make only local deliveries (PA 14:278).

Post Office Tower, London. Two Muggles report seeing an old car flying over this building (CS 5:79).

Potions. *Class at Hogwarts.* This class is taught by Prof. Snape in Years 1 through 5 and by Prof. Slughorn in Year 6. The class is held down in the dungeon (SS 8:136). Harry receives an E (Excellent) in his O.W.L. for Potions. Prof. McGonagall tells Harry that Prof. Slughorn takes students with that score in his N.E.W.T.-level Potions class, though Snape insisted on Outstanding students only (HBP 9:175).

"Potter for President." *Magical sign.* Ron, Hermione, Neville Longbottom, Seamus Finnegan, and Dean Thomas make this sign for Harry on a sheet that Scabbers chewed. They show the sign from the stands during Harry's first Quidditch match in Year 1. Dean uses his artistic talent to draw a Gryffindor lion, while Hermione makes the letters flash in different-colored bright lights (SS 11:184).

Potter, Harry James. *Character.* Prof. McGonagall announces that the name Harry Potter will be famous one day, that there will be books written about him, and that every child will know his name (SS 1:13). That a character's predictions within a fictional world should come true in the world outside the novel must seem uncanny to J. K. Rowling and her readers. Harry sometimes noticed strange things before Hagrid told him that he was a wizard. For example, he once found himself sitting on the chimney over the school's kitchen and did not know how he got there. When Aunt Petunia Dursley cut his shaggy hair very short, leaving the boy almost bald, it mysteriously grew back overnight. When she tried to put him in one of Dudley's old sweaters, it became smaller and smaller until it was too little to go over Harry's head (SS 2:24–25).

At Hogwarts Harry is sorted into Gryffindor House, but the Sorting Hat also gives him the opportunity to go into Slytherin. Harry chooses Gryffindor, which marks his courage and honesty. Harry has no feelings about bloodline, and even tells Ernie Macmillan that he does not care what kind of blood

Daniel Radcliffe as Harry Potter in *Harry Potter and the Sorcerer's Stone* (2001). Rowling's charming and brave boy wizard delighted millions of readers around the world in the years immediately before and after the turn of the millennium. Courtesy of Warner Bros./Photofest.

(magical or Muggle) Ernie has (CS 11:200). He is friendly toward everyone, unless the person treats him or someone he knows poorly. Harry believes he is better at Quidditch than Ron, but he is not better than Ron at other things (OP 9:166).

Harry's famous unruly hair is frustrating for Mrs. Weasley when she tries to comb it before his hearing at the Ministry (OP 7:123). He wears glasses that were repaired in Year 1 on the Hogwarts Express by Hermione Granger, whom he had just met. Harry is not perfect. He is a normal wizard boy who also happens to have lived through a tragedy and come out of it famous—in this and other traits, he shares much in common with his creator, J. K. Rowling.

Potter, James. *Character.* Hagrid tells Harry that his father is famous and was a talented wizard (SS 4:50–51). James Potter was Head Boy (SS 4:53). Prof. Snape tells Harry he is very much like his father in that he allows his talent in the Quidditch stadium to translate into arrogance off the field; Snape says that, like James Potter, Harry likes to break Hogwarts rules (PA 14:284). Snape tells Harry that James Potter and his friends played a joke on him that would have killed him had James not backed out at the last minute to save his own skin (in Snape's view) (PA 14:285). After the Triwizard Tournament, Hagrid tells Harry that he performed as his father would have done, and Harry regards this is as high praise (GF 37:719).

Harry sees one of Snape's memories in which James Potter is a bully. James is taking his O.W.L.s; he looks much like Harry. After the test he goes out with his friends to the grounds and turns Snape upside down so that his robes fly down, revealing gray underwear. It is not a flattering image of James, and Harry is surprised to see him as a bully (OP 28:641–49). Harry talks to Sirius Black about his father's treatment of Snape. Sirius defends him as a typical fifteen-year-old, but also one who was constantly being cursed by Snape and who did not approve of the Dark Arts that Snape was so heavily involved in (OP 29:670–71). James Potter became an Animagus whose Patronus is a stag, earning him the nickname Prongs among his friends.

Potter, Lily Evans. *Character.* Hagrid tells Harry that his mother is famous and was a talented witch (SS 4:50–51). She was Head Girl at Hogwarts (SS 4:53). In Snape's worst memory that Harry sees in the Pensieve, Lily is sympathetic toward Snape for the bullying he endures from James Potter, but her sympathy ends when Snape calls her a Mudblood (OP 28:648). Horace Slughorn tells Harry that Harry's mother was one of the best students he ever had and was also lively and charming. Slughorn was surprised to learn that Lily was a half-blood since her strong magical ability suggested otherwise (HBP 4:70). Voldemort tells Harry that his mother did not have to die; he would not have killed her and only wanted baby Harry (HBP 22:489).

Powers You Never Knew You Had and What to Do With Them Now You've Wised Up. *Magical book.* Harry and friends consult this book to prepare him for the second task of the Triwizard Tournament, but they find nothing of use in it (GF 26:488).

Practical Defensive Magic and Its Use Against the Dark Arts. *Magical book.* Harry receives this book from Sirius Black and Prof. Lupin for Christmas in Year 5 (OP 23:501).

Prang, Ernie. *Character.* The driver of the Knight Bus (PA 3:35). The character is named for Rowling's grandfather, Ernie Rowling.

Predicting the Unpredictable: Insulate Yourself Against Shocks. *Magical book.*
Harry sees this book at Flourish and Blotts (PA 4:53).

Predictions. *Magical findings.* Prof. Trelawney makes several predictions in Divination
class, some of which appear to come true. In Year 3, she predicts that someone from the
class will leave near Easter, and this happens when Hermione drops the class (PA
15:299). Though predictions are mentioned in the series, there seems to be little faith
placed in them. Even the greatest prediction of all—the Prophecy—is undercut by
Dumbledore's advice to Harry that prophecies need not be accepted or carried out if
those involved do not wish to do so; Dumbledore also says that prophecies may actually
become self-fulfilling rather than predictors of the future.

Prefect. *Magical honor.* In the fifth year at Hogwarts, one boy and one girl from each
house is chosen to be the student leader of the house. During Harry's first year, Percy
Weasley is the boy prefect for Gryffindor House (SS 6:96). The prefect helps monitor
student behavior and can impose penalties such as deducting house points. Prefects have
their own bathroom on the fifth floor as Harry finds out when he seeks clues to the
second task of the Triwizard Tournament (GF 23:431).

Hermione and Ron become prefects in Book 5 (OP 9:161–62). Ron is the fourth
prefect in the Weasley family and makes his mother proud (OP 9:169). Remus Lupin was
a prefect in James and Lily Potters' days at Hogwarts (OP 9:170).

Prefects' bathroom. *Magical place.* Located on the fifth floor, four doors down to the left of
the statue of Boris the Bewildered (GF 23:431). The room is very luxurious. It is made of all
white marble with a chandelier of candles in the ceiling. The center has a rectangular
swimming pool for a tub, complete with diving board and about a hundred taps made of gold
and set with a jewel. The taps emit different kinds of bubbles, from pink and blue football-sized
bubbles, to white foam bubbles, to purple bubbles. One large painting hangs on the wall—it is
a portrait of a blonde mermaid snoring on a rock with her hair covering her face. Long white
curtains grace the windows and thick white towels are stacked in the corner (GF 25:459–60).

Prejudice. *See* Race

Prentice, Mr. *Character.* A neighbor of Mrs. Figg's on Wisteria Walk (OP 2:21).

Presents. *See* Gifts/gift-giving

President. *Character.* This person is about to call the Prime Minister of Muggles at the
beginning of *Half-Blood Prince* when he is visited by the Minister of Magic, Cornelius
Fudge. The President is from a country a long ways away and is described as a "wretched
man." Fudge tells the Prime Minister that they will take care of the President's memory
and make it so that he will call tomorrow evening instead (HBP 1:1, 3). Speculation in
Britain and the United States suggested that the President might represent the American
president, but Rowling has never confirmed any direct connections between the political
figures in the series and those in the real world.

Prewett, Fabian. *Character.* A member of the original Order of the Phoenix. It took
five Death Eaters to kill Fabian Prewett and his brother Gideon; they were heroes (OP
9:174). Antonin Dolohov is convicted in relation to the murder (OP 25:543).

Prewett, Gideon. *Character.* A member of the original Order of the Phoenix. It took five Death Eaters to kill Gideon Prewett and his brother Fabian; they were heroes (OP 9:174). Antonin Dolohov is convicted in relation to the murder (OP 25:543).

Prewett, Jill. A friend of Rowling's in Portugal. Rowling dedicates *Prisoner of Azkaban* in part to this friend and apparently names two famous wizards after her.

Prewetts. *Characters.* Hagrid tells Harry that Voldemort killed these people, who were among the best witches and wizards of their time; yet Harry, as an infant, survived Voldemort's attack (SS 4:56). Jill Prewett was a friend of Rowling's in Portugal.

Pride of Portree. *Magical sports team.* Cho Chang thinks Oliver Wood joined this professional Quidditch team after Hogwarts, but Harry corrects her (OP 25:557). The team was founded in 1292 and comes from the Isle of Skye (QA 36).

Prime Minister of Muggles. *Character.* Readers are introduced to the Prime Minister of Muggles in the opening of *Half-Blood Prince*; he is not given a name (HBP 1:1).

Prince, Eileen. *Character.* Severus Snape's mother. As a fifteen-year-old student at Hogwarts, she was captain of the Hogwarts Gobstones Team. In the photograph Hermione finds of her in an old *Daily Prophet* from the library, she appears skinny, unattractive, and seems to be irritated and glowering at the same time. She has heavy eyebrows and a long face (HBP 25:537). She married Muggle Tobias Snape, making Severus a "half-blood," hence, the "Half-Blood Prince" (HBP 30:637).
See also Advanced Potion-Making; Snape, Prof. Severus

"The Principles of Rematerialization." *Magical essay.* Ron looks over Hermione's essay on this subject (HBP 10:195).

Pringle, Apollyon. *Character.* The Hogwarts caretaker during Mr. and Mrs. Weasley's days at Hogwarts (GF 31:616).

"Prior Incantato!" *Incantation.* This incantation causes a wand to reveal its previous spells in reverse order, starting with the most recent (GF 9:136). The phrase may be translated as "prior incantations."

Pritchard, Graham. *Character.* A Slytherin student three years behind Harry (GF 12:180).

Privet Drive, Number Four. *See* Number Four, Privet Drive

Probity Probe. *Magical object.* The security device put up Arkie Philpott's bottom at Gringotts Bank (HBP 6:108). Some readers have interpreted the device as a parody on security measures put in place following the terrorist attacks of September 11, 2001.

Prongs. *Magical nickname.* James Potter's nickname that comes from his Animagus form as a stag. Prongs is one of the creators of the Marauder's Map (PA 14:287).

The Prophecy. *Magical object and document.* Harry's name is on a glass ball in the Department of Mysteries at the Ministry. When he first sees it, he hears Lucius Malfoy's voice behind him asking him to hand over the Prophecy (OP 34:780). The Prophecy states that neither Voldemort nor his opponent can live while the other survives. The opponent will be someone with a birthday at the end of July whose parents confronted Voldemort three times. This leaves either Neville Longbottom or Harry Potter as possibilities. The Prophecy also states that Voldemort will choose which one of these is his equal, and Voldemort has chosen Harry.

Dumbledore counsels Harry that he need not fulfill a prophecy just because it was made. He always has a choice about what he does. Rowling commented in interviews that her use of prophecy in the series echoes the one made by the witches in Shakespeare's *Macbeth*.

See also Choice vs. destiny; Predictions; Shakespeare, William

Protean Charm. *Magical spell.* This is a N.E.W.T.-level skill that Hermione knows. She uses it in her communication system for Dumbledore's Army; when Harry changes the date and time on his Galleons, the date and time on the other members' Galleons will change accordingly (OP 19:398). In mythology Proteus was a sea god, the son of Oceanus and Tethys. From Poseidon, Proteus received the power to change shapes and to prophesy.

"Protego!" *Incantation.* Harry uses this incantation for Occlumency in his lesson with Prof. Snape (OP 26:591). He uses it again in the Room of Prophecy against Bellatrix Lestrange (OP 35:783). In Latin the word means "to cover over."

Proudfoot. *Character.* When Harry arrives in Year 6, Nymphadora Tonks tells him that Proudfoot is at Hogwarts (HBP 8:158).

Ptolemy. *Character.* One of two cards Ron needs to complete his five hundred-card collection of famous witches and wizards from inside packages of Chocolate Frogs. The other one he is missing is Agrippa (SS 6:102).

Pucey, Adrian. *Character.* Slytherin Chaser in Quidditch (SS 11:186).

Puddlemere United. *Magical sports team.* A reserve Quidditch team that Oliver Wood signs onto after leaving Hogwarts (GF 7:84). Harry corrects Cho Chang when she mistakenly thinks Oliver joined the Pride of Portree (OP 25:557). Albus Dumbledore wishes the team the best in his foreword to QA, most likely because his former student, Oliver Wood, is on the team (QA viii). The Puddlemere United is the oldest Quidditch team in the League. Founded in 1163, it has won the League championship twenty-two times (QA 36).

See also Quidditch Through the Ages

Puffapod. *Magical plant.* Harry and Hermione work on the same Puffapod in Herbology in Year 3. The class task involves taking full pink pods from the plants and emptying out the glossy beans from them (PA 8:147).

Puffskein. *Magical creature.* From *Fantastic Beasts*. Classified 2X by the MM. In his foreword to *Fantastic Beasts*, Dumbledore suggests that readers may use the book to learn how to cure their pet puffskein's habit of drinking out of the toilet (FB vii). Puffskeins are small, furry, and round with a long, thin tongue that can extend out of the puffball for some distance in search of food. They are quiet and friendly and a favorite pet with wizard children (FB 34). There is also a miniature variety of puffskein, and they are found around the world.

Ron Weasley owned one as a pet until his brother Fred used it as a Bludger for Quidditch practice; he notes this in his and Harry's copy of *Fantastic Beasts* (FB 34). A nest of dead puffskeins is found under the drawing room sofa at Number Twelve, Grimmauld Place (OP 6:101)

See also Fantastic Beasts and Where to Find Them

Puking Pastille. *Magical candy.* One of the varieties of Skiving Snackboxes. These purple and orange sweets are used to make one ill enough to get out of class (HBP 5:88).

See also Candy and sweets; Weasleys' Wizard Wheezes

Pullman, Philip (1946–). A British contemporary of Rowling's, Pullman is best known for his Dark Materials trilogy, a fantasy series composed of *The Golden Compass*, *The Subtle Knife*, and *The Amber Spyglass*. His art is considered high fantasy, closer to that of J.R.R. Tolkien than J. K. Rowling, though Rowling disagrees that his work shares much in common with either of them or with C. S. Lewis, who is also frequently mentioned in relation to Pullman's books. Because Pullman and Rowling are contemporaries and are both popular British novelists, however, they are often compared. In an interview on Powells.com, Pullman says that he is glad the Harry Potter books absorb a lot of popular attention at the same time he is publishing his books. It allows his books to enter the marketplace more quietly.

In a 2002 interview in *Guardian Unlimited*, Pullman said, "Harry Potter has his place. I'm glad Rowling is inventing him." In a 2003 interview in *The Independent*, he admitted that he had only read one of the Potter books, *Chamber of Secrets*, which he thought "funny and inventive." Pullman appears in the documentary about Rowling's life, *Harry and Me*.

Pullman has won the Whitbread Prize in Britain for his work. He is the first children's author to do so.

Further Reading: Robertson, Mel. "Harry Potter or The Lord of the Rings." *The Independent*, November 5, 2003; "There Has to Be a Lot of Ignorance in Me When I Start a Story." *Guardian Unlimited*, February 18, 2002. http://www.books.guardian.co.uk/departments/childrenandteens/story/0,6000,650988,00.html.

"Pumbles." *Wrong word.* Arthur Weasley's mispronunciation of the Muggle word "plumbers" (OP 7:133).

Pumpkin Pasties. *Magical treat.* One of the treats on the Hogwarts Candy Cart that Harry shares with Ron on their first meeting (SS 6:101–102). By the time the Sorting Hat Ceremony is over, it seems to Harry like a long time since he has had Pumpkin Pasties (SS 7:122).

See also Candy and sweets

Punching telescope. *Magical object.* One of the Weasley twins' less-than-successful inventions. Hermione gets punched by the telescope in their room when she visits the Burrow in the summer before Year 6 (HBP 6:118).

Purkiss, Mrs. Doris. *Character.* Mrs. Purkiss lives at 18 Acanthia Way, Little Norton, and claims in an article in *The Quibbler* that Sirius Black is actually Stubby Boardman.

See also Black, Sirius; Boardman, Stubby

Put-Outer. *Magical object.* The first magical device shown in the series. The Put-Outer is something like a silver cigarette lighter, but with the opposite function. Prof. Dumbledore puts out twelve streetlights on Privet Drive with the Put-Outer then waits for Hagrid to bring baby Harry to the Dursleys' doorstep (SS 1:9).

Pye, Augustus. *Character.* The trainee healer in the Dai Llewellyn Ward on the day that Harry and the Weasleys visit (OP 22:487). Augustus Pye tries the Muggle treatment of stitches on Arthur, much to Molly's disapproval (OP 23:506–7).

Pygmy Puffs. *Magical creatures.* Cute and popular miniature puffskeins sold at Weasleys' Wizard Wheezes. Ginny Weasley buys a purple one she names Arnold (HBP 6:121).
  See also Puffskein

✦ Q ✦

Quaffle. *Magical sports ball.* Used in Quidditch, the Quaffle is a large red leather ball thrown by the three Chasers on each side. The ball must be thrown through one of six hoops to score (SS 10:167). It is approximately twelve inches in diameter. Older Quaffles had straps or holes for the fingers (QA 20–21).
See also Quidditch; *Quidditch Through the Ages*

Quaffle-pocking. *Magical game penalty.* From QA. This is a penalty held against a Chaser who does anything to the Quaffle, such as poking holes in it, to make it fly erratically (QA 30).
See also Quidditch Through the Ages

Quality Quidditch Supplies. *Magical place.* A store on Diagon Alley. Ron covets a set of Chudley Cannon robes in the window (CS 4:58). This is Harry's favorite store on the street (PA 4:50).

Queerditch Marsh. *Magical place.* From QA. Quidditch matches may have derived their name from Gertie Keddle, who recorded in her diary a game played near this marsh in the eleventh century (QA 7–8).
See also Quidditch Through the Ages

The Quibbler. *Magical magazine.* Luna Lovegood is reading *The Quibbler* upside down on the Hogwarts Express when Harry meets her (OP 10:185). Hermione discounts the publication as garbage until Luna says that her father is the editor (OP 10:193).

Quiberon Quafflepunchers. *Magical sports team.* From QA. A professional Quidditch team from France (QA 40).
See also Quidditch Through the Ages

Quick-Quotes Quill. *Magical object.* A green quill pen that automatically takes notes on parchment during an interview. Rita Skeeter uses it when she interviews Harry before the first task of the Triwizard Tournament (GF 18:304).

"Quid agis." *Magic words.* A password into Gryffindor Tower, Year 6 (HBP 24:533).

Quidditch. *Magical sport.* Rowling has said that she invented the game of Quidditch in a small room at the Bournville Hotel in Didsbury, Manchester, after having an argument with her then-boyfriend. Harry Potter first hears of Quidditch in Madam Malkin's robe shop when Draco Malfoy speaks to Harry about the game before he knows who Harry is (SS 5:77); Harry later asks Hagrid about Quidditch (SS 5:79). On the Hogwarts Express, Ron begins to explain the game to Harry—that it involves seven players on a team and four balls (SS 6:108). Oliver Wood instructs Harry in the basics of the game, including the balls and other equipment (SS 10:167–68). Oliver tells Harry that a game of Quidditch continues until the Seeker on one team or the other catches the Golden Snitch. The longest game on record went for three months (SS 10:169).

In reading *Quidditch Through the Ages*, Harry finds out that there are 700 possible ways to commit a foul in the game, and this number was reached once, in the 1473 World Cup. He also learns that the Seeker is usually small and fast and risks the most injuries of any player on the team. Players rarely die in the sport, but some referees have occasionally disappeared and resurfaced months later in the Sahara Desert (SS 11:181).

Harry is the youngest player in over a century (CS 7:106). He ends up catching the Snitch by swallowing it in his first game, and Gryffindor wins against Slytherin, 170 points to 60 (SS 11:191). Harry is made captain of the Gryffindor Quidditch team in his sixth year at Hogwarts. The honor is the same level as that of a prefect (HBP 6:106–7). Playing the sport is the one thing that Harry admits he may do better than other people, though as he matures he begins to recognize his talent for Defense Against the Dark Arts as well.

Quidditch Cup. *Magical award.* The trophy for Quidditch at Hogwarts; it is very large and silver (PA 8:144). Argus Filch makes Ron polish the cup fourteen times in the Trophy Room during his detention (CS 7:121). The Gryffindor team wins the cup in Year 3 with a dangerous final match against Slytherin House where Harry beats Draco Malfoy in catching the Snitch (PA 15:312).

Quidditch fouls. *Magical game penalties.* There are 700 fouls described in the records of the Department of Magical Games and Sports. The full list, however, has not been released to the public. The only game in which all 700 fouls were committed was the final match of the first World Cup in 1473. Quidditch fouls include: Blagging, Blatching, Blurting, Bumphing, Cobbing, Flacking, Haversacking, Quaffle-pocking, Snitchnip, and Stooging (QA 29–30).

See also Quidditch Through the Ages

Quidditch League. *Magical sports organization.* From QA. In 1674 Britain and Ireland formed a league of the thirteen best teams in the area, and the other teams were dissolved. The teams compete each year for the League Cup (QA 32).

See also Quidditch Through the Ages

Quidditch rules. *Magical game regulations.* From QA. *Quidditch Through the Ages* outlines the rules of the game, which were set by the Department of Magical Games and Sports in 1750 (QA 27–28).

See also Quidditch Through the Ages

Quidditch Teams of Britain and Ireland. *Magical book.* Hermione gives this book to Harry in Year 4 for Christmas (GF 23:410). He packs it up when the Order of the Phoenix guard comes to take him to Headquarters (OP 3:52).

Quidditch Through the Ages. *Magical/actual book.* This book was written by Kennilworthy Whisp, and published by Whizz Hard Books in 1952. Hermione checks the book out of the Hogwarts Library and reads playing tips to Harry during their first year (SS 9:144). The book is later produced in facsimile by Rowling as a fund-raiser for Comic Relief, U.K. in 2001.

The actual book is approximately 15,000 words long and contains the following sections: review "blurbs" from various characters in the series; an About the Author section; a foreword by Albus Dumbledore; and ten chapters about the origins, history, rules, and equipment of the game. The book is a facsimile of a Hogwarts Library book, complete with a warning from Irma Pince, Hogwarts librarian, inside the front cover. There is also a chart where students put their name and the date due. Students who have "checked out" the book before Harry (who last checked it out with a due date of March 11) include: O. Wood, B. Dunstan, M. Flint, C. Diggory, A. Johnson, E. Macmillan, T. Boot, S. Fawcett, K. Bundy, K. Bell, C. Warrington, J. Dorny, T. Nott, S. Capper, M. Bulstrode, F. Weasley, H. Granger. Interestingly, many of the due dates are in July and August when, presumably, students would not be at Hogwarts or have access to its library. Dumbledore's "Foreword" claims that the book is one of the most popular in the library (QA vii).

Topics in the book include the development of the flying broomstick; first broomstick games; the game's crude origins at Queer Ditch Marsh as witnessed and recorded by Gertie Keddle in her diary in the eleventh century; the story of how the Golden Snitch became part of the game; ways the wizarding world has kept Muggles from catching sight of their games; basic changes in the game over the last 600 years; a history of each of the balls and other equipment of the game; a listing of ten of the 700 known fouls possible; descriptions of professional Quidditch teams from Europe and around the world; evolution of the racing broom; and a description of thirteen famous plays in modern-day Quidditch.

Rowling illustrated *Quidditch Through the Ages* herself with sketches of the pitch and various equipment, as well as a sketch of the Starfish and Stick play (QA 54). The book also contains simulated historic archival material and artifacts, such as Gertie Keddle's eleventh-century diary, ancient broomsticks, and old *Daily Prophet* articles, most of which are said to be displayed or stored at the Museum of Quidditch in London.

Quidditch Through the Ages, along with *Fantastic Beasts and Where to Find Them*, has raised over $28.7 milllion (£15.7 million) for Comic Relief, U.K.

See also Comic Relief, U.K.; Fantastic Beasts and Where to Find Them; Quidditch

Quidditch World Cup. *Magical event.* Something like the World Cup for soccer, this event features two professional Quidditch teams from different countries and is a world event on the wizarding scene. In her letter requesting to take Harry with her family, Molly Weasley writes to the Dursleys that the event has not been hosted by Britian for thirty years (GF 3:30). The match Harry goes to is between Ireland and Bulgaria (GF 3:35). He is told that the previous year's match went on for five days (GF 5:64). Around

100,000 witches and wizards attend (GF 6:69). The first World Cup was held in 1473 and is held every four years (QA 39–40).

"Quietus." *Incantation.* Ludo Bagman uses this incantation to turn his wand back from a microphone into a wand (GF 8:116).

Quigley. *Character.* A player on the Ireland National Quidditch Team in the World Cup (GF 8:105).

Quijudge. *Magical sports position.* From QA. An old name for the Quidditch referee (QA 18).
  See also Quidditch Through the Ages

Quintaped. *Magical creature.* From *Fantastic Beasts.* Classified 5X by the MM. The Quintaped is also known as Hairy MacBoon. The beast especially likes humans. It is only found on Scotland's Isle of Drear. The beast is the result of a duel between two Scottish wizarding families, the McCliverts and the MacBoons. The MacBoons were transformed into Quintapeds by the McCliverts in retribution for their clan chief, Dugald McClivert, being killed by Quintius MacBoon. The MacBoon creatures then killed off all of the McCliverts, which meant there was no one to transform them back to human form (FB 34–35).
  See also Fantastic Beasts and Where to Find Them

Quintessence: A Quest. *Magical book.* A book assigned in Charms class (HBP 15:304).

Quirke, Orla. *Character.* A Ravenclaw student three years behind Harry (GF 12:180).

Quirrell, Prof. *Character.* The Defense Against the Dark Arts teacher in Harry's first year at Hogwarts. Harry first meets him at the Leaky Cauldron in London, where he recognizes Harry immediately. He wears a turban and stutters; sometimes he wears a turban of a different color, such as the purple one he wears at Harry's Sorting Hat Ceremony (SS 7:122). Hagrid tells Harry that Quirrell was a smart wizard. However, he met werewolves and got into trouble with a hag in the Black Forest during a year off from teaching; Quirrell has been fearful of his pupils and his subject matter ever since (SS 5:70–71). Later in the novel, it is shown that Quirrell's body has been possessed by Voldemort to do his bidding. He unwraps his turban to reveal Voldemort's sickly, snakelike face on the back side of his head (SS 17:293).

Quodpot. *Magical game.* From QA. Originating in the United States, it is a derivation of Quidditch begun by eighteenth-century wizard Abraham Peasegood. Instead of seven players on a side, there are eleven. Players toss the Quod (which is a ball adapted from an accident involving a Quaffle and Peasegood's wand in his traveling trunk) from player to player to get it into the pot before it blows up. The pot is a cauldron holding a potion that keeps the Quod from exploding. Once a score is made, a new Quod is played in the pitch (QA 44).
  See also Quidditch Through the Ages

ᐧ R ᐧ

Rabnott, Madam Modesty. *Character.* From QA. A witch who writes to her sister Pru in 1269 an eyewitness account of Snidget-hunting and Quidditch (which she spells "Cuaditch"). When the players abandon the game to hunt down the Snidget, she casts a Summoning Charm, hides the bird in her robes, and runs away to release it in the woods. She loses her home to pay the fine of 10 Galleons for disrupting the game. A preserve for the birds was named in her honor in Somerset in the fourteenth century (QA 12–13).
   See also Snidget-hunting

Race. Racial bigotry exists in the series in the characters who seek to know and foster the existence of "purebloods." In Harry's magical world, purebloods are those people who are all-magical and come from all-magical families that have not intermarried with nonmagical people called Muggles. Ron tells Harry that none of these pure bloodlines actually still exist in the wizard community. Purebloods have had to intermarry with Muggles or they would have died out completely. The source of the racial bigotry at Hogwarts was Salazar Slytherin, one of the four original founders. Over time he thought only purebloods should be admitted to the school. The other founders disagreed and admitted students based on their magical abilities or signs of talent rather than on their blood backgrounds. This resulted in Slytherin hiding the Basilisk in the Chamber of Secrets for a descendant to come back and unleash as his revenge.
   As one might expect, racial bigotry was handed down through Slytherin families. The Blacks dislike Muggles and any mixed-blood witches and wizards. So do the Malfoys. Draco Malfoy, Harry's contemporary at Hogwarts, goes so far as to use a racial slur against Hermione Granger, who is Muggle-born. He calls her a "Mudblood," the magical equivalent of the "n-word." Her blood is "muddied" or "soiled" with Muggle blood. Draco is clearly repeating what his father and others have taught him about the different kinds of people in the world. In Flourish and Blotts, Draco's father, Lucius Malfoy, has a confrontation with Arthur Weasley over associating with Hermione and other Muggle-borns and mixed-bloods.

In interviews Rowling has made occasional references to Adolf Hitler and World War II. It is evident that her books' focus on bloodlines alludes to Hitler's genocide against the Jews and quest for domination of the world. Dumbledore, the great wizard of the series, embraces magical people, Muggle people, and mixed-blood people of all kinds, even those who combine human characteristics with creature characteristics, such as giants, merpeople, goblins, and house-elves. Tolerance is part of the theme of love in the books. Racial intolerance is portrayed as cruel and wrong; tolerance, compassion, and acceptance are portrayed positively.

See also Slavery

Rackharrow, Urquhart. *Character.* Urquhart Rackharrow invented the entrail-expelling curse. He lived from 1612 to 1697, and his portrait hangs at St. Mungo's Hospital (OP 22:487). Rowling may have gotten the name Urquhart from Jane Urquhart, a fellow author whose work is published by Bloomsbury.

Radcliffe, Daniel.. *See* Films

Radulf. *Character.* From QA. A blacksmith who played the old game of "Kwidditch." He was hit in the head with a "Blooder," a precursor to the Bludger (QA 9).
See also Quidditch Through the Ages

Ragnok. *Character.* A goblin who was deceived in gambling with Ludo Bagman and received leprechaun gold (OP 5:86).

Railview Hotel. *Muggle place.* The hotel in Cokeworth where Uncle Vernon Dursley initially takes the family to escape the letters arriving for Harry from Hogwarts. They stay in Room 17 (SS 3:42).

Ramora. *Magical creature.* From *Fantastic Beasts.* Classified 2X by the MM. Silver fish that live in the Indian Ocean; they guard sailors and can anchor ships (FB 36).
See also Fantastic Beasts and Where to Find Them

Rat tonic. *Magical substance.* The witch at Magical Menagerie gives Ron a small red bottle of rat tonic to help Scabbers perk up after his trip to Egypt (PA 4:59).

Ravenclaw House. *Magical school organization.* One of the four student houses of Hogwarts. Hermione mentions to Harry and Ron that she hopes she will be sorted into Gryffindor, but Ravenclaw might not be so bad (SS 6:106). Ravenclaw was founded by Rowena Ravenclaw and its current head is Prof. Flitwick, who teaches Charms. Its students are characterized by intelligence and wit. Its colors are blue and bronze, and its emblem is a golden eagle on a blue shield. The Ravenclaw quarters are located in their own tower at the west side of the castle. Their Quidditch robes are blue. Its ghost is presumed to be the Grey Lady (based on interviews, the films, and other information), though she is not mentioned specifically in Books 1 through 6.

Notable characters from Ravenclaw include: Luna Lovegood; Cho Chang; Padma Patil; and Roger Davies.

Ravenclaw, Rowena. *See* Ravenclaw House

Readings, public and private. Rowling has given few public readings in recent years, but she did give more earlier in her career. Probably the two most noteworthy readings took place during her North American book tour for *Goblet of Fire* in 2000. She read in Toronto at the Sky Dome to 12,000 fans and in Vancouver to nearly the same number. The theory was that reading to large numbers of people at once would keep the time away from her daughter to a minimum. She was a single parent at the time. In 2005, for the launch of *Half-Blood Prince*, she gave a reading at Edinburgh Castle in Scotland. She read from the chapter about Fred and George Weasley's new shop on Diagon Alley rather than from the first chapter as she had originally planned. She made this choice as a sensitive response to the terrorist bombings that had occurred in London just over a week prior to the publication date. Chapter one of *Half-Blood Prince* contains a scene in which the Prime Minister speaks with the Minister of Magic about evil and strange happenings around the country and what might be causing them. Occasionally news reports tell of small, selected public readings Rowling has given around Scotland and other areas, mostly as benefits for charity.

Rowling has said in an interview that when she reads privately to her oldest daughter, she goes into different voices for the characters at full tilt with no inhibitions, unlike the more steady voice she maintains in public readings. In those instances with her daughter, her Prof. Dumbledore, she says, sounds a bit like John Gielgud—elderly and stately. Prof. McGonagall sounds—upper class, clipped and quick, or like a governess who works around the wealthy. She agrees with a caller on a radio show that Margaret Thatcher is a good model for McGonagall's voice. Hagrid, in her mind and in the voice she makes in her readings, sounds like someone from the West Country where she grew up. Perhaps most telling is that when an interviewer asked what Harry's voice sounds like in Rowling's private readings, the author said that Harry sounds like herself. She uses her own voice when reading Harry's dialogue to her family.

Further Reading: Lyndon, Christopher. "J. K. Rowling Interview." *The Connection* (WBUR Radio, Boston), October 12, 1999.

Reasonable Restriction of Underage Sorcery. *Magical law.* This law keeps young people under age seventeen from practicing magic away from school (OP 2:21).

Reception Committee. *Magical group.* Seven friends and members of the Order of the Phoenix meet Harry at King's Cross to escort him over to the waiting Dursleys; they are to let the Dursleys know that they must not let anything happen to Harry over the summer. The seven members of the committee are: Mad-Eye Moody, Nymphadora Tonks, Mr. and Mrs. Weasley, Rufus Lupin, and Fred and George Weasley. Harry is very grateful to have their support and seems ready to deal with the summer at Privet Drive after their warnings to the Dursleys (OP 38:867, 70).

Red Caps. *Magical creatures.* From *Fantastic Beasts.* Classified 3X by the MM. Red Caps are most common in northern Europe and are especially dangerous to Muggles (FB 36). They are goblinlike creatures that hang around bloody areas such as battlefields (PA 8:141). They are part of Prof. Lupin's DADA final exam in Year 3 (PA 16:318). Mad-Eye Moody makes sure that the students have gone over Red Caps in DADA class before he teaches them the Unforgivable Curses (GF 14:211).

Red card. *Muggle game penalty.* Dean Thomas keeps trying to relate Quidditch to soccer by calling for a red card when Marcus Flint fouls Harry in his first match. Ron has to keep reminding him that Quidditch is not soccer (SS 11:188).

"Reducio." *Incantation.* The anti-curse to the "Engorgio!" incantation (GF 14:215).

"Reducto!" *Incantation.* Incantation for the Reductor Curse. Several DA members use this spell in the Room of Prophecy. It smashes shelves (OP 35:787).

Reductor Curse. *Magical spell.* This spell smashes solid objects; the incantation is "Reducto!" (GF 31:608).

Re'em. *Magical creature.* From *Fantastic Beasts.* Classified 4X by the MM. They are huge oxen that live in the wild in North America and the Far East (FB 36).
   See also Fantastic Beasts and Where to Find Them

Referee. *Magical sports position.* From QA. The judge in a Quidditch match. Referees are chosen in Britain by the Department of Games and Sports. A referee's broom was turned into a Portkey that sent him or her to the Sahara Desert partway through a match (QA 30–31).
   See also Quidditch Through the Ages

Registry of Proscribed Charmable Objects. *Magical record.* An area of the Ministry of Magic that proclaimed flying carpets to be Muggle objects (GF 7:91).

Regurgitating toilet. *Bewitched Muggle object.* Anti-Muggle pranksters have rigged public toilets so that they flush up instead of down. The pranksters need to be taken care of by the Magical Law Enforcement Patrol (OP 7:133).

"Relashio!" *Incantation.* A charm that causes something or someone to be released (GF 26:496). Bob Ogden uses it on Marvolo Gaunt when Gaunt violently goes after his daughter (HBP 10:211).

Remedial Potions. *Fake magical class.* Snape gives Harry the following instructions: Anyone who wants to know why Harry is going to Snape's classroom after school to study Occlumency is to be told that Harry is going there for Remedial Potions (OP 24:519).

Remembrall. *Magical object.* Neville Longbottom receives a Remembrall in his first year at Hogwarts. It is a marble-sized glass ball with a white, smoky interior that glows red when its owner has forgotten something (SS 9:145). Draco Malfoy steals it from Neville during their first Flying Lesson, but Harry gets it back for him (SS 9:148–49). It is banned from the examination room during O.W.L. exams (OP 31:709).

"Reparo!" *Incantation.* This incantation fixes what is broken (GF 11:169). Harry uses it to fix a bowl (OP 15:329). Bob Ogden uses it to fix Merope Gaunt's broken pot (HBP 10:206). Harry fixes a bowl in Herbology (HBP 14:282).

Repelling Spells. *Magical spells.* From QA. The crowds at the old Quidditch games with real Snidgets for Golden Snitches used Repelling Spells on the tiny birds so they could not fly away (QA 12).

Restricted Section. *Magical place.* An area of the Hogwarts Library that is off-limits to students unless they have a signed note from a teacher to look at or check out books from the area. The section contains books about the Dark Arts (SS 12:198).

Reusable Hangman. *Magical object.* A popular game at Weasleys' Wizard Wheezes, it is like the Hangman spelling game in the Muggle world except that it is made up of a small wooden man and a real gallows. The man works his way up the steps toward the gallows as words are misspelled in the game. The losing speller will make him "swing." The man apparently survives to be "swung" again (HBP 6:117).

Revealer. *Magical object.* The Revealer looks like a bright red eraser. It can sometimes make invisible ink visible. Hermione tries a Revealer she bought on Diagon Alley on Tom Riddle's diary, but it does not work (CS 13:233).

Reverse Pass. *Magical sports play.* One Chaser tosses the Quaffle to a teammate over his or her shoulder. It is an imprecise move (QA 53).

Rickman, Alan.. *See* Films

"Rictusempra!" *Incantation.* In Latin *rictus* means "open mouth, especially from laughing." This is the incantation for the Tickling Charm. Harry hits Draco Malfoy with the spell during Dueling Club lessons (CS 11:192).

"Riddikulus!" *Incantation.* The incantation for the Laughing Charm that repels bog-garts (PA 7:134). A pun on "ridiculous."

Riddle Family. The elderly couple, Mr. and Mrs. Riddle, and their grown son, Tom, Sr. (Voldemort's father) were all murdered at the Riddle House in Little Hangleton. Police reports indicated that there was no apparent sign of the cause of the death on the bodies; they appeared to be in fine health (GF 1:4). Gardener Frank Bryce is charged with the crime, but is later let go. Tom Marvolo Riddle (Lord Voldemort) actually did the dastardly deed.

The Riddle House. *Magical place.* The large, old manor where the Riddle family lived, overlooking the village of Little Hangleton. It used to be the largest and finest building around. At the time of the novels, fifty years after the murders of three Riddles occurred there, it has boarded up windows, ivy grown wild across the front, and missing roof tiles. Locals think the house is "creepy" (GF 1:1).

Riddle, Tom Marvolo. *Character.* Tom Marvolo Riddle won several awards at Hogwarts, including one for Special Services to the School and the Medal for Magical Merit; he was also Head Boy and prefect (CS 13:234). The boy was taken to an orphanage after his Muggle father deserted his mother, who died after he was born. His mother lived long enough to name him Tom after his father and Marvolo after his grandfather (CS 13:244). Tom Riddle tells Harry that he has always had a way with charming those he needs, and he was able to do so with Ginny Weasley through his diary (CS 17:310). Dumbledore confirms that Tom Riddle is the last surviving descendant of Salazar Slytherin (CS 18:332). His house is visible on the hill from the graveyard (GF 33:646). Mrs. Cole of the orphanage tells Dumbledore that he was given the name Tom in honor of his father's father and Marvolo in honor of his mother's father (HBP 13:266).

When Dumbledore takes the young orphan Tom to Hogwarts, he must first tell Tom to return anything he has stolen at the orphanage. In his box, he has a yo-yo, a mouth organ, and a silver thimble (HBP 13:273). Tom was a promising student while he was at Hogwarts, as Dumbledore tells Harry. Dumbledore tells Harry there were three main reasons why Tom Riddle wanted to teach at Hogwarts: it was his home; it holds ancient magic within its walls; and he could influence a new generation of witches and wizards to turn to the Dark Side (HBP 20:431).

See also Voldemort, Lord

Riddle, Tom, Sr. *Character.* Voldemort's father, a squire's son. He was a wealthy Muggle and was loved by a Squib witch, Merope Gaunt (HBP 10:212). Dumbledore thinks Merope gave him a love potion to make him marry her; when it wore off, as Dumbledore thinks Merope allowed to happen, Tom immediately left her, even though she was pregnant (HBP 10:213–15). His grave has a large marble headstone and is what Wormtail threw Harry against in the graveyard (GF 32:638).

The Rise and Fall of the Dark Arts. *Magical book.* A book Hermione has read that explains the Dark Mark (GF 9:141).

Robards, Gawain. *Character.* Rufus Scrimgeour tells Harry that this person is the new Head of the Auror office (HBP 16:345).

Roberts (child). *Character.* A Muggle child who is spun upside down sixty feet in the air during the Death Eaters' rowdy torture of Muggles after the World Cup (GF 9:120).

Roberts, Mr. *Character.* Muggle in charge of the campsites for the first field at the Quidditch World Cup (GF 7:76). He is tortured by Death Eaters after the match when he is hung upside down in the air (GF 9:120). His memory of the event is erased (GF 9:142).

Roberts, Mrs. *Character.* Mr. Roberts's wife; Mr. and Mrs. Roberts and their children are dangled upside down in midair by the Death Eaters after the Quidditch World Cup. Her nightgown falls to reveal large bloomers, and she tries to cover herself up while the crowd below laughs (GF 9:120). Her memory of the event is erased (GF 9:142).

Robins, Demelza. *Character.* A new Chaser on the Gryffindor Quidditch team the year Harry captains. She exhibits skill at avoiding Bludgers (HBP 11:224). She delivers the message from Snape to Harry about his detention (HBP 11:235–36). The name Demelza may be Rowling's tribute to Harry Potter actor Daniel Radcliffe, whose favorite charity, Demelza House, is a children's hospice in London.

Rock Cakes. *Magical "treat."* Hagrid's very tough cakes with raisins that nearly break Harry's and Ron's teeth (SS 8:140).

Romania. Charlie Weasley, one of Ron's older brothers, is in Romania studying dragons (SS 6:107). In early 2006, Rowling went there to launch her participation in the Children's High Level Group, an organization established to help institutionalized children.
See also Children's High Level Group

Romanian Longhorn. *Magical creature.* From *Fantastic Beasts.* A breed of dragon with green scales and long, gold horns. The powdered horns are valuable as ingredients in potions (FB 14).

Ronan. *Magical creature.* One of the three centaurs Harry meets in the Forbidden Forest. Ronan has a deep voice and predicts that innocents will die young. He reads the planets and says that Mars is shining brightly (SS 15:253). He is not happy to hear Hermione say that she hoped the centaurs would drive away Umbridge for her and the other students (OP 33:756).
See also Centaurs

Rookwood, Augustus. *Character.* Augustus Rookwood worked at the Department of Mysteries at the Ministry. His name is given up by Igor Karkaroff as a spy leader for the Death Eaters (GF 30:590). He has a pocked face and greasy hair and was convicted of leaking information from the Ministry to Voldemort (OP 25:543–44). Harry has a vision about him through Voldemort's eyes (OP 26:585). He is present at the attack in the Department of Mysteries (OP 35:788).

Room of Requirement. *Magical place.* The Room of Requirement is also called the Come and Go Room. Dobby tells Harry about this room that transforms into whatever the first person entering it wants it to be (OP 18:386). It is on the seventh floor of Hogwarts; one must walk past the tapestry of Barnabas the Barmy three times thinking of what is needed in a room (OP 18:389). The Room of Requirement is where Harry holds his DA meetings and DADA lessons and where Draco Malfoy seems to be going to do something mysterious in Year 6 (HBP 21:452).

"Roonil Wazlib." *Wrong words.* Ron writes "Roonil Wazlib" as his name on an essay when his Spell-Checking quill runs out of spell; Hermione fixes it for him (HBP 21:449).

Rosier, Evan. *Character.* Rosier was the last name of a friend of Prof. Snape's when he was a student at Hogwarts; he was killed by Aurors the year before Voldemort was defeated (GF 27:531). Harry sees Rosier's name mentioned by Igor Karkaroff and Barty Crouch, Sr. in the vision he has in Dumbledore's pensieve. Barty Crouch, Sr. says that Rosier is dead after struggling to go quietly. Mad-Eye Moody says Rosier took some of him on his way down (GF 30:589). There is another Rosier who is one of Voldemort's original Death Eaters (HBP 20:444).

Rosmerta, Madam. *Character.* Curvaceous and pretty, Madam Rosmerta serves drinks at the Three Broomsticks pub in Hogsmeade. It is rumored that Dumbledore orders 800 barrels of her mulled mead for the Yule Ball (GF 22:391). Dumbledore drinks her finest mead matured in oak at the beginning of Book 6 and offers some to Harry and the Dursleys (HBP 3:48). Rosmerta plays a major role on the night Dumbledore and Harry visit the cave to go after a Horcrux. Dumbledore says he is going to the Three Broomsticks when he takes Harry to Hogsmeade, but she later tells Harry she saw them when they Apparated. She informs Dumbledore of the Dark Mark when Harry comes back with Dumbledore, who is in a weakened condition. She lends them broomsticks to get to the castle more quickly, since it is not possible to Apparate within its walls (HBP 27:580–83). Dumbledore and Harry learn that Draco Malfoy put her under the Imperius Curse to do his bidding during the school year, and this was how Katie Bell got the cursed necklace and how the poisoned mead reached Hogwarts (HBP 27:388–89).

Rotfang Conspiracy. *Magical rumor.* Luna Lovegood tells Harry that she does not think he should be an Auror because they are part of the Rotfang Conspiracy to bring down the Ministry through Dark Magic and gum disease (HBP 15:320).

Rowling, Anne Volant. J. K. Rowling's mother, who died from multiple sclerosis in 1990 when the author was twenty-five. She was the daughter of Frieda and Stan Volant. Anne liked to read books of all sorts, popular and literary, and shared them with her daughters. She kept a clean house and worked as a lab assistant for chemistry classes at Wydean Comprehensive, where her daughters went to school. In 1980 she was diagnosed with multiple sclerosis and battled the disease, though her health quickly deteriorated. She died on December 30, 1990. She was 45.

Rowling and her sister Di were close to their mother. Some observers have said that Rowling wrote the series indirectly as a means of helping herself cope with her mother's loss. After her mother died, Rowling found that she had greater empathy for Harry's loss and related in a different way to the story, especially with the scene of the Mirror of Erised.

Rowling, Dianne. J. K. Rowling's younger sister. In 1993, when Dianne was a fairly new bride in Edinburgh, she took her sister in for a while after she arrived in Scotland from Portugal. Dianne was the first to hear Harry's story, and the author claims that had her sister not liked it right away, the first book would likely not have been completed. Dianne married Roger, co-owner of Nicolson's Café, the famous establishment where Rowling wrote much of the books while sipping coffee and tending to her sleeping daughter in a stroller beside her. Rowling has said that her sister gave up nursing to become an attorney.

See also Nicolson's Café

Rowling, Ernie. Rowling's paternal grandfather. He owned a store in Dorset called Glenwood Stores and used to allow his granddaughters to play in it when it was not busy. Rowling pays tribute to him by naming a minor character in the series, Ernie Prang, the driver of the Knight Bus, after him. Ernie Macmillan, a student at Hogwarts, also shares his name.

Rowling, Janet Gallivan. Over two years after the death Anne Volant Rowling, the author's father, Peter Rowling, married his former secretary, Janet Gallivan, on April 2, 1993.

Rowling, Jessica Isabel. Rowling's first child. Jessica Isabel Rowling was born on July 27, 1993, in Oporto, Portugal. The daughter of Rowling and her first husband, journalist Jorge Arantes, Jessica was named after one of Rowling's favorite authors, human rights activist Jessica Mitford. Rowling gave her new daughter a copy of Mitford's book *Hons and Rebels* as a memento. When the girl was only a few months old, she went with her mother to Edinburgh, Scotland, when the author left her husband due to marital difficulties.

In the well-publicized story of Rowling being on the dole, Jessica was the infant that Rowling took with her to cafés while the author wrote in notebooks until her baby woke up again. Rowling dedicated *Sorcerer's Stone* to "Jessica, who loves stories," as well as to her mother and sister.

Rowling, J. K. J. K. Rowling was born in Yate, England, near Chipping Sodbury on July 31, 1965. Her sister Di was born at home in 1967. She spent her young childhood in Winterbourne, where she played with neighbor children, Ian and Vikki Potter, from whom Harry gets his last name. Rowling began school at St. Michael's Church of England School in 1970. When she was about nine, the family moved to Church Cottage in Tutshill, where she and her sister attended the Tutshill Church of England Primary School, which was located next door to their home. In 1976 she began attending Wydean Comprehensive School in nearby Sedbury and graduated as Head Girl in 1983.

Throughout school, the author wrote and told stories to her friends around the lunch table, but she did not make her desire to become a writer a public career choice.

The author enrolled at Exeter University in 1983, majoring in French and classics (ancient Greek and Roman studies). She spent one year in France, teaching in Paris from 1985 to 1986. In 1987 she graduated from Exeter and moved to London, where she took a job at Amnesty International and enrolled in a course in secretarial skills. She moved to Manchester, where she had short stints in clerical jobs at the university and chamber of commerce. In 1990, on a train from Manchester to London, she imagined Harry Potter, whom she has said arrived in her imagination "fully formed."

Rowling's mother passed away on December 30, 1990, and in 1991 Rowling moved to Portugal to teach English as a second language. There, she met and married Jorges Arantes and they had a daughter, Jessica, born on July 27, 1993. The marriage broke up soon thereafter, and Rowling brought her daughter and her Harry Potter manuscript to Edinburgh, Scotland, to be near her sister. In Edinburgh she took more course work in order to be certified

J. K. Rowling holding a copy of *Harry Potter and the Half-Blood Prince* at the book's worldwide launch at Edinburgh Castle, July 15, 2005. Her fame is second only to Harry's. © Adrian Dennis/AFP/Getty Images.

to teach French in Scotland. For a few months in the meantime, she lived on public assistance. All the while she continued to write Harry Potter's story.

In 1997 she received an £8,000 (approximately $4,500) grant from the Scottish Arts Council, and the first Harry Potter novel was published by Bloomsbury. Scholastic purchased the American rights to the book for an unprecedented $105,000, launching curiosity on both sides of the Atlantic as to who this author was and why her first novel was worth such a large investment. Rowling's fame, awards, and wealth continued to grow as the books appeared one at a time and were made into films almost as quickly. Her awards include the O.B.E. and honorary doctorate degrees from Exeter University in the U.K. and Dartmouth College in the United States.

In 2001 she married Dr. Neil Murray and the couple has had two children in addition to Jessica: David Gordon, born March 23, 2003; and Mackenzie Jean, born January 23, 2005. J. K. Rowling and her family make their home in Edinburgh, Scotland.

Rowling, Kathleen. Rowling's paternal grandmother. Rowling took the initial "K" from her grandmother when Barry Cunningham asked her to use only her initials on the covers of the books. Kathleen Rowling was her favorite grandmother, and she died when the author was still adjusting to her early years in Tutshill. Kathleen and her husband Ernie ran a store and used to allow their granddaughters to play store when they visited, including running the cash register.

Rowling, Peter James. J. K. Rowling's father came of age in the 1960s and married Anne Volant on March 14, 1965. He worked as an engineer at the Rolls-Royce airplane engine plant in Bristol, England, when Rowling and her sister Di were growing up. His influence on Rowling's imagination included reading to her the children's fantasy *Wind in the Willows*, by Kenneth Grahame, when she was sick with the measles. He also moved the family to a stone cottage in Tutshill, near Chepstow, Wales, close to the rather magical Forest of Dean. Readers of the series who are familiar with the author's biography notice that Rowling's father and Harry Potter share the same middle name, James, and that Peter Pettigrew, a less than savory character in the series, bears her father's first name. Rowling dedicated *Goblet of Fire* to her father and others in 2000.

Runespoor. *Magical creature.* From *Fantastic Beasts.* Classified 4X by the MM. The Runespoor is a three-headed snake that can grow to seven feet long. It used to be a favorite creature of Dark wizards. Runespoors live in the small African country of Burkina Faso (FB 36–37).

See also Fantastic Beasts and Where to Find Them

Rushdie, Salman (1947–). The award-winning author famous for, among other things, needing to go into hiding after worldwide death threats resulted from his novel *The Satanic Verses.* Rushdie endorsed Rowling's contribution to world literature in New York City in 2005. Speaking at the first PEN World Voices festival in a forum entitled "The Power of the Pen: Does Writing Change Anything?" Rushdie answered the question in the affirmative. He said, "*Uncle Tom's Cabin* changed attitudes toward slavery, and Charles Dickens's portraits of child poverty inspired legal reforms, and J. K. Rowling changed the culture of childhood, making millions of boys and girls look forward to 800-page novels." Rushdie is the author of six novels, including *Midnight's Children*, for which he won the Booker Prize, as well as *The Satanic Verses*, which won the Whitbread. Like Rowling's and many other authors' works, Rushdie's books have been banned in many places around the world. In 1989 this censorship was taken to a further extreme when Rushdie was condemned to death by the Iranian spiritual leader, Ayatollah Ruhollah Khomeini. The edict resulted in Rushdie's famed hiding, which lasted for years, from those around the globe who sought to carry out this sentence.

Further Reading: Smith, Dinitia. "A Crowd That's Seldom at a Loss for Words." *New York Times*, April 23, 2005. http://www.nytimes.com/2005/04/23/arts/23pen.html.

Ryan, Barry. *Character.* A Keeper on the Ireland National Quidditch Team in the World Cup (GF 8:105). He makes a play against Poland that Ron Weasley duplicates fairly well for Gryffindor (OP 19:400).

· S ·

Sahara. From QA. Quidditch referees have occasionally turned up in the Sahara months after a match when their brooms were turned into Portkeys; these referees disappeared partway through a match (QA 30).

See also Africa; *Quidditch Through the Ages*

St. Brutus's Secure Center for Incurably Criminal Boys. *Muggle place.* The detention center Uncle Vernon Dursley tells Harry to pretend he attends when Aunt Marge is visiting (PA 2:19). Aunt Marge is particularly interested in knowing whether or not they use the cane at St. Brutus's, and Harry plays along, saying that he has had it used on him many times (PA 2:24).

St. Michael's Church of England School. Rowling's primary school in Winterbourne, England. She attended from the age of five in 1970 until her family moved to Tutshill when she was around nine years old. The principal at the time Rowling attended was named Alfred Dunn, causing some observers to speculate whether he may have inspired any elements of the famous headmaster of Hogwarts who bears the same initials.

St. Mungo's Hospital for Magical Maladies and Injuries. *Magical hospital.* Cornelius Fudge tells Arthur Weasley at the World Cup that Lucius Malfoy gave a generous donation to this wizard hospital. Malfoy's scheming generosity has apparently been rewarded when Fudge makes him his guest in the Top Box at the Quidditch World Cup (GF 8:101).

The hospital is located in London, aboveground. Mad-Eye Moody explains its appearance to Harry. It is in a large, red-brick building that looks abandoned. It used to be an old-fashioned department store called Purge and Dowse Ltd., but there are signs across the doors saying it is closed for renovation. The store still has mannequins in the windows, but they are chipped and their wigs are crooked. The clothes on display are at least a decade out of date. To enter, one must lean into the glass in front of a particularly ugly dummy wearing green nylon (OP 23:505) and announce whom one is there to see.

The dummy nods, crooks a finger, and the visitors walk right into the glass and disappear into what is a reception area in the hospital (OP 22:482–83).

St. Mungo's treats different kinds of injuries and maladies on different floors. The ground floor handles accidents with artifacts, such as injuries from exploding cauldrons, wands that backfire, and crashes with brooms. The first floor handles injuries from creatures, including bites, stings, burns, bones, and spines that become embedded in one's body. The second floor handles contagious magical ailments such as dragon pox, vanishing sickness, and something called scrofungulus. On the third floor, health care workers treat poisons from plants and potions that cause rashes, vomiting, uncontrollable laughing, and so forth. Damage done by spells is treated on the fourth floor. These include hexes, jinxes that cannot seem to be reversed, and charms that were not correctly applied. The fifth floor is where the shop and tea room are located for visitors (OP 22:485–86).

In the real London, St. Mungo's is the largest organization in the city that offers shelter to homeless people. Mungo is the patron saint of the Glasgow Cathedral in Glasgow, Scotland. Mungo means "dear one."

"Saint Potter, the Mudblood's Friend." *Magical nickname.* Malfoy refers to Harry by this nickname when speaking to Harry and Ron, who are disguised as Vincent Crabbe and Gregory Goyle (CS 12:223).

Salamander. *Magical creature.* From *Fantastic Beasts.* Classified 3X by the MM. The Salamander is a lizard that lives in fires; its blood has curing properties (FB 38).
  See also Fantastic Beasts and Where to Find Them

Sanguini. *Character.* A Vampire friend of Eldred Worple who goes to Slughorn's Christmas party with Eldred (HBP 15:315).

Saturn. Prof. Trelawney tells Harry that he must have been born under this planet because of his dark hair, early tragedies, and strength. This means that he would have been born in midwinter, but Harry tells her that he was born in July (GF 13:201).

Saucy Tricks for Tricky Sorts. *Magical book.* Harry rests his head on this book while researching what he should do for the second task of the Triwizard Tournament (GF 26:486).

Savage. *Character.* Nymphadora Tonks tells Harry that Savage is at Hogwarts when he arrives in Year 6 (HBP 8:158).

Scabbers. *Magical animal.* Ron Weasley's rat that was handed down to him from his brother Percy (SS 6:100, 104). Ron tries to turn Scabbers yellow in a spell demonstration on the Hogwarts Express, but it does not work and Hermione Granger is unimpressed (SS 6:105). Scabbers chews Ron's sheets during his first night at Hogwarts (SS 7:130) and does not fare well after the Weasley family's trip to Egypt (PA 4:58). Scabbers is missing a toe, and the witch in the Magical Menagerie points out to Ron that it is unusual for a common rat like Scabbers to live much past three years (PA 4:59). Ron thinks that Hermione's cat Crookshanks has eaten Scabbers, but he turns up in Hagrid's Hut (PA 16:329). Everyone learns in *Prisoner of Azkaban* that Scabbers was Peter Pettigrew in Animagus form.

Scamander, Newt. *Character.* Rowling's pseudonym as the "author" of *Fantastic Beasts and Where to Find Them.* Newt Scamander's full name is Newton Artemis Fido Scamander, and the author's profile in *Fantastic Beasts* states that he was born in 1897. His mother bred hippogriffs and encouraged his interest in fantastic beasts. After graduating from Hogwarts, the author worked in the Office for House-Elf Relocation, a part of the Department for the Regulation and Control of Magical Creatures at the Ministry of Magic. He later worked in the Beast Division, where he was quickly promoted because of his expertise in the subject. Besides writing *Fantastic Beasts*, Scamander's accomplishments include: creating the Werewolf Register in 1947; seeing the Ban on Experimental Breeding passed; and working with the Dragon Research and Restraint Bureau. Scamander is retired and lives with his wife Porpentina in Dorset. They have three kneazles—Hoppy, Milly, and Mauler (FB vi).

Scamander, Porpentina. *Character.* The wife of Newt Scamander. She lives with him in retirement in Dorset (FB vi).

Scars. *Magical marks.* Harry Potter and Prof. Albus Dumbledore both have scars that are mentioned in the series. Harry's is a lightning-shaped mark left on his forehead by Lord Voldemort on the night Voldemort killed Harry's parents (SS 1:15). When Harry was young, Aunt Petunia Dursley falsely explained to him that he received his scar in the car accident that killed his parents. Hagrid explains the scar to Harry in the Hut-on-the-Rock (SS 4:55); a scar like Harry's is left when an evil curse touches the person. News about this marking circulates far and wide in the wizard world, and when Harry rides the Hogwarts Express, several of his comrades come to his cabin to see it as proof that he is the legendary Harry Potter they have heard about.

Harry is not always pleased to get attention for the scar that is a constant reminder of his parents' tragic end. The scar also hurts Harry quite literally several times throughout the books. It burns with pain after he is sorted into Gryffindor House in the first year. It also throbs, or even sears, with pain at times of danger or worry, or at the impending arrival of Voldemort. At the end of Year 1, after he has seen Voldemort drinking unicorn blood in the Forbidden Forest, Harry's scar hurts him a great deal (SS 16:264). It also pains him when Voldemort kills Frank Bryce (GF 2:16). Dumbledore tells Harry that he is connected to Voldemort through the scar—it is not an ordinary scar (GF 30:600). In *Order of the Phoenix*, Harry's scar often hurts, particularly when he thinks about or is around Dumbledore (OP 9:157) because Voldemort can read Harry's mind and see Dumbledore.

Prof. Dumbledore claims to have a scar above his left knee that is an accurate map of the London Underground, which he has found useful (SS 1:15). For years as the series unfolded, Rowling said in interviews that she has always had the end of the seven books clearly in her mind, down to the last word, which she said would be the word "scar." After the publication of Book 6, Rowling left the door open in interviews, saying that the last word may change.

Schmidt, Bruno. *Character.* From *Fantastic Beasts.* The six-year-old wizard child who survived an attack from an Erkling by hitting it with his father's collapsible cauldron (FB 15).
    See also Erkling

Scholastic Books. Rowling's American publisher is the largest publisher of children's books in the United States. Its imprint, Arthur A. Levine Books, is the company that purchased the American rights to the first novel for the unprecedented sum of $105,000.

After changing the title from *Harry Potter and the Philosopher's Stone* to *Harry Potter and the Sorcerer's Stone*, the company first published the book in the United States in 1998. In 2005 the company reported that the American edition of *Harry Potter and the Half-Blood Prince* sold 11 million copies in the first nine weeks following its release, and 6.9 million copies in the first twenty-four hours. Over 116.5 million copies of the American editions of the first six novels are in print. Headquartered in New York City, Scholastic has more than 10,000 employees around the world working in several divisions related to books and other media.

See also Klein, Cheryl; Levine, Arthur A.

Further Reading: Arthur A. Levine Books website: http://arthuralevine.com; Scholastic website: http://www.scholastic.com.

School song. *Magical song.* Prof. Dumbledore has the school sing the song after dessert at the Start-of-Term Banquet in Harry's first year (SS 7:128).

School story. *See Tom Brown's Schooldays* (Hughes)

Schools of witchcraft and wizardry. *Magical places.* Besides Hogwarts, there are several other schools of witchcraft and wizardry. Most of these become known in *Goblet of Fire*, when other schools come to Hogwarts to compete in the Triwizard Tournament. Durmstrang Institute, for example, is smaller and is located somewhere in Northern Europe, or perhaps Germany. It has extensive grounds. Beauxbatons Academy is presumed to be located in France.

See also Beauxbatons Academy of Magic; Durmstrang Institute

Scotland. Rowling's romance with Scotland began with family folklore. Her parents met on a train on their way to Arbroath. Peter Rowling was on his way to join the Royal Navy, and Anne Volant was on her way to join the W.R.N.S., the Women's Royal Naval Service, a women's group that supported the Royal Navy. They met on the train from London's King's Cross Station in the 1960s. Later, when Rowling's sister Di lived in Edinburgh with her new husband, the author went to that city with her child when she returned from Portugal. The Scottish Arts Council gave Rowling a writing grant that helped her make ends meet until *Philosopher's Stone* was published and while she completed the next book in the series. She has said that this gift meant the world to her at the time, and it is something she will never forget. Even after the success of her books, Rowling makes her home near Edinburgh.

It is perhaps no accident that her Harry Potter novels appear to be set primarily in Scotland as well. As Harry and Ron follow the Hogwarts Express due north of London's King's Cross Station for several hours, the location of Hogwarts is presumed to be the Scottish countryside. In *Fantastic Beasts*, the Isle of Drear off the northern coast of Scotland has been made unplottable because of the presence of the carnivorous Quintaped (FB 34–35).

Scottish Quidditch Team. *Magical sports team.* This team lost badly to Luxembourg in the run-up to the World Cup (GF 5:63).

"Scourgify." *Incantation.* The incantation for the Cleaning charm (OP 3:53). Harry sees in Snape's worst memory that James Potter put the spell on Snape after he used foul language; soap bubbles came out of Snape's mouth (OP 28:646).

Screaming Yo-yos. *Magical object.* Dumbledore tells students at the Start-of-Term Banquet in Year 4 that Argus Filch has banned Screaming Yo-yos from Hogwarts (GF 12:183).

Scrimgeour, Brutus. *Character.* Author of *The Beaters' Bible*. Brutus Scrimgeour provides a blurb on QA featured in the QA frontispiece. He wrote the first rule for Quidditch which involves removing the Seeker (QA 27). He may be related to Rufus Scrimgeour.

Scrimgeour, Rufus. *Character.* The new Minister of Magic in Book 6, succeeding Cornelius Fudge. Rufus Scrimgeour has a lionlike mane and a rough-featured face (HBP 1:16). Harry grows to dislike him when he tries to lure Harry into a useless position in the Ministry; Scrimgeour wants to make it look like the government is doing something productive in its duty to protect the wizarding world from Voldemort. He was formerly the head of the Auror office in the Department of Magical Law Enforcement (HBP 3:40). Dumbledore is evasive in answering Harry's question about whether he thinks Scrimgeour stands for goodness, but he admits that Scrimgeour is a more dynamic leader than Fudge (HBP 4:61). At Dumbledore's funeral Scrimgeour again asks Harry to work for the Ministry and receives Harry's repeated statement of loyalty to the great wizard Dumbledore (HBP 30:648–49).

Scrivenshaft's Quill Shop. *Magical place.* A store in Hogsmeade. Hermione goes there to buy a new black-and-gold quill after the first DA meeting at the Hog's Head. The quill cost her 15 Sickles and 2 Knuts (OP 16:348).

"Scurvy cur." *Magical password.* Password for entry into Gryffindor Common Room during Sir Cadogen's watch, Year 3 (PA 11:230).

Scurvy-grass. *Magical plant.* Used in Confusing and Befuddlement Draughts (OP 18:383).

Sea Serpent. *Magical creature.* From *Fantastic Beasts*. Classified 3X by the MM. The Sea Serpent has the head of a horse and the body of a snake with humps. It has never been known to harm humans, though appearances have been reported by Muggles in the Atlantic and Pacific Oceans and the Mediterranean Sea (FB 38).
  See also Fantastic Beasts and Where to Find Them

Second. *Magical position.* During a Wizards' Duel, the competitor's second takes over for his or her side if the competitor dies (SS 9:154).

Secrecy Sensor. *Magical object.* A golden, antennalike device that vibrates when it is around deceit and lies. Mad-Eye Moody shows it to Harry (GF 20:343). There are some Secrecy Sensors in the Room of Requirement for use by Dumbledore's Army (OP 18:390). Hogwarts students are scanned by Secrecy Sensors when they come to school (HBP 11:234–35). Argus Filch uses one when students go to Hogsmeade (HBP 21:463).

Secret-Keeper. *Magical person.* A friend or other person whom someone entrusts with his or her secrets. Sirius Black was James Potter's Secret-Keeper, but he convinced the Potters to make Peter Pettigrew their Secret-Keeper as a bluff to Voldemort. The bluff

Seventeenth-century depiction of a sea serpent. According to *Fantastic Beasts and Where to Find Them*, sea serpents in Harry's new world have the heads of horses and do not harm human beings. They are given a 3X danger ranking by the Ministry of Magic. Courtesy of the Library of Congress.

backfired when Pettigrew/Wormtail proved to be untrustworthy and led Voldemort straight to the Potters (PA 10:205). Snape explains to Bellatrix Lestrange that he cannot reveal the location of the Headquarters for the Order of the Phoenix because he is not the Secret-Keeper for the Order (HBP 2:30).

Secret passageways. *Magical places.* There are seven secret passageways at Hogwarts (PA 10:198).

"Sectumsempra!" *Incantation.* Harry sees this incantation written in his Potions book in Year 6. It is labeled by the Half-Blood Prince as an incantation for enemies (HBP 21:448–49). The hex slices through the skin as though striking it with an invisible sword; Harry casts this spell on Draco before he realizes how violent it is (HBP 21:522). Harry uses it in the cave against the Inferi, but they have no blood to spill (HBP 26:575).

Seeker. *Magical sports position.* There is one Seeker on each team in Quidditch. The Seeker's task is to catch the Snitch, which ends the game and awards his or her side 150 points (SS 10:169). Before his first game, Seamus Finnigan heightens Harry's uneasiness by telling him that the Seeker is often the player most physically hurt by the other team (SS 11:184).

The position derived from that of the "Hunter" in the game's early form in the thirteenth century (QA 13). The Hunter was the player whose only task was to catch the living Snidget bird. The Seeker is usually the quickest flier on the team and the lightest in weight (QA 26).

Figuratively, Harry is also a Seeker in the sense that he is searching for his identity, knowledge, enlightenment, and truth.

See also Quidditch; *Quidditch Through the Ages*

Seer. *Magical being.* One who can see the future. Prof. McGonagall tells Harry and his friends that Seers are rare and that Prof. Trelawney may not be one (PA 6:109).

Self-Correcting Ink. *Magical substance.* Self-Correcting Ink is banned in the O.W.L. examination room (OP 31:709).

Self-Defensive Spellwork. *Magical book.* A book in the Room of Requirement that Harry uses for Dumbledore's Army lessons (OP 18:390).

Self-Fertilizing Shrubs. *Magical plant.* Prof. Sprout assigns an essay on Self-Fertilizing Shrubs in Herbology (OP 14:288).

Self-Inking quills. *Magical objects.* These pens are sold at Weasleys' Wizard Wheezes (HBP 6:117).

Self-Shuffling Playing Cards. *Magical game.* Ron has these cards in his bedroom at the Burrow (CS 3:40).

Self-Straightening Brush. *Magical object.* From QA. A feature on the Twigger 90 racing broom that made it more expensive than useful (QA 51).

Selkies. *Magical beings.* From *Fantastic Beasts.* Merpeople of Scotland (FB 29).

"Serpensortia!" *Incantation.* This incantation causes a snake to shoot out of the tip of one's wand. Draco Malfoy casts it at Harry during the Dueling Club lesson (CS 11:194).

Severing Charm. *Magical spell.* A spell used for cutting. Ron uses it to cut off the lace on his hand-me-down dress robes before the Yule Ball (GF 23:411).

Shacklebolt, Kingsley. *Character.* A tall member of the Order of the Phoenix; he bows to Harry when he is introduced (OP 3:49). In his low voice he tells Harry that he has heard that Harry flies well (OP 3:51). He is bald and wears an earring (OP 3:57). He is a spy in the Ministry, presumably searching for Sirius Black and giving false information that he has been spotted in Tibet (OP 5:95). Harry and Mr. Weasley see him at work in Auror Headquarters at the Ministry, but Harry must pretend he has never met him before (OP 7:131). Shacklebolt wonders why Dumbledore did not make Harry prefect (OP 9:172). He is in Dumbledore's office when Harry is called in by Dolores Umbridge and confronted about the DA (OP 27:610). Shacklebolt is an Auror who has been stationed as the secretary at the Prime Minister's office. His job is to protect the Prime Minister from harmful wizarding spells, such as the Imperius Curse, as well as to keep an eye on things for the Ministry (HBP 1:17).

Shakespeare, William (1564–1616). Rowling has pointed out comparisons between the Harry Potter series and Shakespeare's play *Macbeth.* In Macbeth, three witches called the Weird Sisters (Rowling makes a pun on this name by using it for the rock band that plays at the Hogwarts Yule Ball) make a prophecy to Macbeth, which sets in motion a series of tragic events. Had the characters not sought to fulfill the prophecy, the events need not have occurred. Free will, choice versus destiny, and fate are some of the themes

British playwright, poet, and actor, William Shakespeare (1564–1616). J. K. Rowling may have borrowed the theme of prophecy from Shakespeare's *Macbeth* and the name Hermione from a character in *The Winter's Tale*. Courtesy of the Library of Congress.

of the play that also run a strong current through the Potter books. In *Order of the Phoenix*, Dumbledore tells Harry about the Prophecy concerning Harry and Voldemort, but he also tells Harry that the prophecy need only come true if the participants think it must. The theme is likely to be one of the major threads of the series once all of the books are completed. Scotland ties Harry Potter, Macbeth, and Rowling together as well, since both fictional stories are set there and the country is Rowling's adopted home.

Another tie between Rowling and Shakespeare is their use of the name Hermione. The name comes from a central character in Shakespeare's play *The Winter's Tale*. Rowling saw the play performed at Stratford-upon-Avon when she was about thirteen years old. In the play, Hermione is a strong female character who turns into a statue for sixteen years, then reemerges.

Sherbet balls. *Magical sweet.* Ron says Honeydukes sells these treats, which make people rise up off the ground while they melt in their mouths (PA 5:76).

See also Candy and sweets

Shield Charm. *Magical charm.* This charm puts up a protective barrier that wards off smaller curses (GF 31:608). The charm deflects a minor jinx back onto the attacker. In the DA, Neville and Hermione are good at Shield Charms (OP 25:553). George comments that even people in the Ministry are not always capable of conjuring good ones the way Harry can (HBP 6:119).

Shield Cloaks. *Magical objects.* A popular clothing item sold at Weasleys' Wizard Wheezes at a time when people are worried about protecting themselves against the Dark Arts and Voldemort (HBP 6:119).

Shield Gloves. *Magical objects.* A popular clothing item sold at Weasleys' Wizard Wheezes at a time when people are worried about protecting themselves against the Dark Arts and Voldemort (HBP 6:119).

Shield Hats. *Magical objects.* A popular clothing item sold at Weasleys' Wizard Wheezes at a time when people are worried about protecting themselves against the Dark Arts and Voldemort (HBP 6:119).

Shock Spells. *Magical spells.* Hermione reads a letter that arrives after *The Quibbler*'s article about Harry and the rise of Voldemort. The letter recommends that Harry learn Shock Spells at St. Mungo's (OP 26:579).

Shooting Star. *Magical object.* Ron Weasley's broomstick model (CS 4:46). After Harry's broom breaks, he rides one of these models from the school supply of brooms (PA 10:190). First manufactured by Universal Brooms, Ltd. in 1955, the model is the least expensive racing broom ever made, but it loses power with age. The models stopped being made in 1978 when the company went out of business (QA 50).
See also Broomsticks; *Quidditch Through the Ages*

Shrake. *Magical creature.* From *Fantastic Beasts*. Classified 3X by the MM. A spiny fish in the Atlantic Ocean (FB 38–39).
See also Fantastic Beasts and Where to Find Them

Shrieking Shack. *Magical place.* Hermione says she has read in *Sites of Historical Sorcery* that this is the most haunted dwelling in Britain (PA 5:77). Ron says that Nearly Headless Nick told him that a bad crowd of ghosts hangs out there, and the Hogwarts ghosts stay away from the place (PA 14:279). The shack consists of one dusty room with peeling wallpaper, broken and gnawed-looking furniture, and a stained floor (PA 17:337). Prof. Lupin later tells the trio that the shack was built for him to go to when he transforms into a werewolf. He goes there for his own protection and for the protection of everyone else around him (PA 18:353).
See also Hogsmeade

Shrinking Solution. *Magical substance.* Gryffindor and Slytherin students practice making this substance in Potions class (PA 7:124).

Shrivelfig. *Magical plant.* An ingredient in the Shrinking Solution (PA 7:124).
See also Abysinnian Shrivelfigs

Shrunken head. *Magical object.* A Shrunken head is taken from Vincent Crabbe after he is scanned for security at Hogwarts (HBP 11:235).

Shunpike, Stan. *Character.* Conductor on the Knight Bus. Harry notices that Stan is not much older than himself, perhaps eighteen or nineteen. He has pimples and ears that are big and stick out (PA 3:34). After the World Cup, Harry and friends see Stan trying to impress the Veela by saying that he is going to be the next Minister of Magic (GF 9:126). He is still the conductor when Harry and friends ride the bus back to Hogwarts after the holidays at Grimmauld Place. Stan tells Harry that he is from outside of Birmingham (OP 24:525). In Year 6 Stan is arrested at his house in Clapham and charged as a Death Eater; Harry does not believe it (HBP 11:221).

Shuntbumps. *Magical game.* From QA. This is an ancient broomstick game that is akin to jousting; players try to knock each other off their brooms. The last player still on his or her broom is the winner. The game was especially popular in Devon, England, and survives as a game played by children (QA 6).

Sickles. *Magical money.* Harry first sees mention of Sickles on his first visit to Diagon Alley, where dragon liver is advertised at 17 Sickles per ounce (though he does not yet know the conversion factor or what they are) (SS 5:72).

Side-Along-Apparition. *Magical move.* Apparating with a witch or wizard who is of age. Harry does this with Dumbledore (HBP 17:356).

Silencing Charm. *Magical spell.* This spell makes a creature go quiet (FB 18). The incantation is "Silencio!" (OP 18:375).

"Silencio!" *Incantation.* This is the incantation for the Silencing Charm. Hermione tells Ron that one must jab with the wand rather than wave it to produce the charm effectively (OP 18:375).

Silver Arrow. *Magical object.* A broomstick invented by Leonard Jewkes. It was the forerunner of the racing broom (QA 49). In Harry's time it is an older style (PA 13:254).
   See also Broomsticks

Sin. When Prof. Dumbledore catches Harry looking into his Pensieve in his office, he tells Harry that curiosity is not a sin, but one must be careful with it. The use of the word "sin" is one of the few direct biblical or theological references in the series (GF 30:398).
   See also Christian responses

Singing Valentine. *Magical message.* A Singing Valentine was sent to Harry in Year 2 by Ginny Weasley (CS 13:237–39).

Sinistra, Prof. *Character.* Astronomy teacher. Prof. Sinistra helps Prof. Flitwick carry Justin Finch-Fletchley to the hospital after he is petrified (CS 11:204). She is one of the professors rarely seen in the series. In Latin *sinistra* means "the left hand"; *sinister* means "wrong, perverse."

Sir Cadogen. *See* Cadogen, Sir

Sites of Historical Sorcery. *Magical book.* A book Hermione reads about the history of Hogsmeade (PA 5:77).

62442. *Magical number.* The phone number required to go to the Ministry of Magic from the telephone booth in London (OP 33:768). The numbers suggest a date of June 24, 1942, but Rowling has not confirmed whether this is a clue.

1612 Goblin Rebellion. *Magical event.* Hermione tells Harry and friends that an inn in Hogsmeade was the headquarters for the 1612 Goblin Rebellion (PA 5:77).

Skeeter, Rita. *Character.* A reporter at the *Daily Prophet* (GF 10:147). Rita Skeeter wears jeweled glasses, tight curls in her hair, and often carries a crocodile-skin purse (GF 18:303). Bill Weasley comments that she makes everyone in her articles look bad. She once wrote a piece on Charm Breakers that made fun of Bill's long hair (GF 10:152). Her other articles include an attack on Arthur Weasley and Mad-Eye Moody for raising an alarm from the Ministry (it later proved not to be a false alarm, but was probably a response to the presence of Barty Crouch, Jr., on the scene) (GF 13:203). She interviews Harry before the first task of the Triwizard Tournament in a broom closet to avoid detection by Dumbledore; of course, the article misrepresents what Harry says (GF 18:303). When she tests her Quick-Quotes Quill, it writes that she is blonde and age forty-three (GF 18:304). She interviews Hagrid about Blast-Ended Skrewts (GF 21:369).

In beetle form, Rita Skeeter listens to conversations undercover and reports them in her articles. She is the beetle on the stone reindeer's back when Harry and Ron hear Hagrid talking privately with Madame Maxime after the Yule Ball (GF 23:427). She is also the beetle on the windowsill when Harry passes out in Divination class (GF 29:576).

Harry explains "bugging" in the Muggle world (with wire taps and so forth) (GF 28:546) to Hermione and Ron. This later gives Hermione an idea, and she figures out that Rita Skeeter is an unregistered Animagus in the form of a beetle (GF 37:727). After Hermione holds this knowledge over Rita's head, she enlists Rita to write an article about Harry that will be published in *The Quibbler*. The article will tell the story of the rise of Voldemort and of Cedric Diggory's death, and it will clear Harry's name (OP 25:564–69). Rita Skeeter writes a less than flattering blurb for *Quidditch Through the Ages* in the QA frontispiece.

Skele-Gro. *Magical substance.* This substance makes bones grow. Madam Pomfrey gives Harry some of this concoction when Prof. Lockhart removes his bones instead of healing his broken arm after a Quidditch match in Year 2 (CS 10:174). The regrowth process takes some time and is painful, making Harry's arm feel as though it were full of big splinters. Madam Pomfrey says he has thirty-three bones to grow back (CS 10:176).

Skiving Snackboxes. *Magical candy.* These are sweets invented by Fred and George Weasley. They are orange on one end and purple on the other. The orange end gets the victim slightly ill, and the purple end brings him or her back to health. They are useful to students for getting out of class. For example, Puking Pastilles make people throw up; eating the purple end stops this and makes them feel fine enough to do whatever they may like with the extra time. While testing the product on each other, Fred admitted that they were not yet able to stop vomiting long enough to eat the purple end (OP 6:104).

The Weasley twins later test the product on first-year students at Hogwarts, much to Hermione's dismay. After the twins leave the school, many students begin appearing sick in class, using the candy in protest against Dolores Umbridge (OP 30:678). They are sold at Weasleys' Wizard Wheezes in a variety of flavors. Varieties include: Blood Blisterpods, Fainting Fancies, Fever Fudge, Nosebleed Nougat, and Puking Pastilles (HBP 6:116).

See also Candy and sweets

Slavery. Though the appearance of house-elves such as Dobby, Winky, and Kreacher in the series may at first seem to provide an avenue for dramatization of the social problem of slavery, the lack of development of Hermione's S.P.E.W. (Society for the Promotion of Elfish Welfare) organization and its diminished integration into the story weakens the possibilities that may have existed for a fuller exploration of this theme. Like Harry and Ron, readers and apparently most of the other students at Hogwarts, can easily sympathize with the house-elves' plight, yet they also view Hermione's efforts to help house-elves as misguided. Even good-hearted advisors to the trio, such as Hagrid, tell Hermione that house-elves want to serve families and are not happy unless they do so. Winky and Kreacher both appear to put loyalty to their masters above any desire for individual comfort. Only Dobby seems grateful to Harry Potter for freeing him. After struggling to find paid work, he is happy to be employed by Dumbledore at Hogwarts for an arrangement of wages and days off that he negotiates in Dumbledore's favor rather than his own.

The magical world blurs the definition of a house-elf in that it is unclear whether their "nature" is to want to serve their masters, just as the nature of a Dementor is to suck the souls out of people and treat them unkindly. In other words, it is not clear whether house-elves are to be regarded as humans with inalienable and equal human rights befitting all people, or whether they are some other kind of creature with very different needs. One could argue that this is precisely the argument given for slavery in the United States and elsewhere throughout history—that the basic nature of blacks in Western society was defined by others in power over them; these people thought of them as property to be bought and sold, not as human beings with inherent rights equal to their own. The Fountain of Brethren contains a representation of house-elves which suggests that they are more like humans than anything else. Nevertheless, in a story full of goblins, giants, centaurs, and other magical beings, the nature of a house-elf, what makes a house-elf happy, and what ought to be a house-elf's rightful destiny remains unclear.

The ambiguity the house-elf presents to some readers may reflect the uncertainties and complexities of the issue of slavery in general, demonstrating the kinds of problems that American abolitionists faced in their arguments for the freedom of slaves. Thomas Jefferson, for example, joined other slave owners in arguing that slavery may be wrong but that freeing all of the slaves at one time would do them a disservice in terms of disrupting their livelihoods and ways of life.

Harry's approach to freeing Dobby as an individual seems to have worked much more effectively as a catalyst for change within the house-elf community than Hermione's school political campaign. Perhaps this is Rowling's way of signifying that change must come slowly through experience, opportunity, and understanding of those who are oppressed, and is not best achieved through buttons and slogans. Hermione's approach of knitting hats for the house-elves (which only Dobby collects each night) demonstrates her continued misunderstanding of the house-elves' needs. She has not asked them what they want, and she has neither listened to their stories nor fully understood the complexity and history of their situation. In the Hogwarts kitchen scene, she seems frustrated that the elves do not want what she thinks they should want. She blindly makes a quilt for Kreacher as a peace offering (whether he wants it or not) before she knows the full details of the evil deeds that he has committed. However well intentioned, Hermione imposes her own views of what she thinks the house-elves should have rather than seeking to understand and effect real change on their behalf.

Human rights is undeniably a concern of Rowling's, given that she once worked for Amnesty International, one of the most prominent human rights organizations in the world. In addition, she wrote two books for the purpose of donating the proceeds to Comic Relief, U.K. to benefit the poor. She continues to make significant financial donations to charities of her choice. The house-elves are as much a part of Rowling's effort to make a statement about human rights as S.P.E.W. is Hermione's effort to do the same. It remains to be seen with the series' conclusion whether the gesture in the novels rings any truer than Hermione's organization has thus far.

Sleekeazy's Hair Potion. *Magical substance.* Hermione uses this potion to smooth down her frizzy hair for the Yule Ball, but she finds it too bothersome to use on a daily basis (GF 24:433).

Sleeping Draught. *Magical substance.* Hermione concocts this substance and puts it inside two chocolate cakes for Harry and Ron to feed to Vincent Crabbe and Gregory Goyle. This is done in an effort to find out if Draco Malfoy is the Slytherin heir (CS 12:213). Hagrid tells Harry that the organizers used this substance on the many dragons at Hogwarts for the Triwizard Tournament (GF 19:327).

Sleeping Potion. *Magical substance.* Dumbledore asks that Harry take Sleeping Potion after his traumatic experience in the third task of the Triwizard Tournament (GF 36:699). Madam Pomfrey tells him that it will give him a deep sleep with no dreams (GF 36:701).

Sloper, Jack. *Character.* Jack Sloper becomes a Beater on the Gryffindor team when Prof. Umbridge bans Fred and George Weasley from playing (OP 21:453). Ron says Jack has less talent than even he has (OP 25:556). He delivers a note to Harry from Dumbledore and asks Harry as captain of the Gryffindor Quidditch team when try-outs are to be held (HBP 9:181).

Sloth Grip Roll. *Magical sports play.* Angelina Johnson has the Quidditch team practice this move in Year 5 (OP 17:351). It involves holding onto the broomstick with both hands and feet while hanging upside down. The move is often used to avoid getting hit by a passing Bludger (QA 54).

The Slug Club. *Magical group.* The name given to those students chosen by Prof. Horace Slughorn to attend his private parties (HBP 7:147). Ron jokes that Harry and Hermione could be King and Queen Slug (HBP 14:282).

Slughorn, Prof. Horace. *Character.* An older wizard brought out of hiding and re-tirement by Prof. Dumbledore to teach Potions class when Prof. Severus Snape is moved to the Defense Against the Dark Arts faculty position in Year 6 (HBP 4:66–80). Slug-horn used to be Head of Slytherin when he was on the faculty at Hogwarts in Harry's parents' time (HBP 4:70). Harry tells his friends that Slughorn looks something like a walrus (HBP 5:90). In his youth Slughorn had hair the color of straw and a ginger-blond mustache (HBP 23:494). He likes treats such as crystallized pineapple (HBP 24:494). Slughorn likes to rub elbows with the rich, powerful, and influential, and frequently drops the names of former students whom he believes fall into this category.

Slugs. *Magical creatures.* Ron tries to defend Hermione when Draco Malfoy calls her a Mudblood in Year 2, but Ron's spell backfires and he belches up large, slimy slugs for several hours (CS 7:113).

Slytherin House. *Magical school organization.* Harry first hears of Slytherin House when Draco Malfoy speaks to him at Madam Malkin's on Diagon Alley (SS 5:77). Ron tells Harry that it was the house that Voldemort lived in (SS 6:107). It is one of the four student resident houses at Hogwarts. The house was founded by Salazar Slytherin and is headed through most of the series by Prof. Severus Snape, who teaches Potions, then DADA. At the end of *Half-Blood Prince*, when Snape departs, the Head post is taken over by Horace Slughorn, who teaches Potions when Snape is given the DADA post in Year 6. Students of Slytherin are characterized by cunning and the desire to achieve their goals through any means. The Slytherin quarters are located under the lake in a dungeonlike area. Their colors are green and silver, and their emblem depicts a silver snake on a green background. The Slytherin ghost is the Bloody Baron. Their Quidditch robes are green. Notable Slytherin characters include: Draco Malfoy, Vincent Crabbe, Gregory Goyle, Pansy Parkinson, and others.

Slytherin, Salazar. *See* Slytherin House

Smart-Answer quills. *Magical objects.* Pens that give correct answers on tests and homework; they are sold at Weasleys' Wizard Wheezes (HBP 6:117).

Smeltings. *Muggle place.* The private school that Vernon and Dudley Dursley both attended. The uniforms consist of maroon tailcoats, orange knickerbockers, and flat straw hats. Each student is also given a knobbly stick that they use to strike one another with when the teachers are looking the other way (SS 3:32).

Smethley, Veronica. *Character.* Another of Gilderoy Lockhart's fans that requires a response while Harry is in detention in his second year. When Harry addresses her letter, it feels like the 1,000th letter (CS 7:120).

Smethwyck, Elliot. *Character.* From QA. Inventor of the Cushioning Charm for broomsticks (QA 47).
   See also Quidditch Through the Ages

Smethwyck, Hippocrates. *Character.* The Healer-in-Charge, or head doctor, in the Dai Llewellyn Ward of serious bites the day that Harry and the Weasleys visit Arthur (OP 22:487). He finds the antidote to the snake's poison (OP 24:522).

Smith, Dame Maggie.. *See* Films

Smith, Hepzibah. *Character.* A very old witch from Tom Riddle's younger days. She has many possessions and Tom Riddle visits her to acquire her goblin-made armour (HBP 20:435). It turns out, however, that she also owns what is supposed to be Helga Hufflepuff's original cup and the Slytherin locket. Hokey, her house-elf, was blamed for her poisoning, which was clearly the work of Tom Riddle (HBP 20:436–38).

Smith, Zacharias. *Character.* A student at Hogwarts who challenges Harry about how he knows that Voldemort is back (OP 16:340). He chides Harry for taking "Remedial Potions" with Prof. Snape, saying that he must be very bad at the subject since Snape rarely offers extra help (OP 24:527). Ginny Weasley puts the Bat-Bogey Hex on Zacharias on the Hogwarts Express (HBP 7:146). He commentates the Quidditch match between Gryffindor and Slytherin in Year 6 (HBP 14:296). Harry dislikes Zacharias and is sickened when Hermione tells him she almost asked him to Slughorn's Christmas party instead of Cormac McLeggan in her effort to make Ron jealous (HBP 15:317). In Year 6 he plays Chaser on the Hufflepuff team (HBP 19:409). After Dumbledore's death, his arrogant-looking father comes to take him from the school (HBP 30:633).

Snakes. Beginning with the snake Harry unintentionally sets free from the zoo, the creatures continue to slither their way through the books of the series. Harry makes friends with the snake at the zoo on Dudley Dursley's birthday; it is a boa constrictor supposedly from Brazil, but bred in captivity (SS 2:27–28). Harry later learns that he is a Parseltongue—one who can speak with snakes. There is a snake carved into one of the taps in Moaning Myrtle's bathroom, and this is how Harry figures out how to reach the Chamber of Secrets (CS 16:300). In *Chamber of Secrets* he battles the king of the serpents, the Basilisk in the Chamber (CS 17:318–20). However, that is not the end of the snakes in the series. The Slytherin House mascot is a snake and the symbol turns up, explicitly or implicitly, whenever house members are around. When the Dueling Club has a practice, Draco Malfoy makes a black snake come out of his wand and go after Harry. Harry speaks to it, scaring all of the other students who are there (CS 11:194–95). In *Half-Blood Prince* there is a snakeskin nailed to the Gaunt family hut (HBP 10:209).

Snape, Prof. Severus. *Character.* Severus Snape is perhaps the most complex and mysterious character in the Harry Potter series. The name Snape may come from a small town in England that has the same name. In Latin, *severus* means strict, stern, and grave, and is the root of the English words severe, severity, and also sever, meaning to cut. Severus is also a Roman family name. Cornelius Severus was a fellow poet and friend to Ovid at the time of Caesar Augustus. Septimius Severus was emperor from A.D. 193–211, and Aurelius Alexander Severus ruled as emperor from A.D. 222–234. Severus mons is a mountain in the Sabine, a section of the Apennines.

Prof. Snape has stringy, greasy black hair and a hooked nose (SS 7:126). His eyes are black with a cold appearance (SS 8:136). In Years 1–5, he is the Potions professor at Hogwarts, but in Year 6, he is finally assigned the position he has coveted for years—teaching Defense Against the Dark Arts (HBP 8:166). Snape is the head of Slytherin House and tends to favor Slytherin students in the classroom (SS 8:135). The most difficult aspect about Snape for Harry is that Harry's encounters with him almost always result in his distrusting the professor. These experiences leave him wondering why Snape seems to dislike him so vehemently. Harry's feelings are complicated by Dumbledore's complete trust in Snape for reasons he will not reveal to Harry. This causes much uncertainty and frustration for the boy wizard.

Harry first sees Prof. Snape at the Head Table during the Start-of-Term Banquet in his first year at Hogwarts (SS 7:126). Harry sees Snape speaking with Prof. Quirrell. Suddenly, Snape turns to look directly in Harry's eyes, making the scar on Harry's forehead hurt. Percy Weasley tells Harry that Snape knows a

Alan Rickman as Severus Snape in *Harry Potter and the Prisoner of Azkaban* (2004). In the series, Snape protects Harry one moment and treats him unkindly the next, making him one of Rowling's most complex and intriguing characters. Courtesy of Warner Bros./Photofest.

lot about the Dark Arts (SS 7:126). In his first Potions class, Harry receives an early sample of Snape's wrath. While reading the roll, the professor pauses at Harry's name and makes a snide remark about him being a celebrity (SS 8:136). Snape tells the class that he can teach them to "bottle fame, brew glory, even stopper death" (SS 8:137). Then he immediately asks Harry a question about ingredients for the Draught of Living Death. Harry is taken off guard; he does not know the answer. He suggests that Prof. Snape might allow Hermione Granger to answer, since her hand is raised enthusiastically. Instead, Snape takes a point from Gryffindor House for what he says is Harry's boldness (SS 8:137–38).

Readers find that things are not always as they seem with Snape. For example, when Harry sees Snape staring at him during a Quidditch match his first year at the school, Harry's broomstick begins acting erratically, and he suspects Snape has jinxed it. However, it turns out that it was Prof. Quirrell, not Snape, who was attempting to jinx Harry's broom. Snape, in fact, was saying a counter-curse against Quirrell's jinx to help Harry (SS 17:288–89). Dumbledore trusts Snape for reasons that Harry and others cannot understand. In a scene in *Prisoner of Azkaban*, Cornelius Fudge remarks to Dumbledore that he should watch out for Snape because Snape must be out of his mind. Dumbledore says to Fudge, however, that Snape is not insane—he has simply experienced a bad disappointment (PA 22:240). That disappointment remains a secret until the last book in the series.

Severus Snape's past is mysterious, and Harry and the reader learn more about it in small portions. Snape was enemies with Sirius Black, for example, back in their student days at Hogwarts (GF 12:175). In *Goblet of Fire*, Mad-Eye Moody and Snape have a confrontation. Moody says that he thinks some people have spots that never come off, no matter how trusting Dumbledore is of them, referring to the Dark Mark tattoo on Snape's forearm. This causes the tattoo, a Death Eater symbol, on Snape's arm to hurt him (GF 25:472). Moody tells Harry that Snape has been given a second chance from something that he would like to know about. When Harry tells this to Ron and Hermione, Hermione reiterates that Dumbledore trusts Snape (GF 26:481).

Sirius Black tells Harry a bit about Snape's student years at Hogwarts. He says that Snape was never caught as a Death Eater, but was known to have a fascination with the Dark Arts while in school and was seen hanging out with a group of Slytherins who almost all became Death Eaters. Snape came to the school already knowing a lot of Dark Magic, even more than most seventh-year students at Hogwarts (GF 27:531). Harry discovers that Severus actually once was a Death Eater by viewing one of Dumbledore's memories in the Pensieve. From that vision of Igor Karkaroff's hearing, Harry learns that Snape was cleared by the Council from evidence given previously by Dumbledore, and that he has been spying for the good side with great risk to himself, according to Dumbledore. Snape switched sides before Voldemort was brought down (GF 30:591). When Harry wants to press Dumbledore about what makes him trust Snape so much, Dumbledore closes the subject by saying that it is a private matter between him and the Potions professor (GF 30:604).

Snape shows Cornelius Fudge the Dark Mark on his arm in an effort to convince him that Voldemort called his Death Eaters the night of the Triwizard Tournament's third task. Snape claims this is also a sign that the Dark Lord has returned (GF 36:710). At this news, Dumbledore tells Snape that it is time to set in motion what Snape knows he must do (GF 36:713). Whether or not this is some prearranged plan made between Dumbledore and Snape remains unclear to readers until the last book in the series.

In *Order of the Phoenix*, although he does not stay or eat at the Order's headquarters at Number Twelve, Grimmauld Place, Snape apparently continues to work as a double-agent behind the scenes on their behalf. He tells Sirius Black, for example, that Lucius Malfoy recognized him in his dog form at the train platform (OP 24:520). When Harry and Ron question Snape's loyalties yet again, Hermione reminds Ron once more that Dumbledore trusts him, and that this should be enough for all of them (OP 25:555).

Dumbledore assigns Snape the task of teaching Harry Occlumency in *Order of the Phoenix*. During one lesson, Harry sees memories of Snape's childhood that show a man with a hooked nose yelling at a woman who is huddled with a young, cowering Snape crying in a corner. A teenaged Snape zaps flies on the ceiling with apparent disinterest. Harry sees a girl laughing while a Snape-like figure attempts to get on a bouncing broomstick (OP 26:592). Snape does not seem happy to be giving the Occlumency lessons to Harry, but he is even less pleased when he discovers that Harry has seen some of his memories in the Pensieve.

In one lesson, Harry gains important insight not only into Snape's past but also into his own father's character as a teenager. He sees Snape's worst memory. Harry sees Snape being teased by a teenage James Potter and Sirius Black. Lily Evans, Harry's mother, is also there. She tries to stick up for Snape but Snape snaps at her. James casts Snape's wand away and turns him upside down in mid-air, showing the crowd Snape's underwear (OP 28:640–50). Seeing the memory of James bullying Snape in such a cruel way confuses Harry's feelings for his father.

Snape's history with the Potters may help explain his mixed actions toward Harry. Not only was James Potter cruel to Snape when they were both students at Hogwarts, but James also once saved Snape's life. Although Dumbledore has told Harry this in general terms (SS 17:300), Remus Lupin explains the story in more detail in *Prisoner of Azkaban*. On a lark in their student days, young Sirius Black once told a curious Snape how to follow Lupin and find out where he disappeared to mysteriously once a month. When Snape entered the secret corridor at the Whomping Willow and headed toward Lupin, who was in his dangerous werewolf form, James Potter came quickly and got Snape out of the tunnel before he was killed (PA 18:357). Snape claims that James saved him only to save himself and Sirius Black from being expelled (OP 14:285). Even so, Dumbledore suggests to Harry that Snape may be helping Harry in order to ease some of his feelings of indebtedness toward James's memory (SS 17:300).

As much as Snape seems to dislike Harry because he reminds him of James Potter on the one hand, he also continues to act on the boy's behalf perhaps for the same reason. For example, he is less than cooperative with Umbridge when she orders Snape to make more Veritaserum to use against Harry. As a result of his reluctance to help her, Umbridge puts Snape on probation (OP 32:744). Late in *Order of the Phoenix*, Dumbledore explains to Harry the importance of Snape's role in finding Sirius Black and sending the Order to help Harry at the Room of Prophecy (OP 37:830). Even at this point, though it seems that Snape is working as a double agent between Voldemort and Dumbledore; neither readers nor Harry trust Snape without reservation.

Whether Snape lived at Spinner's End at one time is unclear, but it is there that he meets Narcissa Black Malfoy and Bellatrix Lestrange at the opening of *Half-Blood Prince* (HBP 2:22). There, he makes an Unbreakable Vow to save Draco Malfoy and spare his life if Draco cannot perform the task Voldemort has in store for him. At the climax of the novel at the battle on the Astronomy Tower, Snape appears and honors his Unbreakable Vow with Narcissa Black. Seeing that Draco cannot kill Dumbledore on

Voldemort's apparent orders, Snape commits the deed himself (HBP 27:595–96). It is unclear whether Dumbledore's plea to Snape is to kill Dumbledore and protect Draco Malfoy by doing so, or to spare Dumbledore's life.

Throughout the series, and especially at the end of Book 6, Snape is a conundrum for readers. Like Harry, Ron, and Hermione, readers do not know whether to trust Snape or not, nor why Dumbledore ever trusted the very wizard who would eventually kill him. The question in readers' minds at the end of *Half-Blood Prince* remains: On whose side do Snape's loyalties really lie—Dumbledore's, Voldemort's, or his own?

Snape, Tobias. *Character.* Severus Snape's father. He was a Muggle who married Eileen Prince (HBP 30:637).

Snargaluff stumps. *Magical plant.* This plant is part of a term project in Herbology (HBP 14:279).

Sneakoscope. *Magical object.* Like a spinning top made of glass, the Sneakoscope sounds alerts by spinning, glowing, and whistling when someone nearby is being dishonest. Harry receives a pocket version from Ron for his thirteenth birthday. There are some of these in the Room of Requirement for use by Dumbledore's Army (OP 18:390). Horace Slughorn uses a Freezing Alarm rather than a Sneakoscope to get into Muggle houses (HBP 4:68). Sneakoscopes are sold at Weasleys' Wizard Wheezes. In Year 6 Arthur Weasley confiscates cursed Sneakoscopes that were probably tainted by the Death Eaters (HBP 5:85).

Sneezewort. *Magical plant.* Sneezewort is used in Confusing and Befuddlement Draughts (OP 18:383).

Snidget. *Magical creature.* From *Fantastic Beasts.* Classified 4X by the MM due to the harsh penalties associated with capturing it or harming it, not because it is dangerous. The Snidget is a rare, small, round bird with a long, thin beak and garnet-like eyes. The Golden Snidget was hunted years ago for its feathers and eyes and is the precursor of the Quidditch Snitch (FB 39).
See also Fantastic Beasts and Where to Find Them; Quidditch Through the Ages

Snidget-hunting. *Magical sport.* From QA. An old sport among witches and wizards beginning in the early twelfth century. A tapestry from that period depicts hunters engaged in the sport (QA 10).
See also Quidditch Through the Ages

Snitch. *Magical sports equipment.* The small, fast-flying golden ball with wings that the Seeker in Quidditch tries to catch for 150 points, ending the game. Because the point value is so high for catching it, the side that catches it usually wins.
See also Quidditch

Snitchnip. *Magical game penalty.* From QA. A penalty imposed if any player other than the Seeker touches the Golden Snitch (QA 30).

"Snivellus." *Nickname.* Sirius Black calls Snape "Snivellus" when he tells Snape that he does not trust him (OP 24:520).

"**Snuffles.**" *Magical nickname.* Sirius Black tells Harry and friends to call him this nickname to avoid people finding out that he was around (GF 27:534). He apparently thinks of it as his name when in dog form (OP 6:115).

Society for the Protection of Ugly Goblins (S.P.U.G.). Ron teases Hermione that she could start a group called S.P.U.G. (GF 24:449).

Socks. Whether intentionally highlighted by Rowling or not, there are several scenes with socks mentioned in the series—enough so that they have become a kind of literary motif. In the first instance Harry is looking for socks when he wakes up on Dudley Dursley's birthday. He finds a pair in his cupboard under the stairs and must pull a spider off of one of them (SS 2:19). Harry receives an old pair of Uncle Vernon's socks and a coat hanger from the Dursleys for his tenth birthday (SS 3:43). Dumbledore says he would see socks if he looked in the Mirror of Erised (SS 12:214). Mrs. Weasley is concerned about the condition of Harry's socks before he goes back to Hogwarts his second year (CS 4:42). Dobby says that the gift of clothes from one's master will free a house-elf, but so far the Malfoys have not given him even a sock (CS 10:177). Harry and Ron run in their socks to Moaning Myrtle's bathroom in order to stay undetected (CS 12:225). Dobby is freed when Harry puts Tom Riddle's diary into a smelly sock and gives it to Lucius Malfoy, who flings the sock off the book so that it lands on Dobby (CS 18:337–38). Ron puts Harry's pocket Sneakoscope in an old pair of Vernon's socks to muffle its whistle so that it will not wake Prof. Lupin on the Hogwarts Express (PA 5:76).

Harry says he never wears socks if he can avoid it (PA 11:226). Mrs. Weasley washes all of Harry's socks before he heads off to Hogwarts in Year 4 (GF 10:155). Hagrid is mending his socks with yellow yarn and a huge needle made of bone when Harry and friends go to see him (GF 16:265). The day of the first task of the Triwizard Tournament, Harry goes to put his foot in a hat, not a sock (GF 20:337).

Dobby's favorite clothing is socks. Ron gives him a pair of purple socks that his mother made him for Christmas, along with a sweater she made (GF 23:409). Dobby makes socks for Harry Potter from wool purchased with his wages as a free house-elf; one sock is red with broomsticks on it, and the other is green with Golden Snitches on it (GF 23:409). For helping him with the gillyweed for the second task of the Triwizard Tournament, Harry buys Dobby socks for every day of the year (GF 26:508). Dobby is thrilled and quite moved when he receives them (GF 28:535).

Mundungus Fletcher's pipe smoke smells like burning socks (OP 5:81). Ron wraps his prefect badge in maroon socks before going to Hogwarts (OP 9:168). Seamus Finnigan leaves the dormitory before Harry can get his socks on at the beginning of Year 5 (OP 12:221). Dobby wears the hats Hermione is making, plus several pairs of socks, when he returns Hedwig to Harry (OP 18:385). Harry hides his small bottle of luck potion, Felix Felicis, inside a pair of socks in his trunk (HBP 9:193). When Mrs. Weasley points out the fine gifts the twins buy her for Christmas, George Weasley tells his mother that he and Fred appreciate her more now that they wash their own socks (HBP 16:339). Harry gives Ron a pair of socks that have Felix Felicis wrapped in them in case Ron or Hermione needs it (HBP 25:552).

Many of the characters also knit in the series. Hagrid and Hermione knit, and Dumbledore is interested in knitting patterns in magazines. Close readers ponder the significance, if any, of this motif of socks and knitting.

See also Clothing

Somerset. The Modesty Rabnott Snidget Reservation is located in Somerset (QA 14). Cornelius Fudge tells the Muggle Prime Minister that members of the Regulation and Control of Magical Creatures are combing this area looking for the giant who may have been involved with the Death Eater "hurricane" incident (HBP 1:13).

Sonnets for a Sorcerer. *Magical book.* This book makes everyone who reads it speak in limericks for the rest of their lives (CS 13:231). It appears to be the only book of poetry in the series.

"Sonorus!" *Incantation.* This incantation allows one's voice to be heard like a microphone (GF 26:493).

Sorcerer's Stone. *Magical object.* Also called in England the Philosopher's Stone. Harry, Ron, and Hermione find out that Voldemort is after the Sorcerer's Stone that Nicolas Flamel made; Voldemort wants the stone so that he might have eternal life. The Elixir of Life may be made from the stone (SS 16:267). The stone is described as being the color of blood (SS 17:292).

Sorting Hat Ceremony. Prof. McGonagall explains to first-year students about the four student houses and the Sorting Ceremony upon their arrival (SS 7:114). The hat is a raggedy, black, pointed hat that talks through a slit near the brim which opens like a mouth. During the ceremony the hat sings a song relating character traits of students in each of the four houses of Gryffindor, Hufflepuff, Ravenclaw, and Slytherin. Each first-year student's name is called alphabetically, and he or she sits atop a three-legged stool while the hat sits atop the student's head. The hat then announces to the whole school which house the student will go into, and the student jumps off and joins that house's table (SS 7:117–22).

When Harry gets sorted, the hat takes awhile to decide his house. It speaks to Harry with a small voice in his ear, unable to decide, but Harry thinks very hard and asks not to be put in Slytherin. The hat asks if he is sure, because Harry has the capacity to do great things, and Slytherin House would help him achieve greatness. Finally, the hat relents and places him into Gryffindor House.

Harry sees the hat again in Prof. Dumbledore's office (CS 12:205). It becomes clear from the new Sorting Hat Song in Year 4 that the hat once belonged to Godric Gryffindor (GF 12:177). There is a new song every year (GF 12:178). In fifth year, the song advises that all of the student houses need to work together (OP 11:204–7).

Spattergroit. *Magical malady.* A medieval wizard hollers out to Ron at St. Mungo's that he must have this affliction of the skin, but he is referring to Ron's freckles (OP 23:508).

Special Award for Services to the School. *Magical award.* Tom Riddle received this award fifty years ago. Ron spits slugs on the award and then has to polish it during his detention with Argus Filch in Year 2 (CS 7:121). Harry and Ron both receive this award from Dumbledore after solving the mystery of the Chamber of Secrets (CS 18:331).

"Special Effects" Sweets. *Magical candy.* A line of candy sold at Honeydukes. It includes Droobles Best Blowing Gum, Toothflossing Stringmints, Pepper Imps, Ice Mice, toad-shaped peppermint creams, sugar quills, and Exploding Bonbons (PA 10:197).

"Specialis Revelio!" *Incantation*. This incantation makes an object reveal any spells that were put on it; it does not work, however, when Hermione tries it on Harry's Potions textbook (HBP 9:193).

Spectrespecs. *Magical object*. Spectrespecs come free in an issue of *The Quibbler*. Luna Lovegood wears them in Harry's cabin on the Hogwarts Express in Year 6. They make her eyes look large and owlish (HBP 7:137–38).

Spell-Checking quills. *Magical objects*. Spell-Checking quills are sold at Weasleys' Wizard Wheezes (HBP 6:117).

Spellman's Syllabary. *Magical book*. Hermione reads this book (OP 26:575). She seems to carry it in her bag (HBP 24:517).

Spellotape. *Muggle office supply*. This is the British term for what Americans commonly call Scotch tape (CS 5:95).

S.P.E.W. *Magical society*. Society for the Promotion of Elfish Welfare. Hermione founds this student organization when she becomes aware that house-elves serve at Hogwarts. The slogan she once thought of using was "Stop the Outrageous Abuse of Our Fellow Magical Creatures and Campaign for a Change in Their Legal Status" (GF 14:224). Hermione makes Harry secretary and Ron treasurer. She charges 2 Sickles to join, which pays for the badge and the leaflets she hopes to distribute (GF 14:225). Hermione runs into trouble getting others to join. Hagrid refuses, saying that it would be unkind of them to free the house-elves (GF 16:265). Though readers hear less about her cause, Hermione has apparently not given up on it entirely at the time of the Order of the Phoenix's reorganization (OP 4:76). When Ron says he feels like a house-elf from cleaning Grimmauld Place for so long, Hermione suggests that he might want to spend more time with S.P.E.W. (OP 9:159).

See also Race; Slavery

Sphinx. *Magical creature*. From *Fantastic Beasts*. Classified 4X by the MM. A mythological creature with the head of a woman and the body of a lion; found in Egypt. The Sphinx enjoys puzzles (FB 39). Harry encounters a Sphinx in the maze during the third task of the Triwizard Tournament. He solves the Sphinx's riddle with the word "spider" (GF 31:628–29).

See also Fantastic Beasts and Where to Find Them

Sphinx in front of the Pyramid at Giza. Harry encounters a sphinx in the maze of the Triwizard Tournament. Bill Weasley works as a curse breaker in Egypt for Gringotts Wizarding Bank. Courtesy of Getty Images/PhotoDisc.

Sphinx's Riddle. Harry solves the riddle with the word "spider" (GF 31:629). The legendary Riddle of the Sphinx (different from the one Harry solves) is: "What goes on four feet, on two feet, on three, / But the more feet it goes on the weaker it be?" Another wording of this same riddle is: "What has four legs in the morning, three in the afternoon, and two in the evening?" The answer to this most famous riddle of the Sphinx is "man." In mythology, the famous riddle is solved by Oedipus.

Spiders. Spiders are first mentioned as being something Harry does not fear; he saw them all the time in his days living in the cupboard under the stairs at the Dursleys. They resurface in a major way in *Chamber of Secrets*. First, Harry and his friends notice many tiny spiders climbing out of a window. Ron mentions that he does not like the way living spiders move, and Hermione thinks this is funny. He goes on to tell her that his brother Fred once turned his teddy bear into a big, hairy spider after he broke his toy broomstick. Hermione tries not to laugh (CS 9:154). When Hagrid is led off to Azkaban in Year 2, he hints to Harry and Ron that they should follow the spiders to help solve some of the mysteries of that year (CS 14:264).

See also Acromantula; Aragog; Mosag

Spies/spying. There are a few spies in the series, but most often readers hear about those who turn out to work for Voldemort against their will (PA 10:204). Draco Malfoy clearly keeps his father (a Death Eater) informed of the goings-on at Hogwarts. Prof. Quirrell ends up being more than a spy; his head is shared by the grotesque face of Voldemort. Argus Filch appears to spy on all of the students at Hogwarts, but for what reason no one is quite sure. One of the big questions left unresolved by *Half-Blood Prince* is whether or not Severus Snape is a spy or perhaps a double agent.

Peter Pettigrew has been a spy for Voldemort all along, posing as Scabbers the rat (PA 19:369). Sirius Black and Remus Lupin apparently mistook one another for spies when the Potters were killed (PA 19:373). Sirius indicates that Pettigrew was spying for Voldemort for a year before he sold out the Potters (PA 19:374). Once the series is complete, readers will no doubt enjoy rereading the books to watch the spies' actions that they missed before.

Spine of lionfish. *Magical substance.* While Harry is at the World Cup, Mrs. Weasley buys more spine of lionfish for his potions kit (GF 10:155).

Spinner's End. Death Eaters Bellatrix Lestrange and Narcissa Black Malfoy go to speak with Snape at the abandoned house on Spinner's End. It is one of several abandoned brick houses in a mill town (HBP 2:21). Spiders, spinning, and knitting may be important motifs in the story, but their significance, if any, are not clear through Book 6.

Spinnet, Alicia. *Character.* The Gryffindor Chaser in Harry's first Quidditch match (SS 11:189). She is two years above Harry (CS 7:107) and is nearly asleep at Oliver Wood's pre-dawn practice in Year 2. She angrily asks Malfoy how he dares call Hermione a Mudblood (CS 7:112). She asks Wood to request an inquiry when she sees the bewitched Bludger attacking Harry in a match in Year 2 (CS 10:170). Snape says that Alicia Spinnet must have had a Hair-Thickening Charm placed on her when her eyebrows grow so thick and long that she cannot see. Fourteen witnesses tell him that Miles Bletchley, Slytherin Keeper, put a jinx on Alicia in the library (OP 19:400).

Splinching. *Magical error.* When one does not Apparate correctly, half of the body is left behind, and this is called splinching (GF 6:67). Instructor Wilkie Twycross explains to Harry's class that this happens when the person is not determined enough (HBP 18:385).

Sprout, Prof. Pomona. *Character.* Herbology teacher (SS 8:133). She is the Head of Hufflepuff House. Her first name is not given in the series but was released by Rowling in a set of collector's cards. Sprout's name suits the class she teaches since she works with plants all day in the greenhouses at Hogwarts. Her work is not limited to being an instructor for the students; she also tends to the magical plants needed for potions and cures at the school.

S.P.U.G. *See* Society for the Protection of Ugly Goblins (S.P.U.G.)

Squib. *Kind of character.* A person born into a wizard family who shows no magical abilities at all. Argus Filch is a Squib, and Neville Longbottom fears he is nearly one (CS 11:185). Squibs are rare (CS 9:145). Mrs. Figg is a Squib, though Harry did not know she was from the wizarding world at all while he was growing up on Privet Drive. Squibs can see Dementors, as Mrs. Figg informs the Wizengamot at Harry's expulsion hearing (OP 8:143).

Squid, Giant. *Magical creature.* The creature lives in the Hogwarts lake, and students like to watch it float across when they are outside relaxing (PA 16:314).

Stag. This is the form of Harry's Patronus that drives away the hundred Dementors at Hogwarts lake. Harry initially thinks the Patronus is his father since it is a stag, but he later explains to Hermione that it was he himself who conjured the highly technical and powerful spell to defeat the Dementors (PA 21:411–12).

The Standard Book of Spells, Grade 1. *Magical book.* A book by Miranda Goshawk. First-year textbook (SS 5:66).

The Standard Book of Spells, Grade 2. *Magical book.* A book by Miranda Goshawk. Second-year textbook (CS 4:43).

The Standard Book of Spells, Grade 4. *Magical book.* A book by Miranda Goshawk. Fourth-year textbook. Hermione reads it at the Burrow in the last days of summer before Year 4 at Hogwarts (GF 10:152) and she continues reading on the Hogwarts Express (GF 11:167).

The Standard Book of Spells, Grade 5. *Magical book.* A book by Miranda Goshawk. Fifth-year textbook. Harry mentions at Grimmauld Place that this book and one other book are the only two new textbooks needed that year (OP 9:160).

The Standard Book of Spells, Grade 6. *Magical book.* Prof. Snape says that Hermione nearly quotes this book word-for-word when she answers his question about nonverbal spells (HBP 9:178–79).

Starfish and Stick. *Magical sports play.* From QA. A defensive move for Keepers; it involves hanging from the broom by one hand and foot and keeping the other arm and leg outstretched so that as much of the Keeper's body hangs before the goals, blocking as much as possible. *Quidditch Through the Ages* notes that the Starfish Without Stick play should not be tried (QA 54). Rowling drew the illustration for this dangerous play in the book.

Start-of-Term Banquet. *Magical event.* The feast held in the Great Hall after the Sorting Hat Ceremony that begins the school year at Hogwarts (SS 8:136).

Statues. *Magical sculptures.* As might be expected, statues in the series do not always remain stationary and often have other magical qualities. Statues range from gargoyles outside gates and doorways at Hogwarts, to busts of wizards, to full-length statues and elaborate fountains containing many figures.

Harry hides behind a stone griffin the night the troll enters Hogwarts in Year 1; he does this so that he can remind Ron that Hermione does not know about the troll (SS 10:173). Stone boars guard the gates of Hogwarts. Gargoyle statues keep watch over both the staff room and Dumbledore's office. There is a magic passageway to Honeydukes from Hogwarts that may be reached by climbing into a hump on the back of a statue of a witch. Wilfred the Wistful is a statue located on the way to the Owlery; Mrs. Norris hides behind this statue while following Harry (OP 14:281). There is a bust of a medieval wizard located near the hallway to Dolores Umbridge's office at Hogwarts; the statue mumbles to itself (OP 32:738). The Fountain of Magical Brethren at the Ministry of Magic comes to life during the battle at the Hall of Prophecy when Dumbledore arrives via the fountain; he then uses it as a Portkey to transport Harry back to the safety of his office.

Statute of Secrecy. *Magical legislation.* Also known as the International Statute of Secrecy and the International Confederation of Warlocks' Statute of Secrecy. Mafalda Hopkirk cites Section 13 of this law in her letter to Harry about the Hover Charm that Dobby casts at Privet Drive (CS 2:21). Harry receives another letter from Mafalda regarding this statute after he conjures a Patronus to ward off the Dementors in Little Whinging (OP 2:21). Sirius Black thinks that there is a clause in the statute that allows magic to be performed in self-defense when one's life is in danger (OP 6:115). Prof. Lupin tells Sirius that this clause also applies to underage wizards (OP 7:123). Section 13 of this law is also cited for illegal use of magic at the Wizengamot court (OP 8:140). Dumbledore points out to the court that it is Clause 7 of the Decree that allows the practice of magic in self-defense when the wizard's life may be in danger (OP 8:148).

Stealth Sensoring Spells. *Magical spells.* Prof. Umbridge tells Harry she set these spells around her doors (OP 32:742).

Stebbins. *Character.* Hufflepuff student whom Snapes catches in the bushes with Fawcett after the Yule Ball (GF 23:426).

Stimpson, Patricia. *Character.* A student in Fred and George Weasley's year. She keeps fainting with anxiety the year they take their O.W.L.s (OP 12:226).

Stinging Hex. *Magical spell.* This spell stings its victim, putting a burn mark where it strikes (OP 24:534).

Stink pellets. *Magical objects.* Fred Weasley wants to buy more Stink pellets at Zonko's Joke Shop in Hogsmeade (PA 8:145). Argus Filch threatens the students with whipping for using Stink pellets after Dolores Umbridge takes charge of Hogwarts (OP 28:628). After Fred and George Weasley leave Hogwarts, many students set these off in an effort to cause more havoc for Umbridge (OP 30:677).

Stinksap. *Magical substance.* Stinksap squirts out of Neville Longbottom's *Mimbulus mibletonia* plant; it is green and slimy and smells like manure. Though it is definitely foul, it is not poisonous (OP 10:187).

Stitches. The trainee Healer at St. Mungo's, Augustus Pye, conspires with Arthur Weasley to try using this Muggle remedy on his snake bite, but it does not work well. Molly Weasley is incredulous that the method involves sewing the skin back together (OP 23:506–7).

Stitchstock. *Magical game.* From QA. The ancient German flying broom game involving an inflated dragon bladder; it fell out of favor by the fourteenth century. The game is recorded in an 1105 painting, *Günther der Gewalttätige ist der Gewinner* ("Gunther the Violent Is the Winner") (QA 4).

Stoatshead Hill. *Magical place.* Location of the Portkey near the Burrow, outside of Ottery St. Catchpole (GF 6:70).

Stonewall High. *Muggle place.* The public high school Harry Potter would have attended had he not gone to Hogwarts (SS 3:32).

Stonewall Stormers. *Magical sports team.* From QA. Quidditch team from Canada (QA 43).

Stooging. *Magical game penalty.* Only one Chaser is allowed in the scoring area at a time. This penalty occurs if more than one player enters the scoring area (QA 30).

Stouffer, Nancy.. *See* Lawsuits

Streeler. *Magical creature.* From *Fantastic Beasts*. Classified 3X by the MM. The Streeler is a giant snail that leaves a poisonous trail in its path (FB 40).
  See also Fantastic Beasts and Where to Find Them

Strengthening Solution. *Magical substance.* A potion made in Potions class (OP 15:309). One of its ingredients is salamander blood; Hermione reminds Harry about this as she takes away the pomegranate juice he was about to use (OP 17:363). Harry still concocts it wrong, and Snape takes out his anger over Dolores Umbridge's evaluation of him by making Harry write an essay about how the potion should be made (OP 17:364).

Stretching Jinxes. *Magical spell.* In Book 6, Mrs. Weasley says that Harry and Ron look as though they have had Stretching Jinxes put on them because they have grown so much (HBP 5:83).

Strout, Miriam (Healer). *Character.* A nurse (Healer) at St. Mungo's Hospital. She delivers a plant to Broderick Bode that she thinks is a Flitterbloom, but it turns out to be a Devil's Snare that kills him (OP 25:546).

Stubbs, Billy. *Character.* One of the orphan children at the orphanage where Tom Riddle lived as a boy (HBP 13:264). Tom Riddle hung Billy Stubbs's rabbit as a child (HBP 13:267).

A *Study of Recent Developments in Wizardry*. *Magical book.* Harry and friends go searching for information about Nicolas Flamel in this book (SS 12:198; SS 13:220).

Stump, Grogan. *Character.* From *Fantastic Beasts*. Minister of Magic in 1811. He began the three divisions in the Department for the Regulation and Control of Magical Creatures: Beast, Being, and Spirit Divisions (FB xii).

Stunners. *Magical weapon.* Amos Diggory says that his Stunner, along with others', went through trees and must have worked on some of the intruders at the World Cup (GF 9:131). Ron uses a Stunner in the escape from the Inquisitorial Squad (OP 33:760).

Stunning Charm. *Magical spell.* The incantation is "Stupefy!" The charm stuns the victim, making him or her fall to the ground. Hagrid and several other wizards put this spell on the dragons who are at Hogwarts for the Triwizard Tournament (GF 19:326). Sirius tells Harry that one wizard would not be enough to do this; at least half a dozen are required (GF 19:334). Harry and others see someone attempt to Stun Hagrid at his hut the night of Harry's Astronomy practical O.W.L. (OP 31:720).

"Stupefy!" *Incantation.* The incantation for the Stunning Charm. About twenty witches and wizards yell this incantation into the air over Harry's head to try to stop the Death Eaters after the World Cup (GF 9:129).

Substantive Charm. *Magical spell.* Seamus Finnigan studies the definition of the Substantive Charm in preparing for O.W.L.s (OP 31:710).

Sugar quills. *Magical object.* Pens that taste like sugar on the end. They are sold at Honeydukes. Students tasting the ends of the quills during school look like they are thinking hard (PA 5:77). There are extra large ones in Honeydukes when Harry and friends go to Hogsmeade in Year 6 (HBP 12:244).

Sumbawanga Sunrays. *Magical sports team.* From QA. Quidditch team from Tanzania, Africa (QA 43).

Summerby. *Character.* Hufflepuff Seeker (OP 26:575).

Summoning Charm. *Magical spell.* Hermione studies this charm in a textbook on the way to Hogwarts (GF 11:167). After Mad-Eye Moody speaks to Harry about the first task of the Triwizard Tournament, he asks Hermione to train Harry on this charm (GF 20:345). Harry practices on a dictionary, books, quills, chairs, old Gobstones, and Neville's toad Trevor (GF 20:346). Madam Modesty Rabnott of Kent uses a Summoning

Charm to get hold of the living Snidget bird in a thirteenth-century game of Quidditch so that she can run off and set it free (QA 13).

"Sunny Jim." *Magical name.* A gargoyle calls Harry "Sunny Jim" (OP 17:357).

Surrey. Number Four, Privet Drive, Little Whinging, is located in Surrey (SS 3:34).

Sweden. The summer after Year 5, Luna Lovegood's family plans to go to Sweden to try to catch a Crumple-Horned Snorkack (OP 38:848). Sweden was the location of the annual broom race, an early flying broom game (QA 3).
See also Annual broom race

Swedish Short-Snout. *Magical creature.* The Swedish Short-Snout is one of the many dragons that comes to Hogwarts for the Triwizard Tournament; it is blue-gray in color (GF 19:327). This is the breed that Cedric Diggory chooses to get past for the first task of the Triwizard Tournament (GF 20:350). It is not considered as dangerous to human beings as many other varieties, but this may be because it lives in the mountains, away from most human life (FB 14). The silver trophy of the ancient Swedish flying broom game was shaped like a Swedish Short-Snout and given to the fastest survivor who flew 300 miles through the dragons' territory (QA 4).

Sweetwater All-Stars. *Magical sports team.* From QA. A professional Quidditch team from Texas (QA 45).
See also Americans; *Quidditch Through the Ages*

Swelling Solution. *Magical substance.* Swelling Solution makes parts of the body, such as the nose, expand. Harry's solution is too thin when he tries to concoct it in Potions class. Gregory Goyle's potion gets all over everyone when Harry tosses a Filibuster Firework in his cauldron (CS 11:186).

Swiftstick. *Magical object.* From QA. A racing broom manufactured by Ellerby and Spudmore in 1952. It is faster than their previous model, the Tinderblast, but loses acceleration on rising, so it is not used in professional Quidditch (QA 50).

"Swish and Flick." *Magical movement.* Prof. Flitwick tries to teach Harry and the other first-years how to use their wands by having them focus on these movements (SS 10:171).

Switching Spells. *Magical spells.* Hermione discourages Harry from going to the Wizards Duel with Draco Malfoy because he will lose the house points she gained from knowing Switching Spells in Prof. McGonagall's class (SS 9:155). Hermione discusses Switching Spells for dealing with the first task of the Triwizard Tournament (GF 20:338). Harry forgets the definition of these spells in his theoretical Transfiguration O.W.L. (OP 31:714).

Swivenhodge. *Magical game.* From QA. Another ancient British broomstick game. It started in Herefordshire. It was something like tennis; players used broomsticks to bat an inflated pig's bladder back and forth across a hedge (QA 6).

Sykes, Jocunda. *Character.* From QA. Jocunda Sykes made the first Atlantic crossing on a broomstick in 1935 (QA 48).

· T ·

Tapestry. *Magical object.* There is a secret passageway behind the tapestry that leads to the Charms corridor (SS 9:158). Gryffindor students must pass through a door behind another tapestry on their way to the staircase to their tower (GF 12:190).

See also Black Family Tapestry

"Tapeworm." *Magic word.* Password to Gryffindor Tower, Year 6 (HBP 23:493).

"Tarantallegra!" *Incantation.* This charm makes one's legs jerk around like a tarantula. Draco Malfoy performs this charm on Harry during Dueling Club lessons (CS 11:192). The incantation appears to be a combination of "tarantula" and "leg."

Tarapoto Tree-Skimmers. *Magical sports team.* From QA. Professional Quidditch team from Peru (QA 46).

Tawny owl. *Magical creature.* The owl sent from Hagrid to deliver Harry's card and present for his thirteenth birthday (PA 1:7).

Tchamba Charmers. *Magical sports team.* From QA. Quidditch team from Togo, Africa (QA 43).

Tebo. *Magical creature.* From *Fantastic Beasts*. Classified 4X by the MM. The Tebo is a warthog that can become invisible. It is valuable to wizards for its hide, which can be made into shields and clothing (FB 40).

See also Fantastic Beasts and Where to Find Them

Ted. *Character.* A news anchor on the Muggle evening news. Mr. Dursley watches Ted the night Harry Potter arrives on his doorstep. Ted reports the unusual occurrence of hundreds of owls flying in all directions across Britain in the daytime (SS 1:6).

Tents. *See* Camping, Wizard

"Tergeo!" *Incantation. Tergeo* is Latin for "to clean." Hermione uses the incantation to clean the blood off Harry after Draco Malfoy steps on his nose on the train (HBP 8:162).

Theories of Transfiguration. *Magical book.* Dumbledore mentions that he accidentally doodled in this library book. He soon found the book hitting him over the head, presumably from a jinx that Madam Pince put on it (QA viii).

Thestrals. *Magical creatures.* Winged horses that are invisible except to those who have witnessed death; this makes them seem unlucky to wizards. Thestrals are very rare (FB 42).

Harry begins seeing the thestrals that pull the Hogwarts carriages in Year 5, after he has witnessed the death of Cedric Diggory in Year 4. Luna Lovegood can also see them (OP 10:196–99). Harry also sees them several times flying out of the Forbidden Forest before he is told what they are (OP 14:282). Hagrid tells Harry and friends that he has the only domestic herd in Britain. He is saving them to bring to class one day before O.W.L.s (OP 20:439). Thestrals like to live in dark places (OP 21:443). They make a loud cry, have a face something like a dragon, and a black body with wings and a long tail. Their eyes are white. When Hagrid shows one to his class, it is eating a cow (OP 21:444–45). Luna remembers Hagrid's lesson that they are good at finding places their riders want to go, so she suggests they use them to get to the Department of Mysteries at the Ministry (OP 33:762).

Thickey, Janus. *Character.* A wizard who falsely claimed to have been attacked by a Lethifold when he had really taken off to live with the landlady of the Green Dragon Inn (FB 27). There is a Janus Thickey residential ward at St. Mungo's that is for patients suffering with permanent spell damage; Gilderoy Lockhart lives there, as do Neville Longbottom's parents (OP 23:510–14).

See also Fantastic Beasts and Where to Find Them; Lethifold

Thief's Curse. *Magical spell.* Prof. Dumbledore informs readers that *Fantastic Beasts and Where to Find Them* has been protected by this curse, so they should not be tempted to steal it and deny Comic Relief, U.K. its rightful and needed donation (FB viii).

Thomas, Dean. *Character.* A student in Harry's year who is sorted into Gryffindor (SS 7:122). He shares a dormitory with Harry and Ron. During their first year Ron is always poking at Dean's Muggle poster of the West Ham soccer team to see if the players will move (SS 9:144). Dean Thomas is among those who congratulate Ron and Harry for their brilliant entrance to Hogwarts in the Ford Anglia in Year 2 (CS 5:85). He is good at forgeries and offers to sign Uncle Vernon Dursley's name on the release form for Harry to go to Hogsmeade (PA 8:151). Dean is with Seamus Finnigan at the Irish campsite outside the Quidditch World Cup playing field when they see Harry and friends (GF 7:82). His parents are Muggles, so they do not read the lies printed about Harry in the *Daily Prophet* (OP 11:219). In Book 5, Ginny Weasley tells Harry and friends that she has chosen to go out with Dean (OP 38:866).

Thompson, Emma. *See* Films

A *Thousand Magical Herbs and Fungi*. *Magical book.* Ron returns this book to Harry (HBP 25:539). It is named earlier in the series as *One Thousand Magical Herbs and Fungi*.

Three Broomsticks. A pub in Hogsmeade where butterbeer is sold (PA 8:158). When Harry goes there in disguise, he and his friends see several Hogwarts faculty members order drinks. Prof. McGonagall has a small gillywater; Hagrid orders four pints of mulled mead; Prof. Flitwick has a cherry syrup and soda with ice and an umbrella; and Cornelius Fudge orders red currant rum (PA 10:202).

Thundelarra Thunderers. *Magical sports team.* From QA. Quidditch team from Australia (QA 42).

Tiara. *Magical object.* Harry hides the Potions book belonging to the Half-Blood Prince in the Room of Requirement. He puts it in a cabinet on which he places a bust with a wig and a tarnished tiara so that he can find it again when he returns (HBP 24:527). When Fleur Delacour proves she still wants to marry Bill Weasley after he has suffered the bites from Greyback, Mrs. Weasley tells her about a beautiful, goblin-made tiara owned by their Great-Auntie Muriel that would look lovely in her hair on her wedding day (HBP 29:623). Some readers awaiting Book 7 pondered whether the tiara might be a Ravenclaw Horcrux.

Tiberius, Uncle. *Character.* Cormac McLaggen's uncle who hunted Nogtails in Norfolk with Cormac, Bertie Higgs, and Rufus Scrimgeour (HBP 7:144–45).

Tickling Charm. *Magical spell.* The incantation for this spell is "*Rictusempra!*" Harry hits Malfoy with the spell during Dueling Club lessons (CS 11:192).

Time Room. *Magical place.* A room in the Department of Mysteries at the Ministry of Magic (OP 35:795).

Time-Turner. *Magical object.* The Ministry of Magic grants Hermione use of the Time-Turner in Year 3 at Prof. McGonagall's recommendation; Hermione needs the Time-Turner because she wants to take classes that meet at the same time. She uses it with Harry to alter the events that will allow Sirius Black to escape and Buckbeak to avoid execution. The Time-Turner is a tiny hourglass on a chain that she wears about her neck, and Hermione turns an indicated number of times. Dumbledore tells her that three turns should be enough to go back in time and save Sirius Black and Buckbeak (PA 21:394–95). Changing time is breaking one of the most important wizard laws; in order for no harm to come of it, those who are traveling through time must not be seen (PA 21:398). There are several Time-Turners in a cabinet in the Time Room at the Department of Mysteries (OP 35:794–95); Hermione tells Hagrid that they were all destroyed during the battle at the Hall of Prophecy (HBP 11:231).

Timeline of the series. Whether or not Rowling intended for the events of the series to be rigidly tied to any external or internal timeline remains unclear. However, close readers quickly began trying to figure out dates and years as early as the publication of *Chamber of Secrets* when Nearly Headless Nick celebrates his 500th Death Day Party. Nick's cake in the shape of a tombstone informs readers that he died on Halloween in

1492, placing the night of the party at October 31, 1992 (CS 8:133). This date has been used as a cornerstone from which further dates before and afterward have been extrapolated. For example, Harry's birthday is July 31 (the same as Rowling's), and he had just turned eleven when he was invited to Hogwarts. This would make him twelve in the second book when he attends Nick's party. Extrapolating backward twelve years, Harry's date of birth would be July 31, 1980. Close readers and fans have found discrepancies in the timelines they have drawn up, making it uncertain whether adhering to a timeline is important to Rowling as a writer of fiction.

Two elements tied to time that do seem important are the connections to Dumbledore defeating the evil wizard Grindelwald in 1945 (about the same time as the end of World War II) and the generational shifts of characters at Hogwarts. There has to be enough time for former students to mature, marry, and have children who take their places in the classrooms at the school. The current generation of students has parents who knew each other as students, and these had ancestors who knew each other as well. In the Pensieve Harry sees visions of past events among other generations through both Dumbledore's and Prof. Snape's memories. Parallels through time among the generations are also evident, such as the antagonism between Lucius Malfoy and James Potter and their sons Draco Malfoy and Harry Potter.

Though there are discrepancies in the timeline, much of it does work out. This suggests that it may be one detail Rowling will resolve should she ever revise the entire series when all the books are published.

See also Death Day Party

Timms, Agatha. *Character.* Agatha Timms bets half the shares of her eel farm against Ludo Bagman that the World Cup match will last a week (GF 7:88).

Tinderblast. *Magical object.* From QA. A racing broom manufactured in 1940 by Ellerby and Spudmore (QA 50).

"Tiptoe Through the Tulips." Uncle Vernon Dursley manically sings this song while he boards up the house so that no more letters can come for Harry from Hogwarts (SS 3:40).

"Toffee éclairs." *Magic words.* The password into Dumbledore's office in Year 6 (HBP 23:493).

Tofty, Prof. *Character.* Prof. Tofty is one of the ancient O.W.L. examiners. He administers Harry's practical Charms O.W.L. exam. Harry thinks he looks like the oldest of all the examiners; he is bald. He recognizes Harry's famous name (OP 31:713). Tofty takes Harry out of his History of Magic O.W.L. when he falls out of his chair after a Voldemort vision. Tofty thinks Harry fainted due to nerves over the exams (OP 32:729).

Tolkien, J.R.R. (1892–1973). The British author and linguistic scholar best known for his *Lord of the Rings* fantasy trilogy. John Ronald Reuel Tolkien was a professor of Old English at Oxford University. He published his trilogy in the 1950s and they enjoyed a resurgence and cult following in the 1960s, particularly among those who had become newly conscious and proactive about saving the environment. Some observers compare

British author J.R.R. Tolkien (1892–1973). J. K. Rowling's series has occasionally been compared to Tolkien's *Lord of the Rings* trilogy, which she read in college. Most readers observe, however, that Tolkien's fantasy world is more complex. Courtesy of the Library of Congress.

Rowling's fantasy series to Tolkien's. Obvious connections are that both authors are British, wrote fantasies in a series of books, have an interest in language, and use initials in their pen names.

Rowling has admitted reading the *Lord of the Rings* books when she was in college. In an online chat in March 2001 hosted by the BBC, she said she thinks she was about twenty when she read them and liked them a great deal back then. However, she has not reread the series, which, she said, is a telling detail for her. She tends to reread books several times when she particularly enjoys them. Tolkien invented a world, language, and a mythology in his books, which Rowling admits is quite different from what she is trying to do. She has called his books "an incredible achievement." In an interview in 2000 with Scholastic, she said that she read *The Hobbit* only after the first Potter book was written. She called comparisons between her work and Tolkien's "superficial."

Further Reading: "About the Books: Transcript of J. K. Rowling's Live Interview." Scholastic.com, October 16, 2000; Red Nose Day Chat, BBC Online, March 12, 2001.

Tom. *Character.* The bartender and innkeeper at the Leaky Cauldron (SS 5:68–69). Tom takes care of Harry, giving him room and board after Cornelius Fudge makes arrangements for Harry to spend the last two weeks of his summer vacation at the Leaky Cauldron (PA 3:42–47).

***Tom Brown's Schooldays* (Hughes).** Along with the genres of mystery/detective series and fantasy, the Harry Potter books fall into another genre popular in children's books, and that is the genre of the school story. Rowling was not the first author to set her plot at a boarding school with student houses and competitions. The earliest known example of the developed school story is *Tom Brown's Schooldays* by Thomas Hughes, which was first published in England in 1857.

Similarities between this novel and Harry Potter include a boy protagonist enrolled at boarding school; a kindly headmaster who takes him under his wing; some questionable teachers with controversial tactics; school bullies; sports matches and championship tournaments; and experiences through which the boy discovers much about himself. In his *New York Times Book Review* article about *Goblet of Fire* in 2000, Stephen King wrote,

"The Harry Potter series is a supernatural version of *Tom Brown's Schooldays*, updated and given a hip this-is-how-kids-really-are shine."

Further Reading: Hughes, Thomas. *Tom Brown's Schooldays* (1857). Oxford: Oxford University Press, 1999; King, Stephen. "Wild about Harry: The Fourth Novel in J. K. Rowling's Fantastically Successful Series about a Young Wizard." *New York Times Book Review*, July 23, 2000: 13–14.

Ton-Tongue Toffee. *Magical candy.* One of Fred and George Weasley's inventions. They had been looking for someone to test it on all summer. Dudley Dursley eats a piece of the toffee, which causes his tongue to grow to a foot long before the Weasley brothers leave the house using Floo Powder (GF 5:51). Dudley's tongue grows to four feet long before the Dursleys allow Mr. Weasley to work magic on it to shrink it back to its normal size (GF 5:53).

Tonks, Andromeda Black. *Character.* Sister to Bellatrix Black Lestrange and Narcissa Black Malfoy. Andromeda married Muggle Ted Tonks and so was disowned by the Black family. She is Nymphadora Tonks's mother and Sirius Black's favorite cousin. Her name was burned out of the Black Family Tree Tapestry (OP 6:113).

Tonks, Nymphadora. *Character.* A member of the Order of the Phoenix. She prefers to go by the name Tonks because she does not approve of the first name her mother gave her. She has purple hair when Harry first meets her. Tonks is a Metamorphmagus, which means she can change her appearance whenever she desires; it is a trait she was born with, and it is a rare ability. At the party to celebrate Ron and Hermione becoming prefects, Tonks changes her hair so that it is long and red, and she looks as though she could be Ginney Weasley's sister (OP 9:170). She changes into an old woman with gray hair and a purple hat to escort Harry and the Weasleys to the train (OP 10:181).

Tonks is an Auror, and she tells Harry that she received top grades in Concealment and Disguise in Auror training. Because Harry is interested in a career as an Auror himself, he is fascinated with Tonks. She seems a bit younger in age, or at least in attitude, than the other members of the Order. She has just passed her qualifications to be an Auror a year before Harry meets her and tells him that she nearly failed Stealth and Tracking because she is clumsy (OP 3:52). She envies Harry's Firebolt broomstick and says she still rides a Comet Two Sixty (OP 3:53). When Harry arrives at King's Cross at the end of Year 5, Tonks is there as a member of the Order to protect him, and she has bright bubble-gum–pink hair, patched jeans, and a purple Weird Sisters T-shirt (OP 38:867).

Tonks is at the Burrow in Year 6 when Harry and Dumbledore first arrive (HBP 5:81). She is part of the Order that joins the fight against Voldemort and the Death Eaters at the Hall of Prophecy (OP 35:801). Dumbledore tells Harry that she is expected to make a full recovery at St. Mungo's (OP 37:822).

In the summer before Year 6, Tonks is unhappy partly because Sirius Black is dead, but in particular because she did not save him from Bellatrix Lestrange. Hermione says that Tonks has survivor's guilt and is having trouble with Metamorphosing (HBP 5:94–95). Tonks is in love with Remus Lupin, who has been telling her that he is not whole and that he is too poor and too old for her. When Fleur Delacour demonstrates her love for Bill Weasley after he is attacked, there seems to be new hope for Tonks and Lupin (HBP 29:624).

Tonks, Ted. *Character.* A Muggle who married Andromeda Black, thus removing her from the pureblood-obsessed Black family and causing her name to be removed from the family tapestry at Grimmauld Place. Their daughter is Nymphadora Tonks, a member of the Order of the Phoenix. His wife was Sirius Black's favorite cousin (OP 6:113).

See also Black Family Tapestry

Toothflossing Stringmints. *Magical sweet.* A treat from Honeydukes (PA 10:190). They are something like flavored toothpicks (PA 10:197).

Towler, Kenneth. *Character.* A student in Fred and George Weasleys' year. He broke out in boils, not from anxiety over O.W.L.s as Fred first recalls, but from the Bulbadox Powder in his pajamas that George remembers Fred putting there (OP 12:226).

Toyohashi Tengu. *Magical sports team.* From QA. A professional Quidditch team from Japan (QA 46).

Transfiguration. *Class at Hogwarts.* Taught by Prof. Minerva McGonagall, this is the magical skill of turning one thing into another, such as turning a cup into a mouse. Prof. McGonagall describes the skill to Harry's first-year class as one of the most difficult and dangerous (SS 8:134). For one exam in the subject, the students had to transform a teapot into a tortoise (PA 16:317). Hermione does well in the subject; Prof. McGonagall says she is the only one by Year 4 who can turn a hedgehog into a pincushion (GF 15:233). Hermione laments that they will not learn human Transfiguration until sixth year, so she cannot use it to help Harry with the Triwizard Tournament (GF 26:482).

Transfiguration Today. *Magical magazine.* During his two weeks at the Leaky Cauldron, Harry watches old and wise wizards discuss articles from this magazine while he eats his breakfast (PA 4:49).

Transfiguration Torture. *Magical curse.* Gilderoy Lockhart claims to have seen Transfiguration Torture used often. If he had been at the scene when Mrs. Norris was petrified, he claims he could have counteracted it (CS 9:141).

Translations. According to a BBC article that was published at the release of *Half-Blood Prince* in July 2005, the Harry Potter books have sold more than 265 million copies in 200 countries and have been translated into 62 languages. Languages include French, German, and Spanish, and also Indonesian, Portuguese, and Norwegian. There are editions in Latin and ancient Greek, which Rowling finds particularly intriguing, and also Irish Gaelic. There are traditional Chinese translations; Japanese; Italian; Vietnamese; Urdu; Welsh; braille; and many more.

Converting Rowling's humor into different lanuages can be a particular challenge to translators, especially working with the many puns and wordplays she engages in with the English language. Occasionally Rowling's representatives take action against illegal translations, such as a Bengali translation in India in 2003 that was not authorized. While English readers may believe that a lot gets lost in translation of the Harry Potter series to other languages, the books sell well around the world in English, and they continue to do well when they appear in a country's mother tongue.

Transylvania. From QA. The Quidditch World Cup between Transylvania and Flanders was recorded as the most violent in history (QA 40).

Transylvanian Tackle. *Magical sports move.* From QA. The Transylvanian Tackle is when one player pretends to hit another in the nose. It was first witnessed at the 1473 World Cup, but it has rarely been seen since because it is difficult to execute while both players are flying quickly on broomsticks (QA 54).

Travels With Trolls. *Magical book.* A book by Gilderoy Lockhart. It is a second-year "textbook" (CS 4:44). Lockhart picks up Neville Longbottom's copy in the first Defense Against the Dark Arts class in Year 2 and shows the class his picture on the front as a way of introduction (CS 6:99). Harry absentmindedly walks over some loose pages from this book after his room has been ransacked for the Riddle diary (CS 14:252).

Travers. *Character.* Igor Karkaroff gives up Travers as a Death Eater in the hearing that is in Dumbledore's Pensieve. Travers was said to have aided in the killing of the McKinnons (GF 30:590).

Trelawney, Prof. Sibyll Patricia. *Character.* The teacher of Divination class. She is thin and wears thick glasses that make her eyes look huge. She also wears many beads and bangle bracelets (PA 6:102). She is the great-great-granddaughter of Cassandra Trelawney, who was a famous Seer (OP 15:314). Prof. Umbridge puts Prof. Trelawney on probation after sixteen years of service at Hogwarts (OP 17:366). Prof. Trelawney is eventually fired by Umbridge and becomes very upset because Hogwarts has become her home. Dumbledore confronts Umbridge calmly and informs her that he still has the power to say who may reside at Hogwarts, and he wishes for Prof. Trelawney to stay (OP 26:594–96).

Trevor. *Magical animal.* Trevor is Neville Longbottom's toad that he is always losing (SS 6:112). In Potions class Hermione helps Neville with his Shrinking Solution so that when Snape tests it on Trevor, the toad turns into a tadpole. Gryffindor loses five points because Hermione helped Neville (PA 7:128).

Trick wands. *Magical objects.* Weasleys' Wizard Wheezes contains barrels of these. The most expensive versions hit the unsuspecting user about the head and neck; the least expensive turn into rubber chickens or underwear when waved about (HBP 6:117).

Trip Jinx. *Magical spell.* Draco Malfoy puts this spell on Harry, making him stumble (OP 27:609).

Triwizard Cup. *Magical object.* The cup at the center of the maze in the third task of the Triwizard Tournament. It was bewitched to be a Portkey that transports both Harry and Cedric Diggory to a graveyard where Voldemort is waiting (GF 31:635–36).

Triwizard Tournament. *Magical event.* Begun seven hundred years ago, the tournament was designed to foster international relations among the three largest schools of witchcraft and wizardry in Europe; these include Hogwarts, Beauxbatons, and Durmstrang. Students who are of age to compete (seventeen or older) may enter their names on slips of paper into the Goblet of Fire. The goblet then selects one student from each school to enter the competition. These competitors are called "champions." The champions compete in accomplishing three sophisticated magical tasks over the duration of the school year. Though the tournament did encourage good relations among students from different countries, the deaths resulting from the tournament caused it to be discontinued in the past. The event was resurrected in Harry's fourth year because the Departments of International Magical Cooperation and Magical Games and Sports at the Ministry of Magic thought it was time to try offering the tournament again and worked hard all summer to make it a safe event for all. Three champions were hurt during a tournament in 1792 from cockatrice gone loose. This resulted in a new rule that one representative from each school be a judge (GF 15:238). The winner of the tournament is the one who gets the most points after all three tasks are accomplished. The winnings are 1,000 Galleons for the winner to use as he or she pleases, and the prestigious Triwizard Cup for the winning school (GF 12:187–88).

Beauxbatons and Durmstrang arrive at Hogwarts at 6:00 P.M. on October 30 (GF 15:235). The Goblet of Fire chooses Viktor Krum of Durmstrang, Fleur Delacour of Beauxbatons, and Cedric Diggory of Hogwarts as champions. It also chooses Harry Potter as fourth champion who will have to compete (GF 16:269–70). Because of their work for task preparation, champions do not have to sit for final exams in any of their subjects (GF 17:287). Champions are not supposed to ask for help with their tasks from teachers or classmates (GF 17:281), but cheating always happens anyway (GF 20:343). The wands of all of the champions are weighed before the first task.

The first task takes place on November 24 and is designed to test the champions' courage. They are to capture a golden egg and get past a dragon (GF 17:281). The second task is held at 9:30 A.M. on February 24 (GF 20:361). It involves swimming to the bottom of the lake at Hogwarts and rescuing one hostage held there by the Merpeople (GF 26). The third task takes place on June 24 at dusk, and the champions are not told what it is until one month before (GF 26:507). It is a hedge maze set up inside the Quidditch field. The first one to get to the center and touch the Triwizard Cup wins the task (GF 28:551). The hedge is twenty feet high (GF 31:620).

Harry gives his 1,000 Galleon winnings from the Triwizard Tournament to the Weasley twins to start up their joke shop (GF 37:733).

Troll. *Magical being.* From *Fantastic Beasts.* Classified 4X by the MM. A troll may be up to twelve feet tall and weigh over one ton. There are mountain, forest, and river trolls. Mountain trolls have gray skin, are bald, and are the most dangerous. Forest trolls have green skin and some hair. River trolls have purple skin, horns, and can be hairy. Trolls are ignorant creatures with tiny heads and brains. They carry clubs and wreak havoc wherever they go. In their shared copy of *Fantastic Beasts*, either Harry or Ron has sketched a troll's head next to this entry and written a note about it being a smelly Gregory Goyle (FB 40–41).

A troll is allowed into Hogwarts in Year 1 as part of Voldemort's diversionary tactics. Harry and Ron save Hermione from it, and they become friends forever after the incident when Hermione takes the blame for their all being in the girls' bathroom (SS 10:172). Newt Scamander claims that trolls are less intelligent than human beings or even unicorns and have no magical power; they are simply strong because of their size (FB x). Trolls are also mentioned in *A History of Magic* (FB xi).

See also Fantastic Beasts and Where to Find Them

Tropical birds. *Magical creatures.* Sirius Black sends messages to Harry in the summer before Year 4 using tropical birds instead of the customary owl; this indicates to Harry that Black is in hiding in an exotic place (GF 2:24).

See also Birds, birdlike, and flying creatures; Owls

Troublemakers-in-Chief. *Student role.* After Fred and George Weasley leave Hogwarts, several other students try to fill the role of Troublemakers-in-Chief (OP 30:677).

Troy. *Character.* Chaser on the Ireland National Quidditch Team in the World Cup (GF 8:105).

"Tuck in." *Words.* At Harry's fourth-year Start-of-Term Banquet, Dumbledore has only these two words to say before they eat (GF 12:180).

Turpin, Lisa. *Character.* A student in Harry's year; sorted into Ravenclaw (SS 7:122).

Tutshill, England. Rowling lived in Tutshill from the time she was about nine years old until she left for college. The small town is located in Gloucestershire on the border with Wales in the West Country of England, and is located near the Wye and Severn Rivers and the Forest of Dean. The area is known for its outstanding natural beauty. The closest town of any size where residents may do their shopping is Chepstow, Wales. At the time that Rowling lived there through her adolescence, she was dissatisfied with its slower, rural lifestyle and admired the quicker pace and forward thinking of the Londoners she read and heard about. Her parents, however, had been Londoners themselves and relished the opportunity to live in a more rural and natural setting.

See also Church Cottage; Forest of Dean

Tutshill Primary School of England. Before she went to high school, Rowling attended this school (formerly Tutshill Church of England Primary School) near her home after the family's move to the village. It was old-fashioned to the point that modern-day children might not understand. There were still old wooden desks with places for inkwells, and the seats were lined in rows. The school dates from the nineteenth century. Rowling has said it reminds her of something out of a Charles Dickens novel. When Rowling first attended, her teacher, Mrs. Sylvia Morgan, gave the class a quiz on fractions. When they got their papers back, the students were rearranged in rows. Rowling soon discovered that Mrs. Morgan had seated them by how much she thought they knew. Since she had never studied fractions before, Rowling was seated in the "dumb row." Once she learned them, the teacher moved her across the room to the "bright row." The move made her sit away from the first friends she had made at the school. Rowling has said that she patterned some of Prof. Snape's characteristics from her least favorite teachers. Perhaps some of the fear and discomfort she felt starting a new school in Mrs. Morgan's classroom poured itself into Snape.

In Year 10 Rowling had Mrs. Morgan's husband, John Morgan, as a teacher. While she feared he would be as strict as his wife, this proved not to be the case. The Morgans were well regarded in the community.

Tutshill Primary School still exists and has renovated its interior to make it more modern. Perhaps one of the influences Rowling's history has had on the school is that it emphasizes to students the value of charity. The school once sponsored class projects supporting Comic Relief, U.K., one of Rowling's charities of choice.

Tutshill Tornados. *Magical sports team.* The *Quibbler* reports that the Tutshill Tornados are winning the Quidditch League by devious means such as blackmail, torture, and tampering with brooms (OP 10:193). The team won the League Cup five years in a row in the early twentieth century (QA 37). They are named after the town where Rowling grew up.

See also Tutshill, England; Tutshill Primary School of England

"Tweak!" *Word.* One of the "few words" Professor Dumbledore speaks before the Start-of-Term Banquet in Harry's first year. The other few words are "Blubber!" "Nitwit!" and "Oddment!" (SS 7:123).

"Twenty-five Ways to Mingle With Muggles." *Fake headline.* Rita Skeeter says that Luna Lovegood's father must run a newspaper that runs headlines such as this (OP 25:568).

Twigger 90. *Magical object.* From QA. A racing broomstick first made in 1990 by Flyte and Barker to compete with the Nimbus company brooms. Since the Twigger 90 warps at high velocity, however, and has features no one needs, it has not succeeded in pushing Nimbus brooms out of the top spot. The Twigger 90 is regarded as more expensive than it is worth (QA 51).

See also Broomsticks

Twilfitt and Tatting's. *Magical place.* Another shop on Diagon Alley that sells clothing, including student robes for Hogwarts; it is a competitor to Madam Malkin's (HBP 6:114).

Twitchy Ears. *Magical malady.* Harry gets Twitchy Ears as a consequence of not dodging one of Mad-Eye Moody's hexes properly in DADA class (GF 28:547).

Two-Way Mirror. *Magical object.* Though he never unwrapped it in time, Harry was given a dirty, old, square-shaped mirror by Sirius Black to contact him if he ever needed him. A note on the back explains that Sirius has the other mirror; if Harry speaks Sirius's name into his mirror, then Harry will appear in Sirius's mirror and Sirius will be able to talk to him. Sirius and James Potter used the mirrors when they were in detention at the same time but in different rooms. Unfortunately, Harry opens the package only after Sirius has died. He tries to see if it will still work, hoping to reach Sirius as he grieves, but it does not (OP 38:857–58).

Twycross, Wilkie. *Character.* The Ministry Apparition instructor; he is whispy and transparent (HBP 18:382).

· U ·

U-No-Poo. *Magical substance*. When Harry and friends first go to Weasleys' Wizard Wheezes, they see a flashing sign in the window for this constipation-inducing joke product (HBP 6:116).

Ugga. *Character*. From QA. An older player on Goodwin Kneen's "Kwidditch" team who played the equivalent position of Beater (QA 9).
   See also Kneen, Goodwin

Ukrainian Ironbelly. *Magical creature*. From *Fantastic Beasts*. The breed of dragon that is the largest of all; it can weigh up to six tons. In 1799 it took off with an empty sailboat from the Black Sea (FB 14–15).

Umbridge, Prof. Dolores Jane. *Character*. The name is likely to be a play on the word "umbrage," which means "a feeling of being offended." To take umbrage is to take offense, and Dolores Umbridge's behavior is certainly offensive. She is Senior Undersecretary to the Minister and an Interrogator at Harry's expulsion hearing at the Wizengamot court (OP 8:139). She looks to Harry like a huge, pale toad with bulging eyes. She is short and broad with very little neck and a wide face. Harry is surprised that her voice is so high-pitched and girlish when she questions Dumbledore at his hearing (OP 8:146). She has curly brown hair that she sometimes wears pulled back in a hairband (OP 11:203). She becomes the fifth DADA teacher during Harry's time at Hogwarts and gives a very long, boring speech after Dumbledore introduces her at the Start-of-Term Banquet (OP 11:211–14).

When she is DADA teacher, her office desk and other surfaces are covered in lace doilies and vases of dried flowers. The walls are hung with decorative plates featuring kittens wearing bows of different colors (OP 13:265). Sirius Black tells Harry that Prof. Lupin really dislikes her because she wrote antiwerewolf legislation. Umbridge hates merpeople, werewolves, and other part-humans (OP 14:302). Hermione leads Umbridge into the Forbidden Forest as a ruse to escape her after she discovers

Dumbledore's Army. Umbridge insults the centaurs and gets driven away by Grawp (OP 33:158–59). Later, Dumbledore, who has earned the respect of the centaurs, retrieves her from the forest, though no one, including her, discusses how (OP 38:848). Umbridge attends Dumbledore's funeral, but her expression of grief appears less than genuine (HBP 30:642).

Umbridge-itis. *Make-believe illness.* Students get sick in class or do not come to class to protest Umbridge. Many students use the Weasley twins' Skiving Snackboxes to become sick (OP 30:678).

Umfraville, Quintius. *Character.* From QA. The author of *The Noble Sport of Warlocks*, written in 1620. The book features a diagram of a Quidditch pitch from the seventeenth century (QA 18–19).

Umgubular Slashkilter. *Magical object.* Something owned by Cornelius Fudge that Luna Lovegood is talking about when they run out of time for DADA class (OP 18:395).

Unbreakable Charm. *Magical spell.* The Firebolt broomstick has this feature which keeps it from breaking (PA 4:51). Hermione casts this charm on the jar in which she put Rita Skeeter in her beetle form (GF 37:728).

Unbreakable Vow. *Magical spell.* Narcissa Black Malfoy asks Prof. Snape to make an Unbreakable Vow with her. The vow requires him to protect Draco and do the deed Voldemort has asked Draco to do if Draco proves that he cannot carry it out. Making such a vow requires a witness whom wizards call the Bonder. A rope of fire goes around the hands of the wizard making the vow. The wizard must have his or her hand clasped with the one he or she is making the promise to. The Bonder casts another rope of fire around both of their hands to seal the vow (HBP 2:35–37). When Harry overhears Snape tell Draco that he made an Unbreakable Vow with his mother, Harry asks Ron about it. Ron tells him that the person who breaks this kind of vow will die. Fred and George tried to get Ron to make an Unbreakable Vow when they were small, but his father luckily stopped them in time (HBP 16:326).

Undetectable Poisons. *Magical substances.* Prof. Snape assigns an essay on Undetectable Poisons for Potions class (PA 12:244).

Unfogging the Future. *Magical book.* A book by Cassandra Vablatsky. It is Harry's Divination class textbook. The manager of Flourish and Blotts tells him it is a good book about basic techniques such as reading crystal balls, palms, and bird entrails (PA 4:53). Ron and Harry look through the book for examples of predictions to fake in their Divination homework (GF 14:222).

Unforgivable Curses. *Magical Dark Magic spells.* The three Unforgivable Curses are: Imperius, Cruciatus, and Avada Kedavra curses. They are illegal in the magical world and mean lifetime imprisonment in Azkaban if one is found guilty of casting them (GF 14:213–15). The Imperius Curse makes the victim do the caster's bidding; the Cruciatus Curse tortures the victim with pain; and the Avada Kedavra Curse is the Killing Curse.
See also "Avada Kedavra"; Cruciatus Curse; Imperius Curse

Unicorns. *Magical creatures.* From Latin, *unum cornu,* "one horn." From *Fantastic Beasts.* Classified 4X by the MM because of the respect the wizarding community gives them, not because they are dangerous. Mythical creatures, unicorns are beautiful white horses with horns on their heads, found in northern Europe. Their horns, blood, and hair have magical qualities (FB 41).

They live in the Forbidden Forest outside Hogwarts, but they are preyed upon in Book 1 by Voldemort. He is drinking their blood in an effort to come back to life. Harry sees Voldemort doing so during the boys' detention in the forest in Year 1 (SS 15:256). Prof. Grubbly-Plank teaches a lesson in unicorns in Care of Magical Creatures class when she substitutes for Hagrid. She encourages only the girls to work with the large white unicorn in the paddock because she says that unicorns prefer females (GF 24:436). When Hagrid returns to teaching, he continues unicorn lessons and presents the students with a pair of two-year-old foals that are all gold. He says they do not grow their horns until they are four and they turn white when they reach adulthood at age seven. They are more trusting of others at a younger age, so they will allow the boys near them (GF 26:484).

In legends from the Middle Ages, the unicorn was thought to be tamed only by virgins.

In medieval folklore, the unicorn had the tail of a lion, the legs of a buck, and the body and head of a white horse with a horn. The image of the unicorn has simplified in recent years to a graceful white horse with a horn. Courtesy of Dover Pictorial Archive.

Universal Brooms Ltd. *Magical business.* From QA. Universal Brooms Ltd. manufactured the Shooting Star beginning in 1955. The racing broom was the least expensive on the market but lost power with age. The company went out of business in 1978 (QA 50).

See also Broomsticks

Unplottable. *Magical condition.* A place that has been enchanted so that it is not possible to mark its location on a map (FB xix; GF 11:166–67). Number Twelve, Grimmauld Place is unplottable (OP 6:115). Dumbledore is unsure if it is still unplottable after Sirius Black's death (HBP 3:50).

Unspeakable. *Magical occupation.* An employee of the Ministry of Magic whose work is top secret; no one knows what the unspeakable's job is (GF 7:86). These employees work in the Department of Mysteries (OP 24:539).

Uranus. Ron and Harry joke about this and other planets in Divination class. Ron asks Lavender Brown if he can see Uranus on her charts (GF 13:201).

"Urg the Unclean." *Made-up name.* Ron Weasley makes up this name during his History of Magic exam in Year 4. He says that Urg the Unclean is one of the goblins in the Goblin Rebellion.

Uric the Oddball. *Character.* Prof. Binns teaches about this historical figure in History of Magic (SS 8:133). In *Fantastic Beasts*, it is said that Uric the Oddball once slept with fifty Augureys (FB 3). He also experimented with Fwooper song to see if, instead of bringing on insanity, it might actually be good for one's health. The experiment apparently failed, as evidenced by his appearance at the Wizards' Council to report his findings wearing a dead badger for a toupee and nothing else (FB 18).

Urquhart. *Character.* Captain of the Slytherin Quidditch team in Year 6 (HBP 14:295). The name may come from Bloomsbury author, Jane Urquhart.

Vaisey. *Character.* A Chaser on the Slytherin Qudditch team in Year 6 (HBP 14:294).

Valentine's Day. In Harry's second year Gilderoy Lockhart uses this holiday to boost the students' morale after all the petrifications related to the Chamber of Secrets mystery. He decorates the Great Hall with pink flowers and heart-shaped confetti. A dozen rough-looking dwarfs with gold wings and harps are enlisted to deliver Valentines to students throughout the day (CS 13:235–36). Lockhart recommends that students ask for Love Potions in Prof. Snape's class and Entrancing Enchantments from Prof. Flitwick. He thanks the students for the forty-six cards he received; one was from Hermione (CS 13:235–38).

Valentine's Day is also the occasion in Book 3 when Harry has his first date in Hogsmeade with Cho Chang.

See also Chang, Cho

Vampires. Luna Lovegood tells Harry that her father says Rufus Scrimgeour is a vampire (HBP 15:314).

Vance, Emmeline. *Character.* A member of the original Order of the Phoenix who comes with others to Privet Drive to fly Harry to Headquarters. She is statuesque and wears a green shawl (OP 3:49). She is murdered sometime in the summer between Harry's fifth and sixth year at Hogwarts (HBP 1:4, 14; HBP 4:77).

Vane, Romilda. *Character.* A bold girl who likes Harry in his sixth year. She has big, dark eyes, a prominent chin, and long, black hair. Harry does not like her (HBP 7:138). She tries to influence his feelings by offering him gillywater and Chocolate Cauldrons, which Hermione warns him may have been spiked with love potion (HBP 15:308–9).

Vanishing cabinet. *Magical object.* Argus Filch finds the vanishing cabinet useful (CS 8:128). Fred and George Weasley put Montague into the cabinet after he tries to take points away from Gryffindor, and Montague disappears (OP 28:627). Harry finds the cabinet in the Room of Requirement when he sees how Draco Malfoy has been using the room in Year 6 (HBP 24:526–27). There is a pair of vanishing cabinets, and Draco gets the one at Hogwarts repaired so that the other at Borgin and Burkes may symbolically connect to it and make a secret passageway between Hogsmeade and Hogwarts (HBP 27:586–87).

Vanishing Spell. *Magical spell.* Harry wishes he knew a Vanishing Spell when Prof. Lockhart keeps approaching him in Year 2 about how to manage his fame (CS 6:98). In Year 5 Prof. McGonagall tells the students to practice Vanishing Spells for homework (OP 13:264). She wants to discuss the Vanishing Spell in class when Dolores Umbridge is there doing her faculty evaluation. It is apparently more difficult to make the spell work on more complicated animals (OP 15:320–21).

Vault 713. *Magical place.* The vault where Prof. Dumbledore's Sorcerer's Stone is kept at Gringotts. Griphook illustrates how the high security vault would trap any individual other than a goblin who tried to break into it. When Harry asks, Griphook says that the vaults are only checked every ten years for any intruders that may have become locked inside (SS 5:76).

Vauxhall Road, London. The name of a variety store on Vauxhall Road is printed on the back of Tom Riddle's diary. This is a clue to Ron that Tom Riddle must have been Muggle-born (CS 13:231–32).
See also Diary, Tom Riddle's

Vector, Prof. *Character.* The witch who teaches Arithmancy. Hermione takes this class, but Ron and Harry do not (PA 12:244). Prof. Vector is nearly knocked over by an upset Hagrid who has just found out that Dolores Umbridge has put him on probation (OP 25:549). Like Prof. Sinistra, Prof. Vector is rarely seen in the series.

Veela. *Magical beings.* Very beautiful women who dance quickly and mesmerize any male watching them. They are the mascots of the Bulgarian National Quidditch Team at the World Cup (GF 8:103). When things heat up during the game, the Veela charge the Leprechauns from the Ireland Team with handfuls of fire. When the Veela are angry, their appearance changes dramatically—they look like ugly, mean birds with scaly wings. Mr. Weasley tells the young wizards sitting near him that this is why it is never good to judge people by looks alone (GF 8:111–12).

After the World Cup match, young wizards are found talking and trying to impress the Veela. One says he is a vampire hunter who has killed ninety vampires; the dishwasher at the Leaky Cauldron claims to be a dragon killer for the Committee for the Disposal of Dangerous Creatures; and Stan Shunpike claims that he is going to be the next Minister of Magic. Ron yells to the Veela in passing that he has invented a new kind of broomstick that will fly to Jupiter (GF 9:126).

In Eastern European folklore Veela are spirits of the woods, streams, and lakes. They are beautiful women with long, flowing hair who are guardians of the woods. They have healing skills for which they use the herbs of the forest. They enjoy music and dancing by the light of the moon. They are normally kind to humans, but if they are seen while dancing, they may bring bad luck to the person who saw them. Men who see them become so entranced that they pine away for them until they die. The Veela are similar to the Dryads of Greek mythology.

Further Reading: Willis, Roy. *Dictionary of World Myth.* London: Duncan Baird, 1995.

Veil. *Magical object.* The veil is the black curtain found in the Department of Mysteries; it hangs from the stone archway on the dais in the center of the circular room (OP 34:773). In fighting with Bellatrix Lestrange, Sirius Black falls behind the veil and dies (OP 35:806).

Venomous Tentacula. *Magical plant part.* Poisonous teeth in a young, teething Mandrake (CS 6:93).

Venus. Ron and Harry create predictions based on this and other planets to speed up their Divination homework (GF 14:222). Harry mislabels Venus for Mars in his O.W.L. exam but tries to correct it as noise erupts at Hagrid's hut (OP 31:720).

Veritaserum. *Magical substance.* Truth Potion. It is very powerful, and three drops make a person tell the truth about everything he or she knows. Its use is regulated by the Ministry of Magic (GF 27:517). Dumbledore uses some of the potion, provided by Snape, on Barty Crouch, Jr., who then reveals his entire elaborate plot involving his father and many others (GF 35:683–91). Hermione warns Harry not to talk to Sirius Black or else Dolores Umbridge will force him to drink Veritaserum and answer all of her questions (OP 29:660). Prof. Slughorn tells his students that the potion has no color or odor (HBP 9:184).

Verity. *Character.* The blond clerk at Weasleys' Wizard Wheezes; she calls both Fred and George "Mr. Weasley," and that surprises Harry (HBP 6:120).

Vibration control. *Magical feature.* The Cleansweep broomstick Ron wants after he becomes prefect has built-in vibration control (OP 9:173).

Violet. *Character.* The Fat Lady's friend (GF 17:284).
See also Fat Lady

Vipertooths. *Magical creatures.* From *Fantastic Beasts.* Dragons indigenous to Peru (FB 46).

Volant, Frieda. The author's maternal grandmother. It does not appear that Rowling was particularly close to her growing up. Rowling remembers Frieda liking dogs more than children. This memory fed the character of Aunt Marge Dursley, the mean aunt who breeds boxers and whom Harry blows up in *Prisoner of Azkaban.*

Volant, Stan. Rowling's maternal grandfather. He is said to have had a dreamy disposition and liked to tinker in his shed in Tufnell Park. He worked as an engineer, then as a hospital mail carrier. His marriage to Frieda was not an especially happy one. Rowling pays tribute to her grandfather by naming Stan Shunpike, the young Knight Bus conductor, after him.

Voldemort, Lord. *Character.* The villain of the series. In the first novel readers encounter the name when Prof. Dumbledore tells Prof. McGonagall that she should call Voldemort by his real name, not "You-Know-Who" (SS 1:11). Hagrid tells Harry about him at the Hut-on-the-Rock (SS 4:54). "I am Lord Voldemort" is a sixteen-letter anagram for "Tom Marvolo Riddle" (CS 17:314). In *Chamber of Secrets,* Voldemort points out similarities between himself and Harry Potter—they both were orphans; both are half-bloods; and both were brought up by Muggles; Voldemort even thinks they look somewhat alike (CS 17:317). He obtains all the ingredients he needs to rise again by the time of the Triwizard Tournament (GF 32:643). What Voldemort wants is to live forever (GF 33:653).

When Voldemort appears in the Hall of Prophecy, readers have their first chance to see him one-on-one with the powerful wizard Dumbledore. Although Dumbledore is effective in fighting him, once Voldemort inhabits Harry's mind Dumbledore is virtually defeated in his efforts against Voldemort. It is only through Harry's own emotions (thinking of Sirius Black and wanting to see him, even if it means Harry has to die to do so) that Harry is freed at once of Voldemort's power (OP 36:814). Horace Slughorn points out that Voldemort has never looked for a fight with Dumbledore since Voldemort fears Dumbledore more than any other wizard (HBP 4:72).

In *Half-Blood Prince,* Dumbledore shows Harry a great deal of Tom Riddle's past. Some observers have commented that Voldemort's history matches the typical profile of a psychopath, including rejection by parents, solitude, feelings of inadequacy, and the mistreatment of animals. Oddly enough, though Voldemort is the true villain of the series (he has clearly gone against nature by splitting his soul and wanting to cheat death), readers are often more intrigued by Severus Snape, whose loyalties and ambitions remain unclear through Book 6.

See also Riddle, Tom Marvolo

Volkov. *Character.* Beater on the Bulgaria National Quidditch Team in the World Cup (GF 8:105).

Voyages With Vampires. *Magical book.* A book by Gilderoy Lockhart. It is a second-year "textbook" (CS 4:44). Hermione is reading the book on the morning after Harry and Ron's disastrous arrival at Hogwarts in Year 2 (CS 6:86). She stops reading when Ron receives a Howler from his mother (CS 6:88) but is seen with the book again later on (CS 6:96, 97).

Vratsa Vultures. *Magical sports team.* From QA. A Quidditch team from Bulgaria (QA 40).

Vulchanov. *Character.* Beater on the Bulgaria National Quidditch Team in the World Cup (GF 8:105).

"Waddiwasi!" *Incantation.* Prof. Lupin uses this incantation to remove wad of chewing gum from a keyhole; Peeves was the one who put the gum in the keyhole. The gum goes up Peeves's left nostril. The act makes Dean Thomas and others have more respect for Lupin (PA 7:131).

Wagga Wagga Werewolf. *Magical creature.* Harry is made to reenact Prof. Lockhart's "defeat" of the Wagga Wagga Werewolf with the Homorphus Charm; afterwards, the students are assigned to write a poem about it (CS 10:162).

Wailing Widow from Kent. *Character.* An out-of-town guest at Nearly Headless Nick's Death Day Party (CS 8:135).

Wales. Harry asks while riding the Knight Bus if they are somewhere in Wales, and Ernie Prang says that they are (PA 3:36). J. K. Rowling grew up in Tutshill, on the Welsh border.

Wands. *Magical object.* Perhaps no book about witches and wizards could be considered credible if it did not contain magic wands; the Harry Potter series is full of them. Harry first learns about wands from Mr. Ollivander when Hagrid takes him to Ollivanders to buy his first wand. Lily Potter's wand, Harry is told, was $10\frac{1}{4}$ inches long, swishy, made of willow, and good for working charms. James Potter's wand was mahogany, 11 inches, pliable and powerful, and good for Transfiguration. Voldemort's wand is yew, $13\frac{1}{2}$ inches, phoenix feather, and very powerful. Hagrid's is 16 inches and made out of oak. Mr. Ollivander tells Harry that each wand contains a magical feature that consists of unicorn hair, dragon heartstrings, or phoenix tail feathers. He says that rather than the wizard choosing the wand he or she likes, it is really the wand that selects the wizard (SS 5:82–85).

Harry makes several failed attempts to find the right wand. He tries a 9-inch flexible beechwood with dragon heartstring; a whippy 7-inch maple with phoenix feather; and a springy $8\frac{1}{2}$-inch ebony with unicorn hair (SS 5:84). Finally, he tries a supple, 11-inch holly with phoenix feather wand, and the warmth of it tells him that this is the right one. When he waves it, gold and red sparks (Gryffindor House colors) fly out of the tip. Mr. Ollivander tells him that the phoenix feather inside of it came from the same bird as the one inside Voldemort's wand; their wands are brothers. Harry pays 7 Galleons for his wand (SS 5:85).

Characters' wands often do seem to suit their personalities. Fleur Delacour's wand is rosewood, $9\frac{1}{2}$ inches, not flexible, and contains the hair of her grandmother Veela; it was not purchased at Ollivanders (GF 18:308). Cedric Diggory's Ollivander wand is $12\frac{1}{4}$ inches, ash, springy, with a single tail-hair from a very large male unicorn that stood seventeen hands tall (GF 18:309). Viktor Krum's wand was made by Gregorovitch; it is $10\frac{1}{4}$ inches long and is made of thick hornbeam with a dragon heartstring inside (GF 18:309).

Other wands in the series include Ron Weasley's, which is a hand-me-down from his brother Charlie; it has been beaten up and contains unicorn hair in it that is almost sticking out (SS 6:100, 105). Ron makes things worse when the wand cracks as the flying Ford Anglia crashes into the Whomping Willow (CS 5:74). After Mr. Weasley wins the *Daily Prophet* prize money, Ron gets a new wand—a 14-inch willow that contains a hair from the tail of a unicorn (PA 4:56).

Wands can malfunction if they are damaged. Ron's wand sent out a charge in Charms class that hit Prof. Flitwick and left a boil on his forehead (CS 7:104). Hagrid's broken wand, which he hides in a pink umbrella, comes in handy for him at times even though he is not supposed to use it. He uses an Engorgement Charm on his pumpkins to make them larger (CS 7:117–18).

The phoenix feathers in Harry's and Voldemort's wands both came from Fawkes. Ollivander informed Dumbledore of Harry's purchase immediately (GF 36:697). One of the more striking events involving wands occurs in *Goblet of Fire* when Voldemort attempts to duel with Harry and they each cast spells at the same time. Since their wands are brothers, a thin gold line forms between the wands; the line holds a bead that Harry must mentally push toward Voldemort's wand (GF 34:664).

Neville Longbottom gets a new wand from his grandmother after his heroic role in the fight at the Hall of Prophecy. The wand is cherry with a unicorn hair inside. It is the last wand sold by Ollivander before he disappears (HBP 7:137).

See also Ollivanders

War. Dumbledore tells the Dursleys that the wizard world is engaged in a war (HBP 3:55). Firenze tells his Divination students that the positioning of the planet Mars has indicated a second war has been coming for some time. In interviews Rowling alludes to World War II; the connection through Book 6 is unclear, other than that Voldemort's rise is causing a second war in the wizarding world. Book 7 resolves all questions about a war.

Warbeck, Celestina. *Character.* A singer who recorded the Puddlemere United team song as a fund-raiser for St. Mungo's Hospital (QA 36). She is Mrs. Weasley's favorite singer. At Christmas in the Burrow, everyone hears Celestina Warbeck sing songs on the radio such as "A Cauldron Full of Hot, Strong Love" and "You Charmed the Heart Right Out of Me" (HBP 16:330).

Warlock. *Magical being.* Harry sees warlocks at the Leaky Cauldron when he stays there for two weeks before Year 3 (PA 4:49). In folklore a warlock is an evil wizard, but warlocks do not seem to function that way in the series.

Warlocks' Convention of 1709. *Magical event.* This convention voted to make dragon-breeding illegal (SS 14:230).

Warner Bros. *See* Films

Warning Whistle. *Magical object feature.* From QA. A feature on the Twigger 90 racing broom that makes it more expensive than useful (QA 51).
See also Broomsticks

Warrington. *Character.* A player on the Slytherin Quidditch team in Year 3 (PA 15:306). He is large and looks like a sloth. Dean Thomas tells Harry that he thinks Warrington got up early to put his own name into the Goblet of Fire as a candidate for the Triwizard Tournament (GF 16:261). As a member of the hated Inquisitorial Squad under Dolores Umbridge, Warrington develops a strange, cornflake skin condition (OP 30:677). He brings Ron to Umbridge's office when Harry is caught in the office trying to communicate with Sirius Black (OP 32:742).

Wartcap powder. *Magical substance.* Sirius Black is bitten by a silver snuffbox while cleaning Grimmauld Place and his hand turns brown and crusty. He says that the box must have been filled with Wartcap powder to have caused that reaction (OP 6:116).

Watson, Emma. *See* Films

"Wattlebird." *Magical password.* Gryffindor password that Ron and Harry do not hear because they arrive late in the second year (CS 5:84).

Weasley, Arthur. *Character.* Arthur Weasley is curious and compassionate and provides Harry with a father figure in the series. He is nearly bald, but the hair he does have is bright red like the rest of the family's. He is soft-hearted with creatures like garden gnomes; they come back because he is not strict about keeping them out; he thinks they are amusing (CS 3:38). He gives Ginny a reminder about the advice he has given all of the children more than once: never trust something that appears to think for itself unless you can see where its brain is located (CS 18:329).

Arthur Weasley writes to Harry in Little Whinging after Harry casts the Patronus to fight off two Dementors. He tells Harry that he should stay where he is and not turn over his wand to the authorities (OP 2:28). Arthur is fascinated by the automatic ticket machines at the Underground on his way to taking Harry to his hearing (OP 7:124). Arthur is attacked by a venomous snake, an event that Harry witnesses in a vision as though he were looking through the snake's eyes. It is Harry who runs to tell Dumbledore about the incident and indirectly saves Arthur's life.

When Arthur goes to Grimmauld Place after his recovery from the attack, he finds Sirius Black and Severus Snape in a confrontation (OP 24:521). He is with Molly at King's Cross to meet and protect Harry after Year 5 is over (OP 38:867). In Harry's sixth year, Arthur is promoted to Head of the Office for the Detection and Confiscation of Counterfeit Defensive Spells and Protective Objects (HBP 5:84).

Many readers point out that Mr. Weasley bears the name of King Arthur from legends.

Weasley, Bill. *Character.* Bill Weasley works for Gringotts Wizarding Bank in Africa (SS 6:107). He also works as a Curse-Breaker in Egypt (PA 1:8). When Harry finally meets Bill for the first time after hearing about him from Ron for several years, he thinks that he is "cool." He has a ponytail and an earring with a fang hanging from it (GF 5:52). Bill's mother questions him about both his hair and the earring, but he tells her that the bank is happy with him as long as he keeps bringing back valuables from his work in Egypt (GF 5:62).

At the battle of Astronomy Tower, Bill Weasley is roughed up by werewolf Fenrir Greyback and will not look the same ever again (HBP 29:612). Prof. Lupin does not think Bill will become a werewolf because Greyback was not in wolf form when he attacked; however, Bill will have some wolfish traits that he will have to live with for good (HBP 29:613). Bill is engaged to Fleur Delacour, and they still plan to marry after his attack.

Weasley, Charlie. *Character.* Charlie Weasley works with dragons in Romania (SS 6:107); he is short and stocky (GF 5:52). He needed to take his Apparition test twice since he appeared five miles from where he was supposed to be the first time atop an old lady doing her shopping (GF 6:67). In Oliver Wood's opinion, Charlie was such a good Quidditch player in his days at Hogwarts that he could have gone on to play professionally for England (SS 10:170).

Weasley Family. *Characters.* Harry first encounters the friendly Weasley family at King's Cross Station in London when he is attempting to figure out how to catch his first Hogwarts Express (SS 6:92). Mrs. Molly Weasley is rounding up her boys while tending to young Ginny who is still too young to go to school, despite Ginny's protests to the contrary. The whole family has red hair. Twin boys, Fred and George, tease their mother by switching identities. Harry sees that they have carts similar to his, including an owl, and this clues him in that perhaps they can help him. Mrs. Weasley spots Harry and teaches him the technique of disappearing through the platform barrier to get to the Hogwarts Express (SS 6:92–93).

Ron tells Harry of the legacy of the family at Hogwarts; he is the youngest boy of six brothers and he has one younger sister. Bill and Charlie Weasley have already left Hogwarts (SS 6:99). Bill was Head Boy and Charlie was captain of the Gryffindor Quidditch team. Fred and George get acceptable grades, but they are jokesters who are popular at school.

The Weasley family is what Draco Malfoy would call a "pureblood" wizard family, but Draco still looks down on them because of their financial status; they have little money because there are so many children to support on Arthur Weasley's salary from the Ministry of Magic. Ron gets stuck with hand-me-downs such as Bill's robes, Charlie's wand, and Percy's rat (SS 6:100). Ron tells Harry that Mrs. Weasley may have a second cousin who is an accountant (whom they don't speak about), but the rest are wizards (SS 6:99). Fred and George almost attack Draco Malfoy when he calls Hermione Granger a Mudblood, but Marcus Flint moves in front of Draco to protect him (CS 7:112).

Whenever Harry is with the any of the Weasleys, he seems to respond as though he is with family.

Weasley, Fred and George. *Characters.* The mischievous, red-haired Weasley twins; they are two years ahead of Harry and Ron at Hogwarts. Harry gives them his 1,000 Galleon winnings from the Triwizard Tournament to start up their joke shop. He also asks them to buy Ron a new set of dress robes as a gift from them; they do this before the start of Ron's fifth year (OP 12:228).

Fred and George get three O.W.L.s each and do not want to go to Hogwarts for their seventh year. They return, however, because their mother is already suffering from Percy ignoring the family, and they think it would hurt her too much to have them leave school at the same time. They decide to do market research that year so their time is not wasted (OP 12:227). It appears that the only person they are afraid of in their antics is their mother. When Hermione threatens them for experimenting with their products on first-year students, the thought of detention does not deter them, but when she says that she will write to their mother, they fold to her wishes (OP 13:254).

Harry wonders why Fred and George only got three O.W.L.s each since they know business so well; Hermione claims that they only know about things that do not matter. Ron tells her that they have made 26 Galleons so far with their mail-order business (OP 17:369). When Dumbledore escapes Hogwarts, Fred and George no longer care about being expelled with Dolores Umbridge as Head, and they decide to unleash a full dose of their mayhem on the school to honor Dumbledore before they leave (OP 28:627).

The twins get caught by the Inquisitorial Squad when they create a Portable Swamp of Stinksap as a distraction that will allow Harry to talk to Sirius Black. When Argus Filch gets ready to whip the twins under Umbridge's new rules, they defy Umbridge by casting a Summoning Charm on their brooms, and then they fly away. Before they do, however, they yell to the students below the address of their new shop on Diagon Alley and offer a discount to any student using their products to get rid of Umbridge. They say they have "outgrown full-time education" and call out their famous refrain in protest of Umbridge: "Give her hell from us, Peeves." Peeves, who never obeyed anyone except the Bloody Baron, takes off his hat in salute as the Weasley twins fly out the open doors of the school (OP 29:673–75).

Harry finally admits to Hermione that the twins got the money to open their shop from Harry's Triwizard Tournament winnings (OP 30:680). When they meet Harry as part of the welcoming committee at King's Cross Station after Year 5, they are already wearing new jackets of green dragon skin—their business has taken off (OP 38:867). Harry and the Weasley family visit their new store in Book 6, and it is clear that they are content, well established, and their business is booming.

Weasley, Ginevra (Ginny) Molly. *Character.* Ginevra is the Italian form of Guinevere, meaning "fair one." Ginny is the Weasleys' youngest child of seven and the only daughter; she is the first female born in the Weasley family in several generations. From early in the series, she is fascinated with Harry Potter. In Book 1 she wants to see him when she is still too young to go to Hogwarts and must stay home with her mother. Harry is told at the Burrow that she has been talking about him all summer (CS 3:35). Finally at Hogwarts, she is sorted into Gryffindor House, but Ron misses her ceremony due to the Whomping Willow incident (CS 5:82). Ginny loves cats and is quite upset when Mrs. Norris gets petrified in Year 2 (CS 9:146). Ginny is taken to the Chamber of the Secrets by Voldemort, who has bewitched her through Tom Riddle's diary. Harry rescues her (CS 16:293).

Ginny is good at imitations and does one of Dolores Umbridge's annoying *"hem, hem"* at the first DA meeting at the Hog's Head (OP 16:345). She takes over Harry's position as Seeker on the Quidditch team when he is banned from the game by Umbridge (OP 22:453). When Harry uses the *"Sectumsempra!"* spell, Hermione chastises him for using something from the Half-Blood Prince's Potions book before he knows what it is; Ginny defends him (HBP 24:530). After the Quidditch match against Ravenclaw in sixth year when Harry has detention with Prof. Snape, Ginny plays Seeker for him against Cho

Chang. When he gets to the Gryffindor Common Room after the match, Ginny runs into his arms, and he kisses her as the most natural reaction in the world (HBP 24:533). At Dumbledore's funeral, Ginny seems to understand that Harry feels he must find Voldemort, and she shares his steely resolve (HBP 30:646–47).

"Weasley Is Our King." *Magical song.* The Slytherins make up this song, along with badges and signs, to mock Ron Weasley in his new position as Keeper on the Gryffindor Quidditch team (OP 19:404–10). The song turns into a chant of triumph by Ron's supporter's when Ron helps win a big game against Slytherin (OP 30:702).

Weasley, Molly Prewett. *Character.* Mrs. Molly Weasley serves as a mother figure to Harry. When she gives him a second hug at King's Cross while sending him off with her own children, he is embarrassed but pleased (PA 5:72). She is thrilled when Ron becomes prefect (OP 9:163). She is there at King's Cross to meet and protect Harry after his eventful Year 5 (OP 38:867). Molly is good at homemaking and taking care of her large family. When Harry has no family who will come watch him in the third task of the Triwizard Tournament, Molly Weasley and her son Bill come to support him (GF 31:615).

Weasley, Percy Ignatius. *Character.* The oldest Weasley boy attending Hogwarts with Harry is Percy, who is a prefect in Harry's first year. He becomes Head Boy in Harry's Year 3, and he is only the second Weasley to earn this title (PA 1:10). Fred and George tease him for being the talk of the family all summer as a result of this honor (SS 6:95–96). Percy Weasley is ambitious, with hopes of becoming Minister of Magic one day (CS 4:58). He gets top grades in his N.E.W.T. exams (PA 22:430).

In Year 4 Percy has joined the Ministry, where he works at the Department of International Magical Cooperation (GF 3:36). He is working on a report about a variance in cauldron thicknesses, which is obviously busy work, but which he thinks is an important task assigned to him by Bartemius Crouch, Sr. (GF 5:56). Barty Crouch calls Percy Weasley "Weatherby" in error, showing that he does not know Percy as well as the ambitious young employee would like (GF 7:90). Fred and George send dragon dung to Percy's office at the Ministry under the ruse that it needs inspection; Percy believes it is a real task (GF 5:64). Crouch, Sr., tells Dumbledore that Percy is a bit too ambitious (GF 17:281). Percy and his father have a falling out over Voldemort's return and Cornelius Fudge's treatment of Dumbledore; Percy does not believe in Voldemort's second rise (OP 4:70–72). Percy serves as Court Scribe during Harry's hearing at the Ministry (OP 8:139).

At Christmas in Year 5, Mrs. Weasley cries when Percy sends back his traditional sweater without even enclosing a note. Percy neither visits his father at St. Mungo's nor asks how he is (OP 23:502). Percy is in Dumbledore's office when Harry is brought there and questioned about the DA (OP 27:610).

Weasley, "Peter." *Mistaken identity.* Draco Malfoy erroneously calls Percy "Peter" when he talks with Harry and Ron (thinking they are Vincent Crabbe and Gregory Goyle) about him (CS 12:220).

Weasley, Ronald (Ron) Bilius. *Character.* Harry's best friend (OP 9:167). Ron is sorted into Gryffindor (SS 7:122). Ron has a winning sense of humor. He is kind to Harry. The boys meet on the train to Hogwarts in Year 1 when they share candy from

Ron Weasley (Rupert Grint), Harry Potter (Daniel Radcliffe), and Hedwig the owl fly to Hogwarts in a Ford Anglia in *Harry Potter and the Chamber of Secrets* (2002). Courtesy of Warner Bros./Photofest.

the vendor's cart (SS 6:102). Ron shows great courage when he plays wizard chess with life-sized figures to help Harry get the sorcerer's stone and keep it from falling in the wrong hands (SS 16:281–84). Much to the surprise of everyone, Ron receives a letter from Hogwarts that he has been made prefect of Gryffindor in his fifth year (OP 9:161). Ron asks his mother for a new Cleansweep broomstick as a gift for his accomplishment (OP 9:165). He is the fourth prefect in the family (OP 9:169). He tries out to be Gryffindor Keeper on the Quidditch team after he receives his new Cleansweep broom (OP 13:271). Captain Angelina Johnson tells Harry that Ron is not that good, but she is banking on his improving (OP 13:276). Ron's birthday is in March (HBP 17:355). Prof. Slughorn keeps calling Ron by the wrong name, suggestive of the fact that he does not consider him important or influential enough to be worth knowing; examples include: "Ralph" (HBP 18:397) and "Rupert" (HBP 22:485). Ron tells Hermione he loves her when she tells him she can fix the misspelled words in his essay. He says it very naturally, and Hermione blushes and tells him not to let Lavender Brown hear him say so. He says it would help him get rid of Lavender if Hermione did tell her what he said (HBP 21:449). Not unexpectedly, Ron pledges loyalty to Harry in Harry's decision to defeat Voldemort (HBP 30:651).

Weasleys' Wildfire Whiz-Bangs. *Magical objects.* Fred and George Weasley make a statement against Dolores Umbridge in their final prank at the school when they set off their own brand of fireworks all over the buildings and grounds. These fireworks include dragons, Catherine wheels, rockets, stars, and sparklers writing swear words in the air. Umbridge is helpless against them, and even Hermione congratulates the twins on their protest. They tell her they used up all of their stock for the fabulous display, but she can add her name to the list to receive a Basic Blaze box for 5 Galleons or the Deflagration Deluxe for 20 (OP 28:632–34). Harry tells them their fireworks will put Dr. Filibuster out of business. George hopes that Umbridge will try a Vanishing Charm on the fireworks because they multiply tenfold if someone tries do so (OP 28:633). Harry sees flying, winged piglets outside the Gryffindor Tower as the fireworks continue into the night (OP 28:636).

Weasleys' Wizard Wheezes. *Magical place.* The joke shop that Fred and George Weasley establish on Number 93 Diagon Alley with the money Harry gives them from winning the Triwizard Tournament (OP 29:675). They dropped out of Hogwarts to start the store, but business seems good and they appear happier than they were as students (HBP 6:115). They began the company as a mail-order business, using forms they distributed at school for their inventions made at home and at Hogwarts. Mrs. Weasley is not at all pleased when she finds the price lists and order forms (GF 5:54). However, she feels guilty after the events at the World Cup, and fears that her scolding the twins for their actions may have been the last conversation she ever had with them (GF 10:146). She and the boys laugh over it later; but they seem to be working on their order forms again (GF 10:153).

"Weatherby." *Wrong name.* Barty Crouch, Sr., calls Percy Weasley by this name in error, showing that he does not know Percy as well as the ambitious young employee would like (GF 7:90).

Website, J. K. Rowling's. In early 2004 Rowling established an official author website on the Internet. The site contains information about the author's biography; notes and sketches that were not used in the books; comments from Rowling about current or recent events related to the books; announcements; a section where she dispels rumors or misconceptions that have risen; links to her favorite charities and to her publishers and agent; and games and other information. The address for the site is: www.jkrowling.com. Occasionally she will hide secrets or information on the site that requires the reader to solve a puzzle in order to find and access the information. One of the locations of these secrets is behind a closed door with a sign hanging from the handle saying "Do Not Disturb."

Wedding. Fleur Delacour and Bill Weasley plan to marry in Year 7. Fleur says that there will be two bridesmaids—Gabrielle Delacour and Ginny Weasley. She decides on a color scheme of light gold because she thinks pink would clash with Ginny's hair (HBP 7:131). At the end of Book 6, Harry's spirits lift when he thinks about the wedding that he will attend with Ron and Hermione, which will possibly be the last peaceful and pleasant day he will have with them (HBP 30:652).

The Weird Sisters. *Magical musical group.* Hogwarts students who listen to WWN (Wizarding Wireless Network) are excited that Dumbledore booked this famous group for the Yule Ball. Harry has never heard of them (GF 22:391). Their instruments include drums, several guitars, a lute, a cello, and bagpipes. Their bodies are hairy and their costumes consist of long, black robes torn in stylized ways (GF 23:419). Harry reads an article about one of them getting married in the *Daily Prophet* (OP 14:286).

The Weird Sisters undoubtedly get their name from the three witches in Shakespeare's play *Macbeth*.

See also Shakespeare, William

Weird Wizarding Dilemmas and Their Solutions. *Magical book.* Hermione consults this book to help Harry with his second task in the Triwizard Tournament, but she wonders why anyone would want help making their nose hair grow into ringlets (GF 26:487).

Welfare/Dole. *See* Rowling, J. K.

Wellington boot. *Muggle object*. Crookshanks chases a garden gnome into a Wellington boot at the Burrow (GF 5:60).

Wellington, New Zealand. From QA. The location of the New Zealand Ministry of Magic (QA 41).

Welsh Quidditch Team. *Magical sports team*. This team lost to Uganda in the run-up to the Quidditch World Cup (GF 5:63).

Wendelin the Weird. *Character*. A witch who is written about in A *History of Magic*. She enjoys being burned because of the defense mechanism, the Flame Freezing Charm, that tickles rather than burns. She allows herself to be caught forty-seven times under different disguises so she can keep enjoying the experience (PA 1:2).

Werewolf. *Magical creature*. From *Fantastic Beasts*. Classified 5X by the MM. According to *Fantastic Beasts*, these creatures spend most of their existence as human wizards or Muggles, but they turn into violent, four-legged creatures once a month. They are creatures that can maim and kill, and they have no conscience (FB x). The cure for the condition is unknown but it can be treated with potions so that its violent side is not quite as strong (FB 41–42). In their shared copy of *Fantastic Beasts*, either Harry or Ron scribbles that werewolves "aren't all bad," alluding to their beloved teacher, Prof. Remus Lupin (FB 41).

Harry asks Hagrid if a werewolf might be attacking the unicorns in the Forbidden Forest, but Hagrid tells him that werewolves are not fast enough (SS 15:251). Prof. Snape wants to teach Lupin's DADA class about them when Lupin is out ill (PA 9:171). Mad-Eye Moody makes sure that the students have gone over werewolves in DADA class before he teaches them the Unforgivable Curses (GF 14:211).

In folklore werewolves particularly like children, which probably explains Fenrir Greyback's attraction to them (HBP 27:593). Greyback attacked Lupin when he was young (HBP 16:334–35). Bill Weasley also gets attacked by Greyback, and time will tell how severe his symptoms become (HBP 29:612).

Werewolf Capture Unit. *Magical office*. Located in the Beast Division of the Department for the Regulation and Control of Magical Creatures in the Ministry of Magic (FB xiii).

Werewolf Code of Conduct, 1637. *Magical event*. Hermione is glad she did not have to know about this for her Year 1 History of Magic exam (SS 16:263).

Werewolf Register/Registry. *Magical record*. From *Fantastic Beasts*. Newt Scamander started this registry in 1947 (FB vi). It is maintained in the Beast Division of the Department for the Regulation and Control of Magical Creatures at the Ministry of Magic (FB xiii).

Werewolf Support Services. *Magical office*. This office exists in the Being Division of the Department for the Regulation and Control of Magical Creatures at the Ministry of Magic (FB xiii).

West Country, England. The region of England where Rowling grew up. The southwest of the country is called the West Country. It has a romantic sound to many

Londoners' ears like J. K. Rowling's parents, since the area is known for its natural beauty and rural scenery.

West Country Hurricane. *See* Hurricane

West Ham Soccer Team. *Muggle sports team.* Dean Thomas's favorite soccer team. Ron Weasley is always poking a stick at Dean's Muggle poster of the team to see if the players will move like they do in magical posters, but they do not (SS 9:144). After the Quidditch World Cup, Thomas has a poster of Viktor Krum pinned up next to this poster (GF 12:191).

West Tower. *Magical place.* A tower at Hogwarts. Buckbeak flies as high as this tower before he leaves with Sirius Black on his back (PA 21:415).

Whalley, Eric. *Character.* One of the orphan children at the orphanage where Tom Riddle was a boy (HBP 13:264). There is an Eric, whose last name is not identified, who works as a security guard at the Ministry of Magic.

"Wheezy." Dobby's nickname for Ron Weasley (GF 26:490).

Where There's a Wand, There's a Way. *Magical book.* Harry falls asleep consulting this book the night before the second task of the Triwizard Tournament and ends up arriving late for the task (GF 26:490).

Which Broomstick. *Magical magazine.* Harry borrows this magazine from Oliver Wood and looks at the different broom models after his Nimbus 2000 breaks during his fall (PA 10:190). The editor provides a blurb on *Quidditch Through the Ages* in the QA frontispiece.

Whisp, Kennilworthy. *Character.* From QA. Fictional author of *Quidditch Through the Ages*. He is the author of *The Wonder of Wigtown Wanderers, He Flew Like a Madman*, and *Beating the Bludgers—A Study of Defensive Strategies in Quidditch*. He likes backgammon, vegetarian cooking, and vintage broomstick collecting (QA v).

Whitby, Kevin. *Character.* A Hufflepuff student three years behind Harry (GF 12:180).

Whizz Hard Books. *Magical place.* From QA. The fictional publisher of *Quidditch Through the Ages*. The company is located at 129B Diagon Alley, London.

Whizzing Worms. *Magical objects.* Argus Filch asks Harry why he is not going to Hogsmeade to buy Whizzing Worms and other joke products (PA 8:153).

Whomping Willow. *Magical plant.* A large, very old tree on the Hogwarts grounds that is something like a wheeping willow except that its branches are thick. The tree does not take kindly to Ron and Harry crashing the flying Ford Anglia into it, so it attacks them (CS 5:75). Afterwards, Prof. Sprout bandages up the tree and puts its branches in slings (CS 6:89). When Harry falls off his broomstick during a Quidditch match, his broom falls into the Whomping Willow and is destroyed (PA 9:182). The Whomping Willow was planted the year Remus Lupin came to Hogwarts as a student. A secret passageway led under it to the Shrieking Shack, where Lupin could go each month to transform safely into werewolf form (PA 18:353).

Widdershin, Willy. *Character.* He is the culprit behind the regurgitating toilets that Arthur Weasley investigates. His jinx backfired with one toilet and left him unconscious until he was found and arrested (OP 22:489). He was bandaged up and sitting in the Hog's Head pub in Hogsmeade when Harry had his first DA meeting. Prof. McGonagall thinks that his act of spying on the DA must be the reason he was never prosecuted for his crime by the Ministry (OP 27:613–14).

Wigtown Wanderers. *Character.* From QA. The seven children of butcher Walter Parkin founded this team in 1422; Parkin descendants still appear on the team from time to time (QA 37).

Wilfred the Wistful. *Magical statue.* This statue is located on the way to the Owlery at Hogwarts. Mrs. Norris hides behind it while following Harry (OP 14:281).

Wilkes. *Character.* A friend of Prof. Snape's in his days as a student at Hogwarts; Wilkes was killed by Aurors (GF 27:531).

Will. *Character.* A colleague of Mundungus Fletcher's in the stolen goods business (OP 5:86). It is unclear whether he is the same character as Williamson.

Williamson. *Character.* Cornelius Fudge asks Williamson to go to the Department of Mysteries to check on the Death Eaters that Dumbledore has put in the Death Chamber (OP 36:817).

Wimple, Gilbert. *Character.* Gilbert Wimple has horns and is with the Committee on Experimental Charms (GF 7:86).

"Wingardium Leviosa." *Incantation.* This is the incantation for a Levitation Charm. In Latin *levo* means "to raise." Hermione tries to help Ron pronounce the incantation properly and gets a scowl in return. She is successful in raising a feather in Charms class (SS 10:171). Ron returns Hermione's favor, however, when he uses the charm to fling the club out of a troll's hand that is threatening Hermione (SS 10:176). Harry uses the charm during the attack in the Room of Prophecy (OP 36:809).

Winged horse. *Magical creature.* From *Fantastic Beasts.* Classified 2X to 4X by the MM, depending on the breed. Breeds include: Abraxan, Aethonan, Granian, and Thestral. Owners often must use Disillusionment Charms when moving them about to prevent Muggles from seeing them (FB 42).
    See also Abraxan horses; Aethonan horses; *Fantastic Beasts and Where to Find Them;* Granian horses; Thestrals

Winged keys. *Magical objects.* Flying keys that are another obstacle to Harry, Ron, and Hermione in their quest to find the Sorcerer's Stone. Harry flies quickly among them and finds the right one to unlock the door (SS 16:279).

Winky. *Character.* A female house-elf who works for Barty Crouch, Sr. Harry meets her at the World Cup; she wears a tea towel (GF 8:98; GF 9:131). Harry and his friends find Winky in the Hogwarts kitchen, where she is very unhappy no longer being the house-elf for Barty Crouch, Sr. (GF 21:377). She admits to keeping his secrets (GF 28:538). Dobby tells Harry that Winky is still drinking too much in Year 5 (OP 18:385).

Winterbourne, England. J. K. Rowling lived at 35 Nicholls Lane in this town from 1967 to the mid-1970s, when the family moved to Tutshill. Family friends the Potters—Ruth and Graham and their two children, Ian and Vikki—lived nearby at 29 Nicholls Lane. Ian and Vikki were playmates in the neighborhood with sisters Joanne and Dianne Rowling. J. K. Rowling is said to have liked their surname and years later adopted it for the name of her magical hero. Ian Potter once indicated that they liked to play wizards as children, but Rowling has denied this claim. Rowling attended her first school in September 1970, at St. Michael's Church of England Primary School at High Street in Winterbourne. By all accounts, her early childhood years spent in Winterbourne were happy ones.

Further Reading: Kirk, Connie Ann. *J. K. Rowling: A Biography.* Westport, CT: Greenwood, 2003.

Winterbourne Wasps. *Magical sports team.* From QA. Founded in 1312, the Wasps earned their name in a game opposite the Appleby Arrows. One of the Wasp Beaters whacked a bees' nest at an Arrows Seeker for whom the bees' stings were so damaging that he needed to retire. The Wasps won the game and took on the bee as their mascot (QA 38).

J. K. Rowling spent her early childhood in Winterbourne.

See also Winterbourne, England

Wisteria Walk. *Muggle place.* The street where Mrs. Figg lives near the Dursleys (OP 1:2, 13).

Wit-Sharpening Potion. *Magical substance.* Prof. Snape's Potions class makes this potion (GF 27:513).

"Witch Burning in the Fourteenth Century Was Completely Pointless." *Magical assignment.* An essay assigned over the summer between Years 2 and 3 for Prof. Binns's History of Magic Class (PA 1:1).

Witch Weekly. *Magical magazine.* Gilderoy Lockhart is proud that he has received the Most Charming Smile Award from this magazine five times in a row (CS 6:91).

Witch with a hairy chin. *Character.* This witch was actually the one to banish the Bandon Banshee described in Lockhart's book (CS 16:297).

Witches/wizards. The Harry Potter series received much attention from those concerned with the devil and evil spirits. The books are populated with boys and girls who are, after all, going to a school to learn how to be wizards and witches. Rowling has said in interviews that she does not believe in witchcraft and is not out to promote it in any form. The series appears to use witches and wizards metaphorically in the magical fantasy world in which Harry finds himself. There are wands, broomsticks, and cauldrons in the books, and indeed there are evil characters who practice the Dark Arts, but the children at Hogwarts learn how to defend themselves against these evil ways; they are not encouraged to learn the ways themselves or to practice them. Occupations for individuals after Hogwarts tend to be predominantly in the civic areas of healing, teaching, banking, law enforcement, and government.

The word "witch" comes from Middle English *witche,* derived from Old English *wicca, wicce,* and *wiccian,* meaning "to work sorcery." The Indo-European root, *weik,* relates to magic and religion. The word "wizard" is derived from the Middle English *wis,* meaning "wise." The term "wizard" first appeared in 1440 to refer to wise women and wise men. After 1825 "witch" and "wizard" came to be used interchangeably, with "witch" representing a female and "wizard" a male.

As with black and white magic, throughout history there were witches who believed in performing good acts just as there were those who at-

The Harry Potter series adds a new chapter to a long tradition of tales about wizards and magic in world literature. Courtesy of Dover Pictorial Archive.

tempted to work hexes and curses for unsavory purposes. The Western view of witches and wizards working for the devil or evil spirits goes back to the ancient Hebrews, Greeks, and Romans. Witches were thought to possess the evil eye. Ovid and Plutarch wrote of witches whose looks could kill because they had poison in their eyes. In the Middle Ages and Renaissance, the Bible was used to hold trials against women and men who were thought to be practicing magic. Accusers cited the Bible passage Exodus 22:18, "Thou shalt not suffer a witch to live." Other translators differed in their understanding of "witch" in the scripture and explained it to mean diviners, astrologers, or something else.

The famous Salem witch trials of 1692 and 1693 mark a point in American history when fear of witchcraft resulted in rash actions against many young girls who started out in some cases playing a game that turned deadly. During the trial period 141 females and males were arrested as suspects. Of those, nineteen were tried in unfair proceedings and were hung; one man was pressed to death by being forced to lie under a wooden plank on which stones were piled until he expired. The furor that arose out of the injustice of the trials did much to change the political and religious atmosphere of New England.

The image of Merlin the wizard seems to have first appeared in literature in *The Prophecies of Merlin,* written in the 1130s by Welsh cleric Geoffrey of Monmouth. The foundation of the story of the twelve knights of the Round Table comes from a later book, *History of the Kings of Britain* completed by Monmouth in approximately 1135 or 1136.

King Arthur uses the wizard Merlin as an advisor in the French poetic version of Monmouth's *History* and in Sir Thomas Malory's *Le Morte d'Arthur*. This is the famous tale of young Arthur proving his right to the throne by pulling the sword Excalibur from a stone. Whether the Merlin of legend actually existed is unknown. A series of wizards may have held the name. Merlin may have been a poet or a prophet; some evidence suggests that he may have lived at the end of the fifth century.

It is worth noting that the contemporary popular image of witches tends to be of ugly old hags with humped backs, scratchy voices, and long fingernails hovering over a blazing cauldron in the woods. The image of wizards tends to be of kindly, wise, old Merlin-figure men with long, flowing beards and spectacles, experimenting with alchemy in laboratories and giving good counsel to the young.

Rowling employs folklore in the series to her own devices, and this includes the stories and history surrounding witches and wizards.

Further Reading: Guiley, Rosemary Ellen. *The Encyclopedia of Witches and Witchcraft*, 2nd ed. New York: Facts on File, 1999.

Witherwings. *Magical creature.* The alias given to Hagrid's hippogriff friend Buckbeak to protect him from the Ministry of Magic, which wanted his head on the chopping block in Year 3. After Sirius Black's death, Buckbeak remained under Hagrid's care with Harry's approval (HBP 3:53; HBP 6:109). Hagrid tells Harry that Buckbeak is enjoying being back outside again (HBP 6:109).

Wizard Chess. *Magical game.* Ordinary chess played in a violent manner with extraordinary, living pieces that make the game like war. Ron teaches Harry how to play with his grandfather's set. Because the set is old, Ron has learned the chess pieces well and can make them do as he wishes. Seamus Finnigan lends Harry his set, but the pieces do not trust Harry (SS 12:199). Harry receives his own new set from the Wizard Crackers he opens at Christmas (SS 12:204).

At the close of Year 1, Ron directs Harry and Hermione in a dramatic life-sized game of Wizard Chess so that Harry may continue on his way toward the Sorcerer's Stone (SS 16:281–84). Harry and Ron play the game on the Hogwarts Express after Year 5 (OP 38:865).

Wizarding Examinations Authority. *Magical office.* Griselda Marchbanks is head of this office which includes a group of examiners. Various old witches and wizards from this office come to Hogwarts to administer O.W.L.s (OP 31:709).

Wizarding Wireless Network (WWN). *Magical radio station.* Many Hogwarts students know about the Weird Sisters from listening to them on this radio station (GF 22:391).

The Wizards' Council. *Magical organization.* From *Fantastic Beasts*. The previous name for the Ministry of Magic (FB x).

Wizards Duel. *Magical competition.* Two wizards compete against one another by attacking each other with only their wands and magical abilities. No touching is allowed. Draco Malfoy challenges Harry to a Wizards Duel in their first year (SS 9:153).

Wizengamot Administration Services. *Magical office.* Located on the second floor of the Ministry of Magic, it is part of the Department of Magical Law Enforcement (OP 7:130).

Wizengamot Charter of Rights. *Magical law.* At Harry's court hearing, Prof. Dumbledore cites this law as allowing the accused to present witnesses on his or her behalf (OP 8:142).

Wolfbane. *Magical plant.* A plant used in potions. It also goes by the names aconite and monkshood. Harry does not know this information when Prof. Snape questions him on it during his first Potions Class (SS 8:138).

Wolfbane's Potion. *Magical substance.* A recently discovered potion that allows werewolves to keep their heads when they transform if they take the potion during the week before the full moon (PA 18:353).

"Won-Won!" *Nickname.* This is what Lavender Brown calls Ron when they are in their snogging phase in Year 6 (HBP 17:351).

WonderWitch products. *Magical objects.* Bright pink beauty products sold at Weasleys' Wizard Wheezes that are popular with some witches. One example is a ten-second pimple vanisher that removes blackheads and boils (HBP 6:120).

Wood, Oliver. *Character.* He is a fifth-year student and captain of the Gryffindor Quidditch team in Harry's first year. Oliver Wood is the student Prof. McGonagall pulls out of Charms class to introduce to Harry as the team's new Seeker (SS 9:150). Oliver teaches Harry about the game of Quidditch (SS 10:167–68). It is Oliver who wakes Harry up at dawn in Year 2 to train on the field, only to be met by the Slytherin team (CS 7:110). In a pep talk to the team in Year 2, he tells Harry to catch the Snitch or die trying. This also happens to be the game when Harry must fight against a Bludger that has been bewitched to go after him (CS 10:170). Oliver is pleased with the eventual win, even though Harry suffers a broken arm as a result (CS 10:172). In Harry's third year Wood desperately wants to win the Quidditch Cup since Gryffindor has not won it for seven years, and this is his last chance to win it before he leaves the school (PA 8:143). After leaving Hogwarts, Oliver signs with the Puddlemere United reserve professional team (GF 7:84).

Woollongong Shimmy. *Magical sports play.* From QA. A zigzagging flying maneuver designed to evade Chasers from the other team; developed by the Austrailian Woollongong Warriors (QA 55).

Woollongong Warriors. *Magical sports team.* From QA. Quidditch team from Australia (QA 42).

Worme, Augustus. *Character.* Publisher of Obscurus Books. Newt Scamander explains that Augustus Worme was the one who invited him to write the book *Fantastic Beasts and Where to Find Them* (FB ix).

Wormtail. *Magical nickname.* Peter Pettigrew's nickname. A contemporary of James Potter's at Hogwarts, Wormtail's Animagus form is a rat that turns out to be Ron's pet,

Scabbers (PA 14:287). After an altercation at the Shrieking Shack where he is almost killed but receives mercy from Harry Potter instead, Wormtail shrinks back to rat form and disappears. He reappears in the Riddle House as a servant of Voldemort at the opening of *Goblet of Fire* (GF 1:7). He is present in the Little Hangleton graveyard and kills Cedric Diggory on Voldemort's order (GF 32:638). After humiliating Wormtail (because of his previous disloyalty) in front of the other Death Eaters who gather at the cemetery, Voldemort restores Wormtail's severed hand with a silver metallic one (GF 33:649). Wormtail is in the background of Snape's worst memory (OP 28:646). He is at Spinner's End when Snape is visited by Bellatrix Black Lestrange and Narcissa Black Malfoy; Snape tells them that the Dark Lord sent Wormtail there to work for him (HBP 2:23).

Wormwood. *Magical substance.* One of the ingredients for the Draught of Living Death. Harry does not know this information when Prof. Snape asks him about the substance in his first Potions Class (SS 8:137–38).

Worple, Eldred. *Character.* One of Prof. Slughorn's previous students; he is the author of *Blood Brothers: My Life Amongst the Vampires.* Eldred Worple is short and chubby with glasses, and he asks Harry if he might be interested in having him write a biography of Harry. Harry tells him that he has no interest (HBP 15:315–16).

Wrackspurt. *Magical creature.* An invisible insect that floats into the brain through the ears and blurs one's thinking (HBP 7:140).

Wright, Bowman. *Character.* From QA. Inventor of the Golden Snitch; he lived in Godric's Hollow (QA 14).

Wronski (Defensive) Feint. *Magical game play.* A defensive move by a Seeker in Quidditch, perfected by Viktor Krum of the Bulgaria National Team. It involves diving toward the ground, then making a sharp turn upward just in time. The move normally fakes out the Seeker from the other team to the point where the other player hits the ground (GF 8:108–9). Harry thinks about learning how to do it (GF 9:118). Hermione calls it the "Wonky-Faint thing" (GF 19:317). The move was named after Josef Wronski, a Polish player (QA 55).
See also Wronski, Josef

Wronski, Josef. *Character.* From QA. The inventor of the Wronski Feint defensive play. He was a Seeker on Poland's Grodzisk Goblins Quidditch team (QA 41).

WWN (Wizarding Wireless Network). *See* Wizarding Wireless Network (WWN)

Wyedean Comprehensive. Rowling attended this school in Sedbury from 1976 until 1983. While there, she was an excellent student who impressed her favorite English teacher, Lucy Shepherd, and became Head Girl. Wyedean's dissimiliarities to Hogwarts do not end with it being a "Muggle" school rather than a magical one. Wyedean is a public school, not private, and it is not a boarding school. Rowling's mother Anne worked as a lab assistant in the chemistry department, so Rowling, her mother, and her sister frequently went to school together in the mornings. Her typical classes included chemistry and physics (with which she struggled), gym (which she did not particularly enjoy), and other subjects in the practical arts, or what Americans might call "shop." In that class she once made a flat spoon that she gave to her mother.

During her years at Wyedean, Rowling befriended Sean Harris, who was new to the school and felt a bit out of place, as she often did. He had an old turquoise and white Ford Anglia that he used to take her for rides. At Wyedean Rowling encountered bullies, but she worked hard at her studies. In the evenings and on weekends, she and the other adolescents of her town struggled to find suitable entertainment when very little was available to them. She took to sitting underneath the Severn Bridge with Sean Harris, smoking cigarettes and dreaming of getting out of Tutshill to somewhere like London where much more was happening. Before she graduated in 1983, Rowling had dreams of going to Oxford and even sat for some of the entrance exams. The results, for whatever reason, did not end up with her admittance to the school. She went to Exeter instead. Rowling's years at Wyedean became the backdrop, whether intentionally or not, for the seven years of Harry Potter's experience at Hogwarts. While filled with some of the same adolescent journeys toward identity and self-discovery that Rowling's years in school surely were, she made certain that Harry's high school years were anything but boring.

See also Ford Anglia

·Y, Z·

Yate, England. Though Rowling has said that she was born in the more interestingly-named town of Chipping Sodbury, the Sean Smith book, *J. K. Rowling: A Biography*, produced a facsimile of her birth certificate identifying Yate as her official place of birth. The towns are very close to one another. Yate is the more modernized of the two, though some have called it rather nondescript compared to the older and more charming Chipping Sodbury.

Yaxley. *Character.* A Death Eater. When Bellatrix Lestrange charges that Snape did not look for Voldemort when the villain disappeared, Snape counters with the assertion that neither did other Death Eaters, such as Yaxley (HBP 2:26).

Year With the Yeti. *Magical book.* A book by Gilderoy Lockhart. It is a second-year "textbook" (CS 4:44).

Yeti. *Magical creature.* From *Fantastic Beasts*. Classified 4X by the MM. Other names for the Yeti are Bigfoot and the Abominable Snowman. It is a native of Tibet and similar to a troll. It is white and furry and stands up to fifteen feet tall. It is afraid of fire (FB 42).
  See also Fantastic Beasts and Where to Find Them

Yolen, Jane (1939–). The American author of nearly 300 books for children, young adults, and adults, and someone who has been called "the Hans Christian Andersen of America," by *Newsweek* magazine. Yolen is a Rowling contemporary who remarked publicly about the Harry Potter series in an online interview in *Newsweek* on August 12, 2005. Yolen admitted to reading the first three novels but stopped somewhere in *Goblet of Fire* and never went back. Yolen has written fantasy books for children for several decades, including a novel called *Wizard's Hall* that shares many uncanny resemblances to Harry Potter, though it was published six years earlier in 1991. In a Barnes & Noble interview in March 1999, Rowling was asked about this novel and she said that she never read it. Yolen comments about the Potter books, "I just don't feel like they're well written." She clarified her comments on her website a day or two after the *Newsweek* article appeared, saying that Rowling is "a strong storyteller, but her prose style is not really very good."

The reaction from fans, critics, and readers around the world to Yolen's comments spanned a wide range. On the one end readers were suspicious of sour grapes on the part of Yolen; she is an award-winning but primarily mid-list fantasy author who has been writing for four decades with great popularity, but not with the superstardom of J. K. Rowling. Observers at the other end of the spectrum regard Yolen as a longtime respected author and educator, as well as an ambassador for children's literature; these people feel that she is stepping out and saying publicly what many critics and readers have believed about the Harry Potter series for a long time, but have not had the courage to say aloud.

Further Reading: Springen, Karen. "Writing Dynamo." *Newsweek*, August 12, 2005. Online: http://www.msnbc.msn.com/id/8917828/site/newsweek/; Yolen, Jane. Official website. www.janeyolen.com.

Yorkshire. During the evening news Mr. Dursley watches on the night Harry is left on his doorstep, weather forecaster Jim McGuffin reports people seeing a downpour of shooting stars as far away as Yorkshire, rather than the showers he predicted (SS 1:6). This is also where Goodwin Kneen lives when he writes to his Norwegian cousin Olaf about "Kwidditch" (QA 8–10).

"You-Know-Who." *Character.* Lord Voldemort's nickname among the witches and wizards who dare not speak his name (SS 1:10). Hagrid tells Harry that the only wizard Voldemort is afraid of is Dumbledore (SS 4:55).

See also Voldemort, Lord

Youdle, Cyprian. *Character.* From QA. A Quidditch referee from Norfolk who died during a match in 1357, possibly due to a curse from a member of the crowd (QA 30).

Yule Ball. *Magical event.* A formal dance held at 8:00 P.M. on Christmas night for fourth-year Hogwarts students and above; these students may invite younger students (GF 22:386). The champions of the Triwizard Tournament are expected to attend with partners and to open the dance. Prof. McGonagall tells Harry that this will be expected of him when he tells her that he does not dance (GF 22:387). Although Harry invites Cho Chang, she is already going to go with Cedric Diggory (GF 22:397), so Harry impulsively asks Parvati Patil (GF 22:401). Fred Weasley takes Angelina Johnson from the Quidditch team (GF 22:394). Hermione goes with Viktor Krum (GF 22:399); Lavender Brown goes with Seamus Finnigan; and Ron goes with Padma Patil (GF 22:402). Fleur Delacour goes with Ravenclaw Quidditch player Roger Davies (GF 23:412–13) and Pansy Parkinson goes with Draco Malfoy (GF 23:413).

The dance proceeds like most formal dances in schools—most of the couples are more interested in attending the event with friends than accompanying their dates. Though Harry dances the required first dance with Parvati Patil, he and Ron mostly ignore their dates and wind up secretly listening to Hagrid sharing his past with Madam Maxime.

Yvonne. *Character.* A friend of Aunt Petunia Dursley's who is vacationing in Majorca and cannot watch over Harry on Dudley's birthday (SS 2:22).

Zabini, Blaise. *Character.* A student in Harry's year; he is in Slytherin House (SS 7:122). He has lunch with Harry and others in Prof. Slughorn's train compartment on the way to Hogwarts in Year 6 (HBP 7:143). Blaise is on Slughorn's favored list because of his beautiful mother (HBP 7:145). He is in the train compartment with Draco Malfoy when Harry spies on him with his Invisibility Cloak (HBP 7:149–54).

Zamojski, Ladislaw. *Character.* The best Chaser on the Polish International Quidditch team (OP 19:400).

Zeller, Rose. *Character.* A first-year student in Harry's fifth year. She is sorted into Hufflepuff (OP 11:208).

Zograf. *Character.* Keeper on the Bulgaria National Quidditch Team who plays in the World Cup (GF 8:109).

Zombie. *Magical being.* Prof. Quirrell is said to have acquired his turban from an African prince after the professor helped rid the prince of a zombie. In folklore a zombie is a dead person restored to life by a sorcerer. The zombie has no will of its own but does the bidding of the sorcerer. The term may come from the Congo word *nzambi*, meaning "the spirit of a dead person."

Zonko's. *Magical place.* The joke shop in Hogsmeade (PA 8:145). Treats that Harry and Ron buy at Zonko's include Dungbombs, Hiccup Sweets, Frog Spawn Soap, and Nose-Biting Teacups (PA 14:278). The store is closed in Year 6 (HBP 12:243). Fred Weasley tells Harry that he and George are thinking of buying Zonko's as a Hogsmeade branch of their Weasleys' Wizard Wheezes (HBP 19:399).

Hogwarts School of Witchcraft and Wizardry

Hogwarts Faculty and Staff

Professor Binns, History of Magic
Albus Percival Wulfric Brian Dumbledore, Headmaster
Argus Filch, Caretaker
Firenze, Divination
Filius Flitwick, Charms
Wilhelmina Grubbly-Plank, Care of Magical Creatures (temporary)
Rubeus Hagrid, Keeper of the Keys and Grounds; Care of Magical Creatures (temporary)
Madam Rolanda Hooch, Flying instructor and Quidditch referee
Professor Kettleburn, Care of Magical Creatures (retired)
Gilderoy Lockhart, Defense Against the Dark Arts (temporary)
Remus Lupin, Defense Against the Dark Arts (temporary)
Minerva McGonagall, Transfiguration; Deputy Headmistress
Alastor "Mad-Eye" Moody, Defense Against the Dark Arts (temporary; actually not Moody, but Barty Crouch, Jr.—"Faux Moody"—in disguise)
Madam Irma Pince, librarian
Madam Poppy Pomfrey, school nurse
Professor Sinistra, Astronomy
Severus Snape, Potions
Pomona Sprout, Herbology
Sibyll Patricia Trelawney, Divination
Dolores Jane Umbridge, Defense Against the Dark Arts (temporary)
Vector, Arithmancy

Gryffindor House

Founder: Godric Gryffindor
Colors: Red and gold
Mascot: Lion

Quidditch robes: Red
Common traits: Courageous
Head: Professor Minerva McGonagall
Ghost: Nearly Headless Nick (Sir Nicholas de Mimsy-Porpington)
Quarters: Gryffindor Tower, 7th floor entrance

Gryffindor House Members Past and Present

Abercrombie, Euan
Bell, Katie
Black, Sirius
Brown, Lavender
Creevey, Colin
Creevey, Dennis
Dumbledore, Albus Percival Wulfric Brian
Evans, Lily
Finnegan, Seamus
Frobisher, Victoria (Vicky)
Granger, Hermione
Hagrid, Rubeus
Hooper, Geoffrey
Johnson, Angelina
Jordan, Lee
Kirke, Andrew
Longbottom, Neville
Lupin, Remus
McDonald, Natalie

McGonagall, Minerva
Patil, Parvati
Pettigrew, Peter (possibly)
Potter, Harry
Potter, James
Sloper, Jack
Spinnet, Alicia
Stimson, Patricia
Thomas, Dean
Weasley, Arthur
Weasley, Bill
Weasley, Charlie
Weasley, Fred
Weasley, George
Weasley, Ginny
Weasley, Molly Prewett
Weasley, Percy Ignatius
Weasley, Ronald Bilius (Ron)
Wood, Oliver

Hufflepuff House

Founder: Helga Hufflepuff
Colors: Yellow and black
Mascot: Badger
Quidditch robes: Yellow
Common traits: Hardworking, just, patient, and loyal
Head: Professor Pomona Sprout
Ghost: The Fat Friar
Quarters: Exact location unknown, but they are downstairs off the main hall and the quarters
    have the appearance of a cellar

Hufflepuff House Members Past and Present

Abbott, Hannah
Bones, Susan
Branstone, Eleanor
Cauldwell, Owen
Diggory, Cedric
Finch-Fletchley, Justin
Hopkins, Wayne

Jones, Megan
Macmillan, Ernie
Madley, Laura
Smith, Zacharias
Whitby, Kevin
Zeller, Rose

Ravenclaw House

Founder: Rowena Ravenclaw
Colors: Blue and bronze
Mascot: Eagle
Quidditch robes: Blue
Common traits: Wise, witty, learned
Head: Professor Filius Flitwick
Ghost: The Grey Lady (presumed)
Quarters: West side, Ravenclaw Tower

Ravenclaw House Members Past and Present

Ackerley, Stewart
Boot, Terry
Bradley
Brocklehurst, Mandy
Chambers
Chang, Cho
Clearwater, Penelope
Corner, Michael
Davies, Roger
Edgecombe, Marietta
Fawcett, S.
Goldstein, Anthony
Lovegood, Luna
McDougal, Morag
Patil, Padma
Quirke, Orla
Turpin, Lisa

Slytherin House

Founder: Salazar Slytherin
Colors: Green and silver
Mascot: Snake
Quidditch robes: Green
Common traits: Cunning; will use any means to achieve desired ends
Head: Professor Severus Snape
Ghost: The Bloody Baron
Quarters: Under the lake; low ceilings; looks like a dungeon with green-tinted chairs and lamps

Slytherin House Members Past and Present

Avery
Baddock, Malcolm
Black (Malfoy), Narcissa
[Black], Phineas Nigellus
Bletchley, Miles
Bole
Bulstrode, Millicent
Crabbe, Vincent
Derrick
Flint, Marcus
Goyle, Gregory
Greengrass, Daphne
Higgs, Terence
Lestrange, Bellatrix Black
Lestrange, Rastaban
Lestrange, Rodolphus
Malfoy, Draco
Malfoy, Lucius
Montague
Nott, Theodore
Parkinson, Pansy
Pritchard, Graham
Pucey, Adam
Riddle, Tom Marvolo (Voldemort)
Rosier, Evan
Snape, Severus
Warrington, C.
Wilkes
Zabini, Blaise

The Ministry of Magic

Ministers of Magic:	Grogan Stump (in 1811) (FB xii) Millicent Bagnold Cornelius Oswald Fudge Rufus Scrimgeour
Senior Undersecre- tary to the Minister:	Dolores Umbridge
Employees (Support):	Eric (security) (OP 7:128)
Support Depart- ments:	Magical Maintenance Security

Phone Booth Access

Location:	Level 1 (street level). Levels descend from the street.

Department of Magical Law Enforcement

Location:	Level 2 (OP 7:130)
Head:	Amelia Susan Bones (until Year 6) (OP 7:123) Bartemius Crouch, Sr. (in Tom Riddle's time) (GF 27:526)

Employees:	Malfalda Hopkirk (Improper Use of Magic Office) (CS 2:20–21;
	   OP 2:27)
	Perkins (Misuse of Muggle Artifacts) (CS 3:31)
	Arthur Weasley (Misuse of Muggle Artifacts [OP 7:132]; promoted
	   to Head of the Office for the Detection and Confiscation
	   of Counterfeit Defensive Spells and Protective Objects
	   [HBP 5:84])

Includes:	Improper Use of Magic Office Auror Headquarters

Wizengamot Administration Services (OP 7:130)
Misuse of Muggle Artifacts (OP 7:132)
Office for the Detection and Confiscation of Counterfeit Defensive
Spells and Protective Objects (HBP 5:84)

Department of Magical Accidents and Catastrophes

Location: Level 3 (OP 7:130)
Department Head: Unknown
Employees: Gilbert Wimple (Committee on Experimental Charms) (GF 7:86)
                       Arnold (Arnie) Peasegood (Obliviator) (GF 7:86)
Includes: Accidental Magic Reversal Squad (OP 7:130)
                       Muggle-Worthy Excuse Committee (OP 7:130)
                       Obliviator Headquarters (OP 7:130)

Department for the Regulation and Control of Magical Creatures

Location: Level 4 (OP 7:130)
Department Head: Unknown
Employees: Amos Diggory (GF 6:71)
                       Bob (OP 7:129)
                       Walden Macnair (Executioner, Committee for the Disposal
                          of Dangerous Creatures) (PA 16:328)
                       Cuthbert Mockridge (Office head, Goblin Liaison Office)
Includes: Beast, Being, and Spirit Divisions (OP 7:130)

> *Beast Division:* Centaur Liaison Office; Werewolf Registry;
>   Werewolf Capture Unit (FB xiii)
> *Being Division:* Werewolf Support Services (FB xiii)

                       Goblin Liaison Office (OP 7:130)
                       Pest Advisory Bureau (OP 7:130)
                       Office for House-Elf Relocation (FB vi)
                       Dragon Research and Restraint Bureau (FB vi)

Department of International Magical Cooperation

Location: Level 5 (OP 7:130)
Department Head: Bartemius (Barty) Crouch, Sr.
Employee: Percy Weasley (GF 3:36)
Includes: International Magical Trading Standards Body (OP 7:130)
                       International Magical Office of Law (OP 7:130)
                       International Confederation of Wizards, British Seats (OP 7:130)

Department of Magical Transport

Location: Level 6 (OP 7:129)
Department Head: Unknown

Employees:	Basil (manages Portkeys at the Quidditch World Cup) (GF 7:75) Madam Edgecombe (Floo Network) (OP 27:612)
Includes:	Apparition Test Center Broom Regulatory Control Floo Network Authority Portkey Office (OP 7:129)

Department of Magical Games and Sports

Location:	Level 7 (OP 7:129)
Department Head:	Ludovic (Ludo) Bagman
Employee:	Bertha Jorkins
Includes:	British and Irish Quidditch League Headquarters Official Gobstones Club Ludicrous Patents Office (OP 7:129)

Atrium

Location:	Level 8 (OP 7:127–29)

Department of Mysteries

Location:	Level 9
Head:	Unknown
Employees:	Broderick Bode (Unspeakable) (GF 7:86) Croaker (Unspeakable) (GF 7:86) Augustus Rookwood (spy for Voldemort) (OP 25:543–44)
Includes:	Time Room (OP 35:795) Death Chamber (OP 36:817)

Dungeon/Courtroom Ten

Location:	Level 10 (furthest below street level; can only be reached by stairs from Level 9) (OP 7:135)
Includes:	Courtroom Ten

Bertie Bott's Every Flavor Beans

Baked bean (SS 6:104)
Booger (according to George Weasley) (SS 6:104)
Chocolate (SS 6:103)
Coconut (SS 6:104)
Coffee (SS 6:104)
Curry (SS 6:104)
Ear wax (SS 17:300–301)
Grass (SS 6:104)
Liver (SS 6:104)
Marmalade (SS 6:103)
Pepper (SS 6:104)
Peppermint (SS 6:103)
Sardine (SS 6:104)
Spinach (SS 6:104)
Sprouts (SS 6:104)
Strawberry (SS 6:104)
Toast (SS 6:104)
Toffee (SS 17:300–301)
Tripe (SS 6:104)
Vomit (SS 17:300–301)

Books in the Books

Advanced Potion-Making, by Libatius Borage (HBP 9:183–84)
The Adventures of Martin Migg, the Mad Muggle (CS 3:40)
An Anthology of Eighteenth Century Charms (GF 26:488)
An Appraisal of Magical Education in Europe (GF 9:123)
Basic Hexes for the Busy and the Vexed (GF 20:339)
The Beaters' Bible, by Brutus Scrimgeour (QA frontispiece)
Beating the Bludgers—A Study of Defensive Strategies in Quidditch, by Kennilworthy Whisp
   (QA v)
A Beginner's Guide to Transfiguration, by Emeric Switch (SS 5:66)
Blood Brothers: My Life Amongst the Vampires, by Eldred Worple (HBP 15:315)
Break With a Banshee, by Gilderoy Lockhart (CS 4:43)
Broken Balls: When Fortunes Turn Foul (PA 4:53)
A Charm to Cure Reluctant Reversers (PA 2:27)
Charm Your Own Cheese (CS 3:34)
Common Magical Ailments and Afflictions (GF 2:21)
A Compendium of Common Curses and Their Counter-Actions (OP 18:390)
Confronting the Faceless (HBP 9:177)
*Curses and Countercurses: Bewitch Your Friends and Befuddle Your Enemies with the Latest
   Revenges: Hair Loss, Jelly-Legs, Tongue-Tying and Much, Much More*, by Professor Vindictus
   Viridian (SS 5:80)
The Dark Arts Outsmarted (OP 18:390)
The Dark Forces: A Guide to Self-Protection, by Quentin Trimble (SS 5:67; GF 14:210)
Death Omens: What to Do When You Know the Worst Is Coming (PA 4:54)
Defensive Magical Theory, by Wilbert Slinkhard (OP 9:160)
Dragon Breeding for Pleasure and Profit (SS 14:233)
A Dragon Keeper's Guide (SS 14:230)
Dragon Species of Great Britain and Ireland (SS 14:230)
Dreadful Denizens of the Deep (GF 26:488)
The Dream Oracle, by Inigo Imago (OP 12:237)
Enchantment in Baking (CS 3:34)

Encyclopedia of Toadstools (CS 4:63)

Fantastic Beasts and Where to Find Them, by Newt Scamander (SS 5:67)

Flesh-Eating Trees of the World (HBP 14:283)

Flying With the Cannons (GF 2:18)

Fowl or Foul? A Study of Hippogriff Brutality (PA 15:300)

From Egg to Inferno (SS 14:230)

Gadding With Ghouls, by Gilderoy Lockhart (CS 4:43)

Great Wizarding Events of the Twentieth Century (SS 6:106)

Great Wizards of the Twentieth Century (SS 12:197)

A Guide to Advanced Transfiguration (GF 20:340)

A Guide to Medieval Sorcery (GF 26:488)

Hairy Snout, Human Heart, by anonymous; published by Whizz Hard Books, 1975 (FB 41)

Handbook of Do-It-Yourself Broomcare (PA 1:12)

Handbook of Hippogriff Psychology (PA 15:300)

He Flew Like a Madman (biography of Dai Llewellyn), by Kennilworthy Whisp (QA v)

Hélas, Je me suis Transfiguré Les Pieds ("Alas, I've Transfigured My Feet"), by Malecrit (QA 39)

A History of Magic, by Bathilda Bagshot; Little Red Books, 1947 (SS 5:66; PA 1:1)

Hogwarts, A History (CS 9:147)

Holidays with Hags, by Gilderoy Lockhart (CS 4:43)

Home Life and Social Habits of British Muggles (PA 13:264)

Important Modern Magical Discoveries (SS 12:198)

Intermediate Transfiguration (PA 4:54)

Invisible Book of Invisibility (PA 4:53)

Jinxes for the Jinxed (OP 18:390)

Madcap Magic for Wacky Warlocks (GF 26:488)

Magical Drafts and Potions, by Arsenius Jigger (SS 5:66)

Magical Hieroglyphs and Logograms (OP 26:574)

Magical Me, by Gilderoy Lockhart (CS 4:58)

Magical Theory, by Adalbert Waffling (SS 5:66)

Magical Water Plants of the Mediterranean (GF 14:220)

Magick Moste Evile (HBP 18:381)

Men Who Love Dragons Too Much (GF 20:338)

Modern Magical History (SS 6:106)

The Monster Book of Monsters (PA 1:13)

Moste Potente Potions (CS 9:160)

Muggles Who Notice, by Blenheim Stalk (FB xvi)

Nature's Nobility: A Wizarding Genealogy (OP 6:116)

New Theory of Numerology (OP 23:503)

The Noble Sport of Warlocks, by Quintius Umfraville (QA 18–19)

Notable Magical Names of Our Time (SS 12:197)

Numerology and Gramatica (PA 16:315)

Olde and Forgotten Bewitchments and Charmes (GF 26:486)

One Minute Feasts—It's Magic! (CS 3:34)

One Thousand Magical Herbs and Fungi, by Phyllida Spore (SS 5:66; SS 14:229)

The Philosophy of the Mundane: Why the Muggles Prefer Not to Know, by Professor Mordicus Egg (Dust & Mildeewe, 1963)

Powers You Never Knew You Had and What to Do With Them Now You've Wised Up (GF 26:488)

Practical Defensive Magic and Its Use Against the Dark Arts (OP 23:501)

Predicting the Unpredictable: Insulate Yourself Against Shocks (PA 4:53)

✦ APPENDIX E ✦
Addresses

To Write to J. K. Rowling

J. K. Rowling
c/o Bloomsbury Publishing Plc.
38 Soho Square
London W1D 3HB
UNITED KINGDOM

J. K. Rowling
c/o Christopher Little Literary Agency
10 Eel Brook Studios
125 Moore Park Road
London SW6 4PS
UNITED KINGDOM

J. K. Rowling
c/o Scholastic Books, Inc.
557 Broadway
New York, NY 10012
USA

Organizations Important to J. K. Rowling

Amnesty International, UK
The Human Rights Action Centre
17–25 New Inn Yard
London EC2A 3EA
UNITED KINGDOM

Children's High Level Group
c/o Baroness Nicholson of Winterbourne
    MEP
The House of Lords
2 Millbank
London SW 1A 0PW
UNITED KINGDOM

Comic Relief, UK
Fifth Floor
89 Albert Embankment
London SE1 7TP
UNITED KINGDOM

Multiple Sclerosis Society
MS National Centre
372 Edgware Road
Staples Corner
London NW2 6ND
UNITED KINGDOM

National Council for One Parent Families
255 Kentish Town Road
London NW5 2LX
UNITED KINGDOM

Bibliography

Works by J. K. Rowling

Rowling, J. K. "Biography." http://www.jkrowling.com/biography.
———. "Foreword." *Families Just Like Us: The One Parent Families Good Book Guide*. London: Young Book Trust and National Council for One Parent Families, 2000.
———. *Harry Potter and the Chamber of Secrets*. London: Bloomsbury, 1998.
———. *Harry Potter and the Chamber of Secrets*. New York: Scholastic, 1998.
———. *Harry Potter and the Goblet of Fire*. London: Bloomsbury, 2000.
———. *Harry Potter and the Goblet of Fire*. New York: Scholastic, 2000.
———. *Harry Potter and the Half-Blood Prince*. London: Bloomsbury, 2005.
———. *Harry Potter and the Half-Blood Prince*. New York: Scholastic, 2005.
———. *Harry Potter and the Order of the Phoenix*. London: Bloomsbury, 2003.
———. *Harry Potter and the Order of the Phoenix*. New York: Scholastic, 2003.
———. *Harry Potter and the Philosopher's Stone*. London: Bloomsbury, 1997.
———. *Harry Potter and the Prisoner of Azkaban*. London: Bloomsbury, 1999.
———. *Harry Potter and the Prisoner of Azkaban*. New York: Scholastic, 1999.
———. *Harry Potter and the Sorcerer's Stone*. New York: Scholastic, 1998.
———. "I Miss My Mother So Much" (reprint). *InsideMS* 20, no. 3 (Summer 2002). http://www.nationalmssociety.org//IMSSu02-MyMother.asp.
———. "J. K. Rowling's Diary." *Sunday Times*, July 26, 1998.
———. "A Kind of Magic." *The Daily Telegraph* (London), June 9, 2002.
———. "Let Me Tell You a Story." *Sunday Times* (London), May 21, 2000.
———. "My Fight by J. K. Rowling." *The Sunday Times* (London), February 5, 2006. http://www.timesonline.co.uk/article/0,,2092-2025101_1,00.html.
———. "The Not Especially Fascinating Life So Far of J. K. Rowling." 1998. http://web.archive.org/web/19991012045509/http:/okukbooks.com/harry/rowling.htm.
———. Official Website. http://www.jkrowling.com.
[Newt Scamander, pseud.]. *Fantastic Beasts and Where to Find Them*. London: Bloomsbury and Obscurus Books, 2001.
[Newt Scamander, pseud.]. *Fantastic Beasts and Where to Find Them*. New York: Scholastic and Obscurus Books, 2001.

[Kennilworthy Whisp, pseud.]. *Quidditch Through the Ages*. London: Bloomsbury and Whizz Hard Books, 2001.

[Kennilworthy Whisp, pseud.]. *Quidditch Through the Ages*. New York: Scholastic and Whizz Hard Books, 2001.

Secondary and Related Works

Abanes, Richard. *Harry Potter and the Bible: The Menace Behind the Magick*. Camp Hill, PA: Horizon Books, 2001.

Abel, Katy. "Harry Potter Author Works Her Magic." *Family Education* (Summer 1999).

About the Books: Transcript of J. K. Rowling's Live Interview on Scholastic.com. October 16, 2000.

Acocella, Joan. "Under the Spell." *The New Yorker*, July 31, 2000: 74–78.

Adler, Bill, ed. *Kids' Letters to Harry Potter from Around the World*. New York: Carroll & Graf, 2001.

Adler, Margot. "Harry Potter." *All Things Considered* (NPR Radio), December 3, 1998. http://www.npr.org/templates/story/story.php?storyId=1032154.

———. J. K. Rowling interview. *All Things Considered* (NPR Radio), October 13, 1999. http://www.npr.org/templates/story/story.php?storyId=1065272.

Ahuja, Anjana. "Harry Potter's Novel Encounter." *London Times*, June 27, 2000.

Alderson, Brian. "A View from the Island: Harry Potter, Dido Twite, and Mr. Beowulf." *The Horn Book* 76 (May/June 2000): 349.

Anatol, Giselle Liza, ed. *Reading Harry Potter: Critical Essays*. Westport, CT: Praeger, 2003.

Anelli, Melissa, and Emerson Spartz. The Leaky Cauldron/MuggleNet Interview. July 16, 2005. http://www.the-leaky-cauldron.org/extras/aa-jointerview1.html.

Assuras, Thalia. "J. K. Rowling Discusses the Adventures of Harry Potter." *CBS News This Morning*, June 28, 1999.

Austen, Jane. *Emma* (1815). Oxford: Oxford University Press, 1992.

———. *Mansfield Park* (1814). New York: Penguin, 1996.

———. *The Oxford Illustrated Jane Austen: Emma*. Oxford: Oxford University Press, 1988.

———. *Pride and Prejudice* (1813). New York: Penguin, 1996.

Baggett, David, and Shawn Klein, ed. *Harry Potter and Philosophy: If Aristotle Ran Hogwarts*. Chicago: Open Court, 2004.

Barker, Raffaella. "Harry Potter's Mum." *Good Housekeeping* (October 2000).

Barnes & Noble chat transcript. Barnes&Noble.com, September 8, 1999. http://www.quick-quote-quill.org/articles/1999/0999-barnesnoble-staff.htm.

Barnes & Noble Chat with J. K. Rowling. October 20, 2000. http://www.quick-quote-quill.org/articles/2000/1000-livechat-barnesnoble.html.

Barnes & Noble Interview, March 19, 1999. http://www.quick-quote-quill.org/articles/1999/0399-barnesandnoble.html.

Beech, Linda Ward. *Scholastic Literature Guide: Harry Potter and the Chamber of Secrets by J. K. Rowling*. New York: Scholastic, 2000.

———. *Scholastic Literature Guide: Harry Potter and the Goblet of Fire by J. K. Rowling*. New York: Scholastic, 2000.

———. *Scholastic Literature Guide: Harry Potter and the Sorcerer's Stone by J. K. Rowling*. New York: Scholastic, 2000.

Bernstein, Richard. "Examining the Reality of the Fantasy in the Harry Potter Stories." *New York Times*, December 2, 1999: B1.

Bertodano, Helena de. "Harry Potter Charms a Nation." *Electronic Telegraph*, July 25, 1998.

Bethune, Brian. "The Rowling Connection: How a Young Toronto Girl's Story Touched an Author's Heart." *Maclean's*, November 6, 2000: 92.

Blacker, Terence. "Why Does Everyone Like Harry Potter?" *The Independent* (London), July 13, 1999: 4.

Bloom, Harold. "Can 35 Million Book Buyers Be Wrong? Yes." *Wall Street Journal*, July 11, 2000: A26.

Blume, Judy. "Is Harry Potter Evil?" *New York Times*, October 22, 1999: A27.

Bock, Linda. "'Harry Potter' Magic Draws Thousands." *Telegram & Gazette* (Worcester, MA), October 12, 1999.

Boekhoff, P. M., and Stuart A. Kallen. *J. K. Rowling*. San Diego, CA: Kidhaven Press, 2003.

"Book Written in Edinburgh Café Sells for $100,000." *The Herald* (Glasgow), July 8, 1997.

Borges, Jorge Luis, with Margarita Guerrero. *The Book of Imaginary Beings*. New York: Dutton, 1969.

Boyle, Fiona. *A Muggle's Guide to the Wizarding World: Exploring the Harry Potter Universe*. Toronto: ECW Press, 2004.

Bradley, Ed, and Lesley Stahl. "Harry Potter Book Sales Skyrocket Around the World." *60 Minutes*, September 12, 1999.

Bradman, Tony. "Mayhem Wherever He Flits." *London Times Literary Supplement*, December 22, 2000.

Brewer, Ebenezer Cobham, et al. *The Dictionary of Phrase and Fable*, 16th ed. New York: HarperCollins, 2000.

Bridger, Francis. *The Spirituality of Potterworld*. Image Books, 2002.

Briggs, Julia. "Fighting the Forces of Evil." *London Times Literary Suppplement*, December 22, 2000.

Brody, Leslie. "Students Meet the Real Wizard Behind the Harry Potter Craze." *The Record* (Bergen-Hackensack, NJ), October 14, 1999.

Bruce, Ian S. "Wizard Read Lives Up to Hype." *Sunday Herald* (UK), July 9, 2000.

Buchanan, Ben. *My Year with Harry Potter: How I Discovered My Own Magical World*. New York: Lantern Books, 2001.

Burkart, Gina. *A Parent's Guide to Harry Potter*. Downer's Grove, IL: InterVarsity Press, 2005.

Campbell, Joseph. *The Hero with a Thousand Faces*. Princeton, NJ: Princeton University Press, 1968.

Carey, Joanna. "Who Hasn't Met Harry?" *Guardian Unlimited*, February 16, 1999.

"Children Pick Winner of £2,500 Literary Prize." *The Herald* (Glasgow), November 19, 1997.

Clute, John, and John Grant. *The Encyclopedia of Fantasy*. New York: St. Martin's, 1999.

Cochrane, Lynne. "Harry's Home." *Sunday Times* (London), July 2, 2000.

Cohen, Witaker E. "Hands Off Harry!" Letter to the editor, *New Yorker*, October 18–25, 1999: 16.

Colbert, David. *The Magical Worlds of Harry Potter: A Treasury of Myths, Legends, and Fascinating Facts*. Wrightsville Beach, NC: Lumina Press, 2001.

———. *The Magical Worlds of Harry Potter: A Treasury of Myths, Legends, and Fascinating Facts, Revised and Updated*. New York: Penguin, 2004.

Collins, Gail. "An Ode to July." *New York Times*, July 11, 2000: A31.

Compson, William. *J. K. Rowling*. New York: Rosen Central, 2003.

Couric, Katie. Interview with J. K. Rowling on NBC's *Today Show*, October 20, 2000.

Cowell, Alan. "All Aboard the Harry Potter Promotional Express; an Author's Promotional Juggernaut Keeps Rolling On." *New York Times*, July 10, 2000.

Cox, Rose. "Harry Potter Books Inspire New Love for Literature." *Anchorage Daily News*, January 26, 2002.

Craig, Amanda. "*Harry Potter and the Prisoner of Azkaban*." *New Statesman*, July 12, 1999: 74.

Crittenden, Daniele. "Boy Meets Book." *Wall Street Journal*, November 26, 1999: W13.

Cunningham, Barry. "Discovering Harry Potter." *Fortune Magazine*, June 27, 2005.

Dahl, Roald. *Charlie and the Chocolate Factory* (1964, revised 1973). New York: Alfred A. Knopf, 1983.

———. *James and the Giant Peach* (1961). New York: Puffin Books, 1988.

Demetrius, Danielle. "Harry and the Source of Inspiration." *Daily Telegraph* (London), July 1, 2000: 3.

Dick, Sandra. "That Magical Day When Barry Met Harry." *The Scotsman*, September 15, 2005.

Dirda, Michael. "*Harry Potter and the Chamber of Secrets*." *Washington Post*, July 4, 1999.

Donahue, Deirdre. "'Goblet of Fire' Burns Out." *USA Today*, July 10, 2000: 1D.

———. "Harry Potter's Simplicity Lures Kids of All Ages." *USA Today*, June 9, 2000: 10B.

———. "Phenom Harry Potter Casts a Spell over His Author, Too." *USA Today*, September 9, 1999.

Dowd, Maureen. "Dare Speak His Name." *New York Times*, October 22, 2000: 15.

———. "Veni, Vidi, Voldemort." *New York Times*, December 9, 2001.

Dubail, Jean. "Finding Children's Magic in World of Harry Potter." *The Plain Dealer* (Cleveland), June 13, 1999: 10I.

Dunbar, Robert. "Simply Wizard." *The Irish Times*, July 17, 1999.

———. "Volumes of Choices for the Holidays." *The Scotsman*, June 28, 1997: 15.

Dunn, Elizabeth. "From the Dole to Hollywood." *Electronic Telegraph*, August 2, 1997.

Egan, Kelly. "Potter Author Thrills 15,000: J. K. Rowling Leads 'Revolution.'" *The Ottawa Citizen*, October 25, 2000: A3.

Edinburgh "Cub Reporter" Press Conference. ITV, July 17, 2005. http://news.bbc.co.uk/cbbcnews/hi/newsid_4690000/newsid_4690800/4690885.stm.

Ezard, John. "Harry Potter's Real Life Model Was No Sluggard on Tricks." *The Guardian* (London), July 12, 1999.

Feldman, Roxanne. "The Truth about Harry." *School Library Journal*, September 1999.

Fraser, Lindsey. *Conversations with J. K. Rowling*. New York: Scholastic, 2001.

———. "Harry Potter—Harry and Me." *The Scotsman*, November 2002.

———. "J. K. Rowling at the Edinburgh Book Festival, August 15, 2004." http://www.jkrowling.com/textonly/en/news_view.cfm?id=80.

———. *Telling Tales: An Interview with J. K. Rowling*. London: Mammoth, 2000.

Gaines, Ann Graham. *J. K. Rowling: A Real-Life Reader Biography*. Bear, DE: Mitchell Lane Publishers, Inc., 2002.

Galloway, Jim. "Harry Potter: School Lets Hero Off Hook." *Atlanta Journal and Constitution*, October 13, 1999: 1B.

Gibb, Eddie. "Tales from a Single Mother." *The Sunday Times* (London), June 29, 1997.

Gibbons, Fiachra. "Harry Potter Banned from Paper's Bestseller List." *The Guardian*, July 17, 1999: 6.

Gibbs, Nancy. "Harry Is an Old Soul." *Time*, December 25, 2000.

Gilson, Nancy. "*Sorcerer's Stone* Looks Like a Real Page-Turner." *Columbus Dispatch Weekender*, September 17, 1998: 20.

Giselle, Liza Anatol, ed. *Reading Harry Potter: Critical Essays*. Westport, CT: Praeger, 2003.

Gish, Kimbra Wilder. "Hunting Down Harry Potter: An Exploration of Religious Concerns about Children's Literature." *Horn Book*, May–June 2000: 263–71.

Glaister, Dan. "Debut Author and Single Mother Sells Children's Book for £100,000." *The Guardian* (London), July 8, 1997.

Gleick, Elizabeth. "The Wizard of Hogwarts." *Time*, April 12, 1999.

Gleick, Peter H. "Harry Potter, Minus a Certain Flavour." *New York Times*, July 10, 2000: A25.

Glitz, Michael. "They're Wild about 'Harry': A Popular Series Aimed at Kids Works Its Magic on Adults." *Entertainment Weekly*, July 9, 1999.

Goring, Rosemary. "Harry's Fame." *Scotland on Sunday*, January 17, 1999.

Goudge, Elizabeth. *The Little White Horse* (1946). Cutchogue, NY: Buccaneer Books, 2001.

Grahame, Kenneth. *The Wind in the Willows* (1908). New York: Charles Scribner's Sons, 1983.

Granger, John. *The Hidden Key to Harry Potter: Understanding the Meaning, Genius, and Popularity of Joanne Rowling's Harry Potter Novels*. Zossima Press, 2002.

———. *Looking for God in Harry Potter*. Wheaton, IL: Tyndale House Publishers, 2004.

Gray, Paul. "Wild About Harry." *Time*, September 20, 1999.

Grossman, Lev. "J. K. Rowling Hogwarts And All." *Time*, July 27, 2005. http://www.time .com/time/archive/preview/0,10987,1083935,00.html.

Grybaum, Gail A. "The Secrets of Harry Potter." *San Francisco Jung Institute Library Journal* 19, no. 4 (2001): 17–48.

Guiley, Rosemary Ellen. *The Encyclopedia of Ghosts and Spirits*. New York: Facts on File, 2000.

———. *The Encyclopedia of Witches and Witchcraft*, 2nd ed. New York: Facts on File, 1999.

Hainer, Cathy. "Second Time's Still a Charm." *USA Today*, May 27, 1999: 1D.

———. "Third Time's Another Charmer for 'Harry Potter.'" *USA Today*, September 8, 1999: 1D.

Hall, Dinah. "Children's Books: Junior Fiction." *Sunday Telegraph* (London), July 27, 1997: 14.

———. "Children's Books for Summer: Fiction." *Sunday Telegraph* (London), July 19, 1998: 12.

Harrington-Lueker, Donna. "Harry Potter Lacks for True Heroines." *USA Today*, July 11, 2000: 17A.

"Harry Potter Author Defends Her Work." Associated Press, October 14, 1999.

Hartman, Donna. "Imagining Harry: Sarasota Artist Mary GrandPré Brings Boy Wizard to Life Through Books' Illustrations." *Herald Today* (Bradenton/Sarasota, FL), September 25, 2005. http://www.bradenton.com/mld/bradenton/entertainment/12724363.htm.

Hattenstone, Simon. "Harry, Jessie, and Me." *The Guardian* (Manchester), July 8, 2000: 32.

Hauck, Dennis William. *Sorcerer's Stone: A Beginner's Guide to Alchemy*. New York: Citadel Press, 2004.

Heilman, Elizabeth E., ed. *Harry Potter's World: Multidisciplinary Perspectives*. New York: Routledge, 2003.

Hensher, Philip. "Harry Potter, Give Me a Break." *The Independent* (London), January 25, 2000: 1.

Higgins, Charlotte. "From Beatrix Potter to Ulysses . . . What the Top Writers Say Every Child Should Read." *The Guardian* (London), January 31, 2006. http://www.guardian .co.uk/uk_news/story/0,,1698548,00.html.

Highfield, Roger. *The Science of Harry Potter: How Magic Really Works*. New York: Penguin, 2003.

Hill, Mary. *J. K. Rowling*. New York: Welcome Books, 2003.

Hines, Barry. *A Kestrel for a Knave* (1968). New York: Penguin, 2000.

Holt, Karen Jenkins. "Spreading the Potter Magic." *Brill's Content*, April 2001: 98.

Hughes, Thomas. *Tom Brown's Schooldays* (1857). Oxford: Oxford University Press, 1999.

Iyer, Pico. "The Playing Fields of Hogwarts." *New York Times Book Review*, October 10, 1999: 39.

J. K. Rowling Interview. *The Connection* (WBUR Radio, Boston), October 12, 1999.

"J. K. Rowling's World Book Day Chat." March 4, 2004.

Jerome, Helen M. "Welcome Back, Potter." *Book*, May–June 2000: 40–45.

Johnson, Daniel. "Go for Good Writing." *The Times* (London), August 23, 1997.

———. "Just Wild about Harry." *The Times* (London), April 23, 1999.

———. "The Monster of Children's Books J. K. Rowling Shows Originality and Imagination: Why Then Has She Inspired Such Vitriol?" *Daily Telegraph* (London), January 29, 2000: 24.

Johnson, Syrie. "From Café Girl to Hit Writer." *The Evening Standard* (London), July 10, 1998.

Johnstone, Anne. "Fun is Brought to Book." *The Herald* (Glasgow), July 4, 1998: I4.

———. "Happy Ending, and That's for Beginners." *The Herald*, June 24, 1997.

———. "A Kind of Magic." *The Herald Saturday Magazine* (Glasgow), July 8, 2000: 8–12.

———. "Oh, to Hide behind a Cloak of Secrecy." *The Herald* (Glasgow), August 27, 1999.

———. "We Are Wild about Harry." *The Herald*, January 26, 1999.

Jones, Malcolm. "Magician for Millions." *Newsweek*, August 23, 1999.

———. "The Return of Harry Potter!" *Newsweek*, July 10, 2000: 52–60.

Judah, Hettie. "Harry is Pure Magic." *The Herald* (Glasgow), July 15, 1999.

Judge, Elizabeth. "Rowling Rejects Tory's Family 'Norm.'" *The Times* (London), December 6, 2000.

Kakutani, Michiko. "Harry Potter Works His Magic Again in a Far Darker Tale." *New York Times*, July 16, 2005. http://www.nytimes.com.

King, Stephen. "Wild about Harry: The Fourth Novel in J. K. Rowling's Fantastically Successful Series about a Young Wizard." *New York Times Book Review*, July 23, 2000: 13–14.

Kipen, David. "J. K. Rowling's Fantasy Series Hits an Awkward Teenage Phase with 'Goblet.'" *San Francisco Chronicle*, July 10, 2000.

Kirk, Connie Ann. "Imagi(c)nation in *Harry Potter and the Philosopher's Stone*." In Steve VanderArk, ed., *The Harry Potter Lexicon*. http://www.hp-lexicon.org/essays/essay-imagicnation.html.

———. "Is Harry Potter 5th Beatle?" *Harrisburg Patriot-News* (PA), July 2003: A7.

———. *J. K. Rowling: A Biography*. Westport, CT: Greenwood Press, 2003.

Kronzck, Allan Zola, and Elizabeth Kronzck. *The Sorcerer's Companion: A Guide to the Magical World of Harry Potter*. New York: Broadway Books, 2001.

Levi, Jonathan. "Pottermania." *Los Angeles Times Book Review*, July 16, 2000: 1.

Levine, Arthur A., with Doreen Carvajal. "Why I Paid so Much." *New York Times*, October 13, 1999: C14.

Lewis, C. S. *Chronicles of Narnia*. New York: HarperCollins 2005.

Lively, Penelope. "Harry's in Robust Form, Although I'm Left Bug-Eyed." *The Independent* (London), July 13, 2000: 5.

Lockerbie, Catherine. "Just Wild about Harry." *The Scotsman*, July 9, 1998.

———. "Magical Mystery Tour de Force." *The Scotsman*, July 10, 1999: 11.

———. "Mischief with a Magical Allure." *The Scotsman*, June 27, 1998.

———. "Spell of Best-Seller Magic." *The Scotsman*, November 28, 1998.

Loer, Stephanie. "All about Harry Potter from Quidditch to the Future of the Sorting Hat." *Boston Globe*, October 18, 1999.

———. "Harry Potter Is Taking Publishing World by Storm." *Boston Globe*, January 3, 1999: M10.

Lurie, Alison. "Not for Muggles." *New York Review of Books*, December 16, 1999.

Lyndon, Christopher. "J. K. Rowling Interview." *The Connection* (WBUR Radio, Boston), October 12, 1999.

Macdonald, Hugh. "Potter's Deal . . . Or the Importance of Being Harry." *The Herald Saturday Magazine* (Glasgow), July 8, 2000: 8–12.

Macguire, Gregory. "Lord of the Golden Snitch." *New York Times Book Review*, September 5, 1999: 12.

Macmonagle, Niall. "The Season of the Wizard." *The Irish Times*, July 15, 2000: 69.

"Magic, Mystery, and Mayhem: An Interview with J. K. Rowling." Amazon.com (early Spring 1999).

Mangino, Andrew. "'Harry Potter' Editor Comes to Silliman." *Yale Daily News*, September 27, 2005.

Maslin, Janet. "At Last, the Wizard Gets Back to School." *New York Times*, July 10, 2000: E1.

Mayes-Elma, Ruthann Elizabeth. "The Feminist Literary Criticism Approach to Representations of Women's Agency in *Harry Potter*." PhD diss. Miami University, 2003.

McCann, John. "Writer Tops Bestselling List with Children's Novel." *The Scotsman*, July 9, 1998.

McCarthy, Shaun. *J. K. Rowling*. Chicago, IL: Raintree, 2004.

McCrum, Robert. "Plot, Plot, Plot That's Worth the Weight." *The Observer* (London), July 9, 2000.

McGarrity, Mark. "A Wizard of Words Puts a Spell on Kids—'Potter' Author Visits School in Monclair." *The Star-Ledger* (Newark, NJ), October 14, 1999.

McGee, Chris. "The Mysterious Childhood: The Child Detective from the Hardy Boys to Harry Potter." PhD diss. Illinois State University, 2004.

Mehren, Elizabeth. "Upward and Onward Toward Book Seven—Her Way." *Los Angeles Times*, October 25, 2000: E1.

Merrill, Trista Marie. "Crossing Boundaries on a Bolt of Lightning: Mythic, Pedagogical, and Techno-Cultural Approaches to *Harry Potter*." PhD diss. Binghamton University, 2003.

Mitford, Jessica. *Hons and Rebels* (1960). London: Orion Books, 2000.

Moore, Sharon, ed. *Harry Potter, You're the Best! A Tribute from Fans the World Over*. New York: St. Martin's, 2001.

Moyes, Jojo. "The Myths of Single Mothers, as Told by J. K. Rowling." *The Independent* (London), October 5, 2000.

Mutter, John, and Jim Milliot. "Harry Potter and the Weekend of Fiery Sales." *Publishers Weekly*, July 17, 2000: 76.

National Press Club. Reading and Question-and-Answer Session. October 20, 1999. Book-TV and C-SPAN2.

Naughtie, James. "James Naughtie Talks to JK Rowling about One of Her Novels, *Harry Potter and the Philosopher's Stone*." *Radio 4's Book Club Programme*, August 1, 1999.

Neal, Connie. *The Gospel According to Harry Potter: Spirituality in the Stories of the World's Most Famous Seeker*. Louisville, KY: Westminster John Knox Press, 2002.

———. *What's a Christian to Do With Harry Potter?* Colorado Springs, CO: WaterBrook Press, 2001.

Nel, Philip. *J. K. Rowling's Harry Potter Novels: A Reader's Guide*. New York: Continuum, 2001.

———. "You Say 'Jelly,' I Say 'Jell-O'? Harry Potter and the Transfiguration of Language." In Lana A. Whited, ed., *The Ivory Tower and Harry Potter: Perspectives on a Literary Phenomenon*. Columbia: University of Missouri Press, 2002.

Nigg, Joseph. *The Book of Fabulous Beasts: A Treasury of Writings from Ancient Times to the Present*. New York: Oxford University Press, 1999.

"Now It's Doctor Rowling." *Post and Courier* (Charleston, SC), July 15, 2000: 2A.

Oakes, Margaret J. "Flying Cars, Floo Powder, and Flaming Torches: The High-Tech, Low-Tech World of Wizardry." In Giselle Liza Anatol, ed., *Reading Harry Potter: Critical Essays*. Westport, CT: Praeger, 2003.

O'Donnell, Rosie. Interview with J. K. Rowling. *The Rosie O'Donnell Show*, WB, June 21, 1999.

Ogden, Tom. *Wizards and Sorcerers: From Abracadabra to Zoroaster*. New York: Facts on File, 1977.

Olsen, Kirstin. *All Things Austen: An Encyclopedia of Austen's World*. Westport, CT: Greenwood, 2005.

O'Malley, Judy. "Talking with . . . J. K. Rowling." *Book Links* (July 1999).

"Online Chat with J. K. Rowling." Scholastic.com. February 3, 2000. http://www.scholastic.com.

Parravano, Martha P. "J. K. Rowling, *Harry Potter and the Chamber of Secrets*." *Horn Book* (July–August 1999): 74.

Paxman, Jeremy. "JK's OOTP Interview." *BBC Newsnight*, June 19, 2003.

Pennick, Nigel. *The Complete Illustrated Guide to Runes*. Boston: Element Books, 1999.

Phelan, Laurence. "Books: Christmas Dystopia: Parents, Ghosts, the Future, Bullying and Lemonade." *The Independent* (London), December 6, 1998: 12.

Plummer, William, and Joanna Blonska. "Spell Binder." *People*, July 12, 1999.

Power, Carla, with Shehnaz Suterwalla. "A Literary Sorceress." *Newsweek*, December 7, 1998: 7.

Prynn, Jonathan. "Potter to Join Pooh and Classics." *The Evening Standard* (London), October 6, 1999: 23.

Radosh, Daniel. "Why American Kids Don't Consider Harry Potter an Insufferable Prig." *The New Yorker*, September 20, 1999: 54, 56.

Randall, Jessy. "Wizard Words: The Literary, Latin, and Lexical Origins of Harry Potter's Vocabulary." *Verbatim: The Language Quarterly* 26, no. 2 (Spring 2001): 1–7.

Red Nose Day Chat. BBC Online, March 12, 2001.

Reynolds, Nigel. "$100,000 Success Story for Penniless Mother." *The Telegraph* (London), Spring 1997.

Robertson, Mel. "Harry Potter or The Lord of the Rings?" (Philip Pullman interview). *The Independent*, November 5, 2003.

Rogers, Shelagh. "Interview: J. K. Rowling." Canadian Broadcasting Company, October 23, 2000.

Rollin, Lucy. "Among School Children: The Harry Potter Books and the School Story Tradition." *South Carolina Review* 34, no. 1 (Fall 2001): 198–208.

Rose, Matthew, and Emily Nelson. "Potter Cognoscenti All Know a Muggle When They See One." *Wall Street Journal*, October 18, 2000: A1, A10.

Rosenberg, Liz. "A Foundling Boy and His Corps of Wizards." *Boston Globe*, November 2, 1998: L2.

———. "Harry Potter's Back Again." *Boston Globe*, July 18, 1999: K3.

———. "Making Much of Memories." *Boston Globe*, September 19, 1999: H2.

"A Rowling Timeline." *Book* (May–June 2000): 40–45.

Russell, Jeffrey B. *A History of Witchcraft*. London: Thames and Hudson, 1980.

Safire, William. "Besotted with Potter." *New York Times*, January 27, 2000: A27.

Savill, Richard. "Harry Potter and the Mystery of J. K.'s Lost Initial." *The Daily Telegraph* (London), July 19, 2000: 3.

Sawyer, Kem Knapp. "Orphan Harry and His Hogwarts Mates Work Their Magic Stateside." *St. Louis Post-Dispatch*, June 13, 1999: F12.

Sayid, Ruki. "The Million-Hers; 50 Top Earning Women in the British Isles." *The Mirror*, October 18, 1999: 11.

Schafer, Elizabeth D. *Beacham's Sourcebooks for Teaching Young Adult Fiction: Exploring Harry Potter*. Osprey, FL: Beacham, 2000.

Schoefer, Christine. "Harry Potter's Girl Trouble." *Salon.com*, January 23, 2000: 1.

Shakespeare, William. *Macbeth*. Folger Shakespeare Library. New York: Washington Square Press, 2004.

———. *A Winter's Tale*. New York: Viking/Penguin, 1999.

Shapiro, Marc. *J. K. Rowling: The Wizard Behind Harry Potter*. New York: St. Martin's, 2000.

"£60,000 for Novel Written in Café." *Western Morning News* (Devon, UK), July 8, 1997.

Smith, Dinitia. "A Crowd That's Seldom at a Loss for Words." *New York Times*, April 23, 2005. http://www.nytimes.com/2005/04/23/arts/23pen.html.

Smith, Sean. *J. K. Rowling: A Biography*. London: Michael O'Mara Books, 2001.

"Something about Harry." *Vanity Fair*, October 2001: 300–321.

Springen, Karen. "Writing Dynamo." *Newsweek*, August 12, 2005. http://www.msnbc .msn.com/id/8917828/site/newsweek/.

Stahl, Lesley. "Profile of J. K. Rowling." *60 Minutes*, September 12, 1999.

Stanton, Jim, and Jennifer Veitch. "Maggie's Is Magic, Says Creator of Harry." *Evening News* (Scotland), October 4, 1999.

Steffens, Bradley. *J. K. Rowling*. People in the News Series. San Diego, CA: Lucent Books, 2002.

Sutton, Roger. "Potter's Field." *Horn Book* (September–October 1999): 500–501.

Taylor, Alan. "We All Know about the Hype but is J. K. Rowling Really up with the Greats?" *Scotland on Sunday*, July 11, 1999: 15.

"There Has to Be a Lot of Ignorance in Me When I Start a Story" (Q&A with Philip Pullman). *Guardian Unlimited*, February 18, 2002. http://www.books.guardian.co.uk/departments/childrenandteens/story/0,6000,650988,00.html.

Thompson, Tanya. "First Attempt at Fantasy becomes a $100,000 Reality." *The Scotsman*, July 8, 1997.

Till, Lawrence, and Barry Hines. *Kes: Play*. London: Nick Hern Books, 2000.

Tisdell, Timothy Michael. "'Harry Potter' and the World of Internal Objects: An Object Relations Analysis." PhD diss. The Wright Institute, 2002.

Tolkien, J.R.R. *The Hobbit* (1937). New York: Houghton Mifflin, 2002.

———. *The Lord of the Rings* (1954–1955). New York: Houghton Mifflin, 1994.

Treneman, Ann. "Joanne Rowling's Secret Is Out." *The Independent* (London), November 21, 1997.

Trueland, Jennifer. "Author's Ex-Husband Gets in on the Harry Potter Act." *The Scotsman*, November 15, 1999: 3.

Tucker, Nicholas. "The Rise and Rise of Harry Potter." *Children's Literature in Education* 30, no. 4 (December 1999): 221–34.

"Turning a Page at the Book Review." *New York Times Inside*, Fall 2000: 1–3.

"U.K.'s Number One Bestseller, 'Harry Potter and the Sorcerer's Stone,' Tops Bestseller Charts in U.S." *Business Wire*, December 7, 1998.

VanderArk, Steve, ed. "Differences Between U.K. and U.S. Versions." *The Harry Potter Lexicon*. http://www.i2k.com/~svderark/lexicon/help.html#Language.

Walker, Andrew. "Edinburgh Author Is Elated as America Goes Potty over Potter." *The Scotsman*, October 29, 1998: 7.

———. "Harry Potter Is Off to Hollywood—Writer a Millionairess." *The Scotsman*, October 9, 1998.

Wasserman, Dan. "I Can Already See How It Ends—The Dark Forces Win." *Washington Post National Weekly Edition*, no. 24 (July 2000): 28.

Waters, Galadriel, and Astre Mithrandir. *Ultimate Unofficial Guide to the Mysteries of Harry Potter*. Niles, IL: Wizarding World Press, 2003.

Weir, Margaret. "Of Magic and Single Motherhood." *Salon*, 1999.

"We're Off to See the Wizards." *Nickelodeon*, October 2001: 52–54.

"What if Quidditch, the Enchanted Sport of Wizards and Witches Featured in the Harry Potter Books, Were Regulated by the NCAA?" *Sports Illustrated*, August 21, 2000: 33.

Whited, Lana A., ed. *The Ivory Tower and Harry Potter: Perspectives on a Literary Phenomenon*. Columbia: University of Missouri Press, 2002.

Wiener, Gary, ed. *Readings on J. K. Rowling*. San Francisco, CA: Greenhaven Press, 2004.

Will, George F. "Harry Potter: A Wizard's Return." *Washington Post*, July 4, 2000: A19.

Williams, Rhys. "The Spotty Schoolboy and Single Mother Taking the Mantle from Roald Dahl." *The Independent* (London), January 29, 1999.

Willis, Roy. *Dictionary of World Myth*. London: Duncan Baird, 1995.

Willis, Scott. "Could You Turn That Down? I'm Trying to Read!" *San Jose Mercury News*, July 12, 2000.

Winerip, Michael. "Children's Book." *New York Times Book Review*, February 14, 1999.

Woods, Judith. "Coffee in One Hand, Baby in Another—A Recipe for Success." *The Scotsman*, November 19, 1997.

Wyman, Max. "'You Can Lead a Fool to a Book but You Can't Make Them Think': Author Has Frank Words for Religious Right." *The Vancouver Sun* (British Columbia), October 26, 2000. http://www.canada.com/vancouversun.

Wynee-Jones, Tim. "Harry Potter and the Blaze of Publicity: On the Whole, the Junior Wizard Deserves It All." *The Ottawa Citizen*, July 16, 2000: C16.

Yeats, W. B., ed. *A Treasury of Irish Myth, Legend, and Folklore*. New York: Random House, 1986.

Yolen, Jane. *Wizard's Hall*. New York: Harcourt, 1991.

Zipes, Jack. *Sticks and Stones: The Troublesome Success of Children's Literature from Slovenly Peter to Harry Potter*. New York: Routledge, 2001.

Internet Sources

Official Websites

Arthur A. Levine Books: http://www.arthuralevinebooks.com.

Bloomsbury: http://www.bloomsbury.com/harrypotter.

Christopher Little Literary Agency: http://www.christopherlittle.net.

Jim Dale: http://www.jim-dale.com.

J. K. Rowling Official Website: http://www.jkrowling.com.

Scholastic: http://www.scholastic.com/harrypotter.

Stephen Fry: http://www.stephenfry.com.

Warner Bros. Harry Potter Website (films): http://harrypotter.warnerbros.co.uk/main/home page/home.html.

Rowling-Endorsed Fan Websites

The following fan websites have been endorsed by J. K. Rowling through her official website.

Godric's Hollow: http://www.godrics-hollow.net.

Harry Potter Automatic News Aggregator (HPANA): http://www.hpana.com.

Harry Potter Lexicon: http://www.hp-lexicon.org.

Immeritus: http://www.immeritus.org.

The Leaky Cauldron: http://www.the-leaky-cauldron.org.

MuggleNet: http://www.mugglenet.com.

Other Relevant Websites

Amnesty International: http://www.amnesty.org.

Comic Relief: http://www.comicrelief.com.

MS Society (Scotland): http://www.mssocietyscotland.org.uk.

Index

About the Author

CONNIE ANN KIRK is an author and independent scholar specializing in American and children's literature and the poet Emily Dickinson. Her previous books from Greenwood Press include *J.K. Rowling: A Biography*, *Emily Dickinson: A Biography*, *Mark Twain: A Biography*, *Sylvia Plath: A Biography*, and *The Companion to American Children's Picture Books*.